FOURTH EDITION

STUDY GUIDE AND
SELF-EXAMINATION REVIEW

FOR

SYNOPSIS OF

PSYCHIATRY

COMPREHENSIVE TEXTBOOK OF

PSYCHIATRY

SENIOR CONTRIBUTING EDITOR

ROBERT CANCRO, M.D., MED.D.Sc.

Professor and Chairman, Department of Psychiatry,
New York University School of Medicine;
Director, Department of Psychiatry, Tisch Hospital,
the University Hospital of the
New York University Medical Center, New York, New York;
Director, Nathan S. Kline Institute for
Psychiatric Research, Orangeburg, New York

CONTRIBUTING EDITOR

ROBIN SEGAL, M.D.

Clinical Instructor in Psychiatry,
Director of the Clinical Clerkship and Senior Elective Program in Psychiatry,
New York University School of Medicine, New York, New York

FOURTH EDITION

STUDY GUIDE AND SELF-EXAMINATION REVIEW

FOR

SYNOPSIS OF

PSYCHIATRY

AND

COMPREHENSIVE TEXTBOOK OF

PSYCHIATRY

HAROLD I. KAPLAN, M.D.

Professor of Psychiatry, New York University School of Medicine;
Attending Psychiatrist, Tisch Hospital, the University Hospital of
the New York University Medical Center;
Attending Psychiatrist, Bellevue Hospital, New York, New York

BENJAMIN J. SADOCK, M.D.

Professor and Vice Chairman, Department of Psychiatry,
New York University School of Medicine;
Attending Psychiatrist, Tisch Hospital, the University Hospital of
the New York University Medical Center; Attending Psychiatrist,
Bellevue Hospital, New York, New York

WILLIAMS & WILKINS
BALTIMORE • HONG KONG • LONDON • MUNICH
PHILADELPHIA • SYDNEY • TOKYO

Editor: Michael G. Fisher
Associate Editor: Carol Eckhart
Designer: Norman W. Och
Illustration Planner: Lorraine Wrzosek
Production Coordinator: Charles E. Zeller
Cover Designer: Dan Pfisterer

Copyright © 1991
Williams & Wilkins
428 East Preston Street
Baltimore, Maryland 21202, USA

Accurate indications, adverse reactions, and dosage schedules for drugs are provided in this book, but it is possible that they may change. The reader is urged to review the package information data of the manufacturers of the medications mentioned.

Printed in the United States of America

First edition 1983   Second edition 1985   Third edition 1989

Library of Congress Cataloging-in-Publication Data

Kaplan, Harold I., 1927–
    Study guide and self-examination review for Synopsis of psychiatry and Comprehensive textbook of psychiatry / Harold I. Kaplan, Benjamin J. Sadock.—4th ed.
        p.   cm.
    Rev. ed. of: Study guide and self-examination review for Synopsis of psychiatry. 3rd ed. ©1989.
    Study guide to Comprehensive textbook of psychiatry/V / editors, Harold I. Kaplan, Benjamin J. Sadock. 5th ed. ©1989, and Synopsis of psychiatry / Harold I. Kaplan, Benjamin J. Sadock. 6th ed. ©1991.
    Includes bibliographical references.
    Includes index.
    ISBN 0-683-04535-0
    1. Mental illness—Examinations, questions, etc. 2. Psychiatry—Examinations, questions, etc. I. Sadock, Benjamin J., 1933–   . II. Kaplan, Harold I., 1927–   . Study guide and self-examination review for Synopsis of psychiatry. III. Kaplan, Harold I., 1927–   . Synopsis of psychiatry. 6th ed. IV. Comprehensive textbook of psychiatry/V. V. Title.
    [DNLM: 1. Mental Disorders—examination questions. 2. Psychiatry—examination questions. WM 18 K17s]
RC454.K36   1991
616.89'0076—dc20
DNLM/DLC
for Library of Congress   90-12969
                                                                CIP

                                                    92   93   94
                            3   4   5   6   7   8   9   10

Dedicated to our wives,
Nancy Barrett Kaplan
and
Virginia Alcott Sadock,
without whose help and sacrifice
this textbook would not have been possible

☐ Preface

This is the fourth edition of the *Study Guide and Self-Examination Review for Synopsis of Psychiatry and Comprehensive Textbook of Psychiatry*. The book is keyed to the new sixth edition of *Synopsis of Psychiatry* and, in a major modification, is also keyed to the fifth edition of *Comprehensive Textbook of Psychiatry*.

Significant changes have been made to improve this text so that it meets the needs of medical students, psychiatrists, neurologists, and others who require a review of the behavioral sciences and clinical psychiatry.

Among the unique aspects of this edition are the following: All nosology terms follow the most current revised third edition of the American Psychiatric Association's *Diagnostic and Statistical Manual of Mental Disorders* (DSM-III-R), which was published in May 1987. The authors have added many new questions and have modified the questions and answers from earlier editions. Answers have been carefully researched and defined, and certain phrases have been italicized to emphasize the main idea encompassed by the question. In addition, the authors have added extensive case material derived from the newly published *DSM-III-R Case Book*, published by the American Psychiatric Association and used with permission.

Because this book is a study guide, each chapter begins with an introduction that directs students to areas of special significance used in their studying. The authors have prepared special lists of helpful hints that present key terms and concepts essential to a basic knowledge of psychiatry. Students should be able to define and discuss each of the terms in depth as preparation for examinations. In their review, students should emphasize each term.

The *Study Guide* forms one part of a comprehensive system developed by the authors to facilitate the teaching of psychiatry and the behavioral sciences. The keystone is *Comprehensive Textbook of Psychiatry*, now in its fifth edition (1989), which is global in depth and scope and encyclopedic in breadth of information. This part of the system is accompanied by *Synopsis of Psychiatry*, a thoroughly eclectic and fully integrated textbook covering both the behavioral sciences and clinical psychiatry. Another segment, *Pocket Handbook of Clinical Psychiatry*, is a newly written book by the authors with outstanding collaborators from New York University School of Medicine; it covers the diagnosis and the treatment of psychiatric disorders and is a handy reference on clinical issues compactly designed to be carried in the pocket of the clinical clerk or practicing physician. The last part is the authors' newly published *Comprehensive Glossary of Psychiatric and Psychological Terms*, which provides simply written definitions of terms used frequently by psychiatrists, other physicians, medical students, and mental health professionals.

The *Study Guide* will be especially useful for students preparing for certification examinations, such as the National Board of Medical Examiners, the American Board of Psychiatry and Neurology, and the Federation of Licensing Examination of the Commission on Foreign Medical Graduates. It will also be useful for physicians who wish to update their general psychiatric knowledge or to identify areas of weakness and of strength. The allocation of questions has been carefully weighted, with subjects of both clinical and theoretical importance taken into account.

To use this book most effectively, the student should attempt to answer all questions in a particular chapter. By allowing about one minute for each answer, the student can approximate the time constraints of an actual examination. The answers should then be verified by referring to the corresponding answer section in each chapter. The page numbers indicate a major discussion of the topic in *Synopsis of Psychiatry* or in *Comprehensive Textbook of Psychiatry*. The student can then refer to the appropriate pages for a more extensive and definitive discussion of the material. We wish to thank Robert J. Campbell, M.D., and his publishers, Oxford University Press, for giving us permission to derive some of the definitions used in this text from his book, the fifth edition of *Psychiatric Dictionary*.

In the preparation of this edition, we have been most fortunate to enlist the assistance of Robin Segal, M.D., Clinical Instructor of Psychiatry and Director of the Clinical Clerkship and Senior Elective Programs in Psychiatry at New York University School of Medicine, who served as contributing editor. She assumed the major and key role in the revision of this book and contributed immensely to its present form. Her dedication, enthusiasm, and academic and clinical skills were invaluable. The authors wish to thank her for her incalculable contribution.

We also wish to thank Richard Perry, M.D., Clinical Associate Professor of Child Psychia-try, and Rebecca Jones, M.D., Research Assistant Professor of Psychiatry, at New York University Medical Center for their help. Lynda Abrams, M.A., an important member of our staff performed a variety of tasks in an outstanding, dedicated, and devoted manner that contributed to the publication of this book. We also thank Joan Welsh for her invaluable help in editing this textbook. Virginia A. Sadock, M.D., Clinical Professor of Psychiatry and Director of Graduate Education in Human Sexuality at the New York University School of Medicine, also played an important role in planning and implementation.

Robert Cancro, M.D., Professor and Chairman of the Department of Psychiatry at New York University Medical Center, participated as senior contributing editor of this edition. He is also senior contributing editor of both *Synopsis of Psychiatry* and *Comprehensive Textbook of Psychiatry*. Dr. Cancro's support, encouragement, and inspiration have been of inestimable value. He is a personal friend, colleague, and mentor whose collaboration has contributed immeasurably to the new ideas and directions shaping these books. He is one of America's leading psychiatrists, and it is our privilege to be associated with this outstanding clinician, researcher, and educator.

New York University Medical Center
New York, New York
February, 1991

Harold I. Kaplan, M.D.
Benjamin J. Sadock, M.D.

☐ Contents

1

The Doctor-Patient Relationship

The doctor-patient relationship remains the keystone in the practice of medicine. The relationship should be one of understanding and trust between doctor and patient. After establishing rapport, the patient feels that the physician accepts him or her and that the physician can recognize both assets and weaknesses. This feeling enables the physician to enlist the patient's cooperation and participation in treatment. A receptive and nonjudgmental physician gains the greatest understanding of the patient and of the patient's disease.

Obtaining a mental status, eliciting a history of the patient's present illness and past life, and carrying out therapy depend on a perceptively conducted interview that begins with the initial contact between patient and physician. An understanding of the patient in health and in sickness comes chiefly from the patient's account of life events, attitudes, and emotions and from the development of the patient's symptoms. The diagnosis and the prognosis are based on these data, together with additional information obtained from the patient's relatives, the physical examination, psychological tests, and any other special examinations that are indicated. With this knowledge, the physician can formulate treatment objectives and institute a realistic plan of therapy for the patient.

Failure of the physician to establish good rapport accounts for much of the ineffectiveness in the care of patients. The young physician too frequently loses sight of the whole person and, instead, regards the patient as the corpse dissected by the anatomist, the cells and fluids studied by the physiologist, or the consciousness observed by the psychiatrist.

"The secret of the care of the patient is in caring for the patient," once remarked Francis Peabody, a talented teacher, clinician, and researcher. It is essential that all physicians understand the critical factors that influence the doctor-patient relationship and the importance of this relationship in caring for the patient.

In *Synopsis VI*, Chapter 1, "The Doctor-Patient Relationship," factors that influence that relationship are discussed. Students should also review Section 9.1 in *CTP V*, "The Psychiatric Interview, History, and Mental Status Examination," and then test their knowledge of the subject by studying the questions and answers below.

HELPFUL HINTS

The key terms listed below should be known by the student as they apply to the doctor-patient relationship.

personality	unresolved conflicts	listening
therapeutic limitations	individual experience	distortion
psychodynamics	cultural attitudes	emotionally charged statements
rapport	socioeconomic background	misrepresentation
transference	"good patients"	misperception
countertransference	aggression and counteraggression	early social pressures
identification	sublimation	emotional reactions
empathy	unconscious guilt	biopsychosocial model
authority figures	defensive attitudes	illness behavior
active versus passive patients	belligerent patient	sick role
mutual participation	overcompensatory anger	
compliance versus noncompliance	humor	

QUESTIONS

DIRECTIONS: The incomplete statement below is followed by five suggested completions. Select the *one* that is best.

1.1. In the initial interview, the patient complains that previous visits to several psychiatrists had not effected any improvement. You should
A. ask whether payment for services was involved
B. ask why the patient thought no improvement occurred
C. ask why the patient is seeking treatment again in spite of the previous experiences
D. suggest that the patient may have been resistant to therapy
E. acknowledge that there are incompetent psychiatrists

DIRECTIONS: For each of the incomplete statements below, *one or more* of the completions given are correct. Choose answer

A. if only *1, 2, and 3* are correct
B. if only *1 and 3* are correct
C. if only *2 and 4* are correct
D. if only *4* is correct
E. if *all* are correct

1.2. The model of mutual participation is most applicable to such diseases as
1. diabetes
2. hypertension
3. multiple sclerosis
4. pharyngitis

1.3. Commonly held negative beliefs by patients about physicians are that physicians
1. do not have the time or the inclination to listen to and consider the patients' feelings
2. do not have enough knowledge of the emotional factors that affect health
3. do not know or care about the socioeconomic background of the family
4. increase anxiety by giving explanations in technical language

DIRECTIONS: Each set of lettered headings below is followed by a list of numbered phrases. For each numbered phrase, select the best lettered heading. Each heading can be used once, more than once, or not at all.

Questions 1.4–1.6
A. Transference
B. Countertransference

1.4. The physician avoids issues that are important to the patient because the physician finds them boring or has difficulty dealing with them

1.5. On speaking to a doctor for the first time over the telephone, the patient experiences intensely negative feelings toward the doctor

1.6. During an initial consultation session, the physician experiences intensely erotic feelings toward the patient

Questions 1.7–1.8
A. Reflection
B. Facilitation
C. Interpretation
D. Self-revelation
E. Reassurance

1.7. Provision of verbal and nonverbal cues that encourage the patient to continue talking

1.8. Repetition to the patient, in a supportive manner, of something that the patient has said

Questions 1.9–1.10
A. Sick role
B. Illness behavior

1.9. The patient's reactions to the experience of being sick

1.10. The societal attribute conveyed to a sick person

ANSWERS

The Doctor-Patient Relationship

1.1. The answer is B (*Synopsis VI*, pages 6–7; *CTP V*, pages 450–451).

All the responses to the patient who, during the initial interview, complained that previous visits to psychiatrists had not effected any improvement have merit. However, the best initial response of the interviewer is to ask why the patient thought *no improvement occurred*. Such a question is open-ended and is likely to elicit the most information, such as the patient's fantasies and expectations about therapy. To respond initially with a question about fees may indicate that the doctor is concerned about payment for the present services and is not relevant. The discussion of money is entirely appropriate but is ill timed at this point. It is germane to ask *why the patient is seeking treatment again* in spite of having had negative experiences with psychiatrists. Have life events made the current situation intolerable? Have symptoms worsened? The fact that a patient is willing to see a psychiatrist is a favorable sign; however, some patients go from one psychiatrist to another, seeking a particular solution or confirmation of a delusional belief. The interviewer may gain clues as to whether it is true in this case by asking why the patient believes therapy was not successful in the past.

Resistance is the opposition to the uncovering of unconscious factors that must be overcome if psychotherapy is to be successful. It is best attended to as part of the therapeutic process, and it is premature to discuss resistance as an issue in the initial interview. In addition, unless the concept is clearly defined, the patient may have no idea what the interviewer means by the term. Finally, although there are *incompetent psychiatrists*, there is no indication on the basis of what was said that the patient had consulted such a person, and it is not necessary for the interviewer to make such an inference. A patient may go to several psychotherapists before finding the right therapist-patient fit. Similarly, the psychiatrist may decide that the patient would be served best by working with another therapist and appropriately refer the patient to a colleague.

1.2. The answer is A (1, 2, 3) (*Synopsis VI*, page 2; *CTP V*, pages 450–454).

Individual patients react differently to physicians according to their underlying personalities and their particular needs. Some patients are most comfortable with a form of passive compliance in which the doctor is clearly in charge and the patient does as

directed. Other patients need a different relationship with the doctor, one in which the patient actively contributes to self-care and is treated by the doctor as an equal and a respected adult. The doctor-patient model of mutual participation, in which both doctor and patient are equally involved in treatment, is more applicable to chronic diseases that require a patient's clear understanding of and compliance with treatment, such as *diabetes, hypertension*, and *multiple sclerosis*. With acute illnesses, such as *pharyngitis*, it is not as critical to apply the mutual participation model, although, for some patients, compliance in more acute conditions clearly occurs only within this model. The more chronic the disease, the more essential is the need for doctor-patient mutuality in management issues and the decision-making process.

1.3. The answer is E (all) (*Synopsis VI*, page 2; *CTP V*, pages 1446–1450).

Individual experiences, as well as patients' cultural attitudes, affect their reactions to doctors and the delivery of health care. Surveys have shown that some patients hold negative beliefs about their physicians. They feel that physicians do not have the *time or the inclination to listen* to or to consider their feelings, that physicians do not have *enough knowledge of their emotional problems* and of the *socioeconomic background* of their families, and that physicians increase fear by giving *explanations in technical language*. Clearly, psychosocial and economic factors exert a profound influence on human relations; it is desirable for the physician to have as much understanding as possible of the patient's emotional state and cultural background. Differences between doctors and patients in social, intellectual, and educational status have been found to seriously interfere with rapport. Understanding or lack of understanding of a patient's beliefs, use of language, and attitudes toward illness influence both the character of the physician's examination and the patient's reaction to the examination.

1.4–1.6

1.4. The answer is B (*Synopsis VI*, page 3; *CTP V*, pages 1446–1448).

1.5. The answer is A (*Synopsis VI*, pages 2–3; *CTP V*, pages 1446–1448).

1.6. The answer is B (*Synopsis VI*, pages 2–3; *CTP V*, pages 1446–1448).

The physician needs to consider not only the implications of the patient's conscious, realistic statements and interactions but also the unconscious or transference aspects. *Transference* is defined as the reactivation outside the patient's awareness of attitudes and feelings toward people who have been important to the patient and the projection of these reactions onto the physician. The physician may, in turn, develop *a countertransference*, the converse of the transference, in which the patient represents someone from the physician's past and serves to help alleviate the physician's own conflicts and feelings. The physician must constantly undergo self-criticism and self-appraisal and must be alert to such feelings and attitudes that may adversely affect the relationship with the patient and, thus, impair clinical judgment.

When a physician avoids issues important to the patient because of the physician's own sensitivities, prejudices, or peculiarities, it is considered to be a countertransferential reaction. A physician experiencing an intensely erotic feeling toward a patient is also considered to be experiencing a countertransferential reaction. It is a reaction determined by the doctor's inner needs, rather than by the patient's needs, and may reinforce the patient's earlier traumatic history if not checked by the therapist. A patient who has a relatively realistic attitude about the physician's desire and ability to deliver adequate care, leading to a cooperative and informed working relationship, is not displaying a transferential reaction to the physician. A transferential reaction is one that is not based on a realistic assessment of the doctor but on the patient's unconscious needs and conflicts. A patient who has an intensely negative reaction to a physician as a result of a single telephone conversation is most likely experiencing a transference response based more on a repetition of attitudes toward other authoritative persons who have figured prominently in the patient's life than on a realistic attitude toward the physician.

1.7–1.8

1.7. The answer is B (*Synopsis VI*, page 7; *CTP V*, page 451).

1.8. The answer is A (*Synopsis VI*, page 7; *CTP V*, page 451).

Different interviewing techniques are useful in assessing different aspects of the patient's history and current functioning so that the physician may formulate an accurate diagnosis and treatment plan. *Reflection* is a technique in which the doctor repeats to the patient, in a supportive manner, something that the patient has said. This technique assures the physician that he or she correctly understands what the patient is trying to say, and it lets the patient know that the physician is actively listening and understands the patient's concerns. Reflection is not an exact repetition but, rather, a paraphrase that indicates that the doctor has perceived what the patient is saying.

Facilitation is the provision of verbal and nonverbal cues that encourage the patient to continue talking. Examples are nodding one's head, leaning forward in one's seat, and saying "Yes and then?"

Interpretation is the technique in which the psychiatrist states something about the patient's behavior or thoughts that the patient may not be aware of, based on careful listening to the underlying themes and patterns in the patient's story. This sophisticated technique, in general, should be used only after the physician has established a rapport with the patient and has a good understanding of these underlying themes.

Self-revelation is limited, discrete, self-disclosure by the physician. The psychiatrist chooses to answer a personal question or to volunteer some personal fact because this information will further the patient's care. Often, self-revelation is not warranted, so the physician should try to understand the hidden concern behind the patient's personal question.

Reassurance that is real and truthful is experienced by the patient as the empathic response of a concerned physician and can lead to increased trust and compliance.

1.9–1.10

1.9. The answer is B (*Synopsis VI*, pages 1–2; *CTP V*, pages 1287–1288).

1.10. The answer is A (*Synopsis VI*, pages 1–2; *CTP V*, pages 284, 622, 1265–1267).

The *sick role* is the societal attribute conveyed to a sick person. The sick role includes such factors as being excused from responsibility, receiving special treatment, and being perceived as having special talents or sensitivities. Cultural attitudes about dependency and illness influence the sick role.

Illness behavior is a term that describes a patient's reactions to the experience of being sick. Edward Suchman has described five stages of illness behavior. They are

1. the symptom-experience stage, in which a decision is made that something is wrong
2. the assumption-of-the-sick-role stage, in which a decision is made that one is sick and needs professional care
3. the medical-care-contact stage, in which a decision is made to seek professional care
4. the dependent-patient-role stage, in which a decision is made to transfer control to the doctor and to follow prescribed treatment
5. the recovery or rehabilitation stage, in which a decision is made to give up the patient role

2 |||||

Human Development Throughout the Life Cycle

Developmental theorists have looked at human maturation throughout the life cycle. They have developed many criteria to define and describe the phases of life from birth to death. Developmental theories can provide a comprehensive and integrated view of the sequence of cognitive, emotional, and psychosocial landmarks.

Jean Piaget concentrated on the cognitive development of children and offered striking evidence of the evolution of thought at different ages. Sigmund Freud focused on the psychosexual aspect of development through adolescence and opened the door to profound discoveries about the nature of infantile sexuality and its relation to the unconscious and to adult behavior. Erik Erikson provided a psychosocial developmental perspective, expanding on the discoveries of Freud to include characteristic maturational crises that correlate with the issues confronted psychosexually. Margaret Mahler described development in terms of the separation-individuation process and the development of object constancy, which emphasize the issues of both attachment and autonomy in development.

When all these theories are considered together, a dynamic and vibrant picture of the growing human organism emerges. More recent theorists, such as Daniel Levinson and Theodore Lidz, have contributed to the understanding of what is confronted and worked through in the course of the life cycle. The student who understands the basic tenets of different life-cycle theories and how they interrelate will have not only a clear image of normal development but a more lucid sense of dysfunctional development as well; knowing what can go wrong in early phases of development helps clarify different forms of psychopathology later in life. For instance, the student who understands Mahler's normative theories of the development of object constancy has a richer understanding of the dynamic causes of personality disorders. An even deeper dynamic understanding of these disorders is possible if the student is also aware of the potential points of dysfunction in cognitive, psychosexual, and psychosocial development.

Students should review Chapter 2, "Human Development Throughout the Life Cycle," in *Synopsis VI* and Section 32.2, "Normal Child Development," and Section 32.3, "Normal Adolescent Development," in *CTP V* and then test their knowledge of the subject by studying the questions and answers below.

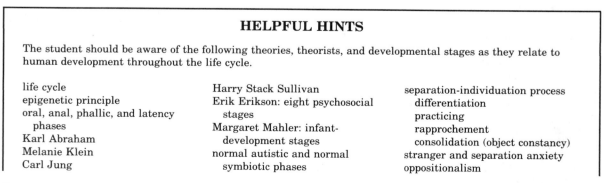

HELPFUL HINTS

The student should be aware of the following theories, theorists, and developmental stages as they relate to human development throughout the life cycle.

life cycle
epigenetic principle
oral, anal, phallic, and latency
  phases
Karl Abraham
Melanie Klein
Carl Jung

Harry Stack Sullivan
Erik Erikson: eight psychosocial
  stages
Margaret Mahler: infant-
  development stages
normal autistic and normal
  symbiotic phases

separation-individuation process
  differentiation
  practicing
  rapprochement
  consolidation (object constancy)
stranger and separation anxiety
oppositionalism

Jean Piaget
characteristics of thought
   sensorimotor phase (object
   permanence)
   preoperational phase
   concrete operations
   formal operations
Daniel Levinson
George Vaillant
concepts of normality as health,
   utopia, average, and process;
   psychoanalytic concepts
Heinz Hartmann
autonomous ego functions
Anna Freud
Daniel Offer
Thomas Szasz
social and community psychiatry
Alexander Leighton
Roy Grinker
pregnancy and childbirth
postpartum mood disorders and
   psychosis
pregnancy and marriage
Madonna complex
family size
inborn errors of metabolism
fetal development
genetic counseling: principles and
   conditions
prenatal diagnosis
drug effects and hazards
perinatal complications
maternal behavior
feeding and infant care
maternal neglect
failure to thrive
neural organization of infancy
ethology
imprinting
Harry Harlow
surrogate mother
John Bowlby
bonding
attachment
René Spitz
social deprivation syndromes
   (anaclitic depression-
   hospitalism)
fathers and attachment
temperament
parental fit
spacing of children
birth order
Arnold Gesell
developmental landmarks

smiling
negativism
toilet training
anal personality
gender identity
sibling rivalry
play and pretend
imaginary companions
egocentrism
Oedipus complex
castration anxiety
Electra complex
superego
ego ideal
penis envy
identification
school adjustment, behavior,
   refusal
learning problems
psychosexual moratorium
socially decisive stage
dreams in children
language development
imagery and drawings
somnambulism
effects of divorce
stepparents and siblings
foster parents
adoption
puberty
primary and secondary sex
   characteristics
Masters and Johnson
masturbation
cults
peer group
formal operations and morality
menarche
body image
crushes
adolescent homosexuality
dependency
identity
religious behavior
normative crisis
reactions to authority
intimacy
generativity
integrity
gender expectations
dual-career families
vocation and unemployment
core identity
racism, prejudice
mutuality

age 30 transition
parenthood
middle age
mid-life crisis
climacterium
vasomotor instability
empty-nest syndrome
marriage
divorce
remarriage
separation
alimony
spouse and child abuse
single-parent home
parental-right doctrine
custody
adultery
geriatric period
biological landmarks of aging
average life expectancy
sex in the aged
age-related cell changes
retirement
senility
cognitive decline
handicaps
pseudodementia
suicide in the aged
thanatology
Elisabeth Kübler-Ross
pain management
DNR
living wills
brain dead
death and children
sibling and parental death
grief
mourning
bereavement
survivor guilt
linkage objects
John Bowlby's stages of
   bereavement
affectional bond
bereavement in children
delayed, inhibited, and denied
   grief
anticipatory grief
grief versus depression
self-blame, worthlessness
Mourning and Melancholia
uncomplicated bereavement
hospice
Dame Cicely Saunders
burnout

QUESTIONS

DIRECTIONS: Each of the incomplete statements below is followed by five suggested completions. Select the *one* that is *best* in each case.

2.1. The main characteristic of Margaret Mahler's differentiation subphase is
A. separation anxiety
B. stranger anxiety
C. rapprochement
D. castration anxiety
E. none of the above

2.2. A child is generally able to conceptualize the true meaning of death by age
A. 3 years
B. 5 years
C. 7 years
D. 10 years
E. 12 years

2.3. In an infant, social smiling is elicited preferentially by the mother at age
A. under 4 weeks
B. 4 to 8 weeks
C. 8 to 12 weeks
D. 3 to 4 months
E. more than 4 months

2.4. A patient, on being told he or she has a fatal illness, may respond with
A. depression
B. anger
C. denial
D. bargaining
E. all the above

2.5. Erik Erikson used the term "generativity versus stagnation" to describe the conflict occurring in
A. childhood
B. adolescence
C. young adulthood
D. middle adulthood
E. late adulthood

2.6. The percentage of people between the ages of 65 and 85 living in nursing homes is
A. 5 percent
B. 10 percent
C. 15 percent
D. 20 percent
E. more than 25 percent

DIRECTIONS: For each of the incomplete statements below, *one or more* of the following completions given are correct. Choose answer

A. if *only 1, 2, and 3* are correct
B. if *only 1 and 3* are correct
C. if *only 2 and 4* are correct
D. if *only 4* is correct
E. if *all* are correct

2.7. All life-cycle theories assume that
1. development occurs in successive, defined stages
2. each stage of the life cycle is characterized by events that must be resolved for development to proceed
3. each stage contains a dominant feature that distinguishes it from other stages
4. the same developmental criteria are used to define maturation, regardless of theory

2.8. Some features of the hospice program include
1. the control of pain as a primary goal
2. the avoidance of narcotics to prevent addiction
3. an organized routine providing care for both the patient and the family
4. costs that are equivalent to those of a general hospital

2.9. The separation-individuation process, as described by Margaret Mahler,
1. begins in the fourth or fifth month of life
2. is completed by the age of 6 years
3. consists of four subphases
4. includes the normal autistic and normal symbiotic phases

2.10. True statements about Erik Erikson's theory of development include the following:
1. There are eight stages, ranging from infancy to old age
2. Each stage has both positive and negative aspects that lead to a characteristic crisis
3. Ideally, the crisis of each stage is resolved when the person achieves a new level of functioning at the end of the stage
4. Most people fall more toward the negative end of the spectrum than toward the positive end

2.11. During pregnancy, sexual behavior may change because of
1. physiological changes in the woman
2. psychological factors in the woman
3. psychological factors in the man
4. fear, on the part of either partner, of harming the developing fetus

2.12. People most prone to a mid-life crisis tend to come from families characterized by
1. parental discord
2. withdrawal by the same-sex parent
3. anxious parents
4. impulsive parents

2.13. Firstborn children, as compared with their siblings,
1. perform better academically
2. receive the least amount of attention in the home
3. are more authoritarian
4. have the greatest need to develop strong peer relationships

2.14. John Bowlby's stages of bereavement include
1. protest
2. yearning
3. despair
4. reorganization

2.15. Congenital differences among human infants are expressed through
1. temperament
2. autonomic reactivity
3. responses to stimulation
4. distractibility

2.16. In the second and third years of life, the child
1. has a degree of control over personal actions because of the ability to walk
2. is in a negativistic stage
3. requires the setting of limits on acceptable behavior
4. must be protected from stressful challenges

2.17. In the fourth year of life, the child
1. is capable of anticipating events
2. can experience conflicts over initiative
3. is curious about sex
4. is preoccupied with the issues involved in toilet training

2.18. Postpartum emotional disturbances
1. affect 10 percent of the population
2. affect only women
3. are caused only by psychological factors
4. range from mild dysphoria to frank psychosis

DIRECTIONS: Each group of questions below consists of five lettered headings followed by a list of numbered words or statements. For each numbered word or statement, select the *one* lettered heading that is most associated with it. Each lettered heading may be selected once, more than once, or not at all.

Questions 2.19–2.23
A. Basic trust versus mistrust
B. Integrity versus despair
C. Initiative versus guilt
D. Intimacy versus isolation
E. Identity versus role diffusion

2.19. Oral-sensory (infancy)

2.20. Late adulthood or old age

2.21. Early childhood

2.22. Early adulthood

2.23. Puberty and adolescence

Questions 2.24–2.28
A. Magical thinking
B. Thinking about one's thoughts
C. Object permanence
D. Symbolic thought
E. Cause and effect

2.24. 9 to 12 months

2.25. 2 to 7 years

2.26. 7 to 11 years

2.27. 11 years through adolescence

2.28. 18 to 24 months

Questions 2.29–2.33
A. Distress
B. Shame
C. Anger
D. Sadness
E. Guilt

2.29. Birth

2.30. 3 to 4 months

2.31. 8 to 9 months

2.32. 18 months

2.33. 3 to 4 years

Questions 2.34–2.38
A. 18 months
B. 2 years
C. 3 years
D. 4 years
E. 6 years

2.34. Copies a triangle

2.35. Copies a cross

2.36. Walks up stairs with one hand held

2.37. Puts on shoes

2.38. Refers to self by name

Questions 2.39–2.43
A. Birth to 6 months
B. 7 to 11 months
C. 12 to 18 months
D. 54 months on
E. None of the above

2.39. Plays at making sounds and babbles (repeats a series of sounds)

2.40. Plays language games (pat-a-cake, peek-a-boo)

2.41. Understands up to 150 words and uses up to 20 words

2.42. Speech is 100 percent intelligible

2.43. Uses language to tell stories and share ideas

DIRECTIONS: The lettered headings below are followed by a list of numbered phrases. For each numbered phrase, select

A. if the item is associated with *A only*
B. if the item is associated with *B only*
C. if the item is associated with *both A and B*
D. if the item is associated with *neither A nor B*

Questions 2.44–2.47
A. Normal grief
B. Major depression

2.44. Psychomotor retardation or agitation

2.45. Anorexia with weight loss

2.46. Marked feelings of worthlessness

2.47. Suicide attempts

ANSWERS

Human Development Throughout the Life Cycle

2.1. The answer is B (*Synopsis VI*, pages 18–19; *CTP V*, page 399).

Margaret S. Mahler (1897–1985) was a Hungarian-born psychoanalyst who practiced in the United States and who studied early childhood object relations. She described the separation-individuation process, resulting in a person's subjective sense of separateness and the development of an inner object constancy. The separation-individuation phase of development begins in the fourth or fifth month of life and is completed by the age of 3 years.

As described by Mahler, the characteristic anxiety during the differentiation subphase of separation-individuation is *stranger anxiety*. The infant has begun to develop a more alert sensorium and has begun to compare what is and what is not mother. This subphase occurs between 5 and 10 months. A fear of strangers is first noted in infants at 26 weeks of age but does not fully develop until about 8 months. Unlike babies exposed to a variety of caretakers, babies who have only one caretaker are more likely to have stranger anxiety. But, unlike stranger anxiety, which can occur even when the infant is in the mother's arms, *separation anxiety*—which is seen between 10 and 16 months, during the practicing subphase—is precipitated by the separation from the person to whom the infant is attached. The practicing subphase marks the beginning of upright locomotion, which gives the child a new perspective and a mood of elation, the "love affair with the world." The infant learns to separate as it begins to crawl and to move away from the mother but continues to look back and to return frequently to the mother as home base. Between the ages of 16 and 24 months, the *rapprochement* subphase occurs, with the characteristic event being the rapprochement crisis, during which the infant's struggle becomes one between wanting to be soothed by the mother and not wanting to accept her help. The symbol of rapprochement is the child standing on the threshold of a door in helpless frustration, not knowing which way to turn. *Castration anxiety*, as described by Freud, is a characteristic anxiety that arises during the oedipal phase of development, ages 3 to 5 years, concerning a fantasized loss of or an injury to the genitalia.

2.2. The answer is D (*Synopsis VI*, page 58; *CTP V*, pages 1349–1350).

By *the age of 10 years*, the child is able to conceptualize the true meaning of death—something that may happen to the child, as well as to the parent. At that time, the child shows a great tendency for logical exploration to dominate fantasy and shows a more fully developed understanding of feelings and interactions in relationships. The child has well-developed capacities for empathy, love, and compassion, as well as emerging capacities for sadness and love in the context of concrete rules. As opposed to parents in some other parts of the world, middle-class adults in the United States tend to shield children from a knowledge of death. The air of mystery with which death is surrounded in such instances may unintentionally create irrational fears in children. Attending funerals, then, is recommended for children if the adults present are trustworthy and reasonably composed. That event may act as an introduction into the adult world of crises and tribulations, on the way to a full transition into other phases of development.

The preschool child under age 5 years is beginning to be aware of death, not in the abstract sense but as a separation similar to sleep. Between the ages of 5 and 10 years, the child shows a developing sense of inevitable human mortality; the child first fears that the parents may die and that the child will be abandoned.

Discussing death with an inquiring child requires simplicity and candor. Adults are cautioned not to invent answers when they have none. Basically, death must be conveyed as a natural event that cannot be avoided but that causes pain because it separates people who love each other.

2.3. The answer is B (*Synopsis VI*, pages 31–32; *CTP V*, page 1702).

Arnold Gesell, a developmental psychologist and physician, has described developmental schedules that outline the qualitative sequence of motor, adaptive, language, and personal-social behavior of the child from the age of 4 weeks to 6 years. Gesell's is a normative approach, viewing development as the unfolding of a genetically determined sequence. According to his schedules, at birth, all infants have a repertoire of reflex behaviors—breathing, crying, and swallowing. By 1 to 2 weeks of age, the infant smiles. The response is endogenously determined, as evidenced by smiling in blind infants. By 2 to 4 weeks of age, visual fixation and following are evident. By 4 to 8 weeks, social smiling is elicited preferentially by the face or the voice of the caretaker.

2.4. The answer is E (*Synopsis VI*, pages 56–57; *CTP V*, pages 1340–1341).

Elisabeth Kübler-Ross described five psychological stages that a dying person may experience on being told of the prognosis. Although Kübler-Ross presented the five stages in the sequential order of denial, anger, bargaining, depression, and acceptance, she clearly did not intend that this order be taken literally. From her work with dying patients, she recognized that the experience of these stages was fluid and individual; one person may initially react with anger, then denial, then depression, then anger again; another person may respond with a more immediate acceptance, whereas another may never experience the acceptance stage.

Kübler-Ross's description of these stages has been extremely important to the understanding of the emotional life of a dying person. *Denial* is the first stage, when a patient may first appear dazed and then refuse to believe the diagnosis. *Anger* is often characterized by the response "Why me?" The *bargaining* stage occurs when the patient attempts to negotiate with the physician, friends, or even God, by promising to fulfill certain bargains in return for a cure. *Depression* may result as a reaction to the reality of impending death or to the debilitating effects of illness. *Acceptance* is the stage when a patient is able to come to terms with the inevitability of death and with the losses associated with death. In this stage, a patient may be more able to talk about death and to face the unknown.

2.5. The answer is D (*Synopsis VI*, pages 15 and 18–21; *CTP V*, page 408).

Erik Erikson accepted Sigmund Freud's theory of infantile sexuality, but Erikson also saw the developmental potential of all stages of life. In each of Erikson's eight stages, a maturational crisis arises. During *middle adulthood*, each person has the opportunity to become *generative*, productive through his or her contributions to society, or to become *stagnant*, preoccupied only with his or her own well-being. Erikson's stages are outlined in Table 2.1.

2.6. The answer is A (*Synopsis VI*, page 55; *CTP V*, page 2058).

More than 25 million Americans are over age 65, and, although a myth persists that most elderly people live in nursing homes, only *5 percent* of persons between the ages of 65 and 85 are so institutionalized. With increasing age, however, the rate of institutionalization does increase. Over the age of 85, 20 percent of people live in nursing homes.

2.7. The answer is A (1, 2, 3) (*Synopsis VI*, pages 14–15; *CTP V*, pages 399–402).

The idea of a life cycle suggests that there is an underlying order in the temporal sequence of the life course from conception through old age and that the meanings of particular events and relationships are deeply colored by the life-cycle phase in which they

Table 2.1
Erikson's Eight Stages of Development

BASIC TRUST VERSUS BASIC MISTRUST (ORAL SENSORY) (birth to 1 year)
- Social trust demonstrated in ease of feeding, depth of sleep, bowel relaxation
- Dependence on consistency and sameness of experience provided by caretaker
- Second six months' teething and biting moves infant from getting to taking
- Weaning leads to nostalgia for lost paradise
- If basic trust is strong, child maintains hopeful attitude

AUTONOMY VERSUS SHAME AND DOUBT (MUSCULAR-ANAL) (1 to 3 years)
- Biologically includes learning to walk, feed self, talk
- Muscular maturation sets stage for holding on and letting go
- Need for outer control, firmness of caretaker prior to development of autonomy
- Shame occurs when child is overtly self-conscious about negative exposure
- Self-doubt can evolve if parents overly shame child (e.g., about elimination)

INITIATIVE VERSUS GUILT (LOCOMOTOR GENITAL) (3 to 5 years)
- Initiative arises in relation to tasks for the sake of activity, both motor and intellectual
- Guilt may arise over goals contemplated (especially aggressive)
- Desire to mimic adult world; involvement in oedipal struggle leads to resolution through social role identification
- Sibling rivalry frequent

INDUSTRY VERSUS INFERIORITY (LATENCY) (6 to 11 years)
- Child is busy building, creating, accomplishing
- Receives systematic instruction, as well as fundamentals of technology
- Danger of sense of inadequacy and inferiority if child despairs of his or her tools, skills, and status among peers
- Socially decisive age

IDENTITY VERSUS ROLE DIFFUSION (ADOLESCENCE) (11 years through end of adolescence)
- Struggle to develop ego identity (sense of inner sameness and continuity)
- Preoccupation with appearance, hero worship, ideology
- Group identity (peers) develops
- Danger of role confusion, doubts about sexual and vocational identity
- Psychosocial moratorium, stage between morality learned by the child and ethics to be developed by the adult

INTIMACY VERSUS SELF-ABSORPTION or ISOLATION (EARLY ADULTHOOD) (end of adolescence to 40 years)
- Period of courtship and early family life
- Characterized by options for occupation, marriage, and other commitments; may be tentative
- Attainment of intimacy includes ability to share with and care for others without fear of losing self
- Failure to achieve intimacy results in self-absorption and isolation

GENERATIVITY VERSUS STAGNATION (MIDDLE ADULTHOOD) (40 to 65 years)
- Prerequisite to attainment of generativity is successful achievement of identity
- Generativity may be achieved by the childless with development of sense of altruism and creativity
- Attainment of generativity is characterized by feelings of concern about others beyond family (e.g., nature of society and world in which future generations will live)
- Failure to attain generativity results in stagnation and self-concern

Table 2.1
Continued

INTEGRITY VERSUS DESPAIR AND ISOLATION (LATE ADULTHOOD OR OLD AGE) (over 65 years)
- Achievement of intimacy and generativity allows for feelings of peace and contentment, prerequisite to mastering task of integrity
- Attainment of integrity includes sense of self-satisfaction with one's life
- Failure to achieve integrity results in despair, the feeling that one's life had little purpose or meaning

occur. The imagery of the life cycle suggests that the life course evolves through a sequence of definable forms. The fundamental assumption of all life-cycle theories is that development occurs in *successive, clearly defined stages* and in a constant order. A second assumption is the principle of epigenesis. Epigenesis is concerned with systems, with process rather than with structure, and with the network of events within which behavior occurs. Within the life-cycle concept, epigenesis implies that each stage of the life cycle is characterized by events or crises that must be satisfactorily *resolved* in order for development to proceed smoothly. A third assumption is that each stage contains a *dominant feature* or complex of features that distinguishes it from other stages that it either precedes or follows.

Change goes on within each stage, and a transition is required for the shift from one stage to the next. Every stage has its own time; it is important in its own right and needs to be understood in its own terms. The most significant differences among various models of the human life cycle involve the *developmental criteria* used, which are not all the same. To study the course of a life, one must take into account stability and change, continuity and discontinuity, and orderly progression, as well as stasis and fluctuation. Thus, research on the life cycle has included investigation into many aspects of living—inner wishes and fantasies, love relationships, involvement in family and work, and bodily changes. Among criteria that have been cited are biological maturity, which relates to stages of completed growth; psychological capacities, which relate to potential mental abilities; adaptive techniques, which relate to behavior that increases the person's ability to adjust to a situation; defense mechanisms, which relate to the unconscious process acting to relieve conflict and anxiety; role demands, which relate to patterns of behavior developed under the influence of significant persons in one's environment; and cognitive development, which relates to the progressive acquisition of conscious thought and problem-solving abilities.

2.8. The answer is B (1, 3) (*Synopsis VI*, pages 61–62; *CTP V*, page 1344).

A hospice is a facility devoted to the care of the terminally ill. It is neither a fully equipped acute hospital nor a nursing facility that offers little more

than custodial service and medication. It usually means an inpatient service or home care by experienced medical personnel. The consistent *control of pain* is a primary goal, and *narcotics* are given without fear of the patient's becoming addicted. Primary emphasis is on the psychosocial unit of family and patient; intensive *care* is provided to *the patient and the family* through a supervised organized routine. The routine and the emphasis have led to a prevention of social isolation and neglect, as well as to the possible prevention of morbid grief reactions among the survivors. Governmental agencies have supported various hospices, because hospices and home care are *more economical* than hospitalization.

2.9. The answer is B (1, 3) (*Synopsis VI*, pages 15 and 18–21; *CTP V*, pages 399–401).

Margaret Mahler described a separation-individuation process, which begins in the *fourth or fifth month* of life. This process consists of *four subphases*, including differentiation (5 to 10 months), practicing (10 to 16 months), rapprochement (16 to 24 months), and object constancy or consolidation (24 to 36 months). The separation-individuation process *is completed by the age of 3 years*. It is preceded by two phases, termed the *normal autistic* (birth to 4 weeks) and the *normal symbiotic* (3 to 4 weeks to 4 to 5 months). Table 2.2 lists a description of the subphases of separation-individuation.

2.10. The answer is A (1, 2, 3) (*Synopsis VI*, pages 15–22; *CTP V*, pages 405–409).

Erik Erikson made a major contribution to the psychoanalytic concept of development in his study of the relationship between instinctual zones and the development of specific modalities of ego functioning. In his 1950 book, *Childhood and Society*, Erikson postulated a parallel relationship between specific phases of ego or psychosocial development and specific phases of individual development.

Erikson believes that human development can be understood only if the social forces that interact with the developing person are taken into account. He focuses on the fact that the development of the ego is not merely a matter of intrapsychic vicissitudes but also a matter of mutual regulation evolving between the growing child and the traditions of society. Erikson describes a program of ego development that reaches from birth to death: the person passes through *eight psychosocial phases or stages* of the life cycle by meeting and resolving a series of developmental psychosocial crises. Each stage has two possible outcomes—*one healthy or positive and the other unhealthy or negative*. Ideally, each crisis is resolved when a *higher level of functioning* is achieved at the more positive end of each stage. Successful resolution at any level lays the foundation for engaging in the next developmental crisis. Erikson believes that most people fall more toward the *positive* than toward the negative pole. Table 2.1 lists Erikson's eight stages.

Table 2.2
Margaret Mahler's Stages of Infant Development

THE SUBPHASES OF SEPARATION-INDIVIDUATION PROPER:
FIRST SUBPHASE: DIFFERENTIATION
(5 to 10 months)
- Process of hatching from autistic shell (i.e., developing more alert sensorium that reflects cognitive and neurological maturation)
- Beginning of comparative scanning (e.g., comparing what is and what is not mother)
- Characteristic anxiety: stranger anxiety, which involves curiosity and fear (most prevalent around 8 months)

SECOND SUBPHASE: PRACTICING
(10 to 16 months)
- Beginning of this phase marked by upright locomotion—child has new perspective and also mood of elation
- Mother used as home base
- Characteristic anxiety: separation anxiety

THIRD SUBPHASE: RAPPROCHEMENT
(16 to 24 months)
- Infant now a toddler—more aware of physical separateness, which dampens mood of elation
- Child tries to bridge gap between self and mother—concretely seen as bringing objects to mother
- Mother's efforts to help toddler often not perceived as helpful, temper tantrums typical
- Characteristic event: rapprochement crisis: wanting to be soothed by mother and yet not be able to accept her help
- Resolution of crisis occurs as child's skills improve and child is able to get gratification from doing things

FOURTH SUBPHASE: CONSOLIDATION AND OBJECT CONSTANCY
(24 to 36 months)
- Child is better able to cope with mother's absence and to engage substitutes
- Child can begin to feel comfortable with mother's absences by knowing she will return
- Gradual internalization of image of mother as reliable and stable
- Through increasing verbal skills and better sense of time, child can tolerate delay and endure separations

Adapted from table by Sylvia Karasu, M.D., and Richard Oberfield, M.D.

2.11. The answer is E (all) (*Synopsis VI*, pages 23–24; *CTP V*, pages 558, 1335).

During pregnancy, a couple's sexual activity may increase or decrease. *Physiological changes in the woman*, including pelvic vasocongestion, help some women become more sexually responsive than before pregnancy, but symptoms such as nausea, vomiting, and fatigue lead some women to less frequent sexual activity.

Psychological factors affect both the man and the woman. Women may exhibit more interest in sex because of the resolution of their ambivalent feelings regarding birth control or because of their subjective sense of being more attractive while pregnant. Alternatively, a woman may associate pregnancy as an asexual period, or she may feel unattractive because of the changes in her body proportions.

Psychological factors similarly affect men. Some men find their pregnant partners more attractive; others find their partners ugly or become fearful of defiling a pregnant woman. The *Madonna complex* is exhibited by some men who view the pregnant woman as sacred.

Fear, on the part of either partner, of harming the developing fetus is common and may be due to misinformation. The physician can reassure the couple that most obstetricians advise the couple to abstain from sex only in the last four to six weeks of pregnancy.

2.12. The answer is E (all) (*Synopsis VI*, pages 47–48; *CTP V*, pages 1412–1413).

The mid-life crisis consists of sudden, drastic changes in work or marriage, severe depression, and increased use of alcohol or drugs. Men and women most prone to a mid-life crisis tend to come from families characterized by parental *discord* and *withdrawal* by the same-sex parent and by *anxiety, impulsivity*, and depression, with little concern or sense of responsibility for each family member.

The idea of an inevitable and normative mid-life crisis is controversial. Daniel Levinson reported that 70 to 80 percent of a sampling of men experienced a moderate to severe crisis during their mid-40s or early 50s. Levinson saw these crises as developmental ones brought on by a difficulty in dealing with the developmental tasks of the period. He refers to the mid-life crisis as "becoming one's own man." His sampling has not included women. The term "mid-life crisis" has also been used to define the inner turmoil related to confronting the idea of death. Some studies, however, do not support the concept of a crisis in middle age.

2.13. The answer is B (1, 3) (*Synopsis VI*, page 31; *CTP V*, page 413).

The effects of birth order vary. As compared with second- and third-born children, firstborns are more achievement oriented, *perform better academically*, and tend to be the *most authoritarian*. Parents are more anxious about caretaking with firstborn children than with second and third children, who have the advantage of the parents' previous experience. Children who are spaced too closely do not get enough lap time in many cases. The arrival of new children in the family affects not only the parents but also the siblings. Firstborn children may resent the birth of a new sibling, who threatens their sole claim on parental attention. In some cases, such regressive behavior as encopresis, enuresis, or thumb sucking is seen.

In general, the oldest child achieves the most and is the most authoritarian; the middle child usually receives the *least attention* in the home and may *develop strong peer relationships* to compensate; and the youngest child may receive the most attention from older siblings, siblings' friends, and parents. Alfred Adler (1870–1937), a Viennese-born psychiatrist who was a part of Freud's circle for nine years, made some interesting observations on the significance of the birth order. Adler said that the firstborn, having lost the position of only child, is often conservative, feeling that those in power should remain in power. The second child, wanting to equal the first, often wants power to change hands. The youngest can never be displaced and will always be the youngest. Adler believed that the birth order can be played out in many different ways, but early responses to one's birth-order position become part of one's life-style.

Studies of children from large families (four to five children) show that they are more likely to develop conduct disorders and have slightly lower levels of verbal intelligence than children from small families. Decreased parental interaction and discipline may account for these findings.

2.14. The answer is E (all) (*Synopsis VI*, page 59; *CTP V*, page 891).

The British psychoanalyst John Bowlby (1907–1990) is best known for his theory of attachment, which has had an immense effect on the understanding of normal and abnormal child development. Bowlby identified specific phases that occur in children who are separated from their mothers, comparing these phases to mourning and bereavement in adults.

There are four stages of bereavement. Stage 1, called *protest*, is characterized by outbursts of distress, fear, or anger. Stage 2 is characterized by *yearning* and searching for the lost figure. This stage may last for several months or even years and is marked by preoccupation with the dead person to the point that the griever actually believes that the deceased is present. Stage 3 occurs as a result of a gradual recognition and integration of the reality of death, leading to a sense of disorganization and *despair*. In this stage, the bereaved person may be restless and aimless and make only ineffective and inefficient efforts to resume normal patterns of living. Stage 4 is the final stage, in which, ideally, the person begins to resolve grief and to *reorganize*, with a gradual recession of the grief and a replacement with cherished memories. These stages are not discrete, and there is a tremendous variability among persons. In general, normal grief resolves within one or two years as the person experiences the calendar year at least once without the lost person.

2.15. The answer is E (all) (*Synopsis VI*, page 30; *CTP V*, pages 554, 1355, 1692).

Considerable evidence suggests that congenital differences exist among infants. For example, *autonomic reactivity* is one expression of these differences. The studies of Alexander Thomas and Stella Chess demonstrated nine *temperamental* characteristics in infants. (See Table 2.3.) Among these characteristics are a high or low threshold of *response to stimulation* and a high or low level of *distractibility*. The ratings on individual children showed that tem-

Table 2.3
Temperamental Characteristics of Infants

1. **Activity level**—the motor component present in a given child's functioning
2. **Rhythmicity**—the predictability of such functions as hunger, feeding pattern, elimination, and sleep-wake cycle
3. **Approach or withdrawal**—the nature of the response to a new stimulus, such as a new food, toy, or person
4. **Adaptability**—the speed and ease with which a current behavior is able to be modified in response to altered environmental structuring
5. **Intensity of reaction**—the amount of energy used in mood expression
6. **Threshold of responsiveness**—the intensity level of stimulation required to evoke a discernible response to sensory stimuli, environmental objects, and social contacts
7. **Quality of mood**—pleasant, joyful, friendly behavior as contrasted with unpleasant, crying, unfriendly behavior
8. **Distractibility**—the effectiveness of extraneous environmental stimuli in interfering with or in altering the direction of ongoing behavior
9. **Attention span and persistence**—the length of time a particular activity is pursued by the child (attention span) and the continuation of an activity in the face of obstacles (persistence)

Table derived from data by Stella Chess, M.D., and Alexander Thomas, M.D.

peramental factors correlated at 3 months and at 2 years, but much lower correlations existed at 5 years.

2.16. The answer is E (all) (*Synopsis VI*, pages 35–36; *CTP V*, pages 1701–1708).

The second and third years of life are marked by accelerations in motor and intellectual development. The *ability to walk* confers on toddlers a degree of control over their own actions, which allows them to determine when to approach and when to withdraw. Normal milestones in the second year include progressing from clumsy to coordinated walking and even to running and climbing stairs. In the third year, coordinated gross motor activity consists of running and climbing stairs without holding on. The acquisition of speech profoundly extends the child's horizons. Near the end of the second year and into the third, the use of short sentences is sometimes possible. By the third year, the toddler can name many objects, use personal pronouns, and make needs known verbally. Typically, children learn to say "No" before they learn to say "Yes." The *negativism* of the toddler is a vital stage in individuation. The balance between dependency and autonomy may shift for a brief time to dependency. Power struggles may intermittently dominate relationship patterns. Dominant issues are basic dependency, need for security, and fear of separation.

This period poses changing tasks for parents, as well as toddlers. Whereas in infancy the major responsibility for parents is to meet the infant's needs in a sensitive and giving fashion, without overanticipating and without overfulfilling those needs so that the baby never experiences tension, at the toddler stage the parental task includes a requirement for firmness in *setting limits* on acceptable behavior and the encouragement of the progressive emancipation of the child. The dyadic relationship with the primary caretaker evolves into a balance between need fulfillment and emerging autonomy. Children must be allowed to do for themselves as far as they are able, but they must be *protected* and assisted when the challenges are beyond them.

2.17. The answer is A (1, 2, 3) (*Synopsis VI*, pages 35–37; *CTP V*, pages 406, 1701, 1708).

By the time children reach the age of 4 years, their basic attitudes reflect a curiosity about the world. Their capacities, however, still run well behind their aspirations, so they often undertake things they cannot complete successfully. They are *capable of anticipating* events and are learning to postpone immediate gratification. Concentration and self-regulation are possible with appropriate context and support. There is a flowering of the imagination, as revealed in controlled fantasy and play. Play is a central psychological activity for this period. It serves the function of releasing tension and energy. The trial roles children assay in dramatic play allow them to try out the adult identities they one day will have to understand and assume.

Erikson's stage of initiative versus guilt (3 to 5 years) encompasses the fourth year of life, and it is during this period that a child's sense of self-initiative can result in feelings of accomplishment or of guilt. *Conflicts over initiative* may lead to future problems with self-initiation and ambition. Relationship patterns become more complicated, both in content (language and symbolic modes) and in form (e.g., rivalries, intrigue, secrets, jealousies, and triangular envy begin to emerge). Pride and joy in psychological and bodily self, especially the sexual organs, further emerge. Children exhibit active *curiosity about sex.* If this curiosity is recognized as healthy and is met with honest and age-appropriate replies, they acquire a sense of the wonder of life and are comfortable about their own roles in it. If the subject of sex is taboo and children's questions are rebuffed,they respond with shame and discomfort. *Toilet training*, a central issue in the second and third years of life, is generally resolved by the age of 4 years.

2.18. The answer is D (4) (*Synopsis VI*, page 23; *CTP V*, pages 852–858, 1219).

Postpartum emotional disturbances affect 20 to 40 percent of women after childbirth. The disturbances *range from mild dysphoria to frank psychosis*, but most women affected experience only the postpartum blues, consisting of sadness, tearfulness, and increased dependency. Rarely does a postpartum disorder develop into psychosis (1 to 2 cases per 1,000 deliveries). The postpartum emotional changes that women may experience have been attributed to the rapid hormonal shifts at the time of delivery and to

the physical stress of childbirth, in addition to psychological factors.

Women are not alone in experiencing postpartum emotional changes. Some men show mood changes during their partner's pregnancy or after delivery. The father is affected by many factors: emotional, such as feeling forgotten, left out, or less important to his spouse; financial, as concerns about providing the necessary care for the new family member are taken into account; and psychosexual, as the man perceives that his partner is less available sexually because of the demands of caring for the newborn.

2.19–2.23

2.19. The answer is A (*Synopsis VI*, pages 18–21; *CTP V*, pages 405–408).

2.20. The answer is B (*Synopsis VI*, pages 18–21; *CTP V*, pages 405–408).

2.21. The answer is C (*Synopsis VI*, pages 18–21; *CTP V*, pages 405–408).

2.22. The answer is D (*Synopsis VI*, pages 18–21; *CTP V*, pages 405–408).

2.23. The answer is E (*Synopsis VI*, pages 18–21; *CTP V*, pages 405–408).

The first of Erik Erikson's developmental phases, *oral-sensory* (infancy—birth to 1 year), is characterized by the first psychosocial crisis the infant must face, that of *basic trust versus mistrust.* The crisis takes place in the context of the intimate relationship between infant and mother. The infant's primary orientation to reality is erotic and centers on the mouth. The successful resolution of this phase includes a disposition to trust others, a basic trust in oneself, a capacity to entrust oneself, and a sense of self-confidence.

During *early childhood*, approximately ages 3 to 5 years, the crisis addressed by the child is *initiative versus guilt.* As the child struggles to resolve the oedipal struggle, guilt may grow because of aggressive thoughts or wishes. Initiative arises as the child begins to desire to mimic the adult world and as the child finds enjoyment in productive activity.

The phase of *puberty and adolescence* (age 11 years through the end of adolescence) is characterized by *identity versus role diffusion*, during which the adolescent must begin to establish a future role in adult society. This particular psychosocial crisis is peculiarly vulnerable to social and cultural influences.

Early adulthood (end of adolescence to 40 years) is characterized by *intimacy versus self-absorption or isolation. Late adulthood or old age* (65 and older) is characterized by *integrity versus despair and isolation.* The intimacy versus isolation crisis is characterized by the need to establish the capacity to relate intimately and meaningfully with others in mutually satisfying and productive interactions. The failure to achieve a successful resolution of this crisis results in a sense of personal isolation. The crisis of integrity versus despair implies and depends on the successful resolution of all the preceding crises of psychosocial growth. It means the acceptance of oneself and of all the aspects of life and the integration of their elements into a stable pattern of living. The failure to achieve ego integration often results in a kind of despair and an unconscious fear of death. The person who fails in integrity lives in basic self-contempt.

For a further explanation of Eriksonian theory, see Table 2.1.

2.24–2.28

2.24. The answer is **C** (*Synopsis VI*, pages 18–21; *CTP V*, pages 258–262, 399–407).

2.25. The answer is **A** (*Synopsis VI*, pages 18–21; *CTP V*, pages 258–262, 399–407).

2.26. The answer is **E** (*Synopsis VI*, pages 18–21; *CTP V*, pages 258–262, 399–407).

2.27. The answer is **B** (*Synopsis VI*, pages 18–21; *CTP V*, pages 258–262, 399–407).

2.28. The answer is **D** (*Synopsis VI*, pages 18–21; *CTP V*, pages 258–262, 399–407).

Jean Piaget made a major contribution to the understanding of human cognitive development. During the first stage of sensorimotor development, the child develops *object permanence*. By *9 to 12 months*, the child has the ability to retain an object in his or her mind when the object is no longer in view. At this time, peek-a-boo becomes a game joyfully played with the child. The end of the sensorimotor period is marked by the attainment of *symbolic thought* by the child of *18 to 24 months* of age. With the acquisition of symbolic thought, the whole world of symbolic play is now open to the child. Ages *2 through 7 years* mark the years of preoperational thought. This is the stage of prelogical thinking; it is non-reversible. The child believes in immanent justice—that a bad deed will inevitably be punished. The child also believes in *magical thinking*, the idea that thoughts or wishes—good or bad—can come true. Magical thinking has positive and negative repercussions. After some ill has befallen a loved one, for example, the child may blame himself or herself because of "bad" wishes. Happily, some children believe they are gaining a new sibling because they have wished for it, and they can view a new baby as a present.

Ages *7 to 11 years* are the years of concrete operational thinking. The child is now able to understand classifications and *cause and effect*. At this time the child is also able to take another's point of view, and in games children can take turns and follow rules.

Formal operational thinking is entered at about age *11 years through adolescence*. This is the time of the acquisition of abstract logic. In addition to being able to hypothesize and make deductions, the person can now comprehend probabilities and can now *think about his or her thoughts*.

2.29–2.33

2.29. The answer is **A** (*Synopsis VI*, page 33; *CTP V*, pages 1704–1705).

2.30. The answer is **C** (*Synopsis VI*, page 33; *CTP V*, pages 1704–1705).

2.31. The answer is **D** (*Synopsis VI*, page 33; *CTP V*, pages 1704–1705).

2.32. The answer is **B** (*Synopsis VI*, page 33; *CTP V*, pages 1704–1705).

2.33. The answer is **E** (*Synopsis VI*, page 33; *CTP V*, pages 1704–1705).

Mood or general emotional tone is an internal judgment based on the way children look and behave, as well as on their content of speech. During the first 12 months, mood is highly variable and is intimately related to internal states, such as hunger. Toward the second third of the first year, mood is also related to external social cues. When the child is internally comfortable, a sense of interest and pleasure in the world and in the primary caretakers should prevail. From 3 to 5 years, Freud's oedipal phase and Erikson's psychosocial crisis of initiative versus guilt prevail; thus, the child is capable of experiencing the complex emotions of jealousy and envy, as well as a growing sense of separation and security. At birth, the infant can experience *distress;* at 3 to 4 months, *anger;* at 8 to 9 months, fear and *sadness;* at 12 to 18 months, *shame;* and at 3 to 4 years, *guilt*. Table 2.4 lists the landmarks of emotional development.

2.34–2.38

2.34. The answer is **E** (*Synopsis VI*, pages 31–32; *CTP V*, page 1702).

Table 2.4
Landmarks of Emotional Development

Age	Emotion
Birth	Surprise, distress, disgust, pleasure
6 to 8 weeks	Joy
12 to 16 weeks	Anger
32 to 36 weeks	Fear, sadness
1 to 1½ years	Tenderness, shame
2 years	Pride
3 to 4 years	Guilt
5 to 8 years	Humility, confidence, envy, ingenuity

2.35. **The answer is D** (*Synopsis VI*, pages 31–32; *CTP V*, page 1702).

2.36. **The answer is A** (*Synopsis VI*, pages 31–32; *CTP V*, page 1702).

2.37. **The answer is C** (*Synopsis VI*, pages 31–32; *CTP V*, page 1702).

2.38. **The answer is B** (*Synopsis VI*, pages 31–32; *CTP V*, page 1702).

To understand normal development, one must take a comprehensive approach and have an internal map of the age-expected norms for various aspects of human development. The areas of neuromotor, cognitive, and language milestones have many empirical normative data. The normal child is able to accomplish specific tasks at certain ages. For example, a *cross* can be copied at 4 years, a *square* can be copied at 5 years, and a *triangle* can be copied at 6 years. At 18 months, children can *walk up the stairs* holding someone's hand and, at 2 years, can refer to *themselves by name*. Some children may be able to perform a task at an earlier or later age and still fall within the normal range. Other landmarks of normal behavioral development are listed in Table 2.5.

2.39–2.43

2.39. **The answer is A** (*Synopsis VI*, page 33; *CTP V*, page 1702).

2.40. **The answer is B** (*Synopsis VI*, page 33; *CTP V*, page 1702).

2.41. **The answer is C** (*Synopsis VI*, page 33; *CTP V*, page 1702).

2.42. **The answer is D** (*Synopsis VI*, page 33; *CTP V*, page 1702).

2.43. **The answer is D** (*Synopsis VI*, page 33; *CTP V*, page 1702).

Language development occurs in well-delineated stages. At *birth to 6 months*, the child plays at *making sounds and babbles;* at *7 to 11 months*, the child plays *language games*, such as *pat-a-cake* and *peek-a-boo;* at *12 to 18 months*, the child is *using up to 20 words and understanding up to 150 words;* and from *54 months on*, the child's language is *100 percent intelligible*, and the child is using language to *tell stories and share ideas*. See Table 2.6 for a description of these stages.

2.44–2.47

2.44. **The answer is C** (*Synopsis VI*, page 60; *CTP V*, page 1348).

2.45. **The answer is C** (*Synopsis VI*, page 60; *CTP V*, page 1348).

2.46. **The answer is B** (*Synopsis VI*, page 60; *CTP V*, page 1348).

Table 2.5
Landmarks of Normal Behavioral Development

Age	Motor and Sensory Behavior	Adaptive Behavior	Personal and Social Behavior
Under 4 weeks	Makes alternating crawling movements Moves head laterally when placed in prone position	Responds to sound of rattle and bell Regards moving objects momentarily	Quiets when picked up Impassive face
16 weeks	Symmetrical postures predominate Holds head balanced Head lifted 90 degrees when prone on forearm Visual accommodation	Follows a slowly moving object well Arms activate on sight of dangling object	Spontaneous social smile (exogenous) Aware of strange situations
28 weeks	Sits steadily, leaning forward on hands Bounces actively when placed in standing position	One-hand approach and grasp of toy Bangs and shakes rattle Transfers toys	Takes feet to mouth Pats mirror image Starts to imitate mother's sounds and actions
40 weeks	Sits alone with good coordination Creeps Pulls self to standing position Points with index finger	Matches two objects at midline Attempts to imitate scribble	Separation anxiety manifest when taken away from mother Responds to social play, such as pat-a-cake and peek-a-boo Feeds self cracker and holds own bottle
52 weeks	Walks with one hand held Stands alone briefly	Seeks novelty	Cooperates in dressing

Table adapted from Arnold Gesell, M.D., and Stella Chess, M.D.

Table 2.6
Development of Language

Age and Stage of Development	Mastery of Comprehension	Mastery of Expression
0 to 6 months	Shows startle response to loud or sudden sounds Attempts to localize sounds, turning eyes or head Appears to listen to speakers, may respond with smile Recognizes warning, angry, and friendly voices Responds to hearing own name	Has vocalizations other than crying Has differential cries for hunger and pain Makes vocalizations to show pleasure Plays at making sounds Babbles (repeats a series of sounds)
7 to 11 months *Attending to language stage*	Shows listening selectivity (voluntary control over responses to sounds) Listens to music or singing with interest Recognizes "no," "hot," own name Looks at pictures being named for up to one minute Listens to speech without being distracted by other sounds	Responds to own name with vocalizations Imitates the melody of utterances Uses jargon (own language) Has gestures (shakes head for "no") Has exclamation ("oh-oh") Plays language games (pat-a-cake, peek-a-boo)
12 to 18 months *Single-word stage*	Shows gross discriminations between dissimilar sounds (bell vs. dog vs. horn vs. mother's or father's voice) Understands basic body parts, names of common objects Acquires understanding of some new words each week Can identify simple objects (baby, ball, etc.) from a group of objects or pictures Understands up to 150 words by age 18 months	Uses single words (mean age of first word is 11 months; by age 18 months, child is using up to 20 words) "Talks" to toys, self, or others using long patterns of jargon and occasional words Approximately 25 percent of utterances are intelligible All vowels articulated correctly Initial and final consonants often omitted
55 months on up *True communication stage*	Understands concepts of number, speed, time, space Understands left, right Understands abstract terms Is able to categorize items into semantic classes	Uses language to tell stories, share ideas, and discuss alternatives Increasing use of varied grammar, spontaneous self-correction of grammatical errors Stabilizing of articulation of f,v,s,z,l,r,th, and consonant clusters Speech 100 percent intelligible

Table adapted from Michael Rutter and Lionel Hersov, editors, *Child and Adolescent Psychiatry*. Blackwell Publications, London, 1985, with permission.

2.47.   The answer is B (*Synopsis VI*, page 60; *CTP V*, page 1348).

Although depression as a symptom may occur as a prominent feature of normal bereavement, as well as of a depressive mood disorder, and although both conditions may be precipitated by a loss, some features differentiate grief from depression. The full depressive syndrome may occur in complicated bereavement, although marked preoccupation with *worthlessness*, extended functional impairment, and marked psychomotor retardation are more often observed in a major depression. Sadness, crying, and tension expressed as *psychomotor retardation or agitation* may be seen in both normal grief and depression. Decreased appetite with *weight loss*, decreased libido, and withdrawal may be found in both conditions. The grief-stricken person, however, shows shifts of mood from sadness to a more normal state within a reasonably short time and increasingly finds enjoyment in life as the loss recedes. A key aspect of the distinction between major depression and normal grief is similar to Freud's original distinction between mourning and melancholy; that is, in normal grief a person does not show the marked lowering of self-esteem and the sense of personal badness that may be of delusional proportions in major depression, which may also give rise to *suicide attempts*.

3 ||||

The Brain and Behavior

Neuropsychiatry, the study of psychiatric symptoms associated with neurological conditions and of neurological symptoms associated with psychiatric disorders, requires that the student understand the biology of the brain. By forming an understanding of neuroanatomy, brain imaging, neurochemistry, and neurophysiology, the student can appreciate the biological interface between psychiatry and neurology and can further his or her understanding of the multidimensional aspects of human behavior.

It is possible to divide brain study grossly into neuroanatomy and neurochemistry. This distinction is becoming increasingly unwieldy, however, because neuroanatomists are studying anatomy at molecular (i.e., chemical) levels, and neurochemists are studying the precise localization (i.e., anatomy) of molecules. Nevertheless, the student needs a method of organizing the vast amount of information about the brain, and the division between neuroanatomical and neurochemical is still useful.

To appreciate the current research and theories about mental disorders, the student must have basic information about the major brain areas—cerebral cortex, limbic system, basal ganglia, thalamus, hypothalamus, pituitary, cerebellum, and brain stem. This information should include the anatomical location and the major subdivisions of each area. The student should also know the projections to and from these major areas and the clinical effects of lesions. Distinctions should be drawn between destructive lesions, such as strokes, and excitatory lesions, such as epilepsy. Finally, the student should be able to discuss how various parts of the brain may be involved in the major psychiatric disorders.

It has sometimes been taught that the "higher" brain areas (e.g., the cerebral cortex) were the anatomical localization for "higher" mental functions in humans, but this idea is now considered simplistic. Although all areas of the brain are probably involved in the complex processes that result in thoughts, feelings, and behavior, specific anatomical areas are implicated in major disorders. For example, the frontal lobes of the cerebral cortex, the limbic system, and the basal ganglia are major areas of focus for research into schizophrenia, and the limbic system and the hypothalamus for mood disorder research. The cell bodies for most of the neurons that release biogenic amine neurotransmitters implicated in schizophrenia, mood disorders, and anxiety disorders are located in the brain stem.

Brain imaging has become increasingly sophisticated in the past decade. Imaging techniques can assess both the structure and some aspects of the function of the brain. Brain-imaging techniques such as electroencephalography (EEG), evoked potentials (EPs), polysomnography, computed tomography (CT), and magnetic resonance imaging (MRI) are widely used in clinical settings for diagnostic purposes. Students are encouraged to become knowledgeable in the uses of brain-imaging methods.

Neurochemical research receives its major impetus from the fact that a major modality of modern psychiatry is drug therapy. As most psychiatric drugs act on neurotransmitter receptors in the brain, psychiatrists must understand how neurochemical transmission is accomplished. The student should become completely familiar with the details of neurochemical transmission and of the biogenic amine neurotransmitters and γ-aminobutyric acid (GABA). This information should include the neuroanatomical location of the cell bodies, the major projection tracts, the subtypes of receptors, and the psychoactive drugs that affect each neurotransmitter. A basic knowledge of the differences between peptide neurotransmitters and biogenic amine neurotransmitters is also necessary.

Both the therapeutic and the adverse effects of drugs can be understood in terms of neurochemistry. Many clinicians and researchers are frustrated by the lack of comprehension concerning, for example, how changes in brain chemicals result in changes of mood. Such questions, however, have as much to do with philosophy as with science.

Four frontiers for psychiatry are psychoneuroendocrinology, psychoneuroimmunology, chronobiology, and molecular genetics. It is possible to conceptualize the nervous, endocrine, and immune systems as the three systems in the body that communicate both within themselves and with each other. Chronobiology is the science that describes the regular changes in these systems with time. Neuroendocrinology may eventually explain the mechanisms through which the environment affects brain function—for example, stress acting through the glucocorticoid system. Basic

knowledge of neuroendocrinology includes knowing the major neuroendocrine axes, the nature of the hormonal signals between different levels of the axes, and the clinical symptoms of hypoactivity and hyperactivity of each axis. Neuroimmunology may eventually explain the mechanisms through which psychosomatic disorders, such as asthma and inflammatory bowel disorders, evolve. Societies and journals already exist around such topics as psychoneurocardiology. Finally, many psychiatric disorders seem to have a genetic basis, suggesting that some abnormality of protein structure, function, or regulation almost certainly must be operant and, thus, opening the possibility for definitive diagnosis, treatment, and, perhaps, eradication of mental disorders.

Students should review Chapter 3, "The Brain and Behavior," in *Synopsis VI* and Chapter 1, "Neural Science," in *CTP V* and then test their knowledge of the subject by studying the questions and answers below.

HELPFUL HINTS

The following items, including their structure and function, should be known by the student.

neuroanatomical structures and associated syndromes	CNS location	vasopressin, oxytocin
neurons and glia	neurotransmission	LHRH
cerebral, frontal, temporal, parietal, and occipital lobes; Broca's area; laterality	neuromodulators	melatonin
	neuromessengers, second messengers	pineal gland
epilepsy: complex partial seizures, kindling, anticonvulsant medications, *déjà vu*	neurohormones	estrogen
	receptors	endocrine assessment
	tuning and grading	pituitary challenge
	aplysia experiment	third ventricle enlargement in schizophrenia
aphasia: fluent, receptive, expressive, productive, anomic, thalamic, global	dopaminergic system and associated clinical syndromes; dopamine hypothesis of schizophrenia and mood disorders	psychoneuroimmunology
		neurotoxic virus (AIDS)
amygdala, hippocampus, and limbic system; Papez circuit		neural regulation of immunity
Klüver-Bucy syndrome; Wernicke-Korsakoff's syndrome		β-endorphin
	noradrenergic system and associated clinical syndromes (VMA, MHPG)	stress and T-cell proliferation
		immunoglobulin
basal ganglia and associated clinical syndromes	serotonergic system and associated clinical syndromes (5-HIAA, L-tryptophan)	chronobiology
		ultradian
hypothalamus, pituitary, thalamus		circadian
	cholinergic system and associated clinical syndromes (tardive dyskinesia)	zeitgebers
		phase advance and phase delay
brain-imaging techniques (CT, MRI, EP, PET, CBF)		seasonal affective disorder
	amino acid neurotransmitters (GABA)	genetics
electroencephalography and wave forms		family risk
	peptide neurotransmitters (endorphins)	twin studies (MZ, DZ)
neurochemical and neurophysiological concepts		adoption studies
	psychoendocrinology	genome
	adrenal axis	DNA, tRNA
		RFLPs

QUESTIONS

DIRECTIONS: Each of the questions or incomplete statements below is followed by five suggested responses or completions. Select the *one* that is *best* in each case.

3.1. What is the chemical name of the following structure?

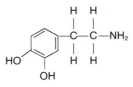

A. Serotonin
B. Acetylcholine
C. γ-Aminobutyric acid (GABA)
D. Dopamine
E. Norepinephrine (NE)

3.2. The corpus striatum of the brain is most closely associated with the highest concentration of
A. norepinephrine (NE)
B. serotonin
C. γ-aminobutyric acid (GABA)
D. dopamine
E. acetylcholine

3.3. Enkephalins are
A. opiatelike peptides
B. tricyclic antidepressants (TCAs)
C. dopamine blocking agents
D. cholinergic agents
E. monoamine oxidase inhibitors (MAOIs)

3.4. The dietary amino acid precursor of serotonin is
A. neurotensin
B. phenylalanine
C. tyramine
D. tryptophan
E. glycine

3.5. Bilateral destruction of the temporal lobes results in
A. psychic blindness
B. hypersexuality
C. hyperphagia
D. docility
E. all the above

DIRECTIONS: For each of the questions or incomplete statements below, *one or more* of the responses or completions given are correct. Choose answer

A. if only *1, 2, and 3* are correct
B. if only *1 and 3* are correct
C. if only *2 and 4* are correct
D. if only *4* is correct
E. if *all* are correct

3.6. The major metabolites of norepinephrine (NE) in the brain are
1. homovanillic acid (HVA)
2. vanillylmandelic acid (VMA)
3. 5-hydroxyindoleacetic acid (5-HIAA)
4. 3-methoxy-4-hydroxyphenylglycol (MHPG)

3.7. The amygdala is
1. located within the temporal lobe
2. part of the limbic system
3. associated with violent behavior
4. a group of neurons

3.8. Monoamine oxidase inhibitors (MAOIs) act by causing synaptic cleft accumulation of
1. norepinephrine (NE)
2. dopamine
3. serotonin
4. acetylcholine

3.9. The neurotransmitter dopamine plays an important role in
1. Parkinson's disease
2. Huntington's chorea
3. schizophrenia
4. Tourette's disorder

3.10. Which of the following are the major brain neurotransmitters?
1. Glycine
2. Norepinephrine (NE)
3. γ-Aminobutyric acid (GABA)
4. Acetylcholine

3.11. The hypothalamus
1. is considered part of the limbic system
2. is involved in appetite and sexual regulation
3. has a major role in the control of biological rhythms and immune system regulation
4. is located in the diencephalon, beneath the thalamus and on either side of the third ventricle

3.12. Syndromes associated with the parietal lobes include
1. Gerstmann syndrome
2. Wernicke's aphasia
3. anosognosia
4. Anton's syndrome

3.13. Neurotransmitters include
1. biogenic amines
2. amino acids
3. peptides
4. catecholamines

DIRECTIONS: Each set of lettered headings below is followed by a list of numbered words or statements. For each numbered word or statement, select the *one* lettered heading that is most closely associated with it. Each lettered heading may be selected once, more than once, or not at all.

Questions 3.14–3.18
A. Klüver-Bucy syndrome
B. Korsakoff's syndrome
C. Parkinson's disease
D. Huntington's chorea
E. Wilson's disease

3.14. Poor short-term memory related to neuropathology in the hippocampal area, including the dentate gyrus

3.15. Atrophy of the caudate nuclei

3.16. Increased copper deposits in the lenticular nuclei

3.17. Bilateral destruction of the amygdala and the temporal lobes

3.18. Destruction of dopaminergic cells in the substantia nigra

Questions 3.19–3.22
A. Frontal lobe
B. Temporal lobe
C. Parietal lobe
D. Occipital lobe
E. Insula

3.19. Disturbed spatial orientation (metamorphopsia)

3.20. Kinesthetic apraxias and astereognosis

3.21. Alexia and agraphia

3.22. Sexual and aggressive behavior

Questions 3.23–3.26
A. Dopamine type-1 (D_1) receptors
B. Dopamine type-2 (D_2) receptors

3.23. Stimulate adenylate cyclase

3.24. Inhibit adenylate cyclase

3.25. Potency of antipsychotics is most clearly correlated with the binding affinity

3.26. Located on presynaptic neurons

Questions 3.27–3.29
A. Supersensitivity
B. Subsensitivity

3.27. Decrease in the number of receptors available for neurotransmitter binding

3.28. Increase in receptor affinity

3.29. Results from a more efficient message translation by the receptor to the neuron

Questions 3.30–3.31
A. Tricyclic antidepressants (TCAs)
B. Monoamine oxidase inhibitors (MAOIs)

3.30. Block reuptake of norepinephrine (NE) and serotonin

3.31. Block degradation of norepinephrine (NE) and serotonin

Questions 3.32–3.36
A. Frontal lobe
B. Superior temporal gyrus
C. Arcuate fasciculus
D. Dominant angular gyrus
E. Left hemisphere

3.32. Conduction aphasia

3.33. Expressive aphasia

3.34. Anomic aphasia

3.35. Receptive aphasia

3.36. Global aphasia

Questions 3.37–3.40
A. Tyrosine hydroxylase
B. Dopamine β-carboxylase
C. Tryptophan hydroxylase
D. Glutamic acid decarboxylase

3.37. Dopamine

3.38. Norepinephrine

3.39. γ-Aminobutyric acid

3.40. Serotonin

ANSWERS

The Brain and Behavior

3.1. The answer is D (*Synopsis VI*, pages 86–87; *CTP V*, page 48).

The illustration is of *dopamine*, the neurotransmitter that is most implicated in the pathophysiology of schizophrenia and movement disorders.

Serotonin, a catecholamine, is also called 5-hydroxytryptamine (5HT). *GABA* is γ-aminobutyric acid, the best studied amino acid neurotransmitter. It has an inhibitory effect on neurotransmission; thus, too little GABA activity may be one basis for anxiety. *Norepinephrine* (NE) is a neurotransmitter that has been implicated in depression. Too little NE results in a depressed mood. *Acetylcholine* is a neurotransmitter that is also implicated in depression. Anticholinergic drugs are used to treat the parkinsonian side effects of antipsychotics.

3.2. The answer is D (*Synopsis VI*, pages 89–94; *CTP V*, pages 42–44).

The corpus striatum is part of the basal ganglia and is the area of the brain with the highest concentration of the neurotransmitter *dopamine*. The corpus striatum is made up of the caudate nucleus, putamen, and globus pallidus, which are large subcortical nuclear masses. Two types of diseases associated with diseases of the corpus striatum are abnormal involuntary movements, known as dyskinesias, and disturbances of muscle tone, such as hypotonia and rigidity. The largest concentration of noradrenergic neurons that contain *norepinephrine* (NE) is the locus ceruleus in the pons. Serotonergic neurons that contain *serotonin* have their cell bodies in the upper pons and midbrain—in particular, the median and dorsal raphe nuclei. The amino acid neurotransmitter *γ-aminobutyric acid (GABA)* is located extensively throughout the brain. *Acetylcholine* is found in cholinergic neurons in the nucleus basalis of Meynert and in the reticular system.

3.3. The answer is A (*Synopsis VI*, page 95; *CTP V*, pages 52–54 and 121).

Enkephalins are *opiatelike peptides* that are found in many parts of the brain and that bind to specific receptor sites. They are opiatelike because they decrease pain perception. They also serve as neurotransmitters.

Cholinergic agents are drugs that cause the liberation of acetylcholine. *Dopamine blocking agents* are drugs, such as the antipsychotic haloperidol (Haldol), that block dopamine receptors on postsynaptic neurons, thus effectively decreasing the functional levels of the neurotransmitter dopamine. Dopamine blockers are most often used to treat psychotic patients whose psychosis is related to a hyperdopaminergic state.

The two major classes of antidepressant drugs are the *monoamine oxidase inhibitors (MAOIs)* and the *tricyclic antidepressants (TCAs)*. MAOIs are a group of agents with widely varying chemical structures that have in common the ability to inhibit monoamine oxidase (MAO). Inhibition of MAO results in a functional increase of the monoamines norepinephrine (NE), dopamine, and serotonin within nerve terminals. When these amines start leaking out into the synaptic cleft, facilitation of the actions of all monoamines occurs. The TCAs are potent inhibitors of the reuptake inactivation mechanism of catecholamine and serotonin neurons. The ability of TCAs to inhibit the reuptake process results in a functional increase of such neurotransmitters as NE and serotonin, leading to the medication's antidepressant activity.

3.4. The answer is D (*Synopsis VI*, page 92; *CTP V*, page 49).

Tryptophan is the dietary amino acid precursor of serotonin. It is hydroxylated by the enzyme tryptophan hydroxylase to form 5-hydroxytryptophan; 5-hydroxytryptophan is decarboxylated to serotonin. Serotonin is destroyed by reuptake into the presynaptic terminal and subsequent metabolism by monoamine oxidase (MAO), which oxidatively deaminates it to 5-hydroxyindoleacetic acid (5-HIAA).

Neurotensin is a neurotransmitter and an amino acid peptide that can lower blood pressure; it acts as an analgesic when injected directly into the brain. *Phenylalanine* is an amino acid in proteins that, when not present in infants, causes mental retardation. *Glycine*, an amino acid, functions as an inhibitory neurotransmitter within the spinal cord.

Tyramine is a sympathomimetic amine that has an action similar to that of epinephrine. It is present in ripe cheese, herring, and other foods. Tyramine-containing substances must be avoided by patients on monoamine oxidase inhibitors (MAOIs), because of the danger of adrenergic potentiation.

3.5. The answer is E (*Synopsis VI*, page 71; *CTP V*, page 148).

Bilateral temporal lobe destruction, which includes ablation of the amygdaloid complex and destruction of major sections of the hippocampus, produces the Klüver-Bucy syndrome. The syndrome includes the following changes in behavior: (1) *psychic blindness*, in which vision is physically intact but the patient has an inability to discriminate between objects in a meaningful fashion, such as food and a menacing animal (sometimes called hypermetamorphosis), and loss of recognition of people also occurs; (2) oral hyperactivity, in which compulsive licking, biting, and examination of all objects by the mouth occurs; (3) *docility* and placidity, in which the patient shows no evidence of fear or anger reactions; (4) altered sexual behavior, such as *hypersexuality*, which is manifest without regard to gender or species of partner; and (5) altered dietary habits, in which *hyperphagia* or bulimia nervosa is seen. Memory defects also can occur. The Klüver-Bucy syndrome is rare in humans but has been produced experimentally in monkeys.

3.6. The answer is C (2, 4) (*Synopsis VI*, pages 89–92; *CTP V*, pages 48–49 and 869–870).

An alcohol derivative called *3-methoxy-4-hydroxyphenylglycol (MHPG)* is the major metabolite of norepinephrine (NE) in the brain. It is formed from the action of monoamine oxidase (MAO) on NE. MHPG can diffuse from the brain to the general circulation and is excreted in the urine. Measurement of urinary MHPG is a valuable tool in estimating functional NE levels. Low urinary MHPG excretion is believed to represent decreased central NE activity, a state associated with clinical depression; monitoring urinary MHPG may have value in predicting a patient's response to antidepressant drugs.

The other metabolite of NE is *vanillylmandelic acid (VMA)*. This metabolite is produced by using two enzymes, MAO and catechol-O-methyltransferase (COMT). This product of NE breakdown leaves the cerebrospinal fluid (CSF) and, like MHPG, is excreted in the urine. VMA levels are measured as an index of sympathetic nervous function and to diagnose norepinephrine- or epinephrine-producing tumors, such as pheochromocytoma and neuroblastoma.

Homovanillic acid (HVA) is one of three breakdown products of dopamine. Other products in smaller quantities are 3,4-dihydroxyphenylacetic acid (DOPAC) and VMA.

Serotonin is destroyed by MAO, which oxidatively deanimates it to the aldehyde, just as MAO does with the catecholamines. The aldehyde formed from serotonin is primarily oxidized to *5-hydroxyindoleacetic acid (5-HIAA)*. Some recent studies have focused on decreased levels of CSF 5-HIAA as a possible chemical indicator of suicide potential.

3.7. The answer is E (all) (*Synopsis VI*, pages 70–71; *CTP V*, pages 31–33).

The amygdala is a *group of neurons located within the temporal lobe*. It is a major component of the *limbic system*, the part of the brain most closely associated with emotional experience, along with the hippocampus, hypothalamus, anterior thalamus, cingulate gyrus, and basal ganglia. The amygdala is a small, discrete nuclear mass located at the inferior end of the caudate nucleus. It projects directly to the hypothalamus, and interruption of these connections gives rise to rage reactions. The amygdala has been most closely associated with *violent behavior*, shown by studies of animals that correlate docility with amygdalar lesions and rage reactions with amygdalar stimulation. The hippocampus is thought to be involved in memory and motivation; see Figure 3.1.

3.8. The answer is A (1, 2, 3) (*Synopsis VI*, pages 89–91; *CTP V*, page 1651).

Antidepressant drugs, in general, are thought to act by facilitating the synaptic effects of the monoamines. Monoamine oxidase inhibitors (MAOIs), in particular, act by inhibiting the degradative enzyme MAO, thus leading to an increase within the synaptic cleft of the biogenic amines normally degraded by MAO. The biogenic amines that accumulate include the catecholamines, such as *norepinephrine* (NE) and *dopamine*, and the indoles, such as *serotonin*.

Acetylcholine is inactivated through hydrolysis by the enzyme acetylcholinesterase. MAOIs do not lead to an accumulation of acetylcholine.

Dopamine, decarboxylated dopa, is a catecholamine neurotransmitter, which is an intermediate compound in tyrosine metabolism and the precursor of NE and epinephrine. It is localized in the basal ganglia (caudate and lentiform nuclei). The dopamine hypothesis of schizophrenia involves the idea that a hyperdopaminergic state leads to psychotic, schizophrenic symptoms.

Norepinephrine (NE), noradrenaline, is a catecholamine neurotransmitter substance liberated by adrenergic postganglionic neurons of the sympathetic nervous system. It is the precursor of epinephrine, possesses the excitatory action of epinephrine, and is present in the adrenal medulla. It is also a major central nervous system (CNS) neurotransmitter. Diminished functional levels of NE are associated with clinical depression, and increased functional levels have been associated with manic states.

Serotonin is 5-hydroxytryptamine (5HT), an endogenous indolamine synthesized from dietary tryptophan and found in the gastrointestinal tract, the platelets, and the CNS. Various functions have been attributed to serotonin, but its chief interest for psychiatry lies in the evidence that serotonin is normally involved as a synaptic agent in the regulation of centers in the brain concerned with wakefulness,

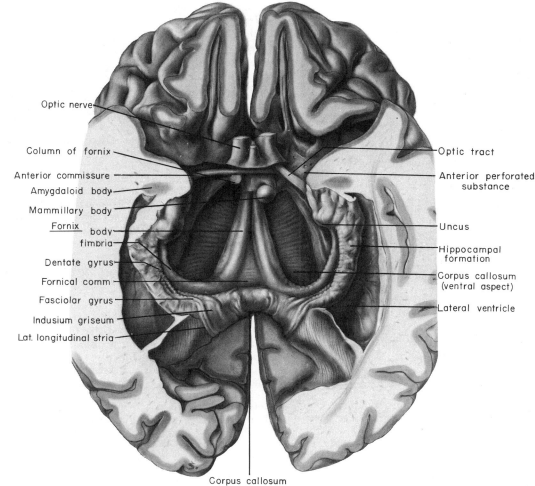

Optic nerve

Column of fornix

Anterior commissure
Amygdaloid body
Mammillary body
Fornix body
fimbria
Dentate gyrus
Fornical comm
Fasciolar gyrus
Indusium griseum
Lat. longitudinal stria

Optic tract

Anterior perforated
substance

Uncus
Hippocampal
formation
Corpus callosum
(ventral aspect)
Lateral ventricle

Corpus callosum
(splenium)

Figure 3.1. Dissection of the inferior surface of the brain showing the configuration of the fornix, the hippocampal formation, the dentate gyrus, and related structures. (Reproduced with permission from F. A. Mettler: *Neuroanatomy*, ed 2. Mosby, St. Louis, 1948.) (From Carpenter and Sutin: *Human Neuroanatomy*. Williams & Wilkins, Baltimore, 1983.)

temperature, blood pressure, and various other autonomic functions. Dysfunction in central serotonergic systems has been proposed as a cause or factor in various mental disorders, including schizophrenia and the mood disorders.

Acetylcholine is believed to be the sole mediator at autonomic synapses and in the transmission of the nerve impulse from motor nerve to skeletal muscle.

3.9. The answer is E (all) (*Synopsis VI*, pages 72–73 and 90; *CTP V*, pages 136, 174, 719–720, and 1870).

The neurotransmitter dopamine is implicated in *Parkinson's disease, Huntington's chorea, Tourette's disorder*, and *schizophrenia*. Schizophrenia is a hyperdopaminergic psychotic disorder. Biological

treatment involves the use of dopamine receptor blockers, such as the butyrophenone haloperidol (Haldol) and the phenothiazine chlorpromazine (Thorazine). Schizophrenia is generally defined as a large group of disorders characterized by disorganization from a previous level of functioning, the presence of some psychotic features during the active illness phase, evidence of chronicity, and disturbances of multiple psychological processes.

Parkinson's disease is a neurological syndrome usually resulting from arteriosclerotic changes in the basal ganglia and is characterized by rhythmical muscular tremors, rigidity of movement, shuffling gait, drooped posture, and a masklike facies. It is a disorder of middle or late life, typically with a gradual progression and a prolonged course. Its cause is unknown, although several discrete dopamine pathways (primarily nigrostriatal) are known to degenerate. A parkinsonian syndrome may develop during the course of therapy with antipsychotic phenothiazine or butyrophenone drugs as a result of the functional decrease in dopamine. Restoration of the depleted dopamine by treatment with its amino acid precursor dihydroxy-L-phenylalanine (levodopa or L-dopa) greatly alleviates the symptoms of Parkinson's disease.

Huntington's chorea is a neurological disease in which there is a heightened response of striatal receptors to dopamine, with a diminished level of acetylcholine. The brain reveals atrophy of certain basal ganglia structures, including the caudate and the putamen. A disease that affects cognitive, emotional, and motor functioning, it is inherited as an autosomal dominant trait, thus affecting 50 percent of every generation.

Tourette's disorder is a stereotyped movement disorder of childhood that begins between ages 2 and 15. It is characterized by facial and vocal tics, including coprolalia (the involuntary yelling of obscenities) in more than half the cases. Marked relief of symptoms has been obtained in many cases with high doses of the dopamine blocker haloperidol, leading researchers to believe that a hyperdopaminergic state is involved in the pathogenesis.

3.10. The answer is B (1, 3) (*Synopsis VI*, page 93; *CTP V*, pages 50–51).

The major neurotransmitters in the brain are *glycine* and *γ-aminobutyric acid (GABA)*. In various brain regions, GABA probably accounts for transmission at between 60 and 70 percent of the synapses. GABA inhibits the firing of neurons and is, therefore, a major inhibitory transmitter. In the spinal cord and the brain stem, the amino acid glycine, in addition to its other metabolic functions, acts as an inhibitory transmitter. Anxiolytics or benzodiazepines, such as diazepam (Valium), act by enhancing the inhibitory neurotransmitters. *Norepinephrine* (NE) and *acetylcholine* account for only a small percentage of synaptic transmissions in the brain.

3.11. The answer is E (all) (*Synopsis VI*, pages 73–75; *CTP V*, pages 5, 9, and 15–16).

The hypothalamus is located in the central and medial region of the *diencephalon* forming the walls of the central half of the third ventricle, delineated from the thalamus by the hypothalamic sulcus. It has afferent and efferent connections with the *limbic system*. The hypothalamus is prominently involved in the functions of the autonomic nervous system (ANS) and in endocrine regulation. It also appears to play a role in the neural mechanism underlying mood and motivational states. It is involved in *appetite* and *sexual regulation* and in the control of *biological rhythms* and immune system regulation.

3.12. The answer is B (1, 3) (*Synopsis VI*, pages 67–68; *CTP V*, pages 147–148, 461, and 606).

The parietal lobes contain the associational cortices for visual, tactile, and auditory input and are involved in the intellectual processing of sensory information. The left parietal lobe has a preferential role in verbal processing, whereas the right lobe has a major role in visuospatial processing. *Gerstmann syndrome*, a symptom complex described by the American neurologist Joseph Gerstmann in 1940, is associated with lesions of the dominant parietal lobe. Presence of the Gerstmann syndrome implies some parietal lobe pathology, usually in the neighborhood of the angular gyrus. Symptoms include agraphia, which is the inability to write; acalculia, which is the inability to perform arithmetic operations; right-left disorientation; and finger agnosia, which is the inability to recognize fingers on testing. A syndrome associated with nondominant parietal lesions includes *anosognosia*, the denial of illness, including complete neglect of the left side of the body. There is a tendency to suppress all knowledge of the disability.

Anton's syndrome is associated with the occipital lobes and with bilateral occlusion of the posterior cerebral arteries, resulting in cortical blindness and denial of blindness. *Wernicke's aphasia* occurs as the result of lesions in Wernicke's area of the temporal lobe and is associated with fluent or receptive aphasias in which there is impaired comprehension, word deafness, and anomia, the disturbed capacity to name objects. The power of using speech is retained but is usually meaningless and confined to parrotlike utterances.

3.13. The answer is E (all) (*Synopsis VI*, page 86; *CTP V*, pages 48–54).

There are three classes of neurotransmitters, which are the chemical messages that convey electrical impulses from one neuron to another. They are the *biogenic amines, amino acids*, and *peptides*. The biogenic amines (or monoamines) are subdivided into the *catecholamines* (dopamine, norepinephrine [NE], and epinephrine), the indoles (tryptophan and serotonin), a quaternary amine (acetylcholine), and an ethylamine (histamine). The biogenic amines account for 5 to 10 percent of synapses, although they may have particular importance in the areas of the brain concerned with emotional behavior. The amino acid neurotransmitters, in particular the inhibitory γ-aminobutyric acid (GABA) and glycine, may account for up to 60 percent of the synapses. A major recent development involves the realization that numerous peptides may also be neurotransmitters. The most studied peptide transmitters are the opiatelike peptides, the enkephalins. Peptide neurotransmitters, also called neuroactive peptides, coexist in axon terminals with the other neurotransmitters. The major difference between peptide neurotransmitters and other neurotransmitters is in their synthesis.

Biogenic amines and amino acids are made in the nerve terminals by the actions of enzymes on available substances; peptides are made in the neuronal cell body through the transcription or translation of genetic message codes on deoxyribonucleic acid (DNA) and are presumably inactivated by enzymatic hydrolysis.

3.14–3.18

3.14. The answer is B (*Synopsis VI*, pages 71–72; *CTP V*, pages 693–694).

3.15. The answer is D (*Synopsis VI*, page 73; *CTP V*, pages 208–209).

3.16. The answer is E (*Synopsis VI*, page 73; *CTP V*, page 211).

3.17. The answer is A (*Synopsis VI*, page 71; *CTP V*, page 148).

3.18. The answer is C (*Synopsis VI*, pages 72–73; *CTP V*, page 211).

Various anatomical structures of the limbic system are associated with emotions, sexual drives, eating behavior, rage, violence, memory, and motivation. Various anatomical structures of the basal ganglia are associated with movement control and such cerebral disorders as psychosis, depression, and dementia.

Korsakoff's syndrome, termed alcohol amnestic disorder in DSM-III-R, is an amnestic syndrome resulting from thiamine deficiency associated with alcoholism. In patients with Wernicke-Korsakoff's syndrome, severe anterograde amnesia occurs, with inability to retain short-term memory, even though immediate memory is unimpaired and remote memory is only mildly impaired. The amnesia may be related to pathology in the hippocampal area, including the dendate gyrus. *Huntington's chorea* is a rare hereditary disorder of the basal ganglia, characterized by atrophy of the caudate nucleus. The disorder is characterized by a deteriorating course of chorea, dementia, depression, and psychosis. *Wilson's disease*, or hepatolenticular degeneration, is an autosomal recessive disorder of copper metabolism characterized by degeneration of the corpus striatum, especially the putamen, and liver cirrhosis. There is decreased serum ceruloplasm and increased urinary excretion of copper and amino acids, with increased cooper deposits in the lenticular nuclei. The lenticular nuclei consist of the putamen, the caudate nucleus, and the globus pallidus. *Klüver-Bucy syndrome* is caused by bilateral destruction of the amygdala and the temporal lobes; it presents with hypersexuality, pica, and docility. *Parkinson's disease* is characterized by degeneration of cells and tracts of the striate bodies and substantia nigra, perhaps secondary to disturbed metabolism of brain amines. Both dopamine and serotonin are decreased in the brain and the urine, related possibly to a deficiency in the enzyme dopadecarboxylase and to a destruction of dopaminergic cells. The characteristic symptoms are cogwheel rigidity, spontaneous tremor, masklike facies, and propulsive gait, among others.

3.19–3.22

3.19. The answer is D (*Synopsis VI*, page 65; *CTP V*, pages 147–150 and 606).

3.20. The answer is C (*Synopsis VI*, pages 65 and 70; *CTP V*, pages 147–150 and 606).

3.21. The answer is C (*Synopsis VI*, pages 65 and 70; *CTP V*, pages 147–150 and 606).

3.22. The answer is B (*Synopsis VI*, page 65; *CTP V*, pages 147–150 and 606).

The cerebral cortex is divided anatomically into four lobes—frontal, temporal, parietal, and occipital. The insula is an oval region of the cerebral cortex lateral to the lenticular nucleus, buried in the depth of the sylvan fissure, which can be seen when the temporal and frontal lobes are separated. It is considered a fifth lobe of the brain by some workers (see Figure 3.2). Cortical injury often leads to major behavioral and psychological symptoms.

Metamorphopsia or disturbed spatial orientation is a condition in which objects appear distorted in various ways. Dysfunctions of the occipital lobe lead to the disturbance. *Kinesthetic apraxias* are disorders of voluntary movement, consisting of an incapacity to execute purposeful movements, although muscular power, sensibility, and coordination are retained. *Astereognosis* is the loss of the ability to judge the form of an object by touch. Apraxias and astereognosis are associated with dysfunctions of the parietal lobe. *Alexia* is the loss of the ability to grasp the meaning of written words; *agraphia* is the loss of the ability to write. Both alexia and agraphia are also associated with dysfunctions of the parietal lobe. Frontal lobe syndrome is associated with lesions of the prefrontal and frontobasilar cortex of the brain, and clinical features are most striking when the disease is bilateral. This syndrome is associated with changes in personality, which can include inappropriate or uninhibited behavior. The temporal lobe includes a heterogeneous array of brain structures, in particular the hippocampus, the amygdala, and the gyrus fornicatus. These structures have been associated with sexual and aggressive behavior.

See Table 3.1 for a more complete description of the functions and potential dysfunctions of each lobe.

3.23–3.26

3.23. The answer is A (*Synopsis VI*, page 89; *CTP V*, pages 50 and 1611).

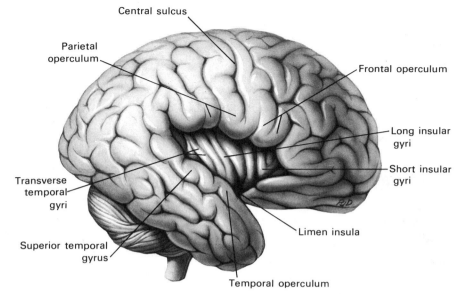

Figure 3.2. View of the right cerebral hemisphere with the banks of the lateral sulcus drawn apart to expose the insula.

Table 3.1
Major Behavioral and Psychological Symptoms of Cortical Injury

Lobe	Functions	Dysfunctions*
Frontal	Reciprocally connected with motor, sensory, and emotional brain areas Controls contralateral movement Produces speech (dominant hemisphere) Critical to personality, abstract thinking, memory, concentration, judgment, and other higher mental functions	Frontal lobe syndrome that may include *inappropriate or uninhibited behavior*, irritability and labile affect, depression and flat affect, lack of motivation, difficulty with attention, memory, and other cognitive deficits *Peculiar facetious sense of humor (witzelsucht)* Aphasia (dominant hemisphere) Ipsilateral motor abnormalities
Temporal	Memory (especially hippocampus) Sexual and aggressive behavior Comprehension of language Interpretation of gustatory and olfactory sensations Major component of limbic system	Memory impairment (bilateral) Language comprehension Control of *sexual and aggressive* drives Fluent aphasia (dominant hemisphere) Klüver-Bucy syndrome

Parietal	Receives and identifies sensory information from tactile receptors
	Processes visual and auditory sensations
	Praxes
		Dominant:
		    Alexia, agraphia, anomia, idiokinetic and kinesthetic apraxias, dyscalculia, right-left disorientation, *astereognosis*
		Nondominant:
		    Impaired spatial abilities, denial of illness (anosognosia), inability to recognize body parts (autotopagnosia), dressing, constructional, and *kinesthetic apraxias*, astereognosis, left spatial neglect

Occipital	Interpretation of visual images Visual memory	*Disturbed spatial orientation* (metamorphopsia) Visual illusions Visual hallucinations Blindness Symptoms may simulate hysteria

*The actual dysfunction is related to the specific area of the lobe that is injured.

3.24. The answer is B (*Synopsis VI*, page 89; *CTP V*, pages 50 and 1611).

3.25. The answer is B (*Synopsis VI*, page 89; *CTP V*, pages 50 and 1611).

3.26. The answer is B (*Synopsis VI*, page 89; *CTP V*, pages 50 and 1611).

Proteins in the neuronal cell membrane that are in part exposed to the extracellular fluid, both presynaptically and postsynaptically, and specifically recognize neurotransmitters are called receptors. Two receptors are linked to the functioning of adenylate cyclase; one is excitatory, and the other is inhibitory.

Receptors that recognize the neurotransmitter dopamine are divided into dopamine type-1 (D_1) and dopamine type-2 (D_2) receptors. The first biochemical means of examining dopamine receptors derives from the observation that dopamine selectively increases cyclic adenosine monophosphate (cAMP) formation by stimulating its biosynthetic enzyme adenylate cyclase in dopamine-rich parts of the brain. The dopamine-sensitive adenylate cyclase is blocked by phenothiazines in proportion to their clinical potencies but is affected only weakly by butyrophenones. Because of this finding, D_1 receptors that are linked to adenylate cyclase are not the receptors through which antipsychotics work. D_2 receptors, which are physically distinct from D_1 receptors, are competed for by antipsychotics in proportion to clinical potency and, thus, are felt to be the receptors blocked by antipsychotics.

D_1 receptors *stimulate* adenylate cyclase; D_2 receptors *inhibit* adenylate cyclase. D_1 and D_2 receptors are both located *postsynaptically*, whereas only D_2 receptors are also found *presynaptically*. The clinical potency of antipsychotics is most closely correlated with their *binding affinity* to D_2 receptors.

3.27–3.29

3.27. The answer is B (*Synopsis VI*, page 87; *CTP V*, page 3).

3.28. The answer is A (*Synopsis VI*, page 87; *CTP V*, page 3).

3.29. The answer is A (*Synopsis VI*, page 87; *CTP V*, page 3).

Supersensitivity and subsensitivity are concepts applied to receptors. An *increase in receptor affinity* is supersensitivity and results from a *more efficient message translation* by the receptor to the neuron. Subsensitivity is characterized by a *decrease* in the number of receptors available for neurotransmitter binding.

Receptors specifically recognize neurotransmitters, and they may be either postsynaptic or presynaptic. Receptors may, at different times, become supersensitive or subsensitive. The concepts of supersensitivity and subsensitivity imply that specific neuronal receptors respond in an increased or decreased way to an unchanging amount of neurotransmitter. The increase or decrease in response could occur as a result of several different changes in receptors. For example, the actual number of receptors may increase or decrease (perhaps as a compensatory response); the affinity of the receptor for a neurotransmitter could increase or decrease; the mechanism by which the receptor translates its message into the neuron could be more or less efficient. All these receptor changes indicate the degree of plasticity inherent in neuronal receptor functioning.

3.30–3.31

3.30. The answer is A (*Synopsis VI*, page 91; *CTP V*, page 71).

3.31. The answer is B (*Synopsis VI*, page 91; *CTP V*, page 71).

Tricyclic antidepressants (TCAs) and monoamine oxidase inhibitors (MAOIs) are used to treat the clinical symptoms of depression. Both act functionally to increase the concentration of biogenic amines (e.g., norepinephrine [NE] and serotonin) available in the synaptic cleft, and, thus, both affect the noradrenergic system. Once in the synaptic cleft, NE interacts with noradrenergic receptors. The two classes of noradrenergic receptors are α and β, each of which has two subtypes, α_1 and α_2 and β_1 and β_2; α_1 stands for postsynaptic receptors, and α_2 stands primarily for presynaptic receptors; β_1 and β_2 receptors are located primarily postsynaptically but may also be located presynaptically. TCAs increase functional levels of biogenic amines by *blocking reuptake of NE and serotonin*, whereas MAOIs acutely *block the degradation of NE and serotonin* by inhibiting the metabolic enzyme MAO. Acutely, both antidepressants block postsynaptic α_1 receptors; this causes sedation and postural hypotension. Neither TCAs nor MAOIs stimulate presynaptic dopamine type-2 (D_2) receptors; α_2 receptors are selectively stimulated by alpha agonists, such as the drug clonidine (Catapres). Clonidine is an antihypertensive agent with central and peripheral actions, but it has also been used with partial success in a variety of neuropsychiatric disorders, including opiate withdrawal. Clonidine should not be confused with clonazepam (Klonopin), which is a benzodiazepine derivative.

3.32–3.36

3.32. The answer is C (*Synopsis VI*, pages 68–69; *CTP V*, pages 146–148).

3.33. The answer is A (*Synopsis VI*, page 68; *CTP V*, pages 146–148).

Table 3.2
Aphasias

Type	Fluency	Comprehension	Repetition	Naming
Broca's	No[a]	Yes[b]	No	No
Wernicke's	Yes	No	No	No
Conduction	Yes	Yes	No	No
Motor transcortical	No	Yes	Yes	No
Sensory transcortical	Yes	No	Yes	No
Mixed transcortical	No	No	Yes	No
Global	No	No	No	No
Anomic	Yes	Yes	Yes	No
Thalamic	Yes	Variable	Yes	No

[a]No = Impaired.
[b]Yes = Relatively spared.

3.34. **The answer is D** (*Synopsis VI*, pages 69–70; *CTP V*, pages 146–148).

3.35. **The answer is B** (*Synopsis VI*, page 68; *CTP V*, pages 146–148).

3.36. **The answer is E** (*Synopsis VI*, page 69; *CTP V*, pages 146–148).

An aphasia is an acquired disorder of language that is not due to a muscular dysfunction. Aphasias may affect comprehension, expression, word choice, and syntax.

Lesions of the arcuate fasciculus result in a *conduction aphasia*. This lesion disconnects the center of language production from the center of language comprehension. Although comprehension and speech production are not severely impaired, the patient is unable to repeat phrases.

Expressive aphasia is due to a lesion in Brodmann's area 44 of the frontal lobe. It is also called Broca's aphasia, anterior aphasia, and motor aphasia. The patient comprehends others but can produce only telegraphic, agrammatical speech. Frequently, patients with expressive aphasia experience depression.

A lesion in the dominant angular gyrus causes an isolated defect in naming, an *anomic aphasia*. Speech is characterized by frequent pauses as the patient searches for words. The patient frequently uses vague words, such as "it" and "thing."

Receptive aphasia—also called Wernicke's aphasia, posterior aphasia, and fluent aphasia—is caused by a lesion in Wernicke's area in the superior temporal gyrus (Brodmann's area 22). Patients with this lesion produce fluent, incoherent speech. The patient is unable to comprehend any language. Wernicke's aphasia may be misdiagnosed as a thought disorder if no other neurological symptoms are present. The psychotic patient can almost always comprehend spoken and written language and can repeat phrases; the aphasic patient has lost these abilities.

Infarction of the entire region of the left hemisphere served by the middle cerebral artery results in *global aphasia*. Virtually all language function is lost, although some patients may still say a few simple phrases, such as "good-bye" and "thank you." These patients almost always have a right hemiparesis and a hemisensory defect.

See Table 3.2 for more information about aphasias.

3.37–3.40

3.37. **The answer is A** (*Synopsis VI*, page 89; *CTP V*, page 49).

3.38. **The answer is B** (*Synopsis VI*, page 91; *CTP V*, page 48).

3.39. **The answer is D** (*Synopsis VI*, page 94; *CTP V*, pages 50–51).

3.40. **The answer is C** (*Synopsis VI*, page 92; *CTP V*, page 49).

Tyrosine hydroxylase is the rate-limiting enzyme for the synthesis of *dopamine*. It is under regulatory control by protein kinases. Tyrosine is converted to 3,4-dihydroxyphenylalanine (DOPA) by this enzyme. DOPA is converted to dopamine by an aromatic amino acid decarboxylase. The noradrenergic terminal uses the same enzymes as the dopaminergic neuron to make dopamine. The noradrenergic neuron also contains dopamine β-carboxylase, which converts dopamine into *norepinephrine*.

The inhibitory amino acid neurotransmitter γ-*aminobutyric acid* (GABA) is synthesized in the GABA-ergic synapse by the enzyme glutamic acid decarboxylase.

To form *serotonin*, also called 5-hydroxytryptamine, tryptophan hydroxylase and an amino acid decarboxylase convert tryptophan.

Contributions
of the Psychosocial Sciences
to Human Behavior

A psychological and social understanding of patients is critical to a full appreciation of human behavior. Data derived from the psychological sciences are crucial toward attaining that end, and much research is being conducted in such areas as cognition, learning, attachment, bonding, epidemiology, and ethology. The student is more likely to read about research in the biological aspects of behavior to the exclusion of research in the psychological sciences, yet perception, cognition, attachment, and learning are clearly psychological and intellectual phenomena affected in all emotional disorders.

Jean Piaget formulated a comprehensive theory of cognitive development that is essential to the understanding of how children learn and how defects in that learning process can contribute to emotional problems later in life.

Attachment theory, developed by John Bowlby, has direct application to the understanding of child-rearing practices, adult affectional ties, and personality disorders.

One of the fastest growing fields in psychiatry, behavioral therapy, is based on the principles of learning theory, and the student should be aware of the tenets of classical and operant conditioning. Learning theory has also been enhanced by neurophysiological advances, which postulate that learning produces changes in the structure and the function of nerve cells.

Aggression is a major problem not only for individuals but for society. The student should be aware of the biological, social, and environmental determinants of aggression. The prevention, prediction, and control of aggression are of major concern to psychiatrists.

Ethology, the study of animal behavior, has had a major effect on the understanding of human behavior. Animal models of psychopathology have helped psychiatrists understand a number of psychiatric disorders, especially depression, which can be induced in primates, as demonstrated by Harry Harlow.

Like ethology, anthropology sheds light on the understanding of human behavior, as the study of culture includes such diverse areas as customs, beliefs, manners, and language. The psychiatrist attempts to understand the person within the context of the person's culture.

In addition, the study of the epidemiology of mental illness helps define and evaluate ways to prevent and control disease. Epidemiologists rely on a variety of assessment instruments to obtain information, and these instruments, to be effective, must be both reliable and valid. The National Institute of Mental Health Epidemiologic Catchment Area program (NIMH ECA) is a federally funded prospective survey being carried out to determine the prevalence and the course of mental disorders in this country.

This chapter also covers community psychiatry and preventive psychiatry, aspects of the field that deal with organized programs for the promotion of mental health and the treatment of mental illness. With regard to the socioeconomics of health care in all medicine, the student needs to be aware of the availability of health care delivery systems and of the major health problems that are the focus of both government and commercial insurance programs.

This broad range of material relevant to human behavior and clinical psychiatry is extremely complex. At times, it may appear to be imprecise; however, findings in this area continue to be translated into knowledge that facilitates theoretical and therapeutic progress in psychiatry.

The reader should refer to Chapter 4, "Contributions of the Psychosocial Sciences to

Human Behavior," in *Synopsis VI* and to Chapter 3, "Contributions of the Psychological Sciences," Chapter 4, "Contributions of the Sociocultural Sciences," Chapter 5, "Quantitative and Experimental Methods in Psychiatry," and Chapter 47, "Community Psychiatry," and the sections on stress in *CTP V*. Studying the questions and answers below will help students assess their knowledge of these subjects.

HELPFUL HINTS

The student should know the following terms, theoreticians, and concepts.

Jean Piaget
genetic epistemology
epigenesis
adaptation
assimilation
accommodation
organization
sensorimotor stage
preoperational stage
concrete operations
formal operations
scheme
object permanence
symbolization
egocentric
phenomenalistic causality
syllogistic reasoning
abstract thinking
John Bowlby
attachment
monotropic
bonding
preattachment stage
René Spitz
hospitalism
anaclitic depression
protest-despair-detachment
imprinting
Mary Ainsworth
learning theory
operant and classical conditioning
Ivan Pavlov
extinction
John B. Watson
B. F. Skinner
primary and secondary reward
    conditioning
escape and avoidance conditioning
respondent behavior
operant behavior
positive and negative
    reinforcement
fixed and variable ratios
punishment

aversive stimuli
Joseph Wolpe
reciprocal inhibition
anxiety hierarchy
systematic desensitization
frustration-aggression hypothesis
tension-reduction theory
learned helplessness
cognitive triad
social learning
reciprocal determinism
Eric Kandel
set
motivation
cognitive dissonance
aggression
Konrad Lorenz
catharsis
ethology
Nickolaas Tinbergen
H. S. Liddell
experimental neurosis
behavior disorders
social isolation and separation
Harry Harlow
contact comfort
surrogate mother
therapist monkeys
sensory deprivation
Ruth Benedict
Margaret Mead
Alexander Leighton
family types, studies
roles of women
national character
acculturation
therapeutic community
illness behavior
culture-bound syndromes
epidemiology
normative
frequency
prevalence
incidence

deviation, significance
lifetime expectancy
variation, average
risk factors
cash registers
indirect surveys
reliability
validity
Type I and Type II errors
bias
double-blind method
use of controls
randomization
basic study design
Faris and Dunham
drift hypothesis
segregation hypothesis
social class and mental disorders
social causation and selection
    theory
Monroe County Study
Midtown Manhattan Study
New Haven Study
Hollingshead and Redlich
Stirling County Study
NIMH ECA
DIS
Holmes and Rahe
vulnerability theory
cross-cultural studies and
    syndromes: amok, latah windigo,
    plibokto, curandero, esperitismo,
    voodoo
Hans Selye
CMHC
primary, secondary, and tertiary
    prevention
deinstitutionalization
hospitals: beds, admissions, length
    of stay
mortality trends
insurance
health care providers

QUESTIONS

DIRECTIONS: Each of the questions or incomplete statements below is followed by five suggested responses or completions. Select the *one* that is *best* in each case.

4.1. The development of object permanence is associated with the
A. latency stage
B. sensorimotor stage
C. preattachment stage
D. stage of concrete operations
E. stage of formal operations

4.2. The concept of operant (instrumental) conditioning is attributed to
A. Ivan Pavlov
B. Clark L. Hull
C. Joseph Wolpe
D. B. F. Skinner
E. Edward L. Thorndike

4.3. According to T. H. Holmes and R. H. Rahe, which one of the following life events causes the greatest stress?
A. Death of a spouse
B. Divorce
C. Marital separation from mate
D. Detention in jail or other institution
E. Death of a close family member

4.4. The intrinsic rule of medical ethics—beneficence—refers to the concept of
A. benefits outweighing costs
B. doing good and avoiding harm
C. respect for persons
D. fair distribution of psychiatric services
E. what is right or wrong

4.5. The drive theory of aggression is associated with
A. Sigmund Freud
B. Konrad Lorenz
C. Mary Ainsworth
D. John Dollard
E. Nikolaas Tinbergen

4.6. Which of the following statements is *not* true?
A. Life-style accounts for about 70 percent of all illness in the United States
B. Lung cancer is the primary cause of cancer death in women between the ages of 55 and 70

C. Regular physical activity can reduce stress
D. The number of adults exercising daily has risen over the past two decades
E. More than half of all school-age children exercise daily

4.7. Hospitals use approximately what percentage of health care costs in the United States?
A. 10 percent
B. 20 percent
C. 30 percent
D. 40 percent
E. 50 percent

4.8. The approximate death rate across all age groups in the United States in 1989, expressed as deaths per 100,000, was
A. less than 100
B. 550
C. 850
D. 1,000
E. more than 1,500

4.9. The most common cause of death among adolescents and young adults (ages 15 to 24) is
A. suicide
B. homicide
C. accidents
D. cancer
E. pneumonia

4.10. The average life expectancy in the United States is approximately
A. 65 years
B. 70 years
C. 75 years
D. 80 years
E. 85 years

4.11. Primary prevention programs
A. attempt to eliminate causative factors
B. detect disease early
C. attempt to rehabilitate patients
D. treat long-term complications of the disorder
E. do none of the above

DIRECTIONS: For each of the questions or incomplete statements below, *one or more* of the numbered responses or completions are correct. Choose answer

A. if only *1, 2, and 3* are correct
B. if only *1 and 3* are correct
C. if only *2 and 4* are correct
D. if only *4* is correct
E. if *all* are correct

4.12. Children in Jean Piaget's stage of preoperational thought characteristically display
1. intuitive thinking
2. egocentric thinking
3. magical thinking
4. animistic thinking

4.13. Attachment to a mothering figure
1. is an instinctive behavior pattern
2. depends on the intensity and the quality of the time spent together
3. develops during the first year of life
4. is a reciprocal affectionate relationship

4.14. Which of the following is associated with the development of object permanence?
1. Looking for a toy that has been hidden
2. The process of symbolization
3. Knowing that an object exists even though it is not present to the senses
4. The final stage of separation-individuation

4.15. Normal phenomena of classical conditioning, as described by Ivan Pavlov, include
1. response by analogy
2. stimulus generalization
3. discrimination
4. experimental neurosis

4.16. Concepts in applied operant conditioning include
1. reinforcement
2. response frequency
3. shaping
4. chaining

4.17. Monkey infants, when separated from their mothers,
1. exhibit a protest stage
2. show a despair stage
3. rapidly reattach when returned to their mothers
4. abolish play

4.18. Punishment
1. is an aversive stimulus
2. is an effective deterrent to aggression
3. reduces the probability of a behavior's recurring
4. is a negative reinforcement

4.19. Informed consent refers to the patient's being made aware of the
1. nature of the illness
2. treatment options
3. side effects of treatment
4. physician's feelings toward the patient

4.20. Culture-bound syndromes associated with Japan include
1. *taijin-kyofusho*
2. *piblokto*
3. *shinkeishitsu*
4. *hi-wa itck*

4.21. Which of the following conditions has a higher prevalence among blacks than among whites?
1. Hypertension
2. Arthritis
3. Diabetes
4. Obesity

4.22. Modeling, learning through imitation, is influenced by
1. status
2. reinforcement
3. intention
4. accident

4.23. Which of the following statements apply to the ways in which hospitals are organized in the United States?
1. The state mental hospital system has about 140,000 beds
2. Investor-owned hospitals are increasing in importance nationally
3. Veterans Administration (VA) hospitals usually have affiliations with medical schools
4. Special hospitals are less regulated than other hospitals

DIRECTIONS: Each group of questions below consists of lettered headings followed by a list of numbered words or statements. For each numbered word or statement, select the *one* lettered heading that is most closely associated with it. Each lettered heading may be selected once, more than once, or not at all.

Questions 4.24–4.27
A. Ivan Pavlov
B. Eric Kandel
C. Konrad Lorenz
D. Harry Harlow

4.24. Imprinting

4.25. Surrogate mother

4.26. Experimental neurosis

4.27. Aplysia

Questions 4.28–4.31
A. John Dollard and Neal E. Miller
B. Aaron Beck
C. John B. Watson
D. O. H. Mowrer

4.28. Little Albert

4.29. Two-factor learning theory

4.30. Tension-reducing theory

4.31. Cognitive behavioral theory of depression

Questions 4.32–4.35
A. Chicago Area Study—Faris and Dunham
B. New Haven Study—Hollingshead and Redlich
C. Stirling County Study—Leighton
D. Midtown Manhattan Study—Rennie and Srole

4.32. Social causation theory

4.33. Relation of social class to prevalence of treated mental illness

4.34. Association of stress to psychological symptoms

4.35. Twenty percent of population in need of psychiatric attention

DIRECTIONS: Each set of lettered headings is followed by a list of numbered phrases. For each numbered phrase select

A. if the item is associated with *A only*
B. if the item is associated with *B only*
C. if the item is associated with *both A and B*
D. if the item is associated with *neither A nor B*

Questions 4.36–4.39
A. Privileged communication
B. Unethical breach of confidentiality

4.36. The communication of private information by the psychiatrist to a third person

4.37. The right of the patient to decide whether or not to admit being in treatment

4.38. Publishing a case report in which the patient can be identified

4.39. Reporting child abuse to the appropriate agency

Questions 4.40–4.44
A. Secondary prevention
B. Tertiary prevention

4.40. Emphasizes rehabilitation

4.41. Reduces residual defect of chronic mental illness

4.42. Early treatment of school phobia

4.43. Dietary deficiency in niacin

4.44. Shortens the course of an illness

ANSWERS

Contributions of the Psychosocial Sciences to Human Behavior

4.1. The answer is B (*Synopsis VI*, pages 104–106; *CTP V*, page 258).

Jean Piaget, the noted Swiss psychologist, formulated a comprehensive theory of cognitive development. He described four major stages leading to the capacity for adult thought: sensorimotor, preoperational, concrete operational and formal operational. Like all developmental theorists, Piaget stipulated that each stage must be successfully traversed for the next stage to have a chance at success.

The critical cognitive achievement of the *sensorimotor stage* of development (birth to 2 years) is the construction of object concepts. The most important of these concepts is object permanence, and its attainment heralds the end of the sensorimotor period. To adults, objects have an existence independent of their immediate experience; a person or an object continues to exist even when it is not immediately present. This capacity is not innate, nor is it simply learned. A sense of object permanence is constructed during the first year or so of life, as the infant becomes progressively more coordinated—visually, motorically, and mentally.

The *latency stage* was described by Freud as a stage of relative quiescence of the sexual drive; this stage occurs after the resolution of the Oedipus complex and extends until pubescence. The *preattachment stage* is a concept of John Bowlby's; it refers to the period during the first two to three months of life. Piaget's stage of *concrete operations* is characterized by deductive or syllogistic reasoning and encompasses approximately the years between 7 and 11. The *formal operations* stage is characterized by the attainment of abstract thought and extends from the age of 11 through the end of adolescence.

4.2. The answer is D (*Synopsis VI*, pages 109–113; *CTP V*, page 262).

An underlying assumption of all behavioral interactions, therapy, and teaching is the idea that, if changes occur in a person's behavior, they have occurred as a result of learning. Learning theory is the study of the variables that contribute to the success of learning as a behavioral change. The leading learning theorists include Ivan Pavlov, Clark L. Hull, Joseph Wolpe, B. F. Skinner, and Edward L. Thorndike. It is common to view conditioning as a form of learning, and most theorists accept a rough dichotomy between two types of conditioning—classical and operant.

The concept of operant (instrumental) conditioning is attributed to *B. F. Skinner* (1904–1990). He concentrated on the frequency and the probability of a specific observable response under specified observable conditions. In operant conditioning a fully moving organism behaves in a way that is instrumental in producing a reward.

Ivan Pavlov (1849–1936), in contrast to operant conditioning, described a form of classical conditioning in which the organism was usually more restrained and the response was elicited by the experimenter. His research was directed toward an analysis of reflex behavior that would occur given certain conditions; for example, the stimulus of the experimenter's footsteps would elicit salivation in dogs, because the footsteps had come to be associated with the food the experimenter brought.

Clark L. Hull (1884–1952) approached learning theory from a mathematical and neurophysiological point of view. He described the learning process as analogous to receptor-effector connections, in which learning consists of strengthening some and not others of these connections or of setting up entirely new connections.

Joseph Wolpe (b. 1915) developed the technique of systematic desensitization based on tenets of learning theory, in which a patient in a relaxed state imagines increasingly anxiety-producing scenes. Wolpe's theory of reciprocal inhibition states that relaxation is incompatible with anxiety and, thus, will effectively decrease the anxiety associated with the anxiety-producing stimulus.

Edward L. Thorndike (1874–1949) described trial-and-error learning. His law of effect emphasized reward as a primary determinant of behavior.

4.3. The answer is A (*Synopsis VI*, pages 141–142; *CTP V*, page 1235).

According to T. H. Holmes and R. H. Rahe, the *death of a spouse* causes the greatest stress. They introduced the notion of life change as a scale of measuring stress in 1967. The Holmes-Rahe Social Readjustment Rating Scale ranks diverse events according to their average expectable effects.

If a certain number of stressful events occur in a one-year period, the risk of illness—such as myocardial infarction, peptic ulcer, or psychiatric disorder—is increased. Some have found the scale useful but simplistic in that it ignores widely disparate significances that may be attached to similar events within different cultures and different persons. Recent studies have examined life changes as pleasant, unpleasant, expected, or unexpected. Those factors also need to be taken into account in evaluating the effects of life events. Table 4.1 lists the 15 life events that produce the most stress.

4.4. The answer is B (*Synopsis VI*, pages 127, 142, 145, 151, and 832; *CTP V*, pages 2125–2126).

The intrinsic rule of medical ethics—beneficence—refers to the concept of *doing good and avoiding harm*, which is protecting the patient from harm. Several additional ethical principles may serve as the basis for psychiatric intervention. The right to be treated and the right to treat encompass the related issue of the right to refuse treatment. Other related ethical principles include utilitarianism, respect for persons, and justice. An integral issue involved in all these principles is that of competence of the patient to decide whether an intervention is justified.

Utilitarianism is the principle that attempts to come to terms with the reality that the physician, even in wanting to do good, cannot always avoid doing harm—for instance, through side effects. Utilitarianism states the principle of the greatest good for the greatest number, the concept that *benefits must outweigh costs*. *Respect for persons* implies the respect for a person's self-determination or decision-making capacity.

The ethical principle of justice implies that health care is a right and can be understood in the current context as a fair application and *distribution of psychiatric services*. The concept of what is *right or wrong* is a general principle that defines the entire field of ethics—a set of moral principles that determine what is right or wrong and good or bad.

Table 4.1
The 15 Life Events Producing the Most Stress

1. Death of spouse
2. Divorce
3. Marital separation from mate
4. Detention in jail or other institution
5. Death of a close family member
6. Major personal injury or illness
7. Marriage
8. Being fired at work
9. Marital reconciliation with mate
10. Retirement from work
11. Major change in the health or behavior of a family member
12. Pregnancy
13. Sexual difficulties
14. Gaining a new family member (through birth, adoption, oldster moving in, etc.)
15. Major business readjustment (merger, reorganization, bankruptcy, etc.)

Table adapted from T Holmes: Life situations, emotions, and disease. J Acad Psychosom Med *19:* 747, 1978.

4.5. The answer is D (*Synopsis VI*, pages 115–117; *CTP V*, pages 447–448).

Aggression is the motor counterpart of the affects of rage, anger, and hostility. Aggression is constructive when it is involved in problem solving and appropriate as a defense against a realistic attack; it is pathological when it is self-destructive, not problem solving, and the outcome of unresolved emotional conflict. Proposed by *John Dollard* and his colleagues in 1939, the drive theory of aggression is an alternative to the instinct views of aggression put forward by Sigmund Freud and Konrad Lorenz. According to Dollard's view, frustration—the blocking of ongoing goal-directed behavior—leads to the arousal of a drive whose primary goal is that of wanting to harm some person or object. This drive, in turn, leads to attacks against various targets, especially against the source of the frustration. The oldest perspective on aggressive behavior is the view that such behavior is mainly instinctive in nature; it occurs because human beings are genetically or constitutionally programmed for such behavior.

Freud viewed aggression as a reaction to the blocking or thwarting of libidinal impulses. *Lorenz* proposed that human aggression springs primarily from a fighting instinct that human beings share with many other organisms. He suggested that greater feelings of love and friendship for others may prove incompatible with the expression of overt aggression, may tend to block such behavior, and, thus, may redirect or control aggression.

The inspirations of classical ethology, the study of animals in their natural habitat and the kind of behavior that is specific to a species, as originally expounded by Konrad Lorenz and *Nikolaas Tinbergen*, were derived from the study of behavior in the context of phylogeny, the evolution of a genetically related group of organisms as distinguished from the development of the individual organism. Tinbergen stressed the relationship between hormonal states and environmental factors in producing so-called instinctive responses.

Mary Ainsworth, expanding on John Bowlby's attachment theory, has shown that, although school was once regarded as a necessary time for weaning from the home, in this modern, technical, and possession-oriented society, parental involvement with children in school and in their learning, at least through the primary grades, may be developmentally vital to both child and parent. Ainsworth has also contributed in the areas of the development of the mother-infant bond, maternal separation, and multiple mothering.

4.6. The answer is E (*Synopsis VI*, page 146; *CTP V*, page 1262).

Less, not more, than half of all *school-age children* are exercising on a daily basis, although the *number of adults* involved in an exercise program has been rising, especially over the past 15 to 20 years. *Lifestyle* and personal habits are major factors in the cause of illness and death in the United States, accounting for about 70 percent of all illness, both mental and physical. For example, obesity, which is directly related to eating habits, is associated with heart disease and diabetes. Many cancer deaths have been related to both poor dietary habits and the chewing and smoking of tobacco. Over the past 20 years the smoking rate for women has been rapidly approaching that for men, and the increase in lung cancer in women has paralleled this rise in smoking behavior. For women 55 to 70 years of age, *lung cancer* is the primary cause of death due to cancer. *Regular physical activity* has a positive effect on stress reduction, and it has been found to be useful in treating and preventing such mental disorders as anxiety and depression.

4.7. The answer is D (*Synopsis VI*, pages 149–150; *CTP V*, pages 2075–2077).

Hospitals use approximately *40 percent* of health care costs in the United States, representing the largest segment of health care dollars, whereas physicians' fees represent approximately 20 percent. The expenditure of public funds and increasing government regulation have affected mental health programs, as well as general health programs. Health care costs are increasingly being paid by third parties. Approximately 10 percent of the United States gross national product (the total value of the nation's annual output of goods and services) is spent for health care. Health care spending continues to escalate, with hospital costs and general medical services rising much faster than physicians' fees.

4.8. The answer is B (*Synopsis VI*, page 148; *CTP V*, pages 1339–1342).

In 1989 the death rate across all age groups in the United States was *524.1 per 100,000*. This was the lowest rate ever recorded. Acquired immune deficiency syndrome (AIDS) was the 11th leading cause of death in 1989. Death rates differ by race and sex, with women having lower mortality rates than men and racial minorities having higher rates than the majority population. Table 4.2 lists the top 10 causes of death in the United States.

Table 4.2
The 10 Leading Causes of Death in the United States

1. Heart disease
2. Cancer
3. Stroke
4. Accidents
5. Chronic obstructive pulmonary disease
6. Pneumonia
7. Diabetes
8. Suicide
9. Cirrhosis
10. Atherosclerosis

National Center for Health Statistics, 1989.

4.9. The answer is C (*Synopsis VI*, page 148; *CTP V*, page 1714).

Accidents are the most common cause of death among adolescents and young adults (ages 15 to 24), with 75 percent of the fatalities occurring in automobile accidents, most of which are associated with alcohol use. *Homicide* and *suicide*, respectively, are the second and third leading causes of death in this age group. Among adolescents a higher suicide rate is associated with subcultures that devalue life, a history of parental suicide, an inability to form stable attachments, and drug or alcohol abuse. Among college students a depressed person's sense of alienation may be aggravated on the college campus by isolation from family, friends, and other support services. Of the 10 leading causes of death of all age groups in the United States, *cancer* is ranked second and *pneumonia* sixth.

4.10. The answer is C (*Synopsis VI*, page 148; *CTP V*, pages 1339–1342).

In 1988 the average life expectancy in the United States was *74.9 years*. Black men are 7½ years behind the average, with a life expectancy of 67.4 years; white men have a life expectancy of 71.5 years; white women have a life expectancy of 78.3 years; and black women have a life expectancy of 75.5 years. Life expectancy for all women is greater than for all men (78.3 years versus 71.5 years), but this difference has been decreasing in recent years.

In the United States the life expectancy of all age, sex, and race groups has been steadily increasing since the turn of the century. At the turn of the century, the average life expectancy was approximately 47 years.

4.11. The answer is A (*Synopsis VI*, page 144; *CTP V*, pages 2067–2068).

One of the basic aspects of a community mental health program is a commitment to prevention, as well as treatment. The commitment to prevention evolved from the public health model, which describes three types of prevention. The first is primary prevention, which *attempts to eliminate causative factors*. With alcohol-related disorders as a paradigm, primary prevention consists of stopping the initial phase of alcohol abuse, thus reducing the incidence of alcohol-related disorders. Secondary prevention is *early detection* and prompt treatment at the beginning of the disease process (e.g., treating gastritis secondary to alcohol abuse). Tertiary prevention consists of *an attempt to rehabilitate* patients after the onset of acute illness, including efforts to care for people with chronic illnesses and to treat *long-term complications* (e.g., alcohol amnestic disorders).

4.12. The answer is E (all) (*Synopsis VI*, pages 104–106; *CTP V*, pages 256–262).

Jean Piaget (1896–1980), the Swiss psychologist, developed a theory of cognition focusing on the development of thought and consisting of four stages: (1) the sensorimotor stage (from birth to 2 years), during which the concept of object permanence is attained; (2) the preoperational stage (from 2 to 7 years), during which thinking and events are linked by juxtaposition, rather than by logic; (3) the concrete operational stage (from 7 to 11 years), during which logical thought, reasoning, and self-regulation begin to develop; and (4) the formal operational stage (from 11 through the end of adolescence), during which abstract thought begins to develop.

Piaget's preoperational stage coincides in time with Sigmund Freud's oedipal phase and Erik Erikson's phase of initiative versus guilt. It is characterized by *intuitive*, as opposed to logical, thought and transductive reasoning. Preoperational children are *egocentric*, believing themselves to be the center of the universe, and assume that whatever they are thinking or talking about is automatically—in fact, *magically*—understood by the other. These children are also observed to engage in thinking that is *animistic* and phenomenalistic. Animistic thinking is characterized by the endowment of inanimate objects with lifelike attributes (e.g., "the chair hates me," "the moon is running"). Phenomenalistic causality is the belief that events that occur in close temporal proximity cause one another (e.g., thinking bad thoughts about mother caused mother to get sick) and is another term for magical thinking. When adults regress under stress, they can return to the stage of preoperational thought.

4.13. The answer is E (all) (*Synopsis VI*, pages 106–108; *CTP V*, pages 1895–1896).

The British psychoanalyst John Bowlby (1907–1990) was concerned with the concept of attachment, its development, and the consequences of its disruption. Bowlby defined attachment as the *reciprocal affectionate relationship* between infant and primary caretaker that gradually *develops during the first year of life*. The development of attachment between infant and caretaker depends on the *intensity, the quality, and the amount of time spent together*.

Bowlby believed that early separation and disruption of attachment have persistent and irreversible effects on personality and intelligence. He pointed to the overt and the dynamic similarities between withdrawn, depressed behavior in infants and young children separated from the primary caretaker and mourning behavior in adults. He viewed smiling in the infant as an *instinctive behavior pattern* and hypothesized that this smiling response increases the infant's chances of survival, as it makes the infant more appealing to the mother. He further suggested that this smiling response has been favorably selected in evolutionary terms and that infants without a strong smiling response have a higher mortality rate.

4.14. The answer is A (1, 2, 3) (*Synopsis VI*, pages 104–105; *CTP V*, page 258).

Object permanence is the cognitive capacity that, once attained, heralds the end of Jean Piaget's sensorimotor stage at approximately 18 months to 2 years of age. Object permanence is the ability to know that an *object continues to exist* even if it is not present to the senses and no longer physically visible to the child; the child has begun to develop mental representations of objects. *Looking for a toy* that has been hidden is a behavioral example associated with a child who has developed object permanence. The development of the *process of symbolization* occurs at approximately the same time as the development of object permanence (18 months to 2 years). Symbolization is the ability of the child to use mental representations or words to signify the real object.

The *final stage of the separation-individuation* process, part of Margaret Mahler's scheme of development, involves the concept of object constancy. The final stage of object constancy occurs at approximately 3 years of age. Object constancy is the capacity to have a steady and secure internal picture of primary caretakers that allows for the maintenance of object relatedness despite frustration. This capacity is probably dependent on the child's earlier attainment of object permanence.

4.15. The answer is A (1, 2, 3) (*Synopsis VI*, pages 109–110; *CTP V*, pages 263–264 and 601–602).

In Ivan Pavlov's learning theory, normal phenomena of classical conditioning include *response by analogy, stimulus generalization,* and *discrimination*. In a typical Pavlovian experiment a stimulus that had no capacity to evoke a particular type of response before training becomes able to do so. Response by analogy occurs when animals respond to stimuli that are similar to but different from the stimulus to which they were originally conditioned. Stimulus generalization is a similar phenomenon in which a conditioned response is transferred from one stimulus to another. Discrimination occurs when an animal is able to distinguish among similar but different stimuli. The term *experimental neurosis* was introduced by Pavlov to describe abnormal behavior of a chronic nature that is produced experimentally.

4.16. The answer is E (all) (*Synopsis VI*, pages 110–112; *CTP V*, pages 264–265 and 439–440).

B. F. Skinner proposed a theory of learning and behavior known as operant or instrumental conditioning. The term "operant" refers to a class of responses that are emitted by the organism, rather than elicited by some known stimulus. Operant responses are also frequently referred to as voluntary, as opposed to involuntary or reflex, behavior. An example of an operant response is reaching for the telephone when it rings. Concepts in applied operant conditioning include *reinforcement, response frequency, shaping*, and *chaining*.

Reinforcement, both positive and negative, is a key concept in operant conditioning. Positive reinforcement is an event that, if it occurs in response to a particular behavior, increases the probability of that behavior's recurring. Negative reinforcement also increases the probability of a response by causing an aversive stimulus to diminish. Negative reinforcement is not synonymous with punishment, which is a negative response to an event, leading to a decrease in the response. Response frequency is the frequency at which a response occurs. Shaping refers to the experimenter's choosing of a final response to be produced. In shaping behavior, the experimenter must specify the responses desired not in general terms but by specific behavior criteria. Chaining is Skinner's technique of building responses on one another to form a behavioral pattern.

4.17. The answer is E (all) (*Synopsis VI*, pages 125–126; *CTP V*, pages 329–330).

Harry and Margaret Harlow studied the effects of various forms of social deprivation on the social development of young monkeys. At initial separation, the monkey infants exhibited a *protest stage*. The protest stage changed to *despair* during the next 48 hours. *Play* was almost abolished during the time of maternal separation and then increased rapidly after reunion with the mother.

A difference observed in human infants when compared with monkey infants is that many human children are rejecting when reunited with their mothers. Bowlby termed this reunion phase detachment. Monkey infants *rapidly reattach* when returned to their mothers. Anaclitic depression is the term used by the Austrian-born psychoanalyst René Spitz (1887–1974) to describe the syndrome exhibited by human infants separated from their primary caretakers for extended periods. Spitz observed a depression in children who were 6 to 8 months old at the time of a separation that lasted about three months. The reaction was seen in full form only in children who had had a good interaction with the caretaker. Spitz found the syndrome to be reversible

if the caretaker was restored to the child within three months.

A summary of the Harlow work is presented in Table 4.3, which lists five types of social deprivation or affectional systems and the effects on behavior.

4.18. The answer is B (1, 3) (*Synopsis VI*, page 120; *CTP V*, pages 266–267).

Punishment is an *aversive stimulus* that is seen in response to a behavior and that *reduces the probability* of that behavior's recurring. Punishment is *not a negative reinforcement*. It weakens or suppresses an undesired response. In the past it was assumed that punishment was a highly effective deterrent to human violence. That punishment is sometimes effective in deterring overt aggression appears obvious; however, the question of whether punishment always or even usually produces such effects remains controversial. Findings suggest that the influence of punishment on aggression is quite complex. Punishment is not always *an effective deterrent* to aggression. Further, its use may involve consequences or side effects that largely counter its deterrent influence (e.g., people who administer punishment may often serve as aggressive models for those receiving the discipline).

Negative reinforcement describes an event that strengthens the behavior that removes it (e.g., a teenager mows the law to avoid the parents' complaints).

4.19. The answer is A (1, 2, 3) (*Synopsis VI*, pages 134–135 and 824–825; *CTP V*, pages 1317–1318).

Informed consent refers to the patient's being told the *nature of the illness*, the various *treatment options*, and their *side effects*. It does not refer to knowing the *physician's feelings* toward the patient.

Patients may refuse treatment, even though such treatment has been proved to be effective and of little risk. But when, for instance, gangrene sets in and the patient is psychotic, treatment even as extreme as amputation may be ordered to save the person's

Table 4.3
Social Deprivation in Nonhuman Primates

Type of Social Deprivation	Effects
Total isolation (not allowed to develop caretaker or peer bond)	Self-orality, self-clasping, fearful with peers, unable to copulate. Females unable to nurture young. If isolation goes beyond six months, no recovery is possible
Mother-only-reared	Fail to leave mother and explore. Terrified when finally exposed to peers. Unable to play or to copulate
Peer-only-reared	Engage in self-orality, grasp one another in clinging manner, easily frightened, reluctant to explore, timid as adults, play is minimal
Partial isolation (can see, hear, and smell other monkeys)	Stare vacantly into space, engage in self-mutilation, stereotyped behavior patterns
Separation (taken from caretaker after bond has developed)	Initial protest stage changing to despair 48 hours after separation; refuse to play. Rapid reattachment when returned to mother

life. Courts require that the physician relate sufficient information to a patient to allow the patient to decide whether a procedure is acceptable in the light of its risks and benefits and the alternatives that are available, including no treatment at all. This duty of full disclosure gave rise to the phrase "informed consent." The consent process contains three elements: information, comprehension, and voluntariness. Uninformed or coerced consent is not considered to be consent under any circumstances.

4.20. The answer is B (1, 3) (*Synopsis VI*, pages 131–133; *CTP V*, pages 843–846).

Psychiatric disorders not found in standard nomenclature include, for example, culture-bound syndromes, which are psychiatric syndromes restricted to specific cultural settings. Culture-bound syndromes associated with Japan include *taijin-kyo-fusho*—which is characterized by anxiety, fear of rejection, blushing, fear of eye contact, and concern about body odor—and *shinkeishitsu*, which is marked by obsessions, perfectionism, ambivalence, social withdrawal, neurasthenia (a state of chronic fatigue and debility), and hypochondriasis. *Piblokto* is found among Eskimos. In the attack (sometimes referred to as Arctic hysteria), which lasts from one to two hours, the patient, usually female, screams, tears off and destroys her clothing, and either throws herself on the snow or runs wildly about on the ice. After the attack the patient appears quite normal and often does not remember it. *Hi-wa itck* afflicts the Mojave American Indian and is characterized by insomnia, anorexia, depression, and suicide as the result of an unwanted separation from a loved one.

4.21. The answer is E (all) (*Synopsis VI*, page 147; *CTP V*, pages 303–304).

The rates of such chronic conditions as *obesity, diabetes*, heart disease, *hypertension*, and *arthritis* are higher among blacks than among whites. Persons between the ages of 20 and 30 and those over age 65 tend to have more illness and health care needs than persons in middle adulthood. Regardless of age, women seek health care and are hospitalized more often than men. Some studies have shown a slightly higher percentage of bipolar disease among higher socioeconomic status (SES) persons and a greater number of persons with schizophrenia in lower SES groups. Approximately 75 percent of all carcinogens come from the environment, contributing to approximately one quarter of today's health problems.

Life-style, age, SES, sex, environment, and race affect the use of health care facilities. In 1984 approximately 10 times as many visits were made to physicians' offices by white persons as by blacks.

4.22. The answer is E (all) (*Synopsis VI*, page 113; *CTP V*, page 269).

A tenet of social learning theory is that human behavior may change because of role modeling. The choice of a role model is subject to a variety of factors, such as the model's *status*, sex, and similarity to oneself. A person learns by observing this role model, either *intentionally* or *accidentally*. However, for the imitated behavior to become part of a person's repertoire, it must be *reinforced* or rewarded.

4.23. The answer is E (all) (*Synopsis VI*, pages 150–151; *CTP V*, pages 283–285).

Hospitals are organized in a variety of ways in the United States. The *state mental hospital* system has about 140,000 beds. State psychiatric hospitals have been markedly reduced in population since the 1960s and 1970s, when deinstitutionalization and effective somatic therapies combined to focus on outpatient treatment of mentally ill persons. *Investor-owned hospitals* are for-profit hospitals and are increasing in importance. *Veterans Administration (VA) hospitals* are usually affiliated with medical schools and with the U.S. Department of Defense, Public Health Service, and other entities. In *special hospitals*, 70 percent of the facility must be designated for treatment of a single condition (not including psychiatric or substance-abuse disorders). See Table 4.4 for an overview of aspects of hospital organization.

4.24–4.27

4.24. The answer is C (*Synopsis VI*, pages 122–123; *CTP V*, page 336).

4.25. The answer is D (*Synopsis VI*, page 125; *CTP V*, page 327).

4.26. The answer is A (*Synopsis VI*, page 123; *CTP V*, pages 263–264).

4.27. The answer is B (*Synopsis VI*, pages 113–114; *CTP V*, pages 270 and 334).

Imprinting has been described as the process by which certain stimuli become capable of eliciting certain innate behavior patterns during a critical period of the animal's behavioral development. This phenomenon is associated with *Konrad Lorenz*, who in 1935 demonstrated that the first moving object (in this case, Lorenz himself) a duckling sees during a critical period shortly after hatching is thereafter regarded as and reacted to as the mother duck.

Harry Harlow is associated with the concept of *surrogate mother* from his experiments in the 1950s with rhesus monkeys. Harlow designed a series of experiments in which infant monkeys were separated from their mothers during the earliest weeks of life. He found that the infant monkeys, if given the choice between a wire surrogate and a cloth-covered surrogate mother, chose the cloth-covered surrogates even if the wire surrogates provided food (Figure 4.1).

Ivan Pavlov coined the term *"experimental neurosis"* to describe disorganized behavior that appears

Table 4.4
Some Aspects of Hospital Organization

Criteria	Investor-Owned Hospitals	State Mental Hospital System	Federal Hospital System	Special Hospitals*
Patient population	All illnesses, although hospital may specialize	Mental illness	All illnesses	70% of facility must be for single diagnosis
Number of hospitals	757	277 (140,000 beds nationally)	342	150
Profit orientation	For profit	Nonprofit	Nonprofit	For profit or nonprofit
Ownership	Private corporation; may be owned by M.D.s	State	Federal government	Private or public
Affiliation	May be owned by large chains, such as Hospital Corporation of America and Humana Corporation	Free-standing or affiliated with various medical schools	Department of Defense (190); Public Health Service, Coast Guard, prison, Merchant Marine, Indian Health Service; VA (129)	Optional affiliation with medical schools
Other	Increasing in importance nationally	Deinstitutionalization—number of patients has been reduced	VA hospitals usually have affiliations with medical schools	Less regulated than other types of hospitals

*Special hospitals include obstetrics and gynecology; eye, ear, nose, and throat; etc. They do not include psychiatric hospitals or substance-abuse hospitals.

Figure 4.1. An infant rhesus monkey clinging to a cloth-covered surrogate mother.

in the experimental subject (in Pavlov's case, dogs) in response to an inability to master the experimental situation. Pavlov described extremely agitated behavior in his dogs when they were unable to discriminate between sounds of similar pitch or test objects of similar shapes.

Eric Kandel contributed to the knowledge of the neurophysiology of learning. He demonstrated in the study of the snail *Aplysia* that synaptic connections are altered as a result of learning.

4.28–4.31

4.28. The answer is C (*Synopsis VI*, page 110; *CTP V*, pages 263 and 977).

4.29. The answer is D (*Synopsis VI*, page 88; *CTP V*, pages 267 and 991).

4.30. The answer is A (*Synopsis VI*, page 112; *CTP V*, pages 447–448).

4.31. The answer is B (*Synopsis VI*, page 113; *CTP V*, pages 891 and 1541–1543).

Learning may be defined as a change in behavior resulting from reinforced practice. Numerous learning theories developed over the years have contributed to a better understanding of how behavior is established, maintained, and modified.

In 1920 *John Watson*, using Pavlov's theory of classical conditioning, reported the frequently quoted case of *Little Albert*, an 11-month-old boy who was conditioned to a fear of rats by an experimenter who struck an iron bar behind the boy just as he was about to touch a rat. The boy's original fear of loud noises was transferred to the rat and even became generalized to other furry objects.

In 1939 *O. H. Mowrer* presented the *two-factor learning theory*, the anxiety-reduction or fear-reduction theory of reinforcement. Mowrer theorized that much learning can be explained on the basis of acquired fear (anxiety) and that responses that reduce this anxiety are learned and maintained. He suggested that anxiety responses are learned by contiguity (proximity, closeness); for example, a stimulus that in itself is not fear-evoking is accidentally presented at the same time as a painful stimulus. By simple conditioning (what Mowrer then called sign learning) the neutral stimulus becomes a conditioned aversive stimulus. Mowrer believed that these anxiety responses, unlike other types of conditioned responses, did not need continued reinforcement to be maintained. Mowrer also assumed in his two-factor theory that fear responses are entirely autonomic.

John Dollard and Neal E. Miller at Yale showed that hostility in animals results from frustration and attempted to correlate learning theories and psychoanalysis. Their *tension-reduction theory* sees behavior as motivated by one's attempt to reduce tension produced by unsatisfied or unconscious drives—such as guilt, anger, and sex—and the need for self-esteem, love, and social approval.

Aaron Beck originated the *cognitive behavioral (CB) theory of depression*, which posits that cognitive dysfunctions are the core of depression and that affective and physical changes and other associated features of depression are consequences of the cognitive dysfunctions. The CB theory consists of a cognitive triad, specific schemes, and cognitive errors or faulty information processing. The cognitive triad consists of negative cognitions regarding oneself, the world, and one's future. First is a negative self-percept, seeing oneself as defective, inadequate, deprived, worthless, and undesirable. Second is a tendency to experience the world as a negative, demanding, and defeating place and to expect failure and punishment. Third is an expectation of continued hardship, suffering, deprivation, and failure.

4.32–4.35

4.32. The answer is A (*Synopsis VI*, page 135; *CTP V*, pages 319–322).

4.33. The answer is B (*Synopsis VI*, page 135; *CTP V*, pages 319–322).

4.34. The answer is D (*Synopsis VI*, page 135; *CTP V*, pages 319–322).

4.35. The answer is C (*Synopsis VI*, page 135; *CTP V*, pages 319–322).

In psychiatry, epidemiology is defined as the study of the prevalence and the distribution of mental disorders within a population. The various applications of epidemiology depend essentially on three sequential levels of investigation: (1) descriptive—studies that produce basic estimates of the rates of disorders in a general population and its subgroups, (2) analytic—studies that explore the basis for the variations in illness rates among different groups in order to identify risk factors that may contribute to the development of a disorder, and (3) experimental—studies that test the presumed association between a risk factor and a disorder and that seek to reduce the occurrence of illness by controlling the risk factor.

Several major North American studies have been directed at testing specific causative hypotheses about the causal relation of social environmental factors to the occurrence of mental disorder—e.g., the Stirling County Study and the Midtown Manhattan Study. Alexander Leighton, leading the Stirling County investigation, studied a sample of 1,010 adult residents in a rural Canadian county of 20,000. Estimates of the lifetime prevalence of mental disorders included rates of 57 percent for all DSM-I conditions, 24 percent for significant impairment, and 20 percent in *need of psychiatric attention*. The Midtown Manhattan Study, led by Thomas Rennie and Leo Srole, sampled 1,600 residents of midtown Manhattan, which had an adult population of 110,000. Associations were found between *stress and psychological symptom* variables: 81.5 percent of the population had at least mild impairment from psychological symptoms, and 23.4 percent had significant impairment.

R. Faris and H. Dunham led the Chicago Area Study, examining 35,000 psychiatric hospital admissions between the years 1922 and 1934. Members of the lowest socioeconomic class had the highest first hospital admissions for schizophrenia; the schizophrenia rates decreased as one moved into more affluent communities. On the basis of their findings, Faris and Dunham postulated a drift hypothesis, impaired persons slid down on the social scale because of their illness; a segregation hypothesis, schizophrenic persons seek the areas of a city where anonymity and isolation can protect them from societal demands; the *social causation theory*, being a member of a lower socioeconomic group is causatively significant; and the social selection theory, having a mental illness leads one to become a member of a lower socioeconomic group.

The *relation of social class to prevalence* of treated mental illness was investigated in the New Haven Study, led by Hollingshead and Redlich. Their findings include the following: neurosis was more prevalent among those in high socioeconomic levels; psychosis was more prevalent among members of low socioeconomic groups; the poor were seen in mental health clinics; and low socioeconomic status, job instability, and downward mobility were associated with a high frequency of psychiatric disability.

The scope of psychological symptoms and the distribution by particular sociodemographic groups have had important policy and public health service implications and have served as a stimulus to generate improved definitions of mental disorder diagnosis.

4.36–4.39

4.36.   The answer is B (*Synopsis VI*, pages 11 and 82; *CTP V*, pages 2118–2120).

4.37.   The answer is A (*Synopsis VI*, pages 153 and 821; *CTP V*, pages 2118–2120).

4.38.   The answer is B (*Synopsis VI*, pages 11 and 821; *CTP V*, pages 2118–2120).

4.39.   The answer is D (*Synopsis VI*, pages 146, 148, and 822; *CTP V*, pages 2118–2120).

Privileged communication is a legal term that refers to the patient's right to keep private all information disclosed to the physician. Only the patient has the *right to decide* whether to disclose the fact of being in treatment. The physician is not allowed to divulge that information without the patient's consent; privilege belongs to the patient. Confidentiality refers to how information, once collected by the doctor, is treated to ensure that no harm will befall the patient. *Communication by the psychiatrist* of private information to a third person is an unethical breach of confidentiality. There are, however, specific critical exceptions to the rule of confidentiality. For example, discussing a particular patient with a psychotherapy supervisor is not an unethical breach of confidentiality. Privilege is not involved in this situation, since the patient is not speaking to the supervisor. Quality control necessitates a review of individual patients and therapists and requires discriminate disclosures.

The psychiatrist may break confidentiality in order to protect the patient or others. In a number of situations, reporting by the physician to the authorities is specifically required by law. An example of mandated reporting, one in which penalties are imposed for failure to report, involves child abuse. By law, therapists are required to report suspected cases of *child abuse* to public authorities. Another area is the reporting of AIDS patients to public health officials, which is required in some states. The Tarasoff case raises further questions about the psychiatrist's responsibility for the safety of not only the patient but others and the obligation to report such concerns. This case is discussed in more detail in Chapter 46 ("Forensic Psychiatry"), but, briefly stated, it refers to the ruling that a physician or a psychotherapist who has reason to believe that a

patient may injure or kill another person must notify the potential victim, relatives, friends, or the authorities.

Publishing of case reports is another area in which the issue of confidentiality arises. If the *patient can be identified*, an unethical breach of confidentiality occurs. By writing, a psychiatrist shares knowledge and experience, providing information that may be useful to both the profession and the public. Writing without breaching confidentiality, however, is not an easy task. Without adequate disguise, the consent of the patient is required.

4.40–4.44

4.40.   The answer is B (*Synopsis VI*, page 144; *CTP V*, pages 2068–2070).

4.41.   The answer is B (*Synopsis VI*, page 144; *CTP V*, pages 2068–2070).

4.42.   The answer is A (*Synopsis VI*, page 144; *CTP V*, pages 2068–2070).

4.43.   The answer is D (*Synopsis VI*, page 144; *CTP V*, pages 2068–2070).

4.44.   The answer is A (*Synopsis VI*, page 144; *CTP V*, pages 2068–2070).

Primary prevention programs in psychiatry are designed to lower the rate of onset of emotional disorder in the community by counteracting the stressful or potentially harmful social conditions that produce mental illness. Correcting a *niacin deficiency* in the diet will prevent pellagra (characterized by dementia, diarrhea, and dermatitis).

Secondary prevention may be defined as the early identification of a disease or disorder, which becomes the prerequisite for prompt treatment. Secondary prevention programs *shorten the course* of an illness and reduce the prevalence (number of existing cases) of the illness. *Early treatment of a school phobia* is an example of secondary prevention.

Tertiary prevention refers to the task of reducing the rate of defective functioning caused by a mental disorder. The goal of tertiary prevention has been described as reducing the *residual defect* of mental illness. Implicit in this task is the role of *rehabilitative* services to patients who have recovered from the acute phase of their mental illness.

Psychology and Psychiatry: Psychometric and Neuropsychological Testing

Psychometric testing can assess intelligence, cognitive functions, and personality. Such tests are used for diagnosis, treatment planning, clinical monitoring, and research. Psychiatrists need a basic working knowledge of commonly used tests so that they can participate actively in consultations with clinical psychologists who are experts in the science of psychometric testing. Because ordering a psychometric test involves both monetary expense and a patient's time, the psychiatrist should know (1) why the specific psychometric test is being ordered, (2) in what group of persons the test was originally standardized, (3) whether the test is reliable and valid, and (4) what advantages the test has over similar tests. Psychometric tests should be ordered using decision trees similar to the ones that should be used when ordering other laboratory tests. The information from psychometric tests complements the mental status examination. However, information from psychometric testing that was not suspected during the clinical examination must be evaluated carefully regarding its accuracy and, in particular, its clinical importance. Psychometric tests are not a substitute for a careful clinical examination of the patient. Furthermore, many but not all psychometric tests are state-dependent; that is, a change in the clinical state or the administration of drugs can affect the results. For example, a personality test and a test of attention are both altered if a patient is under the influence of a sympathomimetic.

Neuropsychological tests (e.g., Luria-Nebraska, Halstead-Reitan) are increasingly important in psychiatric research and practice. Inasmuch as psychiatrists have a renewed interest in localizing the brain regions involved in specific psychiatric disorders, the localizing abilities of psychometric tests can enhance neuroanatomical information from brain-imaging and neuropathological studies. For example, the Wisconsin Card-Sorting Test, a test with some specificity for the dorsolateral prefrontal cortex, has been used in tandem with brain-imaging techniques to test the hypothesis that frontal lobe dysfunction is involved in schizophrenia. The use of neuropsychological tests in clinical practice is particularly important in the organic mental syndromes, mood disorders associated with organic insults (e.g., tumors, strokes), and schizophrenia. The results of such tests can be used to devise specific treatment plans to address cognitive deficits.

This chapter covers both psychological testing of intelligence and personality and neuropsychiatric tests of brain function. Readers should refer to Chapter 5, "Psychology and Psychiatry: Psychometric and Neuropsychological Testing," in *Synopsis VI* and to Section 9.4, "Psychological Assessment of Personality of Adults and Children," Section 9.5, "Neuropsychological and Intellectual Assessment of Adults," and Section 9.6, "Neuropsychological and Intellectual Assessment of Children," in *CTP V*. An accurate assessment of knowledge and understanding in these areas can be gained by studying the questions and answers below.

HELPFUL HINTS

The psychological terms and tests listed here should be defined and memorized.

psychodynamic formulations	representational	dementia
standardization	motivational aspects of behavior	abstract reasoning
validity	SCT	behavioral flexibility
reliability	word-association technique	memory—left versus right
objective tests	stimulus words	hemisphere disease
projective tests	reaction times	orientation
individual and group tests	clang association	temporal orientation
battery tests	perseveration	visual-object agnosia
Alfred Binet	MMPI	dressing apraxia
mental age	accurate profile	DSS
intelligence quotient (I.Q.)	Bender-Gestalt Test	prosody
average I.Q.	maturational levels	fluency
WAIS	Gestalt psychology	dyslexia
verbal subtests	coping phase	dysgraphia
performance subtests	recall phase	attention
full-scale I.Q.	organic dysfunction	catastrophic reaction
bell-shaped curve	DAPT	attention-deficit hyperactivity
scatter pattern	interrogation procedure	disorder
WISC	House-Tree-Person Test	Stanford-Binet
WPPSI	test behavior	learning disability
classification of intelligence	personality functioning	EEG abnormalities
personality testing	inferred diagnosis	manual dexterity
Rorschach test	prognosis	Luria-Nebraska (LNNB)
TAT	primary assets and weaknesses	Halstead-Reitan
Henry Murray and Christiana	neuropsychiatric tests	mental status cognitive tasks
Morgan		

QUESTIONS

DIRECTIONS: Each of the incomplete statements below is followed by five suggested completions. Select the *one* that is *best* in each case.

5.1. An intelligence quotient (I.Q.) of 100 corresponds to an intellectual ability for the general population in the
A. 20th percentile
B. 25th percentile
C. 40th percentile
D. 50th percentile
E. 65th percentile

5.2. The first sign of beginning cerebral disease is often impairment in
A. immediate memory
B. long-term memory
C. remote memory
D. recent memory
E. none of the above

5.3. The correct formula for determining intelligence quotient (I.Q.) is
A. $I.Q. = \dfrac{C.A.}{M.A.} \times 100$
B. $I.Q. = C.A. \times M.A. \times 100$
C. $I.Q. = \dfrac{M.A.}{C.A.} \times 100$
D. $I.Q. = C.A. \times M.A. \div 100$
E. none of the above

5.4. The most likely diagnosis for a 43-year-old college professor who drew the following figure on the Draw-a-Person Test (DAPT) is
A. obsessive-compulsive personality
B. depressive neurosis
C. organic brain damage
D. conversion disorder
E. mania

5.5. The patient was an 82-year-old widow who, over the previous five years, had been hospitalized for three minor strokes, from which she had recovered except for some slurred speech and right-side weakness. Over the past year, her friends had noticed an apathetic attitude toward her previously meticulously maintained apartment. She had some loss of memory about such things as whether she had gone shopping or had bathed, and she showed some lapses in judgment. Her long-term memory was relatively good. When visited by a medical team in her home, the patient was cooperative and cheerful and denied any problems but showed evidence of recent memory loss, disorientation to time, and concrete interpretations of proverbs.

[From *DSM-III-R Case Book*, used with permission.]

The most likely diagnosis, based on these findings, is
A. normal aging
B. primary degenerative dementia (PDD) of the Alzheimer type
C. multi-infarct dementia (MID)
D. major depressive episode
E. amnestic syndrome

DIRECTIONS: For each of the questions or incomplete statements below, *one or more* of the following responses or completions given are correct. Choose answer

A. if only *1, 2, and 3* are correct
B. if only *1 and 3* are correct
C. if only *2 and 4* are correct
D. if only *4* is correct
E. if *all* are correct

5.6. Psychological tests
1. provide an objective picture of a person's intelligence and personality
2. include a psychodynamic formulation of the ways in which the mind functions
3. are used to help in the diagnosis of mental disorders
4. provide guidelines for treatment

5.7. The Bender-Gestalt Test is administered
1. as a means of evaluating maturation levels in children
2. as a screening device for signs of organic dysfunction
3. to test visual and motor coordination
4. as a personality test

5.8 In interpreting the Thematic Apperception Test (TAT), the examiner
1. notes with whom the patient identifies
2. may assume that all the figures are representative of the patient
3. can elicit data pertaining to different areas of the patient's functioning
4. can infer motivational aspects of behavior

5.9. Objective personality tests
1. are typically pencil-and-paper tests
2. present ambiguous stimuli
3. are easily subjected to statistical analysis
4. generally require long and difficult training in application and interpretation

5.10. Disorientation to which of the following is most commonly present in brain-damaged patients?
1. Space
2. Place
3. Person
4. Time

DIRECTIONS: Each group of questions below consists of lettered headings followed by a list of numbered statements. For each numbered statement, select the *one* lettered heading that is most closely associated with it. Each lettered heading may be selected once, more than once, or not at all.

Questions 5.11–5.15

A. Wechsler Adult Intelligence Scale (WAIS)
B. Minnesota Multiphasic Personality Inventory (MMPI)
C. Thematic Apperception Test (TAT)
D. Bender-Gestalt Test
E. None of the above

5.11. Patient is asked to construct stories

5.12. Test of visual-motor coordination

5.13. Eleven subtests, six verbal and five performance, yielding a verbal I.Q., a performance I.Q., and a combined or full-scale I.Q.

5.14. Self-report inventory consisting of 550 statements to which the person has to respond with "True," "False," or "Cannot say"

5.15. A series of sentence stems, such as "I like . . . ," that the patients are asked to complete in their own words

Questions 5.16–5.20

A. Rorschach test
B. Luria-Nebraska Neuropsychological Battery
C. Halstead-Reitan Battery of Neurological Tests
D. Stanford-Binet
E. None of the above

5.16. Consists of 10 tests, including the Trail Making Test and the Critical Flicker Frequency

5.17. Extremely sensitive in identifying such problems as dyslexia

5.18. Consists of 120 items, plus several alternative tests, applicable to the ages between 2 years and adulthood

5.19. Furnishes a description of the dynamic forces of personality through an analysis of the person's responses

5.20. A test of diffuse cerebral dysfunction to which normal children by the age of 7 years respond negatively

Questions 5.21–5.25

A. Frontal lobes
B. Dominant temporal lobe
C. Nondominant parietal lobe
D. Dominant parietal lobe
E. Occipital lobes

5.21. Loss of gestalt, loss of symmetry, distortion of figures

5.22. Can name an object when not camouflaged but cannot name it when camouflaged

5.23. Two or more errors or two or more seven-second delays in carrying out tasks of right-left orientation (e.g., place left hand to right ear, right elbow to right knee)

5.24. Any improper letter sequence in spelling "earth" backward

5.25. Cannot name common objects, gives word approximations, or describes functions, rather than words

Questions 5.26–5.29
A. Wechsler Adult Intelligence Scale (WAIS)
B. Wechsler Intelligence Scale for Children (WISC)
C. Wechsler Preschool and Primary Scale of Intelligence (WPPSI)
D. All the above
E. None of the above

5.26. A scale for children ages 6 through 16

5.27. A scale for children ages 4 to 6½

5.28. Educational background affects the information and vocabulary subtest

5.29. Assesses children from 8 weeks to 2½ years of age

Questions 5.30–5.33
A. Beck Depression Inventory
B. Hamilton Depression Rating Scale
C. Brief Psychiatric Rating Scale

5.30. Emphasis on subjective mood and thoughts

5.31. Self-administered

5.32. Emphasis on neurovegetative symptoms

5.33. Provides a global pathology index

Psychology and Psychiatry: Psychometric and Neuropsychological Testing

5.1.   The answer is D (*Synopsis VI*, page 155; *CTP V*, pages 497–498).

An I.Q. of 100 corresponds to the *50th percentile* in intellectual ability for the general population. Modern psychological testing began in the first decade of the 20th century when Alfred Binet, a French psychologist (1857–1911), developed the first intelligence scale to separate the mentally defective (who were to be given special education) from the rest of the children (whose school progress was to be accelerated). Alfred Binet also introduced the concept of mental age (M.A.), which is the average intellectual level of a particular age. The intelligence quotient (I.Q.) is the ratio of M.A. over chronological age (C.A.) multiplied by 100. When C.A. and M.A. are equal, the I.Q. is 100, or average. One way of expressing the relative standing of an individual within a group is by percentile.

5.2.   The answer is D (*Synopsis VI*, pages 164–165; *CTP V*, pages 568–570).

Impairment in *recent memory*, the inability to recall the past several hours or days, is a prominent behavioral deficit in brain-damaged patients and is often the first sign of beginning cerebral disease. Recent memory is also known as short-term memory. *Remote memory*, also known as *long-term memory*, consists of childhood data or important events known to have occurred when the patient was young or free of illness. *Immediate memory* is memory after five seconds and is the ability to repeat four to seven digits forward and backward. Patients with unimpaired memory can usually recall six or seven digits backward.

Memory is a term that covers the retention of all types of material over different periods of time, involves diverse forms of response, and is an integral part of all thinking and learning. Memory is based on three essential processes: (1) registration, the ability to establish a record of an experience; (2) retention, the persistence or permanence of a registered experience; and (3) recall, the ability to arouse and repeat in consciousness a previously registered experience. A good memory involves the capacity to register swiftly and accurately, to retain for long periods of time, and to recall promptly. Memory is usually evaluated from the view of recent memory and remote memory.

5.3.   The answer is C (*Synopsis VI*, page 155; *CTP V*, page 497).

The intelligence quotient (I.Q.) is the ratio of a person's intelligence to so-called average or normal intelligence for the person's age. To determine I.Q., divide the assigned mental age (M.A.) by the chronological age (C.A.) and multiply by 100:

$$\text{I.Q.} = \frac{\text{M.A.}}{\text{C.A.}} \times 100$$

See Table 5.1 for a summary of the revised third edition of *Diagnostic and Statistical Manual of Mental Disorders* (DSM-III-R) classification of intelligence scores.

Intelligence is a controversial concept. The most widely accepted definition involves the capacity to solve new problems by means of reasoning, to understand the relevant issues in new tasks and think of successful solutions to the tasks. In tests of intelligence, reasoning is stressed because performances are easily influenced by transient emotional stress and by training. The reason for intelligence testing is to determine the role the intellectual level may play in the difficulties the person experiences or to make educational or occupational plans for the future.

5.4.   The answer is C (*Synopsis VI*, page 163; *CTP V*, page 485).

The most likely diagnosis for the 43-year-old college professor who drew the figure on the Draw-a-Person Test (DAPT) is *organic brain damage*.

Table 5.1
Classification of Intelligence by I.Q. Range

Classification	I.Q. Range
Profound mental retardation (MR)*	Below 20 or 25
Severe MR*	20–25 to 35–40
Moderate MR*	35–40 to 50–55
Mild MR*	50–55 to approx 70
Dull normal	80 to 90
Normal	90 to 110
Bright normal	110 to 120
Superior	120 to 130
Very superior	130 and above

*According to DSM-III-R, *Diagnostic and Statistical Manual of Mental Disorders*, ed 3, revised.

Brain-damaged patients often have a great deal of trouble projecting their images of the body into a figure drawing. Experience with the drawing technique allows for recognition of differences in the drawings of brain-damaged patients from drawings by patients with other disorders. The DAPT should be used with other psychological tests to confirm the diagnosis.

Deficiencies that accompany organic brain malfunctioning are frequently highlighted by means of psychological tests. Occasionally they are most apparent in areas ordinarily conceptualized as intellectual—in memory ability, arithmetical skills, and the analysis of visual designs. At other times they are most apparent in graphomotor productions, such as the DAPT, in which such distortions as difficulties in spatial orientation, fragmentation, and oversimplification of the figures can occur. *Obsessive-compulsive* patients in general pay attention to details of anatomy and clothing and show long, continuous lines; *depressed* patients may draw small sizes, heavy lines, few details, and dejected facial expressions; *manics* may draw large, colorful figures with exaggerated features, sometimes filling the whole page; a patient with *conversion disorder* may show exaggeration, emphasis, or, conversely, negligence of body parts involved in the conversion symptom.

5.5.   The answer is C (*Synopsis VI*, pages 164–170; *CTP V*, pages 617–620).

The most likely diagnosis for the patient described is *multi-infarct dementia* (MID) because of her stepwise deterioration associated with focal neurological signs, suggesting that the patient's strokes contributed to the dementia. The salient features of this case are the loss of intellectual abilities of sufficient severity to interfere with functioning (no longer able to maintain apartment or personal hygiene), loss of memory, impaired abstract thinking (concrete interpretation of proverbs), personality change (apathetic attitude), and impaired judgment—all occurring in a clear state of consciousness. Although memory disturbance is prominent, this is not an *amnestic syndrome*, which is defined as an impairment of short-term and long-term memory that is attributed to a specific organic factor. The diagnosis is not made if it is associated with impairment in abstract thinking, impaired judgment, other disturbances of high cortical function, or personality change. *Normal aging* does not involve a global deterioration in intellectual abilities, and in the absence of evidence for a cause other than those associated with aging (e.g., a neoplasm or an endocrine disturbance), the differential diagnosis is between *primary degenerative dementia* (PDD) of the Alzheimer type and MID. In the elderly, apathy, loss of interest, and apparent memory loss may indicate a *major depressive episode*. However, in this case the patient's cheerful mood rules that out.

5.6.   The answer is E (all) (*Synopsis VI*, page 155; *CTP V*, pages 476–486).

A variety of psychological tests may be performed for different purposes. Psychological tests provide an *objective picture* of a person's intelligence and personality. In fact, the norms of every standardized test enable the examiner to evaluate any person's test performance and its implications for performance in life far more objectively than a nonstandardized interview can. The most objective tests are typically paper-and-pencil questionnaires that eliminate almost completely the influence of the examiner in both the administration and the interpretation of the subject's responses.

Psychological tests also include a *psychodynamic formulation* of the ways in which the mind functions. Projective personality tests are perhaps the best designed to elicit a psychodynamic understanding of the patient. These tests are concerned with visual images, elicited by and externalized on ambiguous test stimuli. In projective tests, persons reveal aspects of themselves by making something definite out of an indefinite, ambiguous stimulus (such as a scene or an abstract design). Thus, everything that is definite in a response reflects the person's habitual ways of reacting and provides clues to the patient's underlying dynamics.

Psychological tests are often used to help in the *diagnosis of mental disorder*, as the major psychiatric diagnoses exhibit characteristic features in the testing. Another use of tests is their ability, primarily through diagnostic clarification, to provide *guidelines for treatment*.

Performance on psychological tests, it is assumed, reflects selected performances in real life. Different tests yield information about different psychological aspects and often give information not accessible in direct interviews.

5.7.   The answer is A (1, 2, 3) (*Synopsis VI*, pages 166–167; *CTP V*, pages 485 and 508).

The Bender Visual Motor Gestalt Test, devised by the American neuropsychiatrist Lauretta Bender in 1938, consists of nine geometrical figures that are copied by the subject (Figure 5.1). It is administered as a means of evaluating *maturation levels in children* and of assessing *organic dysfunction*. Its chief applications are to determine retardation, loss of function, and organic brain defects in children and adults. The designs are presented one at a time to the person, who is asked to copy them onto a sheet of paper (Figure 5.2). The person is then asked to draw the designs from memory (Figure 5.3); thus, the Bender designs can be used as a test of both *visual-motor coordination* and immediate visual memory.

The value of the Bender designs as a *personality test* is doubtful at best. Objective scores based on the measurement of deviations of the copied designs from the models do not provide particularly useful information about personality dynamics, but they are useful in the detection of brain disorders.

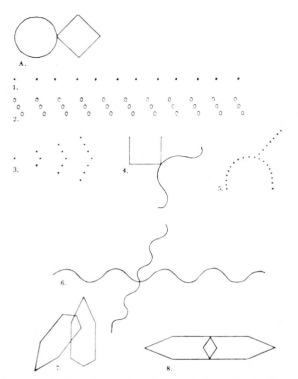

Figure 5.1. Test figures from the Bender Visual Motor Gestalt Test, adopted from Wertheimer. (From Lauretta Bender: *A Visual Motor Gestalt Test and Its Clinical Use.* Research Monograph, no 3, American Orthopsychiatric Association, New York, 1938.)

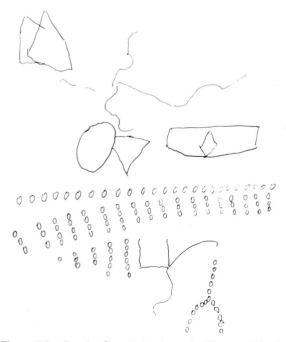

Figure 5.2. Bender-Gestalt drawings of a 57-year-old brain-damaged female patient.

Figure 5.3. Bender-Gestalt recall of the same 57-year-old brain-damaged female patient as in Figure 5.2.

5.8. The answer is E (all) (*Synopsis VI*, pages 160–162; *CTP V*, pages 483–485).

The Thematic Apperception Test (TAT) was introduced by Henry A. Murray in 1935 as a new way of interpreting stories made up by the patient about pictures representing human beings of both sexes and different ages, alone or in a group, and in a variety of surroundings and interactions. Originally, the chief usefulness was seen as revealing drives of which the patient was unaware. However, it became clear that conscious, as well as unconscious, tendencies were revealed by the test. Its aim expanded to include the study of many *different areas of the patient's functioning*, including personality traits, emotions, neurotic defenses, conflicts, intellectual level, ambitions, attitudes toward parental figures, and psychopathology. The patient is shown one picture at a time and asked to tell a complete story, including the interactions occurring, the events leading up to these interactions, the thoughts and feelings of the figures, and the outcome. In interpreting the TAT, the examiner notes, among other factors, with which figures the *patient identifies* and assumes that all the figures may *represent different aspects* of the patient being projected onto the ambiguous scenes and interactions; drives or attitudes that the patient considers as negative may, for instance, be projected onto the figures that are apparently most unlike the patient. The TAT appears to be most useful in helping to *infer motivational aspects* of behavior, as opposed to providing a clear-cut and definitive diagnosis.

As with all projective tests, there are disagreements about the value of the TAT; the foremost seems to be the failure of investigators to duplicate exactly the studies they set out to check. Another reason is the lack of a sufficiently comprehensive, clear, and formalized basis for the interpretations of TAT results. Psychologists and other workers who believe that projective tests are useful maintain that any measure of potential behavior is valuable. Experienced clinical psychologists (who are most likely to administer and interpret a useful TAT) generally agree as to the difficulty in acquiring sufficient skill and experience for satisfactory interpretations of TAT results. It is easy to learn how to administer the test but hard to interpret it well.

5.9. The answer is B (1, 3) (*Synopsis VI*, page 155; *CTP V*, pages 477–482).

Objective personality tests are typically *pencil-and-paper tests* consisting of straightforward questions and instructions, as opposed to projective tests that present *ambiguous stimuli*. Although the application and the interpretation of some projective tests require *long and difficult training*, the objective questionnaires are easily subjected to *statistical analysis*. They eliminate the influence of the examiner almost completely in both application and interpretation, particularly if standardized norms are available. The numerical scores and the profiles of many objective tests make statistical analysis easy. Projective tests, however, are among the most difficult to interpret, and many believe that the skill of the interpreter is as important as the tests themselves.

5.10. The answer is D (4) (*Synopsis VI*, page 165; *CTP V*, pages 505 and 568).

Disorientation to *time* is most commonly present in brain-damaged patients; disorientation to *person* or *place* is not usually impaired unless the patients are severely demented. About 25 percent of nonpsychotic patients with hemispheric cerebral disease are likely to show significant impairment with respect to precision of temporal orientation. Orientation to person is felt to be disturbed in only the most severely impaired patient. *Spatial* orientation refers to the person's awareness of the surroundings and is similar to orientation to place. A general definition of orientation is the recognition of one's environment and the temporal, spatial, and personal relationships within it.

5.11–5.15

5.11. The answer is C (*Synopsis VI*, pages 160–162; *CTP V*, pages 483–485).

5.12. The answer is D (*Synopsis VI*, page 166; *CTP V*, pages 485 and 508).

5.13. The answer is A (*Synopsis VI*, page 156; *CTP V*, pages 498–499).

5.14. The answer is B (*Synopsis VI*, pages 157–159; *CTP V*, pages 478–479).

5.15. The answer is E (*Synopsis VI*, pages 162–163; *CTP V*, page 485).

The Thematic Apperception Test (TAT) consists of a series of 20 pictures of ambiguous figures and events and one blank card. Most patients are shown approximately 10 pictures, the choice of pictures generally depending on the examiner's wish to clarify specific conflict areas. The TAT requires that a patient construct or create a *story* based on the pictures. With the blank card, the patient has to imagine a scene first and then tell a story about it. The

patient is asked to relate the story with a beginning, a middle, and an end. This projective test elicits information regarding a broad spectrum of psychological functioning, including needs, attitudes, and motives. Scoring of the TAT is not standardized. Although scoring systems exist, test interpretation is typically impressionistic and informal. Stories are examined for recurrent themes to provide evidence of mood, conflict, interpersonal relationships, and areas of strengths and weaknesses.

The Bender-Gestalt Test assesses *visual-motor coordination*. It consists of nine separate designs printed against a white background on separate cards. The patient is asked to copy each design, first with the card present and then from memory. This test is most frequently used with adults as a screening device for signs of organic brain dysfunction, but it has also been used to evaluate maturational levels in children.

The Wechsler Adult Intelligence Scale (WAIS) is an intelligence test designed for persons 16 years old or older. It is the best standardized and most widely used intelligence test in clinical practice today. The scale is designed for individual administration and consists of 11 subtests, six verbal and five nonverbal performance tests, yielding *verbal, performance, and full-scale I.Q.s*. Norms are provided for each of the tests, thus eliciting an I.Q. for the verbal test group, for the nonverbal test group, and for the entire scale. The subtests are information, comprehension, arithmetic, similarities, digit span, vocabulary, picture completion, block design, picture arrangement, object assembly, and digit symbol. A person's I.Q. score indicates the degree of deviation of the person's intellectual capacity from the average.

The Minnesota Multiphasic Personality Inventory (MMPI), introduced in 1943 and recently revised (MMPI-2), is the most widely used and most thoroughly researched of the objective personality assessment instruments. The inventory is easy to administer and requires little time or effort on the part of the examiner, as the persons evaluate themselves. This *self-report inventory* consists of 550 statements to which the person has to respond with "True," "False," or "Cannot say." The statements pertain to a great many personality aspects, such as physiological functions, habits, attitudes, and psychopathology, and the person is asked to report whether the statements personally apply. The MMPI gives scores on 10 standard clinical scales, each of which was derived from homogenous-criteria groups of psychiatric patients. Each scale was validated by studying various diagnostic groups to determine whether the scale items truly differentiated between normal controls and medical or psychiatric patients.

The Sentence Completion Test (SCT) is composed of a series of *sentence stems*, such as "I like . . . ," that the patients are asked to complete in their own words with the first words that come to mind. This test is designed to tap a patient's conscious associations to areas of functioning in which the examiner may be interested—for instance, responses that are highly emotional, repetitive, humorous, bland, or factually informative.

5.16–5.20

5.16. The answer is C (*Synopsis VI*, pages 168–169; *CTP V*, pages 511–512).

5.17. The answer is B (*Synopsis VI*, page 168; *CTP V*, page 512).

5.18. The answer is D (*Synopsis VI*, pages 156–157; *CTP V*, pages 516–517).

5.19. The answer is A (*Synopsis VI*, pages 159–160; *CTP V*, page 483).

5.20. The answer is E (*Synopsis VI*, pages 166–167; *CTP V*, pages 485 and 508).

Various neuropsychiatric tests, including the Halstead-Reitan and the Luria-Nebraska batteries, are sometimes useful in bringing to light subtle organic dysfunctions that are undetected in standard psychiatric, psychological, and even neurological assessments. The Halstead-Reitan Battery of Neuropsychological Tests consists of 10 tests, including the *Trail Making Test and Critical Flicker Frequency*, and was developed in an attempt to improve the reliability of the criteria used to diagnose brain damage. Assessment data were gathered on a carefully compiled group of patients with left-hemisphere injury, right-hemisphere injury, and global involvement. The Trail Making Test tests visuomotor perception and motor speed, and the Critical Flicker Frequency (noting when a flickering light becomes steady) tests visual perception.

The Luria-Nebraska Neuropsychological Battery (LLNB) is extremely sensitive in identifying discrete forms of brain damage, such as *dyslexia* (an impairment in the ability to read) and dyscalculia (an inability to perform arithmetical operations), rather than more global forms.

The Stanford-Binet Intelligence Scale is the test most frequently used in the individual examination of children. It consists of 120 items, plus several alternative tests, applicable to the ages *between 2 years and adulthood*. The tests have a variety of graded difficulty, both verbal and performance, designed to assess such functions as memory, free association, orientation, language comprehension, knowledge of common objects, abstract thinking, and the use of judgment and reasoning.

The Rorschach test is a psychological test consisting of 10 ink blots that the person is asked to look at and interpret. Its purpose is to furnish a description of the *dynamic forces of personality* through an analysis of the subject's interpretations.

The face-hand test, devised by Lauretta Bender, is a test of *diffuse cerebral dysfunction* to which normal children by the age of 7 respond negatively. The person, whose eyes are closed, is touched simultaneously on the cheek and the hand; retesting is done with the eyes open. Results are considered positive if the subject fails consistently to identify both stimuli within 10 trials.

5.21–5.25

5.21. The answer is C (*Synopsis VI*, pages 168–169; *CTP V*, pages 505–511).

5.22. The answer is E (*Synopsis VI*, pages 168–169; *CTP V*, pages 505–511).

5.23. The answer is D (*Synopsis VI*, pages 168–169; *CTP V*, pages 505–511).

5.24. The answer is A (*Synopsis VI*, pages 168–169; *CTP V*, pages 505–511).

5.25. The answer is B (*Synopsis VI*, pages 168–169; *CTP V*, pages 505–511).

Numerous mental status cognitive tasks are available to test and localize various brain dysfunctions. Construction apraxia—the *loss of gestalt*, the loss of symmetry, and the distortion of figures—seen in the task of copying the outline of simple objects, is localized to the nondominant parietal lobe. Dysfunction of the occipital lobes is suggested when a patient displays the visual-perceptive defect of not being able to *name a camouflaged object* but being able to name it when it is not camouflaged. Two or more errors or two or more seven-second delays in carrying out tasks of *right-left orientation* are localized to dysfunction of the dominant parietal lobe. A dysfunction in concentration is thought to be localized to the frontal lobes and can be tested by eliciting any *improper letter sequence* in the task of spelling "earth" backward. Anomia is the inability to *name common objects* (e.g., watch, key) and is localized to the dominant temporal lobe. A summary of many of these tasks is found in Table 5.2.

5.26–5.29

5.26. The answer is B (*Synopsis VI*, pages 156–157; *CTP V*, page 497).

5.27. The answer is C (*Synopsis VI*, pages 156–157; *CTP V*, page 517).

5.28. The answer is D (*Synopsis VI*, pages 156–157; *CTP V*, pages 497 and 517).

5.29. The answer is E (*Synopsis VI*, pages 156–157; *CTP V*, pages 497 and 517–518).

The Wechsler Adult Intelligence Scale (WAIS) was originally designed in 1939 and has gone through several revisions since then. It is the test most often used to determine I.Q. in the average adult. A scale for children *ages 6 through 16 years* has been devised—the Wechsler Intelligence Scale for Children (WISC)—as well as a scale for children

Table 5.2
Mental Status Cognitive Tasks

Task	Dysfunction	Abnormal Response	Suggested Localization
Spell "earth" backward	Concentration	Any improper letter sequence	Frontal lobes
Serial 7s	Concentration	One or more errors or longer than 90 seconds	Frontal lobes
Name the day of the week, month, year, location	Global disorientation	Any error	Frontal lobes (if memory intact)
Repeat: "No ifs, ands, or buts," "The President lives in Washington," "Methodist Episcopal," "Massachussetts"	Expressive language	Missed words or syllables; repetition of internal syllables; dropping of word endings	Dominant frontal lobes
Name common objects (e.g., key, watch, button)	Anomia	Cannot name; word approximations; describes functions, rather than word	Dominant temporal lobe, angular gyrus
Conversation during examination	Receptive language	Word approximations, neologisms, word salad, stock words, tangential speech	Dominant temporal lobes
Name fingers	Finger agnosia	Two or more errors; cannot identify after examiner numbers each	Dominant parietal lobe
Calculations	Dyscalculia	Errors in borrowing or carrying over when concentration is intact	Dominant parietal lobe
Write a sentence	Dysgraphia	No longer able to write cursive; loss of word structure; abnormally formed letters	Dominant parietal lobe
In individual steps, copy sentence, read it, and do what it says ("Put the paper in your pocket")	Dysgraphia, dyslexia, comprehension	No longer able to write cursive; loss of sentence structure; loss of word structure; abnormally formed letters	Dominant temporoparietal lobe
Place left hand to right ear, right elbow, right knee; same for right hand	Right-left disorientation	Two or more errors or two or more seven-second delays in carrying out tasks	Dominant parietal lobe
Copy the outline of simple objects (e.g., Greek cross, key)	Construction apraxia	Loss of gestalt, loss of symmetry, distortion of figures	Nondominant parietal lobe
Camouflaged object(s)	Visual-perception deficit	Cannot name when camouflaged, can name when clear	Occipital lobes

Table adapted from M A Taylor: Cognitive tasks in the mental status examination. J Nerv Ment Dis *168:* 168, 1980. © 1980, Williams & Wilkins, Baltimore. Used with permission.

ages 4 to 6½ years—the Wechsler Preschool and Primary Scale of Intelligence (WPPSI). The WISC is an individual test that, like the WAIS, provides separate verbal and performance I.Q.s, based on different sets of tests, and a full-scale I.Q.; it requires a highly trained examiner. The WPPSI, devised in 1967, an individual test, extended the range of assessment downward in age. In practice, the WAIS, the WISC, or the WPPSI is used as part of a battery of psychological tests.

Educational background can clearly affect the information and vocabulary segments of the scales and must be taken into account when evaluating a subject's scores.

The Bayley Infant Scale of Development assesses *children from 8 weeks to 2½ years* of age. The test examines both motor and social functioning. The developmental quotient (D.Q.) obtained is based on standardized norms for the child's age.

5.30–5.33

5.30. The answer is A (*Synopsis VI*, page 161; *CTP V*, pages 456 and 482).

5.31. The answer is A (*Synopsis VI*, page 161; *CTP V*, pages 456 and 482).

5.32. The answer is B (*Synopsis VI*, page 237; *CTP V*, pages 456 and 487–488).

5.33. The answer is C (*Synopsis VI*, page 235; *CTP V*, page 487).

The Beck Depression Inventory is a *self-administered* scale. It emphasizes *subjective mood and thoughts* within the framework of Aaron Beck's cognitive theory of depression. The scale has been criticized because it puts little emphasis on the neurovegetative symptoms of depression.

The Hamilton Depression Rating Scale is administered by the examiner. The patient is rated on signs and symptoms of depression, including psychomotor retardation, changes in sleep and appetite, and weight loss. This scale emphasizes the *neurovegetative symptoms* and has been criticized for giving little attention to the affective and cognitive changes that may occur in patients with major depression.

The Brief Psychiatric Rating Scale provides a *global pathology index*. This scale, filled out by the examiner after the interview, screens for a wide range of psychiatric symptoms, including somatic concern, anxiety, disorganization, guilt, tension, grandiosity, hostility, and suspiciousness. As this scale covers many divergent symptoms, it is best used as a barometer of a patient's global pathology and improvement during treatment.

6 |||||

Theories of Personality and Psychopathology

The term "personality" is used in different ways by different theorists. Generally, it refers to a person's characteristic behavioral interactions with people and his or her environment. Many theories have been proposed to explain the structure and the dynamics of normal and abnormal behavior.

Sigmund Freud's theory of psychoanalysis predominated in the evolution of the psychodynamic approach in psychiatry. Psychoanalytic theory is concerned primarily with the elucidation of those factors that motivate behavior. Because of that theory's influence on psychiatric thought and practice, the student must understand the basic assumptions of Freudian theory, including the concepts of dynamic unconscious, psychic determinism, psychic conflict, infantile sexuality, dream interpretation, and defense mechanisms. Also critical to an understanding of psychoanalytic theory are the techniques Freud used to obtain data about the unconscious forces motivating a person's behavior, such as free association and the development of transference.

At various stages in the evolution of psychoanalysis, several of Freud's colleagues expanded or revised his formulations. These modifications were subsequently incorporated into the body of psychoanalytic theory; however, other innovations produced schisms within the Freudian movement and, in some instances, led to the establishment of new schools of psychoanalysis.

Among the most prominent of the early dissenters were Alfred Adler and Carl Jung, both of whom rejected Freud's belief that sexuality plays a unique role in normal and pathological human behavior. Jung's rejection of Freud's libido theory led to the elaboration of a rather mystical psychoanalytic system. Adler turned to the sociocultural determinants of behavior. Social, cultural, and interpersonal behavioral determinants were also emphasized in the so-called culturalist theories of Karen Horney and Harry Stack Sullivan, among others. Concomitantly, these workers de-emphasized the biological instinctual drives, particularly sexuality, as dominant determinants of behavior.

Other theories of psychopathology did not evolve as direct offshoots of Freudian psychoanalysis. Adolf Meyer, for example, conceived of normal, as well as abnormal, behavior as deriving from a series of adaptive reactions to the environment.

Chapter 6 in *Synopsis VI*, "Theories of Personality and Psychopathology," includes a detailed section on Sigmund Freud, founder of classical psychoanalysis, as well as a section devoted to the schools derived from psychoanalysis and psychology. After a review of that chapter and Chapter 6, "Theories of Personality and Psychopathology: Psychoanalysis," Chapter 7, "Theories of Personality and Psychopathology: Other Psychodynamic Schools," and Chapter 8, "Theories of Personality and Psychopathology: Approaches Derived from Psychology and Philosophy," in *CTP V*, students may test their knowledge by studying the questions and answers below.

HELPFUL HINTS

Know the various theorists, their schools of thought, and their theories.

psychoanalytic theory	topographic theory	Sandor Ferenczi
libido and instinct theories	preconscious	Kurt Goldstein
free association	primary process	Carl Jung
fundamental rule	wish fulfillment	Kurt Lewin
hysterical phenomena	latent dream	Adolph Meyer
psychoneurosis	nocturnal sensory stimuli	Henry Murray
psychosexual development	*The Ego and the Id*	Sandor Rado
reality principle	ego ideal	Wilhelm Reich
The Interpretation of Dreams	reality testing	Heinz Kohut
conscious	object relations	Heinz Hartmann
secondary process	object constancy	defense mechanisms
manifest dream	synthetic functions of the ego	pregenital
dream work	primary autonomous functions	character traits
day's residue	Anna Freud	acting out
structural model	unconscious motivation	analytical process
instinctual drives	conflict	interpretation
ego functions	repression	Karl Abraham
regression	talking cure	Franz Alexander
behaviorism	narcissistic, immature, neurotic,	Gordon Allport
psychodynamic thinking	and mature defenses	Ronald Fairbairn
ego psychology	signal anxiety	Donald Winnicott
psychic determinism	infantile sexuality	Erich Fromm
symbolism	primary and secondary gains	Karen Horney
Joseph Breuer	working through	Melanie Klein
hypnosis	transference	Abraham Maslow
Studies on Hysteria	repetition compulsion	Gardner Murphy
abreaction	Alfred Adler	Frederick S. Perls
resistance	Eric Berne	Otto Rank
narcissism	Raymond Cattell	Harry Stack Sullivan
Eros and Thanatos	Michael Balint	

QUESTIONS

DIRECTIONS: Each of the statements or questions below is followed by five suggested responses or completions. Select the *one* that is *best* in each case.

6.1. The fundamental rule of psychoanalysis is
A. psychic determinism
B. abreaction
C. the concept of the unconscious
D. free association
E. resistance and repression

6.2. According to Freudian theory, neurotic symptoms are most likely to develop as a result of the defense mechanism
A. resistance
B. repression
C. regression
D. suppression
E. isolation

6.3. Freud's concepts about the pleasure and reality principles include all the following *except*
A. the reality principle is an unlearned function
B. the reality principle is related to the maturation of ego functions
C. the pleasure principle is inborn
D. the pleasure principle persists throughout life
E. the pleasure principle is modified by the reality principle

6.4. In phobias the major defense mechanism is
A. identification
B. displacement
C. projection
D. reaction formation
E. undoing

6.5. Which of the following statements about dreams is true as described by Freud?
A. Latent dream content derives from the repressed part of the id
B. Dreams are the conscious expression of an unconscious fantasy
C. Dreams represent wish-fulfillment activity
D. Sensory impressions may play a role in initiating a dream
E. All the above

6.6. Classical psychoanalysis as formulated by Freud includes all the following *except*
A. instinct theory
B. free association
C. libido theory
D. collective unconscious
E. unconscious motivation

6.7. Autonomous functions of the ego include all the following *except*
A. intuition
B. repression
C. learning
D. comprehension
E. thinking

6.8. The defense mechanism that enables a person to channel libidinal impulses toward culturally acceptable or socially valued gratification is termed
A. suppression
B. sublimation
C. repression
D. reaction formation
E. isolation

6.9. In the Freudian theory of anxiety, all the following are true *except*
A. anxiety is viewed as a signal
B. anxiety may be real or neurotic
C. anxiety involves the withdrawal of libido from others and reinvestment in the self
D. anxiety may arise as the result of excessive instinctual stimulation
E. anxiety may arise because the patient recognizes aspects of a situation that were once traumatic

DIRECTIONS: For each of the incomplete statements below, *one or more* of the completions given are correct. Choose answer

A. if only *1, 2, and 3* are correct
B. if only *1 and 3* are correct
C. if only *2 and 4* are correct
D. if only *4* is correct
E. if *all* are correct

6.10. Terms associated with Carl Jung include
1. collective unconscious
2. introversion and extroversion
3. archetypes
4. anima and animus

6.11. Mature defenses, according to George Vaillant, include
1. altruism
2. intellectualization
3. humor
4. rationalization

6.12. According to Freud, neuroses develop when
1. there is a conflict between the id and the ego
2. the ego's defense against instinctual impulses is unsuccessful
3. the drives that seek discharge are repressed from consciousness
4. anxiety becomes manifest

6.13. Secondary gain refers to
1. attention or sympathy
2. monetary compensation
3. freedom from responsibility
4. reduction of tension and conflict

DIRECTIONS: Each group of questions below consists of lettered headings followed by a list of numbered words or statements. For each numbered word or statement, select the *one* lettered heading that is most closely associated with it. Each lettered heading may be selected once, more than once, or not at all.

Questions 6.14–6.18
A. Franz Alexander
B. D. W. Winnicott
C. Karen Horney
D. Melanie Klein
E. Heinz Kohut

6.14. Introduced the concept of the transitional object.

6.15. Theorized that oedipal strivings are experienced during the first year of life and that, during this first year, gratifying experiences with the good breast reinforce basic trust

6.16. Challenged the emphasis on the Oedipus complex and believed that a person's current personality attributes were not so much based on infantile strivings but the result of the interaction between the person and the environment

6.17. Introduced the concept of the corrective emotional experience

6.18. Expanded Freud's concept of narcissism; theories are known as self-psychology

Questions 6.19–6.23
A. Oral stage
B. Anal stage
C. Phallic stage
D. Latency stage
E. Genital stage

6.19. Pathological traits resulting from libidinal fixation at this stage include excessive dependency, envy, and jealousy

6.20. Its resolution gives rise to the superego

6.21. Positive development involves developing a sense of industry and a capacity for mastery

6.22. Sets the stage normally for a fully mature personality with a consistent sense of identity

6.23. Maladaptive characteristics and defenses are most typically seen in obsessive-compulsive neuroses

Questions 6.24–6.28
A. Harry Stack Sullivan
B. Abraham Maslow
C. Wilhelm Reich
D. Kurt Lewin
E. Frederick S. Perls

6.24. Coined the term "group dynamics"

6.25. Introduced the concept of the peak experience

6.26. Introduced the term "participant observer"

6.27. Described character formation and character types

6.28. Applied Gestalt theory to therapy

Questions 6.29–6.33
A. Projection
B. Displacement
C. Reaction formation
D. Suppression
E. Repression

6.29. A patient refuses to stay in bed, stating that he is fully capable of walking and needs to keep busy. The staff try to talk with the man; finally, after much initial difficulty, the patient admits that he is terribly frightened that he will become completely dependent on others, and "part of me just wants to be taken care of like a baby, just curl up and die. If I give in to that, what will become of me?"

6.30. A resident on call starts to insert an intravenous tube, but, as she begins to do so, the patient jerks his arm away, pushes the resident, and yells, "You're making me very angry; get out of my room."

6.31. A young woman who had been raped several hours earlier is unable to remember the details of the assault.

6.32. A young woman who has a serious, long-term illness that has disfigured her face and requires extensive plastic surgery tells the nurses that her surgeon "hates me; I know he can't stand to look at my face another second; he just wants me to leave him alone."

6.33. A patient who has just been raped states, "I can't think about it right now; I have to feel stronger first."

Questions 6.34–6.43
A. Topographic theory
B. Structural theory

6.34. Set forth in *The Interpretation of Dreams* in 1900

6.35. Formulated and presented in *The Ego and the Id* in 1923

6.36. Conscious

6.37. Id, ego, and superego

6.38. Reality principle

6.39. Unconscious

6.40. Primary process

6.41. Characteristic of very young children

6.42. Preconscious

6.43. Secondary process

ANSWERS

Theories of Personality and Psychopathology

6.1. The answer is D (*Synopsis VI*, pages 185–186; *CTP V*, page 1456).

The fundamental rule of psychoanalysis is to verbalize honestly all thoughts and feelings through the method of *free association*. The use of free association in psychoanalysis evolved gradually from 1892 to 1895. Sigmund Freud (1856–1939) began to encourage his patients to verbalize, without reservation or censorship, the passing thoughts in their minds. The conflicts that emerge while fulfilling the task of free association constitute *resistance*, which was first defined by Freud as the reluctance of patients to recount significant memories. Later, Freud realized that resistance was often the result of an unconscious *repression* of conflictual material, the repression leading to an active exclusion of painful or anxiety-producing feelings from consciousness. It was this mechanism of repression that Freud thought was at the core of all symptom formation. *Psychic determinism* is the concept that adult actions can be understood as the end result of a chain of psychological events that have well-defined causes and effects. *Abreaction* is a process in which a memory of a traumatic experience is released from repression and brought into consciousness. As the patient is able to express the affect associated with the memory, the affect is discharged, and the symptoms disappear. The concept of the *unconscious* was one of Freud's most important contributions; it was first used to define mental material not in the field of awareness and, later, to designate a topographic area of the mind where psychic material is not readily accessible to conscious awareness. Table 6.1 gives brief definitions of the most common defense mechanisms.

6.2. The answer is B (*Synopsis VI*, pages 183–185; *CTP V*, page 360).

According to Freudian theory, neurotic symptoms are most likely to develop as a result of the *repression* of unconscious impulses and neuroses. Freud believed that, when the impulses (both sexual and aggressive) are not allowed direct expression, they manifest themselves indirectly as neurotic symptoms. Initially in his theoretical formulations, Freud considered repression to be synonymous with defense; repression was what defended the person from the impulses and the drives of the id in accordance with the demands of external reality. Repression is the selective forgetting of what is too painful or objectionable for the conscious mind to accept. *Suppression* is defined as the control and inhibition of un-

acceptable impulses, emotions, or ideas. Suppression is differentiated from repression in that repression is an unconscious process, whereas suppression is a conscious act. In *isolation* an idea or memory is separated from its emotional charge; for example, a person may recount rageful feelings without affect. *Regression* is the act of returning to some earlier level of adaptation. It is observed in many psychiatric conditions, particularly schizophrenia. *Resistance* is a conscious or unconscious opposition to the uncovering of the unconscious. It is a defense against impulses from the id that are threatening to the ego.

6.3. The answer is A (*Synopsis VI*, page 178; *CTP V*, pages 361–362).

The reality principle is a *learned*, rather than an unlearned, *function* and is related to the *maturation of ego functions*. The reality principle causes the *pleasure principle* to be modified to conform to the demands of the outside world. The pleasure principle is an *inborn* characteristic of the organism, whose sole aim is to seek pleasure through the discharge of tension. It *persists throughout life*, although it is most evident during infancy and childhood.

6.4. The answer is B (*Synopsis VI*, pages 182–185; *CTP V*, pages 376 and 976).

In phobias, fear is avoided by using the defense mechanism of *displacement*, through which the conflict is displaced from the unconscious object or situation to the more acceptable conscious object or situation of the phobia. Displacement is a transferring of an emotion from an original unacceptable idea to another idea or object that is manifestly more tolerable. *Projection* is a defense mechanism in which thoughts, feelings, and impulses that are personally unacceptable are attributed to another. In *identification* a person takes on the characteristics of another, who is sometimes a source of unconscious frustration in reality. In *undoing* a person symbolically acts out in reverse something unacceptable. In *reaction formation* a person acts or thinks in a way that is directly antithetical to what is truly felt.

The pathogenesis of phobias has been described quite differently by proponents of different theoretical orientations. For instance, behaviorists using learning theory are concerned not with the underlying causes of the phobia but, rather, with desensitizing the patient to the anxiety-producing associations maintaining phobic behavior. Psychoanalytically oriented theorists concentrate on the unconscious psychological conflicts being manifested

Table 6.1
Defense Mechanisms

Acting out. An action rather than a verbal response to an unconscious instinctual drive or impulse that brings about the temporary partial relief of inner tension. Relief is attained by reacting to a present situation as if it were the situation that originally gave rise to the drive or impulse. An immature defense.

Altruism. Regard for and dedication to the welfare of others. The term was originated by Auguste Comte (1789–1857), a French philosopher. In psychiatry the term is closely linked with ethics and morals. Freud recognized altruism as the only basis for the development of community interest; Eugen Bleuler equated it with morality. A mature defense.

Anticipation. The act of dealing with, doing, foreseeing, or experiencing beforehand. Anticipation of the future is characteristic of the ego and is necessary for the judgment and planning of suitable later action. Anticipation depends on reality testing—by trying in an active manner and in small doses what may happen to one passively and in unknown doses. This testing affords the possibility of judging reality and is an important factor in the development of the ability to tolerate tensions. A mature defense.

Asceticism. A mode of life characterized by rigor, self-denial, and mortification of the flesh. Asceticism is seen typically as a phase in puberty, when it indicates a fear of sexuality and a simultaneous defense against sexuality. Asceticism is also seen as an extreme type of masochistic character disorder, in which almost all activity is forbidden because it represents intolerable instinctual demands. In such cases the very act of mortifying may become a distorted expression of the blocked sexuality and may produce masochistic pleasure. Examples are eccentrics who devote their lives to the combating of some particular evil that unconsciously may represent their own instinctual demands. A mature defense.

Blocking. The involuntary cessation of thought processes or speech because of unconscious emotional factors. It is also known as thought deprivation. An immature defense.

Controlling. The excessive attempt to manage or regulate events or objects in the environment in the interest of minimizing anxiety and solving internal conflicts. A neurotic defense.

Denial. A mechanism in which the existence of unpleasant realities is disavowed. The term refers to a keeping out of conscious awareness any aspects of external reality that, if acknowledged, would produce anxiety. A narcissistic defense.

Displacement. A mechanism by which the emotional component of an unacceptable idea or object is transferred to a more acceptable one. A neurotic defense.

Dissociation. A mechanism involving the segregation of any group of mental or behavioral processes from the rest of the person's psychic activity. It may entail the separation of an idea from its accompanying emotional tone, as seen in dissociative disorders. A neurotic defense.

Distortion. A misrepresentation of reality. It is based on unconsciously determined motives. A narcissistic defense.

Externalization. A general term, correlative to internalization, referring to the tendency to perceive in the external world and in external objects components of one's own personality, including instinctual impulses, conflicts, moods, attitudes, and styles of thinking. It is a more general term than projec-

tion, which is defined by its derivation, form, and correlation with specific introjects. A neurotic defense.

Humor. The overt expression of feelings without personal discomfort or immobilization and without unpleasant effects on others. Humor allows one to bear, yet focus on, what is too terrible to be borne, in contrast to wit, which always involves distraction or displacement away from the affective issue. A mature defense.

Hypochondriasis. An exaggerated concern about one's physical health. The concern is not based on real organic pathology. An immature defense.

Identification. A mechanism by which one patterns oneself after another person; in the process, the self may be permanently altered.

Identification with the aggressor. A process by which one incorporates within oneself the mental image of a person who represents a source of frustration from the outside world. The classic example of this defense occurs toward the end of the oedipal stage, when a boy, whose main source of love and gratification is his mother, identifies with his father. The father represents the source of frustration, being the powerful rival for the mother; the child cannot master or run away from his father, so he is obliged to identify with him.

Incorporation. A mechanism in which the psychic representation of another person or aspects of another person are assimilated into oneself through a figurative process of symbolic oral ingestion. It represents a special form of introjection and is the earliest mechanism of identification.

Inhibition. The depression or arrest of a function; suppression or diminution of outgoing influences from a reflex center. The sexual impulse, for example, may be inhibited because of psychological repression. A neurotic defense.

Intellectualization. A mechanism in which reasoning or logic is used in an attempt to avoid confrontation with an objectionable impulse and thus defends against anxiety. It is also known as brooding compulsion and thinking compulsion. A neurotic defense.

Introjection. The unconscious, symbolic internalization of a psychic representation of a hated or loved external object with the goal of establishing closeness to and constant presence of the object. In the case of a loved object, anxiety consequent to separation or tension arising out of ambivalence toward the object is diminished; in the case of a feared or hated object, internalization of its malicious or aggressive characteristics serves to avoid anxiety by symbolically putting those characteristics under one's own control. An immature defense.

Isolation. In psychoanalysis a mechanism involving the separation of an idea or memory from its attached feeling tone. Unacceptable ideational content is thereby rendered free of its disturbing or unpleasant emotional charge. A neurotic defense.

Passive-aggressive behavior. When a person shows aggressive feelings in passive ways, such as through obstructionism, pouting, and stubbornness. An immature defense.

Primitive idealization. Through this mechanism, external objects that are viewed as either "all good" or "all bad" are unrealistically endowed with great power. Most commonly,

(Continued)

Table 6.1
Continued

the "all good" object is seen as omnipotent or ideal, while the badness in the "all bad" object is greatly inflated. A narcissistic defense.

Projection. An unconscious mechanism in which one attributes to another the ideas, thoughts, feelings, and impulses that are unacceptable to oneself. Projection protects a person from anxiety arising from an inner conflict. By externalizing whatever is unacceptable, one deals with it as a situation apart from oneself. A narcissistic and immature defense.

Projective identification. Unwanted aspects of the self are deposited into another person such that the person projecting feels at one with the object of the projection. The extruded aspects are modified by and recovered from the recipient. This defense allows one to distance and make oneself understood by exerting pressure on another person to experience feelings similar to one's own. A narcissistic defense.

Rationalization. A mechanism in which irrational or unacceptable behavior, motives, or feelings are logically justified or made consciously tolerable by plausible means. A neurotic defense.

Reaction formation. An unconscious defense mechanism in which a person develops a socialized attitude or interest that is the direct antithesis of some infantile wish or impulse in the unconscious. One of the earliest and most stable defense mechanisms, it is closely related to repression; both are defenses against impulses or urges that are unacceptable to the ego. A neurotic defense.

Regression. A mechanism in which a person undergoes a partial or total return to earlier patterns of adaptation. Regression is observed in many psychiatric conditions, particularly schizophrenia. An immature defense.

Repression. A mechanism in which unacceptable mental contents are banished or kept out of consciousness. A term introduced by Freud, it is important in both normal psychological development and in neurotic and psychotic symptom formation. Freud recognized two kinds of repression: (1) repression proper—the repressed material was once in the conscious domain; (2) primal repression—the repressed material was never in the conscious realm. A neurotic defense.

Schizoid fantasy. The tendency to use fantasy and to indulge in autistic retreat for the purpose of conflict resolution and gratification. An immature defense.

Sexualization. The endowing of an object or function with sexual significance that it did not previously have or that it

possesses to a smaller degree; it is used to ward off anxieties connected with prohibitive impulses. A neurotic defense.

Somatization. The defensive conversion of psychic derivatives into bodily symptoms: a tendency to react with somatic rather than psychic manifestations. Infantile somatic responses are replaced by thought and affect during development (desomatization): regression to earlier somatic forms of response (resomatization) may result from unresolved conflicts and may play an important role in psychological reactions. An immature defense.

Splitting. External objects are divided into "all good" and "all bad" accompanied by the abrupt shifting of an object from one extreme category to the other. Sudden and complete reversal of feelings and conceptualizations about a person may occur. The extreme repetitive oscillation between contradictory self-concepts is another manifestation of this mechanism. A narcissistic defense.

Sublimation. A mechanism in which the energy associated with unacceptable impulses or drives is diverted into personally and socially acceptable channels. Unlike other defense mechanisms, sublimation offers some minimal gratification of the instinctual drive or impulse. A mature defense.

Substitution. A mechanism in which a person replaces an unacceptable wish, drive, emotion, or goal with one that is more acceptable.

Suppression. A conscious act of controlling and inhibiting an unacceptable impulse, emotion, or idea. Suppression is differentiated from repression in that repression is an unconscious process. A mature defense.

Symbolization. A mechanism by which one idea or object comes to stand for another because of some common aspect or quality in both. Symbolization is based on similarity and association. The symbols formed protect the person from the anxiety that may be attached to the original idea or object. A mature defense.

Turning against the self. Changing an unacceptable impulse aimed at others by redirecting it against oneself. An immature defense.

Undoing. A mechanism by which a person symbolically acts out in reverse something unacceptable that has already been done or against which the ego must defend itself. A primitive defense mechanism, undoing is a form of magical action. Repetitive in nature, it is commonly observed in persons with obsessive-compulsive disorder. A neurotic defense.

Compiled from Sigmund and Anna Freud, E. Semrad, W. W. Meissner, G. Vaillant. Narcissistic defenses: used by children and psychotics; Immature defenses: used by adolescents, in depression and obsessive-compulsive disorder (OCD); neurotic defenses: used by adults under stress, OCD, hysteria; mature defenses: used by normal adults.

by the phobic symptoms. According to this orientation, phobias, which are irrational fear responses, are seen as originating in an unconscious conflict. This conflict may result from an increase in sexual or aggressive energy attached to an unconscious object.

6.5.   The answer is E (*Synopsis VI*, pages 179–180; *CTP V*, pages 367–369).

In 1900 Freud published *The Interpretation of Dreams*, which is considered one of his most impor-

tant contributions to the field. The book includes data derived from his clinical experience with patients, as well as the insights gained from his self-analysis and free association to his own dreams. Freud concluded that a dream is the *conscious expression of an unconscious fantasy* or wish. Freud maintained that every dream represents *a wish fulfillment*, albeit disguised and distorted through such mechanisms as symbolism, displacement, and condensation. Dream analysis yields material that has been repressed by the ego's defensive activities. The dream, as it is consciously recalled and experienced, is termed the manifest dream, and its various elements are termed the manifest dream content; the unconscious thoughts and wishes that make up the core meaning of the dream are described as the latent dream content. The latent dream content, which gives rise to manifest dreams, includes the nocturnal sensory stimuli, repressed id impulses, and the day's residue. Nocturnal sensory stimuli are *sensory impressions*, such as pain and thirst, that can play an *initiating role* in dream formation. *Repressed id impulses* are wishes that have their origin in oedipal and preoedipal phases of development, and the latent dream content derives from such impulses. The day's residue comprises thoughts and ideas connected with the activities of the dreamer's waking life. Many of these thoughts and ideas become incorporated into the manifest dream.

6.6. The answer is D (*Synopsis VI*, pages 174, 178, and 188; *CTP V*, pages 359–362, 414–416, and 2140).

The *collective unconscious*, a term introduced by Carl Jung, refers to those psychic contents outside the realm of awareness that are common to humankind in general. Transcending cultural differences, the collective unconscious is derived from the heritable collective experience of the species.

Classical or orthodox psychoanalysis has been dependent in large part on Freud's *libido and instinct theories*, which investigate the various manifestations of the original sexual instinct and the complicated paths they may follow in the course of development. Psychoanalysis is based on the investigative technique of *free association*, in which patients attempt to verbalize, without reservation or censorship, their passing thoughts, ideas, and feelings. This method yielded Freud the data used to formulate such key concepts as *unconscious motivation*, which encompasses Freud's belief that actions and feelings are determined primarily by ideas outside the realm of awareness.

6.7. The answer is B (*Synopsis VI*, pages 180–181; *CTP V*, pages 373–374).

Repression is not considered an autonomous function of the ego; it is a mechanism of defense used by the ego to help mediate conflict between the ego, the superego, and the id. Repression is defined as an unconscious defense mechanism in which unacceptable mental contents are banished or kept out of consciousness.

Heinz Hartmann (1894–1970) is the psychoanalyst most closely associated with the term "primary autonomous ego functions." These autonomous ego functions are so named because they develop outside of conflict with the id, in what Hartmann called the average expectable environment. Hartmann included perception, *intuition, comprehension, thinking*, language, phases of motor development, *learning*, and intelligence among these primary autonomous functions.

6.8. The answer is B (*Synopsis VI*, pages 183–184; *CTP V*, page 376).

Sublimation is a mature defense that allows instincts to be channeled to pleasures that are socially acceptable, rather than to be dammed up or diverted. The instinct can then be satisfied in a desexualized form valued by society. *Suppression* is the conscious or semiconscious decision to postpone attention to an impulse. It, too, is a mature defense.

Neurotic defenses include repression, reaction formation, and isolation. *Repression* operates to keep from conscious awareness an idea or impulse unacceptable to the person. *Reaction formation* is the expression of an unacceptable impulse in its antithetical form. *Isolation* is the intrapsychic separation of affect from content; it can result in the repression of the idea or the affect and the displacement of the affect onto a substitute content.

6.9. The answer is C (*Synopsis VI*, pages 182 and 185; *CTP V*, pages 377–379).

Anxiety, according to Freudian theory as postulated in *Inhibitions, Symptoms, and Anxiety* (1926), is a *signal* of danger. At certain stages of development, the person reacts to characteristic danger situations. Anxiety may be *real*, involving an external danger, or *neurotic*, involving danger precipitated by an unknown or internal source.

Freud identified two types of anxiety-provoking situations. The first type, of which birth is an example, results from *excessive instinctual stimulation* that overwhelms one's capacities. The second type occurs in anticipation of a danger subjectively experienced as similar to a *past traumatic situation*. Narcissism, not anxiety, involves the *withdrawal of libido* from others and reinvestment in the self.

6.10. The answer is E (all) (*Synopsis VI*, page 188; *CTP V*, pages 414–416).

Carl Gustav Jung (1875–1961), a Swiss psychiatrist, founded his own school of analytic psychology after disassociating himself from Freud. He expanded on Freud's concept of the unconscious by describing the *collective unconscious* as "the shared mythological associations; those motives and images which can spring anew in every age and clime, without historical tradition or migration...." Jung defined repressed material as the personal unconscious. The collective unconscious includes *archetypes*, mythological or personalized images and configurations that have universal symbolic meaning. Archetypal figures exist for the mother, the father, the child, and the hero, among others. The archetypal configurations encountered most frequently are, in Jung's terminology, the persona, the shadow, the animus (in women), the anima (in men), and the self. Jung noted two types of personality organization: *introversion and extroversion*. Introversion is defined as that approach to life in which the person's predominant sense of reality derives from the inner world of thoughts, intuitions, emotions, and sensations. Extroversion is the attitude in which the person's concerns with material objects and people predominate. *Anima and animus* are unconscious traits; anima refers to a man's undeveloped femininity, and animus refers to a woman's undeveloped masculinity.

6.11. The answer is B (1, 3) (*Synopsis VI*, page 184; *CTP V*, page 376).

George Vaillant's mature defenses include altruism, anticipation, asceticism, humor, sublimation, and suppression. In the 1970s he published his 30-year follow-up study of people who had gone to Harvard in the 1930s. He delineated the psychological characteristics he considered essential to mental health in this group, including descriptions of defense mechanisms he thought to be healthy and those he thought to be more psychopathological. Vaillant classified four types of defenses: (1) narcissistic defenses, which are characteristic of young children and psychotic adults; (2) immature defenses, which are characteristic of adolescents and are also seen in psychopathological states, such as depression; (3) neurotic defenses, which may be seen in adults under stress; and (4) mature defenses, which are characteristic of adult functioning. At times, some of the defensive categories overlap; for instance, neurotic defenses may be seen in normally healthy, mature adults. *Intellectualization* and *rationalization* are characterized by Vaillant as among the neurotic defenses.

Altruism is a regard for the intents and needs of others. *Humor* is the overt expression of feelings without personal discomfort and without unpleasant effects on others. *Intellectualization* represents the attempt to avoid unacceptable feelings by escaping from emotions into a world of intellectual concepts and words. *Rationalization* is justification, making a thing appear reasonable that otherwise would be regarded as irrational.

6.12. The answer is E (all) (*Synopsis VI*, page 185; *CTP V*, pages 385–386).

According to Freud, neuroses develop when there is a *conflict between the id and the ego*, with the superego taking either side. The ego attempts to defend itself against instinctual impulses; if the *defense against instinctual impulses is unsuccessful*, the original impulse may manage to break through, producing a symptom formation, an intensification of the defense, which constitutes a symptom. There is a constant inner tension between drives needing to be discharged and anxiety about drive explosion, keeping them in check. The *drives that seek discharge are repressed from consciousness*, as is the anxiety that controls them. However, if the drives threaten to break through into consciousness, *anxiety becomes manifest* and presents itself as a neurotic symptom, which is a derivative of the underlying forbidden impulse. Treatment is aimed at revealing the impulse that has led to the defensive anxiety that has fueled the defensive symptom, resulting ideally in a lessening of the anxiety attached to the impulse and, thus, lessening of the defensive symptoms.

6.13. The answer is A (1, 2, 3) (*Synopsis VI*, page 185; *CTP V*, page 386).

Secondary gain is the advantage a person obtains from an illness. Examples include provoking pity to get *attention and sympathy*, receiving *monetary compensation*, and the implication that suffering entitles the patient to *freedom from responsibility*. Freudian theory postulates that neurotic illness can be conceptualized as a person's means of achieving primary and secondary gains. According to this conceptualization, neurotic illness serves a function; warded-off instincts that cannot be tolerated in consciousness lead the ego to form symptoms that act to reduce the urgency of unfulfilled strivings. The *reduction of tension and conflict* is not secondary gain but the revival of infantile longings in the adult and is viewed as the primary gain or purpose of a neurotic symptom. Primary gain is viewed as unconscious, whereas secondary gain is the more conscious or preconscious advantage that the ego obtains from the external world through the illness.

6.14–6.18

6.14. The answer is B (*Synopsis VI*, page 181; *CTP V*, page 382).

6.15. The answer is D (*Synopsis VI*, pages 186–189; *CTP V*, pages 380–381).

6.16. The answer is C (*Synopsis VI*, pages 186–189; *CTP V*, pages 422–424).

6.17. The answer is A (*Synopsis VI*, pages 186–189; *CTP V*, page 1443).

6.18. The answer is E (*Synopsis VI*, pages 186–189; *CTP V*, pages 1448–1489).

D. W. Winnicott (1897–1971) is an influential contributor to object relations theory. He focused on the conditions that make it possible for a child to develop awareness as a separate person. One of the conditions is the provision of an environment termed "good-enough mothering." Good-enough mothering enables the child to be nurtured in a nonimpinging environment that permits the emergence of the true self. The concept of the *transitional object* was introduced by Winnicott. Transitional objects are aids that help the child gradually shift from subjectivity to external reality. These possessions, usually blankets or soft toys, exist in an intermediate realm as a substitute for the mother and as one of the first objects a child begins to recognize as separate from the self or "not-me."

Melanie Klein (1882–1960) modified analytic theory, particularly in its application to infants and very young children. In contrast to orthodox psychoanalytic theory, which postulates the development of the superego during the fourth year of life,

Klein maintained that a primitive superego is formed during the first and second years. Klein further believed that aggressive, rather than sexual, drives are preeminent during the earliest stages of development. She deviated most sharply from classical psychoanalytic theory in her formulations concerning the Oedipus complex. She believed that the onset of the Oedipus complex was in the first two years of life, as opposed to the classical formulation of its occurring between the ages of 3 and 5. She also believed that, during the first year, gratifying experiences with the *good breast* reinforce basic trust and that frustrating experiences can lead to a depressive position.

Karen Horney (1885–1952) was an American psychiatrist who ascribed great importance to the influence of sociocultural factors on individual development. She raised questions about the existence of immutable instinctual drives and developmental phases or sexual conflict as the root of neurosis while recognizing the importance of sexual drives. Rather than focusing on such concepts as the Oedipus complex, Horney emphasized cultural factors and disturbances in interpersonal and intrapsychic development as the cause of neuroses in general.

Franz Alexander (1891–1964) founded the Chicago Institute for Psychoanalysis. He developed the concept of the *corrective emotional experience*. The therapist, who is supportive, enables the patient to master past traumas and to modify the effects of those traumas. Alexander was also a major influence in the field of psychosomatic medicine.

Heinz Kohut (1913–1981) *expanded Freud's concept of narcissism*. In *The Analysis of the Self* (1971), Kohut wrote about a large group of patients suffering from narcissistic personality disorders whom he believed to be analyzable but who did not develop typical transference neuroses in the classical sense. The conflict involves the relation between the self and the archaic narcissistic objects. These objects are the grandiose self and the idealized parent image, the reactivations of which constitute a threat to the patient's sense of integrity. Kohut's theories are known as *self-psychology*.

6.19–6.23

6.19. **The answer is A** (*Synopsis VI*, pages 175–177; *CTP V*, pages 363–364).

6.20. **The answer is C** (*Synopsis VI*, pages 175–177; *CTP V*, pages 364–365).

6.21. **The answer is D** (*Synopsis VI*, pages 175–177; *CTP V*, page 377).

6.22. **The answer is E** (*Synopsis VI*, pages 175–177; *CTP V*, pages 379–380).

6.23. **The answer is B** (*Synopsis VI*, pages 175–177; *CTP V*, page 364).

Freud used the term "libido" to refer to that force by which the sexual instinct, together with its complex process of development and its accompanying physical and mental manifestations, is represented in the mind. This psychosexual instinct is not fully formed at birth but develops in an organized sequence of stages, each of which has many aspects and characteristics separate from the actual event of sexual intercourse. The earliest manifestations of sexuality arise in relation to bodily functions that are basically nonsexual, such as feeding and the development of bowel and bladder control. Psychosexual libido development encompasses oral, anal, urethral, phallic, latency, and genital stages.

The objective of the *oral stage* (birth to 18 months) is to establish a trusting dependence on nursing and sustaining objects. The infant judges reality in terms of whether something will provide satisfaction (and, therefore, will be swallowed) or will create tension (and will be spit out). *Pathological traits* can result from excessive oral gratification or deprivation that leads to libidinal fixations in this stage. Oral characters are often *excessively dependent* on objects for the maintenance of their self-esteem. *Envy* and *jealousy* are also associated with oral traits.

The *anal stage* (1 to 3 years) is essentially an ambivalent period of striving for independence and separation from the dependence on and control of the parent. The child is expected, for the first time, to relinquish one aspect of freedom—to accede to the mother's demand that the child use the toilet for the evacuation of feces and urine. Maladaptive character traits, often apparently inconsistent, are derived from anal eroticism and the defenses against it. Orderliness, obstinacy, and frugality are typical of patients who have regressed to this pregenital phase of development as an expression of their wish to dominate. When defenses against anal traits are less effective, the anal character reveals heightened ambivalence (between the tendency to control and retain the object and the desire to destroy and expel it), lack of tidiness, rage, and sadomasochistic tendencies. Anal characteristics and defenses are most typically seen in *obsessive-compulsive neuroses*.

The fundamental task in finding a love object belongs to the *phallic* stage (3 to 5 years), when the pattern for later object choices is set down. It is now that the child discovers the anatomical differences between the sexes. The penis becomes the organ of principal interest to children of both sexes, with the lack of a penis in the girl being considered evidence of castration. Freud used the term "Oedipus complex" to refer to the intense love relationships formed during this period. The resolution of the Oedipus complex in the phallic phase gives rise to the *superego*, the powerful internal resource that is based on the child's identification with the parental figures.

In the *latency stage* (6 to 11 years), the institution of the superego at the close of the oedipal period and the further maturation of ego functions allow for a considerably greater degree of control over instinctual impulses. Freud believed that the sexual drive was inactive during this period until pubescence.

The child can develop a *sense of industry* and a *capacity for mastery* of objects and concepts that allow autonomous function and a sense of initiative without running the risk of a sense of inferiority.

In the *genital stage* (from age 11 or 12 until young adulthood), the physiological maturation of systems of genital (sexual) functioning and attendant hormonal systems leads to an intensification of drives, especially libidinal ones. It has been stated that in puberty incestuous oedipal feelings in both sexes resurge, and the task of withdrawing libido from the parents and attributing it to other, more suitable love objects becomes critically important. The successful resolution of the genital phase sets the stage normally for a *mature personality* with a self-integrated and consistent sense of identity.

6.24–6.28

6.24. The answer is D (*Synopsis VI*, pages 189–191; *CTP V*, pages 435–436).

6.25. The answer is B (*Synopsis VI*, pages 189–191; *CTP V*, pages 443–444).

6.26. The answer is A (*Synopsis VI*, pages 189–191; *CTP V*, pages 424–427).

6.27. The answer is C (*Synopsis VI*, pages 189–191; *CTP V*, pages 427–428).

6.28. The answer is E (*Synopsis VI*, pages 189–191; *CTP V*, page 442).

Kurt Lewin (1890–1947) adapted the field approach from physics into a concept called field theory. A field is the totality of coexisting parts that are mutually interdependent. Applying field theory to groups, he coined the term *"group dynamics"* and believed that a group was greater than the sum of its parts.

Abraham Maslow (1908–1970) was a developer of the self-actualization theory, which focuses on the need to understand the totality of the person. A *peak experience*, according to this school of thought, is an episodic, brief occurrence in which the person suddenly experiences a powerful transcendental state of consciousness. This powerful experience occurs most often in psychologically healthy persons.

Harry Stack Sullivan (1892–1949) made basic contributions to psychodynamic theory with his emphasis on the cultural matrix of personality development. Sullivan defined psychiatry as the study of interpersonal relations that are manifest in observable behavior of persons. Those relations can be observed inside the therapeutic situation, the process being greatly enhanced when the therapist is one of the participants. The transaction then is between the therapist, who is a *participant observer,* and a client, whose life is disturbed or disordered.

Wilhelm Reich's (1897–1957) major contributions to psychoanalysis were in the areas of *character formation and character types*. Reich placed special emphasis on the influence of social forces in determining character structure, particularly on their repressive and inhibiting effects. Reich's basic concept was that character is a defensive structure, an armoring of the ego against both instinctual forces within and the world without. It is the person's characteristic manner of dealing with these threats. He described four major character types: hysterical, compulsive, narcissistic, and masochistic.

The evolution of *Gestalt therapy* is closely associated with the work of *Frederick S. Perls* (1893–1970), a European émigré trained in the psychoanalytic tradition. Although acknowledging its influences, Perls largely rejected the tenets of psychoanalysis and founded his own school of Gestalt therapy, borrowing the name from gestalt theory. Gestalt theory proposes that the natural course of biological and psychological development of the organism entails a full awareness of physical sensations and psychological needs. Perls believed that, as any form of self-control interferes with healthy functioning, modern civilization inevitably produces neurotic people; thus, the task of the therapist is to instruct the patient in discovering and experiencing the feelings and the needs repressed by society's demands.

6.29–6.33

6.29. The answer is C (*Synopsis VI*, pages 183–184; *CTP V*, pages 375–376).

6.30. The answer is B (*Synopsis VI*, pages 183–184; *CTP V*, pages 375–376).

6.31. The answer is E (*Synopsis VI*, pages 183–184; *CTP V*, pages 375–376).

6.32. The answer is A (*Synopsis VI*, pages 183–184; *CTP V*, pages 375–376).

6.33. The answer is D (*Synopsis VI*, pages 183–184; *CTP V*, pages 375–376).

Neurotic conflict is defined as conflict between the ego, which is responsive to the demands of reality, and the id, which follows the pleasure principle only. The mechanisms of defense develop as a means of controlling the expression of impulses that may lead to such conflicts. Defense mechanisms are essential components of healthy psychological functioning; however, they can be maladaptive, as well as adaptive, especially if they become overly rigid or distorting of reality.

The patient refusing to stay in bed is using the defense mechanism *reaction formation*. Reaction formation is the management of unacceptable impulses by permitting the expression of the impulse in its antithetical form. For instance, an attitude of heightened independence is often the conscious response to unconscious fears of dependency.

The patient who reacted angrily to the resident is exhibiting the defense of *displacement*. Displacement involves a transferring of the emotions from the original ideas to other ideas. Although the object on which feelings are displaced is changed, the instinctual nature of the impulse and its aim remain unchanged. In other words, a patient who is unconsciously angry at the illness and the helplessness may displace his or her anger onto a target that is experienced as a more acceptable one—in this case, the resident.

Repression is the active process of keeping out of consciousness ideas and impulses that are unacceptable. It may operate either by excluding from awareness what was once experienced on a conscious level or by curbing ideas and feelings before they have reached consciousness. The young woman who had been raped but is unable to remember details of the assault is using *repression*.

Projection is the process of throwing out onto another the ideas or impulses that belong to oneself; what is thrown out is considered unacceptable to the one projecting. People who blame others for their own mistakes or seek scapegoats are using projection. The young woman with a disfigured face is attributing to her surgeon her own feelings of self-hatred, which is a form of *projection*.

Suppression is the conscious or semiconscious act of inhibiting an impulse or idea, as in the deliberate attempt to forget something and think no more about it. The patient who has just been raped but consciously decides to postpone thinking about it is using *suppression*.

Review Table 6.1 for further definitions of the various defense mechanisms.

6.34–6.43

6.34. The answer is A (*Synopsis VI*, pages 178–181; *CTP V*, pages 369–371).

6.35. The answer is B (*Synopsis VI*, pages 178–181; *CTP V*, pages 369–371).

6.36. The answer is A (*Synopsis VI*, pages 178–181; *CTP V*, pages 369–371).

6.37. The answer is B (*Synopsis VI*, pages 178–181; *CTP V*, pages 369–371).

6.38. The answer is B (*Synopsis VI*, pages 178–181; *CTP V*, pages 369–371).

6.39. The answer is A (*Synopsis VI*, pages 178–181; *CTP V*, pages 369–371).

6.40. The answer is B (*Synopsis VI*, pages 178–181; *CTP V*, pages 369–371).

6.41. The answer is B (*Synopsis VI*, pages 178–181; *CTP V*, pages 369–371).

6.42. The answer is A (*Synopsis VI*, pages 178–181; *CTP V*, pages 369–371).

6.43. The answer is B (*Synopsis VI*, pages 178–181; *CTP V*, pages 369–371).

The *topographic theory*, set forth in *The Interpretation of Dreams* in 1900, divided the mind into three regions—*unconscious, preconscious,* and *conscious*—differentiated by their relation to consciousness. In general, psychic material not in the immediate field of awareness because it is barred from access to consciousness by an intrapsychic force is in the *unconscious*. The *preconscious* includes psychic material that is not in the immediate field of awareness but that can be recalled to consciousness with effort. The *conscious* refers to mental functioning within the realm of awareness at all times.

The *structural theory* was presented in *The Ego and the Id* in 1923. This theory was formulated when Freud discovered that not all unconscious processes could be attributed to instincts. In the structural theory the psychic apparatus is divided into the *id*, the *ego*, and the *superego*. Each refers to an aspect of human mental functioning, and each is not empirically demonstrable. Freud conceived of the *id* as a completely disorganized, primordial reservoir of energy derived from the instincts and under the domination of the primary process. *"Primary process"* is the term Freud used for the laws that govern unconscious processes. It refers to a type of thinking that is *characteristic of very young children*, the id, and dreams. Primary-process thought lacks any sense of time and uses allusions, condensation, and symbols. It is primitive, prelogical thought, seeking immediate gratification of instinctual drives.

The *ego* is an organized, problem-solving mental apparatus. It is governed by the *reality principle* and uses defense mechanisms to inhibit the immediate discharge of instincts. The ego is governed by *secondary-process* thinking. The secondary process uses judgment, intelligence, logic, and reality testing.

The *superego* is formed by the internalization of parental images. It develops as a result of the resolution of the Oedipus complex. The superego contains the conscience and often imposes itself in mental conflicts in the form of guilt.

7

Clinical Examination of the Psychiatric Patient

No technological advance in diagnosis or treatment will ever replace the central importance of an expertly conducted and rigorously recorded clinical history, psychiatric interview, and mental status examination. The skills of clinical examination most incisively distinguish the differences between the doctor-patient relationship and personal friendship—a difficult distinction to teach and an even harder one for students to grasp with true clinical confidence. The strength and the expertise to conduct an outstanding clinical examination come from practice and from a complete knowledge of the details of this process. The ability to discuss with colleagues or examiners in simple, nonjargon terminology both the process and the content of the clinical examination is a good indication that a person understands the technique.

There is more than one type of clinical interview, and examiners should know the purpose and the format of the interview they are going to conduct before they sit down with a patient. Initial, second, and 50th interviews; bedside and office interviews; unstructured, semistructured, and structured interviews— all are very different. Much like a musician who is about to perform, the interviewer should have a framework of the interview in mind. Although this basic framework will be modified during the interview, the examiner must know at the beginning of the interview what information must be obtained and how the interviewer wants to shape the therapeutic relationship.

Amid the bewildering complexity of the clinical examination, two critical factors emerge— clinical flexibility and therapeutic fit. Clinical situations require adjustment to many time, space, and patient-related variables. Therapeutic fit and therapeutic alliance are somewhat synonymous terms, both referring to the relationship between the physician and the patient. This relationship is particularly important in psychiatry for two reasons. First, the nature of the disorders treated requires psychiatrists to ask extraordinarily personal and sometimes frightening questions. Such topics as sex, money, violence, religion, values, dreams, and fantasies need to be discussed whenever appropriate to the clinical situation. Second, more than in any other branch of medicine, the relationship between physician and patient can have curative properties. The strength of this relationship can also solidify the compliance of the patient with an entire treatment program.

The recording of information gathered during the clinical examination is as important as the information-gathering process. The written record of the clinical examination is a component of the patient's medical record, and it is a legal document. Because complete confidentiality cannot be guaranteed for hospital records, the psychiatrist may have to exercise some judgment about what is to be included in the written record. It is difficult to justify, however, the exclusion of material that would communicate clinical information necessary for other caretakers. The clinical record must be well organized and clearly written; clearly written information reflects clear thinking on the part of the examiner. Succinct summaries, rather than all-inclusive novellas, are usually much more useful and appropriate to the situation. It is a common mistake for students and residents to answer every question about a psychiatric patient by reciting everything they know about the patient. For example, if asked to support a diagnosis, a student may reasonably respond with only the clinical information that is pertinent to the diagnostic requirements in the revised third edition of *Diagnostic and Statistical Manual of Mental Disorders* (DSM-III-R). But, if asked to formulate a case from a psychodynamic perspective, a student may find that details of the patient's childhood become germane. The clinical record itself, however, is best limited to subjective and objective data, rather than to extensive theorizing. The use of precise quotations from the patient and clearly defined terms are better than the use of psychiatric jargon alone. "Looseness of associations" (LOA) is not as descriptive as, "Patient said, 'Bird sees the plug in the newspaper toilet.'" Above all, the examiner must be careful to record all that is important, regardless of the examiner's own approval or disapproval, attraction or disgust, comprehension or confusion.

Although the laboratory has long been used to rule out treatable organic disorders in psychiatric patients, it has only recently been used to rule in psychiatric disorders. The major laboratory tests are the dexamethasone-suppression test (DST), the thyrotropin-releasing-hormone (TRH) stimulation test, electroencephalograms (EEGs) (awake and asleep), evoked potentials (EPs), computed tomographic (CT) scans, and magnetic resonance images (MRIs). The use of psychotherapeutic drug serum levels has also entered standard clinical practice. In the clinical setting, the best guide is to ask whether a specific test result will affect diagnosis and treatment. If the answer is affirmative, then ordering the test is probably warranted. However, the effect of the test result may be subtle. For example, although nonsuppression on the DST does not diagnose depression, it may be an important factor in the physician's attempting an antidepressant trial in a patient with uncharacteristic symptoms.

The student is referred to Chapter 7 of *Synopsis VI,* "Clinical Examination of the Psychiatric Patient," and to Chapter 9 of *CTP V,* "Diagnosis and Psychiatry: Examination of the Psychiatric Patient." After reading these chapters, students can test their knowledge by studying the questions and answers below.

HELPFUL HINTS

The student should know these terms, especially the acronyms and laboratory tests.

rapport	occupational and educational history	concentration, memory, and intelligence
style	social activity	judgment and insight
note taking	sexuality	reliability
data	marital and military history	psychiatric report
transference	LFT	DSM-III-R and Axes I-V
resistance	antipsychotics	prognosis
therapeutic alliance	cyclic antidepressants	psychodynamic formulation
countertransference	lithium	treatment plan
initial interview and greeting	carbamazepine	TFTs
uncovering feelings	polysomnography	TSH
using patient's words	EEG	TRH
stress interview	BEAM	DST
patient questions	SSEP	catecholamines
subsequent interviews	family history	BUN
psychiatric history	current social situation	VDRL
preliminary and personal identification	dreams, fantasies, and value systems	*Treponema pallidum*
chief complaint	mental status examination	VEP
history of present illness; previous illness	appearance, behavior, attitude, and speech	AER
past medical history	mood, feelings, and affect	CSF
prenatal history	appropriateness	NMR
early, middle, and late childhood history	perception	MRI
psychosexual history	thought process	PET
religious background	sensorium and cognition	CT
adulthood	consciousness and orientation	rCBF

QUESTIONS

DIRECTIONS: Each of the incomplete statements below is followed by five suggested completions. Select the *one* that is *best* in each case.

7.1. The most important initial task of the physician performing the psychiatric interview is to
A. make a diagnosis
B. develop a treatment plan
C. contact relevant family members
D. establish rapport
E. give advice

7.2. Perceptual disturbances include all the following *except*
A. hallucinations
B. hypnagogic experiences
C. echolalia
D. depersonalization
E. derealization

7.3. Asking patients what they would do if they received someone else's mail among their own is an example of a test of
A. intelligence
B. abstract thinking
C. insight
D. judgment
E. cognition

7.4. Methods to facilitate the development of rapport include all the following *except*
A. conducting a stress interview
B. asking open-ended questions
C. using the patient's words
D. understanding the patient
E. uncovering feelings

7.5. Asking a patient to interpret a proverb is used as a way of assessing
A. judgment
B. impulse control
C. abstract thinking
D. intelligence
E. insight

7.6. The process by which a patient unconsciously responds to the physician as if he or she were a significant person from the patient's past is termed
A. introjection
B. projection
C. transference
D. countertransference
E. distortion

7.7. Thyroid function tests are of use in clinical psychiatric practice because
A. up to 20 percent of patients with depression have thyroid disease
B. mental retardation is associated with neonatal hyperthyroidism
C. hypothyroidism may be a side effect of lithium
D. a blunted TRH stimulation test is associated with mania
E. a blunted TRH stimulation test may aid in predicting response to treatment of psychotic disorders

7.8. The patient's vocabulary and fund of knowledge on a mental status examination are the best guides to
A. intelligence
B. attention
C. memory and orientation
D. abstract thinking
E. judgment

7.9. An abnormal finding on a dexamethasone-suppression test (DST) means that the patient may
A. have a good response to electroconvulsive therapy (ECT)
B. have disseminated cancer
C. have a good response to cyclic antidepressant medications
D. be receiving high-dosage benzodiazepine treatment
E. have all the above

DIRECTIONS: Each group of questions below consists of five lettered headings followed by a list of numbered words or statements. For each numbered word or statement, select the *one* lettered heading that is most closely associated with it. Each lettered heading may be selected once, more than once, or not at all.

Questions 7.10–7.14
A. Depression
B. Schizophrenia
C. Seizure disorders
D. Sleep apnea
E. Organic mental syndrome

7.10. Positron emission tomography (PET)

7.11. Computed tomography (CT)

7.12. Electroencephalography (EEG)

7.13. Polysomnography (PSG)

7.14. Dexamethasone-suppression test (DST)

Questions 7.15–7.19
A. Tangentiality
B. Anosognosia
C. Dysprosody
D. Erotomania
E. Nominal aphasia

7.15. Disorder associated with denial of physical illness

7.16. Person never gets to the point

7.17. Disturbance in language output

7.18. Disordered rhythm of speech

7.19. Disturbance in content of thought

Questions 7.20–7.24
A. Axis I
B. Axis II
C. Axis III
D. Axis IV
E. Axis V

7.20. Kidney failure

7.21. Borderline personality disorder

7.22. Mental retardation

7.23. Birth of a first child

7.24. Delusional disorder

ANSWERS

Clinical Examination of the Psychiatric Patient

7.1. The answer is D (*Synopsis VI*, pages 2–4 and 193–194; *CTP V*, pages 449–450).

The most important initial task of the physician performing the psychiatric interview is to *establish rapport* by listening to and understanding the patient. Failure to do so will cause difficulties in communication and diminish the effectiveness of even the best *treatment plan*. An accurate *diagnosis* is important, but, without a good doctor-patient relationship, the process of making a diagnosis is much more complicated. *Contacting relevant family members* may become an important part of establishing a more complete picture of the patient, especially in situations in which the patient is psychotic and unable to give a reliable history. In many other situations, it may be inappropriate and a breach of confidentiality to contact family members. *Giving advice* may or may not be appropriate in the context of a psychiatric or therapeutic interview. In most cases, advice should be given only after the physician has a clear sense of what the patient needs and a sense that the advice is warranted within the context of the specific therapeutic interaction.

7.2. The answer is C (*Synopsis VI*, pages 201–202; *CTP V*, pages 473–474).

A disturbance in perception is a disturbance in the mental process by which data—intellectual, sensory, and emotional—are organized. Through perception, people are capable of making sense out of the many stimuli that bombard them. Perceptual disturbances do not include *echolalia*, which is the repetition of another's words or phrases. Echolalia is a disturbance of thought form and communication. Examples of perceptual disturbances include *hallucinations*, which are false sensory perceptions without concrete external stimuli. Common hallucinations involve sights or sounds, although any of the senses may be involved. *Hypnagogic experiences* are hallucinations that occur just before falling asleep. Other disturbances of perception include *depersonalization*, which is the sensation of unreality concerning oneself or one's environment, and *derealization*, which is the feeling of changed reality or the feeling that one's surroundings have changed.

7.3. The answer is D (*Synopsis VI*, pages 202–204; *CTP V*, pages 465 and 475).

Asking patients what they would do if they received someone else's mail among their own is a test of *judgment*. Judgment involves the process of eval-

uating choices within the framework of a given value system for the purpose of deciding on an appropriate course of action. A response that one would hand a misdirected letter back to the letter carrier or drop it into a mailbox reflects appropriate judgment. *Intelligence* is the ability to learn and the capacity to apply what one has learned. *Abstract thinking* is the ability to shift voluntarily from one aspect of a situation to another, to keep in mind simultaneously various aspects of a situation, and to think or to perform symbolically. *Insight* is the power or act of seeing into and recognizing the objective reality of a situation. *Cognition* is the perceptual and intellectual level of mental functioning.

A good question often used by examiners to determine a patient's capacity for social judgment is, "What would you do if you found a stamped, addressed letter on the street?" The appropriate response is that the patient would drop it into a mailbox.

7.4. The answer is A (*Synopsis VI*, pages 2–4 and 194–197; *CTP V*, pages 449–450).

A *stress interview* may occasionally be helpful in evaluating a patient, but it is unusually confrontational and is not a method designed to facilitate the development of rapport. *Asking open-ended questions* or questions that cannot be answered merely with "Yes" or "No" effectively allows the patient to reveal more about the patient's life and usually fosters rapport. *Using the patient's own words* as reassurance that the person is being heard can also be helpful. *Uncovering feelings* by asking patients for specific examples of how and when they felt a certain way also helps establish a sense that the physician is interested in the nuances of their emotional lives. In general, a sense by the patient of being understood, of being listened to and heard, is often the most important element in establishing rapport and providing therapeutic relief.

7.5. The answer is C (*Synopsis VI*, pages 203–204; *CTP V*, pages 464 and 472).

Asking a patient to interpret a proverb is generally used as a way of determining whether the person has the capacity for *abstract thought*. Abstract thinking, as opposed to concrete thinking, is characterized primarily by the ability to shift voluntarily from one aspect of a situation to another, to keep in mind simultaneously various aspects of a situation, and to think symbolically. Concrete thinking is characterized by an inability to conceptualize beyond immediate experience or beyond actual things and events. Psychopathologically, it is most characteristic of persons with schizophrenia or organic mental disorders. *Judgment*, the patient's ability to comprehend the meaning of events and to appreciate the consequences of actions, is often tested by asking how the patient would act in certain standard circumstances—for example, if the patient smelled smoke in a crowded movie theater. *Impulse control* is the ability to control acting on a wish to discharge energy in a manner that is, at the moment, felt to be dangerous, inappropriate, or otherwise ill-advised. *Insight* is a conscious understanding of forces that have led to a particular feeling, action, or situation. *Intelligence* is the capacity for learning, recalling, integrating, and applying knowledge and experience.

7.6.   The answer is C (*Synopsis VI*, pages 183 and 186; *CTP V*, pages 1446–1448).

Transference was first described by Sigmund Freud. The patient responds to the physician as if the physician were a significant person from the patient's past, such as a parental figure. *Introjection* is an immature defense mechanism. The person internalizes characteristics of a loved one with the goal of establishing the constant presence of the loved one. *Projection* is also an immature and narcissistic defense. Through projection, the person attributes his or her own unacknowledged and often consciously unacceptable thoughts and feelings to others. *Countertransference* refers to the physician's reactions to the patient as if the patient were an important person from the physician's past. *Distortion* is a narcissistic defense mechanism. Through this defense the person grossly reshapes external reality to suit inner needs.

7.7.   The answer is C (*Synopsis VI*, page 206; *CTP V*, pages 1213–1215 and 1660–1661).

Thyroid function tests are useful in the diagnosis and the treatment of psychiatric disorders. For example, *up to 10 percent (not 20 percent)* of patients with depression have thyroid disease. Hypothyroidism may develop as a *side effect of lithium treatment*; hyperthyroidism may also occur but far less frequently. Mental retardation is associated with *neonatal hypothyroidism, not hyperthyroidism*. With early diagnosis and treatment, the occurrence of mental retardation is significantly reduced. The thyrotropin-releasing-hormone (TRH) stimulation test is *blunted in depression, not in mania*. A blunted TRH stimulation test may aid in *predicting response to treatment of depressive, not psychotic, disorders*.

7.8.   The answer is A (*Synopsis VI*, pages 202–204; *CTP V*, pages 464 and 474).

The patient's vocabulary and fund of knowledge on the mental status examination are the best guides to *intelligence*. A person's ability to articulate and

use language, the person's past and present academic performance, and the general fund of knowledge displayed are some of the useful rough indicators of intellectual ability. However, the rigorous measurement of intellectual capacity, especially when the results of a patient's differential diagnosis include an organic component or mental retardation, necessitates formal psychological testing. *Attention* is defined as concentration, the aspect of consciousness that relates to the amount and the effort exerted in focusing on certain aspects of an experience. *Memory* is the ability to revive past sensory impressions, experiences, and learned ideas. *Orientation* is the state of awareness of oneself and one's surroundings in terms of person, place, and time. *Abstract thinking* is characterized by the ability to grasp the essentials of a whole and to break a whole into its parts. *Judgment* refers to the ability to evaluate choices within the framework of a given set of values for the purpose of selecting a course of action.

7.9.   The answer is E (*Synopsis VI*, page 206; *CTP V*, pages 873–874).

The dexamethasone-suppression test (DST) can be used to confirm a diagnostic impression of major depression with melancholia. In melancholic depressions, the test result is abnormal in many cases, meaning that there is nonsuppression of endogenous cortisol production after exogenous steroid ingestion. A positive finding, nonsuppression, indicates a hyperactive hypothalamic-pituitary adrenal axis. The DST is sometimes used to predict which patients will have a good response to somatic treatments, such as *electroconvulsive therapy (ECT)* and *cyclic antidepressant medications*. The clinician needs to be aware that false-positive findings can result from a number of factors, such as *disseminated cancer*. A false-negative finding can occur in patients receiving *high-dosage benzodiazepine treatment*. In a false-negative result a diseased person has a normal finding. In a false-positive result a nondiseased person has an abnormal finding.

7.10–7.14

7.10.   The answer is B (*Synopsis VI*, pages 79 and 204; *CTP V*, pages 715–716).

7.11.   The answer is E (*Synopsis VI*, pages 78 and 204; *CTP V*, pages 168–169).

7.12.   The answer is C (*Synopsis VI*, pages 76 and 204; *CTP V*, page 165).

7.13.   The answer is D (*Synopsis VI*, pages 77 and 204; *CTP V*, page 1132).

7.14.   The answer is A (*Synopsis VI*, pages 96 and 204; *CTP V*, pages 873–874).

Positron emission tomography (PET) scans measure cerebral oxygen and glucose metabolism and have demonstrated differences in regional glucose uptake and oxygen consumption in persons with *schizophrenia* compared with persons without schizophrenia, with the schizophrenic patients tending to show relatively diminished function in specific areas. Differences among persons with schizophrenia have also been demonstrated: In inactive or catatonic schizophrenia, a decrease is seen in the volume of blood flow and in oxygen consumption in the precentral regions of the cerebrum, whereas hallucinating patients and patients with thought disorders have relatively high activity in the postcentral, temporal, and latero-occipital regions of the cerebral cortex.

A *computed tomography* (CT) scan of the head is a sophisticated X-ray in which relative tissue densities of thousands of areas within one plane are processed and represented photographically. The cerebral cortex can be visualized, as well as ventricular size and displacement and many lesions. A CT scan is useful in the diagnosis of *organic mental syndrome*, as it reveals intracerebral space-occupying lesions or degenerative changes that may be creating the clinical picture.

Electroencephalography (EEG) measures voltages between electrodes placed in the scalp and provides a description of the electrical activity of the brain and its neurons. It is most helpful in the diagnosis of specific *seizure disorders* and is also useful in diagnosing space-occupying lesions, vascular lesions, and encephalopathies. Characteristic EEG changes are caused by specific drugs.

Polysomnography (PSG) is a battery of tests that include an EEG, an electrocardiogram (ECG), and an electromyogram (EMG). It is often given with tests for penile tumescence, blood oxygen saturation, body movement, and body temperature. It is the diagnostic procedure for *sleep apnea*, which refers to transient cessations of breathing during sleep. It is also useful in the assessment of insomnia, enuresis, impotence, and seizure disorders.

The *dexamethasone-suppression test* (DST) is useful in making the diagnosis of major *depression* with melancholia. The administration of dexamethasone, an exogenous corticosteroid, leads to a suppression of the endogenous production of cortisol in nondepressed people. An abnormal finding on a DST is one in which the plasma patient's cortisol level, generally tested 12 hours after the administration of dexamethasone, has not been suppressed (above 5 mg/dL). Suppression of endogenous cortisol indicates that the hypothalamic-adrenal-pituitary axis is functioning properly.

7.15–7.19

7.15. The answer is B (*Synopsis VI*, pages 203 and 221; *CTP V*, page 147).

7.16. The answer is A (*Synopsis VI*, page 202; *CTP V*, page 561).

7.17. The answer is E (*Synopsis VI*, pages 201 and 221; *CTP V*, page 146).

7.18. The answer is C (*Synopsis VI*, page 201; *CTP V*, page 472).

7.19. The answer is D (*Synopsis VI*, pages 202 and 219; *CTP V*, page 473).

The many typical signs and symptoms of psychiatric illness that the student needs to be able to define and recognize include disturbances of consciousness, emotion, motor behavior, thinking, perception, memory, intelligence, insight, and judgment.

Disturbances in the form of thought involve a disruption in the goal-directed flow of ideas and associations typical of the logical sequence of normal thinking. A formal thought disorder is a disturbance in the form, as opposed to the content, of thought. *Tangentiality* is a specific disorder in the form of thought that involves the patient's thinking in tangents that never return to the idea or question or origin; the *person never gets to the point. Anosognosia* is a disturbance associated with organic brain diseases of the nonlanguage sphere. Anosognosia is the unawareness of a physical disorder. The patient *denies, suppresses, or is unable to recognize a physical disability.* Aphasias refer to *disturbances in language* and comprehension. They include motor (or Broca's) aphasia, characterized by difficulty in speaking with comprehension intact; sensory (or Wernicke's) aphasia, characterized by impaired comprehension with speech relatively fluent; and *nominal aphasia* (the defective use of words and the inability to name objects). *Dysprosody* is the *disordered rhythm of speech* or the loss of normal speech melody and may be caused by a frontal lesion that makes the patient's speech sound odd. *Erotomania,* also known as Clérembault's syndrome, is a delusional belief that another person is in love with the patient. It is an example of a *disturbance in content of thought.* Erotomania has been interpreted psychodynamically as a grandiose fantasy that defends against an underlying belief that the patient is unlovable.

7.20–7.24

7.20. The answer is C (*Synopsis VI*, pages 204–205; *CTP V*, pages 590–591).

7.21. The answer is B (*Synopsis VI*, pages 204–205; *CTP V*, pages 590–591).

7.22. The answer is B (*Synopsis VI*, pages 204–205; *CTP V*, pages 590–591).

7.23. The answer is D (*Synopsis VI*, pages 204–205; *CTP V*, pages 590–591).

7.24. The answer is A (*Synopsis VI*, pages 204–205; *CTP V*, pages 590–591).

DSM-III-R uses a multiaxial scheme of classification consisting of five axes, each of which covers a different aspect of psychological and psychiatric functioning. Each axis should be covered for each diagnosis. Axis I consists of all major clinical syndromes, plus conditions not attributable to a mental disorder. Examples include schizophrenia, mood disorders, and *delusional* (paranoid) *disorders*. Axis II consists of *personality disorders* and developmental disorders, such as *mental retardation*. Axis III consists of any medical or physical illness that may be present. The illness may be causative (e.g., *kidney failure* causing delirium), secondary (e.g., acquired immune deficiency syndrome [AIDS] as a result of a psychoactive substance use disorder), or unrelated. Axis IV consists of a six-point rating scale for assessing the severity of psychosocial stressors that are related to the current psychiatric disorder. The scale ranges from a code of 1 (no acute events or enduring circumstances) to 6 (catastrophic stressor, such as the death of a child or the presence of a chronic life-threatening illness). *Birth of a first child* is coded as 4, a severe stressor. Axis V is a global assessment of functioning scale in which the clinician evaluates the highest level of functioning by the patient in the past year. It consists of a 90-point scale, with 90 representing the highest level of functioning in all areas.

8

Typical Signs and Symptoms of Psychiatric Illness Defined

The signs and symptoms of illness, properly collated, form a basis for diagnosis, prognosis, prevention, and treatment.

It has been argued that the best diagnosis is one based on a knowledge of causes. The cure for malaria, for example, depends on the chemical destruction of the causative protozoa, and the prevention of the disease depends on the elimination of the vector, the anopheles mosquito. On closer scrutiny, even this simple example reveals complexities. South American Indians cured malaria with cinchona bark long before they knew what caused the disease. Complicating this matter, patients with sickle cell anemia develop an immunity to malaria.

Consider another example. The tubercle bacillus is surely the cause of active tuberculosis in some people; yet, with the formation of a harmless fibrotic nodule, it can provide lasting immunity in other people. Thus, the boundary between active disease and healthy adaptation is not always easily identified. In effect, a continuum exists between the patient with an active disease and the healthy, though infected, person.

The clinical manifestations of a psychiatric disorder are the outcome of complex interacting forces—biological, sociocultural, and psychological—and are essentially expressions of a breakdown in adaptational process. Adaptation from a psychiatric point of view refers to a series of changes that occur within the person; as a result, wishes and needs are fulfilled in relation to personal satisfaction and to the realities of the environment. Breakdowns in this process are expressed primarily as abnormalities of thought, feeling, and behavior.

The terms "signs" and "symptoms" refer to specific events. *Signs* are objective findings observed by the clinician (e.g., tachycardia and motor hyperactivity); *symptoms* are subjective complaints listed by the patient (e.g., palpitations and anxiety). Psychological symptoms can be ego-syntonic or ego-dystonic; that is, they can be experienced either as acceptable and compatible or as unacceptable and alien. In general usage, the terms "signs" and "symptoms" tend to be used interchangeably. It is especially difficult to maintain the distinction in psychiatry. A patient may not complain of any symptoms (that is, the symptoms are ego-syntonic), but others believe the patient's behavior is strange, and that strange behavior constitutes the signs of illness. Conversely, a patient experiencing hallucinations may vigorously complain about what the patient seems to be hearing (that is, the symptoms are ego-dystonic), but there are no observable signs of hallucinatory activity. Unlike certain medical conditions, psychiatric disorders have few, if any, signs or symptoms that are pathognomonic. Moreover, physical disease may first present with psychiatric symptoms, thereby compounding the difficult task of making an accurate diagnosis. A syndrome is a group of symptoms that occur together and constitute a recognizable condition, and the term "syndrome" is less specific than "disorder" or "disease." Most psychiatric disorders are, in reality, syndromes.

Chapter 8 in *Synopsis VI*, "Typical Signs and Symptoms of Psychiatric Illness Defined," Section 9.3 in *CTP V*, "Typical Signs and Symptoms of Psychiatric Illness," and Chapter 10 in *CTP V*, "Clinical Manifestations of Psychiatric Disorders," should be studied. An assessment of the student's knowledge can be made by studying the questions and answers below.

HELPFUL HINTS

The student should be able to define and categorize the signs and symptoms listed below.

disturbances of consciousness and attention	disturbances of intelligence insight and judgment	phobias noesis
affect and mood	disorientation	agnosias
disturbances of conation	delirium	depersonalization
disturbances in the form and the content of thought	coma distractibility	synesthesia illusions
disturbances in speech	*folie à deux*	*déjà vu*
aphasic disturbances	hypnosis	*déjà pensé*
disturbances of perception, both those caused by organic brain diseases and those associated with psychological phenomena	anxiety panic *cerea flexibilitas* stereotypy	*déjà entendu* *jamais vu* dementia
hallucinations	aggression	pseudodementia
disturbances of memory	delusion	

QUESTIONS

DIRECTIONS: Each of the incomplete statements below is followed by five suggested completions. Select the *one* that is *best* in each case.

8.1. Loss of normal speech melody is known as
A. stuttering
B. stammering
C. aphonia
D. dysprosody
E. dyslexia

8.2. A disharmony between the emotional feeling tone and the idea, thought, or speech accompanying it is known as
A. blunted affect
B. inappropriate affect
C. flat affect
D. labile affect
E. appropriate affect

8.3. Alexithymia is
A. a feeling of intense rapture
B. psychopathological sadness
C. being unaware of one's moods
D. the expression of one's feelings
E. the inability to relate to others

8.4. The disturbance in thought in which a patient believes that thinking something may cause it to happen is known as
A. neologism
B. autistic thinking
C. magical thinking
D. tangentiality
E. circumstantiality

DIRECTIONS: Each group of questions below consists of five lettered headings followed by a list of numbered statements. For each numbered statement, select the *one* lettered heading that is most closely associated with it. Each lettered heading may be selected once, more than once, or not at all.

Questions 8.5–8.8
A. Echolalia
B. Echopraxia
C. Catalepsy
D. Catatonia
E. None of the above

8.5. Agitated, purposeless motor activity, uninfluenced by external stimuli

8.6. Imitation of the movements of another

8.7. Maintaining the body position into which one is placed

8.8. Pathological imitation of words or phrases

Questions 8.9–8.13

A. Neologisms
B. Circumstantiality
C. Flight of ideas
D. Clang associations
E. Loosening of associations

8.9. Indirect speech that is delayed in reaching the point but eventually gets from the original point to the desired goal

8.10. Thoughts that jump rapidly from one idea to the next; the ideas tend to be connected

8.11. New words created by the patient for idiosyncratic psychological reasons

8.12. Flow of thought in which ideas shift from one subject to another in an apparently unrelated way

8.13. Association of words similar in sound but not in meaning

Questions 8.14–8.17

A. Nihilistic delusion
B. Delusion of reference
C. Delusion of control
D. Somatic delusion
E. Pseudologia fantastica

8.14. "My brain is melting"

8.15. The world is nonexistent, threatened, or ending

8.16. Events, actions, and behaviors of others all refer and pertain to oneself

8.17. Thoughts, feelings, and actions are controlled by an external force

Questions 8.18–8.21

A. Synesthesia
B. Paramnesia
C. Hypermnesia
D. Eidetic images
E. Confabulation

8.18. Exaggerated degree of retention and recall

8.19. Unconscious falsification of memory

8.20. Confusion of facts and fantasies

8.21. Sensations or hallucinations that accompany sensations of another modality

Questions 8.22–8.25

A. *Déjà vu*
B. *Déjà entendu*
C. *Déjà pensé*
D. *Jamais vu*
E. Confabulation

8.22. Illusion of auditory recognition

8.23. Incorrectly regarding a new thought as a repetition of an old, previous thought

8.24. False feeling of unfamiliarity with a familiar situation

8.25. Regarding a new situation as a repetition of a previous experience

ANSWERS

Typical Signs and Symptoms
of Psychiatric Illness Defined

8.1. The answer is D (*Synopsis VI*, page 220; *CTP V*, page 472).

Loss of normal speech melody is known as *dysprosody*. A disturbance in inflection and rhythm results in a monotonous and halting speech pattern, which occasionally suggests a foreign accent. It can be the result of an organic brain disease, such as Parkinson's disease, or it can be a psychological defensive device seen in some people with schizophrenia. As a psychological device, it can serve the function of maintaining a safe distance in social encounters.

Stuttering is a speech disorder characterized by repetitions or prolongations of sounds, syllables, and words or by hesitations and pauses that disrupt the flow of speech. It is also known as *stammering*. *Aphonia* is a loss of one's voice. *Dyslexia* is a specific learning disability syndrome involving an impairment of the ability to read that is unrelated to the person's intelligence.

8.2. The answer is B (*Synopsis VI*, page 214; *CTP V*, pages 457 and 464).

Affect is the feeling tone associated with an idea or thought. *Inappropriate affect* is the disharmony between the emotional feeling tone and the idea, thought, or speech accompanying it.

Appropriate affect is present when the emotional tone is in harmony with the accompanying idea, thought, or speech. *Blunted affect* is a disturbance in affect manifested by a severe reduction in the intensity of externalized feeling tone. *Labile affect* is characterized by changeability from one moment to the next. *Flat affect* is an absence or near absence of any signs of affective expression accompanying an idea, thought, or speech.

8.3. The answer is C (*Synopsis VI*, page 217; *CTP V*, pages 470 and 573).

Alexithymia is the *difficulty or inability to describe or become aware of one's emotions or moods*. It is common in depressive states.

Feelings of intense rapture are known as ecstasy and are seen in mania and certain mystical states. *Psychopathological sadness* is seen in depression. The *inability to relate to others* is a common manifestation of many emotional disorders. In general, the *expression of one's feelings* is characteristic of normal mental functioning.

8.4. The answer is C (*Synopsis VI*, page 218; *CPT V*, page 472).

Magical thinking refers to the belief that specific thoughts, verbalizations, associations, gestures, or postures can lead in some mystical manner to the fulfillment of certain wishes or the warding off of certain evils and that thinking something makes it happen. This type of thinking may be found normally in connection with superstitious or religious beliefs that are appropriate in specific sociocultural settings. Young children are prone to such thinking as a consequence of their limited understanding of causality. It is a prominent aspect of obsessive-compulsive thinking and achieves its most extreme expression in schizophrenia.

A *neologism* is a new, nonsensical word or phrase whose derivation cannot be understood. Neologisms are often seen in schizophrenia. *Autistic thinking* is a form of thinking in which the thoughts are largely narcissistic and egocentric, with emphasis on subjectivity, rather than objectivity, and without regard for reality. *Tangentiality* is a disturbance in which the person replies to a question in an oblique, digressive, or even irrelevant manner and the central or goal idea is not communicated. Failure to communicate the central idea distinguishes tangentiality from *circumstantiality*, in which the goal idea is reached in a delayed or indirect manner.

8.5–8.8

8.5. The answer is E (*Synopsis VI*, pages 217–218; *CTP V*, page 471).

8.6. The answer is B (*Synopsis VI*, page 217; *CTP V*, page 471).

8.7. The answer is C (*Synopsis VI*, page 217; *CTP V*, page 471).

8.8. The answer is A (*Synopsis VI*, page 218; *CTP V*, page 471).

Echolalia, echopraxia, and catalepsy are all disturbances in conation, which is the category of mental functioning that includes strivings, wishes, instincts, and cravings, as expressed through a person's behavior or motor activity. Echolalia is the *pathological imitation of words or phrases* of one person by another; it tends to be repetitive and persistent and may be spoken with mocking or staccato intonation. It may be observed in schizophrenia, autism, Alzheimer's disease, and other cerebral degenerative disorders. Echopraxia is the pathological *imitation of movements* of one person by another; it is also observed in cases of catatonic schizophrenia. Catalepsy is the condition in which one *maintains the body position* into which one is placed. Another term often used to describe this phenomenon is *cerea flexibilitas,* waxy flexibility. Catatonia is the term generally reserved for a type of schizophrenia that, as a clinical syndrome, is characterized by abnormal motor manifestations. There may be catatonic stupor, which is characterized by either marked rigidity or immobility, or catatonic excitement, as characterized by *agitated, purposeless motor activity,* seemingly uninfluenced by external stimuli.

8.9–8.13

8.9. The answer is B (*Synopsis VI,* page 218; *CTP V,* page 472).

8.10. The answer is C (*Synopsis VI,* page 219; *CTP V,* page 472).

8.11. The answer is A (*Synopsis VI,* page 218; *CTP V,* page 472).

8.12. The answer is E (*Synopsis VI,* page 219; *CTP V,* page 472).

8.13. The answer is D (*Synopsis VI,* page 219; *CTP V,* page 472).

Disturbances in the form of thought are disturbances in the logical process of thought that often lead to idiosyncratic or autistic modes of communication and use of language. These disturbances include neologisms, circumstantiality, flight of ideas, clang associations, and loosening of associations. Neologisms are *new words created by the patient* with special meaning to the patient and are often formed by the condensation of several different words for idiosyncratic psychological reasons. Circumstantiality is speech that is *delayed in reaching the point* but, unlike tangential speech, eventually gets from the original point to the desired goal; it is characterized by overly detailed and parenthetical remarks. Flight of ideas is a nearly continuous flow of *thoughts that jump rapidly* from one idea to the next but with each idea being more or less related to another. A listener able to keep up with the rapid flow should be able to follow the train of associations. It is most often associated with the manic phase of bipolar disorder. Loosening of associations is a flow of thought in which *ideas shift from one subject to another* in a way that appears completely unrelated to the listener but that seems to make some autistic sense to the person speaking. When severe, speech may seem to be incoherent. Clang associations are associations of *words similar in sound but not in meaning,* which characteristically include rhyming and punning.

8.14–8.17

8.14. The answer is D (*Synopsis VI,* page 219; *CTP V,* page 473).

8.15. The answer is A (*Synopsis VI,* page 219; *CTP V,* page 473).

8.16. The answer is B (*Synopsis VI,* page 219; *CTP V,* page 473).

8.17. The answer is C (*Synopsis VI,* page 219; *CTP V,* page 473).

A delusion is a false, fixed belief that is firmly maintained in the face of contradictory reality. It is not shared by others of the same cultural and religious background but, rather, is an idiosyncratic misinterpretation of reality. It cannot be corrected by reasoning. A nihilistic delusion is the belief that one, others, or *the world is nonexistent, threatened, or ending.* A delusion of reference is the belief that events, actions, and behaviors of others all *refer to and pertain to oneself.*

Persons with a delusion of control believe that their thoughts, feelings, and actions are being *controlled by an external force* that robs them of privacy and free will. Thought withdrawal, insertion, and broadcasting are characteristic of delusions of control. Somatic delusions involve beliefs related to the functioning of the body, most often of a frightening or disturbing nature, such as the belief that one's *brain is melting* or rotting or that one's body is ravaged by cancer. Pseudologia fantastica—a type of uncontrollable, pathological lying in which the person appears to believe in the reality of the lies—is most often associated with Münchausen syndrome. Described in the revised third edition of *Diagnostic and Statistical Manual of Mental Disorders* (DSM-III-R) as a factitious disorder with physical syndromes, Münchausen syndrome is characterized by the intentional production of physical symptoms, which may be totally fabricated or self-inflicted.

8.18–8.21

8.18. The answer is C (*Synopsis VI,* page 221; *CTP V,* page 474).

8.19. The answer is E (*Synopsis VI,* page 221; *CTP V,* page 474).

8.20. The answer is B (*Synopsis VI,* page 221; *CTP V,* page 474).

8.21. The answer is A (*Synopsis VI,* page 221; *CTP V,* page 474).

Synesthesia is a term describing sensations or hallucinations that accompany *sensations of another modality;* for example, an auditory sensation is accompanied by or triggers a visual sensation, or a sound is experienced as being seen or is accompanied by a visual experience. Paramnesia is a disturbance of memory in which real *facts and fantasies are confused*; it leads to a falsification of memory by the distortion of real events by fantasies. Hypermnesia is an *exaggerated degree of retention and recall* or an ability to remember material that is not ordinarily retrievable. Eidetic images, also known as primary memory images, are visual memories of almost hallucinatory vividness. Confabulation is an *unconscious falsification of memory* associated with amnesias of organic cause. Gaps in memory are filled in by fabrications that are elaborated on in great detail and with apparent lucidity.

8.22–8.25

8.22. The answer is B (*Synopsis VI*, page 221; *CTP V*, page 474).

8.23. The answer is C (*Synopsis VI*, page 221; *CTP V*, page 474).

8.24. The answer is D (*Synopsis VI*, page 221; *CTP V*, page 474).

8.25. The answer is A (*Synopsis VI*, page 221; *CTP V*, page 474).

Paramnesia is defined as false recollection. It is a disturbance of memory in which reality and fantasy are confused. It is observed in dreams, certain types of schizophrenia, and organic mental syndromes and is seen periodically in normal persons. Examples of paramnesia are *fausse reconnaissance, déjà vu, déjà entendu, déjà pensé, jamais vu*, confabulation, and retrospective falsification. Confabulation is the unconscious filling in of gaps of memory by imagining experiences that have no basis in fact. Retrospective falsification is the recollection of false memory. *Déjà vu* is the false perception of a new situation as a *repetition of a previous experience* or memory. *Déjà entendu* is an illusion of *auditory recognition. Déjà pensé* is an illusion in which a new thought is incorrectly regarded as a *repetition of an old, previous thought. Jamais vu* is a *false feeling of unfamiliarity* with a familiar situation.

9

Classification in Psychiatry and Psychiatric Rating Scales

The aim of any classification system in psychiatry is to provide clear descriptions of diagnostic criteria that will increase the reliability and the validity of psychiatric diagnoses. Because of the many varied and often contrasting etiological theories proposed to explain psychological and psychiatric pathogenesis, the existing classification system in the United States is phenomenological in nature. The third edition of *Diagnostic and Statistical Manual of Mental Disorders* (DSM-III), published in 1980 by the American Psychiatric Association, was a rigorous attempt to standardize and clarify the criteria by which psychiatrists arrive at diagnoses. DSM-III-R, the revised edition of DSM-III, was published in 1987; it updated DSM-III by incorporating the most recent data collected from field trials and clinical research.

Although the goal of classificatory standardization is critical to a valid and intellectually sophisticated practice of psychiatry, there are potential dangers. Foremost among these dangers is a simplistic approach to psychiatric diagnosis in which the patient loses any semblance of individuality or uniqueness and becomes merely a compilation of behavioral signs. Attention must be directed toward the complex factors that contribute to the development of mental disorders and to the factors that lead to their resolution.

The student needs to be aware of the disagreements within the profession about DSM-III-R and its contents. *Synopsis VI* and *CTP V* attempt to set forth those areas of disagreement when relevant; however, it also attempts to avoid the nosological disagreements that only confuse the reader.

Throughout this *Study Guide* are tables listing the DSM-III-R diagnostic criteria for mental disorders; they represent the current thinking in the field and are criteria with which each student must be completely familiar.

Chapter 9 in *Synopsis VI*, "Classification in Psychiatry and Psychiatric Rating Scales," Section 9.8 in *CTP V*, "Psychiatric Rating Scales," and Chapter 11 in *CTP V*, "The Classification of Mental Disorders," contain descriptions of current diagnostic classifications and address many of the issues in psychiatric classification. The questions below test the student's knowledge of these concepts and issues.

HELPFUL HINTS

The student should be able to define the terms below, especially the diagnostic categories.

classification	differential diagnosis	developmental disorders
validity and reliability	clinical syndromes	ICD-9
predictive validity	personality disorders	residual state
manic-depressive psychosis	competency	global assessment scale
diagnostic criteria	atheoretical	reality testing
disability determination	age of onset	schizophrenia
descriptive approach	course	delusional disorders
associated and essential features	complications	mood disorders
impairment	prevalence	phobias
predisposing factors	familial pattern	gross social norms
sex ratio	multiaxial system	panic disorder

generalized anxiety disorder	ego-dystonic and ego-syntonic	psychosomatic (psychological factors affecting physical condition)
posttraumatic stress disorder	Emil Kraepelin	
physical disorders	dementia precox	
psychosocial stressors	DSM-III, DSM-III-R	agoraphobia
severity-of-stress rating	somatoform disorder	somatization disorder
highest level of functioning	body dysmorphic disorder	conversion disorder
partial and full remission	dissociative disorders	hypochondriasis
psychosis and neurosis	psychogenic fugue	psychogenic amnesia
alcohol withdrawal delirium	depersonalization disorder	multiple personality disorder
obsessive-compulsive disorder	dysthymia	paraphilias
organic mental disorders	sadistic personality disorder	depressive neurosis
sexual dysfunction	self-defeating personality disorder	LLPDD

QUESTIONS

DIRECTIONS: For each of the incomplete statements below, *one* or *more* of the completions given are correct. Choose answer

A. if only *1, 2, and 3* are correct
B. if only *1 and 3* are correct
C. if only *2 and 4* are correct
D. if only *4* is correct
E. if *all* are correct

9.1. New diagnostic entities in DSM-III-R include
1. late luteal phase dysphoric disorder (LLPDD)
2. self-defeating personality disorder
3. sadistic personality disorder
4. anankastic personality disorder

9.2. The cautionary statement in DSM-III-R was formulated to
1. alert clinicians that psychiatric knowledge is based on consensus
2. clarify the criteria for legal responsibility
3. emphasize that the diagnostic criteria are not fixed in stone
4. categorize disability status determination

9.3. DSM-III-R conditions that have been termed neurotic disorders in other classification systems include
1. anxiety disorders
2. dissociative disorders
3. somatoform disorders
4. dysthymia

DIRECTIONS: The statement below is followed by five suggested completions. Select the *one* that is *best*.

9.4. According to the DSM-III-R severity of psychosocial stressors scale, the stress level of marriage is
A. none
B. mild
C. moderate
D. severe
E. extreme

DIRECTIONS: The questions below consist of five lettered headings followed by a list of numbered words or statements. For each numbered word or statement, select the *one* lettered heading that is most closely associated with it. Each lettered heading may be selected once, more than once, or not at all.

Questions 9.5–9.12
A. Axis I
B. Axis II
C. Axis III
D. Axis IV
E. Axis V

9.5. Highest level of functioning

9.6. Developmental language disorder

9.7. Epilepsy

9.8. Organic personality syndrome

9.9. Psychosocial stressors

9.10. Autistic disorder

9.11. Caffeine dependence

9.12. Mood disorder

ANSWERS

Classification in Psychiatry and Psychiatric Rating Scales

9.1. **The answer is A (1, 2, 3)** (*Synopsis VI*, page 234; *CTP V*, pages 1333 and 1385–1387).

Three new diagnostic categories listed in DSM-III-R are late luteal phase dysphoric disorder (LLPDD), self-defeating personality disorder, and sadistic personality disorder. These categories are controversial because not all psychiatrists agree that these syndromes exist as separate, discrete disorders. Among psychiatrists who do believe in their existence, they do not agree as to what criteria are essential to make a diagnosis. The categories are also controversial because some groups think that the new diagnoses are particularly vulnerable to cultural bias, misinterpretation, and abuse. Because of the controversy, all these categories have been placed in an appendix to DSM-III-R, with a statement that they have been included to facilitate further systematic clinical study and research.

LLPDD is described as a condition that affects women in the late luteal phase of the menstrual cycle, occurring in the week before the onset of menses and remitting within a few days after the onset. It is characterized by a variety of physical and emotional changes that represent a pattern of clinically significant and severe symptoms, leading to a marked impairment in functioning. Among the most common symptoms described are emotional lability and persistent feelings of tension and self-deprecation.

Self-defeating personality disorder represents a persistent pattern of self-defeating behavior beginning by early adulthood. Characteristic behavior includes being drawn to situations that will lead to suffering, preventing others from intervening in these situations, and undermining pleasurable experiences.

Sadistic personality disorder is characterized by a persistent pattern of cruel and belittling behavior directed toward other people, reflecting a basic lack of respect or empathy for others. The use of physical violence to establish interpersonal dominance is considered characteristic of many people with this disorder.

Anankastic personality disorder refers to an obsessive-compulsive type of personality. This entity is included in the ninth revision of the World Health Organization's *International Classification of Diseases* (ICD-9) and is not included in DSM-III-R.

9.2. **The answer is B (1, 3)** (*Synopsis VI*, page 223; *CTP V*, page 592).

For the first time, in DSM-III-R a cautionary statement was included to aid in the proper use of the manual. The statement is based on the fact that psychiatric knowledge is based on *consensus* and is *not fixed in stone*. The statement in full is as follows:

The specified diagnostic criteria for each mental disorder are offered as guidelines for making diagnoses, since it has been demonstrated that the use of such criteria enhances diagnostic agreement among clinicians and investigators. The proper use of these criteria requires specialized clinical training that provides both a body of knowledge and clinical skills.

These diagnostic criteria and the DSM-III-R classification of mental disorders reflect a consensus of current formulations of evolving knowledge in our field but do not encompass all the conditions that may be legitimate objects of treatment or research efforts.

The purpose of DSM-III-R is to provide clear descriptions of diagnostic categories in order to enable clinicians and investigators to diagnose, communicate about, study, and treat the various mental disorders. It is to be understood that inclusion here, for clinical and research purposes, of a diagnostic category such as Pathological Gambling or Pedophilia does not imply that the condition meets legal or other nonmedical criteria for what constitutes mental disease, mental disorder, or mental disability. The clinical and scientific considerations involved in categorization of these conditions as mental disorders may not be wholly relevant to legal judgments, for example, that take into account such issues as individual responsibility, disability determination, and competency.

DSM-III-R should not be used to establish *legal responsibility* or to categorize *disability status*.

9.3. **The answer is E (all)** (*Synopsis VI*, pages 227 and 234; *CTP V*, page 595).

A neurosis is defined as an ego-alien (ego-dystonic) nonorganic disorder in which reality testing is intact, anxiety is a major characteristic, and the use of various characteristic defense mechanisms plays a major role. As opposed to ICD-9, which contains a variety of neurotic diagnostic classes, DSM-III-R contains no diagnostic category of neuroses. However, a number of DSM-III-R categories had been termed neurotic disorders in the past, and many clinicians still consider them to represent neurotic behavior. In DSM-III-R several of these disorders are described in parentheses by the older "neurotic" terminology. These disorders include *anxiety disorders* (anxiety and phobic neuroses), *somatoform disorders* (hysterical neurosis, conversion type, or hypochondriacal neurosis), *dissociative disorders* (hysterical neuroses, dissociative type), sexual disorders, and *dysthymia* (depressive neurosis).

9.4. The answer is C (*Synopsis VI*, pages 224–225; *CTP V*, page 587).

Marriage is considered a *moderate* level of stress, according to the DSM-III-R severity of psychological stressors scale. Other moderate stressors include marital separation, loss of job, retirement, and miscarriage. Psychosocial stressors in the patient's life that contribute to the current disorder are coded on Axis IV. Axis IV constitutes a six-point rating scale, ranging from *no stress* to catastrophic stress (code 6). Examples of acute events rated as *mild* stressors on Axis IV are breaking up with a boyfriend or a girlfriend and starting or graduating from school. *Severe* stressors include divorce and the birth of a first child. Examples of *extreme* stressors include death of a spouse, the diagnosis of a serious physical illness, and being the victim of a rape.

9.5–9.12

9.5. The answer is E (*Synopsis VI*, pages 223–226; *CTP V*, pages 588–590).

9.6. The answer is B (*Synopsis VI*, pages 223–226; *CTP V*, pages 588–590).

9.7. The answer is C (*Synopsis VI*, pages 223–226; *CTP V*, pages 588–590).

9.8. The answer is A (*Synopsis VI*, pages 223–226; *CTP V*, pages 588–590).

9.9. The answer is D (*Synopsis VI*, pages 223–226; *CTP V*, pages 588–590).

9.10. The answer is B (*Synopsis VI*, pages 223–226; *CTP V*, pages 588–590).

9.11. The answer is A (*Synopsis VI*, pages 223–226; *CTP V*, pages 588–590).

9.12. The answer is A (*Synopsis VI*, pages 223–226; *CTP V*, pages 588–590).

DSM-III-R is a multiaxial system. *Axis I* lists all the clinical syndromes and the group called conditions not attributable to a mental disorder. *Mood disorder, caffeine dependence,* and *organic personality syndrome* are, therefore, coded on Axis I. Axis II lists developmental disorders and personality disorders, both of which generally begin in childhood or adolescence and persist in a stable form into adult life. Axes I and II constitute the entire classification of mental disorders. The developmental disorders coded on *Axis II* include specific developmental disorders, such as *developmental language disorder*, and the pervasive developmental disorders, including *autistic disorder*. In many instances, the patient has a disorder on both axes. For example, an adult may have bipolar disorder noted on Axis I and borderline personality disorder on Axis II, or a child may have attention-deficit hyperactivity disorder noted on Axis I and developmental reading disorder on Axis II. *Axis III* lists any physical disorder or condition, such as *epilepsy*, that is present in addition to a mental disorder. The physical condition may be the result of the mental disorder, such as gastritis secondary to alcoholism; it may be causative, such as herpes encephalitis causing delirium; or it may be unrelated to the mental disorder. Axis III codes are taken from ICD-9.

Axis IV constitutes a six-point rating scale for coding significant *psychosocial stressors* that contribute to the development of the current disorder. *Axis V* is a global assessment scale according to which a person's *highest level of functioning* over the preceding year is evaluated by the clinician.

10 |||||

Organic Mental Syndromes and Disorders

Organic mental syndromes and disorders describe permanent or temporary changes in the function of the brain. The underlying cerebral disease may originate in the brain or be secondary to a systemic disease; the cerebral disease may be diffuse or focal or both. The growing frequency of organic mental disorders in the aging population and the increased survival of patients with brain damage make it essential that students of psychiatry be thoroughly trained in the diagnosis and the treatment of these disorders.

In the revised third edition of *Diagnostic and Statistical Manual of Mental Disorders* (DSM-III-R) the term "disorder" is used when an organic mental condition is associated with an Axis III medical disorder or known cause, and the term "syndrome" is used to refer to a set of psychological or behavioral signs and symptoms without reference to cause. Although the field of psychiatry continues to differentiate between organic and functional disorders, they should be conceptualized as disorders about which more is known in terms of cause and pathology (i.e., organic) and disorders about which less is known (i.e., functional). This division should not be taken to imply that functional disorders, such as schizophrenia, do not have organic bases.

The major broad areas included in the organic mental syndromes are delirium, dementia, amnestic syndrome, intoxication and withdrawal, organic hallucinosis, organic delusional syndrome, organic mood syndrome, organic anxiety syndrome, and organic personality syndrome. Other disorders of interest include the movement disorders (e.g., Parkinson's disease) and the epilepsies. The psychiatric manifestations of traditional medical disorders (e.g., systemic lupus erythematosus) and neurological disorders are essential knowledge for a psychiatrist. The student must understand the distinction between delirium and dementia. The clinical differences and theoretical similarities between the amnestic disorders and the dissociative disorders must also be clear. The parallel nomenclature regarding organic hallucinosis, organic delusional syndrome, organic mood syndrome, and organic anxiety syndrome simplifies the logic of excluding these diagnoses when considering the functional psychotic, delusional, and mood disorders. It is necessary to know at least the major classes of the medical conditions included in the differential diagnoses for psychiatric symptoms.

In DSM-III-R dementia is classified as an organic mental disorder. With the increasing number of elderly people in the population, the clinical importance of Alzheimer's disease and other brain disorders has increased. The rapid breakthroughs in the understanding of the molecular biology of Alzheimer's disease have made it of central research interest. The student should know the differential diagnosis for dementia occurring in the elderly and be able to discuss approaches to treatable versus untreatable dementias. The treatment approaches to both cognitive and behavioral symptoms in these patients should also be clear to the student.

The reader should refer to Chapter 10 in *Synopsis VI*, "Organic Mental Syndromes and Disorders," and to Chapter 12 in *CTP V*, "Organic Mental Syndromes and Disorders." The questions and answers below should then be studied as a test of the student's knowledge and understanding of these subjects.

HELPFUL HINTS

The student should be able to define the signs, symptoms, and syndromes listed.

organic mental disorder and syndrome
orientation
memory
intellectual functions
delirium
    postoperative
    black-patch
sundowner syndrome
dementia
beclouded dementia
Alzheimer's disease
short-term versus long-term memory loss
abstract attitude
catastrophic reaction
pseudodementia
normal aging
primary degenerative dementia
multi-infarct dementia
amnestic syndrome, transient versus permanent
retrograde versus anterograde amnesia
confabulation
Korsakoff's syndrome

organic hallucinosis
tactile or haptic hallucinations
cocainism
auditory, olfactory, visual hallucinations
Lilliputian hallucinosis
hypnagogic and hypnopompic hallucinations
DTs
organic delusional syndrome
organic mood syndrome
functional illness
organic personality syndrome
organic anxiety syndrome
intoxication and withdrawal
senium and presenium
Pick's disease
Creutzfeldt-Jakob disease
Down's syndrome
senile plaques
neurofibrillary tangles
granulovacuolar degeneration
pseudobulbar palsy
dysarthria
TIA
vertebrobasilar disease

Parkinsonism
Huntington's chorea
kuru
general paresis
normal-pressure hydrocephalus
multiple sclerosis
ALS
SLE
transient global amnesia
intracranial neoplasms
hypoglycemic, hepatic, and uremic encephalopathy
diabetic ketoacidosis
AIP
myxedema
cretinism
Addison's disease
Cushing's syndrome
beriberi
pellagra
pernicious anemia
epilepsy
partial versus generalized seizures
interictal manifestations

QUESTIONS

DIRECTIONS: Each of the questions or incomplete statements below is followed by five suggested responses or completions. Select the *one* that is *best* in each case.

10.1. All the following statements about organic hallucinosis are true *except*
A. it is characterized by prominent persistent or recurrent hallucinations
B. it does not occur exclusively during the course of delirium
C. severe intellectual deficits occur
D. it is most often seen in the context of chronic alcoholism
E. its onset is usually acute, and it lasts on average from days to weeks

10.2. Organic mood syndrome
A. is characterized solely by a depressive mood
B. is not attributed to a clearly defined organic factor
C. does not occur exclusively during the course of delirium
D. antedates the onset of a defined causative organic factor
E. always has an insidious onset

10.3. All the following statements about the clinical differentiation of delirium and dementia are true *except*
A. in delirium, symptoms worsen at night
B. the sleep-wakefulness cycle is disrupted in delirium
C. the onset of delirium is acute
D. the duration of delirium is usually less than one month
E. visual hallucinations and transient delusions are more common in dementia than in delirium

10.4. The electroencephalogram (EEG) shown on page 93 is an example of
A. partial seizure
B. grand mal epilepsy
C. petit mal or absence seizure
D. psychomotor epilepsy
E. none of the above

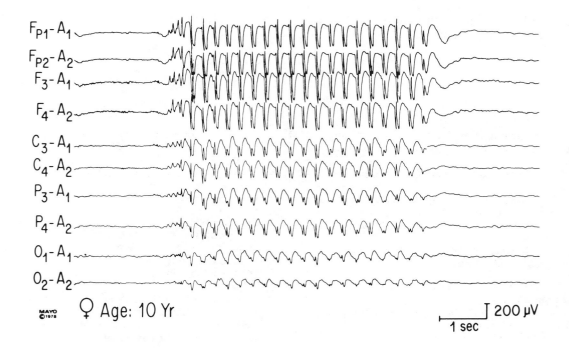

Fp1-A1
Fp2-A2
F3-A1
F4-A2
C3-A1
C4-A2
P3-A1
P4-A2
O1-A1
O2-A2

♀ Age: 10 Yr

200 μV

1 sec

10.5. All the following statements about delirium are true *except*
A. it may be chronic
B. it is a transient disorder
C. diurnal variability is a clinical sign
D. it may first become apparent at night
E. its features include multiple disturbances of attention, memory, orientation, and thinking

10.6. The incidence of delirium after open-heart and coronary-bypass surgery is
A. less than 10 percent
B. 20 percent
C. 30 percent
D. 40 percent
E. greater than 50 percent

10.7. After emerging from a delirium, a patient usually
A. has clear recall of the experiences during the delirium
B. has impaired recall of events before the onset of the delirium
C. has a psychosis
D. refers to the delirium as a nightmare that is clearly remembered
E. has dementia

10.8. The outcome of delirium may be
A. death
B. full recovery
C. dementia
D. delusions
E. all the above

10.9. The most common delusions in organic delusional syndrome are
A. persecutory
B. grandiose
C. jealousy
D. somatic
E. nihilistic

10.10. Which of the following statements about organic delusional syndrome is true?
A. Mild cognitive impairment may be observed
B. The patient may appear confused, disheveled, or eccentric
C. An associated dysphoric mood is common
D. The patient's speech may be incoherent
E. All the above are true

10.11. The important causes of organic personality syndrome include
A. chronic poisoning
B. brain tumor
C. head trauma
D. vascular disease
E. all the above

10.12. According to DSM-III-R, all the following are categorized as organic mental syndromes *except*
A. hallucinosis
B. Tourette's disorder
C. mood syndrome
D. personality syndrome
E. delusional syndrome

DIRECTIONS: For each of the questions or incomplete statements below, *one or more* of the responses or completions given are correct. Choose answer

    A. if only *1, 2, 3* are correct
    B. if only *1 and 3* are correct
    C. if only *2 and 4* are correct
    D. if only *4* is correct
    E. if *all* are correct

10.13. Inpatient cognitive tests that are helpful in the diagnosis of dementia include assessing a patient's
1. ability to remember three objects after five minutes
2. ability to remember the patient's place of birth or what happened yesterday
3. fund of common information, such as past U.S. presidents
4. ability to find similarities and differences between related words

10.14. Characteristic features of the amnestic syndrome include
1. an ability to remember recent events more clearly than remote events
2. an impairment in abstract thinking
3. an impairment in judgment
4. a relatively sudden onset

10.15. According to the DSM-III-R classification, dementias arising in the senium and presenium include
1. the category of primary degenerative dementia (PDD)
2. a category subdivided according to age of onset
3. those classified as being of the Alzheimer type
4. Pick's disease

10.16. Primary degenerative dementia (PDD) of the Alzheimer type
1. is associated with Down's syndrome
2. is seen slightly more frequently in men than in women
3. has been reported to be transmitted in several families through autosomal dominant transmission
4. is associated with an increased amount of acetylcholine in the brain

10.17. Organic personality syndrome tends to
1. persist if it is the result of damage to the brain
2. be permanent
3. evolve into dementia
4. be reversible

10.18. Characteristic clinical features of organic personality syndrome include
1. impaired control of the expression of emotions and impulses
2. euphoria or apathy
3. labile and shallow emotions
4. impaired sensorium

10.19. Susceptibility to organic mental syndromes is increased among people
1. over age 60
2. with preexisting brain damage
3. unable to metabolize drugs
4. in a familiar environment

10.20. True statements about dementia include
1. 5 percent of Americans over 65 have a significant degree of dementia and are unable to care for themselves
2. the most common cause of dementia is multi-infarct dementia
3. about 15 percent of all dementia cases are potentially reversible
4. more than 90 percent of persons in nursing homes have some dementia

10.21. The organic causes of delirium include
1. hypoglycemia
2. hypokalemia
3. migraine headaches
4. infectious mononucleosis

10.22. A 45-year-old man was admitted to a hospital after a series of suicidal gestures, culminating in an attempt to strangle himself with a piece of wire. Four months before his admission, his family had observed that he was becoming depressed: when at home, he spent long periods of time sitting in a chair, slept more than usual, and gave up his habits of reading the evening paper and puttering around the house. Within a month he was unable to get out of bed each morning to go to work. He expressed considerable guilt but could not make up his mind to seek help until forced to do so by his family. He had not responded to two months of outpatient antidepressant drug therapy and had made several half-hearted attempts to cut his wrists before the serious attempt that precipitated the admission.

Physical examination revealed signs of increased intracranial pressure, and a computed tomography (CT) scan showed a large frontal lobe tumor.

[From *DSM-III-R Case Book*. Used with permission.]

The most appropriate diagnosis of the man's condition is
1. organic personality syndrome
2. major depression
3. organic anxiety syndrome
4. organic mood syndrome

10.23. Common causes of organic mood syndrome include
1. antihypertensive medications
2. encephalitis
3. epilepsy
4. hemispheric strokes

10.24. In making the differentiation of dementia and pseudodementia, the psychiatrist must note that in dementia
1. intellectual deficits antedate depression
2. the patient is disturbed by memory impairment and poor intellectual performance and verbalizes this disturbance
3. the patient is usually globally impaired, with consistently poor intellectual performance
4. performance in a sodium amobarbital (Amytal) interview may improve

10.25. Organic hallucinosis is associated with which of the following conditions?
1. Focal cerebral lesion
2. Migraine
3. Temporal arteritis
4. Epilepsy

10.26. In organic personality syndrome
1. many patients exhibit low drive and initiative
2. true sadness and depression are common
3. emotions are typically labile and shallow
4. the expression of impulses is characteristically inhibited

10.27. True statements concerning organic mood syndrome include which of the following?
1. The removal of the cause does not necessarily result in the patient's prompt recovery from the mood disturbance
2. Drugs may trigger an underlying mood disturbance in a patient who is biologically vulnerable; if so, the disturbance is not considered an organic mood syndrome
3. A family history of depression or mania suggests the diagnosis of a nonorganic mood disorder
4. The syndrome may be indistinguishable from manic and depressive episodes that are not attributable to a specific organic factor

10.28. Organic factors or disorders associated with organic mood syndrome include
1. systemic lupus erythematosus
2. parkinsonism
3. infectious mononucleosis
4. use of reserpine

10.29. The diagnosis of multi-infarct dementia (MID) is associated with
1. cerebrovascular disease
2. hypertension
3. a stepwise progression of focal motor symptoms
4. such personality changes as emotional lability and hypochondriasis

10.30. Features of amnestic syndrome are
1. an impairment of memory as the single or predominant cognitive defect
2. retrograde and anterograde amnesia
3. preservation of the ability for immediate recall
4. evidence of a specific causative organic factor

10.31. True statements about organic delusional syndrome include which of the following?
1. The syndrome often lifts after whatever has induced it is resolved
2. Schizophreniformlike psychoses can be produced by lesions of the limbic system
3. The delusions may or may not be systematized
4. A specific causative organic factor need not be found to make the diagnosis

10.32. The DSM-III-R diagnostic criteria for amnestic syndrome include
1. impairment of short-term memory
2. impairment of long-term memory
3. clear consciousness
4. evidence of an organic causative factor

DIRECTIONS: Each group of questions below consists of lettered headings followed by a list of numbered statements. For each numbered statement, select the *one* lettered heading that is most closely associated with it. Each lettered heading may be used once, more than once, or not at all.

Questions 10.33–10.37

A. Creutzfeldt-Jakob disease
B. Normal-pressure hydrocephalus
C. General paresis
D. Huntington's chorea
E. Multiple sclerosis

10.33. Death occurs 15 to 20 years after the onset of the disease, and suicide is common

10.34. Slow virus, with death occurring within two years of the diagnosis

10.35. Manic syndrome with neurological signs in up to 20 percent of cases

10.36. Treatment of choice is a shunt

10.37. More prevalent in cold and temperate climates than in the tropics and subtropics

Questions 10.38–10.41

A. Multi-infarct dementia (MID)
B. Primary degenerative dementia (PDD) of the Alzheimer type

10.38. Occurs more frequently in women than in men

10.39. Accounts for about 10 to 15 percent of all cases of dementia in the elderly

10.40. Most likely to show focal neurological signs

10.41. Onset is sudden

ANSWERS

Organic Mental Syndromes and Disorders

10.1. The answer is C (*Synopsis VI*, pages 256–257; *CTP V*, page 224).

Organic hallucinosis is thought to be a disorder in which mild *intellectual deficits* may occur but in which a severe loss of intellectual abilities is not seen. Organic hallucinosis is defined in DSM-III-R as a mental disorder characterized by *prominent persistent or recurrent hallucinations* in a state of full wakefulness that can be attributed to some specific organic disorder. It does not occur *exclusively during the course* of delirium. Organic hallucinosis is most often seen in the context of *chronic alcoholism* or hallucinogen abuse. Its *onset is usually acute*, and it lasts on average from days to weeks. The DSM-III-R diagnostic criteria are shown in Table 10.1.

10.2. The answer is C (*Synopsis VI*, pages 258–259; *CTP V*, pages 630–633).

Previously called organic affective syndrome, organic mood syndrome is characterized by either (not solely) a *depressive* or a manic mood that is attributed to a *clearly defined organic factor*. According to DSM-III-R, the syndrome does not occur *exclusively* during a course of delirium. Often, a depression accompanies a physical illness and can be viewed as a psychological response to the meaning of the illness to the patient. In those disorders classified under organic mood syndrome, however, a mood syndrome may be induced by some form of direct organic interference with processes regulating normal mood. In these cases the mood disturbance may arise quite separately from the psychological meaning of the illness to the patient. The onset of the syndrome may be acute or *insidious*, and the course varies, depending on the underlying cause; the disturbances are attributed to a clearly defined *organic factor*, the onset of which must antedate the mood syndrome.

Table 10.2 summarizes the DSM-III-R diagnostic criteria for this syndrome.

10.3. The answer is E (*Synopsis VI*, pages 243–244; *CTP V*, pages 623 and 627).

The distinction between delirium and dementia may be quite difficult and, at times, impossible to make, particularly at the transition time between delirium and dementia. *Visual hallucinations and transient delusions* are more common in delirium than in dementia. The *onset of delirium* is generally acute, but prodromal symptoms (e.g., daytime restlessness, anxiety, fearfulness, or hypersensitivity to light or sounds) may occur. Its total *duration* is brief, usually less than one month. Also, in *delirium, symptoms worsen at night,* and the *sleep-wakefulness cycle* is disrupted. Intellectual deterioration of more than one month is more likely to be dementia than delirium. See Table 10.3 for the clinical differentiation of delirium and dementia.

10.4. The answer is C (*Synopsis VI*, pages 263–266; *CTP V*, page 162).

The *petit mal or absence seizure* is associated with a characteristic generalized, bilaterally synchronous, 3-hertz spike-and-wave pattern in the electroencephalogram (EEG) and is often easily induced by hyperventilation. Petit mal (absence) seizures occur predominantly in children. They usually consist of simple absence attacks lasting five to ten seconds, during which there is an abrupt alteration in awareness and responsiveness and an interruption in motor activity. The child often has a blank stare

---

Table 10.1
Diagnostic Criteria for Organic Hallucinosis

A. Prominent persistent or recurrent hallucinations.
B. There is evidence from the history, physical examination, or laboratory tests of a specific organic factor (or factors) judged to be etiologically related to the disturbance.
C. Not occurring exclusively during the course of delirium.

Table from DSM-III-R, *Diagnostic and Statistical Manual of Mental Disorders*, ed 3, revised. Copyright American Psychiatric Association, Washington, DC, 1987. Used with permission.

Table 10.2
Diagnostic Criteria for Organic Mood Syndrome

A. Prominent and persistent depressed, elevated, or expansive mood.
B. There is evidence from the history, physical examination, or laboratory tests of a specific organic factor (or factors) judged to be etiologically related to the disturbance.
C. Not occurring exclusively during the course of delirium.
Specify: manic, depressed, or mixed.

Table from DSM-III-R, *Diagnostic and Statistical Manual of Mental Disorders*, ed 3, revised. Copyright American Psychiatric Association, Washington, DC, 1987. Used with permission.

Table 10.3
Clinical Differentiation of Delirium and Dementia

	Delirium	Dementia
History	Acute disease	Chronic disease
Onset	Rapid	Insidious (usually)
Duration	Days—weeks	Months—years
Course	Fluctuating	Chronically progressive
Level of consciousness	Fluctuating	Normal
Orientation	Impaired, at least periodically	Intact initially
Affect	Anxious, irritable	Labile but not usually anxious
Thinking	Often disordered	Decreased amount
Memory	Recent memory is markedly impaired	Both recent and remote are impaired
Perception	Hallucinations common (especially visual)	Hallucinations less common (except sundowning)
Psychomotor	Retarded, agitated, or mixed	Normal
Sleep	Disrupted sleep-wake cycle	Less disruption of sleep-wake cycle
Attention and awareness	Prominently impaired	Less impaired
Reversibility	Often reversible	Majority not reversible

Note: Demented patients are more susceptible to delirium, and delirium superimposed on dementia is common.

associated with an upward deviation of the eyes and some mild twitching movements of the eyes, eyelids, face, or extremities. Petit mal is usually a fairly benign seizure disorder, often resolving after adolescence.

A *partial seizure* (also known as jacksonian epilepsy) is a type of epilepsy characterized by recurrent episodes of focal motor seizures. It begins with localized tonic or clonic contraction, increases in severity, spreads progressively through the entire body, and terminates in a generalized convulsion with loss of consciousness. *Grand mal epilepsy* is the major form of epilepsy. Gross tonic-clonic convulsive seizures are accompanied by loss of consciousness and, often, incontinence of stool or urine, *Psychomotor epilepsy* is a type of epilepsy characterized by recurrent behavior disturbances. Complex hallucinations or illusions, frequently gustatory or olfactory, often herald the onset of the seizure, which typically involves a state of impaired consciousness resembling a dream, during which paramnestic phenomena, such as *déjà vu* and *jamais vu*, are experienced and the patient exhibits repetitive, automatic, or semipurposeful behaviors. In rare instances, violent behavior may be prominent. The EEG reveals a localized seizure focus in the temporal lobe.

10.5. The answer is A (*Synopsis VI*, pages 241–245; *CTP V*, pages 624–629).

Delirium is, by definition, a *transient disorder*, which implies that the syndrome is never *chronic*. The essential signs and features of delirium include a rapid onset; *multiple disturbances of attention, memory, orientation, and thinking; diurnal variability; and* a disordered sleep-wake cycle. The outcome, however, is not always one of a return to premorbid mental functioning. Delirium lasts, on average, for one week; less often, for several weeks; and, quite rarely, for a few months. It may recur at varying intervals, and, if the underlying cerebral disorder persists, delirium becomes dementia or a more chronic mental syndrome in which there is a relatively stable cognitive impairment. Delirium may *first become apparent at night*, when the patient experiences confusion about his or her whereabouts and situation and the dividing line between dreams and hallucinations.

Table 10.4 outlines the DSM-III-R diagnostic criteria for delirium.

10.6. The answer is C (*Synopsis VI*, page 242; *CTP V*, page 625).

The incidence of delirium after open-heart and coronary-bypass surgery is about *30 percent*. Delirium is the organic psychiatric syndrome encountered most often by psychiatrists who are called to consult on patients in medical and surgical wards. About 10 percent of all hospital inpatients manifest some degree of delirium; 20 to 30 percent of severely burned patients become delirious.

10.7. The answer is B (*Synopsis VI*, page 242; *CTP V*, pages 626–627).

After emerging from a delirium, a patient usually has *impaired recall* of events before the onset of the delirium and impaired registration of current percepts. After the resolution of the delirium, recall of the experiences *during the delirium* is characteristically spotty, and the patient may refer to it as a bad dream or a *nightmare* that is only vaguely (not clearly) remembered. Delirium does not produce *psychosis*, but a psychosis can be exacerbated by an episode of delirium. Delirium may progress into *dementia*, but it is not a usual occurrence.

Table 10.4
Diagnostic Criteria for Delirium

A. Reduced ability to maintain attention to external stimuli (e.g., questions must be repeated because attention wanders) and to appropriately shift attention to new external stimuli (e.g., perseverates answer to a previous question).
B. Disorganized thinking, as indicated by rambling, irrelevant, or incoherent speech.
C. At least two of the following:
1. reduced level of consciousness (e.g., difficulty keeping awake during examination)
2. perceptual disturbances: misinterpretations, illusions, or hallucinations
3. disturbance of sleep-wake cycle with insomnia or daytime sleepiness
4. increased or decreased psychomotor activity
5. disorientation to time, place, or person
6. memory impairment (e.g., inability to learn new material, such as the names of several unrelated objects after five minutes, or to remember past events, such as history of current episode of illness)
D. Clinical features develop over a short period of time (usually hours to days) and tend to fluctuate over the course of a day.
E. Either 1 or 2:
1. evidence from the history, physical examination, or laboratory tests of a specific organic factor (or factors) judged to be etiologically related to the disturbance
2. in the absence of such evidence, an etiologic organic factor can be presumed if the disturbance cannot be accounted for by any nonorganic mental disorder (e.g., manic episode accounting for agitation and sleep disturbance)

Table from DSM-III-R, *Diagnostic and Statistical Manual of Mental Disorders*, ed 3, revised. Copyright American Psychiatric Association, Washington, DC, 1987. Used with permission.

10.8. The answer is E (*Synopsis VI*, page 243; *CTP V*, page 628).

Delirium may have one of four outcomes: (1) a *full recovery* of premorbid functioning (most common), (2) *death*, (3) a transition to *dementia* or another organic mental syndrome, or (4) a transition to a nonorganic mental disorder, such as a *delusional* disorder (most rare).

10.9. The answer is A (*Synopsis VI*, page 257; *CTP V*, pages 634–635).

Persecutory delusions are the most common type seen in organic delusional syndrome. The essential feature of the organic delusional syndrome is the presence of delusions in a state of full wakefulness. The delusions may be systematized or fragmentary, and their content may vary; that is, along with persecutory delusions, delusions of *grandiosity, jealousy*, and others may appear. *Nihilistic* delusions are associated with severe cases of psychotic depression and are characterized by feelings that nothing in life is of value and all is hopeless. *Somatic* delusions involve false, fixed ideas regarding the functioning of the body and body parts—for example, a belief

that one's brain is melting or that one's body is riddled with disease. Somatic delusions are also associated with psychotic depressive states.

10.10. The answer is E (*Synopsis VI*, pages 257–258; *CTP V*, pages 634–635).

In organic delusional syndrome the patient has no change in the level of consciousness, although *mild cognitive impairment* may be observed. The patient may appear *confused, disheveled, or eccentric.* Speech may be tangential or even *incoherent*, and hyperactivity and apathy may be observed. An *associated dysphoric mood* is felt to be common.

10.11. The answer is E (*Synopsis VI*, pages 259–260; *CTP V*, pages 635–638).

Organic personality syndrome is characterized by a marked change in personality caused by a specific organic factor. The important causes of organic personality syndrome include *chronic poisoning, brain tumor, head trauma*, and *vascular disease.* Other conditions associated with organic personality syndrome include temporal lobe epilepsy, Huntington's chorea, multiple sclerosis, endocrine disorders, drugs, neurosyphilis, and systemic lupus erythematosus.

10.12. The answer is B (*Synopsis VI*, page 241; *CTP V*, pages 599–601 and 1867).

As delineated by DSM-III-R, *Tourette's disorder* is a tic disorder, not an organic mental syndrome. Tourette's disorder is a rare illness having its onset in childhood and is characterized by involuntary muscular movements, motor incoordination, echolalia (the repetition of another person's words or phrases), and coprolalia (the use of socially unacceptable, frequently obscene words).

Organic mental syndromes represent clusters of psychological or behavioral abnormalities or symptoms that show a tendency to occur together. These syndromes share a common feature in that a cerebral disorder constitutes a necessary condition for their occurrence. Their essential clinical characteristics, however, differ widely and reflect such variables as the degree of spread, the localization, the rate of onset and progression, and the nature of the underlying pathological process in the brain. The clinical picture displayed by a patient is modified to some extent by his or her personality structure, intelligence, education, emotional state, interpersonal relationships, and other psychological and social factors.

According to DSM-III-R, the organic mental syndromes are delirium, dementia, amnestic syndrome, *organic delusional syndrome, organic hallucinosis, organic mood syndrome*, organic anxiety syndrome, *organic personality syndrome*, intoxication, withdrawal, and organic mental syndrome not otherwise specified (NOS, a residual category). If the cause is known (e.g., delirium caused by pneumonia), the condition is coded on Axis III.

10.13. The answer is E (all) (*Synopsis VI*, pages 246–248; *CTP V*, pages 540, 543, and 549–550).

Dementia is characterized by a loss of cognitive and intellectual abilities that is severe enough to impair social or occupational performance. The diagnostic criteria for dementia include impairment in short-term and long-term memory, which means an inability to learn new information and to remember information that was known in the past. A patient's short-term memory can be assessed by asking the patient to *remember three objects* after five minutes; long-term memory can be assessed by asking the patient to remember past personal information, such as the patient's *place of birth* or what happened yesterday, or assessing the patient's *fund of common information*, such as past U.S. presidents. Other criteria for the diagnosis of dementia include impairment of abstract thinking, which can be indicated by an inability to find *similarities and differences* between related words. See Table 10.5 for the DSM-III-R diagnostic criteria for dementia.

10.14. The answer is D (4) (*Synopsis VI*, pages 254–256; *CTP V*, pages 629–630).

In most cases the onset of amnestic syndrome tends to be relatively *sudden*.

Impairment of memory is the predominant cognitive defect in amnestic syndrome. The memory pathology is of two types: retrograde amnesia (pathological loss of memories established before the onset of the illness) and anterograde amnesia (inability to establish new memories after the onset of the illness). Amnestic syndrome includes an impairment in both short-term and long-term memory, with *remote events* more clearly remembered than recent events. Another criterion is that the amnestic syndrome not meet the criteria for dementia, such as impairment in *abstract thinking or judgment* and no personality change. See Table 10.6 for the DSM-III-R diagnostic criteria for amnestic syndrome.

10.15. The answer is E (all) (*Synopsis VI*, pages 249–252; *CTP V*, page 612).

According to the DSM-III-R classification, dementias arising in the senium and presenium include a single category called *primary degenerative dementia* (*PDD*). The category is subdivided according to *age of onset* and is classified as being of the *Alzheimer type*—PDD of the Alzheimer type, senile onset, and PDD of the Alzheimer type, presenile onset. Dementia associated with Alzheimer's disease was formerly called senile dementia, and *Pick's disease* was formerly called presenile dementia. The distinction no longer applies, as almost all dementias occurring in the senium and presenium are caused by Alzheimer's disease, and the differentiation be-

Table 10.5
Diagnostic Criteria for Dementia

A. Demonstrable evidence of impairment in short- and long-term memory. Impairment in short-term memory (inability to learn new information) may be indicated by inability to remember three objects after five minutes. Long-term memory impairment (inability to remember information that was known in the past) may be indicated by inability to remember past personal information (e.g., what happened yesterday, birthplace, occupation) or facts of common knowledge (e.g., past presidents, well-known dates).
B. At least one of the following:
   1. impairment in abstract thinking, as indicated by inability to find similarities and differences between related words, difficulty in defining words and concepts, and other similar tasks
   2. impaired judgment, as indicated by inability to make reasonable plans to deal with interpersonal, family, and job-related problems and issues
   3. other disturbances of higher cortical function, such as aphasia (disorder of language), apraxia (inability to carry out motor activities despite intact comprehension and motor function), agnosia (failure to recognize or identify objects despite intact sensory function), and "constructional difficulty" (e.g., inability to copy three-dimensional figures, assemble blocks, or arrange sticks in specific designs)
   4. personality change, i.e., alteration or accentuation of premorbid traits
C. The disturbance in A and B significantly interferes with work or usual social activities or relationships with others.
D. Not occurring exclusively during the course of delirium.
E. Either 1 or 2:
   1. there is evidence from the history, physical examination, or laboratory tests of a specific organic factor (or factors) judged to be etiologically related to the disturbance
   2. in the absence of such evidence, an etiologic organic factor can be presumed if the disturbance cannot be accounted for by any nonorganic mental disorder (e.g., major depression accounting for cognitive impairment)
Criteria for severity of dementia:
   Mild: Although work or social activities are significantly impaired, the capacity for independent living remains, with adequate personal hygiene and relatively intact judgment.
   Moderate: Independent living is hazardous, and some degree of supervision is necessary.
   Severe: Activities of daily living are so impaired that continual supervision is required (e.g., unable to maintain minimal personal hygiene; largely incoherent or mute).

Table from DSM-III-R, *Diagnostic and Statistical Manual of Mental Disorders*, ed 3, revised. Copyright American Psychiatric Association, Washington, DC, 1987. Used with permission.

Table 10.6
Diagnostic Criteria for Amnestic Syndrome

A. Demonstrable evidence of impairment in both short- and long-term memory; with regard to long-term memory, very remote events are remembered better than more recent events. Impairment in short-term memory (inability to learn new information) may be indicated by inability to remember three objects after five minutes. Long-term memory impairment (inability to remember information that was known in the past) may be indicated by inability to remember past personal information (e.g., what happened yesterday, birthplace, occupation) or facts of common knowledge (e.g., past presidents, well-known dates).

B. Not occurring exclusively during the course of delirium, and does not meet the criteria for dementia (i.e., no impairment in abstract thinking or judgment, no other disturbances of higher cortical function, and no personality change).

C. There is evidence from the history, physical examination, or laboratory tests of a specific organic factor (or factors) judged to be etiologically related to the disturbance.

Table from DSM-III-R, *Diagnostic and Statistical Manual of Mental Disorders*, ed 3, revised. Copyright American Psychiatric Association, Washington, DC, 1987. Used with permission.

tween the two disorders can be made only by histopathological examination. See Tables 10.7, 10.8, and 10.9 for the DSM-III-R diagnostic criteria for primary degenerative dementia of the Alzheimer type, presenile dementia not otherwise specified, and senile dementia not otherwise specified.

Table 10.7
Diagnostic Criteria for Primary Degenerative Dementia of the Alzheimer Type

A. Dementia.
B. Insidious onset with a generally progressive deteriorating course.
C. Exclusion of all other specific causes of dementia by history, physical examination, and laboratory tests.

Table from DSM-III-R, *Diagnostic and Statistical Manual of Mental Disorders*, ed 3, revised. Copyright American Psychiatric Association, Washington, DC, 1987. Used with permission.

Table 10.8
Diagnostic Criteria for Presenile Dementia Not Otherwise Specified

Dementias associated with an organic factor and arising before age 65 that cannot be classified as a specific dementia (e.g., primary degenerative dementia of the Alzheimer type, presenile onset)

Table from DSM-III-R, *Diagnostic and Statistical Manual of Mental Disorders*, ed 3, revised. Copyright American Psychiatric Association, Washington, DC, 1987. Used with permission.

Table 10.9
Diagnostic Criteria for Senile Dementia Not Otherwise Specified

Dementias associated with an organic factor and arising after age 65 that cannot be classified as a specific dementia (e.g., as primary degenerative dementia of the Alzheimer type, senile onset, or dementia associated with alcoholism)

Table from DSM-III-R, *Diagnostic and Statistical Manual of Mental Disorders*, ed 3, revised. Copyright American Psychiatric Association, Washington, DC, 1987. Used with permission.

10.16. The answer is B (1, 3) (*Synopsis VI*, pages 249–252; *CTP V*, pages 612–617).

The most common type of dementia is primary degenerative dementia (PDD) of the Alzheimer type; its prevalence increases with advancing age, and it is seen slightly *more frequently in women* than in men. The cause of the disease is unknown; however, genetic factors are presumed to be involved, because evidence indicates that it is common for one or more relatives to have the same disorder. In fact, several families have been reported with apparent *autosomal dominant* transmission. Most patients with Down's syndrome who survive into their 30s develop Alzheimer's disease, and recently an anomaly on gene 21, the same gene damaged in Down's syndrome, was found in Alzheimer's disease patients, which may account for the association of Alzheimer's disease and *Down's syndrome*. A decreased (not increased) amount of the neurotransmitter *acetylcholine* has been found in the brains of Alzheimer's patients. Cholinergic neurons that project to the cerebral cortex and limbic system degenerate in Alzheimer's disease.

10.17. The answer is E (all) (*Synopsis VI*, page 261; *CTP V*, pages 635–638).

Both the course and the prognosis of organic personality syndrome depend on its cause. If the syndrome is the result of structural *damage to the brain*, it will tend to persist. The syndrome may follow a period of coma and delirium in cases of head trauma or vascular accident and may be *permanent*. Organic personality syndrome may evolve into *dementia* in cases of brain tumor, multiple sclerosis, or Huntington's chorea. Personality changes produced by chronic intoxication, medical illness, or drug therapy may be *reversible* if the underlying cause is treated.

10.18. The answer is A (1, 2, 3) (*Synopsis VI*, page 260; *CTP V*, pages 635–638).

In organic personality syndrome a change in personality from previous patterns of behavior or an exacerbation of previous personality characteristics is notable. *Impaired control* of the expression of emotions and impulses is a cardinal feature. Emotions are characteristically *labile and shallow*, and *euphoria or apathy* may be prominent. Patients with organic personality syndrome have a clear (not an impaired) *sensorium.*

10.19. The answer is A (1, 2, 3) (*Synopsis VI*, pages 246–248; *CTP V*, page 611).

Susceptibility to organic mental syndromes is increased among persons *over age 60. Preexisting brain damage* of any origin enhances a susceptibility to delirium. Reduced ability to *metabolize drugs* is a factor predisposing elderly patients to the development of delirium in response to even therapeutic doses of medical drugs.

Because social isolation, interpersonal conflicts and losses, and deficient or excessive sensory input may facilitate the occurrence of an organic mental disorder, especially delirium or dementia, a *familiar environment* is beneficial.

10.20. The answer is B (1, 3) (*Synopsis VI*, pages 245–246; *CTP V*, pages 609 and 612).

Dementia occurs most often in old age. One million Americans over age 65 (*5 percent* of the aged population) have a significant degree of dementia and are unable to care for themselves. About 60 percent (not 90 percent) of persons in *nursing homes* have some dementia. The *most common cause* of dementia is primary degenerative dementia of the Alzheimer type (about 65 percent of all cases). The next most common cause is multi-infarct dementia (10 percent of all cases). About 15 percent of all dementia cases are *reversible* if the physician initiates timely treatment, before irreversible damage has taken place.

10.21. The answer is E (all) (*Synopsis VI*, page 242; *CTP V*, page 626).

Delirium has a multitude of organic causes, including *hypoglycemia, hypokalemia, migraine headaches,* and *infectious mononucleosis.* The term "delirium" denotes a transient disturbance characterized by a global impairment of cognitive functions and a widespread disturbance of cerebral metabolism. A large number of cerebral and systemic diseases and toxic agents can lead to delirium.

10.22. The answer is D (4) (*Synopsis VI*, pages 258–259; *CTP V*, pages 630–633).

The most appropriate diagnosis in this case is *organic mood syndrome.* Although the patient's symptoms are identical to those seen in a *major depressive* episode (e.g., depressed mood, suicidal gestures, increased sleep, loss of interest, guilt), it is reasonable to infer that the disturbance is caused by the frontal lobe tumor; thus, the diagnosis of organic mood syndrome is made, which is characterized by either a depressive or a manic mood attributed to a clearly defined organic factor. The frontal lobe tumor would be noted on Axis III. *Organic personality syndrome* is characterized by a marked change in personality style or traits from a previous level of functioning. *Organic anxiety syndrome* is a category new

to DSM-III-R. It is characterized by prominent, recurrent panic attacks or generalized anxiety attributable to some clearly defined organic factor.

10.23. The answer is E (all) (*Synopsis VI*, page 258; *CTP V*, pages 631–633).

Medications, especially *antihypertensives,* are probably the most frequent cause of organic mood syndrome. Drugs such as reserpine and methyldopa (Aldomet) can precipitate a depression by depleting monoamines in more than 10 percent of the persons who take them. Endocrine and cerebral disorders of various causes (e.g., brain tumors, *encephalitis, epilepsy*) have been implicated in the cause of organic mood syndrome. Structural damage to the brain, as with *hemispheric strokes,* is a common cause of the syndrome.

10.24. The answer is B (1, 3) (*Synopsis VI*, pages 248–249; *CTP V*, pages 621–623).

A very important clinical diagnostic problem concerns the differentiation of dementia from pseudodementia, a depressive disorder with cognitive impairment. A number of factors are helpful in making this differentiation, including onset of depressive versus cognitive symptoms, presentation of cognitive deficits, intellectual performance, and sodium amobarbital (Amytal) interviews. In dementia *intellectual deficits antedate depression,* whereas in pseudodementia depressive symptoms antedate cognitive defects. In dementia the patient denies, minimizes, or conceals cognitive deficits; in pseudodementia the patient is disturbed by *memory and intellectual impairment.* The patient with dementia is usually *globally impaired,* with consistently poor intellectual performance, whereas in pseudodementia the dementia is often confined to memory impairment and is inconsistently poor. In a *sodium amobarbital interview,* the performance worsens in dementia and is improved in pseudodementia.

10.25. The answer is A (1, 2, 3) (*Synopsis VI*, page 256; *CTP V*, page 635).

Organic hallucinosis is associated with a variety of conditions. The appearance of hallucinations should prompt the search for organic causative factors. Visual hallucinosis should alert one to the possibility of a *focal cerebral lesion,* hallucinogen abuse, side effects of medical drugs, *migraine,* or *temporal arteritis.* Auditory hallucinosis should raise a question about alcohol abuse. Organic hallucinosis must be distinguished from delirium, which may be accompanied by hallucinations.

Although *epilepsy* may feature auditory hallucinations or visual hallucinations or both, such hallucinations usually occur in a setting of reduced awareness, such as part of an ictal or seizure state. In contrast to a patient with epilepsy, a patient with organic hallucinosis is fully oriented without any impairment of attention or cognitive functioning.

10.26. The answer is B (1, 3) (*Synopsis VI*, pages 259–261; *CTP V*, pages 635–638).

In organic personality syndrome many patients exhibit *low drive* and initiative. Emotions are typically *labile and shallow*, with euphoria or apathy predominating. Apathy may lead one to assume the presence of a depressed mood, but *true sadness and depression* are uncommon. Temper outbursts may occur with little or no provocation, resulting in violent behavior, and the expression of *impulses*, rather than being inhibited, is characteristically disinhibited, resulting in inappropriate jokes, a crude manner, improper sexual advances, or outright antisocial behavior. Evidence of some causative organic factors must antedate the onset of the syndrome.

Table 10.10 summarizes the DSM-III-R criteria for diagnosing organic personality syndrome.

10.27. The answer is E (all) (*Synopsis VI*, page 258; *CTP V*, pages 630–633).

The onset of organic mood syndrome may be acute or insidious, and the course varies, depending on the underlying cause. The *removal of the cause* does not necessarily result in the patient's prompt recovery from the mood disturbance; it may persist for weeks or months after the successful treatment of the underlying physical condition or the withdrawal of the implicated toxic agent. The major differential is between organic and nonorganic mood disorders; the syndrome may be *indistinguishable from manic and depressive episodes* that are not attributable to a specific organic factor. Functional (nonorganic) illness

Table 10.10
Diagnostic Criteria for Organic Personality Syndrome

A. A persistent personality disturbance, either lifelong or representing a change or accentuation of a previously characteristic trait, involving at least one of the following:
   1. affective instability (e.g., marked shifts from normal mood to depression, irritability, or anxiety)
   2. recurrent outbursts of aggression or rage that are grossly out of proportion to any precipitating psychosocial stressors
   3. markedly impaired social judgment (e.g., sexual indiscretions)
   4. marked apathy and indifference
   5. suspiciousness or paranoid ideation
B. There is evidence from the history, physical examination, or laboratory tests of a specific organic factor (or factors) judged to be etiologically related to the disturbance.
C. This diagnosis is not given to a child or adolescent if the clinical picture is limited to the features that characterize attention-deficit hyperactivity disorder.
D. Not occurring exclusively during the course of delirium, and does not meet the criteria for dementia.

Specify explosive type if outbursts of aggression or rage are the predominant feature.

Table from DSM-III-R, *Diagnostic and Statistical Manual of Mental Disorders*, ed 3, revised. Copyright American Psychiatric Association, Washington, DC, 1987. Used with permission.

is usually accompanied by a *family history* of depression or mania, recurrent cycles of depression or mania, and the absence of a specific organic causative factor. *Drugs may trigger* an underlying mood disturbance in a patient who is biologically vulnerable, and, according to DSM-III-R, this would not be an organic mood syndrome. A history of a previous mood disorder in the patient or in relatives suggests that the psychoactive substance merely triggered an existing underlying disorder; the absence of such a history suggests a true organic mood syndrome.

10.28. The answer is E (all) (*Synopsis VI*, pages 258–259; *CTP V*, pages 631–633).

Organic mood syndrome may be caused by a number of organic factors and disorders; its diagnosis depends on the finding of a clearly defined causative organic condition. Many somatic disorders, such as *infectious mononucleosis* and *systemic lupus erythematosus*, and drugs, such as *reserpine*, have been implicated in the causes of depressive and, to a smaller degree, manic disorders. Table 10.2 lists the DSM-III-R diagnostic criteria.

Parkinsonism is a progressive disorder characterized by resting tremor, rigidity, slowed movements, postural abnormalities, and mood changes. Primary parkinsonism—also called paralysis agitans, Parkinson's disease, and idiopathic parkinsonism—is a disorder of middle or late life, typically with a gradual progression and a prolonged course. Its cause is unknown. Secondary parkinsonism may develop during the course of therapy with antipsychotic phenothiazine or butyrophenone drugs. Such drug-induced parkinsonism is reversible when the causative drug is withdrawn or its dosage is reduced.

10.29. The answer is E (all) (*Synopsis VI*, pages 252–254; *CTP V*, pages 617–620).

The diagnosis of multi-infarct dementia (MID) is associated with *cerebrovascular disease*. This disorder affects small- and medium-sized cerebral vessels, producing multiple, widely spread cerebral lesions that result in a combination of neurological and psychiatric symptoms. MID is also associated with *hypertension* and manifests with a *stepwise progression* of focal, sometimes fluctuating, motor symptoms. These symptoms are accompanied by dementia. The clinical description of this disorder includes a variety of symptoms, ranging from headaches, dizziness, and transient focal neurological symptoms to *personality changes*, such as emotional lability and hypochondriasis. Table 10.11 gives the DSM-III-R diagnostic criteria for multi-infarct dementia.

10.30. The answer is E (all) (*Synopsis VI*, pages 254–255; *CTP V*, pages 629–630).

The core feature of the amnestic syndrome, an organic mental syndrome, is the *impairment of memory*, which is the single or predominant cognitive defect. The memory pathology is of two types: (1) *retrograde*, which is a loss of memories of events

Table 10.11
Diagnostic Criteria for Multi-Infarct Dementia

A. Dementia
B. Stepwise deteriorating course with "patchy" distribution of deficits (i.e., affecting some functions, but not others) early in the course.
C. Focal neurologic signs and symptoms (e.g., exaggeration of deep tendon reflexes, extensor plantar response, pseudobulbar palsy, gait abnormalities, weakness of an extremity, etc.).
D. Evidence from history, physical examination, or laboratory tests of significant cerebrovascular disease (recorded on Axis III) that is judged to be etiologically related to the disturbance.

Table from DSM-III-R, *Diagnostic and Statistical Manual of Mental Disorders*, ed 3, revised. Copyright American Psychiatric Association, Washington, DC, 1987. Used with permission.

taking place before the onset of the illness, and (2) *anterograde*, which is the reduced ability to recall current events. Although short-term memory is impaired, there is preservation of the ability for *immediate recall*, as is tested by digit span. As a number of organic pathological factors and conditions can give rise to the amnestic syndrome, *evidence of a specific causative organic factor* is required for the diagnosis.

Table 10.6 lists the DSM-III-R diagnostic criteria for amnestic syndrome.

10.31. The answer is A (1, 2, 3) (*Synopsis VI*, pages 257–258; *CTP V*, pages 634–635).

Organic delusional syndrome is characterized by the predominance of delusions that do not occur exclusively during the course of delirium and are attributable to some clearly defined organic factor. These delusions may or may not be *systematized* (i.e., highly organized, intricate, and detailed), and their content may vary. The syndrome needs to be distinguished from schizophrenia and schizophreniform and delusional disorders, with which it may share various features. To make the diagnosis of organic delusional syndrome, the clinician must find evidence of a *specific organic factor* judged to be causatively significant. A variety of chemical substances and cerebral or systemic diseases may induce the syndrome, and the syndrome often, but not always, *lifts* after the toxic agent is removed or the physical illness is resolved. For instance, amphetamine intoxication appears to be limited to a paranoid-type psychosis, whereas *lesions of the limbic system* appear to be linked to a schizophreniform psychosis. As defined in DSM-III-R, schizophreniform disorder is identical to schizophrenia except that schizophreniform symptoms resolve, with a return to normal functioning within six months. Symptoms must be present for longer than six months to make a diagnosis of schizophrenia.

Table 10.12 summarizes the DSM-III-R diagnostic criteria for organic delusional syndrome.

Table 10.12
Diagnostic Criteria for Organic Delusional Syndrome

A. Prominent delusions.
B. There is evidence from the history, physical examination, or laboratory tests of a specific organic factor (or factors) judged to be etiologically related to the disturbance.
C. Not occurring exclusively during the course of delirium.

Table from DSM-III-R, *Diagnostic and Statistical Manual of Mental Disorders*, ed 3, revised. Copyright American Psychiatric Association, Washington, DC, 1987. Used with permission.

10.32. The answer is E (all) (*Synopsis VI*, page 255; *CTP V*, pages 629–630).

The core DSM-III-R diagnostic criterion for amnestic syndrome is the impairment of memory. Regardless of the cause, there is an impairment of *short-term* and recent memory (a few minutes to a few days) with preservation of the ability for immediate recall, as may be tested by digit span. Memory for learned events from the remote past, such as childhood experiences, is good, but the recall of events of the past decade or longer is defective (*long-term memory*). The sensorium and *consciousness* are clear.

Short-term memory impairment is defined as the inability to learn new information, such that the patient may be unable to learn and remember such information as the name of the hospital or the physician; long-term memory impairment is defined as the inability to remember information that was known in the past.

A number of organic pathological factors and conditions can give rise to the amnestic syndrome, and evidence of an *organic causative factor* is necessary for the diagnosis. Probably the most common cause in this country is thiamine deficiency associated with chronic alcoholism.

In the absence of epidemiological data, no definite statement about the frequency of the various causative associations can be given.

10.33–10.37

10.33. The answer is D (*Synopsis VI*, pages 73 and 246; *CTP V*, pages 208–209 and 1416).

10.34. The answer is A (*Synopsis VI*, page 269; *CTP V*, pages 187–188).

10.35. The answer is C (*Synopsis VI*, page 269; *CTP V*, pages 191 and 2138).

10.36. The answer is B (*Synopsis VI*, pages 63 and 266; *CTP V*, pages 612 and 617).

10.37. The answer is E (*Synopsis VI*, page 269; *CTP V*, pages 191–192).

Huntington's chorea, inherited in an autosomal dominant pattern, leads to major atrophy of the brain with extensive degeneration of the caudate nucleus. The onset is usually insidious and most commonly begins in late middle life. The course is one of gradual progression, with death occurring *15 to 20 years* after the onset of the disease. *Suicide is common.*

Creutzfeldt-Jakob disease is a rare degenerative brain disease caused by a *slow virus* infection. The disease is most common in adults in their 50s, and death usually occurs within two years of the diagnosis. A computed tomography (CT) scan shows cerebellar and cortical atrophy.

General paresis is a chronic dementia and psychosis caused by the tertiary form of syphilis that affects the brain. In approximately 20 percent of cases, presenting symptoms include a *manic syndrome* with euphoria and grandiose delusions and neurological signs.

Normal-pressure hydrocephalus is associated with enlarged ventricles and normal cerebrospinal fluid (CSF) pressure. Along with dementia, the characteristic signs include a gait disturbance and urinary incontinence. The treatment includes *shunting* the CSF from the ventricular space to either the atrium or the peritoneal space. Reversal of dementias and associated signs is sometimes dramatic after treatment.

Multiple sclerosis is characterized by diffuse multifocal lesions in the white matter of the central nervous system (CNS), and its clinical course is characterized by exacerbations and remissions. It has no known specific cause, although research has focused on slow viral infections and autoimmune disturbances. Multiple sclerosis is much more prevalent in *cold and temperate climates* than in the tropics and subtropics, is more common in women than in men, and is predominantly a disease of young adults.

10.38–10.41

10.38.   The answer is B (*Synopsis VI*, pages 249–252; *CTP V*, pages 612–617).

10.39.   The answer is A (*Synopsis VI*, pages 252–254; *CTP V*, pages 617–620).

10.40.   The answer is A (*Synopsis VI*, pages 252–254; *CTP V*, pages 617–620).

10.41.   The answer is A (*Synopsis VI*, pages 252–254; *CTP V*, pages 617–620).

Multi-infarct dementia (MID) is characterized by a stepwise deterioration in cognitive functioning secondary to significant cerebrovascular disease. Primary degenerative dementia (PDD) of the Alzheimer type is a consistently progressive deterioration in cognitive functioning of unknown cause; it occurs *more frequently in women* than in men and accounts for approximately 65 percent of all cases of dementia in the elderly. MID is more common in men and accounts for about *10 to 15 percent* of all cases of dementia in the elderly. It is more likely to show *focal neurological signs* as a result of ischemia in the brain. The *onset of MID is usually sudden.* It has a progressive, though fluctuating, course, as opposed to PDD of the Alzheimer type, which has a more insidious onset and a more continuous progression in deterioration.

11 ▐▐▐

Psychiatric Aspects of Acquired Immune Deficiency Syndrome (AIDS)

Psychiatrists have taken a major role in collaborating with other health care providers to develop programs to reduce the behaviors that transmit human immunodeficiency virus (HIV) infection and to develop effective interventions for those HIV-infected patients who have experienced psychosocial sequelae or psychiatric symptoms.

Physicians must be knowledgeable about acquired immune deficiency syndrome (AIDS), both because of its widespread psychological effects and because AIDS involves the central nervous system (CNS), thereby potentially affecting brain function. Every physician must know the epidemiology of AIDS—how it is transmitted, in which high-risk groups it is found, and how it is diagnosed and treated. Health care workers must also be aware of other groups becoming infected—children of mothers with AIDS, spouses of persons with AIDS, and health care workers themselves.

Mental health professionals must have accurate knowledge concerning HIV infection and the functional and organic psychiatric syndromes that HIV infection may cause. Although depression and dementia are the most common psychiatric presentations of AIDS, this syndrome can present with virtually any set of symptoms described in DSM-III-R. Therefore, the clinician must always consider AIDS in a differential diagnosis. AIDS can result in psychiatric symptoms by three broad mechanisms. First, there is the psychological effect of having a serious illness often associated with social issues regarding alternative life-styles. Second, AIDS patients are susceptible to infections and tumors of the CNS. Third, the virus itself invades and destroys brain tissue. The psychiatrist must know how to approach the differentiation of these possibilities in an individual patient.

The reader is referred to Chapter 11 in *Synopsis VI*, "Psychiatric Aspects of Acquired Immune Deficiency Syndrome (AIDS)," and to Section 26.2 in *CTP V*, "Psychiatric Aspects of Acquired Immune Deficiency Syndrome." An assessment of the student's knowledge can be made by studying the questions and answers below.

HELPFUL HINTS

The following terms relate to AIDS and should be known by the student.

HIV	*Candida albicans*	AIDS in children
Kaposi's sarcoma	tuberculosis	AZT
transmission	ARC	psychopharmacology
ELISA	AIDS dementia complex	psychotherapy
false-positives	AIDS encephalopathy	worried well
seropositive	CNS infections	institutional care
Pneumocystis carinii pneumonia	neuropsychiatric syndromes	Western blot serum test

QUESTIONS

DIRECTIONS: Each of the incomplete statements below is followed by five suggested completions. Select the *one* that is *best* in each case.

11.1. In the psychotherapy of homosexual AIDS patients,
A. therapy with the patient's lover is an unwarranted procedure
B. the discussion of such issues as terminal care and life-support systems should be avoided
C. the patient should be advised not to come out to the family if the patient has not already done so
D. the psychiatrist can help the patient deal with the feeling of being punished for a deviant life-style
E. a discussion of safe-sex practices is not necessary

11.2. The percentage of AIDS patients who develop neuropsychiatric syndromes is
A. less than 10 percent
B. 30 percent
C. 60 percent
D. 80 percent
E. more than 90 percent

11.3. All the following statements about the serum test for the human immunodeficiency virus (HIV) are true *except*
A. false-positives occur in about 1 percent of cases tested
B. the Western blot serum test is less likely to give a false-positive than the enzyme-linked immunosorbent assay (ELISA)
C. blood banks must exclude sera that are ELISA positive
D. a person should be notified immediately if the ELISA is positive
E. 1 to 2 million Americans are seropositive to HIV

11.4. Most of the women infected with HIV are
A. intravenous drug abusers
B. prostitutes
C. homosexuals
D. hemophiliacs
E. health care workers

11.5. The drug of first choice for a depressed AIDS patient with some signs of organic mental syndrome is
A. thioridazine (Mellaril)
B. nortriptyline (Aventyl)
C. lorazepam (Ativan)
D. fluoxetine (Prozac)
E. amitriptyline (Elavil)

11.6. AIDS is associated with
A. cryptococcal meningitis
B. psychosis
C. herpes simplex meningitis
D. dementia
E. all the above

11.7. AIDS dementia complex may present
A. as dysphoric mood, apathy, and social withdrawal
B. acutely, often with a florid psychosis
C. a triad of cognitive, behavioral, and motor symptoms
D. as delirium
E. all the above

ANSWERS

Psychiatric Aspects
of Acquired Immune Deficiency Syndrome (AIDS)

11.1. **The answer is D** (*Synopsis VI*, pages 275–276; *CTP V*, pages 1305 and 1313–1314).

Psychotherapy with homosexual AIDS patients requires great flexibility. The psychiatrist can help such patients *deal with feelings of guilt* regarding behaviors that contributed to AIDS and that are disapproved of by other segments of society, including the feeling that they are being punished for a deviant life-style. Involvement of a homosexual patient's *lover* in couples therapy is warranted in many cases. This includes a discussion of *safe-sex practices*, such as using condoms in anal sex. Difficult health care decisions, as well as *terminal care and life support systems*, should be explored.

Treatment of homosexuals and bisexuals with AIDS often involves both helping the patient to *come out* to the family (i.e., telling the family that the patient is homosexual) and dealing with the possible issues of rejection, guilt, shame, and anger.

11.2. **The answer is C** (*Synopsis VI*, pages 272–274; *CTP V*, page 1305).

Approximately *60 percent* of AIDS patients develop some kind of neuropsychiatric syndrome. The virus directly attacks the central nervous system (CNS) and produces dementia in extreme cases. Other psychiatric syndromes include personality disorders, depression, and psychotic behavior. The usual measures of medical, environmental, and social support should be instituted in these conditions. Psychopharmacological agents have proved useful in managing anxiety, depression, and psychosis.

11.3. **The answer is D** (*Synopsis VI*, pages 270–271; *CTP V*, page 1300).

The serum test used to detect the human immunodeficiency virus (HIV) is the enzyme-linked immunosorbent assay (ELISA). False-positives (nondiseased persons with abnormal findings) occur in about *1 percent* of persons tested with ELISA. If an ELISA result is suspected of being incorrect, the serum can be subjected to a *Western blot serum test*, which is less likely to give a false-positive or false-negative (diseased person with normal findings). A person should *not be notified immediately* of a positive ELISA until a confirmatory test, such as the Western blot, is conducted. *Blood banks*, however, currently must exclude sera that are ELISA positive. About *1 to 2 million Americans* are seropositive to

HIV. That figure has remained steady in the population, although some workers expect it to increase.

11.4. **The answer is A** (*Synopsis VI*, pages 270–271; *CTP V*, pages 1298–1300).

Most of the women infected with HIV are *intravenous drug abusers*, who are usually prostitutes. Although *homosexuals* make up 70 to 80 percent of reported cases, they are mostly men. *Intravenous drug abusers* account for a significant percentage of cases. *Health care workers* have not contracted AIDS, except in very rare cases when they have been exposed to contaminated blood from repeated needle punctures. *Hemophiliacs* contract AIDS from contaminated blood transfusions, but hemophilia occurs almost exclusively in males. Recent studies have found the AIDS virus in cervical secretions, which may account for the transmission of HIV from infected mothers to their newborn infants.

11.5. **The answer is D** (*Synopsis VI*, page 276; *CTP V*, pages 1311–1312).

Antidepressants, particularly those with few anticholinergic side effects, are beneficial in treating depression. If an organic mental syndrome is present, drugs with anticholinergic effects must be used cautiously to prevent atropine psychosis. *Fluoxetine* (Prozac)—a new antidepressant that is unrelated to tricyclic, tetracyclic, and other available antidepressant agents—has few anticholinergic side effects. It is a serotonergic drug that works by blocking the uptake of serotonin. It is considered the drug of first choice so as to avoid anticholinergic actions. Among the other antidepressants, *nortriptyline* (Aventyl) has fewer anticholinergic effects than *amitriptyline* (Elavil). *Thioridazine* (Mellaril) is an antipsychotic, and *lorazepam* (Ativan) is a benzodiazepine; neither has antidepressant effects.

11.6. **The answer is E** (*Synopsis VI*, pages 273–274; *CTP V*, pages 1305–1309).

AIDS is transmitted by a slow retrovirus referred to as human immunodeficiency virus (HIV). HIV causes immunosuppression leading to such central nervous system (CNS) infections as *cryptococcal* and *herpes simplex meningitis*. CNS infection with HIV itself may lead to a subacute encephalopathy, which may progress to *psychosis* or *dementia*. Some degree of dementia has been reported in about 60 percent of patients with AIDS. The diagnosis is made when seropositivity is associated with opportunistic infections. A syndrome known as AIDS-related complex (ARC) occurs in seropositive patients who do not have an opportunistic infection. ARC patients show fatigue, weight loss, fever, night sweats, and lymphadenopathy. About 25 percent of ARC patients eventually get AIDS. Some workers believe that all ARC patients will eventually get AIDS.

11.7. The answer is E (*Synopsis VI*, page 274; *CTP V*, pages 1307–1308).

AIDS dementia complex (ADC) has been reported since 1983. Clinically, ADC is characterized by a *triad of cognitive, behavioral, and motor symptoms.* The range of clinical presentations seen is wide.

Early ADC patients may predominantly exhibit symptoms of *dysphoric mood, apathy, and social withdrawal*, sometimes misdiagnosed as depression. ADC patients may also present acutely, *often with a florid psychosis* or a frank *delirium*. The treatment of ADC is substantially the same as the management of delirium and dementia. The physician should treat all reversible conditions, minimize all medications that have adverse CNS effects, provide frequent orientation and support, and consider the judicious use of low-dose, high-potency antipsychotics. ADC patients with organic psychosis, marked anxiety, and marked lability or agitation may also benefit from the careful use of antipsychotic medications.

Psychoactive Substance-Induced Organic Mental Disorders and Psychoactive Substance Use Disorders

Drug use and the psychiatric disorders that drug use causes are of great concern to all physicians. As yet, physicians, health organizations, and governments have had little effect on the control of illicit drugs and such legal drugs as alcohol and tobacco. These substances are responsible for psychiatric disorders and have grave effects on the person's systemic health because of direct toxicity and risk-taking behaviors that lead to the onset of life-threatening illness. Students must be aware of the social and the epidemiological issues involved in the use of psychoactive substances, in addition to understanding the psychiatric disorders associated with substance use.

The American Psychiatric Association's revised third edition of *Diagnostic and Statistical Manual of Mental Disorders* (DSM-III-R) differentiates psychoactive substance-induced organic mental disorders from psychoactive substance use disorders. The former refers to the direct acute or chronic effects of psychoactive substances on the central nervous system (CNS); the latter refers to maladaptive behavior associated with the regular use of these substances. According to DSM-III-R, the two diagnoses usually coexist. Each drug can produce one or more of the organic syndromes—delirium, dementia, amnestic syndrome, delusional syndrome, hallucinosis, mood disorder, anxiety disorder, and personality disorder. Psychoactive substances can also produce intoxication and withdrawal syndromes.

Although the diagnosis of alcoholism is not included in DSM-III-R, its components are defined under alcohol abuse, alcohol dependence, and the alcohol-induced organic mental disorders. The ingestion of alcohol can result in intoxication, idiosyncratic intoxication, uncomplicated alcohol withdrawal, withdrawal delirium, hallucinosis, amnestic disorder, and dementia. Each of these syndromes has unique symptoms and diagnostic criteria. The psychiatric practitioner must know the epidemiology of alcohol use to assess adequately how the alcohol intake of patients relates to average societal patterns. As a physician, the psychiatrist should know how alcohol affects the peripheral organs, as well as the CNS. There are many treatment approaches to alcohol-related syndromes, and the student should be able to discuss both the merits and the limitations of the different approaches.

The most frequently abused sedative-hypnotics are the barbiturates and the benzodiazepines. Abuse of these drugs can result in intoxication, uncomplicated withdrawal, withdrawal delirium, and amnestic disorder. The student of psychiatry should be clear about the indications for treatment with these drugs and how to manage patients receiving them to reduce the possibility of their abusing the drugs or getting a dependence disorder. Psychiatrists should know how to treat barbiturate withdrawal and should also be aware that it can result in death. Both barbiturates and benzodiazepines are available in forms with a range of half-lives, and the physician should know how to address these differences in both acute intoxication and withdrawal.

Opioids occur naturally (e.g., opium) and can be synthesized (e.g., meperidine [Demerol]); all opioids produce physical and psychological dependence and a characteristic withdrawal syndrome. Urban medical centers usually expend significant resources on treating heroin abuse in the emergency department and in maintaining opioid addicts on methadone in outpatient clinics. General psychiatrists must know the common medical complications accompanying opioid addiction, including the high risk of acquired immune deficiency syndrome (AIDS) in this group, in whom transmission is a result of sharing intravenous needles.

Cocaine abuse in the United States is recognized as both serious and common. Cocaine-related organic syndromes include intoxication, withdrawal, delirium, and delusional disorder. The availability of cocaine in comparatively inexpensive amounts and in forms that can be injected and smoked (crack) has exacerbated the psychiatric, medical, and social problems with this drug. The practicing psychiatrist needs to realize that cocaine abuse is present in all classes and social groups. Cocaine abuse is associated with a variety of medical complications that depend on the route of administration, and the student should be able to describe both the symptoms and the treatment of these complications.

Amphetamines and similarly acting sympathomimetics produce their effects by causing the neuronal release of catecholamines, particularly norepinephrine and dopamine. Amphetamines are used by some persons to increase performance. For example, students, long-distance truck drivers, and athletes are frequent users of amphetamines. When medically indicated, amphetamines must be judiciously prescribed by the physician to prevent a pattern of abuse and consequent morbidity. Abuse of these drugs can result in intoxication, withdrawal syndromes, delirium, and delusional disorder. Amphetamine-induced delusional disorder can be clinically indistinguishable from paranoid schizophrenia. Of particular importance are the so-called designer drugs, often congeners of amphetamine, such as 3,4-methylenedioxymethamphetamine (MDMA, also known as ecstasy), that are being synthesized by illicit drug factories more quickly than the Food and Drug Administration can declare the drugs to be controlled substances.

The hallucinogens (e.g., lysergic acid diethylamide [LSD]) and arylcyclohexylamines (e.g., phencyclidine [PCP]) seem to have episodes of popularity in geographically distinct locales; therefore, clinicians need to be aware that such social phenomena can occur in their practices. These drugs are remarkable for their clinical potency and variety of effects. The clinician needs to know the symptoms of abuse and, particularly, treatment approaches to the acutely intoxicated patient in the emergency department, the most common setting in which these patients are seen.

Although commonly considered innocuous, marijuana use can be associated with intoxication, delusional disorder, and other psychiatric syndromes. More than 40 million Americans have used marijuana at some time in their lives, and 10 million use the drug regularly. Important considerations are whether other drugs are mixed with the marijuana, whether the use pattern is episodic or chronic, and how the use pattern is affecting the user's life.

Caffeine is the psychoactive ingredient in coffee and other preparations; nicotine is the psychoactive component of tobacco. Although these substances are legal and widely used, clinicians have increasingly realized that their excessive use can produce bona fide psychiatric disorders in certain people. Caffeine and nicotine dependence need to be considered in the differential diagnosis of many patients; even if not the primary diagnosis, it may be a secondary diagnosis. The student should know the diagnostic criteria for caffeine intoxication and nicotine withdrawal, as well as the variety of sources of caffeine.

Anabolic or androgenic steroids may be abused by athletes to increase stamina and may produce mania and delusions.

Students are referred to *Synopsis VI*, Chapter 12, "Psychoactive Substance-Induced Organic Mental Disorders and Psychoactive Substance Use Disorders," and to *CTP V*, Chapter 13, "Psychoactive Substance Use Disorders." An assessment can be made of the students' understanding of the various psychoactive substance use disorders by studying the questions and answers below.

HELPFUL HINTS

The student should know each of the terms below and the DSM-III-R syndrome criteria.

intoxication	cocaine intoxication and	dementia
withdrawal	withdrawal	alcohol amnestic disorder
WHO definitions	cocaine delirium	fetal alcohol syndrome
drug dependence	cocaine delusional disorder	disulfiram
patterns of pathological use	cocaine psychosis	Al-Anon
tolerance	amphetamine	sedative-hypnotics
cross-tolerance	psychedelics	DEA
dispositional tolerance	LSD	AIDS
psychological dependence	DPT	opioid intoxication
physical dependence	PCP	MPTP-induced parkinsonism
abuse	MDMA	DMT
misuse	DOM	hallucinogen
psychoactive substance dependence	STP	flashback
psychoactive substance abuse	alcohol intoxication; blood levels	arylcyclohexylamine
pathological alcohol use	alcohol idiosyncratic intoxication	THC
AA	uncomplicated alcohol withdrawal	amotivational syndrome
blackouts	DTs	nitrous oxide
methadone withdrawal	alcohol withdrawal delirium	volatile hydrocarbons
LAMM	alcohol hallucinosis	belladonna alkaloids
opioid antagonists	Korsakoff's and Wernicke's	anticholinergic side effects
opioid withdrawal	syndromes	sympathomimetic signs
		miosis
		mydriasis

QUESTIONS

DIRECTIONS: Each of the questions or incomplete statements below is followed by five suggested responses or completions. Select the *one* that is *best* in each case.

12.1. Each of the following is among the diagnostic criteria for psychoactive substance dependence *except*
A. important social, occupational, and recreational activities given up because of substance use
B. euphoric response to the substance
C. persistent desire or one or more unsuccessful efforts to cut down or to control substance use
D. a great deal of time spent in activities necessary to get the substance
E. marked tolerance

12.2. Alcohol idiosyncratic reaction
A. is a disorder in which the person remains oriented to person, place, and time
B. occurs after the consumption of a small amount of alcohol
C. is less likely to occur in someone taking a hypnotic drug
D. results in behavior that is an exaggeration of the person's normal behavior
E. ends without any effect on the person's memory

12.3. Alcohol abuse and alcohol dependence are
A. two to four times more common in men than in women
B. more common in urban areas than in rural areas
C. highest in the 15- to 21-year-old range
D. about four times more common among children of alcoholics than among children of nonalcoholics
E. associated with a childhood history of separation anxiety disorder

12.4. Which of the following statements about opioid abuse and dependence is true?
A. About 2 percent of the adult population have met the DSM-III diagnostic criteria for opioid use or dependence at some time in their lives
B. There are about a half-million heroin addicts in the United States
C. Most heroin addicts started using heroin in their late 20s to mid-30s
D. Male addicts equal the number of female addicts
E. About a fourth of all American addicts live in the New York City area

12.5. The treatment of cocaine abuse may include
A. hospitalization
B. family and group therapy
C. removal from the setting where the patient obtained the drug
D. medication
E. all the above

12.6. Flashbacks caused by hallucinogens
A. are usually episodes of visual distortion, hallucinations, and misperceptions
B. cause the user to relive intense emotions
C. can be triggered by the use of other drugs
D. continue to cause symptoms for years in 50 percent of persons with flashbacks
E. are distinguished by all the above

DIRECTIONS: For each of the questions or incomplete statements below, *one or more* of the responses or completions given are correct. Choose answer

A. if only *1, 2, and 3* are correct
B. if only *1 and 3* are correct
C. if only *2 and 4* are correct
D. if only *4* is correct
E. if *all* are correct

12.7. Acute phencyclidine (PCP) intoxication is treated with
1. phentolamine (Regitine)
2. cranberry juice
3. diazepam (Valium)
4. phenothiazine

12.8. In alcohol withdrawal syndromes
1. hyperreflexia may be present
2. hallucinations may be present
3. benzodiazepines may be used for treatment
4. bed rest and hydration are indicated

12.9. Possible complications of cocaine use include
1. paranoid ideation
2. delirium
3. formication
4. cardiac arrest

12.10. In alcohol hallucinosis
1. hallucinations are usually tactile
2. hallucinations usually begin within 48 hours after stopping alcohol
3. dependence on alcohol is not a feature
4. a clear sensorium is present

12.11. Clinical effects that may occur with opioid use are
1. dry mouth
2. nose itching
3. flushing
4. anaphylactic shock

12.12. Patterns of pathological alcohol use include
1. the need for the daily use of large amounts of alcohol in order to function adequately
2. regular heavy drinking limited to weekends
3. long periods of sobriety interspersed with binges of heavy alcohol consumption
4. gamma alcoholism

12.13. Patterns of barbiturate use are
1. episodic intoxication
2. intravenous use
3. chronic intoxication
4. incidental to dependence on other drugs

12.14. Which among the following statements are true?
1. Coffee contains 100 to 150 mg of caffeine in a cup
2. Tea contains roughly half as much caffeine as coffee in a cup
3. Cola contains roughly a third as much caffeine as coffee does
4. Some over-the-counter stimulants contain 100 mg of caffeine in each tablet

12.15. Symptoms of caffeinism include
1. nervousness and insomnia—in some people after as little as 250 mg
2. muscle twitching and arrythmias at doses up to 1,000 mg
3. tinnitus and flashing lights with more than 1 g
4. seizures and respiratory failure at very high doses (10 g)

12.16. In hallucinogen use
1. memory impairment is routine
2. physical addiction is common
3. teratogenicity has been evidenced
4. tolerance develops quickly

12.17. The clinical effects of cocaine intoxication may be evidenced by
1. agitation
2. euphoria
3. mydriasis
4. irritability

12.18. In alcohol-produced blackouts
1. remote memory is impaired
2. the amnesia is anterograde
3. complicated acts cannot be performed
4. intellectual faculties are well preserved

12.19. The therapeutic use of amphetamine is currently listed by the Food and Drug Administration for the treatment of
1. mild depression
2. attention-deficit hyperactivity disorder of children
3. augmentation of tricyclic antidepressants
4. obesity

12.20. Opioid
1. tolerance can develop within four doses
2. dependence results in decreased locus ceruleus activity
3. withdrawal responses are intensified when the opioid is rapidly removed from its receptor
4. withdrawal symptoms are exacerbated by clonidine (Catapres)

12.21. Symptoms of barbiturate intoxication include
1. exaggeration of personality traits
2. nystagmus
3. memory impairment
4. hypertonia

12.22. After the last dose, the withdrawal syndrome from
1. heroin begins in six to eight hours
2. methadone begins in one to three days
3. heroin lasts 7 to 10 days
4. methadone lasts three to four weeks

12.23. A 33-year-old advertising executive was picked up by the police at 4:00 A.M. after a traffic accident in which the car he was driving struck a parked vehicle. The police observed him to be extremely talkative and agitated and brought him to the emergency department for evaluation. There he was noted to be sweaty and to have a rapid pulse and widely dilated pupils. He threatened to call his lawyer, "who is a friend of the mayor." He also began physically assaulting the nursing attendant who attempted to quiet him. At one point he became preoccupied with what he said were insects crawling under the skin of his arms. The differential diagnosis would include
1. phencyclidine (PCP) intoxication
2. amphetamine intoxication
3. cocaine intoxication
4. bipolar disorder, manic episode

Questions 12.24–12.25

An 18-year-old high school senior was brought to the emergency room by the police after he was picked up wandering in traffic on the Triborough Bridge. He was angry, agitated, and aggressive and talked of various people who were deliberately trying to confuse him by giving him misleading directions. His story was rambling and disjointed, but he admitted to a police officer that he had been using speed. In the emergency room he had difficulty focusing his attention and had to ask that questions be repeated. He was disoriented as to time and place and was unable to repeat the names of three objects after five minutes. His family gave a history of the patient's regular use of pep pills over the past two years, during which time he was frequently high and did poorly in school. [From *DSM-III-R Case Book.* Used with permission.]

12.24. The clinical effects of central nervous system stimulants include
1. increased libido
2. delirium
3. formication
4. catatonic state

12.25. Abrupt discontinuation of amphetamine produces
1. nightmares
2. agitation
3. muscle cramps
4. dysphoric mood

DIRECTIONS: Each set of lettered headings below is followed by a list of numbered words or phrases. For each numbered word or phrase, select the *best* lettered heading. Each lettered heading may be selected once, more than once, or not at all.

Questions 12.26–12.28
    A. Benzodiazepines
    B. Barbiturates

12.26. Cause rapid eye movement (REM) sleep suppression

12.27. High suicide potential

12.28. Clinically used as muscle relaxants

Questions 12.29–12.31
    A. Withdrawal
    B. Intoxication

12.29. Requires maladaptive behavior as an essential diagnostic criterion

12.31. Follows the recent ingestion and presence in the body of a substance

12.30. Follows the cessation of or the reduction in the intake of a substance

Questions 12.32–12.38
    A. γ-Aminobutyric acid (GABA) receptor system
    B. Opioid receptor system
    C. Glutamate receptor system
    D. Adenosine receptor system
    E. Acetylcholine receptor system

12.32. Ethanol

12.33. Phenobarbital

12.34. Diazepam

12.35. Heroin

12.36. Phencyclidine (PCP)

12.37. Caffeine

12.38. Nicotine

Psychoactive Substance-Induced Organic Mental Disorders and Psychoactive Substance Use Disorders

12.1. The answer is B (*Synopsis VI*, page 282; *CTP V*, pages 642–643).

A *euphoric* response is not included in the DSM-III-R diagnostic criteria for psychoactive substance dependence disorder. The diagnostic criteria for psychoactive substance dependence and intoxication are presented in Tables 12.1 and 12.2.

In DSM-III-R psychoactive substance use disorders are divided into psychoactive substance dependence and psychoactive substance abuse disorders. Table 12.3 contains the DSM-III-R diagnostic criteria for psychoactive substance abuse. According to DSM-III-R, an abuse disorder is most likely to be diagnosed in people who have recently started using psychoactive substances and to involve substances less likely to be associated with marked withdrawal symptoms, such as cannabis and hallucinogens.

Dependence on a drug may be physical or psychological or both. Psychological dependence, also

Table 12.1
Diagnostic Criteria for Psychoactive Substance Dependence

A. At least three of the following:
1. substance often taken in larger amounts or over a longer period than the person intended
2. *persistent desire* or one or more unsuccessful efforts to cut down or control substance use
3. *a great deal of time* spent in activities necessary to get the substance (e.g., theft), taking the substance (e.g., chain smoking), or recovering from its effects
4. frequent intoxication or withdrawal symptoms when expected to fulfill major role obligations at work, school, or home (e.g., does not go to work because hung over, goes to school or work ''high,'' intoxicated while taking care of his or her children) or when substance use is physically hazardous (e.g., drives when intoxicated)
5. important social, occupational, or recreational *activities given up* or reduced because of substance use
6. continued substance use despite knowledge of having a persistent or recurrent social, psychological, or physical problem that is caused or exacerbated by the use of the substance (e.g., keeps using heroin despite family arguments about it, cocaine-induced depression, or having an ulcer made worse by drinking)
7. *marked tolerance:* need for markedly increased amounts of the substance (i.e., at least a 50 percent increase) in order to achieve intoxication or desired effect or markedly diminished effect with continued use of the same amount
Note: The following items may not apply to cannabis, hallucinogens, or phencyclidine (PCP):
8. characteristic withdrawal symptoms (see specific withdrawal syndromes under psychoactive substance-induced organic mental disorders)
9. substance often taken to relieve or avoid withdrawal symptoms
B. Some symptoms of the disturbance have persisted for at least one month or have occurred repeatedly over a longer period of time.

Table from DSM-III-R, *Diagnostic and Statistical Manual of Mental Disorders*, ed 3, revised. Copyright American Psychiatric Association, Washington, DC, 1987. Used with permission.

Table 12.2
Diagnostic Criteria for Intoxication

A. Development of a substance-specific syndrome due to recent ingestion of a psychoactive substance. (**Note:** More than one substance may produce similar or identical syndromes.)
B. Maladaptive behavior during the waking state due to the effect of the substance on the central nervous system (e.g., belligerence, impaired judgment, impaired social or occupational functioning).
C. The clinical picture does not correspond to any of the other specific organic mental syndromes, such as delirium, organic delusional syndrome, organic hallucinosis, organic mood syndrome, or organic anxiety syndrome.

Table from DSM-III-R, *Diagnostic and Statistical Manual of Mental Disorders*, ed 3, revised. Copyright American Psychiatric Association, Washington, DC, 1987. Used with permission.

Table 12.3
Diagnostic Criteria for Psychoactive Substance Abuse

A. A maladaptive pattern of psychoactive substance use indicated by at least one of the following:
1. continued use despite knowledge of having a persistent or recurrent social, occupational, psychological, or physical problem that is caused or exacerbated by use of the psychoactive substance
2. recurrent use in situations in which use is physically hazardous (e.g., driving while intoxicated)
B. Some symptoms of the disturbance have persisted for at least one month or have occurred repeatedly over a longer period of time.
C. Never met the criteria for psychoactive substance dependence for this substance.

Table from DSM-III-R, *Diagnostic and Statistical Manual of Mental Disorders*, ed 3, revised. Copyright American Psychiatric Association, Washington, DC, 1987. Used with permission.

referred to as habituation, is characterized by a continuous or intermittent craving for the substance in order to avoid a dysphoric state. Physical dependence is characterized by the need to take the substance to prevent the occurrence of a withdrawal or abstinence syndrome when the drug is not being used.

Drug abuse and drug misuse are defined differently. Abuse usually refers to the person's illicit use of a substance, whereas misuse usually refers to a physician's prescription drug used by a patient in a medically unacceptable way.

12.2. The answer is B (*Synopsis VI*, pages 287–288; *CTP V*, page 1434).

Alcohol idiosyncratic reaction, also known as pathological intoxication, occurs shortly after the person has consumed a *small amount of alcohol*. The person becomes *dissociated and confused, does not remain oriented*, and may experience hallucinations, illusions, or delusions. The syndrome causes marked behavioral changes, which tend to be atypical, *not merely an exaggeration of the person's normal behavior*.

Alcohol idiosyncratic reaction is more likely, not less likely, to occur in someone taking *hypnotic or sedative drugs*. It is also likely to occur in persons who are fatigued or of advanced age and in those with high levels of anxiety. The disorder usually lasts for a few hours and terminates in a prolonged period of sleep. The person is *unable to recall* the episode.

12.3. The answer is D (*Synopsis VI*, pages 284–285; *CTP V*, pages 324–325 and 690).

Alcohol abuse and alcohol dependence are among the most common substance-abuse diagnoses. The lifetime prevalence of alcohol abuse and alcohol dependence is about 13 percent. Alcohol abuse and alcohol dependence are *five to six times, not two to four times*, more common in men than in women. Alcohol-related diagnoses are *more common in rural areas, not urban areas*. Alcohol abuse and alcohol dependence are *highest among 21-to-34-year-olds, not 15-to-21-year-olds*.

The genetic factor in alcohol-related diagnoses is supported by the finding that *children of alcoholic parents* develop alcoholism about four times more often than children of nonalcoholics, even when they are not raised by their biological parents. Sons of alcoholic parents are more vulnerable than daughters of alcoholic parents to alcoholism. Childhood disorders associated with an increased risk of developing an alcohol-related disorder include attention-deficit hyperactivity disorder and conduct disorder, *not separation anxiety disorder*.

12.4. The answer is B (*Synopsis VI*, page 297; *CTP V*, pages 648–664).

Heroin is the most widely abused opiate in the United States. Epidemiological studies conducted from 1981 to 1983 found that *0.7 percent, not 2 percent*, of the adult population had met the DSM-III criteria for opioid abuse or dependence at some time in their lives. There are *about a half-million heroin addicts* in this country; the estimate ranges from 400,000 to 600,000 people. It is also estimated that *a half, not a fourth*, of all heroin addicts live in the New York City area. Most heroin addicts started using drugs in their *late teens to early 20s, not late 20s to early 30s*. Male heroin addicts do not equal the number of female addicts. *Male addicts outnumber female addicts* in a ratio of 3 to 1.

12.5. The answer is E (*Synopsis VI*, page 304; *CTP V*, pages 672–673 and 1436).

The treatment of cocaine abuse and cocaine dependence requires multidimensional intervention. The most crucial intervention may be social, *removing the person from the setting* from which he or she obtained the drug. Doing so may require *hospitalization* for some patients. *Family and group therapy* are helpful in the treatment of cocaine abuse. These therapies and individual therapy should be directed toward the underlying reasons for the pattern of abuse. *Medications* are also useful in the treatment of cocaine abuse. The two most useful medications are desipramine (Norpramin), a tricyclic antidepressant, and bromocriptine (Parlodel), a dopamine agonist.

12.6. The answer is E (*Synopsis VI*, pages 309–310; *CTP V*, pages 572 and 678).

Hallucinogenic-induced flashbacks are spontaneous transitory recurrences of drug-induced experiences that occur even though the person has not recently ingested the drug. Most flashback episodes include *visual distortion, hallucinations* of sound or vision, *misperceptions* of images, and positive afterimages or halos. Relived *intense emotions*, lasting seconds to minutes, may occur. Flashbacks may be *triggered by other drugs*, such as cannabis, or by emergence from a darkened room. Although 50 percent of those affected by flashbacks have remissions within months, *50 percent of those affected may have symptoms for years*. Suicide, major depression, and panic disorder are major complications. See Table 12.4.

12.7. The answer is A (1, 2, 3) (*Synopsis VI*, page 312; *CTP V*, pages 675–677).

Phenothiazines are not used in the treatment of acute phencyclidine (PCP) intoxication because they have anticholinergic effects that may potentiate the adverse effects of PCP, such as seizures. *Diazepam* (Valium) is of use in reducing agitation. If agitation is severe, however, the antipsychotic haloperidol (Haldol) may have to be used. *Cranberry juice* is used to acidify the urine and promote the elimination of the drug. Ammonium chloride or ascorbic acid also serves the same purpose. *Phentolamine* (Regitine) is

Table 12.4
Diagnostic Criteria for Posthallucinogen Perception Disorder

A. The reexperiencing, following cessation of use of a hallucinogen, of one or more of the perceptual symptoms that were experienced while intoxicated with the hallucinogen (e.g., geometric hallucinations, false perceptions of movement in the peripheral visual fields, flashes of color, intensified colors, trails of images from moving objects, positive afterimages, halos around objects, macropsia, and micropsia).
B. The disturbance in A causes marked distress.
C. Other causes of the symptoms—such as anatomic lesions and infections of the brain, delirium, dementia, sensory (visual) epilepsies, schizophrenia, entoptic imagery, and hypnopompic hallucinations—have been ruled out.

Table from DSM-III-R, *Diagnostic and Statistical Manual of Mental Disorders*, ed 3, revised. Copyright American Psychiatric Association, Washington, DC, 1987. Used with permission.

a hypotensive agent that may be needed to deal with severe hypertensive crises produced by PCP.

12.8. The answer is E (all) (*Synopsis VI*, pages 288–289; *CTP V*, pages 203–204).

Alcohol withdrawal follows the cessation or the reduction of prolonged or heavy drinking. A variety of signs and symptoms develop within hours, including tremors, *hyperreflexia*, tachycardia, hypertension, general malaise, nausea or vomiting, poorly formed *hallucinations*, illusions, vivid nightmares, and disturbed sleep.

Alcohol withdrawal delirium is the most severe form of the withdrawal syndrome and is also known as delirium tremens (DTs). The syndrome is characterized by delirium that occurs within a week after the person stops drinking actively or reduces intake. Other features include (1) autonomic hyperactivity (e.g., sweating, tachycardia, and elevated blood pressure), (2) disturbances in sensorium, (3) visual or tactile hallucinations, and (4) hyperexcitability or lethargy. Treatment is symptomatic and includes a *benzodiazepine*, such as 25 to 50 mg of chlordiazepoxide (Librium) every two to four hours, *bed rest, and hydration*.

Tables 12.5 and 12.6 list the diagnostic criteria for uncomplicated alcohol withdrawal and for alcohol withdrawal delirium.

12.9. The answer is E (all) (*Synopsis VI*, pages 303–304; *CTP V*, page 671).

In high doses, cocaine can induce seizures, depression of the medullary centers, and death from respiratory or *cardiac arrest*. Syncope and chest pain may occur with low doses. Cocaine intoxication is characterized by transient ideas of reference, *paranoid ideation*, increased libido, tinnitus (noises or ringing in the ears), and bizarre behavior, such as sorting objects into pairs. *Delirium* with disorientation and violent behavior may occur. Tactile or haptic hallucinations have been described, in which

Table 12.5
Diagnostic Criteria for Uncomplicated Alcohol Withdrawal

A. Cessation of prolonged (several days or longer) heavy ingestion of alcohol or reduction in the amount of alcohol ingested, followed within several hours by coarse tremor of hands, tongue, or eyelids and at least one of the following:
1. nausea or vomiting
2. malaise or weakness
3. autonomic hyperactivity (e.g., tachycardia, sweating, elevated blood pressure)
4. anxiety
5. depressed mood or irritability
6. transient hallucinations or illusions
7. headache
8. insomnia
B. Not due to any physical or other mental disorder, such as alcohol withdrawal delirium

Table from DSM-III-R, *Diagnostic and Statistical Manual of Mental Disorders*, ed 3, revised. Copyright American Psychiatric Association, Washington, DC, 1987. Used with permission.

Table 12.6
Diagnostic Criteria for Alcohol Withdrawal Delirium

A. Delirium developing after cessation of heavy alcohol ingestion or a reduction in the amount of alcohol ingested (usually within one week).
B. Marked autonomic hyperactivity (e.g., tachycardia, sweating).
C. Not due to any physical or mental disorder.

Table from DSM-III-R, *Diagnostic and Statistical Manual of Mental Disorders*, ed 3, revised. Copyright American Psychiatric Association, Washington, DC, 1987. Used with permission.

the person believes that bugs are crawling just beneath the skin (also known as *formication*).

Tables 12.7 and 12.8 list the DSM-III-R diagnosic criteria for cocaine delirium and for cocaine delusional disorder.

12.10. The answer is C (2, 4) (*Synopsis VI*, pages 289–290; *CTP V*, page 695).

The essential feature of alcohol hallucinosis is an organic hallucinosis with visual or auditory (*not tactile*) hallucinations that usually begin *within 48 hours* after stopping alcohol. The symptoms persist even after the person has recovered from alcohol withdrawal. The disorder can occur at any age; however, the person must have been involved with alcohol over a sufficient period of time so as to become *dependent*. Alcoholic hallucinosis is differentiated from delirium tremens (DTs) by the *presence of a clear sensorium*. The diagnostic criteria for alcohol hallucinosis are listed in Table 12.9.

12.11. The answer is E (all) (*Synopsis VI*, pages 298–299; *CTP V*, pages 649–650 and 654–655).

Clinical effects that may occur with opioid use include a feeling of warmth, a heaviness of the ex-

Table 12.7
Diagnostic Criteria for Cocaine Delirium

A. Delirium developing within 24 hours of use of cocaine.
B. Not due to any physical or other mental disorder.

Table from DSM-III-R, *Diagnostic and Statistical Manual of Mental Disorders*, ed 3, revised. Copyright American Psychiatric Association, Washington, DC, 1987. Used with permission.

Table 12.8
Diagnostic Criteria for Cocaine Delusional Disorder

A. Organic delusional syndrome developing shortly after use of cocaine.
B. Rapidly developing persecutory delusions are the predominant clinical feature.
C. Not due to any physical or other mental disorder.

Table from DSM-III-R, *Diagnostic and Statistical Manual of Mental Disorders*, ed 3, revised. Copyright American Psychiatric Association, Washington, DC, 1987. Used with permission.

Table 12.9
Diagnostic Criteria for Alcohol Hallucinosis

A. Organic hallucinosis with vivid and persistent hallucinations (auditory or visual) developing shortly (usually within 48 hours) after cessation of or reduction in heavy ingestion of alcohol in a person who apparently has alcohol dependence.
B. No delirium as in alcohol withdrawal delirium.
C. Not due to any physical or other mental disorder.

Table from DSM-III-R, *Diagnostic and Statistical Manual of Mental Disorders*, ed 3, revised. Copyright American Psychiatric Association, Washington, DC, 1987. Used with permission.

tremities, and *dry mouth*. The face, particularly the *nose, may itch* and become *flushed* (this effect may occur from a release of histamine). Idiosyncratic responses—such as allergic reactions, *anaphylactic shock*, and pulmonary edema—account for cases of sudden death.

Additional manifestations include analgesia, drowsiness, mood changes, and mental clouding after the ingestion of small amounts of the drug (5 to 20 mg). The analgesic effects peak about 20 minutes after intravenous injection or an hour after subcutaneous injection and last four to six hours, depending on the type of opioid, the dose, and the previous history of drug taking.

12.12. The answer is E (all) (*Synopsis VI*, page 284; *CTP V*, pages 686–698).

According to DSM-III-R, alcohol dependence is characterized by three major patterns of pathological alcohol use: (1) the need for *daily use of large amounts of alcohol* in order to function adequately, (2) regular *heavy drinking limited to weekends*, and (3) long periods of *sobriety interspersed with binges* of heavy alcohol consumption lasting for weeks or months. These patterns encompass such behaviors as (1) the inability to cut down on or stop drinking,

(2) the repeated efforts to control or reduce excessive drinking by going on the wagon (periods of temporary abstinence) or restricting drinking to certain times of the day, (3) going on binges (remaining intoxicated throughout the day for at least two days), (4) the occasional consumption of a fifth of spirits (or its equivalent in wine or beer), (5) amnesic periods for events occurring while intoxicated (blackouts), (6) the continuation of drinking despite a serious physical disorder that the person knows is exacerbated by alcohol use, and (7) drinking of nonbeverage alcohol. In addition, alcoholics show impaired social or occupational functioning, such as violence while intoxicated, absence from work, job loss, legal difficulties (e.g., arrest for intoxicated behavior, traffic accidents while intoxicated), and arguments or difficulties with family or friends because of excessive alcohol use.

Some researchers have divided alcoholism into different patterns of drinking. One example is called *gamma alcoholism*, which is thought to be common in the United States. Gamma alcoholics are unable to stop drinking once they start.

Alcohol is the major psychoactive drug used worldwide. In the United States an estimated 13 million people are classified as alcoholics. Approximately 13 percent of adults have experienced alcohol abuse or dependence at some point in life. After heart disease and cancer, alcoholism is the third largest health care problem in the United States today. Table 12.10 lists the DSM-III-R diagnostic criteria for alcohol intoxication.

12.13. The answer is E (all) (*Synopsis VI*, page 293; *CTP V*, page 1435).

Barbiturates are highly addictive central nervous system (CNS) depressants derived from barbituric acid. The first barbiturate was introduced in 1903. The short-acting barbiturates, such as secobarbital, were developed and came into widespread use during the past 40 years. Currently, pentobarbital, secobarbital, and amobarbital (Amytal) are under the

Table 12.10
Diagnostic Criteria for Alcohol Intoxication

A. Recent ingestion of alcohol (with no evidence suggesting that the amount was insufficient to cause intoxication in most people).
B. Maladaptive behavior changes (e.g., disinhibition of sexual or aggressive impulses, mood lability, impaired judgment, impaired social or occupational functioning).
C. At least one of the following signs:
  1. slurred speech
  2. incoordination
  3. unsteady gait
  4. nystagmus
  5. flushed face
D. Not due to any physical or other mental disorder.

Table from DSM-III-R, *Diagnostic and Statistical Manual of Mental Disorders*, ed 3, revised. Copyright American Psychiatric Association, Washington, DC, 1987. Used with permission.

same federal legal controls as morphine, which may account for the decline in both licit and illicit use.

Almost without exception, persons with a dependence on barbiturates fall into one of these major patterns of use: (1) *chronic intoxication*—occurs for the most part in 30- to 50-year-old middle or upper socioeconomic status persons who initially obtained the prescription from their physicians in response to their complaints of nervousness or difficulty in falling asleep; (2) *episodic intoxication*—users are generally teenagers or young adults who ingest barbiturates for the same purpose as they may consume alcohol, to produce a high or experience a sense of well-being; and (3) *intravenous barbiturate use*—users are mainly young adults who are intimately involved in the illegal drug culture. In addition, some persons use barbiturates *incidentally to their dependence on other drugs* to boost the effects of weak heroin, to relieve tremulousness of alcohol withdrawal, or to avoid the paranoia and agitation experienced by some amphetamine or cocaine abusers.

12.14. The answer is E (all) (*Synopsis VI*, page 316; *CTP V*, pages 683–685).

The following is a rough guide to quantitating caffeine intake:

average cup of *coffee*	*100 to 150* mg
average cup of *tea*	*50 to 75* mg
average *cola* beverage	*35 to 50* mg
over-the-counter stimulants	*100* mg

See Table 12.11 for common sources of caffeine.

12.15. The answer is E (all) (*Synopsis VI*, page 316; *CTP V*, pages 683–685).

The following is a rough guide to some of the symptoms of caffeinism:

250 mg—restlessness, *nervousness*, excitement, *insomnia*, flushing, diuresis, gastrointestinal complaints
1,000 mg—muscle twitching, rambling thought and speech, *arrhythmias*, inexhaustibility, agitation
more than 1 g—tinnitus, flashing light
10 g—seizures, respiratory failure

The DSM-III-R diagnostic criteria for caffeine intoxication are listed in Table 12.12.

12.16. The answer is D (4) (*Synopsis VI*, page 308; *CTP V*, pages 677–678).

Hallucinogens, also known as psychotomimetics and psychedelics, are drugs that produce psychic and behavioral changes that resemble psychoses. Unlike drugs that can produce organic psychoses, hallucinogens *do not produce memory impairment. Tolerance develops quickly*, but long-term use and *physical addiction are rare*. There is *no evidence of teratogenicity* or abnormal fetal development, although the use of these drugs during pregnancy is ill-advised. Lysergic acid diethylamide (LSD) and dipropyltryptamine (DPT) are examples of synthetic psychedelics; psilocybin and mescaline are natural hallucinogens.

Table 12.11
Some Common Sources of Caffeine and Representative Decaffeinated Products

Source	Approximate Amounts of Caffeine per Unit
Beverages and foods	5–6 oz
Fresh drip coffee, brewed coffee	90–140 mg
Instant coffee	66–100 mg
Tea (leaf or bagged)	30–100 mg
Cocoa	5–50 mg
Decaffeinated coffee	2–4 mg
Chocolate bar or ounce of baking chocolate	25–35 mg
Selected soft drinks	8–12 oz
Pepsi, Coke, Tab, Royal Crown, Pepsi Light, Dr. Pepper, Mountain Dew	25–50 mg
Canada Dry Ginger Ale, Coke Caffeine Free, Like, Pepsi Free, 7-Up, Sprite, Squirt, Tab Caffeine Free	0 mg
Cafergot, Migralam	100 mg
Anoquan, Aspir-code, BAC, Brogesic, Darvon, Fiorinal	32–50 mg
Over-the-counter analgesics and cold preparations	
Excedrin	60 mg
Aspirin Compound, Anacin, B-C powder, Capron, Cope, Dolar, Midol, Nilain, Norgesic, PAC, Trigesic, Vanquish	30–32.5 mg
Advil, Aspirin, Empirin, Midol 200, Nuprin, Pamprin	0 mg
Over-the-counter stimulants and appetite suppressants	
Caffin-TD, Caffedrine	250 mg
Vivarin, Verv capsules	200 mg
Quick-Pep	150 mg
Amostat, Anorexin, Appedrine, Nodoz, Wakoz	100 mg

Table 12.12
Diagnostic Criteria for Caffeine Intoxication

A. Recent consumption of caffeine, usually in excess of 250 mg.
B. At least five of the following signs:
   1. restlessness
   2. nervousness
   3. excitement
   4. insomnia
   5. flushed face
   6. diuresis
   7. gastrointestinal disturbance
   8. muscle twitching
   9. rambling flow of thought and speech
   10. tachycardia or cardiac arrhythmia
   11. periods of inexhaustibility
   12. psychomotor agitation
C. Not due to any physical or other mental disorder, such as an anxiety disorder.

Large doses of 3,4-methylenedioxymethamphetamine (MDMA or ecstasy) can produce amphetamine-like toxicity. The DSM-III-R diagnostic criteria for hallucinogen hallucinosis are given in Table 12.13.

12.17. The answer is E (all) (*Synopsis VI*, page 303; *CTP V*, pages 670–671 and 1436).

The clinical effects of cocaine intoxication may be evidenced by extreme *agitation, euphoria, irritability*, impaired judgment, impulsive sexual behavior, aggression, increased psychomotor activity, and manic excitement. Tachycardia (rapid beating of the

Table 12.13
Diagnostic Criteria for Hallucinogen Hallucinosis

A. Recent use of a hallucinogen.
B. Maladaptive behavioral changes (e.g., marked anxiety or depression, ideas of reference, fear of losing one's mind, paranoid ideation, impaired judgment, impaired social or occupational functioning).
C. Perceptual changes occurring in a state of full wakefulness and alertness (e.g., subjective intensification of perceptions, depersonalization, derealization, illusions, hallucinations, synesthesias).
D. At least two of the following signs:
   1. pupillary dilation
   2. tachycardia
   3. sweating
   4. palpitations
   5. blurring of vision
   6. tremors
   7. incoordination
E. Not due to any physical or other mental disorder.

heart), hypertension, and *mydriasis* (dilation of the pupil) are also characteristic of cocaine intoxication. See Table 12.14 for the DSM-III-R diagnostic criteria for cocaine intoxication.

12.18. The answer is C (2, 4) (*Synopsis VI*, page 286; *CTP V*, pages 203 and 691).

Abuse of alcohol may produce amnesia, blackouts. The *amnesia* is *anterograde*—that is, the person cannot remember forward from a point in time. During a blackout, people have relatively *intact (not impaired) remote memory*. However, they experience a specific short-term memory deficit in which they are unable to recall events that happened in the previous five or ten minutes. Because their other *intellectual faculties are well preserved*, they *can perform complicated acts* and appear normal to the casual observer.

12.19. The answer is C (2, 4) (*Synopsis VI*, page 305; *CTP V*, pages 253 and 1184).

Amphetamines, central nervous system stimulants, are sympathomimetic drugs; that is, they mimic the actions of the sympathetic nervous system, the part of the autonomic nervous system that helps a person deal with threatening situations by preparing his or her body for fight or flight.

At present, the therapeutic use of amphetamine is listed by the Food and Drug Administration for the treatment of *attention-deficit hyperactivity* disorder of children, narcolepsy, and *obesity*. Therapeutic effects of amphetamine have been reported in the treatment of *mild depression* and for *augmentation of tricyclic antidepressants* and analgesics.

A 5-mg dose of amphetamine in the average person produces an increased sense of well-being, improves performance on academic tasks, decreases fatigue, reduces the appetite, and elevates the pain threshold.

Table 12.14
Diagnostic Criteria for Cocaine Intoxication

A. Recent use of cocaine.
B. Maladaptive behavioral changes (e.g., euphoria, fighting, grandiosity, hypervigilance, psychomotor agitation, impaired judgment, impaired social or occupational functioning).
C. At least two of the following signs within one hour of using cocaine:
   1. tachycardia
   2. pupillary dilation
   3. elevated blood pressure
   4. perspiration or chills
   5. nausea or vomiting
   6. visual or tactile hallucinations
D. Not due to any physical or other mental disorder.

12.20. The answer is A (1, 2, 3) (*Synopsis VI*, pages 297–298; *CTP V*, pages 649–651).

Opioid tolerance probably develops in humans within the first *four doses*. Withdrawal responses are *intensified* and readily detectable when the opioid is rapidly removed from its receptor, as by an opioid antagonist. The activity of adrenergic neurons in the *locus ceruleus decreases*. Withdrawal symptoms are *blocked (not exacerbated) by clonidine* (Catapres), an adrenergic agonist, which may be explained by its ability to inhibit the activity of neurons in the locus ceruleus.

12.21. The answer is A (1, 2, 3) (*Synopsis VI*, pages 293–294; *CTP V*, pages 205 and 1435).

Mild barbiturate intoxication resembles alcohol intoxication. Neurological effects include *nystagmus* (an involuntary to-and-fro movement of the eyeballs); diplopia (double vision); strabismus (squint); ataxic gait; positive Romberg's sign (swaying of the body when the patient stands with feet together, eyes closed); *hypotonia* (subnormal tension of muscles), *not hypertonia* (extreme tension of the muscles, spacticity, or rigidity); dysmetria (inability to gauge distance for bodily movements); and decreased superficial reflexes.

Other symptoms include sluggishness, incoordination, difficulty in thinking, *poor memory*, slowness of speech and comprehension, faulty judgment, disinhibition of sexual or aggressive impulses, narrowed range of attention, emotional lability, and *exaggeration of basic personality traits*. The sluggishness usually wears off after a few hours, but judgment may remain impaired, mood distorted, and motor skills impaired for as long as 10 to 22 hours. Table 12.15 lists the DSM-III-R diagnostic criteria for sedative, hypnotic, or anxiolytic intoxication.

12.22. The answer is A (1, 2, 3) (*Synopsis VI*, page 300; *CTP V*, page 650).

The heroin withdrawal syndrome begins in *six to eight hours* after the last dose, usually after a one-to-two-week period of continuous use or after the administration of a narcotic antagonist. It reaches its peak intensity during the second or third day and subsides during the next *7 to 10 days*. Methadone withdrawal usually begins *one to three days* after the last dose and is complete in *10 to 14 days*. Table 12.16 lists the diagnostic criteria for opioid withdrawal.

12.23. The answer is E (all) (*Synopsis VI*, pages 280–281; *CTP V*, pages 670–671).

Cocaine, amphetamine, and *phencyclidine (PCP) intoxication* may all present with behavioral manifestations that are also characteristic of *bipolar disorder, manic type*, such as fighting, grandiosity, hypervigilance, psychomotor agitation, impaired judgment, impaired social or occupational functioning, elation, and a decreased need for sleep. The physical findings in this case (sweat, rapid pulse,

Table 12.15
Diagnostic Criteria for Sedative, Hypnotic, or Anxiolytic Intoxication

A. Recent use of a sedative, hypnotic, or anxiolytic.
B. Maladaptive behavioral changes (e.g., disinhibition of sexual or aggressive impulses, mood lability, impaired judgment, impaired social or occupational functioning).
C. At least one of the following signs:
   1. slurred speech
   2. incoordination
   3. unsteady gait
   4. impairment in attention or memory
D. Not due to any physical or other mental disorder.
Note: When the differential diagnosis must be made without a clear-cut history or toxicologic analysis of body fluids, it may be qualified as provisional.

Table from DSM-III-R, *Diagnostic and Statistical Manual of Mental Disorders*, ed 3, revised. Copyright American Psychiatric Association, Washington, DC, 1987. Used with permission.

Table 12.16
Diagnostic Criteria for Opioid Withdrawal

A. Cessation of prolonged (several weeks or more) moderate or heavy use of an opioid or reduction in the amount of opioid used (or administration of an opioid antagonist after a brief period of use), followed by at least three of the following:
   1. craving for an opioid
   2. nausea or vomiting
   3. muscle aches
   4. lacrimation or rhinorrhea
   5. pupillary dilation, piloerection, or sweating
   6. diarrhea
   7. yawning
   8. fever
   9. insomnia
B. Not due to any physical or other mental disorder.

Table from DSM-III-R, *Diagnostic and Statistical Manual of Mental Disorders*, ed 3, revised. Copyright American Psychiatric Association, Washington, DC, 1987. Used with permission.

dilated pupils) raise the question of drug intoxication, as does the tactile hallucination of insects crawling under the skin (formication). For a clear diagnosis, a toxicological analysis of the patient's bodily fluids must be carried out, looking for the presence of cocaine, amphetamine, PCP, and their metabolites in the urine or plasma. Table 12.17 lists the DSM-III-R diagnostic criteria for amphetamine and similarly acting sympathomimetic intoxication. (See also Tables 12.15 and 12.16.)

12.24. The answer is A (1, 2, 3) (*Synopsis VI*, pages 306–307; *CTP V*, pages 670–671).

Both acute amphetamine intoxication and chronic amphetamine use have numerous adverse physical effects (Table 12.17). The psychological effects are also numerous and include restlessness, dysphoria, logorrhea, insomnia, irritability, hostility, anxiety, panic, and, in some cases, psychosis (Table 12.18). When amphetamine is taken intra-

Table 12.17
Diagnostic Criteria for Amphetamine or Similarly Acting Sympathomimetic Intoxication

A. Recent use of amphetamine or a similarly acting sympathomimetic.
B. Maladaptive behavioral changes (e.g., fighting, grandiosity, hypervigilance, psychomotor agitation, impaired judgment, impaired social or occupational functioning).
C. At least two of the following signs within one hour of use:
　1. tachycardia
　2. pupillary dilation
　3. elevated blood pressure
　4. perspiration or chills
　5. nausea or vomiting
D. Not due to any physical or other mental disorder.

Table from DSM-III-R, *Diagnostic and Statistical Manual of Mental Disorders*, ed 3, revised. Copyright American Psychiatric Association, Washington, DC, 1987. Used with permission.

Table 12.18
Diagnostic Criteria for Amphetamine or Similarly Acting Sympathomimetic Delusional Disorder

A. Organic delusional syndrome developing shortly after use of amphetamine or a similarly acting sympathomimetic.
B. Rapidly developing persecutory delusions are the predominant clinical feature.
C. Not due to any physical or other mental disorder.

Table from DSM-III-R, *Diagnostic and Statistical Manual of Mental Disorders*, ed 3, revised. Copyright American Psychiatric Association, Washington, DC, 1987. Used with permission.

venously, there is a characteristic rush of well-being and euphoria. Intoxication with high doses can lead to transient ideas of reference, paranoid ideation, *increased libido*, tinnitus, hearing one's name being called, and *formication* (tactile sensation of bugs crawling on the skin). Stereotyped movements may occur. *Delirium* with episodes of violence may also be seen (Table 12.19). The symptoms of amphetamine delusional disorder may resemble those of paranoid schizophrenia, with predominantly and rapidly developing persecutory delusions; however, the predominance of visual hallucinations, appropriate affect, at times confusion and incoherence, hyperactivity, and the absence of thought disorder helps distinguish amphetamine psychosis from schizophrenia.

Catatonia, also known as waxy flexibility, is not part of amphetamine or other central nervous system stimulant intoxication. In catatonia the person can be molded into a position that is then passively maintained for long periods of time.

12.25. The answer is E (all) (*Synopsis VI*, page 306; *CTP V*, pages 671–672).

Abrupt discontinuation of an amphetamine results in a letdown or crash characterized by the sudden onset of fatigue, *dysphoria, nightmares, muscle cramps*, and *agitation*. According to DSM-III-R, the syndrome may evolve into a withdrawal syndrome

Table 12.19
Diagnostic Criteria for Amphetamine or Similarly Acting Sympathomimetic Delirium

A. Delirium developing within 24 hours of use of amphetamine or a similarly acting sympathomimetic.
B. Not due to any physical or other mental disorder.

Table from DSM-III-R, *Diagnostic and Statistical Manual of Mental Disorders*, ed 3, revised. Copyright American Psychiatric Association, Washington, DC, 1987. Used with permission.

after 24 hours, and within two to three days a depression may develop. The withdrawal depression may be treated with antidepressant medication. The agitation of the immediate letdown syndrome responds to diazepam (Valium). The DSM-III-R diagnostic criteria for amphetamine or similarly acting sympathomimetic withdrawal are listed in Table 12.20.

12.26–12.28

12.26. The answer is B (*Synopsis VI*, pages 292–296; *CTP V*, pages 664–668).

12.27. The answer is B (*Synopsis VI*, pages 292–296; *CTP V*, pages 664–668).

12.28. The answer is A (*Synopsis VI*, pages 292–296; *CTP V*, pages 664–668).

The first of the benzodiazepine derivatives, synthesized in 1957, was chlordiazepoxide (Librium). Various derivatives are currently available in the United States and in foreign markets. Barbiturates were first used in medicine in 1903. Unlike benzodiazepines, *barbiturates cause rapid eye movement (REM) sleep suppression*. An abrupt withdrawal of a barbiturate will cause a marked increase or rebound in REM sleep. Symptoms of withdrawal from both benzodiazepines and barbiturates usually occur within three days. It is far easier to commit *suicide* with barbiturates than with benzodiazepines. Virtually no cases of successful suicide have occurred

Table 12.20
Diagnostic Criteria for Amphetamine or Similarly Acting Sympathomimetic Withdrawal

A. Cessation of prolonged (several days or longer) heavy use of amphetamine or a similarly acting sympathomimetic or reduction in the amount of substance used, followed by dysphoric mood (e.g., depression, irritability, anxiety) and at least one of the following, persisting more than 24 hours after the cessation of substance use:
　1. fatigue
　2. insomnia or hypersomnia
　3. psychomotor agitation
B. Not due to any physical or other mental disorder, such as amphetamine or similarly acting sympathomimetic delusional disorder.

Table from DSM-III-R, *Diagnostic and Statistical Manual of Mental Disorders*, ed 3, revised. Copyright American Psychiatric Association, Washington, DC, 1987. Used with permission.

in patients taking benzodiazepines by themselves. In addition to treating anxiety, benzodiazepines are used in alcohol detoxification, for anesthetic induction, as *muscle relaxants*, and as anticonvulsants.

12.29–12.31

12.29. The answer is B (*Synopsis VI*, pages 278–279; *CTP V*, pages 649–650).

12.30. The answer is A (*Synopsis VI*, pages 278–279; *CTP V*, pages 649–650).

12.31. The answer is B (*Synopsis VI*, pages 278–279; *CTP V*, pages 649–650).

Intoxication is a syndrome that develops after the *recent ingestion and presence in the body* of a substance, whereas withdrawal is the state that *follows the cessation or reduction of intake* of a substance. As with intoxication, the withdrawal syndrome that develops varies according to the substance involved; both are substance-specific. The clinical picture in withdrawal and intoxication does not correspond to any specific organic mental syndrome, and *maladaptive behavior* is listed only as an essential feature for intoxication. The DSM-III-R diagnostic criteria for withdrawal are listed in Table 12.21. (See Table 12.2 for the diagnostic criteria for intoxication.)

12.32–12.38

12.32. The answer is A (*Synopsis VI*, page 286; *CTP V*, pages 664–665).

12.33. The answer is A (*Synopsis VI*, page 293; *CTP V*, pages 664–665).

12.34. The answer is A (*Synopsis VI*, page 296; *CTP V*, pages 664–665).

Table 12.21
Diagnostic Criteria for Withdrawal

A. Development of a substance-specific syndrome that follows the cessation of or reduction in the intake of a psychoactive substance that the person previously used regularly.
B. The clinical picture does not correspond to any of the other specific organic mental syndromes, such as delirium, organic delusional syndrome, organic hallucinosis, organic mood syndrome, or organic anxiety syndrome.

Table from DSM-III-R, *Diagnostic and Statistical Manual of Mental Disorders*, ed 3, revised. Copyright American Psychiatric Association, Washington, DC, 1987. Used with permission.

12.35. The answer is B (*Synopsis VI*, page 297; *CTP V*, page 648).

12.36. The answer is C (*Synopsis VI*, page 308; *CTP V*, pages 51–52 and 675).

12.37. The answer is D (*Synopsis VI*, page 316; *CTP V*, pages 683–685).

12.38. The answer is E (*Synopsis VI*, page 317; *CTP V*, page 680).

Ethanol acts on the gamma aminobutyric acid *(GABA) receptor system* and has been shown to have effects on noradrenergic neurons in the locus ceruleus and on the dopaminergic neurons of the ventral tegmental area. Barbiturates, such as *phenobarbital*, also act primarily on the *GABA system*, specifically on the GABA receptor complex. This receptor complex includes a binding site for the inhibitory amino acid GABA, a regulatory site that binds benzodiazepines, and a chloride ion channel. The binding of the barbiturate results in the facilitation of chloride ion influx into the neuron, making the neuron more negatively charged and less likely to be stimulated.

Diazepam (Valium), a benzodiazepine, affects the *GABA* receptor complex by binding to the site for benzodiazepines. When diazepam or another benzodiazepine binds to this site, the chloride ions flow through the channel, resulting in inhibition of the neuron. The benzodiazepine antagonist flumazenil, which is not available in the United States, reverses the effects of benzodiazepines.

Opioids such as *heroin* bind to specific sites in the brain labeled *opioid receptors*. Changes in the number or the sensitivity of the opioid receptors may occur as the result of continuous exposure to an opioid, producing dependence on the drug. The activity of adrenergic neurons in the locus ceruleus also decreases with chronic use.

Phencyclidine (PCP) binds to specific receptor sites located in the ion channel associated with the receptor for *glutamate*, an excitatory amino acid. Tolerance to PCP does not occur.

The leading theory regarding a mechanism of action for *caffeine* involves antagonism of the *adenosine receptors*. Adenosine appears to function as a neuromodulator, possibly as a neurotransmitter in the brain. Caffeine may also affect dopaminergic systems and adrenergic systems.

Nicotine is believed to exert its effects on the central nervous system through the nicotinic receptors, one subclass of *acetylcholine receptors*. Nicotine affects the nicotinic receptors in the receptor-gated ion channels of the receptor system.

13

Schizophrenia

Schizophrenia is a syndrome that is heterogeneous in cause, pathogenesis, clinical symptoms, response to treatment, and outcome. Many researchers now refer to "the schizophrenias" when describing this clinical disorder. The syndrome is a modestly homogeneous end state that derives from different initial conditions and is influenced by the patient's biopsychosocial environment.

The symptoms of what is now called schizophrenia have fascinated physicians and lay people for thousands of years. The history of the developing understanding of schizophrenia is almost the history of psychiatry itself. To appreciate the diagnostic criteria currently in use, the student needs to understand the historic contributions of Emil Kraepelin, Eugen Bleuler, and Kurt Schneider.

Epidemiological studies of schizophrenia are of both clinical and theoretical interest. Such specifics as populations at risk and suicidality are relevant to individual treatment situations; such information as the cost to society emphasizes the magnitude of this disorder. Other epidemiological data—for example, seasonality of birth—provide the basis for etiological theories.

The major theories regarding the causes of schizophrenia are biological. The practicing psychiatrist must understand the data supporting the dopamine hypothesis of schizophrenia and the shortcomings of this hypothesis. To appreciate neurochemical studies of dopamine function and positron emission tomography (PET) scan data, the psychiatrist must know how details of the dopamine system (e.g., receptor subtypes) relate to the dopamine hypothesis. Other than neurochemical, the major research approaches to schizophrenia are currently brain imaging, electrophysiology, neuropathology, and genetics.

The student should understand these approaches well enough to be able to integrate new research reports into the general thinking about schizophrenia. Basically, however, the frontal lobes, limbic system, and basal ganglia are the major sites of focus in schizophrenia research. The genetic approach to schizophrenia involves two methods. First, researchers assess the incidence of schizophrenia in specific populations (e.g., first-degree relatives of patients with schizophrenia). Second, researchers are using the tools of molecular biology to search for more direct evidence of a genetic disorder (e.g., restriction fragment length polymorphisms).

Although biological theories are the focus of attention, psychosocial approaches to schizophrenia underlie much of the daily therapeutic work with these patients. Students must become familiar with such treatment modalities as directive and supportive individual therapy, group therapy, and social skills training and must acquire a comprehensive knowledge of pharmacotherapy. Family therapy has gained new importance as the role of the family in affecting the course of schizophrenia has been demonstrated in recent research. To develop an integrated treatment program, the psychiatrist must understand the advantages and the uses of all therapies available.

A complete knowledge of the clinical signs and symptoms of schizophrenia includes familiarity with the premorbid symptoms and the myriad presentations on mental status examination. Of slightly more theoretical interest are the types of neurological findings and psychometric test results that are often seen in patients with schizophrenia. The information from the psychiatric examination can help the clinician make predictions regarding course and prognosis. The student should know which specific factors influence good and bad prognoses.

The student should memorize the American Psychiatric Association's revised third edition of *Diagnostic and Statistical Manual of Mental Disorders* (DSM-III-R) diagnosis of schizophrenia, since knowledge of the diagnostic criteria guides the clinical interview. The student should also know the types, based on specific symptoms (e.g., catatonic) and course (e.g., in remission). Knowledge of non-DSM-III-R subtypes, although not likely to be on nationally standardized tests, is important to have when reading research reports that do not adhere to DSM-III-R. The student should also be clear about the approach to the differential diagnosis of schizophrenialike symptoms, including medical-neurological disorders and other psychiatric disorders.

The clinical management of patients with schizophrenia requires a sophisticated knowledge of psychopharmacology and psychosocial interventions. The student should know the different classes of antipsychotic medications available and the strategies to follow if the patient does not respond to traditional medications.

Students are referred to Chapter 13, "Schizophrenia," in *Synopsis VI* and to Chapter 14, "Schizophrenia," in *CTP V* and should then study the questions and answers below to assess their knowledge of this subject.

HELPFUL HINTS

The following terms and their definitions, including the schizophrenic signs and symptoms listed, should be memorized.

Emil Kraepelin
Eugen Bleuler
Benedict Morel
Karl Kahlbaum
Adolf Meyer
Harry Stack Sullivan
Gabriel Langfeldt
Kurt Schneider
dementia precox
manic-depressive psychosis
paranoia
fundamental and accessory
   symptoms
dopamine hypothesis
mesocortical and mesolimbic tracts
neurotransmitters and
   neurodegeneration
brain imaging—CT, PET
electrophysiology—EEG
psychoimmunology and
   psychoendocrinology

RFLPs
genetic hypothesis
psychoanalytic and learning
   theories
Gregory Bateson
double bind
flat affect and blunted affect
hallucinations
delusions
ego boundaries
thought disorders
impulse control, suicide, and
   homicide
orientation, memory, judgment,
   and insight
soft signs
forme fruste
projective testing
disorganized
catatonic
paranoid

undifferentiated
residual
paraphrenia
simple
latent
boufée délirante
oneiroid
pseudoneurotic
autistic disorder
schizoaffective disorder
antipsychotics
CPZ
tardive dyskinesia
ECT
psychosocial treatments and
   therapies
downward-drift hypothesis
social causation hypothesis
seasonality of birth

QUESTIONS

DIRECTIONS: Each of the questions or incomplete statements below is followed by five suggested responses or completions. Select the *one* that is *best* in each case.

13.1. Statistically, schizophrenia has been reported to be highest in the
A. monozygotic twin of a schizophrenic patient
B. dizygotic twin of a schizophrenic patient
C. child of a mother with schizophrenia
D. child of a father with schizophrenia
E. child of two parents with schizophrenia

13.2. A patient who experiences schizophrenic disturbance more or less continuously for six months to two years is classified by DSM-III-R as being
A. subchronic
B. chronic
C. subchronic with an acute exacerbation
D. chronic with an acute exacerbation
E. in remission

13.3. According to current thinking, the term "paraphrenia" is equivalent to
A. latent schizophrenia
B. catatonic schizophrenia
C. disorganized schizophrenia
D. simple schizophrenia
E. paranoid schizophrenia

13.4. Features leading toward a good prognosis in schizophrenia include all the following *except*
A. depression
B. paranoid features
C. family history of mood disorders
D. undifferentiated or disorganized features
E. undulating course

13.5. A 20-year-old man was brought to the hospital lying in a rigid position on a stretcher. He did not speak spontaneously or in response to questions, and his face was immobile. He did not respond to touch and did not obey simple commands. His eyes were open, he made eye contact with the examining physician, and his eye movements tracked events in the hospital room. At times he shut his eyes tightly for a few moments and did not open them at the physician's request. When the physician tried to lift the patient's arm, the patient resisted the movement. This patient is showing signs consistent with which type of schizophrenia?
A. Paranoid
B. Catatonic
C. Hebephrenic
D. Residual
E. Latent

13.6. Schizophrenic hallucinations are most commonly
A. tactile
B. visual
C. olfactory
D. auditory
E. gustatory

13.7. The most useful form of individual psychotherapy in schizophrenia is
A. insight-oriented
B. psychoanalytical
C. supportive
D. short-term
E. none of the above

13.8. The major contraindications to antipsychotic medication include
A. the possibility that the patient has ingested a drug that will interact with an antipsychotic
B. the presence of a severe cardiac abnormality
C. a previously diagnosed seizure disorder
D. narrow-angle glaucoma
E. all the above

13.9. Clozapine (Clozaril)
A. is an appropriate first-line drug for the treatment of schizophrenia
B. is associated with a 10-to-20 percent incidence of agranulocytosis
C. is believed to exert its therapeutic effect by blocking dopamine receptors
D. has not been associated with extrapyramidal side effects
E. requires monthly monitoring of blood indices

13.10. The diagnosis of undifferentiated schizophrenia may be made in patients who do not meet the criteria for paranoid, catatonic, or disorganized type but who present with
A. incoherence
B. grossly disorganized behavior
C. prominent delusions
D. hallucinations
E. all the above

DIRECTIONS: For each of the questions or incomplete statements below, *one* or *more* of the responses or completions given are correct. Choose answer

A. if only *1, 2,* and *3* are correct
B. if only *1* and *3* are correct
C. if only *2* and *4* are correct
D. if only *4* is correct
E. if *all* are correct

13.11. Paranoid schizophrenia most commonly presents with
1. marked loosening of associations
2. flat affect
3. grossly disorganized behavior
4. systematized delusions

13.12. Antipsychotic drugs used in schizophrenia
1. have a clinical potency closely correlated with their binding affinity to dopamine type 1 (D_1) receptors
2. reach the brain quickly
3. are more effective in treating schizophrenic psychoses than psychoses of other types
4. may take as long as six weeks to develop their maximal clinical effects

13.13. Neuropathological studies in schizophrenia indicate
1. decreased numbers of dopamine type 2 (D_2) receptors in the basal ganglia
2. distinguishing changes in dopamine receptors between those caused by schizophrenia and those caused by antipsychotic drug treatment
3. decreased concentrations of brain norepinephrine
4. patterns of degeneration in the limbic forebrain

13.14. The majority of computed tomography (CT) studies of patients with schizophrenia have reported
1. enlarged ventricles in up to 50 percent of patients
2. cortical atrophy in up to 35 percent of patients
3. atrophy of the cerebellar vermis
4. findings that are not the result of treatment

13.15. Thought disorders in schizophrenia are characterized by
1. delusions
2. loss of ego boundaries
3. sexual confusion
4. looseness of associations

13.16. According to DSM-III-R, which of the following signs or symptoms must be present to make a diagnosis of schizophrenia?
1. Characteristic psychotic symptoms, such as delusions and prominent hallucinations
2. Markedly impaired social functioning during the course of the disturbance
3. Signs of the disturbance for at least six months
4. Onset before age 45

13.17. The dopamine hypothesis of schizophrenia is supported by which of the following findings?
1. All effective antipsychotic drugs bind to dopamine receptors
2. The clinical potency of antipsychotic drugs is closely correlated with their binding affinity to dopamine type 2 (D_2) receptors
3. Levodopa (Dopar, Larodopa) administration exacerbates schizophrenic symptoms
4. The clinical effects of dopamine-blocking drugs usually occur within 10 days

13.18. Psychoendocrine findings in schizophrenia include
1. increased prolactin level
2. decreased luteinizing hormone level
3. increased release of thyroid hormone to thyrotropin-releasing hormone stimulation
4. decreased follicle-stimulating hormone level

13.19. Electrophysiological studies of persons with schizophrenia show
1. spikes in the limbic area that correlate with psychotic behavior
2. increased frontal lobe slow-wave activity
3. increased parietal lobe fast-wave activity
4. decreased alpha activity

13.20. Deficit symptoms of schizophrenia include
1. affective flattening
2. hallucinations
3. blocking
4. bizarre behavior

13.21. Signs and symptoms typical of the residual phase of schizophrenia include
1. marked lack of initiative and energy
2. delusions
3. blunted affect
4. peculiar behavior

DIRECTIONS: Each set of lettered headings below is followed by a list of numbered words or statements. For each numbered word or statement, select the *one* lettered heading that is most closely associated with it. Each lettered heading may be selected once, more than once, or not at all.

Questions 13.22–13.24
A. Ewald Hecker
B. Karl Kahlbaum
C. E. Gabriel Langfeldt

13.22. Catatonia

13.23. Hebephrenia

13.24. Schizophreniform psychosis

Questions 13.25–13.29
A. Emil Kraepelin
B. Eugen Bleuler

13.25. Differentiated schizophrenia from manic-depression on the basis of deterioration in course

13.26. Coined the term "schizophrenia"

13.27. Described fundamental and accessory symptoms

13.28. Described the four As of schizophrenia

13.29. Used the term "dementia precox" to describe a severe psychiatric illness with a chronic deteriorating course

Questions 13.30–13.35
A. Schneiderian first-rank symptom
B. Schneiderian second-rank symptom

13.30. Sudden delusional ideas

13.31. Perplexity

13.32. Audible thoughts

13.33. Voices commenting

13.34. Thought withdrawal

13.35. The experience of having one's thoughts controlled

ANSWERS

Schizophrenia

13.1. The answer is A (*Synopsis VI*, pages 327–328; *CTP V*, pages 732–744).

The prevalence of schizophrenia in the general population is 1 percent. Fundamental strategies in the genetic research of schizophrenia are twin and adoptive studies. Statistically, the prevalence of schizophrenia has been reported to be highest in the *monozygotic twin* of a patient with schizophrenia (47 percent). The next highest prevalence of schizophrenia is in the children of *two parents* with schizophrenia (40 percent). The prevalence of schizophrenia in the *dizygotic twin* of a patient with schizophrenia and the prevalence in children with *one parent* with schizophrenia are the same, 12 percent. The prevalence in a nontwin sibling of a patient with schizophrenia is 8 percent. See Table 13.1 for the prevalence of schizophrenia in specific populations.

13.2. The answer is A (*Synopsis VI*, page 333; *CTP V*, pages 767–769).

The *subchronic* form of schizophrenia is described as occurring when the schizophrenic disturbance (including the prodromal, active, and residual phases) lasts more or less continuously for six months to two years. During that time, if prominent signs of psychosis occur, the patient is considered to be *subchronic with an acute exacerbation*. DSM-III-R classifies the *chronic* form of schizophrenia as the episode of disturbance (prodromal, active, and residual phases) lasting more or less continuously for more than two years. *Chronic with an acute exacerbation* is designated with a reemergence of prominent psychotic symptoms during the time of disturbance. The phrase *in remission* is used when the full criteria for the disorder has been met previously but currently only some of the symptoms or signs of the illness are present. "In partial remission" is the term used when there is the expectation that the person will completely recover (or have a complete remission) within the next few years, as in the case of a major depressive episode. "Residual state" is used when there is little expectation of a complete remission or recovery within the next few years, as in the case of autistic disorder or attention-deficit hyperactivity disorder. ("Residual state" should not be used with schizophrenia, since by tradition there is a specific residual type of schizophrenia.) In some cases, the distinction between partial remission and residual state is difficult to make.

In full remission there are no longer any symptoms or signs of the disorder. The differentiation of full remission from recovered (no current mental disorder) requires consideration of the length of time since the last period of disturbance, the total duration of the disturbance, and the need for continued evaluation or prophylactic treatment.

Table 13.2 lists the DSM-III-R classifications of chronicity in schizophrenia.

13.3. The answer is E (*Synopsis VI*, page 337; *CTP V*, pages 770 and 775).

According to current thinking, the term "paraphrenia" is equivalent to *paranoid schizophrenia*. Paraphrenia is not included in DSM-III-R as a diagnostic entity but appears in the ninth edition of the *International Classification of Diseases* (ICD-9). The term is generally used to describe an illness with a chronic downhill course, characterized by well-systematized delusions but with a well-preserved personality.

Latent schizophrenia, as described in ICD-9, is diagnosed in those patients who may have marked schizoid personalities and who show occasional behavioral peculiarities or thought disorders without consistently manifesting any clearly psychotic pathology. The syndrome is also known as borderline schizophrenia. In DSM-III-R the syndrome is subsumed under schizotypal personality disorder. *Simple schizophrenia* is also not a DSM-III-R diagnosis but is in ICD-9 and is characterized by a gradual, insidious loss of drive and ambition. The patient is usually not experiencing hallucinations or delusions, and if these symptoms do occur, they do not persist. The patient withdraws from contact with other people and often stops working. *Catatonic schizophrenia*, both a DSM-III-R and an ICD-9 diagnosis, is a state characterized by muscular rigidity

Table 13.1
Prevalence of Schizophrenia in Specific Populations

Population	Prevalence (%)
General population	1
Nontwin sibling of a schizophrenic patient	8
Child with one schizophrenic parent	12
Dizygotic twin of a schizophrenic patient	12
Child of two schizophrenic parents	40
Monozygotic twin of a schizophrenic patient	47

Table 13.2
Classification of Course in Schizophrenia

1-Subchronic. The time from the beginning of the disturbance, when the person first began to show signs of the disturbance (including prodromal, active, and residual phases) more or less continuously, is less than two years but at least six months.
2-Chronic. Same as above, but more than two years.
3-Subchronic with acute exacerbation. Reemergence of prominent psychotic symptoms in a person with a subchronic course who has been in the residual phase of the disturbance.
4-Chronic with acute exacerbation. Reemergence of prominent psychotic symptoms in a person with a chronic course who has been in the residual phase of the disturbance.
5-In remission. When a person with a history of schizophrenia is free of all signs of the disturbance (whether or not on medication), "in remission" should be coded. Differentiating schizophrenia in remission from no mental disorder requires consideration of overall level of functioning, length of time since the last episode of disturbance, total duration of the disturbance, and whether prophylactic treatment is being given.
0-Unspecified.
Specify late onset if the disturbance (including the prodromal phase) develops after age 45.

Table from DSM-III-R, *Diagnostic and Statistical Manual of Mental Disorders*, ed 3, revised. Copyright American Psychiatric Association, Washington, DC, 1987. Used with permission.

and immobility. *Disorganized schizophrenia*, termed hebephrenic schizophrenia in ICD-9, is characterized by incoherence, marked loosening of associations, or grossly disordered behavior.

See Table 13.3 for the DSM-III-R classification of the different types of schizophrenia.

13.4. The answer is D (*Synopsis VI*, page 332; *CTP V*, page 768).

Features leading toward a good prognosis in schizophrenia include mood symptoms (especially depression), a *family history of mood disorders, paranoid features*, and an *undulating course*. Poor prognostic features include a family history of schizophrenia; poor premorbid social, sexual, and work history; and *undifferentiated or disorganized features*. The range of recovery varies from 10 to 60 percent of patients, and a reasonable estimate is that 20 to 30 percent of all patients are able to lead somewhat normal lives. Approximately 20 to 30 percent of patients continue to experience moderate symptoms, and 40 to 60 percent of patients remain sig-

Table 13.3
Diagnostic Criteria for Types of Schizophrenia

Paranoid Type
A type of schizophrenia in which there are:
A. Preoccupation with one or more systematized delusions or with frequent auditory hallucinations related to a single theme.
B. *None* of the following: incoherence, marked loosening of associations, flat or grossly inappropriate affect, catatonic behavior, grossly disorganized behavior.
Specify stable type if criteria A and B have been met during all past and present active phases of the illness.
Catatonic Type
A type of schizophrenia in which the clinical picture is dominated by any of the following:
1. catatonic stupor (marked decrease in reactivity to the environment and/or reduction in spontaneous movements and activity) or mutism
2. catatonic negativism (an apparently motiveless resistance to all instructions or attempts to be moved)
3. catatonic rigidity (maintenance of a rigid posture against efforts to be moved)
4. catatonic excitement (excited motor activity, apparently purposeless and not influenced by external stimuli)
5. catatonic posturing (voluntary assumption of inappropriate or bizarre postures)
Disorganized Type
A type of schizophrenia in which the following criteria are met:
A. Incoherence, marked loosening of associations, or grossly disorganized behavior.
B. Flat or grossly inappropriate affect.
C. Does not meet the criteria for catatonic type.
Undifferentiated Type
A type of schizophrenia in which there are:
A. Prominent delusions, hallucinations, incoherence, or grossly disorganized behavior.
B. Does not meet the criteria for paranoid, catatonic, or disorganized type.
Residual Type
A type of schizophrenia in which there are:
A. Absence of prominent delusions, hallucinations, incoherence, or grossly disorganized behavior.
B. Continuing evidence of the disturbance, as indicated by two or more of the residual symptoms listed in criterion D of schizophrenia.

Table from DSM-III-R, *Diagnostic and Statistical Manual of Mental Disorders*, ed 3, revised. Copyright American Psychiatric Association, Washington, DC, 1987. Used with permission.

nificantly impaired by their illness for their entire lives. Patients with schizophrenia do worse than patients with mood disorders, although approximately 20 to 25 percent of the mood disorder patients are also severely disturbed at long-term follow-up. See Table 13.4 for a summary of the factors used to assess good and poor prognoses in schizophrenia.

13.5. The answer is B (*Synopsis VI*, pages 332–337; *CTP V*, pages 770 and 773).

The 20-year-old male patient described is showing signs of *catatonic* schizophrenia. DSM-III-R states that essential features of this disorder include stupor, rigidity, posturing, mutism, and negativism. Associated features include stereotypies, mannerisms, and waxy flexibility. Catatonic patients often seem oblivious to the environment but are, in fact, usually aware of what is going on around them. The catatonic patient often resists the passive movement of a body part but may also show catalepsy, in which the patient maintains a posture into which he or she is placed, often for long periods of time. There may be rapid alternation between the extremes of excitement and stupor. During the period of extreme agitation or violent behavior known as catatonic excitement, the patient is dangerous, and physical restraint and antipsychotic medication are indicated.

Paranoid schizophrenia is characterized mainly by delusions of persecution or grandeur, often accompanied by hallucinations. In *residual* schizophrenia the patient is no longer acutely psychotic but has some remaining signs of the illness. Emotional blunting, social withdrawal, eccentric behavior, and illogical thinking are common. *Latent* schizophrenia is not a DSM-III-R diagnosis; it is described as a condition characterized by some schizophrenic symptoms without consistently manifesting any clearly psychotic pathology. This condition most closely resembles the DSM-III-R diagnosis of schizotypal personality disorder. It has been termed borderline schizophrenia in the past. *Hebephrenic* schizophrenia is also not a DSM-III-R diagnosis; the

equivalent schizophrenic subtype in DSM-III-R is disorganized schizophrenia, which is characterized by primitive, disinhibited, and unorganized behavior. Contact with reality is extremely poor, emotional responses are inappropriate, and behavior is best described as wild or silly.

13.6. The answer is D (*Synopsis VI*, pages 329–330; *CTP V*, page 761).

Schizophrenic hallucinations are most commonly *auditory*. Characteristically, the patient hears two or more voices talking about the patient, and the voices may be threatening, obscene, accusatory, or insulting. Many patients with schizophrenia also experience the hearing of their own thoughts, which can be disturbing and distracting.

Visual hallucinations, although not rare, occur less frequently than auditory hallucinations in schizophrenic patients. When visual hallucinations occur in schizophrenia, they are usually seen as nearby, life-size, three-dimensional, moving, and in clearly defined color. Visual hallucinations generally are found in combination with hallucinations involving one of the other senses. *Tactile* (haptic) hallucinations are false perceptions of touch; *olfactory* hallucinations are false perceptions of smell; and *gustatory* hallucinations are false perceptions of taste. All are less common than visual hallucinations; their presence should alert the clinician to the need for ruling out underlying organic causes (e.g., epilepsy, tumors).

13.7. The answer is C (*Synopsis VI*, pages 341–342; *CTP V*, pages 1459–1461).

The most useful form of individual psychotherapy in schizophrenia is *supportive* psychotherapy. Schizophrenic patients can be helped by individual psychotherapy that provides a positive treatment relationship and therapeutic alliance. The relationship between the clinician and the patient is different from that encountered in the treatment of nonpsychotic disorders.

Table 13.4
Features Leading toward Good and Poor Prognoses in Schizophrenia

Good	Poor
Late onset	Young onset
Obvious precipitating factors	No precipitating factors
Acute onset	Insidious onset
Good premorbid social, sexual, and work history	Poor premorbid social, sexual, and work history
Affective symptoms (especially depression)	Withdrawn, autistic behavior
Paranoid or catatonic features	Undifferentiated or disorganized features
Married	Single, divorced, or widowed
Family history of mood disorders	Family history of schizophrenia
Good support systems	Poor support systems
Undulating course	Chronic course
Positive symptoms	Negative symptoms
	Neurological signs and symptoms
	History of perinatal trauma
	No remissions in three years
	Many relapses

Establishing a relationship is often a difficult matter. The patient is desperately lonely yet defends against closeness and trust and is likely to become suspicious, anxious, hostile, or regressed when someone attempts to draw close. Scrupulous observation of distance and privacy, simple directness, patience, sincerity, and adherence to social conventions are preferable to premature informality and the use of first names. Exaggerated warmth or professions of friendship are out of place and are likely to be perceived as attempts at bribery, manipulation, or exploitation. In general, *insight-oriented* psychotherapy and especially classical *psychoanalysis* have no place in the treatment of schizophrenia; classical psychoanalysis is felt to be too rigorous and in depth and runs the risk of leading to psychotic decompensation.

Short-term psychotherapy is usually limited to between 15 and 20 sessions. Patients with schizophrenia benefit from long-term treatment (usually for years), during which a sense of trust can be established. Within the context of a professional relationship, however, flexibility may be essential in establishing a working alliance with the patient. At those times, the therapist may have meals with the patient, sit on the floor, go for a walk, eat at a restaurant, accept and give gifts, play table tennis, remember the patient's birthday, allow him or her to telephone the therapist at any hour, or just sit silently with the patient. The major aim is to convey that (1) the therapist can be trusted and wants to understand the patient and will try to do so and (2) the therapist has faith in the patient's potential as a human being, no matter how disturbed, hostile, or bizarre he or she may be at the moment.

13.8.   The answer is E (*Synopsis VI*, page 340; *CTP V*, pages 1596–1598).

Antipsychotic drugs have a wide margin of safety; if necessary, they may be administered without a full physical diagnostic assessment of the patient. The major contraindications to antipsychotics are the possibility that the patient has previously *ingested* a substance that will interact with the antipsychotic agent, causing central nervous system (CNS) depression or severe anticholinergic symptoms; the presence of a *severe cardiac abnormality*; the presence of a *seizure disorder*; and the presence of *narrow-angle glaucoma*. A past serious allergic response to an antipsychotic is also a contraindication.

13.9.   The answer is D (*Synopsis VI*, page 340; *CTP V*, page 786).

Clozapine (Clozaril) is an antipsychotic medication that is appropriate in the treatment of schizophrenic patients who have not responded to first-line dopamine receptor antagonists or who have developed tardive dyskinesia. It is *not an appropriate first-line drug* for the treatment of schizophrenia. Clozapine has been associated with a *1-to-2 percent (not 10-to-20 percent)* incidence of agranulocytosis and thus requires *weekly, not monthly*, monitoring of blood indices. Clozapine's therapeutic effect is hypothesized to be through the blockade of the *serotonergic, not dopaminergic, receptors*. Since the drug is not a dopamine type 2 (D_2) receptor antagonist, it has not been associated with *extrapyramidal side effects* or tardive dyskinesia.

13.10.   The answer is E (*Synopsis VI*, pages 335–336; *CTP V*, page 774).

According to DSM-III-R, the diagnosis of undifferentiated schizophrenia may be made in patients who do not meet the criteria for paranoid, catatonic, or disorganized schizophrenia but who present with *prominent delusions, hallucinations, incoherence*, or *grossly disorganized behavior*. Paranoid schizophrenia is characterized by persecutory delusions; catatonic, by odd posturing; and disorganized, by extremely regressed behavior.

See Table 13.3, the diagnostic criteria for the types of schizophrenia.

13.11.   The answer is D (4) (*Synopsis VI*, pages 334–335; *CTP V*, page 770).

Paranoid schizophrenia most commonly presents with *systematized delusions*, which may be accompanied by auditory hallucinations that relate to the delusional theme. DSM-III-R explicitly states that paranoid schizophrenia does not present with incoherence, *loosening of associations, flat affect*, catatonic behavior, or *grossly disorganized behavior*. Table 13.3 lists the DSM-III-R diagnostic criteria.

13.12.   The answer is C (2, 4) (*Synopsis VI*, page 340; *CTP V*, pages 1596–1598).

Antipsychotic drugs used in schizophrenia *reach the brain quickly* to block dopamine receptors, but the clinical effects may take as long as *six weeks* to develop maximally. The clinical potency of antipsychotic drugs is closely correlated with their *binding affinity to dopamine type 2 (D_2), not dopamine type 1 (D_1), receptors*. Dopamine antagonists are effective in treating *all psychoses*, not just schizophrenia.

13.13.   The answer is D (4) (*Synopsis VI*, pages 324–327; *CTP V*, pages 705–707).

There have been two main types of neuropathological studies of schizophrenia—studies of neurotransmitters and of neurodegeneration. Many neurotransmitter postmortem schizophrenic studies have reported *increased (not decreased) numbers of dopamine type 2 (D_2) receptors* in the basal ganglia and limbic system (particularly the amygdala, nucleus accumbens, and hippocampus). Although one study found both increased dopamine concentrations and increased number of receptors in the left amygdala, most do not concur. Most studies have also been unable to distinguish *changes in dopamine receptors* related to schizophrenia from the increase of dopamine receptors related to antipsychotic drug treatment. Two studies reported *increased (not decreased)* *concentrations of both norepinephrine* and its metabolites in the nucleus accumbens of chronic paranoid patients.

Recent studies have not produced a single consistent structural defect in schizophrenia; however, there is a consistent *pattern of degeneration in the limbic forebrain* (especially the amygdala and the hippocampus) and the basal ganglia (especially the substantia nigra and the medial pallidum). The specific results of these studies have included increased gliosis in the periventricular diencephalon, a decreased number of cortical neurons in the prefrontal and cingulate regions, and decreased volume of the amygdala, hippocampal formation, and parahippocampal gyrus.

13.14.   The answer is E (all) (*Synopsis VI*, pages 325–326; *CTP V*, pages 707–711).

The majority of computed tomographic (CT) studies of patients with schizophrenia have reported *enlargement of lateral and third ventricles* in 10 to 50 percent of patients and *cortical atrophy* in 10 to 35 percent of patients. Controlled studies have also revealed *atrophy of the cerebellar vermis*, decreased radiodensity of brain parenchyma, and reversals of the normal brain asymmetries. These findings are *not the result of treatment* and are not progressive or reversible. The enlargement of the ventricles seems to be present at the time of diagnosis, before the use of medication. Some studies have correlated the presence of CT scan findings with the presence of negative or deficit symptoms (e.g., social isolation), neuropsychological impairment, more frequent motor side effects from antipsychotics, and poorer premorbid adjustment.

13.15.   The answer is E (all) (*Synopsis VI*, page 330; *CTP V*, pages 761–765 and 560–564).

Disordered thought is characteristic of schizophrenia. Thought disorders may be divided into disorders of content, form, and process. Disorders of content reflect ideas, beliefs, and interpretations of stimuli. *Delusions* are the most obvious example of a disorder of thought content. The delusions may be quite varied—persecutory, grandiose, religious, or somatic. Patients with a thought disorder may have the delusional belief that some outside entity is controlling their thoughts or behavior or, conversely, that they are controlling outside events in some extraordinary fashion (e.g., causing the sun to rise and set, preventing earthquakes).

Loss of ego boundaries describes the patient's lack of a clear sense of where the patient's own body, mind, and influence end and where those of other animate and inanimate objects begin. For example, the content of thought may include ideas of reference that other people, persons on television, or newspaper items are making reference to the patient. Other symptoms include a sense of fusion with outside objects (e.g., a tree, another person) or a sense of disintegration. In this state of mind, patients with schizophrenia may have *sexual confusion* and doubts

as to what sex they are or what their sexual orientation is.

Disorders in thought form or process reflect how thoughts are conveyed. *Looseness of associations*, a disorder of thought form, was once felt to be pathognomonic for schizophrenia; however, this form of thought may be seen in other psychotic states as well. It is characterized by thoughts that are connected to each other by meanings known only to the patient and conveyed in a manner that is diffuse, unfocused, illogical, and even incoherent.

13.16.   The answer is A (1, 2, 3) (*Synopsis VI*, page 333; *CTP V*, page 769).

According to DSM-III-R, the signs and symptoms that must be present to make a diagnosis of schizophrenia include characteristic psychotic symptoms such as *delusions, prominent hallucinations,* flat or grossly inappropriate affect, and marked loosening of associations; markedly *impaired social functioning* during the course of the disturbance; and continuous evidence of *signs for at least six months,* including an active phase. DSM-III-R has eliminated the requirement that the illness begin before age 45; however, if the age of onset is after 45, late onset type should be specified. It is not essential, however, that the age of *onset be before age 45* to make the diagnosis.

13.17.   The answer is A (1, 2, 3) (*Synopsis VI*, page 325; *CTP V*, pages 719–720).

The dopamine hypothesis, the major neurotransmitter hypothesis for schizophrenia, states that there is a hyperactivity of dopaminergic systems in schizophrenia. The major support for this hypothesis is that all effective *antipsychotic drugs bind to dopamine receptors.* The clinical potency of antipsychotic drugs is closely correlated with their *binding affinity to dopamine type 2 (D₂) receptors,* the dopamine receptor subtype that does not stimulate adenylate cyclase. The observation that the administration of amphetamine or *levodopa* (Dopar, Larodopa) *exacerbates the symptoms* of some but not all schizophrenic patients lends additional support to this hypothesis, as levodopa is an agonist of dopamine. However, this hypothesis has three major problems. First, dopamine antagonists are effective in treating all psychoses, not just schizophrenia. Dopaminergic hyperactivity, therefore, is not uniquely associated with schizophrenia. Second, although antipsychotic drugs reach the brain very quickly to block dopamine receptors, the clinical effects can take as long as *six weeks (not 10 days)* to develop completely, thus raising suspicions that other factors beside a straightforward dopamine hypothesis are involved in clinical symptoms and improvement. Third, although some research has demonstrated supportive neurochemical evidence (e.g., increased dopamine metabolites), the majority of studies have not found confirmatory neurochemical data. In spite of this, the dopamine hypothesis remains one of the best explanations of the disorder.

13.18. The answer is C (2, 4) (*Synopsis VI*, page 326; *CTP V*, pages 728–729).

Psychoendocrine dysregulation has been reported in schizophrenia. Although most studies have suggested a normal prolactin axis in schizophrenia, a few studies have found a *decreased (not increased) prolactin level*. The data have been more consistent in demonstrating *decreased levels of luteinizing hormone* (LH) and *decreased follicle-stimulating hormone* (FSH). Two additional abnormalities have been a blunted release of growth hormone (GH) to gonadotropin-releasing hormone (GnRH) and a *blunted release of thyroid hormone to* thyrotropin-releasing hormone (TRH) stimulation.

Hypothalamic pathology (either structural or neurochemical) has been postulated to explain the endocrine dysfunctions seen in schizophrenia. Hyperfunction of dopaminergic systems, for example, could explain the endocrine dysfunctions seen in schizophrenia.

13.19. The answer is E (all) (*Synopsis VI*, page 326; *CTP V*, page 166).

Electrophysiological studies of schizophrenia patients include electroencephalogram (EEG) studies. These studies indicate a higher number of patients with abnormal recordings, increased sensitivity (e.g., more frequent spike activity) to activation procedures (e.g., sleep deprivation), *decreased alpha activity*, increased theta and delta activity, possibly more epileptiform activity, and possibly more left-sided abnormalities. Evoked potential studies have generally shown increased amplitude of early components and decreased amplitude of late components. This difference has been interpreted as indicating that, although schizophrenia patients are more sensitive to sensory stimulation, they compensate for this increased sensitivity by blunting their processing of the information at higher cortical levels.

Other central nervous system (CNS) electrophysiological investigations have included depth electrodes and quantitative EEG (QEEG). One study reported that electrodes implanted in the limbic system of schizophrenic patients show spiking activity that is *correlated with psychotic behavior*; however, no control subjects were examined. QEEG studies of schizophrenia show *increased frontal lobe slow-wave activity* and *increased parietal lobe fast-wave activity*.

13.20. The answer is B (1, 3) (*Synopsis VI*, page 338; *CTP V*, pages 774–775).

A clinically useful system for describing the thought disorders of schizophrenic patients is to divide the disorders into negative (deficit) and positive (productive) symptoms. Deficit symptoms of schizophrenia include *affective flattening, blocking*, poverty of speech, poor grooming, lack of motivation, anhedonia, social withdrawal, cognitive problems, and attentional deficits. Productive symptoms include loose associations, *hallucinations, bizarre behavior*, and increased speech.

Affective flattening is the absence or near absence of emotional expression. Blocking is the involuntary cessation of thought or speech processes. Poverty of speech is monosyllabic speech or a restriction in the amount of speech. Anhedonia is a loss of interest in and withdrawal from pleasurable activities. Loose associations are ideas or thoughts that shift from one subject to another in a way incomprehensible to the listener.

13.21. The answer is E (all) (*Synopsis VI*, page 336; *CTP V*, page 769).

The residual phase of schizophrenia follows the active phase and consists of varied signs and symptoms. A patient in the residual phase commonly shows *affective blunting* or flattening, *peculiar behavior, lack of initiative and energy*, illusions, and delusions.

See Table 13.5 for the complete DSM-III-R diagnostic criteria for schizophrenia. The student should know this chart in great detail and be able to define the terms used.

13.22–13.24

13.22. The answer is B (*Synopsis VI*, page 320; *CTP V*, page 2148).

13.23. The answer is A (*Synopsis VI*, page 320; *CTP V*, page 2148).

13.24. The answer is C (*Synopsis VI*, pages 320–321; *CTP V*, page 837).

Key people in the history of schizophrenia are the following: Karl Kahlbaum (German, 1828–1899) described symptoms of *catatonia*; Ewald Hecker (German, 1843–1909) wrote about the extremely bizarre behavior of *hebephrenia*; and E. Gabriel Langfeldt (Norwegian, 1895–1983) distinguished two groups of schizophrenics—process (nuclear) schizophrenia and the *schizophreniform psychosis*. Process schizophrenia has an insidious onset and a deteriorating course; schizophreniform psychosis has typical schizophrenic characteristics but a relatively well-integrated premorbid personality with an acute onset of illness and a good prognosis.

13.25–13.29

13.25. The answer is A (*Synopsis VI*, page 320; *CTP V*, pages 757–758 and 2149).

13.26. The answer is B (*Synopsis VI*, page 320; *CTP V*, pages 757–758 and 2149).

13.27. The answer is B (*Synopsis VI*, page 320; *CTP V*, pages 757–758 and 2149).

13.28. The answer is B (*Synopsis VI*, page 320; *CTP V*, pages 757–758 and 2149).

Table 13.5
Diagnostic Criteria for Schizophrenia

A. Presence of characteristic psychotic symptoms in the active phase: either 1, 2, or 3 for at least one week (unless the symptoms are successfully treated):
1. two of the following:
   a. delusions
   b. prominent hallucinations (throughout the day for several days or several times a week for several weeks, each hallucinatory experience not being limited to a few brief moments)
   c. incoherence or marked loosening of associations
   d. catatonic behavior
   e. flat or grossly inappropriate affect
2. bizarre delusions (i.e., involving a phenomenon that the person's culture would regard as totally implausible, e.g., thought broadcasting, being controlled by a dead person)
3. prominent hallucinations [as defined in 1b above] of a voice with content having no apparent relation to depression or elation or a voice keeping up a running commentary on the person's behavior or thoughts, or two or more voices conversing with each other
B. During the course of the disturbance, functioning in such areas as work, social relations, and self-care is markedly below the highest level achieved before the onset of the disturbance (or, when the onset is in childhood or adolescence, failure to achieve expected level of social development).
C. Schizoaffective disorder and mood disorder with psychotic features have been ruled out, i.e., if a major depressive or manic syndrome has ever been present during an active phase of the disturbance, the total duration of all episodes of a mood syndrome has been brief relative to the total duration of the active and residual phases of the disturbance.
D. Continuous signs of the disturbance for at least six months. The six-month period must include an active phase (of at least one week or less if symptoms have been successfully treated) during which there were psychotic symptoms characteristic of schizophrenia (symptoms in A), with or without a prodromal or residual phase, as defined below.
Prodromal phase: A clear deterioration in functioning before the active phase of the disturbance that is not due to a disturbance in mood or to a psychoactive substance use disorder and that involves at least two of the symptoms listed below.
Residual phase: Following the active phase of the disturbance, persistence of at least two of the symptoms noted below, these not being due to a disturbance in mood or to a psychoactive substance use disorder.
Prodromal or Residual Symptoms:
1. marked social isolation or withdrawal
2. marked impairment in role functioning as wage-earner, student, or homemaker
3. markedly peculiar behavior (e.g., collecting garbage, talking to self in public, hoarding food)
4. marked impairment in personal hygiene and grooming
5. blunted or inappropriate affect
6. digressive, vague, overelaborate, or circumstantial speech, or poverty of speech, or poverty of content of speech
7. odd beliefs or magical thinking, influencing behavior and inconsistent with cultural norms (e.g., superstitiousness, belief in clairvoyance, telepathy, "sixth sense," "others can feel my feelings," overvalued ideas, ideas of reference)
8. unusual perceptual experiences (e.g., recurrent illusions, sensing the presence of a force or person not actually present)
9. marked lack of initiative, interests, or energy
Examples: Six months of prodromal symptoms with one week of symptoms from A; no prodromal symptoms with six months of symptoms from A; no prodromal symptoms with one week of symptoms from A and six months of residual symptoms.
E. It cannot be established that an organic factor initiated and maintained the disturbance.
F. If there is a history of autistic disorder, the additional diagnosis of schizophrenia is made only if prominent delusions or hallucinations are also present.

Table from DSM-III-R, *Diagnostic and Statistical Manual of Mental Disorders*, ed 3, revised. Copyright American Psychiatric Association, Washington, DC, 1987. Used with permission.

13.29. The answer is A (*Synopsis VI*, page 320; *CTP V*, pages 757–758 and 2149).

Emil Kraepelin (German, 1856–1926) organized seriously mentally ill patients into three diagnoses: dementia precox, manic-depressive psychosis, and paranoia. *Dementia precox* was described as an illness with a chronic deteriorating course, associated with hallucinations and delusions. This illness was distinguished from *manic-depressive* psychosis, which was described as an episodic illness with virtually complete remissions interepisodically. *Eugen*

Bleuler (Swiss, 1857–1939) coined the term "*schizophrenia.*" Bleuler did not believe that deterioration in course was a necessary part of schizophrenia. He did divide schizophrenic symptoms into *fundamental and accessory symptoms*. Fundamental symptoms included the *four As of schizophrenia*: loosening of associations, affective disturbances, autism, and ambivalence. Accessory symptoms included hallucinations and delusions. Both Bleuler and Kraepelin assumed that there was an underlying biological basis for schizophrenia.

13.30–13.35

13.30. The answer is B (*Synopsis VI*, pages 321–322; *CTP V*, pages 768–769).

13.31. The answer is B (*Synopsis VI*, pages 321–322; *CTP V*, pages 768–769).

13.32. The answer is A (*Synopsis VI*, pages 321–322; *CTP V*, pages 768–769).

13.33. The answer is A (*Synopsis VI*, pages 321–322; *CTP V*, pages 768–769).

13.34. The answer is A (*Synopsis VI*, pages 321–322; *CTP V*, pages 768–769).

13.35. The answer is A (*Synopsis VI*, pages 321–322; *CTP V*, pages 768–769).

Kurt Schneider (1887–1967) described a number of first-rank symptoms of schizophrenia that are considered of pragmatic value in making the diagnosis of schizophrenia, although they are not specific to the disease. These symptoms include *audible thoughts*, hearing one's thoughts aloud; *voices* or auditory hallucinations *commenting* on the patient's behavior; *thought withdrawal*, the removal of the patient's thoughts by others; and the experience of *having one's thoughts controlled*. Schneider pointed out that schizophrenia can be diagnosed by second-rank symptoms when accompanied by a typical clinical presentation. Second-rank symptoms include *sudden delusional ideas, perplexity*, and feelings of emotional impoverishment. (See Table 13.6 for Schneider's diagnostic criteria for schizophrenia.)

Table 13.6
Kurt Schneider's Diagnostic Criteria for Schizophrenia

1. First-rank symptoms
   a. Audible thoughts
   b. Voices arguing or discussing or both
   c. Voices commenting
   d. Somatic passivity experiences
   e. Thought withdrawal and other experiences of influenced thought
   f. Thought broadcasting
   g. Delusional perceptions
   h. All other experiences involving volition, made affects, and made impulses
2. Second-rank symptoms
   a. Other disorders of perception
   b. Sudden delusional ideas
   c. Perplexity
   d. Depressive and euphoric mood changes
   e. Feelings of emotional impoverishment
   f. ". . . and several others as well"

14 |||||

Delusional Disorder

Delusional disorders consist of a heterogeneous group of disorders that share the chief features of a delusion. The delusion—a false, fixed belief—may be erotomanic, grandiose, jealous, persecutory, or somatic. These nonbizarre delusions are, in general, well systematized and logically developed. The patient may have little or no impairment in functioning. Previously called paranoid disorders, they are now classified as types of delusional disorder, emphasizing the central role of the delusion and the wide variety of types of delusional disorder.

The old term "paranoid disorders" has been dropped because the delusions do not necessarily have to be paranoid (i.e., persecutory) in character. The historical antecedent to delusional disorder was Emil Kraepelin's concept of paraphrenia. Although delusional disorder is much rarer than either schizophrenia or mood disorders, the secretive and singular nature of the symptoms may result in an underreporting of this disorder.

The cause of delusional disorder is not known, and solid research data for a biological basis are scarce. The psychodynamic formulations regarding delusional disorder, however, are important for the student to know, as they represent important historical markers in the history of psychoanalysis. The major historical case was that of Daniel Paul Schreber, whose life was studied by Sigmund Freud. Students should understand how the concepts of paranoid pseudocommunity and the defense mechanisms of reaction formation, denial, and projection may be involved in this disorder.

The mental status examination of patients with this disorder is striking for the intactness of most cognitive functions accompanying the delusional system. The course is variable and seems to be particularly affected by such major life events as marriage and death. The diagnostic types of this disorder should be familiar to the student. The differential diagnosis of delusional symptoms includes a number of medical and neurological conditions. The psychiatric differential diagnosis requires careful examination of the patient for the presence of symptoms in other areas of the psyche.

The clinical evaluation of a delusional disorder patient requires special attention regarding suicidality and homicidality. The patients are not more likely to be violent; rather, their relative intactness may fool the clinician into underestimating their psychopathology. Treatment, therefore, may require hospitalization. Although antipsychotic medications are used most commonly for this disorder, remarkably little is known about the efficacy of antidepressants, lithium, and carbamazepine (Tegretol). Both individual and family therapy may be of use in delusional disorder.

Students are referred to Chapter 14 of *Synopsis VI*, "Delusional Disorder," and to Chapter 15, "Delusional (Paranoid) Disorders," in *CTP V* and should then study the questions and answers below.

HELPFUL HINTS

Students should know the delusional syndromes and the terms listed.

paranoia	paranoid states	mental status examination
paraphrenia	Clérambault's syndrome	delusions
prevalence	nihilistic delusion	erotomania
incidence	Cotard's syndrome	suicide
age of onset	Capgras's syndrome	homicide
marital status	Fregoli's syndrome	ICD-9
SES	projection	lycanthropy
family studies	denial	neuropsychological testing
limbic system and basal ganglia	Daniel Paul Schreber	EEG and CT scan
neurological conditions	homosexuality	antipsychotic drugs
reduplicative paramnesia	paranoid pseudocommunity	psychotherapy
reaction formation	Norman Cameron	

QUESTIONS

DIRECTIONS: Each of the incomplete statements below is followed by five suggested completions. Select the *one* that is *best* in each case.

14.1. A 45-year-old single woman was brought to the hospital by her parents. Over the preceding year, the patient had begun to believe that her parents and state government officials were involved in a plan to get her to give away a piece of land she owned in the country. She began accusing the officials of putting substances in her food that damaged her hair and caused her to have receding gums. She wrote numerous letters to federal officials complaining of these events, yet all the while she worked efficiently at her job examining income tax forms. She had had no previous contact with mental health professionals. The mental status examination revealed no hallucinations, incoherence, or loosening of associations.
The most likely diagnosis is
A. paranoid personality disorder
B. paranoid schizophrenia
C. delusional disorder
D. mood disorder with psychotic features
E. schizophreniform disorder

14.2. Delusional disorder
A. is less common than schizophrenia
B. is caused by frontal lobe lesions
C. usually begins by age 20
D. is an early stage of schizophrenia
E. is more common in men than in women

14.3. All the following are characteristic of delusional disorder *except*
A. prominent hallucinations
B. mood-congruent ideation
C. paranoid ideation
D. impaired impulse control
E. intact cognition

14.4. The defense mechanism most used in the persecutory type of delusional disorder is
A. denial
B. reaction formation
C. undoing
D. projection
E. sublimation

14.5. All the following are types of delusional disorder *except*
A. persecutory
B. jealous
C. manic
D. somatic
E. grandiose

14.6. The most effective treatment for delusional disorder is
A. carbamazepine (Tegretol)
B. electroconvulsive therapy
C. antidepressant medication
D. psychotherapy
E. lithium

DIRECTIONS: The lettered headings below are followed by a list of numbered phrases. For each numbered phrase, select the *best* lettered heading. Each lettered heading may be used once, more than once, or not at all.

Questions 14.7–14.10
A. Clérambault's syndrome
B. Capgras's syndrome
C. Fregoli's syndrome
D. Cotard's syndrome

14.7. Delusion that familiar people have been replaced by identical imposters

14.8. Delusion that a persecutor is taking on a variety of faces

14.9. Delusion that one has lost everything

14.10. Delusion of erotomania

ANSWERS

Delusional Disorder

14.1. The answer is C (*Synopsis VI*, pages 344–346; *CTP V*, pages 816–829).

Based on the information given, the most likely diagnosis in the case described is *delusional disorder*. The central features are the nonbizarre delusions involving situations that occur in real life—such as being followed, poisoned, and deceived—of at least one month's duration. The average age of onset for delusional disorder is between 40 and 55. Intellectual and occupational functioning is usually satisfactory, whereas social and marital functioning is often impaired. The diagnosis is made only when no organic factor can be found that has initiated or maintained the disorder. If an organic factor is found, the diagnosis of organic delusional syndrome is made.

By definition, delusional disorder patients do not have prominent or sustained hallucinations, and the nonbizarre quality of the delusions cited—for example, substances put in her food—rule out *paranoid schizophrenia* and *schizophreniform disorder*. In addition, as compared with schizophrenia, delusional disorder usually produces less impairment in daily functioning. Another consideration in the DSM-III-R diagnostic criteria for schizophreniform disorder is the specification that the episode lasts less than six months (the patient described had symptoms over one year). The differential diagnosis with *mood disorders with psychotic features* can be difficult, as the psychotic features associated with mood disorders often involve nonbizarre delusions, and prominent hallucinations are unusual. The differential diagnosis depends on the relation of the mood disturbance and the delusions. In a major depression with psychotic features, the onset of the depressed mood usually antedates the appearance of psychosis and is present after the psychosis remits. Also, the depressive symptoms are usually prominent and severe. In delusional disorder, if depressive symptoms occur, they occur after the onset of the delusions, are usually mild, and often remit while the delusional symptoms persist. In *paranoid personality disorder* there are no delusions, although there is paranoid ideation.

14.2. The answer is A (*Synopsis VI*, page 343; *CTP V*, pages 820–824).

Delusional disorder is *less common than schizophrenia*. Its prevalence in the United States is currently estimated to be 0.03 percent—in contrast with schizophrenia, 1 percent, and mood disorders, 5 percent.

The neuropsychiatric approach to delusional disorder derives from the observation that delusions are a common symptom in many neurological conditions, particularly those involving the limbic systems and basal ganglia. There is no evidence linking the disorder to a lesion of the *frontal lobe*. Long-term follow-up of patients with delusional disorder has found that their diagnoses are rarely revised as schizophrenia or mood disorders; hence, delusional disorder is not merely an *early stage* of these other disorders. Moreover, delusional disorder has a later onset than schizophrenia or mood disorder. The mean age of onset is approximately *40 years*, but the age range is from 25 through the 90s. There is a *slight preponderance of female patients*.

14.3. The answer is A (*Synopsis VI*, pages 344–346; *CTP V*, pages 818 and 824).

As defined, delusional disorder patients do not have *prominent or sustained hallucinations*. However, a few delusional patients have rare hallucinatory experiences that are almost always auditory in nature. The patient's mood and delusions are *congruent* with one another; a patient with euphoric mood has grandiose delusions. *Paranoid ideation* with persecutory ideas is the most common type of ideation in delusional disorder. The paranoid delusion may be simple or elaborate, and the patient is often querulous, resentful, and angry. *Impulse control* may be impaired, and all patients must be questioned about their self-destructive violent impulses. *Cognition is usually intact*.

14.4. The answer is D (*Synopsis VI*, page 344; *CTP V*, page 823).

The defense mechanism most used in the persecutory type of delusional disorder is *projection*, in which persons attribute to other people the thoughts, feelings, or impulses that are unacceptable in themselves. Anger and hostility are among the impulses for which the person cannot accept responsibility, and the paranoid person's resentment is projected onto others. A paranoid delusional system is ultimately defensive against such feelings as inferiority and impulses of anger and violence.

Reaction formation is the defense that turns an unacceptable impulse or idea into its opposite, such as love into hate. *Denial* is used to avoid awareness of painful reality. *Undoing* is the defense mechanism by which a person symbolically acts out in reverse something that is unacceptable. Repetitive in nature, undoing is commonly observed in patients with obsessive-compulsive disorder. *Sublimation* is the process of modifying an instinctual impulse in such a way as to conform to the demands of society.

14.5. The answer is C (*Synopsis VI*, pages 345–346; *CTP V*, page 818).

The types of delusional disorder are based on the predominant delusional theme and include erotomanic, *grandiose, jealous, persecutory*, and *somatic*. If no single delusional theme predominates, the unspecified type is noted. There is no *manic* type of delusional disorder. Mania—the euphoric, high-energy phase of bipolar disorder—is classified as a mood disorder.

The persecutory or paranoid type of delusional disorder is one in which the prominent theme of the delusion is that one is being treated in a malevolent way. In the jealous type the predominant theme of the delusion is that one's sexual partner is unfaithful. In the somatic type the predominant theme is that the person has some physical deficit or disease. In the grandiose type the predominant theme of the delusion is one of inflated worth, power, knowledge, identity, or a special relationship with a deity or a famous person. Table 14.1 provides the American Psychiatric Association's revised third edition of *Diagnostic and Statistical Manual of Mental Disorders* (DSM-III-R) diagnostic criteria for delusional disorder and a description of the various types.

14.6. The answer is D (*Synopsis VI*, pages 348–350; *CTP V*, pages 828–829).

Psychotherapy appears to be the most effective treatment for delusional disorder. The essential element is the therapeutic relationship, in which the patient begins to trust the therapist. Over a period of time, as trust develops and defenses are reinforced, the presenting conflicts can begin to resolve. In terms of pharmacotherapy, antipsychotic drugs are currently considered the drugs of choice, although many delusional disorder patients are likely to refuse medication.

Electroconvulsive therapy is not effective in the treatment of delusional disorder. Essentially no data suggest that *antidepressants, lithium*, or *carbamazepine* (Tegretol) is effective in treating delusional disorder. Clinical trials may be warranted in patients with symptoms suggestive of mood disorders or positive family histories of mood disorders.

14.7–14.10

14.7. The answer is B (*Synopsis VI*, page 348; *CTP V*, page 850).

Table 14.1
Diagnostic Criteria for Delusional Disorder

A. Nonbizarre delusion(s) (i.e., involving situations that occur in real life, such as being followed, poisoned, infected, loved at a distance, having a disease, being deceived by one's spouse or lover) of at least one month's duration.
B. Auditory or visual hallucinations, if present, are not prominent [as defined in schizophrenia, A(1)(b)].
C. Apart from the delusion(s) or its ramifications, behavior is not obviously odd or bizarre.
D. If a major depressive or manic syndrome has been present during the delusional disturbance, the total duration of all episodes of the mood syndrome has been brief relative to the total duration of the delusional disturbance.
E. Has never met criterion A for schizophrenia, and it cannot be established that an organic factor initiated and maintained the disturbance.
Specify type: The following types are based on the predominant delusional theme. If no single delusional theme predominates, specify as *unspecified type*.
Erotomanic Type
Delusional disorder in which the predominant theme of the delusion(s) is that a person, usually of higher status, is in love with the subject.
Grandiose Type
Delusional disorder in which the predominant theme of the delusion(s) is one of inflated worth, power, knowledge, identity, or special relationship to a deity or famous person.
Jealous Type
Delusional disorder in which the predominant theme of the delusion(s) is that one's sexual partner is unfaithful.
Persecutory Type
Delusional disorder in which the predominant theme of the delusion(s) is that one (or someone to whom one is close) is being malevolently treated in some way. People with this type of delusional disorder may repeatedly take their complaints of being mistreated to legal authorities.
Somatic Type
Delusional disorder in which the predominant theme of the delusion(s) is that the person has some physical defect, disorder, or disease.
Unspecified Type
Delusional disorder that does not fit any of the previous categories, e.g., persecutory and grandiose themes without a predominance of either; delusions of reference without malevolent content.

Table from DSM-III-R, *Diagnostic and Statistical Manual of Mental Disorders*, ed 3, revised. Copyright American Psychiatric Association, Washington, DC, 1987. Used with permission.

14.8. The answer is C (*Synopsis VI*, page 348; *CTP V*, page 826).

14.9. The answer is D (*Synopsis VI*, page 348; *CTP V*, page 851).

14.10. The answer is A (*Synopsis VI*, page 346; *CTP V*, page 851).

Specific delusions have historically been known by different names. As these names remain in psychiatric literature, it is helpful for the student to be familiar with them. Capgras's syndrome is the delusion that familiar people have been replaced by *identical imposters*. For example, a patient may state, "He looks like my husband and sounds like my husband, but I know he is not my husband." Fregoli's syndrome is the delusion that a persecutor is taking on a *variety of faces*. A patient may state, "I thought I lost him; then I realized that he became the woman on the bus." Cotard's syndrome is a delusion of nihilism. Originally named *délire de négation*, the delusion is that the person believes he or she has *lost everything*. Not only possessions or position but also bodily organs may be believed to be lost. Clérambault's syndrome is a delusion of *erotomania*. The patient believes that he or she is loved by another, usually someone of greater status. The news media have brought attention to several persons who have attempted to contact or harm celebrities who are the objects of such delusions.

15

Psychotic Disorders Not Elsewhere Classified

The diagnostic criteria for schizophrenia, mood disorders, and delusional disorders in the revised third edition of the American Psychiatric Association's *Diagnostic and Statistical Manual of Mental Disorders* (DSM-III-R) do not cover all patients with psychotic conditions, so the category of psychotic disorders not elsewhere classified has been established. The physician may use this residual category for those patients whose symptoms do not conform to other diagnostic criteria.

The psychotic disorders not elsewhere classified include schizoaffective disorder, schizophreniform disorder, brief reactive psychosis, and induced psychotic disorder. DSM-III-R also includes a diagnosis of psychotic disorder not otherwise specified (NOS), also known as atypical psychosis.

Schizoaffective disorder is the most studied of this group of disorders and probably the most common. Patients with schizoaffective disorder have features of both schizophrenia and a mood disorder but cannot be classified as having just one of the two conditions without distorting some aspect of the clinical presentation. Students should be familiar with epidemiology, etiology, clinical signs and symptoms, course and prognosis, diagnostic subtypes, differential diagnosis, and major treatment modalities for patients with schizoaffective disorder.

Schizophreniform disorder is defined in DSM-III-R as differing from schizophrenia only in that the symptoms resolve and that there is a return to normal functioning within six months. Its history, starting with Gabriel Langfeldt, has been one of disagreement until recently. The student should be familiar with this diagnostic category because it is often the most appropriate diagnosis for psychotic patients who do not meet the criteria for either schizophrenia or mood disorder, and it prevents premature diagnosis of patients as suffering from a disorder with a worse prognosis.

Brief reactive psychosis is one of the few DSM-III-R diagnoses for which a specific causative factor, a psychosocial stressor, is specified. The possible relations among this disorder, personality disorders, and defense mechanisms should be known to the student. The features indicating good and bad prognoses should also be studied. Many of these patients are seen in emergency-room settings, so the differential diagnosis should include the usual considerations regarding acute psychosis.

Induced psychotic disorder is the new DSM-III-R diagnostic term for the passive member of what was previously called *folie à deux*. The dominant member of a *folie à deux* receives a diagnosis specific to the signs and symptoms (e.g., schizophrenia). Although induced psychotic disorder is rare, it is an important model for the student to study with regard to psychodynamic formulations of the possible pathological relationship between persons.

The atypical psychoses have many presentations. The most relevant for Western psychiatrists are those that occur only at a particular time (e.g., during the menses or postpartum). The student should know the signs and symptoms of postpartum psychosis and the possible relations with other psychotic and mood disorders. Postpartum psychosis should be differentiated from the other normal and pathological reactions after childbirth.

Finally, a large group of atypical psychoses are restricted to a specific cultural setting; these are known as culture-bound syndromes (e.g., amok, koro). Clinicians attempt to place these disorders, if possible, into one of the more conventional categories of mood disorder or schizophrenia. In some cases, however, the signs and symptoms defy such niceties of classification, and the psychiatrist tries to understand the significance of the varied phenomena those disorders present.

Students are referred to Chapter 15, "Psychotic Disorders Not Elsewhere Classified," in

Synopsis VI and to Chapter 16, "Psychotic Disorders Not Elsewhere Classified," in *CTP V* and should then study the questions and answers below to assess their knowledge.

HELPFUL HINTS

The terms and diagnoses below should be understood.

schizoaffective disorder	*bouffée délirante*	*suk-yeong*
lifetime prevalence	good-prognosis schizophrenia	piblokto
etiology	hysterical psychosis	Arctic hysteria
suicidal incidence	psychodynamic formulation	windigo psychosis
course	induced psychotic disorder	autoscopic psychosis
prognostic variables	shared paranoid disorder	Capgras's syndrome
inclusion and exclusion criteria	*folie à deux*	Cotard's syndrome
subtypes	double insanity	Ganser's syndrome
neuroendocrine function	psychosis of association	postpartum psychosis
DST	passive person and dominant	postpartum blues
TRH stimulation test	person	Cushing's syndrome
schizophreniform disorder	atypical psychoses	atypical cycloid psychoses
Gabriel Langfeldt	culture-bound syndromes	motility, confusional, and anxiety-
lithium	psychotic disorder NOS	blissfulness psychoses
antipsychotics	differential diagnosis	atypical schizophrenia
brief reactive psychosis	amok	periodic catatonia
significant stressor	koro	

QUESTIONS

DIRECTIONS: Each of the incomplete statements below is followed by five suggested completions. Select the *one* that is *best* in each case.

15.1. The main defense mechanism used in induced psychotic disorder is
A. projection
B. regression
C. reaction formation
D. displacement
E. identification with the aggressor

15.2. In schizoaffective disorder all the following variables indicate a poor prognosis *except*
A. no precipitating factor
B. predominance of psychotic symptoms
C. depressive type
D. bipolar type
E. early onset

15.3. Schizophreniform disorder is diagnosed when the duration of the disorder is
A. less than one month
B. less than six months
C. less than eight months
D. less than two years
E. more than two years

15.4. True statements concerning brief reactive psychosis include all the following *except*
A. it may be more common in persons with previously existing personality disorders
B. mood disorders may be more common in the relatives of affected probands
C. prodromal symptoms appear before the onset of the precipitating stressor
D. good prognostic features include a severe precipitating stressor and confusion or perplexity during psychosis
E. the psychosocial stressor must be of sufficient severity to cause significant stress to any person in the same socioeconomic and cultural class

15.5. The category of psychotic disorder not otherwise specified (atypical psychosis) includes
A. disorders with unusual features, such as persistent auditory hallucinations as the only disturbance
B. syndromes that occur only at a particular time, such as the menses
C. disorders that are restricted to a specific cultural setting
D. psychoses about which there is inadequate information
E. all the above

DIRECTIONS: For each of the questions or incomplete statements below, *one or more* of the answers or completions given are correct. Choose

A. if only *1, 2, and 3* are correct
B. if only *1 and 3* are correct
C. if only *2 and 4* are correct
D. if only *4* is correct
E. if *all* are correct

15.6. Induced psychotic disorder occurs most frequently among
1. lower socioeconomic groups
2. women
3. members of the same family
4. the deaf

15.7. Brief reactive psychosis may be common in people with which of the following previously existing personality disorders?
1. Histrionic
2. Borderline
3. Narcissistic
4. Paranoid

15.8. True statements concerning the treatment of induced psychotic disorder include
1. separation of the passive partner from the dominant one is the primary intervention
2. if symptoms persist after separation, the affected partner may eventually meet the diagnostic criteria for delusional disorder or schizophrenia
3. after separation, the passive partner's delusional symptoms tend to remit naturally
4. recovery rates have been reported to be as low as 10 percent

15.9. Schizophreniform patients
1. demonstrate abnormal dexamethasone suppression more often than do patients with schizophrenia
2. have a poor prognosis if they show confusion or disorientation at the height of the psychotic mood
3. have abnormal thyrotropin-releasing hormone findings more often than do patients with schizophrenia
4. have a poorer prognosis than patients with schizophrenia

15.10. Postpartum psychosis
1. symptoms usually occur about the third postpartum day
2. occurs in 1 to 2 per 1,000 deliveries
3. should not be confused with postpartum blues
4. is a psychiatric emergency

15.11. Examples of the atypical psychoses include
1. Capgras's syndrome
2. Cotard's syndrome
3. postpartum psychosis
4. koro

15.12. The validity of schizoaffective disorders as being distinct from schizophrenia has been suggested because
1. close relatives of patients with schizoaffective disorders show a lower prevalence of schizophrenia than do relatives of patients with schizophrenia
2. no sex differences have been reported
3. relatives of patients with schizoaffective disorders show an increased frequency of mood disorder
4. hallucinations and delusions are present

ANSWERS

Psychotic Disorders Not Elsewhere Classified

15.1. The answer is E (*Synopsis VI*, pages 357–359; *CTP V*, page 826).

The main defense mechanism used in induced psychotic disorder is *identification with the aggressor*, the aggressor being the dominant member of the two persons who share the psychosis. The initiator of the psychosis is usually the sicker of the two, often a paranoid schizophrenic, on whom the other person is dependent. This disorder was called shared paranoid disorder in DSM-III and has been termed *folie à deux*.

Identification with the aggressor is an unconscious process by which persons incorporate within themselves the mental image of a person who represents a source of frustration in the outside world. A primitive defense, it operates in the interest and the service of the developing ego.

Projection is an unconscious defense mechanism in which a person attributes to another those generally unconscious ideas, thoughts, feelings, and impulses that are personally undesirable or unacceptable. By externalizing whatever is unacceptable, such persons deal with it as a situation apart from themselves. *Regression* is an unconscious defense mechanism in which a person undergoes a partial or total return to earlier patterns of adaptation. Regression is observed in many psychiatric conditions, particularly schizophrenia. *Reaction formation* is an unconscious defense mechanism in which a person develops an attitude or interest that is the direct antithesis of some unacceptable wish or impulse that the person harbors. *Displacement* is an unconscious defense mechanism by which the emotional component of an unacceptable idea or object is transferred to a more acceptable one. See Table 15.1 for the DSM-III-R criteria for induced psychotic disorder.

Table 15.1
Diagnostic Criteria for Induced Psychotic Disorder

A. A delusion develops (in a second person) in the context of a close relationship with another person, or persons, with an already established delusion (the primary case).
B. The delusion in the second person is similar in content to that in the primary case.
C. Immediately before onset of the induced delusion, the second person did not have a psychotic disorder or the prodromal symptoms of schizophrenia.

15.2. The answer is D (*Synopsis VI*, page 352; *CTP V*, pages 833–834).

The course and the prognosis of schizoaffective disorder are variable. As a group, patients with this disorder have a prognosis intermediate between patients with schizophrenia and patients with mood disorders. Poor prognosis is associated with the *depressive type* of schizoaffective disorder. Poor prognosis is also associated with the following variables: *no precipitating factor, predominance of psychotic symptoms, early or insidious onset*, poor premorbid history, and positive family history of schizophrenia. Schizoaffective disorder, *bipolar type*, is associated with a good prognosis. See Table 15.2 for the DSM-III-R criteria for schizoaffective disorder.

15.3. The answer is B (*Synopsis VI*, page 354; *CTP V*, page 834).

Schizophreniform disorder is diagnosed when an episode of the disturbance—including prodromal, active, and residual phases—lasts *less than six months*. If the episode lasts *less than one month*, it is diagnosed as brief reactive psychosis. The diagnosis for a patient with this disturbance lasting at least six months but *less than two years* is subchronic schizophrenia. If the syndrome lasts for *more than two years* it is labeled chronic schizophrenia. See Table 15.3 for the DSM-III-R criteria for schizophreniform disorder.

Table 15.2
Diagnostic Criteria for Schizoaffective Disorder

A. A disturbance during which at some time there is either a major depressive or a manic syndrome concurrent with symptoms that meet the A criterion of schizophrenia.
B. During an episode of the disturbance, there have been delusions or hallucinations for at least two weeks but no prominent mood symptoms.
C. Schizophrenia has been ruled out (i.e., the duration of all episodes of a mood syndrome has not been brief relative to the total duration of the psychotic disturbance).
D. It cannot be established that an organic factor initiated and maintained the disturbance.
Specify: bipolar type (current or previous manic syndrome)
    or
        depressive type (no current or previous manic syndrome)

Table 15.3
Diagnostic Criteria for Schizophreniform Disorder

A. Meets criteria A and C of schizophrenia.
B. An episode of the disturbance (including prodromal, active, and residual phases) lasts less than six months. (When the diagnosis must be made without waiting for recovery, it should be qualified as "provisional.")
C. Does not meet the criteria for brief reactive psychosis, and it cannot be established that an organic factor initiated and maintained the disturbance.
Specify: without good prognostic features or **with good prognostic features,** i.e., with at least two of the following:
  1. onset of prominent psychotic symptoms within four weeks of first noticeable change in usual behavior or functioning
  2. confusion, disorientation, or perplexity at the height of the psychotic episode
  3. good premorbid social and occupational functioning
  4. absence of blunted or flat affect

Table from DSM-III-R, *Diagnostic and Statistical Manual of Mental Disorders*, ed 3, revised. Copyright American Psychiatric Association, Washington, DC, 1987. Used with permission.

15.4. The answer is C (*Synopsis VI*, pages 355–357; *CTP V*, pages 840–841).

There are *no prodromal symptoms* before the precipitating stressor in brief reactive psychosis. By definition, a significant psychosocial stressor is a causative factor for brief reactive psychosis, and the stressor must be of *sufficient severity* to cause significant stress to any person in the same socioeconomic and cultural class. However, many of these patients also have *preexisting personality disorders*. Although schizophrenia has not been found to be common in the relatives of persons with brief reactive psychosis, *mood disorders may be more common* among these persons. The onset of symptoms is usually abrupt, following the stressor by as little as a few hours. There are several indicators of good prognosis, including good premorbid adjustment, few premorbid schizoid traits, a *severe precipitating stressor*, acute onset, and *confusion or perplexity during psychosis*. See Table 15.4 for the DSM-III-R criteria for brief reactive psychosis.

15.5. The answer is E (*Synopsis VI*, page 359; *CTP V*, pages 842–843).

The category of psychotic disorder not otherwise specified, also called atypical psychosis, includes a diverse group of syndromes. Psychoses with *unusual features*, such as persistent auditory hallucinations as the only disturbance; syndromes that occur only at a *particular time*, such as the menses or postpartum; syndromes that are restricted to a specific *cultural setting*; and psychoses about which there is *inadequate information*—all may be diagnosed as psychotic disorder NOS. The diagnosis can be changed as more information becomes known. The diagnosis cannot be made if a known organic factor initiated and maintained the disturbance. See Table 15.5 for the DSM-III-R diagnostic criteria for this disorder.

Table 15.4
Diagnostic Criteria for Brief Reactive Psychosis

A. Presence of at least one of the following symptoms indicating impaired reality testing (not culturally sanctioned):
  1. incoherence or marked loosening of associations
  2. delusions
  3. hallucinations
  4. catatonic or disorganized behavior
B. Emotional turmoil, i.e., rapid shifts from one intense affect to another, or overwhelming perplexity or confusion.
C. Appearance of the symptoms in A and B shortly after, and apparently in response to, one or more events that, singly or together, would be markedly stressful to almost anyone in similar circumstances in the person's culture.
D. Absence of the prodromal symptoms of schizophrenia, and failure to meet the criteria for schizotypal personality disorder before onset of the disturbance.
E. Duration of an episode of the disturbance of from a few hours to one month, with eventual full return to premorbid level of functioning. (When the diagnosis must be made without waiting for the expected recovery, it should be qualified as "provisional.")
F. Not due to a psychotic mood disorder (i.e., no full mood syndrome is present), and it cannot be established that an organic factor initiated and maintained the disturbance.

Table from DSM-III-R, *Diagnostic and Statistical Manual of Mental Disorders*, ed 3, revised. Copyright American Psychiatric Association, Washington, DC, 1987. Used with permission.

Table 15.5
Diagnostic Criteria for Psychotic Disorder Not Otherwise Specified (Atypical Psychosis)

Disorders in which there are psychotic symptoms (delusions, hallucinations, incoherence, marked loosening of associations, catatonic excitement or stupor, or grossly disorganized behavior) that do not meet the criteria for any other nonorganic psychotic disorder. This category should also be used for psychoses about which there is inadequate information to make a specific diagnosis. (This is preferable to "diagnosis deferred," and can be changed if more information becomes available.) This diagnosis is made only when it cannot be established that an organic factor initiated and maintained the disturbance.
Examples:
  1. psychoses with unusual features (e.g., persistent auditory hallucinations as the only disturbance)
  2. postpartum psychoses that do not meet the criteria for an organic mental disorder, psychotic mood disorder, or any other psychotic disorder
  3. psychoses with confusing clinical features that make a more specific diagnosis impossible

Table from DSM-III-R, *Diagnostic and Statistical Manual of Mental Disorders*, ed 3, revised. Copyright American Psychiatric Association, Washington, DC, 1987. Used with permission.

15.6. The answer is E (all) (*Synopsis VI*, page 357; *CTP V*, page 826).

Induced psychotic disorder is rare but is more common in *women* than in men. Persons in all socioeconomic classes may be affected, although it may be more common in *lower socioeconomic groups*. Patients with such physical disabilities as stroke or *deafness* are also at increased risk because of the dependency relationships that may develop for such people. Over 95 percent of cases involve two members of the *same family*. Approximately a third of the cases involve two sisters; another third involve husband and wife or mother and child. Two brothers, a brother and a sister, and a father and a child have been reported but less frequently.

15.7. The answer is E (all) (*Synopsis VI*, page 356; *CTP V*, pages 840–841).

Brief reactive psychosis may be common in people with previously existing personality disorders— most commonly, *histrionic, narcissistic, borderline, paranoid*, and schizotypal. The incidence, the prevalence, and the sex ratio of brief reactive psychosis have not been definitively studied. Many clinicians believe it is a rare disorder that occurs most often in adolescence and early adulthood. It may be more common in persons in lower socioeconomic classes and in those who have experienced disasters or have undergone major cultural changes.

15.8. The answer is E (all) (*Synopsis VI*, pages 358–359; *CTP V*, page 826).

Separation of the passive partner with induced psychotic disorder from the dominant one usually results in a rapid and dramatic reduction of symptoms. Clinical reports vary, however, and several papers have reported *recovery rates ranging from 10 to 40 percent*. If symptoms persist after separation, the affected partner may eventually meet the diagnostic criteria for *delusional disorder or schizophrenia*. The patient must not have had a psychotic disorder before the inducement of the delusional system. Despite the limitations reported, the recommended approach remains the separation of the affected person from the more dominant source of the delusions. The person with induced psychotic disorder should be supported, usually in a hospital, and observed for the natural *remission* of the delusional symptoms. Pharmacotherapy need not be used unless absolutely necessary to safeguard the patient.

15.9. The answer is B (1, 3) (*Synopsis VI*, pages 354–355; *CTP V*, pages 837–839).

The few available studies done on schizophreniform disorder suggest that a heterogeneous group of patients account for this diagnosis. Some have an illness more similar to schizophrenia, whereas others have an illness more similar to the mood disorders. Several studies have indicated that schizophreniform patients have *better (not poorer) outcomes* than do patients with schizophrenia. There is also a relation to mood disorders, which is supported by the observation that schizophreniform patients demonstrate *abnormal dexamethasone suppression and thyrotropin-releasing hormone findings* more often than do patients with schizophrenia.

The clinical signs and symptoms, as well as the mental status examination, are the same as in schizophrenia. It is important, however, to note the patient's affect and level of confusion or perplexity, as these symptoms are helpful in predicting the course of the disorder. Good prognostic features include *confusion, disorientation*, or perplexity at the height of the psychotic episode and absence of blunted or flat affect. See Table 15.3 for the DSM-III-R criteria for schizophreniform disorder.

15.10. The answer is E (all) (*Synopsis VI*, pages 359–360; *CTP V*, pages 855–857).

Postpartum psychosis occurs in *1 to 2 per 1,000 deliveries*. The risk of a postpartum disorder is increased if the patient or the patient's mother had a previous postpartum illness or if there is a history of mood disorder. The symptoms usually occur about the *third postpartum day* and almost always in the first 30 days after giving birth. The patient begins to complain of insomnia, restlessness, and fatigue and shows lability of mood with tearfulness. Later symptoms include suspiciousness, confusion, incoherence, irrational statements, and obsessive concerns about the baby's health. Delusional material may involve the idea that the baby is dead or defective. The birth may be denied, or ideas of persecution, influence, or perversity may be expressed. Hallucinations may involve voices telling the patient to kill her baby. Postpartum psychosis is a *psychiatric emergency*. In one study, 5 percent of patients killed themselves, and 4 percent killed the baby. Postpartum psychosis should not be confused with *postpartum blues*, which is a normal condition seen in up to 50 percent of women after childbirth and which is self-limited, lasting only a few days. The syndrome is characterized by tearfulness, fatigue, anxiety, and irritability that begins shortly after childbirth and lessens in severity each day postpartum.

15.11. The answer is E (all) (*Synopsis VI*, pages 359–362; *CTP V*, pages 842–851).

Examples of the atypical psychoses include *Capgras's syndrome, Cotard's syndrome, postpartum psychosis*, and *koro*. In general, they are the rare, the exotic, and the unusual mental disorders and include the following: (1) syndromes that occur only at a particular time (e.g., during the menses or postpartum); (2) syndromes that are restricted to a specific cultural setting, culture-bound syndromes; (3) psychoses with unusual features, such as persistent auditory hallucinations; (4) syndromes that seem to belong to a well-known diagnostic entity but that show some features that cannot be reconciled with the generally accepted typical characteristics of that diagnostic category; and (5) psychoses about which information is inadequate to make a more specific diagnosis.

Capgras's syndrome is characterized by the delusional conviction that other persons in the environment are not their real selves but, instead, are doubles who, like imposters, assume the roles of the persons they impersonate and behave like them.

In Cotard's syndrome, patients complain of having lost not only possessions, status, and strength but also the heart, blood, and intestines. The world outside is often reduced to nothingness.

Postpartum psychosis is a syndrome that occurs after childbirth and is characterized by delusions and severe depression. Thoughts of wanting to harm the newborn infant or oneself are common and represent a real danger. Most patients with this disorder have an underlying mental illness—most commonly a bipolar disorder and, less commonly, schizophrenia. A few cases result from an organic mental syndrome associated with perinatal events. Those women with a prior history of schizophrenia or a mood disorder should be classified as having a recurrence of those disorders, rather than an atypical psychosis.

Koro is a culture-bound syndrome characterized by a patient's desperate fear that his penis is shrinking and may disappear into his abdomen. The syndrome is found in Southeast Asia and in some areas of China.

In general, every attempt should be made to place a psychotic syndrome in one of the more conventional diagnostic categories if possible, before a diagnosis of atypical psychosis is made. See Table 15.5 for the DSM-III-R criteria for atypical psychosis.

15.12.   The answer is B (1, 3) (*Synopsis VI*, pages 351–352; *CTP V*, pages 834–835).

The validity of schizoaffective disorders as being distinct from schizophrenia has been suggested. Close relatives of patients with schizoaffective disorders show a *lower prevalence of schizophrenia* than is seen in relatives of persons with schizophrenia; instead, the relatives of patients with schizoaffective disorders evince an increased frequency of uncomplicated, straightforward *mood disorders*. They also present an increased frequency of schizoaffective conditions.

Two kinds of psychotic symptoms define schizoaffective disorders. The first kind includes those symptoms that are part of the DSM-III-R criteria for schizophrenia, such as *delusions* of control and certain types of auditory *hallucinations*, that would suggest schizophrenia if there were no accompanying mood syndrome. The second kind includes those symptoms that arise in the context of a mood syndrome without an apparent relation to depression or elation. Otherwise, the clinical features consist of various mixtures of mood and schizophreniclike symptoms.

No striking *sex differences* in the frequency of schizophrenia and schizoaffective disorders have been reported, and thus sex is not helpful in distinguishing schizoaffective disorders from schizophrenia.

16 |||||

Mood Disorders

Descriptions of mood disorders have been recorded since antiquity. The mood disorders have in common a disturbance of mood accompanied by related cognitive, psychomotor, and physiologic changes and interpersonal difficulties. Mood is defined as a pervasive sustained, internal emotional state that affects the total personality. Affect is defined as the external expression of the person's internal emotional state. Alterations of affect are not the critical pathological changes in mood disorders; however, changes in affect may occur. The pathology of these disorders is the pathology of mood.

The major types of mood disorders are bipolar, cyclothymic, depressive, and dysthymic. Cyclothymia and dysthymia are sometimes referred to as subaffective disorders to emphasize the fact that, although they are similar to bipolar and depressive disorders, their cross-sectional symptoms may be less severe. The student needs to understand the various theoretical relations between depression and mania—two ends of a continuum. The Kraepelinian and psychoanalytic theories regarding the mood disorders are necessary to know to understand the history and the current theoretical formulations of these disorders.

Among the biological research data regarding the mood disorders, the data concerning biogenic amines, neuroendocrine dysregulations, and sleep abnormalities are probably the most important at this time. The effects of the antidepressant drugs on adrenergic and serotonergic receptors, the types of dysregulations seen in the adrenal and thyroid neuroendocrine axes, and the disorders of sleep architecture should be studied. All these data should be integrated according to how they imply pathology in the limbic system and hypothalamus in the mood disorders. The data from family genetic studies, molecular genetic studies, and lineage studies should also be familiar to the student.

An appreciation of how life events and environmental stress may be etiologically related to the mood disorders is necessary for the understanding of some treatment approaches. The theories implicating premorbid personality factors, behavioral factors (i.e., learned helplessness), and cognitive factors also serve as the foundations for specific psychological treatment approaches.

The two basic symptom patterns are those for depression and for mania. The variations of these symptoms seen in children and adolescents are also important. The disorders of thought and the potential for suicide and other violence are important parts of the mental status examination for all clinicians. The statistics for length of episodes, chance of relapse, and long-term prognosis represent significant information that the physician may want to share with the patient.

The signs and symptoms and the American Psychiatric Association's *Diagnostic and Statistical Manual of Mental Disorders*, revised third edition (DSM-III-R), diagnostic criteria for depressive and manic syndromes are important to know. Special attention should be given to the melancholic depressive, seasonal-pattern depressive, and mixed bipolar types. The medical and neurological differential diagnoses for both depressive and manic symptoms are extensive, yet it is in the special purview of psychiatrists to be completely capable of considering these organic disorders in their diagnostic consideration.

The variety of potentially effective treatment approaches makes the clinical management of the mood disorders possibly the most complex in psychiatry. The details of treatment of depression with antidepressants, monoamine oxidase inhibitors (MAOIs), sympathomimetics, serotonergic agonists, lithium, carbamazepine (Tegretol), and L-triiodothyronine (T_3) (Cytomel) should be clear to the student. The various psychotherapeutic approaches to depression—interpersonal, cognitive, behavioral, family, and psychoanalytic therapies—should be considered by the student in terms of indications, predictors of success, and efficacy.

Dysthymia is characterized by chronic, nonpsychotic signs and symptoms of depression that meet specific DSM-III-R diagnostic criteria but do not meet the criteria for major depressive disorder. A critical and difficult concept regarding dysthymia concerns the differential diagnosis, because so many psychiatric disorders can include mild depressive features. The differential diagnosis is essential, because the diagnosis of an alternative specific disorder often indicates a specific treatment approach that would also resolve the depressive symptoms.

Cyclothymia is generally considered a less severe form of bipolar disorder. Although the prevalence of cyclothymia has been reported as less than 1 percent, it is likely that this disorder actually has a considerably greater prevalence in clinical practice than is generally appreciated. Therefore, its clinical signs and symptoms should be consciously assessed during clinical interviews of psychiatric patients, particularly outpatients who may have relatively high levels of functioning. The variety of treatment approaches, including both biological and psychological, should be known to the clinician, and the appropriateness of different approaches should be carefully considered.

Students should refer to *Synopsis VI*, Chapter 16, "Mood Disorders," and to *CTP V*, Chapter 17, "Mood (Affective) Disorders." After completing these chapters, they can test their knowledge by studying the questions and answers below.

HELPFUL HINTS

The following terms that relate to mood disorders should be known.

mood	REM latency, density	differential diagnosis
affect	hypothalamus	pseudodementia
vegetative functions	genetic studies	clinical management
major depressive disorder, unipolar depression	RFLPs	thymoleptics
	life events and stress	HCA
unipolar mania, bipolar disorder	premorbid factors	euthymic
hypomania	Heinz Kohut	T_3
cyclothymia	learned helplessness	lithium
dysthymia	cognitive theories	amphetamine
folie circulaire	melancholia	MAOIs
folie à double forme	age-dependent symptoms	ECT
Karl Kahlbaum	MSE	antipsychotics
Emil Kraepelin	mood-congruent and mood-incongruent psychotic features	carbamazepine
incidence and prevalence		rapid cycling
sex ratios of illnesses	depression rating scales	IPT
biogenic amines	suicide	cognitive, behavioral, family, and psychoanalytic therapies
GABA	depressive equivalent	
LHPA	*forme fruste*	dysthymia (early and late onset)
DST	seasonal pattern	cyclothymia
TSH, TRH	melatonin	double depression
GH	phototherapy	hypomania
LH, FSH	bipolar types: I, II	

QUESTIONS

DIRECTIONS: Each of the incomplete statements below is followed by five completions. Select the *one* that is *best* in each case.

16.1. A 21-year old single male student was admitted for evaluation after an accident in which he wrecked his car. He had been driving at high speed, late at night, feeling "extremely energetic," with no need for sleep. Before the accident the student had felt high and on the verge of a great sexual experience. He reportedly had taken off all his clothes and had run naked through the dormitory. On the day of admission, he heard voices telling him that his parents were evil and not to trust them.
   The most likely diagnosis in this patient is
A. bipolar disorder, manic, with psychotic features (mood-incongruent)
B. bipolar disorder, manic, with psychotic features (mood-congruent)
C. bipolar disorder, mixed, with psychotic features (mood-congruent)
D. bipolar disorder, depressed, with psychotic features (mood-congruent)
E. cyclothymia

16.2. Major depression
A. has a lifetime prevalence of approximately 20 percent
B. is four times more common among women than among men
C. has its onset between the ages of 20 and 50 in 75 percent of patients
D. may be more common in rural areas than in urban areas
E. occurs as often among patients who are divorced or separated as among patients who are married

16.3. The animal model of learned helplessness has been used to explain the cause of
A. mania
B. depression
C. hypomania
D. schizoaffective disorder
E. none of the above

16.4. Vegetative signs in depression include all the following *except*
A. weight loss
B. abnormal menses
C. obsessive rumination
D. decreased libido
E. fatigability

16.5. The drug treatment indicated for most cases of acute mania is
A. lithium and nortriptyline (Aventyl)
B. haloperidol (Haldol) and nortriptyline
C. haloperidol and lithium
D. phenelzine (Nardil) and lithium
E. chlordiazepoxide (Librium) and lithium

16.6. A patient who initially presents with an episode of mania is classified as suffering from
A. cyclothymia
B. hypomania
C. schizoaffective disorder
D. unipolar disorder
E. bipolar disorder

16.7. Depressive symptoms may be associated with
A. schizophrenia
B. cyclothymia
C. alcoholism
D. anxiety disorders
E. all the above

16.8. The percentage of depressed patients who eventually commit suicide is estimated to be
A. 0.5 percent
B. 5 percent
C. 15 percent
D. 25 percent
E. 35 percent

16.9. All the following statements about bipolar disorder are true *except*
A. bipolar disorder most often starts with depression
B. approximately 10 to 20 percent of patients experience only manic episodes
C. an untreated manic episode lasts about three months
D. as the illness progresses, the amount of time between episodes often increases
E. rapid cycling is much more common among women than among men

16.10. Life events
A. may contribute to the onset and the timing of a specific episode of depression
B. are most associated with the development of depression in later life when a parent is lost before age 11
C. are most associated with the onset of a depressive episode when a spouse is lost
D. are not significantly related to the onset and the timing of a specific episode of mania
E. are characterized by all the above

16.11. The diagnostic criteria for melancholia include all the following *except*
A. loss of interest or pleasure in all or almost all activities
B. depression regularly worse in the evening
C. psychomotor retardation or agitation
D. significant anorexia or weight loss
E. no significant personality disturbance before first major depressive episode

16.12. All the following statements about cyclothymia are true *except*
A. 50 to 75 percent of patients have an onset between ages 15 and 25
B. 30 percent of cyclothymic patients have positive family histories for bipolar disorder
C. the cycles of cyclothymia tend to be much longer than they are in bipolar disorder
D. drug-dependency disorders develop in approximately 5 to 10 percent of cyclothymic patients
E. approximately 60 percent of patients respond to treatment with lithium

16.13. L-Tryptophan
A. is the amino acid precursor to serotonin
B. has been used as an adjuvant to antidepressants and to lithium
C. has been used as a hypnotic
D. has been associated with eosinophilia-myalgia syndrome
E. is characterized by all the above

16.14. Guidelines for the pharmacological treatment of depression include
A. the dosage should be maintained at the maximum recommended levels for at least two weeks
B. if a patient has not responded to the drug after an adequate trial at maximal dosage, augmentation with levothyroxine (T_4) (Synthroid) is recommended
C. tricyclic antidepressants are almost always the first drug of choice
D. antidepressant treatment should be maintained for at least six months or the length of the previous episode, whichever is longer
E. the only tricyclic antidepressant known to have a therapeutic window is maprotiline (Ludiomil)

DIRECTIONS: For each of the questions or incomplete statements below, *one or more* of the answers or completions given are correct. Choose

A. if only *1, 2, and 3* are correct
B. if only *1 and 3* are correct
C. if only *2 and 4* are correct
D. if only *4* is correct
E. if *all* are correct

16.15. A 40-year-old man was brought to the psychiatric emergency room after becoming involved in a fistfight at a bar. He was speaking rapidly, jumping from one thought to another in response to simple, specific questions (e.g., "When did you come to New York?" "I came to New York, the Big Apple, it's rotten to the core, no matter how you slice it, I sliced a bagel this morning for breakfast . . ."). The patient described experiencing his thoughts as racing. He was unable to explain how he got into the fight other than to say that the other person was jealous of the patient's obvious sexual prowess, the patient having declared that he had slept with at least 100 women. He made allusions to his father as being God, and he stated that he had not slept in three days. "I don't need it," he said. The patient's speech was full of amusing puns, jokes, and plays on words.

Associated findings consistent with this patient's probable diagnosis are
1. nocturnal electroencephalographic (EEG) changes
2. emotional lability
3. hallucinations
4. delusions

16.16. Age-associated features of major depression include
1. separation anxiety
2. antisocial behavior
3. running away
4. dementia syndrome of depression (pseudodementia)

16.17. Which of the following statements concerning bipolar disorder are true?
1. Bipolar disorder has a worse prognosis than major depressive disorder
2. The presence of psychotic symptoms during manic episodes implies a poor prognosis
3. Patients with pure manic symptoms do better than do patients with depressed or mixed symptoms
4. On long-term follow-up, at least 50 percent of patients are well

16.18. Mood-congruent depressive delusions include those of
1. guilt
2. terminal somatic illnesses
3. poverty
4. thought insertion

16.19. Drugs that may precipitate mania are
1. levodopa (Larodopa, Dopar)
2. amphetamine
3. bromide
4. tetracycline

16.20. Major depression
1. is more common in women than in men
2. has a mean age of onset around age 40
3. does not differ according to race
4. occurs more often in divorced or separated persons than in married persons

16.21. On the mental status examination of a patient classified as bipolar, manic phase, which of the following symptoms may be present?
1. Mood-congruent hallucinations
2. Neologisms
3. Clang associations
4. Mood-incongruent delusions

16.22. Neuroendocrine markers of depression include
1. a blunted release of thyroid-stimulating hormone on administration of thyroid-releasing hormone
2. a decreased release of growth hormone to noradrenergic stimulation with clonidine (Catapres)
3. decreased prolactin release to L-tryptophan administration
4. increased nocturnal secretion of melatonin

16.23. Mood disorders appear to involve pathology of the
1. limbic system
2. basal ganglia
3. hypothalamus
4. corpus callosum

16.24. Objective rating scales of depression include the
1. Zung
2. Raskin
3. Hamilton
4. Holmes-Rahe

16.25. Personality types at greatest risk for depression include
1. oral-dependent
2. obsessive-compulsive
3. hysterical
4. paranoid

16.26. The DSM-III-R diagnostic criteria for the seasonal pattern subtype of mood disorders include
1. a regular temporal relation between the onset of a mood disorder and a particular 60-day period of the year
2. full remissions within a particular 60-day period
3. at least three episodes of mood disturbance in three separate years that demonstrate the temporal seasonal relationship
4. a temporal seasonal mood disturbance in at least two of three consecutive years

16.27. In major depressive disorder
1. approximately 50 to 85 percent of patients have a second depressive episode
2. many patients have their second episode in the four to six months after the resolution of the first episode
3. men are more likely than women to experience a chronically impaired course
4. the risk of recurrence is increased by a young age at onset

16.28. Biological markers of depression include
1. decreased testosterone levels in males
2. decreased basal levels of follicle-stimulating hormone and luteinizing hormone
3. hypersecretion of cortisol
4. hyperactivity of the hypothalamic-pituitary-adrenal axis

16.29. The course of a major depressive disorder usually includes
1. an episode of depression lasting 6 to 13 months if untreated
2. an episode of depression lasting approximately three months if treated
3. the return of symptoms after the withdrawal of antidepressants before three months have elapsed
4. an average of five to six episodes over a 20-year period

16.30. A manic episode is differentiated from a schizophrenic episode by
1. quality of mood
2. psychomotor activity
3. family history
4. speed of onset

16.31. Which of the following medications may produce depressive symptoms?
1. Analgesics
2. Antibacterials
3. Antipsychotics
4. Antihypertensives

16.32. The biogenic amine hypothesis of mood disorders is supported by the observation that
1. monoamine oxidase inhibitors increase brain catecholamines in the synaptic cleft
2. imipramine (Tofranil) binding sites in platelets have been reported to be decreased in depressed patients
3. 3-methoxy-4-hydroxyphenylglycol (MHPG) is decreased in the urine of some depressed patients
4. amphetamine elevates mood

DIRECTIONS: The lettered headings below are followed by a list of numbered phrases. For each numbered phrase, select the lettered heading most closely associated with it. Each lettered heading may be used once, more than once, or not at all.

Questions 16.33–16.35
    A. Major depression
    B. Dysthymia

16.33. Episodic periods of depression

16.34. DSM-III-R defines types based on onset before and after age 21

16.35. May have psychotic symptoms

Mood Disorders

16.1. The answer is A (*Synopsis VI*, pages 366–369 and 386–387; *CTP V*, page 908).

In the case of the 21-year-old single male student, the most likely diagnosis is *bipolar disorder, manic, with psychotic features (mood-incongruent)*. The characteristic features of a manic episode are present in this patient: elevated mood (feeling high), increased energy, decreased need for sleep, and involvement in activities with a high potential for painful consequences (reckless driving). The reference to being on the verge of a great sexual encounter suggests the presence of grandiosity. In DSM-III-R the presence of a manic episode, even without a history of a depressive episode, is sufficient to make a diagnosis of bipolar disorder, manic, as the familial history, course, and treatment response of unipolar mania are apparently the same as in illnesses with both manic and major depressive episodes.

The presence of the persecutory hallucinations is noted by including "with psychotic features." Since the content has no apparent connection with themes of either inflated worth, power, knowledge, identity, or a special relationship to a deity or famous person, the hallucinations are mood-incongruent. This can be indicated in parentheses, as in "bipolar disorder, manic, with psychotic features (mood-incongruent)."

Bipolar disorder, mixed, with mood-congruent psychotic features, involves the full symptomatic picture of both mania and depression intermixed or rapidly alternating every few days, with psychotic features congruent with manic and depressed moods. *Bipolar disorder, depressed*, with mood-congruent psychotic features, involves a current presentation of a major depressive episode in a previously manic patient. The mood-congruent psychotic features involve depressive themes, such as guilt, poverty, nihilism, and somatic concerns.

Cyclothymia is a chronic disorder, of at least two years' duration, characterized by both hypomanic episodes and numerous periods of depressed mood or loss of interest or pleasure. In cyclothymia there is an absence of psychotic features, and it is considered a less severe mood disorder than bipolar disorder.

16.2. The answer is D (*Synopsis VI*, page 364; *CTP V*, pages 863–865).

Major depression is among the most common psychiatric disorders. The lifetime prevalence is approximately *6 percent, not 20 percent*. It is estimated, however, that only 50 percent of patients with major depression receive treatment. Major depression is *two times, not four times, more common among women than among men*. This observation is independent of country. Although major depression may occur at any age, *50 percent, not 75 percent*, of patients have the onset between ages 20 and 50, the mean age being about 40. The prevalence of mood disorders does not differ by race or social class. Major depression may be *more common in rural areas* than in urban areas. In general, major depression occurs more often in people who have no close interpersonal relationships. It is *more common among persons who are divorced or separated* than among those who are married.

16.3. The answer is B (*Synopsis VI*, page 366; *CTP V*, pages 330–331).

The animal model of learned helplessness has been used to explain the cause of human *depression*. In some animal experiments in which dogs were exposed to electric shocks from which they could not escape, the dogs reacted with helplessness and made no attempt to escape future shocks. They learned to give up and appeared to be helpless. In humans with depressive mood disorders, one can find a similar state of helplessness. If a depressed patient can gain a sense of control and mastery of the environment, the depression frequently lifts. Similarly, behavioral techniques of reward and positive reinforcement from one's environment can often help the patient overcome depression.

Other important factors observed in the animal models of learned helplessness are reduced voluntary response initiation, a hopeless attitude about the potential effectiveness of one's own responses, decreased aggressive response, diminution of appetite and sex drive, and physiological decrease in norepinephrine. *Mania* represents the mood disorder associated with a grossly expansive or elevated mood. *Hypomania* is an episode of manic symptoms that does not meet the full DSM-III-R criteria for a manic episode. Patients with *schizoaffective disorder* have features of both schizophrenia and mood disorders but cannot be classified as having just one of the two conditions without distorting some aspect of the clinical presentation.

16.4. The answer is C (*Synopsis VI*, pages 366–367; *CTP V*, page 575).

Vegetative signs in depression include *weight loss, abnormal menses, decreased libido, and fati-*

gability. Obsessive rumination is a state of tension in which a patient has a persistent thought that serves no adaptive purpose. It is seen in depression but is more common in obsessive-compulsive disorders and is usually classified not as a vegetative sign but as a disorder of thought content. Vegetative signs usually refer to functions that relate to the autonomic nervous system, which provides innervation to the blood vessels, heart, glands, viscera, and smooth muscles. Signs that point toward a slowing of the organism, rather than to a quickening, are also known as vegetative (e.g., decreased libido). In the case of decreased libido, the clinician's failure to recognize the underlying depressive disorder can sometimes lead to such inappropriate referrals as marriage or sex therapy.

Almost all depressed patients (97 percent) complain about decreased energy resulting in fatigability, difficulty in finishing tasks, school and work impairment, and decreased motivation in undertaking new projects. Approximately 80 percent of patients complain of trouble in sleeping, especially early-morning awakening. Many patients have decreased appetite and weight loss, although some have an increase in appetite, gain weight, and sleep longer than usual. The various changes in food intake and rest can aggravate coexisting medical illnesses, such as diabetes, hypertension, and chronic obstructive lung and heart diseases. Abnormal menses may present as either amenorrhea or hypermenorrhea.

16.5. The answer is C (*Synopsis VI*, page 382; *CTP V*, pages 1438 and 1656–1657).

The drug of choice for the treatment of acute mania is lithium. However, because lithium takes at least 8 to 10 days to begin to have clinical effects, acute manic episodes are most often treated with a combination of *lithium and haloperidol* (Haldol), an antipsychotic. Once the acute manic symptoms begin to subside, the dosage of the antipsychotic can be tapered down and the patient eventually maintained on lithium alone.

Monoamine oxidase inhibitors (MAOIs), such as *phenelzine* (Nardil), are antidepressants and are not indicated for the treatment of mania. MAOIs lead to a functional increase of biogenic amines, such as norepinephrine (NE), in the synaptic cleft and tend to worsen acute manic symptoms, rather than ameliorate them.

Tricyclic antidepressants, such as *nortriptyline* (Aventyl), also increase the functional level of NE in the synaptic cleft and are not indicated for the treatment of mania. Nortriptyline appears to be stimulating and may aggravate anxiety, tension, and mania.

Minor tranquilizers, such as the benzodiazepines (*chlordiazepoxide* [Librium]), are used for the treatment of anxiety and are not indicated for the control of acute psychotic manic symptoms.

16.6. The answer is E (*Synopsis VI*, pages 374–375; *CTP V*, page 893).

Patients with both manic and depressive episodes and patients with manic episodes alone are said to have *bipolar disorder*. Depression and mania are grouped together as mood disorders in DSM-III-R. Patients who present only with major depressive episodes are said to have major depressive disorder, what was termed *unipolar disorder* in the past. *Cyclothymia* is a DSM-III-R diagnosis that represents a less severe form of bipolar disorder; it includes episodes of *hypomania*. Hypomania is an episode of maniclike symptoms that does not meet the full DSM-III-R criteria for a manic episode. *Schizoaffective disorder* is a psychotic disorder with signs and symptoms compatible with both mood disorder and schizophrenia.

16.7. The answer is E (*Synopsis VI*, page 376; *CTP V*, pages 900–902).

Depressive symptoms may be associated with or superimposed on any other psychological disorder. *Cyclothymic* disorder is a syndrome of depressive and hypomanic symptoms not severe enough to be classified as depressive or manic episodes. *Schizophrenia* presents with hallucinations or delirium, and in many cases depressive symptoms also occur. Significant depressive symptoms may also be present in patients with *alcoholism* (especially when there is a family history of both depression and alcoholism) and *anxiety disorders*. Whenever a patient presents with a history of alcohol abuse or anxiety, one must question whether depressive symptoms are also present. Similarly, when a patient presents with depression, one must always question the possibility of concurrent alcohol abuse or an anxiety disorder.

16.8. The answer is C (*Synopsis VI*, pages 369–371; *CTP V*, page 897).

Approximately two thirds of depressed patients have suicidal ideation, and approximately *10 to 15 percent* do eventually commit suicide. Patients with depression are at increased risk of suicide as they begin to improve and regain the energy needed to plan and carry out a suicide (paradoxical suicide). The clinician is prudent in prescribing only a small amount of antidepressants, especially tricyclics (TCAs), on discharging a depressed patient from the hospital. In this way, a potentially suicidal patient is not given a lethal dose of antidepressant and is more likely to return for reevaluation and refills of medication.

16.9. The answer is D (*Synopsis VI*, pages 372–373; *CTP V*, pages 893–894).

The natural history of bipolar disorders is such that it is often useful to make a graph of a patient's illness and to keep the graph up-to-date as treatment proceeds. Although cyclothymia is sometimes diagnosed retrospectively in bipolar patients, no identified personality traits are specifically associated with this disorder. Bipolar disorder *most often starts with depression* (75 percent of the time in females, 67 percent in males). Bipolar disorder is a recurring illness. Most patients experience both depression and mania, although approximately *10 to 20 percent experience only manic episodes.* The manic episodes typically have a rapid onset (hours or days), but they may evolve over a few weeks. An untreated manic episode lasts about *three months*; therefore, it is unwise to discontinue drugs before that time. As the illness progresses, the amount of *time between episodes often decreases, not increases.* After approximately five episodes, however, the interepisode interval often stabilizes at about six to nine months. Some patients develop rapidly cycling bipolar disorder episodes. Rapid cycling is *much more common in women than in men*, although it is not related temporally to the menstrual cycle. Rapid cycling may be associated with treatment with tricyclic antidepressants, and patients receiving those medications often respond to combination therapies of lithium and MAOIs.

16.10. The answer is E (*Synopsis VI*, page 366; *CTP V*, pages 299–300, 1235–1236, and 1988).

Some clinicians believe that life events play the primary or principal role in depression; others are more conservative, limiting the role of life events to contributing to *the onset and the timing of a specific episode of depression.* The research data to support this relationship, however, are inconclusive. The most robust data indicate that the life event most associated with the later development of depression is *loss of a parent* before age 11. The environmental stressor most associated with the onset of an episode of depression is the *loss of a spouse.* Although reasonable data suggest some relationship between life events and the onset of depression, almost no data support a significant relationship between life events and the *onset of a manic episode.*

16.11. The answer is B (*Synopsis VI*, pages 366–367; *CTP V*, pages 392–393).

DSM-III-R distinguishes a type of major depressive episode based on the symptoms of melancholia. These symptoms include: *loss of interest* or pleasure in all or almost all activities; depression regularly worse in the *morning, not evening; psychomotor retardation or agitation*; significant *anorexia or weight loss*; and *no significant personality disturbance* before first major depressive episode. Several studies suggest that patients with these symptoms are particularly likely to respond to antidepressant medications. See Table 16.1 for the DSM-III-R diagnostic criteria for melancholic type.

16.12. The answer is C (*Synopsis VI*, pages 386–388; *CTP V*, pages 907 and 909).

Cyclothymia is generally considered to be a less severe form of bipolar disorder. The lifetime preva-

Table 16.1
Diagnostic Criteria for Melancholic Type

The presence of at least five of the following:
1. loss of interest or pleasure in all or almost all activities
2. lack of reactivity to usually pleasurable stimuli (does not feel much better, even temporarily, when something good happens)
3. depression regularly worse in the morning
4. early-morning awakening (at least two hours before usual time of awakening)
5. psychomotor retardation or agitation (not merely subjective complaints)
6. significant anorexia or weight loss (e.g., more than 5 percent of body weight in a month)
7. no significant personality disturbance before first major depressive episode
8. one or more previous major depressive episodes followed by complete or nearly complete recovery
9. previous good response to specific and adequate somatic antidepressant therapy, e.g., tricyclics, ECT, MAOI, lithium

Table from DSM-III-R, *Diagnostic and Statistical Manual of Mental Disorders*, ed 3, revised. Copyright American Psychiatric Association, Washington, DC, 1987. Used with permission.

lence has been estimated as less than 1 percent. However, this is probably an underestimate. Approximately 50 to 75 percent of patients have an onset between *ages 15 and 25.* The female-to-male ratio is approximately three to two. Approximately 30 percent of cyclothymic patients have positive *family histories* for bipolar disorder, a rate similar to patients with bipolar disorder. The prevalence of cyclothymia in the relatives of bipolar patients is much higher than the prevalence of cyclothymia in the relatives of patients with other psychiatric disorders and in healthy persons.

The cycles of cyclothymia tend to be much *shorter, not longer*, than they are in bipolar disorder. The changes in mood are irregular, sometimes occurring within hours. Approximately one half of all cyclothymic patients have depression as their major symptom.

Marital difficulties, instability of relationships, and sociopathic behaviors are common complaints among cyclothymic patients. *Drug-dependency disorders* develop in approximately 5 to 10 percent of cyclothymic patients. Patients commonly use these agents to self-medicate or to achieve further stimulation when they are hypomanic.

The pharmacological treatment of cyclothymia is *lithium.* Approximately 60 percent of patients respond when serum lithium levels are in the 0.7 to 1.0 mEq per liter range. Individual psychotherapy is often useful in helping patients become aware of their mood swings and of the consequences of their behavior when they are in either a hypomanic or a depressive state. See Table 16.2 for the diagnostic criteria for cyclothymia.

Table 16.2
Diagnostic Criteria for Cyclothymia

A. For at least two years (one year for children and adolescents), presence of numerous hypomanic episodes (all of the criteria for a manic episode, except criterion C that indicates marked impairment) and numerous periods with depressed mood or loss of interest or pleasure that did not meet criterion A of major depressive episode.
B. During a two-year period (one year in children and adolescents) of the disturbance, never without hypomanic or depressive symptoms for more than two months at a time.
C. No clear evidence of a major depressive episode or manic episode during the first two years of the disturbance (one year in children and adolescents).
   Note: After this minimum period of cyclothymia, there may be superimposed manic or major depressive episodes, in which case the additional diagnosis of bipolar disorder or bipolar disorder NOS should be given.
D. Not superimposed on a chronic psychotic disorder, such as schizophrenia or delusional disorder.
E. It cannot be established that an organic factor initiated and maintained the disturbance (e.g., repeated intoxication from drugs or alcohol).

Table from DSM-III-R, *Diagnostic and Statistical Manual of Mental Disorders*, ed 3, revised. Copyright American Psychiatric Association, Washington, DC, 1987. Used with permission.

16.13. The answer is E (*Synopsis VI*, page 382; *CTP V*, pages 49 and 1591).

L-Tryptophan, the *amino acid precursor to serotonin*, has been used as an *adjuvant to both antidepressant drugs and to lithium* treatment of bipolar disorder. L-Tryptophan has also been used alone as an antidepressant and a *hypnotic*. Recently, L-tryptophan and L-tryptophan-containing products have been recalled in the United States because of an outbreak of *eosinophilia-myalgia syndrome* (EMS) associated with use of L-tryptophan. The symptoms of EMS include fatigue, myalgia, shortness of breath, rashes, and swelling of the extremities. Congestive heart failure and death can also occur. Although several studies have shown that L-tryptophan is an efficacious adjuvant in the treatment of mood disorders, this drug should not be used for any purpose until the problem with EMS is resolved. Current evidence points to a contaminant in the manufacturing process.

16.14. The answer is D (*Synopsis VI*, pages 380–381; *CTP V*, pages 919–921).

General clinical guidelines have been set forth for the pharmacological treatment of depression. The most common clinical mistakes leading to an unsuccessful trial of an antidepressant drug are the use of too low a dosage for too short a time. Unless adverse effects prevent it, the dosage of an antidepressant should be raised to the maximum recommended levels and maintained at those levels for *at least four weeks, not two weeks*, before a drug trial is considered unsuccessful. If a patient is improving on a low dosage of the drug, the dosage should not be raised unless clinical improvement stops before maximal benefit is obtained. If a patient seems not to be responding to appropriate doses of a drug after one to two weeks, a clinician may decide to obtain a plasma concentration of the drug if the test is available for the particular drug being used. This test may indicate either noncompliance or a particularly unusual pharmacokinetic disposition of the drug, thereby suggesting altering the dosage. If a patient has not responded to the drug after four weeks, then the clinician can consider supplementation of the drug with L-*triiodothyronine (T_3) (Cytomel), not levothyroxine (T_4) (Synthroid)*, or with lithium for an additional two to three weeks. Until recently, *tricyclic antidepressants* (TCAs) were almost always the first drug of choice. This is no longer necessarily the rule, as the newer antidepressants, such as fluoxetine (Prozac) and trazodone (Desyrel), have been shown to be equally effective, with fewer side effects than TCAs.

Antidepressant treatment should be maintained for *at least six months* or the length of the previous episode, whichever is longer. Long-term treatment may be indicated as prophylaxis against depression in patients with a history of recurrent serious depression. The only tricyclic antidepressant known to have a therapeutic window is *nortriptyline (Pamelor), not maprotiline (Ludiomil)*. A plasma level of more than 150 mg per mL may reduce the efficacy of nortriptyline. Maprotiline, a tetracyclic antidepressant, has been associated with an increased incidence of seizures if the dose is raised too quickly or is maintained at too high a level.

16.15. The answer is E (all) (*Synopsis VI*, pages 368–369; *CTP V*, pages 905–907).

The patient was experiencing a manic episode, characterized by a predominantly elevated, expansive, or irritable mood. The mood may be *emotionally labile*, with rapid shifts to brief depression from mania. The essential feature of a manic disorder is a distinct period of intense psychophysiological activation with a number of accompanying symptoms, such as lack of judgment of the consequences of actions, pressure of speech, flight of ideas, inflated self-esteem, and, at times, hypersexuality. *Delusions* of grandiosity, *hallucinations*, and ideas of reference also may be present. *Nocturnal electroencephalography (EEG)* findings in mania have shown a decreased total sleep time, a decreased percentage of dream time, and an increased dream latency. These findings have been interpreted as indicating that circadian rhythm activities are delayed in mania because the activity of the intrinsic pacemaker is increased. In DSM-III-R, the diagnosis of manic episodes does not require a specific duration, such as three days, but, rather, only a distinct period of abnormally and persistently disordered mood. Table 16.3 lists the DSM-III-R diagnostic criteria for manic episode.

Table 16.3
Diagnostic Criteria for Manic Episode

Note: A "manic syndrome" is defined as including criteria A, B, and C below. A "hypomanic syndrome" is defined as including criteria A and B, but not C, i.e., no marked impairment.
A. A distinct period of abnormally and persistently elevated, expansive, or irritable mood.
B. During the period of mood disturbance, at least three of the following symptoms have persisted (four if the mood is only irritable) and have been present to a significant degree:
1. inflated self-esteem or grandiosity
2. decreased need for sleep, e.g., feels rested after only three hours of sleep
3. more talkative than usual or pressure to keep talking
4. flight of ideas or subjective experience that thoughts are racing
5. distractibility, i.e., attention too easily drawn to unimportant or irrelevant external stimuli
6. increase in goal-directed activity (either socially, at work or school, or sexually) or psychomotor agitation
7. excessive involvement in pleasurable activities which have a high potential for painful consequences, e.g., the person engages in unrestrained buying sprees, sexual indiscretions, or foolish business investments
C. Mood disturbance sufficiently severe to cause marked impairment in occupational functioning or in usual social activities or relationships with others, or to necessitate hospitalization to prevent harm to self or others.
D. At no time during the disturbance have there been delusions or hallucinations for as long as two weeks in the absence of prominent mood symptoms (i.e., before the mood symptoms developed or after they have remitted).
E. Not superimposed on schizophrenia, schizophreniform disorder, delusional disorder, or psychotic disorder NOS.
F. It cannot be established that an organic factor initiated and maintained the disturbance. **Note:** Somatic antidepressant treatment (e.g., drugs, ECT) that apparently precipitates a mood disturbance should not be considered an etiologic organic factor.

Table from DSM-III-R, *Diagnostic and Statistical Manual of Mental Disorders*, ed 3, revised. Copyright American Psychiatric Association, Washington, DC, 1987. Used with permission.

16.16. The answer is E (all) (*Synopsis VI*, pages 249 and 368; *CTP V*, page 902).

There are certain age-associated features of major depression. Excessive clinging to parents and school phobia, both of which reflect *separation anxiety*, may be symptoms of depression in children. In latency and in early adolescent boys especially, negative and *antisocial behavior* may occur (depressive equivalents). Sexual acting out, truancy, and *running away* are seen in older boys and girls. In the elderly, *pseudodementia*—that is, depression presenting primarily as a loss of intellectual functioning—must be carefully differentiated from true dementia caused by organic mental disorder. DSM-III-R refers to pseudodementia as the *dementia syndrome of depression*.

According to DSM-III-R, abnormalities of mood in dementia are less frequent and, when present, less pervasive than in depression. Cognitive defects in depression usually take place at about the same time as the depression itself, and the patient expresses concern about the memory defect. Symptoms usually progress more rapidly than in true dementia. In dementia, however, depression usually follows the patient's intellectual deterioration, which the patient then rationalizes or denies. Also, in pseudodementia the patient may have a history of previous mood disorder. DSM-III-R states that, in the dementia syndrome of depression, the depression unmasks an underlying structural abnormality in the central nervous system, resulting in clinical features of dementia. DSM-III-R also states that, in the absence of a specific organic cause, if the symptoms of depression are at least as prominent as those suggesting dementia, it is best to diagnose a major depressive episode and to assume that the symptoms suggesting dementia are secondary to the depression.

16.17. The answer is B (1, 3) (*Synopsis VI*, page 373; *CTP V*, pages 893–894).

Bipolar disorder has a *worse prognosis* than major depressive disorder. Patients with *pure manic symptoms* do better than patients with depressed or mixed symptoms. The presence of *psychotic symptoms* during manic episodes does *not imply a poor prognosis*. Patients may have from 2 to 30 episodes of mania (with a mean of 9), but 40 percent have more than 10 episodes on long-term follow-up, *15 percent of patients are well*, 45 percent are well but have had multiple relapses, 30 percent are in partial remission, and 10 percent are chronically ill.

16.18. The answer is A (1, 2, 3) (*Synopsis VI*, page 369; *CTP V*, page 904).

Depressed patients with delusions or hallucinations are said to have major depression with psychotic features. Delusions and hallucinations that are consistent with a depressed mood are said to be mood-congruent. Mood-congruent delusions include those of *guilt*, sinfulness, worthlessness, *poverty*, failure, persecution, and *terminal somatic illnesses* (e.g., cancer, "rotting" brain). The content of the mood-incongruent delusions is either not consistent with a depressed mood or, in essence, mood-neutral. Examples of mood-incongruent delusions are *thought insertion*, thought withdrawal, and thought broadcasting.

16.19. The answer is A (1, 2, 3) (*Synopsis VI*, page 378; *CTP V*, page 631).

Many pharmacological agents, such as *amphetamine* and *bromide*, may precipitate mania, as can antidepressant treatment or withdrawal. *Levodopa* (Larodopa, Dopar), an agonist of dopamine that has been found to produce manic symptoms, has also been implicated as a pharmacological cause of depressive symptoms. *Tetracycline* is just one example of the many drugs associated with depression (not mania). See Table 16.4 for a list of the drugs associated with manic symptoms.

Table 16.4
Drugs Associated with Manic Symptoms

Amphetamines
Baclofen (Lioresal)
Bromide
Bromocriptine (Parlodel)
Captopril (Capoten)
Cimetidine (Tagamet)
Cocaine
Corticosteroids (including ACTH)
Cyclosporine
Disulfiram (Antabuse)
Hallucinogens (intoxication and flashbacks)
Hydralazine
Isoniazid
Levodopa (Larodopa, Dopar)
Methylphenidate (Ritalin)
Metrizamide (following myelography)
Opiates
Procarbazine (Matulane)
Procyclidine (Kemadrin)
Yohimbine (Yocon)

16.20.   The answer is E (all) (*Synopsis VI*, page 364; *CTP V*, pages 863–866).

Major (unipolar) depression is *more common in women than in men*. The reasons for this difference are unknown but may include varying stresses, childbirth, learned helplessness, hormonal differences, and masked depression in men. The difference is not the result of socially biased diagnostic practices. In bipolar disorder the prevalence is only slightly higher in women than in men (about 1.2 to 1).

Major depression can begin from childhood through senescence, but 50 percent of patients have the onset between ages 20 and 50, with a *mean of around 40*. Bipolar disorder begins at a somewhat earlier age, with a range from childhood to 50 and a mean of 30.

The prevalence of mood disorder *does not differ according to race*. There is, however, a clinical tendency to underdiagnose mood disorders and overdiagnose schizophrenia in patients who are from a racial or cultural background different from the examiner's background. White psychiatrists, for example, tend to underdiagnose mood disorders in black and Hispanic patients.

In general, major depression occurs more often in persons who do not have a close interpersonal relationship or who are *divorced or separated*. Bipolar disorder may be more common in divorced and single persons than in married persons.

16.21.   The answer is E (all) (*Synopsis VI*, page 371; *CTP V*, pages 905–907).

On the mental status examination of a patient classified as bipolar, manic phase, one may see both *mood-congruent* and *mood-incongruent hallucinations and delusions, neologisms*, and *clang associations*. Mood-congruent hallucinations and delusions

involve grandiose themes, and mood-incongruent psychotic features involve such ideas as thought withdrawal, insertion, and broadcasting. The more disorganized the thought process in acute mania, the more likely it is that the patient exhibits such features as neologisms (new words created by the patient, often from condensations of two or more actual words) and clang associations (associations based on the sounds of words, rather than on meaning).

16.22.   The answer is A (1, 2, 3) (*Synopsis VI*, page 365; *CTP V*, pages 874–877).

A variety of neuroendocrine dysregulations have been reported in people with mood disorders. It is likely that neuroendocrine abnormalities reflect dysregulations in biogenic amine input to the hypothalamus.

Neuroendocrine markers of depression include a *blunted release of thyroid-stimulating hormone* (TSH) on administration of thyroid-releasing hormone (TRH); a *decreased release of growth hormone* (GH) to noradrenergic stimulation with clonidine (Catapres), an agonist that selectively stimulates presynaptic α_2-receptors; *decreased prolactin release* to L-tryptophan administration; and *decreased (not increased) nocturnal secretion of melatonin*. Although a neuroendocrine dysregulation may be the primary cause of mood disorders, at the present time it is best to consider neuroendocrine testing as a window into the brain.

16.23.   The answer is A (1, 2, 3) (*Synopsis VI*, page 365; *CTP V*, pages 868–878).

Both the symptoms of the mood disorders and biological research findings support the hypothesis that mood disorders involve pathology of the *limbic system*, the *basal ganglia*, and the *hypothalamus*. Pathology of the *corpus callosum* has not been implicated in the etiology of mood disorders. Neurological disorders of the basal ganglia and the limbic system are likely to present with depressive symptoms. The limbic system and the basal ganglia are intimately connected, and a major role in the production of emotions is hypothesized for the limbic system. Dysfunction of the hypothalamus is suggested by the alterations in sleep, appetite, and sexual behavior and by the biological changes in endocrine, immunological, and chronobiological measures. The stooped posture, motor slowness, and minor cognitive impairment seen in depression are similar to disorders of the basal ganglia, such as Parkinson's disease and other subcortical dementias.

16.24.   The answer is A (1, 2, 3) (*Synopsis VI*, page 371; *CTP V*, pages 911–913).

Objective rating scales of depression include the *Zung, Raskin*, and *Hamilton* scales and can be useful in clinical practice for the documentation of clinical state in depressed patients. The Zung Self-Rating Scale is a 20-item report scale. A normal score is 34 or less, and a depressed score is 50 or above. This scale provides a global index of the intensity of depressive symptoms. The Raskin Severity of Depression Scale is a clinician-rated scale measuring severity of depression as reported by the patient and observed by the physician on a five-point scale of three dimensions: verbal report, behavior displayed, and secondary symptoms. It has a range of 3 to 13; normal is 3; depressed is 7 or above. The Hamilton Depression Scale is a widely used scale with 24 items, each of which is rated 0 to 4 or 0 to 2, with a maximum range of 0 to 76. The ratings are derived from a clinical interview with the patient in which questions about feelings of guilt, suicide, sleep habits, and other symptoms are evaluated. The *Holmes-Rahe Scale* is a scale correlating stressful life events with medical illness. Certain events carry more points on a stress scale than do others, and a cumulated number of stress points in a year is correlated with a certain increased risk of medical illness.

16.25. The answer is A (1, 2, 3) (*Synopsis VI*, page 366; *CTP V*, pages 888–890, 934–936, and 1543).

No single personality trait or type has been established as being uniquely predisposed to depression. All humans, of whatever personality pattern, can and do become depressed under appropriate circumstances. However, certain personality types may be at greater risk for depression. These include the *oral-dependent, obsessive-compulsive*, and *hysterical* personality types. Personality types who use projection and other externalizing modes of defense may be at lower risk. They include the antisocial and *paranoid* personality types.

Psychoanalytic theories of depression are of interest. Karl Abraham thought that episodes of depression are precipitated by the loss of a libidinal object. In a regressive process the ego retreats from its mature functioning state to one in which the infantile trauma of the oral-sadistic stage of libidinal development dominates because of a fixation process in earliest childhood. In Freud's structural theory the introjection of the lost object into the ego leads to the typical depressive symptoms characteristic of a lack of energy available to the ego. Unable to retaliate against the lost object, the superego flails out at the psychic representation of the lost object, now internalized in the ego as an introject. When the ego overcomes or merges with the superego, there is a release of energy that was previously bound in the depressive symptoms, and mania supervenes with the typical symptoms of excess.

16.26. The answer is E (all) (*Synopsis VI*, pages 373–374; *CTP V*, pages 895–896).

The DSM-III-R diagnostic criteria for the recently described subtype of mood disorder, the seasonal pattern subtype, include a *regular temporal relation* between the onset and remission of a mood disorder (either bipolar or major depression) and a particular 60-day period of the year (e.g., depression regularly occurring between the beginning of October and the end of November, depression lifting from mid-February to mid-April) and by *at least three episodes in three separate years,* with *at least two of the years being consecutive* and *a full remission within a particular 60-day period.* The seasonal pattern of depression is often described as being characterized by psychomotor slowing, hypersomnia, and hyperphagia. The seasonal pattern of mania presents similarly to a typical manic episode. The seasonal pattern mood disturbances may be associated with abnormal melatonin regulation and often respond to treatment with sleep deprivation or exposure to light. Table 16.5 lists the diagnostic criteria for seasonal pattern.

16.27. The answer is A (1, 2, 3) (*Synopsis VI*, page 372; *CTP V*, pages 893–894).

Major depressive disorder is fundamentally a cyclic disorder with periods of illness separated by periods of mental health. Approximately 50 to 85 percent of patients have a *second depressive episode,* very often in the *four to six months* after the resolution of the first episode. The risk of recurrence is increased by coexisting dysthymia, alcohol and drug abuse, anxiety, and *old (not young) age of onset.* At long-term follow-up, approximately 20 percent have significant impairment, with *men being more likely than women* to experience a chronically impaired course.

16.28. The answer is E (all) (*Synopsis VI*, page 365; *CTP V*, pages 872–874).

The biological markers of depression include a variety of neuroendocrine dysregulations. Neuroen-

Table 16.5
Diagnostic Criteria for Seasonal Pattern

A. There has been a regular temporal relationship between the onset of an episode of bipolar disorder (including bipolar disorder NOS) or recurrent major depression (including depressive disorder NOS) and a particular 60-day period of the year (e.g., regular appearance of depression between the beginning of October and the end of November).
Note: Do not include cases in which there is an obvious effect of seasonally related psychosocial stressors, e.g., regularly being unemployed every winter.
B. Full remissions (or a change from depression to mania or hypomania) also occurred within a particular 60-day period of the year (e.g., depression disappears from mid-February to mid-April).
C. There have been at least three episodes of mood disturbance in three separate years that demonstrated the temporal seasonal relationship defined in A and B; at least two of the years were consecutive.
D. Seasonal episodes of mood disturbance, as described above, outnumbered any nonseasonal episodes of such disturbance that may have occurred by more than three to one.

Table from DSM-III-R, *Diagnostic and Statistical Manual of Mental Disorders*, ed 3, revised. Copyright American Psychiatric Association, Washington, DC, 1987. Used with permission.

docrine markers of depression in some patients include decreased basal levels of *follicle-stimulating hormone (FSH)* and *luteinizing hormone (LH)*, decreased *testosterone levels* in males, hypersecretion of *cortisol* (which has been used in the dexamethasone-suppression test), and a hyperactivity in general of the *hypothalamic-pituitary-adrenal axis.*

16.29. The answer is E (all) (*Synopsis VI*, pages 371–372; *CTP V*, pages 893–894).

The course of a major depressive disorder usually includes the following: An *untreated episode* of depression lasts *6 to 13 months*; most *treated episodes* last approximately *three months*. The *withdrawal of antidepressants before three months* have elapsed almost always results in the return of symptoms. As patients become older, they tend to have more frequent episodes that last longer. Over a 20-year period the *mean number of episodes is five to six.*

16.30. The answer is E (all) (*Synopsis VI*, pages 376–378; *CTP V*, pages 776–777).

Although it can be difficult to differentiate between a manic episode and a schizophrenic episode, there are a few clinical guidelines: (1) *Quality of mood*: merriment, elation, and infectiousness of mood are much more common in mania than in schizophrenia. (2) *Psychomotor activity*: the combination of an elated mood, rapid or pressured speech, and hyperactivity heavily weighs toward a diagnosis of mania, although hyperactivity can also occur in schizophrenia. (3) *Speed of onset*: the onset in mania, as opposed to schizophrenia, is often more rapid, being a marked change from previous behavior. (4) *Family history*: half of bipolar (manic) patients have a family history of a mood disorder, whereas there is not as high a correlation in schizophrenia.

16.31. The answer is E (all) (*Synopsis VI*, pages 375–377; *CTP V*, page 631).

Many substances used to treat somatic illnesses may trigger depressive symptoms. Commonly prescribed medications associated with depressive symptoms include *analgesics* (e.g., ibuprofen), *antibacterials* (e.g., ampicillin), *antipsychotics* (e.g., phenothiazines), and *antihypertensives* (e.g., propranolol [Inderal]). Certain substances used to treat medical disorders may also trigger a manic response. The most commonly encountered manic response is to steroids. Cases exist in which spontaneous manic and depressive episodes originated some years later in patients whose first illness episode seemed to be triggered by the medical use of steroids. Other drugs are also known to have the potential for initiating a manic syndrome, including amphetamines and tricyclic antidepressants (e.g., imipramine [Tofranil], amitriptyline [Elavil, Endep]). Table 16.6 lists drugs that can cause depression. See also Table 16.4 for drugs associated with manic symptoms.

**Table 16.6
Drugs That Can Cause Depressive Symptoms**

Analgesics, anti-inflammatory
 Ibuprofen (Motrin)
 Indomethacin (Indocin)
 Opiates
 Phenacetin
Antibacterials, antifungals
 Ampicillin (Unasyn)
 Cycloserine (Seromycin)
 Ethionamide (Trecator-SC)
 Griseofulvin (Fulvicin)
 Metronidazole (Flagyl)
 Nalidixic acid (NegGram)
 Nitrofurantoin (Macrodantin)
 Streptomycin
 Sulfamethoxazole (Bactrim)
 Sulfonamides
 Tetracycline (Achromycin)
Antihypertensives, cardiac drugs
 Alphamethyldopa (Aldomet)
 Beta-blockers (propranolol [Inderal])
 Bethanidine
 Clonidine (Catapres)
 Digitalis (Digoxin)
 Guanethidine (Ismelin)
 Hydralazine (Apresoline)
 Lidocaine (Xylocaine)
 Methoserpidine
 Prazosin (Minipress)
 Procainamide (Procan)
 Quanabenzacetate
 Rescinnamine (Moderil)
 Reserpine (Diupres)
 Veratrum
Antineoplastics
 C-Asparaginase (Elspar)
 6-Azaduridine
 Azathioprine (AZT) (Imuran)
 Bleomycin (Blenoxane)
 Trimethoprim
 Vincristine (Oncovin)
Neurological, psychiatric
 Amantadine (Symmetrel)
 Antipsychotics (butyrophenones [Haldol], oxyindoles, phenothiazines)
 Baclofen (Lioresal)
 Bromocriptine (Parlodel)
 Carbamazepine (Tegretol)
 Levodopa (Larodopa)
 Phenytoin (Dilantin)
 Sedatives, hypnotics (barbiturates, benzodiazepines, chloral hydrate)
 Tetrabenazine
Steroids, hormones
 Corticosteroids (including ACTH)
 Danazol
 Oral contraceptives
 Prednisone
 Triamcinolone (Aristocort)
Miscellaneous
 Acetazolamide (Diamox)
 Choline
 Cimetidine (Tagamet)
 Cyproheptadine (Periactin)
 Diphenoxylate
 Disulfiram (Antabuse)
 Methysergide (Sansert)
 Stimulants (amphetamines, fenfluramine [Pondimin])

Table 16.7
Diagnostic Criteria for Dysthymia

A. Depressed mood (or can be irritable mood in children and adolescents) for most of the day, more days than not, as indicated either by subjective account or observation by others, for at least two years (one year for children and adolescents).
B. Presence, while depressed, of at least two of the following:
  1. poor appetite or overeating
  2. insomnia or hypersomnia
  3. low energy or fatigue
  4. low self-esteem
  5. poor concentration or difficulty making decisions
  6. feelings of hopelessness
C. During a two-year period (one-year for children and adolescents) of the disturbance, never without the symptoms in A for more than two months at a time.
D. No evidence of an unequivocal major depressive episode during the first two years (one year for children and adolescents) of the disturbance.
  Note: There may have been a previous major depressive episode, provided there was a full remission (no significant signs or symptoms for six months) before development of the dysthymia. In addition, after these two years (one year in children or adolescents) of dysthymia, there may be superimposed episodes of major depression, in which case both diagnoses are given.
E. Has never had a manic episode or an unequivocal hypomanic episode.
F. Not superimposed on a chronic psychotic disorder, such as schizophrenia or delusional disorder.
G. It cannot be established that an organic factor initiated and maintained the disturbance (e.g., prolonged administration of an antihypertensive medication).
Specify primary or **secondary type:**
  Primary type: the mood disturbance is not related to a preexisting, chronic, nonmood, Axis I or Axis III disorder, e.g., anorexia nervosa, somatization disorder, a psychoactive substance dependence disorder, an anxiety disorder, or rheumatoid arthritis.
  Secondary type: the mood disturbance is apparently related to a preexisting, chronic, nonmood, Axis I or Axis III disorder.
Specify early onset or **late onset:**
  Early onset: onset of the disturbance before age 21
  Late onset: onset of the disturbance at age 21 or later

Table from DSM-III-R, *Diagnostic and Statistical Manual of Mental Disorders*, ed 3, revised. Copyright American Psychiatric Association, Washington, DC, 1987. Used with permission.

16.32. The answer is E (all) (*Synopsis VI*, page 364; *CTP V*, pages 869–872).

The causes of mood disorders are unknown, but there are many etiological theories, including biological hypotheses. One such hypothesis involves the biogenic amines, which include three catecholamines—dopamine, norepinephrine (NE), and epinephrine. Other biogenic amines include the indoleamine serotonin and acetylcholine. The biogenic amine hypothesis is based, in part, on the observa-

tions that such drugs as tricyclic antidepressants (TCAs) and *monoamine oxidase inhibitors (MAOIs)* potentiate or increase brain amines, cause behavior stimulation and excitement, and have an antidepressant effect. Conversely, drugs that deplete or inactivate central amines produce sedation or depression. *Imipramine* (Tofranil) binding sites (a neurochemical label of serotonin reuptake sites) in platelets have been reported to be decreased in depressed patients and in all postmortem brains of patients who committed suicide. Some studies have shown that there may be a functional shortage of brain NE in depression. An NE metabolite, *3-methoxy-4-hydroxyphenylglycol (MHPG)*, has been found to be decreased in the cerebrospinal fluid and urine of some depressed patients. Drugs that reduce NE levels, such as methyldopapropranolol and reserpine (Serpasil), may cause depression; and *amphetamine*, which leads to a functional increase of NE, causes elevated mood.

16.33–16.35

16.33. The answer is A (*Synopsis VI*, page 372; *CTP V*, pages 902–904).

16.34. The answer is B (*Synopsis VI*, pages 383–386; *CTP V*, pages 902–904).

16.35. The answer is A (*Synopsis VI*, page 373; *CTP V*, pages 902–904).

Dysthymia does not include patients who have *episodic periods of mild depression*. By definition, dysthymic patients do not have any *psychotic symptoms*. Dysthymia is characterized by chronic (not episodic) nonpsychotic signs and symptoms of depression that meet specific diagnostic criteria but do not meet the diagnostic criteria for major depression. Approximately 5 to 10 percent of patients with *major depression may have psychotic symptoms*, including both delusions and hallucinations. Major depression is fundamentally a cyclic disorder with periods of illness separated by periods of health. Many patients with major depression have a positive family history for mood disorders, and 70 to 80 percent of acute major depressions are responsive to antidepressant medication. It is also true that some patients with dysthymia have a positive family history for mood disorders, decreased rapid eye movement latency, and a positive therapeutic response to antidepressants. These dysthymic patients seem to have a subaffective or submood syndrome that shares a genetic and pathophysiological basis with major depression. A new addition to the description of dysthymia appears in DSM-III-R, a categorization of two types of dysthymia based on *onset before and after age 21*. See Table 16.7 for the DSM-III-R diagnostic criteria for dysthymia.

17

Anxiety Disorders (or Anxiety and Phobic Neuroses)

Psychiatrists recognize anxiety as a psychological entity of paramount importance. Under the terms "anxiety state," "anxiety reaction," and "anxiety neurosis," the syndromes in which anxiety is a prime feature have been given recognition as a group of disorders that represent one of the most prevalent mental health problems today.

Among psychiatric symptoms, the distinction between normal and pathological anxiety is probably one of the most difficult to make. The student should be familiar with the range of normal anxiety and its adaptive functions. The psychodynamic concept of defense mechanisms is intimately tied to the concept of anxiety, and the student should be able to define and give examples of defense mechanisms (e.g., denial, projection). In addition to knowing psychodynamic formulations regarding anxiety, the student should understand the behavioral, existential, and biological theories regarding both normal and abnormal anxiety. In the biological theories the student should appreciate the putative roles of norepinephrine and γ-aminobutyric acid (GABA) in anxiety and how the locus ceruleus and the limbic system, in particular, may be involved.

The American Psychiatric Association's revised third edition of *Diagnostic and Statistical Manual of Mental Disorders* (DSM-III-R) has probably had a greater effect on the conceptualization of anxiety disorders than on any other class of psychiatric disorders. In DSM-III-R anxiety disorders include panic disorder with and without agoraphobia, agoraphobia without a history of panic disorder, social and simple phobias, obsessive-compulsive disorder (OCD), posttraumatic stress disorder (PTSD), generalized anxiety disorder, and anxiety disorder not otherwise specified (NOS). Anxiety can often be a symptom of an underlying med-

ical or neurological disorder, and the student should know how to approach the differentiation of these nonpsychiatric diseases.

The hallmark symptom of panic disorder is spontaneous, episodic, and intense periods of anxiety, often resulting in the development of agoraphobia as an additional symptom. The student should understand the interrelationships of these two disorders and the history of how they came to be associated in the nomenclature. Students who are aware of their epidemiology, signs, and symptoms are more likely to recognize these disorders in the emergency room and in general practice. The research data involving lactate infusions and the coexistence of mitral-valve prolapse in anxious patients should be known to the student, who should also recognize the major pharmacological treatments for the disorders and how psychosocial approaches, such as behavior therapy, are often necessary to address residual symptoms, including agoraphobia.

The student should be able to describe how agoraphobia, social phobia, and simple phobia are different in their clinical features and epidemiology. Phobias are important clinical disorders to understand in terms of both psychoanalytic and behavioral formulations. A variety of pharmacological treatments may also be effective in social phobias.

Obsessive-compulsive disorder is an example of how psychodynamic formulations can be used to describe an illness. This disorder is also interesting to psychiatrists because of its responsiveness to particular pharmacological treatments. Obsessive-compulsive disorder can result in various symptom patterns, of which the student should be able to give clinical examples. The student should understand the data regarding the relation between OCD and premorbid personality disorders and various pathological defense mechanisms. The student should also know the biological data that suggest some pathophysiological overlap between OCD and the mood disorders.

The psychiatric problems of veterans returning from Vietnam was the major impetus for psychiatry to increase its interest in understanding and effectively treating PTSD. This disorder is present in a wide range of people who have experienced some extreme psychosocial stressor, so it should be of general interest to physicians, and its subtle shadings of symptoms should be familiar to all clinicians. As with all the anxiety disorders, both psychodynamic and biological theories should be known, and both the pharmacological and the psychosocial therapies applicable to this disorder should be appreciated.

For the diagnosis to be made, generalized anxiety disorder should meet the specific diagnostic criteria set forth in DSM-III-R. The disorder should not be confused with anxiety disorder NOS, and other psychiatric and medical diagnoses should also be carefully ruled out before making this diagnosis. Generalized anxiety disorder is a major indication for treatment with antianxiety drugs for which the student should know the appropriate prescribing information. Students should read Chapter 17 of *Synopsis VI*, "Anxiety Disorders (or Anxiety and Phobic Neuroses)," and Chapter 18 of *CTP V*, "Anxiety Disorders (Anxiety and Phobic Neuroses)," which cover the anxiety disorders. By studying the questions and answers below, students can test their knowledge of these areas.

HELPFUL HINTS

The names, cases, terms, and acronyms related to anxiety should be known.

anxiety	lactate infusions	cleanliness
fear	PET	ambivalence
Charles Darwin	MVP	magical thinking
stress	panic attacks	dysthymia
conflict	imipramine (Tofranil)	clomipramine (Anafranil)
repression	anticipatory anxiety	aversive conditioning
panic disorders	Little Hans	thought stopping
phobias: agoraphobia, social, simple	Little Albert	soldier's heart
	counterphobic attitude	Da Costa
obsessive-compulsive disorder	Otto Fenichel	shell shock
posttraumatic stress disorder	John B. Watson	trauma
generalized anxiety disorder	ego-dystonic	sleep EEG studies
Sigmund Freud	propranolol (Inderal)	secondary gain
ANS	Joseph Wolpe	numbing
GABA	systematic desensitization	dissociative states
norepinephrine	flooding	MMPI, Rorschach
MHPG	hypnosis	time-limited psychotherapy
DBI	implosion	depression
serotonin	isolation	benzodiazepines
aplysia	undoing	dopamine
limbic system	reaction formation	adrenergic
cerebral cortex	aggression	

QUESTIONS

DIRECTIONS: Each of the questions or incomplete statements below is followed by five suggested responses or completions. Select the *one* that is *best* in each case.

Questions 17.1–17.3

A 28-year-old housewife sought psychiatric treatment because of a fear of storms that had

become progressively more disturbing to her. Although she was frightened by storms since she was a child, the fear had seemed to abate somewhat during her adolescence but had been increasing in severity over the past few years. This gradual exacerbation of her anxiety, plus the fear that she might pass it on to her children, led her to seek treatment.

She recognized the irrational nature of her fear of thunder. She reported that she began to feel anxiety long before a storm arrived. A weather report predicting a storm later in the week could cause her anxiety to increase to the point that she worried for days before the storm. During a storm she did several things to reduce her anxiety. Being with another person reduced her fear, so she often made plans to visit friends or relatives or to go shopping when a storm was threatening. Sometimes, if a storm was forecast and her husband was away, she stayed overnight with a relative. During a storm she covered her eyes or moved to a part of the house far from windows, where she could not see the lightning.

The patient was in good physical health. At the time she entered treatment, there were no unusually stressful situations in her life or other psychiatric difficulties. [From *DSM-III-R Case Book*. Used with permission.]

17.1. This patient is best classified as suffering from
A. simple phobia
B. agoraphobia
C. schizoid personality
D. social phobia
E. avoidant disorder

17.2. Which of the following drugs may be of use in managing this patient?
A. Propranolol (Inderal)
B. Phenelzine (Nardil)
C. Diazepam (Valium)
D. Imipramine (Tofranil)
E. All the above

17.3. All the following techniques of behavioral therapy may be used in the treatment of this patient *except*
A. standing outside in a thunderstorm
B. hearing a tape recording of a thunderstorm
C. exploring aspects of the behavior's secondary gain
D. being hypnotized before the occurrence of a thunderstorm
E. visualizing a thunderstorm

Questions 17.4–17.18

17.4. The most common type of phobia for which treatment is sought is
A. photophobia
B. thanatophobia
C. acrophobia
D. agoraphobia
E. nyctophobia

17.5. All the following are among the drugs used in the treatment of panic disorder *except*
A. imipramine (Tofranil)
B. phenelzine (Nardil)
C. desipramine (Norpramin)
D. propranolol (Inderal)
E. buspirone (BuSpar)

17.6. A 49-year-old man, Roger, came to a Montreal psychiatric outpatient clinic and said that his family thought he needed help. He did not have any specific complaints but acknowledged that, because of "perfectionism and immobility," he had been unable to work for about seven years.

Roger had been reared in a professional family in a small city in British Columbia. He reported that he had had "a happy childhood" and did well in school. However, his wife, whom he had met in the sixth grade, claimed he was "methodical and slow" even in his teens. He graduated from the university but was a semester late because he was unable to complete his written assignments on time.

Roger worked for a small company in an administrative capacity for four years, then left to join a medium-sized real estate development company. Initially, he did well; but, as time went on, he found it increasingly difficult to get to work on time, primarily because, while he was getting dressed, articles of clothing had to be arranged in a special way before he could put them on. He began to miss deadlines for reports. He had no difficulty in starting the reports but was often unable to complete them because he wanted them to be "perfect." In addition, he had difficulty keeping up with opening the mail at home and paying bills. He was aware that they had to be paid, but he somehow could not get around to doing it.

In his early 30s Roger settled into a routine of getting up later than he intended. Even though he knew he would be late for work, he insisted that he have exactly the same breakfast of orange juice, cereal, and eggs every day; while eating, he read the paper; then he took a shower, shaved, and dressed. No matter how late he was, he was unable to shower in less than 45 minutes or to dress in less than 30 minutes. Frequently, he was not ready to leave the house before noon. Nevertheless, when he was at work, he generally did a good job except for his difficulty with finishing reports.

His wife reported that he had gradually become slower in completing tasks. After losing his position at the development company, he was able to run his own real estate company for a few years; but after a large deal fell through, he stayed at home most of the time and finally lost his business and source of income. At the time of the clinic interview, he was facing disciplinary proceedings from the real estate board in his city because he had completed a deal for a friend but had not gotten around to paying his real estate broker license fee.

When Roger came for help, he had unfinished tasks that went back 14 years. He had mail that had been unopened for more than 10 years, yet he refused to allow anyone to touch the mail because they would "not do it properly." His wife decided that she would deal with any accounts that she could identify in the mail and leave the rest of the mail to him. For the first month after delivery, the letters would remain in the hallway; then they would be moved to the dining room table and, after about a year, to a steadily growing pile in the basement for "proper sorting." Roger's old car, which was rusted out, remained in the driveway for seven years before he got around to calling someone to tow it away.

Roger's wife went back to work to support the family. Roger was left alone in the house in the morning and had an unvarying daily routine. He woke up at 7 AM but was unable to shower and get dressed before 11 or 12. He then made his standard breakfast and read the paper. Those activities usually took until 4 or 5 PM. After accomplishing nothing during the day, he watched television in the evening and eventually went to bed at 2 or 3 AM. In contrast to his inability to initiate or complete tasks on his own, he was able to help others in writing reports and was often helpful to neighbors with real estate problems.

Roger denied ever having any checking rituals or other typical compulsions, such as repetitively washing his hands. Although he denied having a depressed mood and symptoms commonly seen in depressive disorder, he described his thinking as "sticky." [From *DSM-III-R Case Book*, used with permission.]

The most likely diagnosis in this case was
A. obsessive-compulsive disorder
B. agoraphobia
C. generalized anxiety disorder
D. temporal lobe epilepsy
E. depression with obsessive thoughts

17.7. The principal neurotransmitter associated with anxiety that mediates presynaptic inhibition in the central nervous system is
A. endogenous opioids
B. γ-aminobutyric acid (GABA)
C. norepinephrine
D. histamine
E. adenosine

17.8. A 30-year-old executive had severe distress whenever he thought about having to travel alone to another city on business. He got dizzy, became nauseated, and felt chest pain, and sometimes his surroundings took on an unreal and unfamiliar quality. As a result, he refused to accept travel assignments that required him to be away from home. The disorder most likely to account for this clinical picture is
A. panic disorder
B. generalized anxiety disorder
C. simple phobia
D. agoraphobia
E. social phobia

17.9. The most effective pharmacological treatment for obsessive-compulsive disorder is
A. imipramine (Tofranil)
B. clomipramine (Anafranil)
C. amitriptyline (Elavil)
D. phenelzine (Nardil)
E. tranylcypromine (Parnate)

17.10. Counterphobic attitudes may be represented by
A. parachute jumping
B. rock climbing
C. hunting
D. para-sailing
E. all the above

17.11. Generalized anxiety disorder is characterized by
A. a duration of six weeks or longer
B. a single issue as the focus of anxiety
C. symptoms of autonomic hyperactivity
D. realistic worry about life circumstances
E. all the above

17.12. The likelihood of posttraumatic stress disorder developing is influenced by
A. age
B. severity of the stressor
C. availability of social support
D. preexisting psychiatric disorders
E. all the above

17.13. Obsessive-compulsive disorder
A. has a lifetime prevalence of 20 to 24 percent
B. most often begins in adolescence and early adulthood
C. affects females two times more frequently than males
D. is less prevalent among persons who are divorced or separated than among married persons
E. is associated with increased growth hormone secretion

17.14. The organic differential diagnosis for panic disorder includes
A. hyperthyroidism
B. hypoglycemia
C. pheochromocytoma
D. carcinoid tumor
E. all the above

17.15. Mitral-valve prolapse is
A. present in 20 percent of the general population
B. more common in men than in women
C. present in 20 percent of patients with panic disorder
D. present in 50 percent of patients with panic disorder
E. a contraindication in the use of tricyclic antidepressants

17.16. Anxiety, by definition, is
A. always pathological
B. a response to an external threat
C. a response to an internal signal
D. usually an interference with a person's ability to function
E. all the above

17.17. Anxiety may be classified into which of the following categories:
A. superego anxiety
B. castration anxiety
C. separation anxiety
D. impulse anxiety
E. all the above

17.18. A patient with obsessive-compulsive disorder
A. does not realize the irrationality of the obsession
B. must have both an obsession and at least one compulsion
C. experiences the obsession and the compulsion as ego-syntonic
D. carries out the compulsive act in an attempt to decrease anxiety
E. is characterized by all the above

DIRECTIONS: For each of the questions or incomplete statements below, *one or more* of the responses or completions given are correct. Choose

  A. if only *1, 2, and 3* are correct
  B. if only *1 and 3* are correct
  C. if only *2 and 4* are correct
  D. if only *4* is correct
  E. if *all* are correct

17.19. Features associated with posttraumatic stress disorder include
1. reexperiencing of the trauma through dreams
2. emotional numbing
3. autonomic instability
4. cognitive difficulties

17.20. Therapy for phobias may include
1. flooding
2. propranolol (Inderal)
3. systematic desensitization
4. phenelzine (Nardil)

17.21. Pharmacological treatment of generalized anxiety disorder includes
1. alprazolam (Xanax)
2. buspirone (BuSpar)
3. propranolol (Inderal)
4. benzodiazepines

17.22. Panic disorder can be diagnosed when
1. caffeine intake precipitates the symptoms
2. schizophrenia is present
3. anticipatory anxiety alone is present
4. depersonalization or derealization is present

17.23. Studies of the sea snail aplysia demonstrate that
1. behavior can be classically conditioned
2. the snail can be sensitized by random shocks
3. there are measurable changes in presynaptic facilitation
4. the snail reacts to danger by increasing its feeding

17.24. Biological findings in panic disorder patients show
1. increased sympathetic tone
2. abnormal dexamethasone-suppression test
3. blunted growth-hormone response to clonidine (Catapres)
4. an increased thyroid-stimulating hormone response to thyrotropin-releasing hormone

17.25. Biological abnormalities reported in groups of obsessive-compulsive patients include
1. higher incidence of nonspecific electroencephalographic (EEG) abnormalities
2. higher incidence of left-handedness
3. decreased rapid eye movement latency
4. nonsuppression on the dexamethasone-suppression test

17.26. Phobias
1. are ego-syntonic
2. usually persist into adulthood
3. are defended against by isolation
4. are treated by exposure to the phobic situation

17.27. Which of the following statements about panic disorder are true?
1. Sodium lactate infusions induce panic at equal rates in panic patients and in normals
2. Carbon dioxide (CO_2) inhalation induces panic at equal rates in panic patients and in normals
3. Mitral-valve prolapse occurs at equal rates in panic patients and in normals
4. The concordance rate for panic disorder in monozygotic twins is 80 to 90 percent

17.28. Posttraumatic stress disorder
1. results from an event outside the range of usual human experiences
2. results from a stress that would be distressing to anyone
3. is associated with biological vulnerability
4. is associated with decreased rapid eye movement latency

17.29. Which of the following statements about generalized anxiety disorder are true?
1. Sleep electroencephalographic (EEG) studies have reported changes similar to the changes seen in depression
2. There is no genetic evidence of heritability
3. The ratio of females to males is one to one
4. Male relatives are more likely to have an alcohol-related disorder than generalized anxiety disorder

17.30. Medications used to treat posttraumatic stress disorder include
1. imipramine (Tofranil)
2. phenelzine (Nardil)
3. amitriptyline (Elavil)
4. clonidine (Catapres)

17.31. Social phobias
1. are less common than simple phobias
2. are more common in women than in men
3. include phobias about eating in public
4. include phobias about spiders

17.32. In the therapy of panic disorder
1. pharmacological treatment usually leads to the amelioration of agoraphobic symptoms, too
2. patients usually respond to much lower antidepressant dose levels than the levels needed to treat depression
3. patients should be maintained on medication for about one year after initial recovery
4. insight-oriented psychotherapy is of little or no benefit

DIRECTIONS: Each group of questions below consists of lettered headings followed by a list of numbered statements. For each numbered statement, select the *one* lettered heading that is most closely associated with it. Each lettered heading may be used once, more than once, or not at all.

Questions 17.33–17.37
A. Simple phobia
B. Panic disorder
C. Obsessive-compulsive disorder
D. Posttraumatic stress disorder
E. Generalized anxiety disorder

17.33. Episodic anxiety unattached to any object

17.34. Chronic and persistent anxiety

17.35. Anxiety experienced after a specific event outside the range of normal experience

17.36. Anxiety attached to a specific object that leads to avoidance behavior

17.37. Anxiety attached to disturbing, unwanted, anxiety-provoking thoughts with repetitive impulses to perform acts

Questions 17.38–17.42
A. Walter Cannon
B. James Lange
C. Otto Rank
D. Harry Stack Sullivan
E. Melanie Klein

17.38. Birth trauma

17.39. Transmission of maternal anxiety

17.40. Adrenal release of epinephrine

17.41. Anxiety in response to peripheral phenomena

17.42. Primitive superego anxiety

Questions 17.43–17.45
A. Obsessions
B. Compulsions

17.43. Acts or behaviors

17.44. Ideas or sensations

17.45. Designed to neutralize or prevent a dreaded event or discomfort

ANSWERS

Anxiety Disorders
(or Anxiety and Phobic Neuroses)

17.1. The answer is A (*Synopsis VI*, pages 398–404; *CTP V*, page 978).

The patient has an excessive fear of thunder, which she recognizes as irrational (ego-dystonic). Because the fear is persistent and circumscribed, it is diagnosed as a *simple phobia* (Table 17.1). *Agoraphobia* is characterized by a fear of open places, of being outside the home alone, or of being in places from which escape may be difficult. The patient does not have those symptoms. Her fear of thunder does not involve a fear of humiliation or embarrassment in social situations, which rules out a diagnosis of *social phobia* (Table 17.2). *Avoidant disorder* is characterized by a fear of being with unfamiliar persons or even peers. *Schizoid personalities* are withdrawn and isolated and are unable to form close relationships with others. Avoidant disorder or schizoid personality would not be diagnosed in the patient described.

17.2. The answer is E (*Synopsis VI*, page 403; *CTP V*, page 983).

A variety of pharmacological treatments have been used with phobias. *Propranolol* (Inderal) appears to be of use in social phobias, such as fear of public speaking. The evidence supporting the use of propranolol in treating simple phobias, such as this patient's fear of thunderstorms, is less extensive. However, therapeutic trials may be warranted in severe cases. Propranolol is a beta-blocker that blocks the peripheral effects of anxiety, such as tremulousness. A single dose of propranolol is taken prophylactically immediately before the phobic situation is encountered. *Phenelzine* (Nardil) is a monoamine oxide inhibitor (MAOI) that has been useful in panic attacks. It may also be of help in this patient because it prevents anticipatory anxiety, represented by the patient's feeling anxiety long before a storm arrived. *Imipramine* (Tofranil) is a tricyclic antidepressant (TCA) that is indicated in depression and panic attacks. Like phenelzine, it prevents anticipatory anxiety. The full maximum dose of phenelzine or imipramine may be required to obtain relief from the panic symptoms. It may take two to four weeks for panic attacks to decrease with treatment. After recovery, patients should be maintained on the drug for 6 to 12 months; then an attempt may be made to taper off slowly. If symptoms return, the drug treatment should be reinstated. Finally, *diazepam* (Valium) is a benzodiazepine that

Table 17.1
Diagnostic Criteria for Simple Phobia

A. A persistent fear of a circumscribed stimulus (object or situation) other than fear of having a panic attack (as in panic disorder) or of humiliation or embarrassment in certain social situations (as in social phobia).
Note: Do not include fears that are part of panic disorder with agoraphobia or agoraphobia without history of panic disorder.
B. During some phase of the disturbance, exposure to the specific phobic stimulus (or stimuli) almost invariably provokes an immediate anxiety response.
C. The object or situation is avoided, or endured with intense anxiety.
D. The fear or the avoidant behavior significantly interferes with the person's normal routine or with usual social activities or relationships with others, or there is marked distress about having the fear.
E. The person recognizes that his or her fear is excessive or unreasonable.
F. The phobic stimulus is unrelated to the content of the obsessions of obsessive-compulsive disorder or the trauma of posttraumatic stress disorder.

Table from DSM-III-R, *Diagnosis and Statistical Manual of Mental Disorders*, ed 3, revised. Copyright American Psychiatric Association, Washington, DC, 1987. Used with permission.

can be used to treat specific symptoms of anxiety both before and during thunderstorms. Treatment with benzodiazepines should be particularly time-limited in most cases because of their potential for addiction.

17.3. The answer is C (*Synopsis VI*, page 403; *CTP V*, pages 982–983).

A variety of behavioral treatment techniques have been used in the treatment of phobias, the most common being systematic desensitization, a method pioneered by Joseph Wolpe. In this method the patient is exposed serially to a predetermined list of anxiety-provoking stimuli graded in a hierarchy from the least to the most frightening (e.g., first having the patient imagine an overcast day, then a gentle rain, and then a more torrential rain and finally having the patient *visualize a thunderstorm*). Patients are taught first how to induce in themselves both mental and physical repose. Once they have mastered the relaxation techniques, patients are instructed to use them to include a sense of calm in the face of each anxiety-provoking stimulus. As they

Table 17.2
Diagnostic Criteria for Social Phobia

A. A persistent fear of one or more situations (the social phobic situations) in which the person is exposed to possible scrutiny by others and fears that he or she may do something or act in a way that will be humiliating or embarrassing. Examples include: being unable to continue talking while speaking in public, choking on food when eating in front of others, being unable to urinate in a public lavatory, hand-trembling when writing in the presence of others, and saying foolish things or not being able to answer questions in social situations.
B. If an Axis III or another Axis I disorder is present, the fear in A is unrelated to it, e.g., the fear is not of having a panic attack (panic disorder), stuttering (stuttering), trembling (Parkinson's disease), or exhibiting abnormal eating behavior (anorexia nervosa or bulimia nervosa).
C. During some phase of the disturbance, exposure to the specific phobic stimulus (or stimuli) almost invariably provokes an immediate anxiety response.
D. The phobic situation(s) is avoided, or is endured with intense anxiety.
E. The avoidant behavior interferes with occupational functioning or with usual social activities or relationships with others, or there is marked distress about having the fear.
F. The person recognizes that his or her fear is excessive or unreasonable.
G. It the person is under 18, the disturbance does not meet the criteria for avoidant disorder of childhood or adolescence.
Specify generalized type if the phobic situation includes most social situations, and also consider the additional diagnosis of avoidant personality disorder.

Table from DSM-III-R, *Diagnostic and Statistical Manual of Mental Disorders*, ed 3, revised. Copyright American Psychiatric Association, Washington, DC, 1987. Used with permission.

become desensitized to each stimulus in the scale, the patients move up to the next stimulus until, ultimately, what previously produced the most anxiety is no longer capable of eliciting the painful affect.

Other behavioral techniques that have recently been used involve intensive exposure to the phobic stimulus through desensitization in vivo—having the patient hear a tape *recording of a thunderstorm*. In flooding, as opposed to systematic desensitization, patients are exposed to the greatest possible phobic stimulus for as long as they can tolerate the fear until they reach a point at which they can no longer feel it. There is no gradual desensitization to the stimulus but, rather, an immediate exposure to the most anxiety-provoking situation. Flooding (also known as implosion when it occurs in the imagination as opposed to in vivo) requires patients to experience the actual phobic stimulus, such as having the patient *stand outside in a thunderstorm*.

The use of *hypnosis* before a thunderstorm is meant to enhance the therapist's suggestion that the phobic object or situation is not dangerous, and it can be taught as self-hypnosis to the patient as a method of relaxation to use when confronted with the feared object.

Exploring aspects of the behavior's *secondary gain* (e.g., obtaining the family's attention) is associated with insight-oriented psychotherapy and is not a behavioral approach.

17.4.   The answer is D (*Synopsis VI*, pages 394 and 397; *CTP V*, pages 979–980).

Agoraphobia, which is the dread of being in places or situations from which escape may be difficult, is the most common type (60 percent) of all phobic disorders for which treatment is sought; however, accurate information about the relative incidence and prevalence of phobias is not entirely reliable. Agoraphobia is one of the most disabling of all phobias because its victims are usually confined to their homes and rarely go outside and then only if accompanied by somebody. As a group, phobic disorders make up about 5 percent of all disorders for which treatment is sought.

Photophobia is hypersensitivity to light and usually refers to a symptom associated with eye disease, such as conjunctivitis. It can also be defined as a neurotic fear or avoidance of light. *Thanatophobia* is a fear of death; *acrophobia*, a fear of high places; and *nyctophobia*, a fear of night or of darkness.

17.5.   The answer is E (*Synopsis VI*, pages 398–399; *CTP V*, pages 970–972).

The principal treatment of panic disorder is pharmacological—tricyclic antidepressants (TCAs) and monomamine oxidase inhibitors (MAOIs). *Buspirone* (BuSpar), an anxiolytic drug, is not effective in the treatment of panic disorder. *Imipramine* (Tofranil) has been the drug most frequently used, although there are several reports that *desipramine* (Norpramin) is as effective and has fewer side effects. Both imipramine and desipramine are TCAs. There are also many reports that *phenelzine* (Nardil), an MAOI, is effective. Other TCAs and MAOIs may be effective; *propranolol* (Inderal) and alprazolam (Xanax) may be tried in patients who either are not responsive to TCAs and phenelzine or cannot tolerate these drugs because of adverse effects. Serotonergic agonists have been useful in some cases (e.g., fluoxetine [Prozac]).

17.6.   The answer is A (*Synopsis VI*, pages 404–409; *CTP V*, pages 984–985).

Roger was most likely suffering from *obsessive-compulsive disorder*. He spent a great deal of time in repetitive behaviors, such as showering for 45 minutes and arranging his clothing in a certain way so that dressing took 30 minutes each morning. Roger's indecisiveness, perfectionism, preoccupation with details, and hoarding of worthless objects made it likely that he also had compulsive personality disorder. The two disorders may coexist. *Agoraphobia* is ruled out, as Roger did not evidence fear of being alone in a public place or in a place from which escape might be difficult or embarrassing. *Depressed* patients often develop obsessions, but this patient did not present with depressed mood. *Generalized anxiety disorder* presents with diffuse, nonremitting anxiety, and ritualistic behavior is rare. Patients with *temporal lobe epilepsy* may have obsessive behavior, but the behavior is not usually complex (e.g., a hair-grooming ritual).

17.7. The answer is B (*Synopsis VI*, pages 392–393; *CTP V*, page 966).

γ-*Aminobutyric acid* (GABA) is the principal neurotransmitter associated with anxiety that mediates presynaptic inhibition in the central nervous system (CNS). GABAergic neurons synapse onto presynaptic terminals and cause a reduction in the amount of neurotransmitter released by those terminals. The GABA receptor complex consists of a GABA binding site, a site that binds benzodiazepines, and a chloride channel. Stimulation of the GABA receptor causes chloride ions to flow into the neuron, thereby hyperpolarizing and inhibiting that neuron. Benzodiazepines increase the affinity of GABA for its binding site, causing more chloride to enter the neuron.

Data defining a pathological role for norepinephrine in human anxiety are inconsistent. Drugs affecting *norepinephrine* (e.g., tricyclics and monamine oxide inhibitors) are effective in treating several of the anxiety disorders. Some studies have reported increased norepinephrine metabolites (e.g., 3-methoxy-4-hydroxyphenylglycol [MHPG]) in urine; others have not. It has been suggested that the *endogenous opioids* may interact with α_2-adrenergic binding sites and so may be involved in anxiety. Treatment of anxiety patients with opioid agonists and antagonists has not yet been demonstrated to be effective. The anxietylike withdrawal symptoms of heroin addicts, however, are reduced by clonidine (Catapres), and α_2-adrenergic agonist. Other neurotransmitters implicated in anxiety include *histamine*, acetylcholine, and *adenosine*. Adenosine receptors, in fact, may be the site of action for the anxiogenic effects of caffeine.

17.8. The answer is D (*Synopsis VI*, pages 394–399; *CTP V*, pages 979–980).

Patients who fear being in situations in which they may experience severe anxiety or panic (e.g., traveling alone to another city) are suffering from *agoraphobia*. Agoraphobic patients generally become immobilized when they are forced into situations in which they may be subjected to the sense of helplessness or humiliation that results from the eruption of the panic attacks to which they are prone. In addition to open, public places, agoraphobic patients are threatened by, for example, crowded stores, public transportation, elevators, and theaters—situations from which they can find no immediate escape. Although they may feel more comfortable when accompanied by a friend or a relative, they tend to avoid what they believe to be dangerous situations by restricting their activities and excursions to an increasingly smaller area and in extreme cases may confine themselves to their homes.

Generalized anxiety disorder is a DSM-III-R classification of anxiety disorder characterized by severe anxiety not attached to any particular idea, object, or event. A *panic disorder* is an episode of acute, intense anxiety. *Social and simple phobias* are discrete phobic disorders. Social phobia is defined by DSM-III-R as a persistent fear of one or more situations in which the person is exposed to possible scrutiny by others; simple phobia is a residual category that includes phobias not covered by agoraphobia or social phobia. Among the social phobias are fears of public speaking, blushing, eating in public, writing in front of others, and urinating in public lavatories. The classic example of a simple phobia is an irrational, overly intense belief in the danger of spiders.

DSM-III-R specifies two types of agoraphobic states—with panic disorder and without a history of panic disorder. Agoraphobia may occur as a pure syndrome; however, if the disorder is associated with panic disorder, the patient reports that severe anxiety or panic arises at unexpected times and is not triggered by any particular thought or situation. Thus, in the case presented, if the patient had several discrete periods of intense fear or discomfort that had no precipitating event, a more appropriate diagnosis would be panic disorder with agoraphobia. In the case described, the DSM-III-R criteria are consistent with agoraphobia without a history of panic disorder. The criteria for the two types of agoraphobia are listed in Tables 17.3 and 17.4.

17.9. The answer is B (*Synopsis VI*, page 408; *CTP V*, page 999).

Clomipramine (Anafranil) (or chlorinated imipramine) appears to be the most effective pharmacological treatment for obsessive-compulsive disorder (OCD). The drug is available in the United States. The effects of clomipramine may be delayed for as long as two months, and it is most effective when specific compulsions are present. Other tricyclics, such as *imipramine* (Tofranil) and *amitriptyline* (Elavil), have been reported effective, although clinicians believe they are much less useful than clomipramine. Monoamine oxide inhibitors (MAOIs) such as *phenelzine* (Nardil) and *tranylcypromine* (Parnate) are also effective in many cases. Treatment should be continued for 6 to 12 months before an attempt is made to stop the medication. Many patients relapse when medication is discontinued. Fluoxetine (Prozac) has also been reported to be useful in obsessive-compulsive disorder.

17.10. The answer is E (*Synopsis VI*, pages 400–401; *CTP V*, page 981).

Many activities may mask phobic anxiety, which can be hidden behind attitudes and behavior patterns that represent a denial, either that the dreaded object or situation is dangerous or that one is afraid of it. Basic to this phenomenon is a reversal of the situation in which one is the passive victim of ex-

Table 17.3
Diagnostic Criteria for Panic Disorder with Agoraphobia

A. Meets the criteria for panic disorder.
B. Agoraphobia: Fear of being in places or situations from which escape might be difficult (or embarrassing) or in which help might not be available in the event of a panic attack. (Include cases in which persistent avoidance behavior originated during an active phase of panic disorder, even if the person does not attribute the avoidance behavior to fear of having a panic attack.) As a result of this fear, the person either restricts travel or needs a companion when away from home, or else endures agoraphobic situations despite intense anxiety. Common agoraphobic situations include being outside the home alone, being in a crowd or standing in a line, being on a bridge, and traveling in a bus, train, or car.
Specify current severity of agoraphobic avoidance:
Mild: Some avoidance (or endurance with distress), but relatively normal life-style (e.g., travels unaccompanied when necessary, such as to work or to shop; otherwise avoids traveling alone).
Moderate: Avoidance results in constricted life-style (e.g., the person is able to leave the house alone, but not to go more than a few miles unaccompanied).
Severe: Avoidance results in being nearly or completely housebound or unable to leave the house unaccompanied.
In partial remission: No current agoraphobic avoidance, but some agoraphobic avoidance during the past six months.
In full remission: No current agoraphobic avoidance and none during the past six months.
Specify current severity of panic attacks:
Mild: During the past month, either all attacks have been limited symptom attacks (i.e., fewer than four symptoms), or there has been no more than one panic attack.
Moderate: During the past month, attacks have been intermediate between "mild" and "severe."
Severe: During the past month, there have been at least eight panic attacks.
In partial remission: The condition has been intermediate between "in full remission" and "mild."
In full remission: During the past six months, there have been no panic or limited symptom attacks.

Table from DSM-III-R, *Diagnostic and Statistical Manual of Mental Disorders*, ed 3, revised. Copyright American Psychiatric Association, Washington, DC, 1987. Used with permission.

Table 17.4
Diagnostic Criteria for Agoraphobia Without History of Panic Disorder

A. Agoraphobia: Fear of being in places or situations from which escape might be difficult (or embarrassing) or in which help might not be available in the event of suddenly developing a symptom(s) that could be incapacitating or extremely embarrassing. Examples include: dizziness or falling, depersonalization or derealization, loss of bladder or bowel control, vomiting, or cardiac distress. As a result of this fear, the person either restricts travel or needs a companion when away from home, or else endures agoraphobic situations despite intense anxiety. Common agoraphobic situations include being outside the home alone, being in a crowd or standing in a line, being on a bridge, and traveling in a bus, train, or car.
B. Has never met the criteria for panic disorder.
Specify with or without limited symptom attacks.

Table from DSM-III-R, *Diagnostic and Statistical Manual of Mental Disorders*, ed 3, revised. Copyright American Psychiatric Association, Washington, DC, 1987. Used with permission.

ternal circumstances to a position of attempting actively to confront and master what one fears. The counterphobic person seeks out situations of danger and rushes enthusiastically toward them. The devotee of dangerous sports—such as *parachute jumping, rock climbing, hunting, and para-sailing*—may be exhibiting counterphobic behavior. Such patterns may be secondary to neurotic phobic anxieties or may be used as a normal means of dealing with a realistically dangerous situation.

17.11. The answer is C (*Synopsis VI*, pages 412–415; *CTP V*, page 953).

Generalized anxiety disorder is defined as a chronic disorder lasting longer than *six months (not*

six weeks). It is characterized by *unrealistic (not realistic) or excessive worry*. The anxiety is focused on *two or more life circumstances, not a single issue*. The symptoms of generalized anxiety disorder include those that are due to *autonomic hyperactivity*, motor tension, and vigilance and scanning. See Table 17.5 for the DSM-III-R criteria for generalized anxiety disorder.

17.12. The answer is E (*Synopsis VI*, pages 409–410; *CTP V*, pages 1001–1004).

The likelihood of posttraumatic stress disorder (PTSD) developing is influenced by many factors. The *severity of the stressor* is a major consideration. The more severe the stressor is, the more likely it is that the syndrome will develop and be severe. The *age* of the person is also a factor in the development of PTSD. The very young and the very old have more difficulty coping with traumatic events than do those in mid-life. Children are not likely to have adequate coping mechanisms, and old people are likely to have rigid coping mechanisms, and so both are more vulnerable than are others to the emotional effects of the trauma. Because of the nature of the most frequent events—wartime combat, assault, and rape—the disorder is most prevalent in young adults. The availability of *social support* may also influence the development, the severity, and the duration of posttraumatic stress disorder. In general, the disorder is not likely to develop in patients who have a good network of social support; if the disorder does develop, the patients are not likely to experience it in its most severe forms. The disorder is more likely to occur in those who are single, divorced, widowed, economically handicapped, or socially deprived than in stable, married persons. *Preexisting psychiatric disorders* also increase the likelihood that PTSD will develop.

Table 17.5
Diagnostic Criteria for Generalized Anxiety Disorder

A. Unrealistic or excessive anxiety and worry (apprehensive expectation) about two or more life circumstances (e.g., worry about possible misfortune to one's child who is in no danger and worry about finances for no good reason, for a period of six months or longer, during which the person has been bothered more days than not by these concerns. In children and adolescents, this may take the form of anxiety and worry about academic, athletic, and social performance).
B. If another Axis I disorder is present, the focus of the anxiety and worry in A is unrelated to it, e.g., the anxiety or worry is not about having a panic attack (as in panic disorder), being embarrassed in public (as in social phobia), being contaminated (as in obsessive-compulsive disorder), or gaining weight (as in anorexia nervosa).
C. The disturbance does not occur only during the course of a mood disorder or a psychotic disorder.
D. At least 6 of the following 18 symptoms are often present when anxious (do not include symptoms present only during panic attacks):

Motor tension
1. trembling, twitching, or feeling shaky
2. muscle tension, aches, or soreness
3. restlessness
4. easy fatigability

Autonomic hyperactivity
5. shortness of breath or smothering sensations
6. palpitations or accelerated heart rate (tachycardia)
7. sweating, or cold clammy hands
8. dry mouth
9. dizziness or lightheadedness
10. nausea, diarrhea, or other abdominal distress
11. flushes (hot flashes) or chills
12. frequent urination
13. trouble swallowing or "lump in throat"

Vigilance and scanning
14. feeling keyed up or on edge
15. exaggerated startle response
16. difficulty concentrating or "mind going blank" because of anxiety
17. trouble falling or staying asleep
18. irritability

E. It cannot be established that an organic factor initiated and maintained the disturbance (e.g., hyperthyroidism, caffeine intoxication).

Table from DSM-III-R, *Diagnostic and Statistical Manual of Mental Disorders*, ed 3, revised. Copyright American Psychiatric Association, Washington, DC, 1987. Used with permission.

17.13. The answer is B (*Synopsis VI*, page 404; *CTP V*, pages 985–986).

The prevalence of obsessive-compulsive disorder (OCD) is now recognized as being much higher than was previously thought. The lifetime prevalence of obsessive compulsive disorder is *2.0 to 2.4 percent, not 20 to 24 percent*. The disorder begins most often in *adolescence and early adulthood*. OCD affects *males and females equally*. The prevalence of this disorder is higher (not lower) among persons who are *divorced, separated,* or unemployed than among married persons. There is no evidence of increased *growth hormone secretion* in OCD; however, one

third of patients show decreased growth hormone secretion with clonidine (Catapres) infusions.

17.14. The answer is E (*Synopsis VI*, pages 398–399; *CTP V*, pages 968–969).

The organic differential diagnosis for panic disorder is lengthy and includes drug intoxication and withdrawal and such disorders of the endocrine system as *hyperthyroidism, hypoglycemia, pheochromocytoma* and *carcinoid tumor*. Other organic disorders—including diseases of the cardiovascular, pulmonary, and neurological systems—may first appear as panic disorder or another anxiety disorder.

17.15. The answer is D (*Synopsis VI*, page 395; *CTP V*, page 969).

Mitral-valve prolapse is a heterogeneous syndrome consisting of the prolapse of one of the mitral-valve leaflets, resulting in a midsystolic click on cardiac auscultation. Mitral-valve prolapse is commonly seen in connective tissue diseases such as Marfan's syndrome and Ehlers-Danlos syndrome. It is present in as many as *50 percent of patients with panic disorder* but only *5 percent of the general population*. Although the mitral-valve prolapse is asymptomatic in approximately *20 percent* of patients with prolapse, the cardiac and respiratory symptoms usually associated with it are similar to those seen in panic disorder. Mitral-valve prolapse and panic disorder seem to have a genetic component, and both are *more common in women than in men*. Mitral-valve prolapse and the occasionally coexisting ventricular ectopic foci seen on electrocardiograms are *not contraindications* to treatment with antidepressants. Imipramine, in fact, may be of benefit in treating such cardiac disorders. Nevertheless, consultation with a cardiologist and frequent electrocardiograms are indicated when treating a mitral-valve prolapse patient with antidepressants. The basis and the significance of the association between mitral-valve prolapse and panic disorder is unknown.

17.16. The answer is C (*Synopsis VI*, page 389; *CTP V*, pages 952–954).

Anxiety is a diffuse, highly unpleasant, often vague feeling of apprehension accompanied by one or more bodily sensations—for example, an empty feeling in the pit of the stomach, tightness in the chest, pounding heart, perspiration, headache, and the sudden urge to void. Restlessness and a desire to move around are also common. Anxiety is an alerting signal; it warns of impending danger and enables the person to take measures to deal with a threat. Fear, a similar alerting signal, is differentiated from anxiety as follows: fear is in response to a threat that is known, *external*, definite, or nonconflictual in origin; anxiety is in response to a threat that is unknown, *internal*, vague, or conflictual in origin.

Since it is clearly to one's advantage to respond with anxiety in certain threatening situations, one can speak of normal anxiety in contrast to abnormal or *pathological* anxiety. Anxiety is normal for infants threatened by separation from parents or by the loss of love, for children on their first day in school, for adolescents on their first date, for adults contemplating old age and death, and for anyone faced with illness. Anxiety is a normal accompaniment of growth, of change, of experiencing something new and untried, and of finding one's own identity and meaning in life. Pathological anxiety, on the other hand, is an inappropriate response to a given stimulus by virtue of either its intensity or its duration.

Anxiety usually leads to actions designed to remove or reduce a threat. This action may be constructive, in which case a person uses coping mechanisms if the action is mainly conscious or deliberate (such as studying for an examination) or uses defense mechanisms if the person's behavior is largely determined by unconscious forces (such as repressing or pushing out of awareness a threatening impulse or idea).

When evaluating a patient complaining of anxiety, the clinician must distinguish between normal and pathological anxiety. Pathological anxiety may be differentiated from normal anxiety by the patient's subjective state, behavior, and decreased *ability to function*. Patients with pathological anxiety require full evaluation and individually tailored treatment. Anxiety can be a component of depression and of many medical disorders.

17.17. The answer is E (*Synopsis VI*, pages 391–392; *CTP V*, pages 952–954).

In psychoanalytic theory, anxiety is seen as falling into four major categories, depending on the nature of the feared consequences: *superego anxiety, castration anxiety, separation anxiety,* and id or *impulse anxiety*. These varieties of anxiety are believed to develop at various times during early growth and development. Id or impulse anxiety is seen as related to the primitive, diffuse discomfort of infants when they feel themselves overwhelmed with needs and stimuli over which their helpless state provides no control. Separation anxiety refers to the stage of older but still preoedipal children, who fear the loss of love or even abandonment by their parents if they fail to control and direct their impulses in conformity with their parents' standards and demands. The fantasies of castration that characterize oedipal children, particularly in relation to their developing sexual impulses, are reflected in the castration anxiety of the adult. Superego anxiety is the direct result of the final development of the superego that marks the passing of the Oedipus complex and the advent of the prepubertal period of latency.

17.18. The answer is D (*Synopsis VI*, page 404; *CTP V*, pages 984–985).

An obsession is a recurrent and intrusive mental event that can be a thought, a feeling, an idea, or a sensation. A compulsion is a conscious, standardized, recurrent behavior, such as counting, checking, or avoiding. A patient with obsessive-compulsive disorder (OCD) *realizes the irrationality* of the obsession. A patient with OCD *may have an obsession or a compulsion or both.* The compulsive act is carried out in an attempt to *reduce anxiety*. Both obsessions and compulsions are experienced as *ego-dystonic, not ego-syntonic*—that is, the patient's ego wants to rid itself of the unwanted thought or behavior.

17.19. The answer is E (all) (*Synopsis VI*, page 409; *CTP V*, page 1001).

Posttraumatic stress disorder (PTSD) develops in persons who have experienced emotional or physical stress that would be extremely traumatic for virtually anyone. The major features associated with PTSD are the *reexperiencing of the trauma through dreams* and waking thoughts; *emotional numbing* to other life experiences, including relationships; and associated symptoms of *autonomic instability*, depression, and *cognitive difficulties*, such as poor concentration.

17.20. The answer is E (all) (*Synopsis VI*, page 403; *CTP V*, pages 982–983).

Both pharmacological and behavioral techniques have been used in treating phobias. The most common behavioral technique is *systematic desensitization*, in which the patient is exposed serially to a predetermined list of anxiety-provoking stimuli graded in a hierarchy from the least to the most frightening. Patients are taught to self-induce a state of relaxation in the face of each anxiety-provoking stimulus. In *flooding*, patients are exposed to the phobic stimulus (actual [in vivo] or through imagery) for as long as they can tolerate the fear until they reach a point at which they can no longer feel it. The social phobia of stage fright in performers has been effectively treated with β-adrenergic antagonists such as *propranolol* (Inderal), which blocks the physiological signs of anxiety (e.g., tachycardia). *Phenelzine* (Nardil), a monoamine oxidase inhibitor, is also of use in treating social phobia.

17.21. The answer is E (all) (*Synopsis VI*, pages 414–415; *CTP V*, pages 982–983).

A variety of drugs are useful in generalized anxiety disorders. *Benzodiazepines* have been the drugs of choice for this disorder. In generalized anxiety disorder these drugs can be prescribed on an as-needed basis so that the patients take a rapidly acting benzodiazepine when they feel particularly anxious. The alternative approach is to prescribe a standing dose of benzodiazepines for a limited period of time, during which psychosocial therapeutic approaches are implemented. Approximately 25 to 30 percent of patients fail to respond, and tolerance and dependency may occur. Some patients may also experience impaired alertness while taking these drugs. *Buspirone* (BuSpar), a nonbenzodiazepine anxiolytic, may be an alternative drug for these patients. Although its onset of effects is delayed, it lacks some of the problems associated with benzodiazepines (e.g., sedation). β-Adrenergic-blocking drugs, such as *propranolol* (Inderal), have been used to treat the peripheral symptoms of anxiety. *Alprazolam* (Xanax) has also been used in anxiety disorders, especially when associated with depression in panic attacks.

17.22.   The answer is C (2, 4) (*Synopsis VI*, pages 396–397; *CTP V*, page 953).

Panic attacks are characterized by symptoms of extreme fear and a sense of impending death and doom. The patient may not be able to name the source of the fear and may feel confused and have trouble concentrating. Physical signs often include tachycardia (rapid heartbeat), palpitations, dyspnea (shortness of breath), and sweating. The patient often tries to leave the situation to seek help. The attack generally lasts 20 to 30 minutes and rarely more than an hour. A formal mental status examination during a panic attack may demonstrate rumination (the periodic reconsideration of the same subject), difficulty in speaking (e.g., stammering), and impaired memory. The patient may also experience *derealization* (when ordinarily familiar things seem strange, unreal, or two-dimensional) or *depersonalization* (the loss of one's identity or the loss of the feeling of one's own reality) during an attack. The symptoms may disappear quickly or gradually. Between attacks, the patient may have anticipatory anxiety about having another attack, although this *anticipatory anxiety* is not in itself sufficient to warrant the diagnosis of panic disorder.

Somatic concerns regarding death from a cardiac or respiratory problem may be the major focus of a patient's attention during a panic attack. The patient may believe that the palpitations and chest pains indicate that he or she is about to die from a heart attack. As many as 20 percent of these patients actually have syncopal episodes (fainting spells) during a panic attack. It is common for such patients to go to emergency rooms; they are young, physically healthy persons who insist that they are about to die from a heart attack. Rather than immediately judging such patients to be hypochondriacs, the emergency room physician should consider a diagnosis of panic disorder. Hyperventilation may produce respiratory alkalosis and additional signs or symptoms. The age-old treatment of breathing into a paper bag sometimes helps in this situation. Mitral-valve prolapse, a heterogeneous syndrome consisting of the prolapse of one of the mitral-valve leaflets, may be an associated condition but does not preclude the diagnosis of panic disorder.

Panic disorder may occur in conjunction with *schizophrenia*, in which case both disorders should be diagnosed. If the attack is precipitated by *caffeine*, amphetamine, or cocaine, an organic anxiety syndrome is diagnosed.

See Table 17.6 for the DSM-III-R criteria for panic disorder.

Table 17.6
Diagnostic Criteria for Panic Disorder

A. At some time during the disturbance, one or more panic attacks (discrete periods of intense fear or discomfort) have occurred that were (1) unexpected, i.e., did not occur immediately before or on exposure to a situation that almost always caused anxiety, and (2) not triggered by situations in which the person was the focus of others' attention.

B. Either four attacks, as defined in criterion A, have occurred within a four-week period, or one or more attacks have been followed by a period of at least a month of persistent fear of having another attack.

C. At least four of the following symptoms developed during at least one of the attacks:
1. shortness of breath (dyspnea) or smothering sensations
2. dizziness, unsteady feelings, or faintness
3. palpitations or accelerated heart rate (tachycardia)
4. trembling or shaking
5. sweating
6. choking
7. nausea or abdominal distress
8. depersonalization or derealization
9. numbness or tingling sensations (paresthesias)
10. flushes (hot flashes) or chills
11. chest pain or discomfort
12. fear of dying
13. fear of going crazy or of doing something uncontrolled

Note: Attacks involving four or more symptoms are panic attacks; attacks involving fewer than four symptoms are limited symptom attacks (see agoraphobia without history of panic disorder).

D. During at least some of the attacks, at least four of the C symptoms developed suddenly and increased in intensity within 10 minutes of the beginning of the first C symptom noticed in the attack.

E. It cannot be established that an organic factor initiated and maintained the disturbance, e.g., amphetamine or caffeine intoxication, hyperthyroidism.

Note: Mitral valve prolapse may be an associated condition, but does not preclude a diagnosis of panic disorder.

Table from DSM-III-R, *Diagnostic and Statistical Manual of Mental Disorders*, ed 3, revised. Copyright American Psychiatric Association, Washington, DC, 1987. Used with permission.

17.23.   The answer is A (1, 2, 3) (*Synopsis VI*, page 393; *CTP V*, page 334).

A neurotransmitter model for anxiety has been proposed based on the study of aplysia, a sea snail that reacts to danger by moving away, withdrawing into its shell, and *decreasing (not increasing) its feeding behavior*. These behaviors can be *classically conditioned* so that the snail responds to a neutral stimulus as if it were a dangerous stimulus. The snail can also be *sensitized by random shocks* so that it exhibits a flight response in the absence of real danger. Parallels have been drawn between the classically conditioned model and human phobic anxiety. The classically conditioned aplysia demonstrates measurable changes in *presynaptic facilitation*, resulting in the release of increased amounts of neurotransmitter. Although the sea snail is a simple animal, this work illustrates an experimental approach to complex neurochemical processes potentially involved in anxiety.

17.24. The answer is B (1, 3) (*Synopsis VI*, page 394; *CTP V*, pages 965–967).

The autonomic nervous systems of some panic disorder patients have been reported to exhibit *increased sympathetic tone*, to adapt more slowly to repeated stimuli, and to respond excessively to moderate stimuli. Neuroendocrine investigations have generally found *no abnormality in the dexamethasone-suppression test* (DST) in panic disorder but have reported a *blunted growth-hormone (BGH) response to clonidine* (Catapres) stimulation and a decreased prolactin and *decreased (not increased) thyroid-stimulating hormone* (TSH) response to infusions of thyrotropin-releasing hormone (TRH).

17.25. The answer is E (all) (*Synopsis VI*, pages 404–405; *CTP V*, pages 991–993).

A variety of biological abnormalities have been reported in groups of obsessive-compulsive patients. The major biological abnormalities seen in this disorder have been reported from electroencephalogram (EEG), sleep EEG, neuroendocrine, and computed tomographic (CT) studies. There is a *higher incidence of nonspecific EEG abnormalities* in obsessive-compulsive patients. It has been hypothesized that these abnormalities may be located in the left hemisphere, which is supported by the observation that there is a *higher incidence of left-handedness* in these patients. Sleep EEG studies have demonstrated abnormalities similar to those seen in depression, such as *decreased rapid eye movement (REM) latency*. Neuroendocrine studies have also found some similarities to depression, such as *nonsuppression on the dexamethasone-suppression test* (DST) in about one third of OCD patients and decreased growth-hormone (GH) secretion with clonidine (Catapres) infusions. Finally, some controversial studies report that severely ill patients may have enlarged ventricles detectable on CT.

17.26. The answer is D (4) (*Synopsis VI*, pages 400–404; *CTP V*, pages 982–983).

Sigmund Freud recognized that psychotherapists had to go beyond their analytic roles and urge the phobic patients to seek out the phobic situations and master the anxiety by using their acquired insight. Since then psychiatrists have agreed that a measure of activity on the part of the therapist is often required to treat phobic anxiety. In a type of treatment called flooding, the patient is *exposed to the phobic situation* directly until the anxiety diminishes. Phobic patients consciously realize that their fears are unfounded and irrational; therefore, the fears are *ego-dystonic, not ego-syntonic*. Simple phobias that begin in childhood usually remit spontaneously and *do not usually persist into adulthood. Isolation is not

one of the typical defense mechanisms seen in phobia. The primary defense involves the use of displacement, in which an unconscious conflict is displaced from the object or situation that evokes the conflict to a seemingly unimportant, irrelevant object or situation, which then has the power to arouse the entire constellation of anxious affects.

17.27. The answer is D (4) (*Synopsis VI*, page 395; *CTP V*, pages 965–967).

There is strong evidence of a genetic basis for panic disorder. About 15 to 17 percent of first-degree relatives of patients with panic disorder are affected. The concordance rate for monozygotic twins is *80 to 90 percent*, as compared with 10 to 15 percent for dizygotic twins. *Sodium lactate infusions* and *carbon dioxide (CO_2) inhalation* both induce panic at significantly higher (not equal) rates in panic disorder patients than in normals. *Mitral-valve prolapse* is present in as many as *50 percent of panic disorder* patients, as opposed to 5 percent of the general population.

17.28. The answer is E (all) (*Synopsis VI*, pages 409–410; *CTP V*, pages 1001–1004).

The stress that precipitates a posttraumatic stress disorder (PTSD) is usually *outside the range of usual human experiences*, such as from earthquakes, flood, and war. It is also a stress that would be considered *distressing to anyone*. The fact that a person finds the stressor disagreeable is not a sign of psychological abnormality. Each person, however, has his or her threshold for developing symptoms of a PTSD, based on the character traits of the victim, *biological vulnerability*, and the nature of the stressor. The more severe the stressor, the more likely it is that the syndrome will develop and be severe. When the trauma is comparatively mild—for example, a minor auto accident—few of the victims develop a PTSD. Recent research on biological theories of posttraumatic stress disorder have demonstrated labile autonomic nervous system reactions to stress, *decreased rapid eye movement (REM) latency* periods, and increased endogenous opioid secretion.

17.29. The answer is D (4) (*Synopsis VI*, pages 412–413; *CTP V*, pages 954–959).

According to DSM-III-R, generalized anxiety disorder is a chronic (longer than six months) disorder characterized by unrealistic or excessive anxiety about two or more life circumstances. The ratio of *females to males* suffering from this disorder is approximately two to one. *Sleep electroencephalographic* (EEG) studies have reported changes that are different from (not similar to) those seen in depression. In generalized anxiety disorder, increased sleep discontinuity, decreased delta sleep, decreased stage 1 sleep, and reduced rapid eye movement (REM) complement are seen. There is *genetic evidence* that some aspects of this disorder may be inherited. Approximately 25 percent of first-degree relatives are affected, female relatives more often than males. Male relatives are more likely to have an *alcohol-related disorder* than generalized anxiety disorder.

17.30. The answer is E (all) (*Synopsis VI*, pages 414–415; *CTP V*, pages 1007–1008).

Tricyclic antidepressants, especially *amitriptyline* (Elavil) and *imipramine* (Tofranil), and the monoamine oxidase inhibiter *phenelzine* (Nardil) are the drugs most often used to treat posttraumatic stress disorder (PTSD). They are particularly indicated when depression or panic symptoms are present. Increasing numbers of clinicians report therapeutic success with *clonidine* (Catapres), and a few reports suggest that propranolol (Inderal) is an effective treatment. Antipsychotic medications may be necessary for brief periods during treatment if behavior is particularly agitated.

17.31. The answer is B (1, 3) (*Synopsis VI*, page 400; *CTP V*, page 980).

Social phobias are *less common* than simple phobias. Social phobias affect 3 to 5 percent of the population; they are *equally common* in women and men. The onset is usually in the early to late teens, although it can begin at any age. DSM-III-R defines social phobia as the fear of humiliation or embarrassment in public places. Social phobias include phobias about *eating in public*, urinating in public restrooms, public speaking, and public musical performances. According to some studies, the fear of public speaking is the most common social phobia.

The six-month prevalence of simple phobia varies from 5 to 12 percent in different studies. Females are more often affected than males. Simple phobia is a residual category that includes specific phobias, such as an irrational and overly intense belief about the danger of *spiders*. The following objects and situations are listed in descending frequency of appearance in simple phobia: animals, storms, heights, illness, injury, and death.

17.32. The answer is B (1, 3) (*Synopsis VI*, pages 398–399; *CTP V*, pages 969–972).

Pharmacological therapy for panic disorder with antidepressant medication usually requires the *same (not lower) dose levels* as are necessary to treat depression. After the patient's initial recovery, most clinicians recommend that the patient be maintained on *medication for about one year*, at which point the drug can be tapered off. Pharmacological treatment of patients with panic attacks associated with agoraphobia usually leads to both symptom complexes being *ameliorated* at the same time. *Insight-oriented psychotherapy* is of benefit in the treatment of panic disorder and agoraphobia. Treatment focuses on helping the patient understand the unconscious meaning of the anxiety.

17.33–17.37

17.33. The answer is B (*Synopsis VI*, pages 394–397; *CTP V*, page 955).

17.34. The answer is E (*Synopsis VI*, pages 412–415; *CTP V*, pages 958–959).

17.35. The answer is D (*Synopsis VI*, pages 409–412; *CTP V*, pages 1004–1006).

17.36. The answer is A (*Synopsis VI*, pages 401–403; *CTP V*, page 979).

17.37. The answer is C (*Synopsis VI*, pages 406–408; *CTP V*, pages 993–995).

Panic disorder is characterized by the experience of *episodic anxiety* unattached to any object, whereas generalized anxiety disorder is experienced as a *chronic and persistent anxiety*. In posttraumatic stress disorder (PTSD) the anxiety is experienced after a specific event that is *outside the range of normal experience*. In simple phobia the anxiety is attached to a specific object and leads to *avoidance behavior*. In obsessive-compulsive disorder (OCD) the anxiety is attached to *disturbing, unwanted, anxiety-provoking thoughts* with repetitive impulses to perform acts to counteract those thoughts. All the disorders are subsumed in DSM-III-R under the heading of anxiety disorders. Table 17.7 lists the full classification of anxiety disorders as described in DSM-III-R.

17.38–17.42

17.38. The answer is C (*Synopsis VI*, page 392; *CTP V*, pages 420–421).

17.39. The answer is D (*Synopsis VI*, page 392; *CTP V*, pages 424–427).

17.40. The answer is A (*Synopsis VI*, page 392; *CTP V*, pages 1159 and 1236).

17.41. The answer is B (*Synopsis VI*, pages 392–393; *CTP V*, pages 1159 and 1236).

Table 17.7
Anxiety Disorders (or Anxiety and Phobic Neuroses)

Panic disorder
  with agoraphobia
  without agoraphobia
Agoraphobia without history of panic disorder
Social phobia
Simple phobia
Obsessive-compulsive disorder (or obsessive-compulsive neurosis)
Posttraumatic stress disorder
Generalized anxiety disorder
Anxiety disorder NOS

17.42. The answer is E (*Synopsis VI*, pages 189 and 391–392; *CTP V*, pages 418–420).

There are differences of opinion in psychoanalytic theory about the sources and the nature of anxiety. Otto Rank, for example, traced the genesis of all anxiety back to the processes associated with the *trauma of birth*. Harry Stack Sullivan placed emphasis on the early relationship between mother and child and the importance of the *transmission of the mother's anxiety* to her infant. Regardless of the particular school of psychoanalysis, however, treatment of anxiety disorders within this model usually involves long-term, insight-oriented psychotherapy or psychoanalysis directed toward the formation of a transference that then allows the reworking of the developmental problem and the resolution of the neurotic symptoms. Melanie Klein described four basic functions of the ego, all of which start with the beginning of life: (1) the experience of and defense against anxiety, (2) processes of introjection and projection, (3) object relations, and (4) integration and synthesis. According to Klein, the first consequence of the operation of the death instinct is anxiety. She considered the ego to be the seat of anxiety; anxiety constitutes the ego's response to the expression of the death instinct. Anxiety is also reinforced by the separation caused by birth and by the frustration of bodily needs. Anxiety becomes fear of persecutory objects and later, through reintrojection of aggression in the form of internalized bad objects, the fear of outer and inner persecutors. Inner persecutors constitute the origin of *primitive superego anxiety*. The content of paranoid fears varies according to the level of psychosexual development. At first, there are oral fears of being devoured and then anal fears of being controlled and poisoned; those early contents later shift into oedipal fears of castration.

Walter Cannon demonstrated that cats exposed to barking dogs exhibited behavioral and physiological signs of fear that were associated with the *adrenal release of epinephrine*. The James Lange theory hypothesized that subjective anxiety was a *response to peripheral phenomena*. It is now generally thought that central nervous system anxiety precedes the peripheral manifestations of anxiety except where there is a specific peripheral cause (e.g., pheochromocytoma—a catecholamine-secreting tumor). Many anxiety disorder patients, especially those with panic disorders, have an autonomic nervous system that exhibits increased sympathetic tone, adapts more slowly to repeated stimuli, and responds excessively to moderate stimuli.

17.43–17.45

17.43. The answer is B (*Synopsis VI*, page 404; *CTP V*, pages 993–995).

17.44. The answer is A (*Synopsis VI*, page 404; *CTP V*, pages 993–995).

17.45. The answer is B (*Synopsis VI*, page 404; *CTP V*, pages 993–995).

Obsessions and compulsions have certain features in common: (1) An idea or an impulse intrudes insistently and persistently into the person's conscious awareness; (2) a feeling of anxious dread accompanies the central manifestation and frequently leads the person to take countermeasures against the initial idea or impulse; (3) the obsession or compulsion is ego-alien; that is, it is experienced as being foreign to the person's experience of himself or herself as a psychological being; (4) the person recognizes the obsession or compulsion as absurd and irrational; and (5) the person suffering from obsessions and compulsions feels a strong desire to resist them. Obsessions are thoughts, feelings, *ideas, or sensations*. Compulsions are *acts or behaviors* designed to *neutralize or prevent* a dreaded situation or discomfort. The compulsive act, however, does not always reduce the anxiety and the obsessional thinking and may, in fact, increase them. Neither obsessions nor compulsions are ego-syntonic. A patient with obsessive-compulsive disorder recognizes the irrationality of the obsession, which means that both the obsession and the compulsion are ego-dystonic.

18 ‖‖‖

Somatoform Disorders

Somatoform disorders are characterized by physical symptoms that suggest physical disease, although no demonstrable organ pathology or pathophysiological mechanism can be identified. In this group of disorders there is clear evidence or a strong presumption that the symptoms are linked to psychological factors. Somatoform disorders differ from factitious disorders and from malingering in that the patient has no voluntary control over the symptoms.

In the revised third edition of *Diagnostic and Statistical Manual of Mental Disorders* (DSM-III-R), somatoform disorders include body dysmorphic disorder, conversion disorder, hypochondriasis, somatization disorder, somatoform pain disorder, undifferentiated somatoform disorder, and somatoform disorder not otherwise specified (NOS). The student should know how some of these somatoform disorders are related to more classically described neurotic disorders.

Patients with body dysmorphic disorder believe that they are physically misshapen or defective in some way, although their appearance is objectively unremarkable. Body dysmorphic disorder should be differentiated from delusional disorder and anorexia nervosa.

In conversion disorder there is a loss or a change in bodily functioning that results from a psychological conflict or need. The theoretical psychodynamic cause of this disorder is important for the student to understand, and alternate etiological theories for conversion disorder should be studied. All clinicians should be familiar with this disorder and its many symptoms, since it may be most commonly seen in medical and surgical practices. The student should also be familiar with the associated features of primary and secondary gain, *la belle indifférence*, and identification.

Hypochondriasis is a disorder characterized by excessive concern about disease and a preoccupation with one's health. As with conversion disorder, physicians should be familiar with this disorder, as its fairly high prevalence in general practices can result in unnecessary treatment regimens and operations. Because of this clinical reality, the signs, symptoms, and differential diagnosis of hypochondriasis are practical for the student to know.

Somatization disorder is a chronic syndrome of multiple somatic symptoms that cannot be explained medically and that is associated with psychosocial distress and medical help-seeking. Since this diagnosis is often used too loosely, the student should know the basic outline of the diagnostic requirements for diagnosis in DSM-III-R. As with hypochondriasis, the student should emphasize the study of the clinical symptoms and differential diagnosis in the study of this disorder.

In somatoform pain disorder the predominant disturbance is severe and prolonged pain for which there is no medical explanation. In fact, it is often impossible to prove that there is no organic basis for many pain syndromes, such as low back pain and headache. Therefore, the emphasis in the study of this disorder should be not only on the various pharmacological approaches to treatment but also on the psychological theories and treatment strategies, such as psychoanalytic, learning, and interpersonal theories.

Students are referred to Chapter 18, "Somatoform Disorders," in *Synopsis VI* and to Chapter 19, "Somatoform Disorders," in *CTP V*. Studying the questions and answers below tests students' knowledge of this area.

HELPFUL HINTS

The somatoform disorder terms listed below should be defined.

somatization disorder
hysteria
Briquet's syndrome
somatosensory input
antisocial personality disorder
conversion disorder
instinctual impulse
depression
stocking-and-glove anesthesia
hemianesthia
conversion blindness
pseudocyesis

astasia-abasia
primary gain and secondary gain
la belle indifférence
identification
Amytal interview
somatoform pain disorder
psychogenic pain
endorphins
major depression
antidepressants
biofeedback
hypochondriasis

undoing
generalized anxiety disorder
body dysmorphic disorder
dysmorphophobia
symbolization and projection
anorexia nervosa
pimozide (Orap)
undifferentiated somatoform
    disorder
somatoform disorder NOS
secondary symptoms
functional symptoms

QUESTIONS

DIRECTIONS: Each of the incomplete statements below is followed by five suggested completions. Select the *one* that is *best* in each case.

18.1. Conversion disorder
A. is 10 times more common in women than in men
B. occurs most commonly in middle age
C. symptoms that are most common are paralysis, blindness, and mutism
D. is not associated with a later diagnosis of any neurological disorder
E. is uncommon in hospitalized patients with organic disease

18.2. A patient with conversion disorder
A. is conscious of a relevant psychological factor
B. may be having a culturally sanctioned response to a psychosocial stress
C. always experiences recurrent episodes
D. is unaware of intentionally producing the symptom
E. usually experiences pain

18.3. All the following are classified as somatoform disorders in DSM-III-R *except*
A. conversion disorder
B. hypochondriasis
C. somatization disorder
D. Munchausen syndrome
E. body dysmorphic disorder

DIRECTIONS: For each of the questions or incomplete statements below, *one or more* of the responses or completions given are correct. Choose answer

A. if only *1, 2, and 3* are correct
B. if only *1 and 3* are correct
C. if only *2 and 4* are correct
D. if only *4* is correct
E. if *all* are correct

18.4. In body dysmorphic disorder
1. the belief in a defect of appearance may take on delusional intensity
2. the average age of patients with the disorder is 30 years
3. patients are normal in appearance
4. anorexia nervosa is a consistent concomitant diagnosis

18.5. Medical disorders to be considered in a differential diagnosis of somatization disorder include
1. multiple sclerosis
2. systemic lupus erythematosus
3. acute intermittent porphyria
4. hyperparathyroidism

18.6. In the treatment of hypochondriasis
1. frequent physical examinations should be performed
2. any underlying psychiatric disorder should be treated
3. most patients are found to be resistant to psychotherapy
4. patients respond better to group psychotherapy than to individual therapy

18.7. Which of the following signs and symptoms are among the best indicators for possible somatization disorder?
1. Pain in the extremities
2. Diarrhea
3. Difficulty in swallowing
4. Impotence

18.8. Psychiatric disorders that occur with higher than expected frequency in somatization disorder patients are
1. antisocial personality disorder
2. alcohol abuse
3. drug abuse
4. suicide

18.9. Somatoform pain disorder is characterized by
1. preoccupation with pain for at least six months
2. no organic pathology to account for the pain
3. pain complaints grossly exceeding whatever demonstrable pathology is present
4. a peak age of onset in the early 20s

18.10. Characteristic signs of conversion disorder include
1. stocking-and-glove anesthesia
2. hemianesthesia of the body beginning precisely at the midline
3. astasia-abasia
4. normal reflexes

18.11. Favorable prognostic features of hypochondriasis include
1. the concurrent presence of anxiety or depression
2. onset in old age
3. acute onset
4. the presence of organic disease

18.12. Hypochondriasis enables patients to
1. deny the pain of low self-esteem
2. gratify their dependency needs
3. protect themselves from guilt
4. provide themselves with various secondary gains

18.13. Characteristic behavioral features in patients with conversion disorders include
1. somatic compliance
2. *la belle indifférence*
3. autonomic dysfunction
4. sexual disturbances

DIRECTIONS: The lettered headings below are followed by a list of numbered phrases. For each numbered phrase, select the lettered heading *best* associated with it. Each heading may be used once, more than once, or not at all.

Questions 18.14–18.19
A. Hypochondriasis
B. Somatization disorder

18.14. Approximately equal occurrence in men and women

18.15. Peak incidence during the 40s or 50s

18.16. Likely to have a hysterical cognitive and interpersonal style

18.17. Includes disease conviction and disease fear

18.18. Begins before age 30

18.19. By definition, includes at least 13 symptoms

ANSWERS

Somatoform Disorders

18.1. The answer is C (*Synopsis VI*, pages 418–420; *CTP V*, pages 1013–1017).

Conversion disorder is *two to five times, not 10 times*, more common in women than in men. Conversion disorder may occur at any age, but it is most common in *adolescence and young adulthood, not middle age*. *Paralysis, blindness, and mutism* have been reported as the most common conversion disorder symptoms. An association between conversion disorder and a later diagnosis of a *neurological disorder* has been found in several follow-up studies. Those studies indicate that 50 to 70 percent of conversion disorder patients have a diagnosable neurological disorder three to four years after the diagnosis of the conversion disorder. Concomitant *organic disease* is common in hospitalized patients with conversion disorder, and evidence of a current or prior neurological disorder or of a systemic disease affecting the brain has been reported in 18 to 64 percent of such patients. See Table 18.1 for the DSM-III-R criteria for conversion disorder.

18.2. The answer is D (*Synopsis VI*, pages 418–420; *CTP V*, page 1013).

The diagnostic criteria for conversion disorder state that psychological factors are judged to be causatively related to the symptom. The patient is not conscious of the *psychological factor* and is not conscious of *intentionally producing the symptom*. The symptom, furthermore, is not a *culturally sanctioned*

Table 18.1
Diagnostic Criteria for Conversion Disorder

A. A loss of, or alteration in, physical functioning suggesting a physical disorder.
B. Psychological factors are judged to be etiologically related to the symptom because of a temporal relationship between a psychosocial stressor that is apparently related to a psychological conflict or need and initiation or exacerbation of the symptom.
C. The person is not conscious of intentionally producing the symptom.
D. The symptom is not a culturally sanctioned response pattern and cannot, after appropriate investigation, be explained by a known physical disorder.
E. The symptom is not limited to pain or to a disturbance in sexual functioning.
Specify: single episode or **recurrent.**

response to a psychosocial stress and cannot be explained by a known physical disorder. A patient may experience a single episode of a conversion disorder or may go on to have *recurrent episodes*. See Table 18.1 for the DSM-III-R criteria for conversion disorder. *Pain* may be a symptom of conversion disorder but is not invariably present.

18.3. The answer is D (*Synopsis VI*, page 416; *CTP V*, pages 1009–1027).

Somatoform disorders are characterized by physical symptoms that resemble medical diseases, but they exhibit no organic pathology or known pathophysiological mechanism. DSM-III-R categorizes seven types of somatoform disorders: (1) *somatization disorder*, (2) *conversion disorder*, (3) somatoform pain disorder, (4) *hypochondriasis*, (5) *body dysmorphic disorder*, (6) undifferentiated somatoform disorder, and (7) somatoform disorder not otherwise specified (NOS), for disorders that cannot be classified as any of the previous categories. *Munchausen syndrome* is categorized as a factitious disorder with physical symptoms; the essential feature is the ability of patients to present physical symptoms so well that they are able to gain admission to and stay in hospitals. The symptom production in somatoform disorders is not intentional. Conversion disorder is a condition in which psychological factors are judged to be causatively related to a loss or an alteration of physical functioning. Hypochondriasis involves preoccupation with the fear of having a serious disease. Somatization disorder is a chronic, polysymptomatic disorder that begins early in life. Body dysmorphic disorder is characterized by preoccupation with some imagined defect in one's appearance.

18.4. The answer is A (1, 2, 3) (*Synopsis VI*, pages 424–425; *CTP V*, pages 1025–1026).

In body dysmorphic disorder, patients believe that they are physically misshapen or defective in some way, although their appearance is objectively unremarkable; the patients are *normal in appearance*. In such patients the belief in a defect in appearance may take on *delusional intensity*. The average age of patients with body dysmorphic disorder is *30 years*; the sex distribution is unclear. Although distortions of body image occur in *anorexia nervosa*, transsexualism, and some specific types of brain damage, they are not concomitant diagnoses. Body dysmorphic disorder should not be diagnosed when the distortions occur exclusively during the course of these illnesses. See Table 18.2 for the DSM-III-R criteria for body dysmorphic disorder.

Table 18.2
Diagnostic Criteria for Body Dysmorphic Disorder

A. Preoccupation with some imagined defect in appearance in a normal-appearing person. If a slight physical anomaly is present, the person's concern is grossly excessive.
B. The belief in the defect is not of delusional intensity, as in delusional disorder, somatic type (i.e., the person can acknowledge the possibility that he or she may be exaggerating the extent of the defect or that there may be no defect at all).
C. Occurrence not exclusively during the course of anorexia nervosa or transsexualism.

Table from DSM-III-R, *Diagnostic and Statistical Manual of Mental Disorders*, ed 3, revised. Copyright American Psychiatric Association, Washington, DC, 1987. Used with permission.

18.5.   The answer is E (all) (*Synopsis VI*, page 418; *CTP V*, page 1011).

The clinician must always rule out organic causes for the patient's symptoms. Medical disorders that present with nonspecific, transient abnormalities pose the greatest diagnostic difficulty in the differential diagnosis of somatization disorder. The disorders to be considered include *multiple sclerosis, systemic lupus erythematosus, acute intermittent porphyria*, and *hyperparathyroidism*. In addition, the onset of many somatic symptoms late in life must be presumed to be caused by a medical illness until testing rules it out.

18.6.   The answer is E (all) (*Synopsis VI*, page 424; *CTP V*, pages 1020–1021).

In the treatment of hypochondriasis, most patients are found to be *resistant to psychotherapy*. Some hypochondriacs accept psychiatric treatment if it takes place in a medical setting and focuses on stress reduction and education in coping with chronic illness. Such patients respond better to *group psychotherapy than to individual therapy*, perhaps because the group provides the social support and social interaction that these patients need. Individual, insight-oriented, traditional psychotherapy for primary hypochondriasis is generally not successful.

Frequent physical examinations should be performed; they are useful in reassuring patients that they are not being abandoned by their doctors and that their complaints are being taken seriously. Invasive diagnostic and therapeutic procedures, however, should be undertaken only on the basis of objective evidence. When possible, it is best to refrain from treating equivocal or incidental findings.

Pharmacotherapy alleviates hypochondriacal symptoms only when there is an underlying drug-sensitive condition, such as an anxiety disorder or a major depression. When hypochondriasis is secondary to some other primary psychiatric disorder, the *underlying psychiatric disorder* should be treated in its own right. When hypochondriasis is a transient situational reaction, patients must be helped to cope with the stress without reinforcing their illness be-

havior and their use of the sick role as solutions to their problems.

See Table 18.3 for the DSM-III-R diagnostic criteria for hypochondriasis.

18.7.   The answer is B (1, 3) (*Synopsis VI*, pages 416–417; *CTP V*, pages 1010–1011).

Patients with somatization disorder have a multitude of somatic complaints and long, complicated medical histories. Vomiting (other than during pregnancy), *difficulty in swallowing*, pain in the *extremities*, shortness of breath unrelated to exertion, amnesia, and painful menstruation are among the most common symptoms that point to a diagnosis of somatization disorder.

See Table 18.4, which lists the DSM-III-R diagnostic criteria for somatization disorder. The seven items listed in bold type are used to screen for the disorder. *Impotence* and *diarrhea* may occur in a somatization disorder but are not among the best indicators for its diagnosis.

18.8.   The answer is A (1, 2, 3) (*Synopsis VI*, page 417; *CTP V*, page 1011).

Three psychiatric disorders occur in somatization disorder patients with higher than expected frequency: *antisocial personality disorder, alcohol abuse*, and *drug abuse*. Suicide threats are frequent, but actual *suicide* is rare. If suicide does occur, it is usually associated with substance abuse.

18.9.   The answer is A (1, 2, 3) (*Synopsis VI*, page 421; *CTP V*, pages 1021–1024).

In somatoform pain disorder (previously called psychogenic or idiopathic pain disorder), the predominant disturbance is severe and prolonged pain for which there is no medical explanation. Courses of

Table 18.3
Diagnostic Criteria for Hypochondriasis

A. Preoccupation with the fear of having, or the belief that one has, a serious disease, based on the person's interpretation of physical signs or sensations as evidence of physical illness.
B. Appropriate physical evaluation does not support the diagnosis of any physical disorder that can account for the physical signs or sensations or the person's unwarranted interpretation of them, **and** the symptoms in A are not just symptoms of panic attacks.
C. The fear of having, or belief that one has, a disease persists despite medical reassurance.
D. Duration of the disturbance is at least six months.
E. The belief in A is not of delusional intensity, as in delusional disorder, somatic type (i.e., the person can acknowledge the possibility that his or her fear of having, or belief that he or she has, a serious disease is unfounded).

Table from DSM-III-R, *Diagnostic and Statistical Manual of Mental Disorders*, ed 3, revised. Copyright American Psychiatric Association, Washington, DC, 1987. Used with permission.

Table 18.4
Diagnostic Criteria for Somatization Disorder

A. A history of many physical complaints or a belief that one is sickly, beginning before the age of 30 and persisting for several years.

B. At least 13 symptoms from the list below. To count a symptom as significant, the following criteria must be met:

1. no organic pathology or pathophysiologic mechanism (e.g., a physical disorder or the effects of injury, medication, drugs, or alcohol) to account for the symptom or, when there is related organic pathology, the complaint or resulting social or occupational impairment is grossly in excess of what would be expected from the physical findings

2. has not occurred only during a panic attack

3. has caused the person to take medicine (other than over-the-counter pain medication), see a doctor, or alter life-style

Symptom list:

Gastrointestinal symptoms:

1. **vomiting (other than during pregnancy)**
2. abdominal pain (other than when menstruating)
3. nausea (other than motion sickness)
4. bloating (gassy)
5. diarrhea
6. intolerance of (gets sick from) several different foods

Pain symptoms:

7. **pain in extremities**
8. back pain
9. joint pain
10. pain during urination
11. other pain (excluding headaches)

Cardiopulmonary symptoms:

12. **shortness of breath when not exerting oneself**
13. palpitations
14. chest pain
15. dizziness

Conversion or pseudoneurologic symptoms:

16. **amnesia**
17. **difficulty swallowing**
18. loss of voice
19. deafness
20. double vision
21. blurred vision
22. blindness
23. fainting or loss of consciousness
24. seizure or convulsion
25. trouble walking
26. paralysis or muscle weakness
27. urinary retention or difficulty urinating

Sexual symptoms for the major part of the person's life after opportunities for sexual activity:

28. **burning sensation in sexual organs or rectum (other than during intercourse)**
29. sexual indifference
30. pain during intercourse
31. impotence

Female reproductive symptoms judged by the person to occur more frequently or severely than in most women:

32. **painful menstruation**
33. irregular menstrual bleeding
34. excessive menstrual bleeding
35. vomiting throughout pregnancy

Note: The seven items in boldface may be used to screen for the disorder. The presence of two or more of these items suggests a high likelihood of the disorder.

Table from DSM-III-R, *Diagnostic and Statistical Manual of Mental Disorders*, ed 3, revised. Copyright American Psychiatric Association, Washington, DC, 1987. Used with permission.

---

somatoform pain are presumed to be psychological, even though such evidence may not be readily apparent in each case. DSM-III-R requires that there be *six months of preoccupation with pain* and that either there be *no organic pathology* to account for the pain or the *pain grossly exceeds* whatever demonstrable pathology is present. The *peak age of onset* is in the 40s and 50s. (See Table 18.5 for the diagnostic criteria for somatoform pain disorder.)

18.10. The answer is E (all) (*Synopsis VI*, pages 418–419; *CTP V*, pages 1015–1016).

In conversion disorder, anesthesia and paresthesia are common, especially of the extremities. All sensory modalities are involved, and the distribution of the disturbance is inconsistent with that of either central or peripheral neurological disease. Thus, one sees the characteristic *stocking-and-glove anesthesia* of the hands or feet or *hemianesthesia* of the body beginning precisely along the midline. Motor symptoms include abnormal movements and gait disturbance, which often is a wildly ataxic, staggering gait accompanied by gross, irregular, jerky truncal movements and thrashing and waving arms (also known as *astasia-abasia*). *Reflexes remain normal*; there are no fasciculations or muscle atrophy, and electromyography results are normal. See Table 18.1 for the DSM-III-R criteria for conversion disorder.

18.11. The answer is B (1, 3) (*Synopsis VI*, pages 422–424; *CTP V*, page 1020).

Favorable prognostic features of hypochondriasis include the *concurrent presence of anxiety or depression*, *acute onset*, *onset* in youth (not old age), the *absence* (*not presence*) *of organic disease*, the absence of personality disorder, and high socioeconomic status. On long-term follow-up, one fourth of hypochondriacs do poorly, and about two thirds run chronic, fluctuating courses. Most hypochondriacal children, however, have recovered by late adolescence or early adulthood. Treatment helps a significant proportion of patients. (See Table 18.3 for the DSM-III-R diagnostic criteria for hypochondriasis.)

Table 18.5
Diagnostic Criteria for Somatoform Pain Disorder

A. Preoccupation with pain for at least six months.

B. Either 1 or 2:

1. appropriate evaluation uncovers no organic pathology or pathophysiologic mechanism (e.g., a physical disorder or the effects of injury) to account for the pain

2. when there is related organic pathology, the complaint of pain or resulting social or occupational impairment is grossly in excess of what would be expected from the physical findings.

Table from DSM-III-R, *Diagnostic and Statistical Manual of Mental Disorders*, ed 3, revised. Copyright American Psychiatric Association, Washington, DC, 1987. Used with permission.

18.12. The answer is E (all) (*Synopsis VI*, page 423; *CTP V*, page 1018).

Investigators see hypochondriacal symptoms as playing a primarily defensive role in the psychic economy. For Harry Stack Sullivan they represented a protective activity that enabled the person to *deny the pain of low self-esteem*. In other words, persons can substitute an image of themselves as physically ill or deficient for the far more devastating view of themselves as worthless human beings.

Hypochondriasis also enables patients to *gratify their dependency needs, protect themselves from guilt,* and *provide themselves with various secondary gains.* The obvious advantage that persons gain from their illness is secondary gain, such as gifts, attention, and release from responsibility.

The theoretical explanations of hypochondriasis have been constructed from observations made on a small number of patients. They must be viewed cautiously because many of these patients are limited in their ability to reveal the kind of psychological introspections on which psychodynamic formulations must be based and tested. Some workers believe that hypochondriasis is grounded on a narcissistic personality organization, and the continued investigation of hypochondriasis is essential to a deeper understanding of narcissistic phenomena. (See Table 18.3.)

18.13. The answer is E (all) (*Synopsis VI*, pages 419–420; *CTP V*, pages 1015–1016).

The most characteristic behavioral feature in patients with conversion disorder is what the French authors of the 19th century called *la belle indifférence*. Despite what appear to be the most extensive and crippling disturbances in function, the patient is completely unconcerned and may not spontaneously mention such disturbances, which often results in their being overlooked. Unless specifically searched for, *la belle indifférence* is a calm mental attitude of acquiescence and complacency directed specifically at the physical symptom.

Somatic compliance is the degree to which a person's organic structures coincide with the psychological mechanisms in the symptomatic expression of the pathological defenses. In conversion symptoms, for instance, the entire cathexis of the objectionable impulses is condensed onto a definite physical function. The ability of the affected function to absorb the cathexis is its somatic compliance.

Autonomic dysfunctions may be reflected in various visceral symptoms, such as anorexia, vomiting, hiccoughs, and other abdominal complaints, which are considered a part of the classical syndrome of conversion disorders. Sensory disturbances—anesthesias, in particular—are also typical of the physical symptoms of hysterical neurosis.

A history of *sexual disturbances*—especially impotence, anorgasmia, and a lack of desire—is frequently seen along with conversion symptoms. According to psychoanalytic theory, conversion disorder has been linked to a psychosexual conflict arising from the failure to relinquish oedipal ties and to rid the normal adult libido of its incestuous ties.

18.14–18.19

18.14. The answer is A (*Synopsis VI*, page 423; *CTP V*, pages 1017–1020).

18.15. The answer is A (*Synopsis VI*, page 423; *CTP V*, pages 1017–1020).

18.16. The answer is B (*Synopsis VI*, pages 416–417; *CTP V*, pages 1009–1012).

18.17. The answer is A (*Synopsis VI*, page 422; *CTP V*, pages 1017–1020).

18.18. The answer is B (*Synopsis VI*, page 417; *CTP V*, pages 1009–1012).

18.19. The answer is B (*Synopsis VI*, page 416; *CTP V*, pages 1009–1012).

Hypochondriasis, which is an excessive concern about disease and a preoccupation with one's health, is found approximately *equally in men and in women*. Somatization disorder, which is a chronic syndrome of multiple somatic symptoms that cannot be explained medically, is much more common in women than in men. The peak incidence of hypochondriasis is thought to occur during the *40s or 50s*, whereas somatization disorder *begins before age 30*. Somatization disorder patients are more likely to have a *hysterical cognitive and interpersonal style*, as opposed to the more obsessional hypochondriac. Somatization disorder does not include *disease conviction or disease fear*, as does hypochondriasis. Somatization disorder includes *at least 13 symptoms* that, by definition, have caused the person to take medication, see a doctor, or alter life-style; have not occurred only during a panic attack; and do not have an organic pathophysiological mechanism or, when there is organic pathology, greatly exceed what is expected from the physical findings. Hypochondriasis does not include any specific number of symptoms or complaints. See Table 18.4 for the DSM-III-R diagnostic criteria for somatization disorder.

19 ||||||

Dissociative Disorders

The essential feature of the dissociative disorders is a disturbance of or an alteration in the normally integrative functions of identity, memory, and consciousness. Clinicians are advised to become familiar with the psychodynamic theories relevant to the dissociative disorders. Current explanations of the dissociative disorders are based on those concepts. Dissociation is conceived of as a mechanism to protect the patient from emotional pain that has arisen either from external circumstances or from anxiety-provoking internal drives and affects.

The dissociative disorders in the revised third edition of *Diagnostic and Statistical Manual of Mental Disorders* (DSM-III-R) are multiple personality disorder, psychogenic fugue, psychogenic amnesia, depersonalization disorder, and dissociative disorder not otherwise specified (NOS).

Multiple personality disorder is characterized by a person's having two or more distinct and separate personalities, each of which determines the nature of the person's behavior and attitudes during the period when it is dominant. Although this disorder was previously thought to be rare, it is now realized that it may be more common than suspected, both in routine psychiatric practice and in the emergency room. The possible causative roles of a highly traumatic childhood and epilepsy should be familiar to the student.

Psychogenic fugue is defined as sudden, unexpected travel, often far from home, and an inability to remember one's former life or identity. The student should be aware of the psychodynamic causative theories and the association with alcohol abuse. Physicians who work in emergency rooms must recognize the clinical features of the disorder, as it is in the emergency room that psychogenic fugue patients often come to medical attention.

Psychogenic amnesia is defined as a sudden inability to recall important personal information already stored in memory. The study of this disorder is an appropriate place for the student to review the organic causes of amnesia. The psychodynamic explanations for psychogenic amnesia should be studied. Finally, the student should be aware of the clinical varieties of amnesia seen in patients.

Depersonalization disorder is characterized by a persistent or recurrent alteration in the perception of the self to the extent that the feeling of one's own reality is temporarily lost. Studying the psychiatric differential diagnosis of this disorder is a good way to understand the disorder, as depersonalization disorder needs to be differentiated from temporal lobe epilepsy, schizophrenia, panic disorder, and agoraphobia. Differentiation between normal levels and pathological levels of depersonalization may be difficult, but clinicians should be careful to consider this diagnosis in young adults in particular.

Dissociative disorders NOS include such syndromes as Ganser's syndrome and trance states. Students should review the examples of this disorder given in DSM-III-R so that they understand the basic concept enough to know when the diagnosis is appropriate in another clinical example.

Students should refer to Chapter 19 of *Synopsis VI*, "Dissociative Disorders," and to Chapter 20 of *CTP V*, "Dissociative Disorders (Hysterical Neuroses, Dissociative Type)," for an overview of this subject and should then study the questions and answers below.

HELPFUL HINTS

The terms below relate to dissociative disorders and should be defined.

hysterical neuroses	multiple personality	crystal gazing
psychogenic amnesia	dominant personality	highway hypnosis
epidemiology of dissociative	secondary gain	approximate answers
disorders	depersonalization	coercive persuasion
localized amnesia	derealization	brainwashing
selective amnesia	hemidepersonalization	somnambulism
continuous amnesia	paramnesia	dissociation
transient global amnesia	double orientation	denial
anterograde amnesia	reduplicative paramnesia	Korsakoff's syndrome
retrograde amnesia	Ganser's syndrome	malingering
fugue	trance	doubling
wandering	possession state	
temporal lobe functions	automatic writing	

QUESTIONS

DIRECTIONS: Each of the incomplete statements below is followed by five suggested completions. Select the *one* that is *best* in each case.

19.1. Depersonalization disorder is characterized by
A. impaired reality testing
B. ego-dystonic symptoms
C. occurrence in the late decades of life
D. gradual onset
E. a brief course and a good prognosis

19.2. Multiple personality disorder is
A. not associated in first-degree relatives of persons with the disorder
B. not nearly as rare as it has been thought to be
C. most common in early childhood
D. much more frequent in men than in women
E. not a dissociative disorder

19.3. Signs of multiple personality disorder include
A. reports by the patient of being recognized by people whom the patient does not know
B. the use of the word "we" by the patient
C. reports of time distortions and discontinuities
D. changes in behavior reported by a reliable observer
E. all the above

19.4. Dissociative disorders in DSM-III-R include
A. psychogenic amnesia
B. depersonalization disorder
C. multiple personality disorder
D. Ganser's syndrome
E. all the above

19.5. Clinical features of psychogenic amnesia include
A. an abrupt onset
B. retaining the capacity to learn new information
C. some precipitating emotional trauma
D. awareness of the memory loss
E. all the above

DIRECTIONS: For each of the incomplete statements below, *one or more* of the completions given are correct. Choose answer

    A. if only *1, 2, and 3* are correct
    B. if only *1 and 3* are correct
    C. if only *2 and 4* are correct
    D. if only *4* is correct
    E. if *all* are correct

19.6. Psychogenic fugue is
1. rare
2. usually long-lasting
3. characterized by a lack of awareness of the loss of memory
4. characterized by behavior that appears extraordinary to others

19.7. Psychogenic amnesia is
1. the least common type of dissociative disorder
2. more common in men than in women
3. most common in old adults
4. most common during periods of war and during natural disasters

19.8. Patients predisposed to psychogenic fugue states include those with
1. mood disorders
2. borderline personality disorders
3. heavy alcohol abuse
4. schizoid personality disorders

19.9. The differential diagnosis of psychogenic amnesia includes
1. transient global amnesia
2. alcohol amnestic disorder
3. postconcussion amnesia
4. epilepsy

ANSWERS

Dissociative Disorders

19.1. The answer is B (*Synopsis VI*, pages 433–435; *CTP V*, pages 1038–1042).

Depersonalization disorder is characterized by a persistent or recurrent alteration in the perception of the self to the extent that the feeling of one's own reality is temporarily lost. In DSM-III-R it is described as the experience of feeling mechanical, being in a dream, or feeling detached from one's body. All these symptoms are *ego-dystonic*—that is, at variance with the ego. The person, however, maintains *intact reality testing*; he or she is aware of the disturbances. As an occasional isolated experience in the life of any person, depersonalization is a common phenomenon and is not necessarily pathological. Information about the epidemiology of depersonalization of pathological proportions is scanty. In a few studies, depersonalization has been rarely found in persons over 40 years of age. The disorder most often starts between the ages of 15 and 30 years, but it has been seen in patients as young as 10 years of age; it occurs less frequently after age 30 and almost never in the *late decades of life*. In the large majority of patients, the symptoms first appear suddenly; only a few patients report *gradual onset*. A few follow-up studies indicate that, in more than half the cases, depersonalization disorder tends to be a long-term, chronic condition, with a *poor prognosis*. In many patients, the symptoms run a steady course without significant fluctuations of intensity; but they may occur episodically, interspersed with symptom-free intervals. See Table 19.1 for the DSM-III-R diagnostic criteria for depersonalization disorder.

19.2. The answer is B (*Synopsis VI*, page 431; *CTP V*, pages 1036–1037).

Recent reports on multiple personality disorder suggest that it *is not nearly as rare* as it has been thought to be. It is *more common in late adolescence and young adult life* than in childhood and is much *more frequent in women than in men*. Several studies have indicated that this disorder is more common in *first-degree biological relatives* of people with the disorder than in the general population. There has been a great deal of interest in multiple personality disorder, and its incidence is being reappraised. At present, several thousand cases have been reported in the literature. It is classified as a *dissociative disorder*. See Table 19.2 for the DSM-III-R diagnostic criteria for multiple personality disorder.

Table 19.1
Diagnostic Criteria for Depersonalization Disorder

A. Persistent or recurrent experiences of depersonalization as indicated by either 1 or 2:
  1. an experience of feeling detached from, and as if one is an outside observer of, one's mental processes or body
  2. an experience of feeling like an automaton or as if in a dream
B. During the depersonalization experience, reality testing remains intact.
C. The depersonalization is sufficiently severe and persistent to cause marked distress.
D. The depersonalization experience is the predominant disturbance and is not a symptom of another disorder, such as schizophrenia, panic disorder, or agoraphobia without history of panic disorder but with limited symptom attacks of depersonalization, or temporal lobe epilepsy.

Table from DSM-III-R, *Diagnostic and Statistical Manual of Mental Disorders*, ed 3, revised. Copyright American Psychiatric Association, Washington, DC, 1987. Used with permission.

Table 19.2
Diagnostic Criteria for Multiple Personality Disorder

A. The existence within the person of two or more distinct personalities or personality states (each with its own relatively enduring pattern of perceiving, relating to, and thinking about the environment and self).
B. At least two of these personalities or personality states recurrently take full control of the person's behavior.

Table from DSM-III-R, *Diagnostic and Statistical Manual of Mental Disorders*, ed 3, revised. Copyright American Psychiatric Association, Washington, DC, 1987. Used with permission.

19.3. The answer is E (*Synopsis VI*, page 432; *CTP V*, pages 1036–1037).

Multiple personality disorder may be misdiagnosed as a schizophrenic disorder or a personality disorder. The clinician is advised to listen for specific features suggestive of this disorder. Signs of the disorder include reports by the patient of being *recognized by people* whom the patient does not know, the use of the word *"we"* by the patient, reports by the patient of *time distortions and lapses*, and changes in behavior reported by a *reliable observer*. See Table 19.3 for other signs of multiple personality disorder.

Table 19.3
Signs of Multiplicity

1. Reports of time distortions, lapses, and discontinuities
2. Being told of behavioral episodes by others that are not remembered by the patient
3. Being recognized by others or called by another name by people whom the patient does not recognize
4. Notable changes in the patient's behavior reported by a reliable observer; the patient may call himself by a different name or refer to himself in the third person
5. Other personalities are elicited under hypnosis or during Amytal interviews
6. Use of the word "we" in the course of an interview
7. Discovery of writings, drawings, or other productions or objects (identification cards, clothing, etc.) among the patient's personal belongings that are not recognized or cannot be accounted for
8. Headaches
9. Hearing voices originating from within and not identified as separate
10. History of severe emotional or physical trauma as a child (usually before the age of 5 years)

Adapted from GB Greaves. Multiple personality 165 years after Mary Reynolds. J Nerv Ment Dis. *168*: 584, 1980. Copyright 1980. The Williams & Wilkins Company, Baltimore, with permission.

19.4. The answer is E (*Synopsis VI*, pages 428 and 435; *CTP V*, pages 1028–1029).

According to DSM-III-R, the dissociative disorders are a group of syndromes characterized by a sudden temporary alteration in the normally integrated functions of consciousness, identity, and motor behavior, so that some part of these functions is lost. In the past they were known as hysterical neuroses of the dissociative type. There are five major types of dissociative disorder: *psychogenic amnesia*, psychogenic fugue, *multiple personality disorder*, *depersonalization disorder*, and dissociative disorder not otherwise specified (NOS). Dissociative disorder NOS is a residual category for disorders in which the predominant feature is a dissociative symptom that does not meet the criteria for one of the specific dissociative disorders listed above. In DSM-III-R, *Ganser's syndrome* is listed in this residual category of dissociative disorders. Ganser's syndrome is the voluntary production of severe psychiatric symptoms. The syndrome is commonly associated with such dissociative phenomena as amnesia, fugue, and perceptual disturbances. Patients with the syndrome also give approximate answers to questions (e.g., 2 + 2 = 5). See Table 19.4 for the DSM-III-R diagnostic criteria for dissociative disorder not otherwise specified.

19.5. The answer is E (*Synopsis VI*, pages 428–429; *CTP V*, page 1035).

Although some episodes of amnesia occur spontaneously, a careful history usually reveals some *precipitating emotional trauma* charged with painful emotions and psychological conflict. The disorder

Table 19.4
Diagnostic Criteria for Dissociative Disorder Not Otherwise Specified

Disorders in which the predominant feature is a dissociative symptom (i.e., a disturbance or alteration in the normally integrative functions of identity, memory, or consciousness) that does not meet the criteria for a specific dissociative disorder.
Examples:
1. Ganser's syndrome: the giving of "approximate answers" to questions, commonly associated with other symptoms such as amnesia, disorientation, perceptual disturbances, fugue, and conversion symptoms
2. cases in which there is more than one personality state capable of assuming executive control of the individual, but not more than one personality state is sufficiently distinct to meet the full criteria for multiple personality disorder, or cases in which a second personality never assumes complete executive control
3. trance states (i.e., altered states of consciousness with markedly diminished or selectively focused responsiveness to environmental stimuli). In children this may occur following physical abuse or trauma
4. derealization unaccompanied by depersonalization
5. dissociated states that may occur in people who have been subjected to periods of prolonged and intense coercive persuasion (e.g., brainwashing, thought reform, or indoctrination while the captive of terrorists or cultists)
6. cases in which sudden, unexpected travel and organized, purposeful behavior with inability to recall one's past are not accompanied by the assumption of a new identity, partial or complete

Table from DSM-III-R, *Diagnostic and Statistical Manual of Mental Disorders*, ed 3, revised. Copyright American Psychiatric Association, Washington, DC, 1987. Used with permission.

usually has an *abrupt onset*, and the patient is usually *aware of losing his or her memory*. The *capacity to learn new information is retained*. See Table 19.5 for the DSM-III-R diagnostic criteria for psychogenic amnesia.

19.6. The answer is B (1, 3) (*Synopsis VI*, pages 430–431; *CTP V*, page 1035).

Psychogenic fugue is considered *rare* and, like psychogenic amnesia, occurs most often during wartime, after natural disasters, and as a result of per-

Table 19.5
Diagnostic Criteria for Psychogenic Amnesia

A. The predominant disturbance is an episode of sudden inability to recall important personal information that is too extensive to be explained by ordinary forgetfulness.
B. The disturbance is not due to multiple personality disorder or to an organic mental disorder (e.g., blackouts during alcohol intoxication).

Table from DSM-III-R, *Diagnostic and Statistical Manual of Mental Disorders*, ed 3, revised. Copyright American Psychiatric Association, Washington, DC, 1987. Used with permission.

sonal crises with intense conflict. Typical features of psychogenic fugue include the following: The patient wanders, in a purposeful way, usually far from home and sometimes for days at a time. During this period, the patient has complete amnesia for his or her past life but, unlike the patient with psychogenic amnesia, there is a *lack of awareness* of the loss of memory. A patient in a psychogenic fugue does not appear to others to be behaving in an *extraordinary* way, nor is there evidence of acting out any specific memory of a traumatic event. The fugue patient generally leads a quiet, reclusive existence. A fugue is usually *brief*—hours to days. Less commonly, a fugue may last many months and involve extensive travel covering thousands of miles. Generally, recovery is spontaneous and rapid. See Table 19.6 for the DSM-III-R diagnostic criteria for psychogenic fugue.

19.7. The answer is D (4) (*Synopsis VI*, page 428; *CTP V*, pages 1035–1036).

Psychogenic amnesia is defined as a sudden inability to recall important personal information already stored in memory that cannot be explained by ordinary forgetfulness. It is *most common during periods of war and during natural disasters.* Psy-

Table 19.6
Diagnostic Criteria for Psychogenic Fugue

A. The predominant disturbance is sudden, unexpected travel away from home or one's customary place of work with inability to recall one's past.
B. Assumption of a new identity (partial or complete)
C. The disturbance is not due to multiple personality disorder or to an organic mental disorder (e.g., partial complex seizures in temporal lobe epilepsy).

Table from DSM-III-R, *Diagnostic and Statistical Manual of Mental Disorders*, ed 3, revised. Copyright American Psychiatric Association, Washington, DC, 1987. Used with permission.

chogenic amnesia is the *most common type* of dissociative disorder, *occurring most often in adolescents and young adults.* It is *more common in women than in men.*

19.8. The answer is E (all) (*Synopsis VI*, page 430; *CTP V*, pages 1035–1036).

Fugue is defined as sudden, unexpected wandering, often far from home, and an inability to remember one's former life or identity. The person may take on an entirely new identity and a new occupation. Although it is believed that *heavy alcohol abuse* may predispose a person to the disorder, the cause is thought to be basically psychological. The essential motivating factor appears to be a desire to withdraw from emotionally painful experiences. Patients with *mood disorders* and certain personality disorders (e.g., *borderline, schizoid,* and histrionic) are predisposed to fugue states.

19.9. The answer is E (all) (*Synopsis VI*, pages 429–430; *CTP V*, pages 1035, 1037–1038).

The differential diagnosis of psychogenic amnesia includes organic mental disorders in which there is a memory disturbance, especially *transient global amnesia* (TGA). TGA, however, is not related to stress; the memory loss is concentrated on recent, rather than remote, events; and there is rarely a loss of personal identity. TGA is most common in patients over 65 with underlying vascular disease. In *alcohol amnestic disorder,* short-term memory loss occurs; that is, events can be remembered immediately after they occur, but the memory fades after a few minutes. This disorder, also known as Korsakoff's syndrome, is associated with prolonged alcohol abuse. In *postconcussion amnesia,* the memory disturbance follows head trauma, is often retrograde, and usually does not extend beyond one week. *Epilepsy* leads to sudden memory impairment associated with motor and electroencephalogram abnormalities. A history of an aura, head trauma, or incontinence helps in the diagnosis.

20 ||||||

Human Sexuality

Patterns of sexual behavior have varied widely throughout history. Activities accepted as normal and openly engaged in during one era have been severely condemned and considered too abnormal to be tolerated during another. Because sexual behavior, specifically variant sexual behavior, is a subject in which moral and religious issues and cultural value systems are deeply implicated, it is difficult to approach with dispassionate scientific objectivity; nevertheless, such objectivity is essential if the psychiatrist is to deal constructively with the psychosocial problems involved in such behavior.

The pioneering work of William Masters and Virginia Johnson that began 25 years ago has had a profound effect on attitudes about sexual behavior. Sexual problems have been brought out into the open, and new and more effective treatments for sexual disorders have been developed. As a result, professionals are not nearly as worried about fixation points and compulsions as was Sigmund Freud and the generation of psychoanalysts after him, provided the sexual activity is pleasurable and noninjurious to both partners. Hence, although the range of normal sexual behavior has broadened enormously from the restricted one of Freud's time and place, the clinician must always retain a concern for compulsive, stereotyped sexual behavior that limits the freedom and flexibility of the patient. Human sexual processes are affected by a wide variety of conscious and unconscious intrapsychic, interpersonal, moral, aesthetic, religious, and cultural influences. The transmission of acquired immune deficiency syndrome (AIDS) through sexual contact has profoundly influenced sexual behavior, and a careful sexual history needs to be part of every psychiatric or medical examination.

According to the revised third edition of *Diagnostic and Statistical Manual of Mental Disorders* (DSM-III-R), sexual disorders are divided into two major groups: paraphilias, classified by arousal in response to sexual objects or situations that are not part of normal arousal patterns, and sexual dysfunctions, characterized by inhibitions in sexual desire or the psychophysiological changes that characterize the sexual response cycle.

The student should know the normal sexual response cycle in great detail. Each phase of the cycle is associated with one or more sexual dysfunctions. Thus, hypoactive sexual desire disorder, characterized by a deficiency in the desire for sexual activity, is associated with the first phase of the response cycle, known as the appetitive phase. The appetitive phase reflects the person's motivations, drive, and personality.

A broad variety of treatment methods for sexual disorders are now available. Some methods, such as insight-oriented psychotherapy, focus on the exploration of unconscious conflicts, motivation, fantasy, and various interpersonal difficulties. Other treatments, such as dual-sex therapy, focus on educating the sexual partners in the theory and the techniques of sexual functioning on the basis of the techniques of behavior therapy. There are also biological and pharmacological therapies that are of great use.

In addition, five special areas of interest are not sexual disorders per se but have, in many instances, sexual overtones. The first three—rape, spouse abuse, and incest—are appropriately viewed as acts of aggression, violence, and humiliation that may be expressed through sexual means. The last two—infertility and sterilization—are sometimes the result of a sexual disorder (e.g., an unconsummated mar-

195

riage) or may produce a sexual disorder (e.g., the neurotic poststerilization syndrome).

There is a close relation of medical illness (especially AIDS), drug use, contraceptive use, mental illness, and sexual behavior and function. The student needs to be aware of the interactions among these factors to counsel the patient effectively and to recognize and pre-

vent, whenever possible, the consequences of rape and sexual violence.

Readers should refer to Chapter 20, "Human Sexuality," in *Synopsis VI* and to Chapter 21, "Normal Human Sexuality and Sexual Disorders," in *CTP V* and should then study the questions and answers below to assess their understanding of this area.

HELPFUL HINTS

The student should know the following terms and their definitions.

psychosexual stages	transvestic fetishism	inhibited male orgasm
sexual and gender identity	frotteurism	retarded ejaculation
HIV, AIDS	zoophilia	retrograde ejaculation
embryological studies	coprophilia	premature ejaculation
gender role	urophilia	dyspareunia
masturbation	partialism	vaginismus
Alfred Kinsey	necrophilia	Peyronie's disease
William Masters and Virginia	hypoxyphilia	orgasmic anhedonia
Johnson	autoerotic asphyxiation	postcoital headache
tumescence and detumescence	telephone scatology	postcoital dysphoria
excitement	sexual desire disorders	unconsummated marriage
plateau	sexual arousal disorders	Don Juanism
orgasm	orgasm disorders	satyriasis
resolution	sexual pain disorders	sexual orientation distress
sympathetic and parasympathetic	sexual dysfunction NOS	homosexuality
nervous systems	biogenic versus psychogenic	dual-sex therapy
ejaculation and erection	inhibited sexual desire	sensate focus
refractory period	hypoactive sexual desire	spectatoring
DSM-III-R phases of sexual	sexual aversion disorder	squeeze technique
response	vagina dentata	stop-start technique
intimacy	male erectile disorder	desensitization therapy
paraphilias	female sexual arousal disorder	hymenectomy
steal phenomenon	anorgasmia	vaginoplasty
pedophilia	castration	prosthetic devices
exhibitionism	nocturnal penile tumescence	rape (male and female)
sexual masochism and sadism	Doppler effect	statutory rape
moral masochism	TFTs, FH, FSH	spouse abuse
voyeurism	cystometric examination	incest
scoptophilia	penile arteriography	infertility
fetishism	clitoral versus vaginal orgasm	sterilization

QUESTIONS

DIRECTIONS: Each of the questions or incomplete statements below is followed by five suggested responses or completions. Select the *one* that is *best* in each case.

Questions 20.1–20.2

Mr. and Mrs. B. were married for 14 years and had three children, aged 8 through 12. The Bs were both bright and well educated. They presented with the complaint that Ms. B. had been able to participate passively in sex "as a duty" but had never enjoyed it since their wedding.

Before their marriage they had had intercourse only twice. Ms. B. had been highly aroused by kissing and petting and felt that she had used her attractiveness to seduce her husband into marriage. She felt intense guilt about their two episodes of premarital intercourse, and during their honeymoon she began to think of sex as a chore that could not be pleasing. Although she passively complied with intercourse, she had almost no spontaneous desire for sex. She never masturbated, had never reached orgasm, thought of all variations (such as oral sex) as completely repulsive, and was preoccupied with a fantasy of how disapproving her family would be if she ever engaged in any of these activities.

Whenever Ms. B. was close to having a feeling of sexual arousal, numerous negative thoughts came into her mind, such as, "What would my mother say about this?" "What am I, a tramp?" "If I like this, he'll just want it more often." "How could I look myself in the mirror after something like this?" These thoughts almost inevitably were accompanied by a cold feeling and an insensitivity to sensual pleasure. As a result, sex was invariably an unhappy experience. Almost any excuse, such as fatigue or being busy, was sufficient for her to rationalize avoiding intercourse.

Intellectually, Ms. B. wondered, "Is something wrong with me?" She was seeking help to find out whether she was normal. Her husband, although tolerant of the situation, was very unhappy about their sex life and hopeful that help would be forthcoming.

[From *DSM-III-R Case Book*. Used with permission.]

20.1. The most appropriate diagnosis for this patient is
A. hypoactive sexual desire disorder
B. dyspareunia
C. orgasmic anhedonia
D. major depression
E. obsessive-compulsive personality disorder

20.2. All the following are appropriate in the treatment of hypoactive sexual desire disorder *except*
A. behavior therapy
B. dual-sex therapy
C. hypnotherapy
D. squeeze technique
E. minor tranquilizers

20.3. The sequence of the DSM-III-R phases of the sexual response cycle is
A. appetitive, excitement, orgasm, resolution
B. excitement, plateau, orgasm, resolution
C. resolution, appetitive, orgasm, excitement
D. excitement, orgasm, plateau, resolution
E. none of the above

20.4. Which of the following surgical procedures may be used in treating sexual dysfunctions?
A. Insertion of a penile prosthesis
B. Penile revascularization
C. Hymenectomy
D. Vaginoplasty
E. All the above

20.5. A married man with a chief complaint of premature ejaculation is best treated with
A. psychoanalysis
B. cognitive therapy
C. squeeze technique
D. antianxiety agents
E. none of the above

20.6. Primary inhibited female orgasm is associated most often with
A. lack of desire for sex
B. inability to achieve vaginal lubrication
C. inability to achieve orgasm through masturbation
D. impotence in the man
E. premature ejaculation in the man

20.7. Measures used to help differentiate organically caused impotence from functional impotence include
A. monitoring of nocturnal penile tumescence
B. follicle-stimulating hormone determinations
C. testosterone level test
D. glucose tolerance test
E. all the above

20.8. The DSM-III-R category called paraphilia not otherwise specified (NOS) includes
A. coprophilia
B. klismaphilia
C. urophilia
D. zoophilia
E. all the above

20.9. True statements about incest include
A. it is most frequently reported among families of low socioeconomic status
B. father-daughter incest is the most common
C. about 15 million women have been the object of incestuous attention
D. one third of incest cases occur before the age of 9
E. all the above

20.10. Rape is predominately used to express power and anger in all the following cases *except*
A. rape of elderly women
B. homosexual rape
C. rape of young children
D. statutory rape
E. gang rape

20.11. Autoerotic asphyxiation is most commonly associated with
A. adolescent girls
B. middle-aged men
C. no other mental disorder
D. adolescent boys
E. a heightened intensity of orgasm

DIRECTIONS: For each of the questions or incomplete statements below, *one* or *more* of the responses or completions given are correct. Choose answer

A. if only *1*, *2*, and *3* are correct
B. if only *1 and 3* are correct
C. if only *2 and 4* are correct
D. if only *4* is correct
E. if *all* are correct

20.12. Inhibited male orgasm
1. usually has an organic cause
2. may be associated with orgasmic anhedonia
3. is synonymous with retrograde ejaculation
4. has a general prevalence of 5 percent

20.13. Which of the following statements about rape are accurate?
1. Most rapists are between ages 25 and 44
2. Ninety percent of rapists are black
3. Most rapists have a previous police record
4. Black rapists tend to rape white women

20.14. Exhibitionism is associated with
1. the recurrent desire to expose the genitals to a stranger
2. sexual excitement occurring in anticipation of the exposure
3. a wish to surprise or shock the observer
4. physical violence

20.15. Premature ejaculation
1. may result from negative cultural conditioning
2. is often exacerbated by stress
3. is not caused exclusively by organic factors
4. is reported less frequently among college-educated men than among men with less education

20.16. Vaginismus is associated with
1. childhood sexual abuse
2. vaginal pain
3. insufficient lubrication
4. urethritis

20.17. Sensate focus
1. is used in dual-sex therapy
2. refers to focusing on the sensations of the orgasm
3. involves the sense of smell
4. is used during coitus

20.18. Hypoactive sexual desire
1. is experienced only by women
2. can result from depression
3. does not affect frequency of coitus
4. protects against unconscious fears of sex

20.19. Dyspareunia
1. often coincides with vaginismus
2. is caused by tension and anxiety
3. is real pain
4. results from surgical procedures on the female genital area in 5 percent of cases

ANSWERS

Human Sexuality

20.1. The answer is A (*Synopsis VI*, pages 449–450 and 454–455; *CTP V*, page 1050).

As described, Ms. B. suffered from *hypoactive sexual desire disorder*, which is characterized by deficiency or absence of sexual fantasies and desire for sexual activity. *Orgasmic anhedonia* refers to a condition in which there is no physical sensation of orgasm, even though the physiological component (e.g., genital contractions) remains intact. It is unlikely that this patient had ever had an orgasm, considering her history of never having masturbated and rarely having experienced sexual arousal. Her intense guilt at those things that led to her arousal is evidence that her lack of sexual desire represented a pathological inhibition. This woman exhibited no evidence of a *major depression*—for example, suicidal ideas or psychomotor retardation.

Frequently, a personality disorder coexists with a sexual dysfunction and may even be conceptualized as causative. If, with treatment, it becomes apparent that the fear of loss of control is a symptom of a personality disorder, the diagnosis of a psychosexual dysfunction nonetheless prevails. Only when a sexual disturbance is judged to be symptomatic of an Axis I disorder, such as major depression, is the diagnosis of a sexual dysfunction not made. On the basis of the case history provided, Ms. B. did not appear to warrant a diagnosis of *obsessive-compulsive personality disorder*. There is no evidence of recurring unwanted ideas or behaviors that produce anxiety if not thought about or acted on.

This woman showed no evidence of *dyspareunia*, which is characterized by persistent pain before, during, or after intercourse.

20.2. The answer is D (*Synopsis VI*, pages 458–461; *CTP V*, pages 1056–1059).

Of the various methods used in the treatment of hypoactive sexual desire disorder, the *squeeze technique* is not appropriate. This exercise is useful in the treatment of premature ejaculation. The recommended treatment modalities for hypoactive sexual desire disorder include the following:

Behavior therapy. Making the assumption that sexual dysfunction is learned maladaptive behavior, the therapist sees the patient as fearful of sexual interaction. Using traditional techniques (as initially developed for the treatment of phobias), the therapist sets up a hierarchy of anxiety-provoking situations for the patient, ranging from the least threatening to the most threatening situation. Mild anxiety may be experienced at the thought of kissing, and massive anxiety may be felt when imagining penile penetration. The behavioral therapist enables the patient to master the anxiety through a standard program of systematic desensitization. The program is designed to inhibit the learned anxious response by encouraging behaviors antithetical to anxiety. The patient first deals with the least anxiety-producing situation in fantasy and progresses by steps to the most anxiety-producing situation. Medication, hypnosis, or special training in deep muscle relaxation is sometimes used to help with the initial mastery of anxiety.

Hypnotherapy. Hypnotherapists focus specifically on the particular sexual dysfunction. Patients are taught relaxation techniques to be used before having sexual relations. With these methods to alleviate anxiety, the physiological responses to sexual stimulation can more readily result in pleasurable excitation and discharge.

Dual-sex therapy. This method, originated and developed by William Masters and Virginia Johnson, assumes that there is no sick half of a patient couple. Both this patient and her husband were involved in a relationship in which there was sexual distress, and both, therefore, needed to participate in the therapy program. The marital relationship as a whole is treated, with emphasis on sexual functioning as a part of that relationship.

Minor tranquilizers. Hypoactive sexual desire frequently serves as a defense against unconscious anxiety about sex. Antianxiety medications may be useful in treating inhibited desire when it is associated with extreme anxiety during sexual contact.

20.3. The answer is A (*Synopsis VI*, pages 440–442; *CTP V*, pages 1048–1050).

The sequence of the DSM-III-R phases of the sexual response cycle are *appetitive, excitement, orgasm,* and *resolution.*

1. Appetitive. This phase is distinct from the more physiological phases and reflects motivations, drives, and personality. The phase is characterized by sexual fantasies and the desire to engage in sexual activity.

2. Excitement. This phase consists of a subjective sense of sexual pleasure and accompanying physiological changes.

3. Orgasm. This phase consists of a peaking of sexual pleasure, with the release of sexual tension and rhythmic contractions of the perineal muscles and pelvic reproductive organs.

4. Resolution. This phase entails a sense of general relaxation, well-being, and muscular relaxation.

See Tables 20.1 and 20.2 for a thorough survey of the male and female sexual response cycles.

20.4. **The answer is E** (*Synopsis VI*, pages 460–461; *CTP V*, pages 1059–1060).

Surgical procedures that may be used in treating sexual dysfunctions are the insertion of a penile prosthesis, penile revascularization, hymenectomy, and vaginoplasty.

Penile prosthetic devices can be implanted in men with inadequate erectile responses who are resistant

Table 20.1
The Male Sexual Response Cycle*

	I. Excitement Phase (several minutes to hours)	II. Plateau Phase (30 sec–3 min)	III. Orgasmic Phase (3–15 sec)	IV. Resolution Phase (10–15 min; if no orgasm, ½–1 day)
Skin	No change	Sexual flush: inconsistently appears; maculopapular rash originates on abdomen and spreads to anterior chest wall, face, and neck and can include shoulders and forearms	Well-developed flush	Flush disappears in reverse order of appearance; inconsistently appearing film of perspiration on soles of feet and palms of hands
Penis	Erection within 10–30 sec caused by vasocongestion of erectile bodies of corpus cavernosa of shaft. Loss of erection may occur with introduction of a sexual stimulus, loud noise	Increase in size of glans and diameter of penile shaft; inconsistent deepening of coronal and glans coloration	Ejaculation: marked by 3 to 4 contractions at 0.8 sec of vas, seminal vesicles, prostate, and urethra; followed by minor contractions with increasing intervals	Erection: partial involution in 5–10 sec with variable refractory period; full detumescence in 5–30 min
Scrotum and testes	Tightening and lifting of scrotal sac and partial elevation of testes toward perineum	50 percent increase in size of testes over unstimulated state due to vasocongestion and flattening of testes against perineum, signaling impending ejaculation	No change	Decrease to baseline size due to loss of vasocongestion. Testicular and scrotal descent within 5–30 min after orgasm. Involution may take several hours if there is no orgasmic release
Cowper's glands	No change	2–3 drops of mucoid fluid that contain viable sperm	No change	No change
Other	Breasts: inconsistent nipple erection	Myotonia: semispastic contractions of facial, abdominal, and intercostal muscles Tachycardia: up to 175 per min Blood pressure: rise in systolic 20–80 mm; in diastolic 10–40 mm Respiration: increased	Loss of voluntary muscular control Rectum: rhythmical contractions of sphincter Up to 180 heart beats per min 40–100 systolic; 20–50 diastolic Up to 40 respirations per min. Ejaculatory spurt: 12–20 inches at age 18, decreasing with age to seepage at 70	Return to baseline state in 5–10 min

Table prepared by Virginia A. Sadock, M.D., after William Masters and Virginia Johnson data.
*In DSM-III-R the excitement phase and the plateau phase are combined into one phase, the excitement phase, preceded by an appetitive phase.

Table 20.2
The Female Sexual Response Cycle*

	I. Excitement Phase (several minutes to hours)	II. Plateau Phase (30 sec–3 min)	III. Orgasmic Phase (3–15 sec)	IV. Resolution Phase (10–15 min; if no orgasm, ½–1 day)
Skin	No change	Sexual flush inconstant except in fair-skinned; pink mottling on abdomen, spreads to breasts, neck, face, often to arms, thighs, and buttocks—looks like measles rash	No change (flush at its peak)	Fine perspiration, mostly on flush areas; flush disappears in reverse order
Breasts	Nipple erection in two thirds of subjects Venous congestion Areolar enlargement	Flush: mottling coalesces to form a red papillary rash Size: increase one fourth over normal, especially in breasts that have not nursed Areolae: enlarge; impinge on nipples so they seem to disappear	No change (venous tree pattern stands out sharply; breasts may become tremulous)	Return to normal in reverse order of appearance in half hour or more
Clitoris	Glans: half of subjects, no change visible, but with colposcope, enlargement always observed; half of subjects, glans diameter always increased twofold or more Shaft: variable increase in diameter; elongation occurs in only 10 percent of subjects	Retraction: shaft withdraws deep into swollen prepuce; just before orgasm, it is difficult to visualize; may relax and retract several times if phase II is unduly prolonged Intrapreputial movement with thrusting: movements synchronized with thrusting because of traction on labia minora and prepuce	No change Shaft movements continue throughout if thrusting is maintained	Shaft returns to normal position in 5–10 sec; full detumescence in 5–30 min (if no orgasm, clitoris remains engorged for several hours)
Labia majora	Nullipara: thin down; elevated; flatten against perineum Multipara: rapid congestion and edema; increases to two to three times normal size	Nullipara: totally disappear (may reswell if phase II unduly prolonged) Multipara: become so enlarged and edematous, they hang like folds of a heavy curtain	No change	Nullipara; *increase* to normal size in 1–2 min or less Multipara: *decrease* to normal size in 10–15 min
Labia minora	Color change: to bright pink in nullipara and red in multipara Size: increase two to three times over normal; prepuce often much more; proximal portion firms, adding up to ¾ inch to functional vaginal sidewalls	Color change: suddenly turn bright red in nullipara, burgundy red in multipara; signifies onset of phase II; orgasm will then always follow within 3 min if stimulation is continued Size: enlarged labia gap widely to form a vestibular funnel into vaginal orifice	Firm proximal areas contract with contractions of lower third	Return to pink blotchy color in 2 min or less; total resolution of color and size in 5 min (decoloration, clitoral return, and detumescence of lower third all occur as rapidly as loss of the erection in men)
Bartholin's glands	No change	A few drops of mucoid secretion form; aid in lubricating vestibule (insufficient to lubricate vagina)	No change	No change

(Continued)

Table 20.2
Continued

	I. Excitement Phase (several minutes to hours)	II. Plateau Phase (30 sec–3 min)	III. Orgasmic Phase (3–15 sec)	IV. Resolution Phase (10–15 min; if no orgasm, ½–1 day)
Vagina	Vaginal transudate: appears 10–30 sec after onset of arousal; drops of clear fluid coalesce to form a well-lubricated vaginal barrel (aids in buffering acidity of vagina to neutral pH required by sperm) Color change: mucosa turns patchy purple	Copious transudate continues to form; quality of transudate generally increased only by prolonging preorgasm stimulation (increased flow occurs during premenstrual period) Color change: uniform dark purple mucosa	No change (transudate provides maximum degree of lubrication)	Some transudate collects on floor of the upper two thirds formed by its posterior wall (in supine position); ejaculate deposited in this area, forming seminal pool
Upper two thirds	Balloons: dilates convulsively as uterus moves up, pulling anterior vaginal wall with it; fornices lengthen; rugae flatten	Further ballooning creates diameter of 2½–3 in; then wall relaxes in a slow, tensionless manner	No change: fully ballooned out and motionless	Cervical descent: descends to seminal pool in 3–4 min
Lower third	Dilation of vaginal lumen to 1–1¼ in occurs; congestion of walls proceeds gradually, increasing in rate as phase II approaches	Maximum distension reached rapidly; contracts lumen of lower third and upper labia to half or more its diameter in phase I; contraction around penis allows thrusting traction on clitoral shaft by labia and prepuce	3 to 15 contractions of lower third and proximal labia minora at ⅓-sec intervals	Congestion disappears in seconds (if no orgasm, congestion persists for 20–30 min)
Uterus	Ascent: moves into false pelvis late in phase I Cervix: passively elevated with uterus (no evidence of any cervical secretions during entire cycle)	Contractions: strong sustained contractions begin late in phase II; have same rhythm as contractions late in labor, lasting 2+ min. Cervix: slight swelling; patchy purple (inconstant; related to chronic cervicitis)	Contractions throughout orgasm; strongest with pregnancy and masturbation	Descent: slowly returns to normal Cervix: color and size return to normal in 4 min; patulous for 10 min
Others	Fourchette: color changes throughout cycle, as in labia minora	Perineal body: spasmodic tightening with involuntary elevation of perineum Hyperventilation and carpopedal spasms; both are usually present, the latter less frequently and only in female-supine position	Irregular spasms continue Rectum: rhythmical contractions inconstant; more apt to occur with masturbation than with coitus External urethral sphincter: occasional contraction, no urine loss	All reactions cease abruptly or within a few seconds

From *The Nature and Evolution of Female Sexuality* by Mary Jane Sherfey, copyright 1966, 1972 by Mary Jane Sherfey. Reprinted by permission of Random House, Inc.
*In DSM-III-R the excitement phase and the plateau phase are combined into one phase, the excitement phase, preceded by an appetitive phase.

to other treatment methods or who have organically caused deficiencies. Some physicians use *revascularization* of the penis as a direct approach to treating erectile dysfunction attributable to vascular disorders. Such surgical procedures may be indicated in patients with corporal shunts, in which normally entrapped blood leaks from the corporal space, leading to inadequate erections.

Among the surgical approaches to female dysfunctions are *hymenectomy* (excision of the hymen) in dyspareunia or in the treatment of an unconsummated marriage because of hymenal obstruction. *Va-*

ginoplasty (plastic surgery involving the vagina) in multiparous women complaining of lessened vaginal sensations is sometimes used. These surgical procedures have not been carefully studied and should be considered with great caution.

20.5. The answer is C (*Synopsis VI*, page 459; *CTP V*, page 1057).

A married man with a chief complaint of premature ejaculation is best treated with the *squeeze technique*. In that method the woman is instructed to squeeze the coronal ridge of the erect penis just before ejaculation or the time of ejaculatory inevitability. That moment is signaled to the woman by the man in a manner previously agreed to, at which time the woman forcefully applies the squeeze technique. The erection subsides slightly, and ejaculation is postponed. This exercise is repeated several times daily for several days. Eventually, the threshold of ejaculatory inevitability is raised, and the condition thereby improves.

Even though premature ejaculation is accompanied by anxiety, drug therapy with *antianxiety agents* is not indicated. *Psychoanalysis* may reveal unconscious fears of women that contribute to premature ejaculation; however it is not considered the most effective therapy. Psychoanalysis can be used if the patient does not respond to the squeeze technique because of deep-seated psychological conflicts. *Cognitive therapy* is used as a treatment of depression and is of limited use as a primary treatment approach to any of the sexual disorders. If the patient has a depression secondary to the sexual disorder, however, cognitive therapy may be of use.

See Table 20.3 for the DSM-III-R diagnostic criteria for premature ejaculation.

20.6. The answer is C (*Synopsis VI*, pages 452–453; *CTP V*, pages 1053–1054).

Primary inhibited female orgasm is characterized by the absence of the orgasmic experience at any time during a woman's life. It is less common than secondary orgasmic dysfunction, in which the woman has experienced orgasm at some time in her life but later is unable to do so. Accordingly, by definition, the woman is unable to experience *orgasm* either through masturbation or during coitus. Such a woman may have a normal *desire for sex* and usually has no difficulty in achieving *vaginal lubrication* or the plateau phase; she is, however, unable to achieve orgasm. The role of the man in this disorder is complex but not causal. As the woman has never achieved orgasm—even through masturbation by herself or by her partner—the man cannot be blamed for being either *impotent* or a *premature ejaculator*. Those disorders are more commonly implicated in secondary orgasmic dysfunction, in which the woman could not be expected to achieve coital orgasm without sufficient penile stimulation. Some men, however, have these disorders secondarily, after repeated attempts to bring the woman to orgasm. They blame themselves, feel rejected, or otherwise feel inadequate and begin to experience im-

Table 20.3
Diagnostic Criteria for Premature Ejaculation

Persistent or recurrent ejaculation with minimal sexual stimulation or before, upon, or shortly after penetration and before the person wishes it. The clinician must take into account factors that affect duration of the excitement phase, such as age, novelty of the sexual partner or situation, and frequency of sexual activity.

Table from DSM-III-R, *Diagnostic and Statistical Manual of Mental Disorders*, ed 3, revised. Copyright American Psychiatric Association, Washington, DC, 1987. Used with permission.

potence or premature ejaculation. The treatment of primary orgasmic dysfunction most often begins with attempts to teach the woman how to masturbate. Women who have never experienced orgasm usually have many psychological conflicts, and insight-oriented psychotherapy may be necessary to overcome such blocks. A useful and well-established approach is to integrate sex therapy methods with psychodynamic psychotherapy. See Table 20.4 for the DSM-III-R diagnostic criteria for inhibited female orgasm.

20.7. The answer is E (*Synopsis VI*, page 452; *CTP V*, page 1054).

A variety of measures are used to help differentiate organically caused impotence from functional impotence. The monitoring of *nocturnal penile tumescence* is a noninvasive procedure; normally, erections occur during sleep and are associated with rapid eye movements (REM) sleep periods. Tumescence may be monitored with a simple strain gauge; the presence or the absence of an erection can be determined thereby. In most cases in which organic factors account for the impotence, there are no nocturnal erections. Conversely, in most cases of functional or psychogenic impotence, erections do occur during REM sleep.

Table 20.4
Diagnostic Criteria for Inhibited Female Orgasm

A. Persistent or recurrent delay in, or absence of, orgasm in a female following a normal sexual excitement phase during sexual activity that the clinician judges to be adequate in focus, intensity, and duration. Some females are able to experience orgasm during noncoital clitoral stimulation, but are unable to experience it during coitus in the absence of manual clitoral stimulation. In most of these females, this represents a normal variation of the female sexual response and does not justify the diagnosis of inhibited female orgasm. However, in some of these females, this does represent a psychological inhibition that justifies the diagnosis. This difficult judgment is assisted by a thorough sexual evaluation, which may even require a trial of treatment.
B. Occurrence not exclusively during the course of another Axis I disorder (other than a sexual dysfunction), such as major depression.

Table from DSM-III-R, *Diagnostic and Statistical Manual of Mental Disorders*, ed 3, revised. Copyright American Psychiatric Association, Washington, DC, 1987. Used with permission.

Other diagnostic tests that delineate organic bases of impotence include *glucose tolerance tests*, *follicle-stimulating hormone* (FSH) determinations, and *testosterone level tests*. The glucose tolerance curve measures the metabolism of glucose over a specific period of time and is useful in diagnosing diabetes, of which impotence may be a symptom. FSH is produced by the anterior pituitary, which stimulates the secretion of estrogen from the ovarian follicle in women and is also responsible for the production of sperm from the testes in men. An abnormal finding suggests an organic cause for impotence. Testosterone is the male hormone produced by the interstitial cells of the testes. A low testosterone level produces a lack of desire as the chief complaint and may be associated with impotence. If a measure of nocturnal penile tumescence is abnormal, indicating the possibility of organic impotence, a measure of plasma testosterone is indicated.

20.8.   The answer is E (*Synopsis VI*, page 447; *CTP V*, page 1080).

Paraphilia not otherwise specified (NOS) includes a group of atypical paraphilias that are extremely varied and do not meet the criteria for any of the categories of paraphilias listed in DSM-III-R. Included in this category are *coprophilia* (sexual pleasure associated with feces), *klismaphilia* (use of enemas as part of sexual stimulation), *urophilia* (sexual pleasure associated with urine), and *zoophilia* (sexual fantasies or activities in which animals are preferentially incorporated).

20.9.   The answer is E (*Synopsis VI*, page 463; *CTP V*, pages 1101–1103).

Accurate figures of the incidence of incest are difficult to obtain because of the general shame and embarrassment of the entire family. Girls are victims more often than boys. About *15 million women* in the United States have been the object of incestuous attention, and one third of sexually abused persons have been molested *before the age of 9*.

Incestuous behavior is most frequently reported among families of *low socioeconomic status*. This difference may be the result of contact with welfare workers, public health personnel, law enforcement agents, and other reporting officials, and it may not be a true reflection of higher incidence. Incest is more easily hidden by economically stable families than by the poor. *Father-daughter incest* is reported to be more common than either sibling or mother-son incest. Many cases of sibling incest are denied by the parents. Parents often consider exploratory sex play between prepubertal siblings to be a normal interaction.

Social, cultural, physiological, and psychological factors all contribute to the breakdown of the incest taboo. Incestuous behavior has been associated with alcoholism, overcrowding and increased physical proximity, and rural isolation that prevents adequate extrafamilial contacts. Some communities may be more tolerant of incestuous behavior than is

society in general. Major mental illnesses and intellectual deficiencies have been described in some cases of clinical incest. Some family therapists view incest as a defense designed to maintain a dysfunctional family unit. The older and stronger participant in the incestuous behavior is usually male. Thus, incest may be viewed as a form of child abuse or as a variant of rape.

20.10.   The answer is D (*Synopsis VI*, pages 461–463; *CTP V*, pages 1097–1101).

Statutory rape varies dramatically from the other kinds of rape in being nonassaultive and in being a sexual act, not a violent act. Statutory rape refers to intercourse that is unlawful because of the age of the participants. Intercourse is unlawful between a male over 16 years of age and a girl under the age of consent, which ranges from 14 to 21 years, depending on the jurisdiction.

Rape is predominantly used to express power and anger. Studies of convicted rapists suggest that the crime is committed to relieve pent-up aggressive energy against persons of whom the rapist is in some awe. Although these awesome persons are usually men, the retaliatory violence is displaced toward women. Victims of rape can be of any age. Cases have been reported in which the victims were as *young* as 15 months and in which they were *elderly*.

Homosexual rape is much more frequent among men than among women, and it occurs primarily in closed institutions, such as prisons and maximum-security hospitals. The dynamics are identical to those involved in heterosexual rape. The crime enables the rapist to discharge aggression and to aggrandize himself.

Gang rape is an expression of anger and rage, as well as a displacement of aggression toward other men. Gang rape also enhances male bonding and increases feelings of power.

20.11.   The answer is D (*Synopsis VI*, page 456; *CTP V*, page 1056).

Autoerotic asphyxiation is a masturbatory phenomenon most common among *adolescent boys*, not *adolescent girls* or *middle-aged men*. The practice involves hanging oneself by the neck while masturbating to induce hypoxia. Hypoxia does produce a slightly altered state of consciousness, but it does *not heighten the intensity of orgasm*. This practice is associated with *severe mental disorders*. Although death is accidental, an estimated 500 to 1,000 deaths by hanging occur each year as a result of this masturbatory practice. Some apparent suicides by male adolescents through hanging are actually due to autoerotic asphyxiation.

20.12.   The answer is C (2, 4) (*Synopsis VI*, pages 453–454; *CTP V*, page 1054).

In DSM-III-R, inhibited male orgasm is the persistent or recurrent delay in or absence of orgasm in a man after a normal sexual excitement phase during sexual activity that the clinician, taking into account the person's age, judges to be adequate in focus, intensity, and duration. This failure to achieve orgasm is usually restricted to an inability to reach orgasm in the vagina, with orgasm possible with other types of stimulation, such as masturbation.

Inhibited male orgasm may be associated with *orgasmic anhedonia*. Some men ejaculate but complain of a decreased or absent subjective sense of pleasure during the orgasmic experience. The incidence of inhibited male orgasm is much lower than the incidences of premature ejaculation and impotence. Masters and Johnson reported only 3.8 percent in one group of 447 sex dysfunction cases. A *general prevalence of 5 percent* has been reported.

Inhibited male orgasm is synonymous with retarded ejaculation, *not retrograde ejaculation*, in which ejaculation occurs but the seminal fluid passes backward into the bladder. It is usually psychological in origin, but it may have *organic causes*. It can occur after surgery on the genitourinary tract, such as prostatectomy. It may also be associated with Parkinson's disease and other neurological disorders involving the lumbar and sacral sections of the spinal cord. The antihypertensive drug guanethidine monosulfate (Ismelin sulfate), methyldopa (Aldomet), the phenothiazines, and serotonergic agents, such as fluoxetine (Prozac), have been implicated in retarded ejaculation.

See Table 20.5 for the DSM-III-R criteria for inhibited male orgasm.

20.13.   The answer is B (1, 3) (*Synopsis VI*, page 462; *CTP V*, pages 1096–1099).

Statistics show that *most rapists are between ages 25 and 44*; 51 percent are white and tend to rape white women, and *47 percent (not 90 percent) are black* and tend to *rape black (not white) women*; the remaining 2 percent of rapists come from all other races. A composite picture of a rapist drawn from police figures portrays a single, 19-year-old man from the low socioeconomic groups with a *previous police record* of acquisitive offenses. It is estimated that only 1 out of 4 to 1 out of 10 rapes is reported.

Table 20.5
Diagnostic Criteria for Inhibited Male Orgasm

A. Persistent or recurrent delay in, or absence of, orgasm in a male following a normal sexual excitement phase during sexual activity that the clinician, taking into account the person's age, judges to be adequate in focus, intensity, and duration. This failure to achieve orgasm is usually restricted to an inability to reach orgasm in the vagina, with orgasm possible with other types of stimulation, such as masturbation.
B. Occurrence not exclusively during the course of another Axis I disorder (other than a sexual dysfunction), such as major depression.

Table from DSM-III-R, *Diagnostic and Statistical Manual of Mental Disorders*, ed 3, revised. Copyright American Psychiatric Association, Washington, DC, 1987. Used with permission.

Studies of convicted rapists suggest that the crime is committed to relieve pent-up aggressive energies against people the rapist fears. The retaliatory violence is directed toward a woman, even though the rapist's unconscious fear is generally of men. This finding dovetails with feminist theory, which proposes that the woman serves as an object for the displacement of aggression that the rapist cannot express directly toward other men. The woman is considered the property or the vulnerable possession of men and is the rapist's instrument for revenge against other men.

Rape often occurs as an accompaniment to another crime. The rapist always threatens his victim with his fists, a gun, or a knife and frequently harms the woman in both nonsexual and sexual ways. The victim may be beaten or wounded and is sometimes killed.

20.14.   The answer is A (1, 2, 3) (*Synopsis VI*, page 445; *CTP V*, pages 1074–1075).

Exhibitionism is the recurrent urge and desire to *expose the genitals to a stranger* or an unsuspecting person. *Sexual excitement* occurs in anticipation of the exposure, and orgasm takes place through masturbation. Exhibitionists are aware of a wish to *surprise or shock* the observer and, in so doing, assert what they perceive to be a heightened masculinity. Exhibitionism is not generally associated with *physical violence*; exhibitionists are not usually dangerous to the victim. Freud believed that such men had an unconscious fear of castration and that the response of the woman to the exposed genitals reassured the man that his genitals were still intact.

20.15.   The answer is A (1, 2, 3) (*Synopsis VI*, page 454; *CTP V*, pages 1054–1055).

In premature ejaculation the man recurrently achieves orgasm and ejaculation before he wishes to. *Stress* clearly plays a role in exacerbating the condition; for example, in ongoing relationships the partner has been found to have great influence on the premature ejaculator, and a stressful marriage exacerbates the disorder. Difficulty in ejaculatory control may also result from *negative cultural conditioning*. For example, men who experience most of their early sexual contacts with prostitutes who demand that the sexual act proceed quickly or in situations in which discovery would be embarrassing (the back seat of a car or the parental home) may become conditioned to achieve orgasm rapidly.

Premature ejaculation is reported *more (not less) frequently among college-educated men* than among men with less education. This condition is thought to be related to their concern for partner satisfaction, which may induce performance anxiety, or to their greater awareness of the availability of therapy. As with other sexual dysfunctions, premature ejaculation is *not caused exclusively by organic factors*.

See Table 20.3, which lists the criteria for premature ejaculation.

20.16. The answer is E (all) (*Synopsis VI*, pages 455 and 784–785; *CTP V*, page 1055).

Vaginismus is characterized by a spastic contraction of the muscles surrounding the outer third of the vaginal canal. It is usually psychological in origin but may also have physiological causes. An important psychological cause is *childhood sexual abuse*; the trauma of the event is carried into adulthood. Even though the woman consciously desires sexual intercourse, unconscious conflicts manifest themselves by vaginal muscle spasticity. Vaginismus is often associated with *insufficient lubrication* of the vagina and with *vaginal pain* secondary to insufficient lubrication or to spasticity of the muscles. A common physical cause of vaginismus is *urethritis*. Infection of the urethra causes pain, which secondarily causes muscle spasm of the vaginal wall. When the infection is cured, the vaginismus abates. See Table 20.6 for the DSM-III-R criteria for vaginismus.

20.17. The answer is B (1, 3) (*Synopsis VI*, page 459; *CTP V*, page 1057).

Sensate focus refers to specific exercises that are prescribed for the couple as part of *dual-sex therapy* for sexual disorders. Beginning exercises focus on heightening sensory awareness to touch, sight, sound, and *smell*. It does not refer to *focusing on the sensations of the orgasm*. Initially, intercourse is forbidden, and these exercises are *not used during coitus*; the couples learn to give and receive bodily pleasure without the pressure of performance. They learn how to communicate nonverbally in a mutually satisfactory way. Sensate focus exercises reduce anxiety.

20.18. The answer is C (2, 4) (*Synopsis VI*, pages 449–450; *CTP V*, page 1050).

Sexual desire disorders have recently become the focus of much attention. Patients with desire problems often have good ego strengths and use inhibition of desire in a defensive way to *protect against unconscious fears of sex*. Lack of desire can also be the result of chronic stress, anxiety, or *depression*.

Hypoactive sexual desire is experienced by *both men and women*, who may not be hampered by any dysfunction once they are involved in the sex act. Lack of desire may be expressed by *decreased frequency of coitus*, perception of the partner as unattractive, or overt complaints of lack of desire.

The need for sexual contact and satisfaction varies among persons and in the same person over time. In a group of 100 couples with stable marriages, 8 percent reported intercourse less than once a month. In another group of couples, one third reported lack of sexual relations for periods averaging eight weeks. Masters and Johnson believe that lack of desire may be the most common complaint among married couples; the true incidence, however, is not known.

Table 20.7 lists the DSM-III-R diagnostic criteria for hypoactive sexual desire disorder.

20.19. The answer is A (1, 2, 3) (*Synopsis VI*, pages 454–455; *CTP V*, page 1055).

Dyspareunia refers to recurrent and persistent pain during intercourse in either the man or the woman. The dysfunction is related to and often coincides with *vaginismus*, an involuntary muscle contraction of the outer third of the vagina that prevents penile insertion and intercourse. Repeated episodes of dyspareunia may lead to vaginismus, and in both disorders somatic causes must be ruled out. Dyspareunia should not be diagnosed when an organic basis for the pain is found.

Painful coitus may result from *tension and anxiety* about the sex act that causes the woman to involuntarily tense her vaginal muscles. The *pain is real* and makes intercourse unbearable or unpleasant. The anticipation of pain may cause the woman to avoid coitus altogether.

Table 20.6
Diagnostic Criteria for Vaginismus

A. Recurrent or persistent involuntary spasm of the musculature of the outer third of the vagina that interferes with coitus.
B. The disturbance is not caused exclusively by a physical disorder, and is not due to another Axis I disorder.

Table from DSM-III-R, *Diagnostic and Statistical Manual of Mental Disorders*, ed 3, revised. Copyright American Psychiatric Association, Washington, DC, 1987. Used with permission.

Table 20.7
Diagnostic Criteria for Hypoactive Sexual Desire Disorder

A. Persistently or recurrently deficient or absent sexual fantasies and desire for sexual activity. The judgment of deficiency or absence is made by the clinician, taking into account factors that affect sexual functioning, such as age, sex, and the context of the person's life.
B. Occurrence not exclusively during the course of another Axis I disorder (other than a sexual dysfunction), such as major depression.

Table from DSM-III-R, *Diagnostic and Statistical Manual of Mental Disorders*, ed 3, revised. Copyright American Psychiatric Association, Washington, DC, 1987. Used with permission.

Table 20.8
Diagnostic Criteria for Dyspareunia

A. Recurrent or persistent genital pain in either a male or a female before, during, or after sexual intercourse.
B. The disturbance is not caused exclusively by lack of lubrication or by vaginismus.

Table from DSM-III-R, *Diagnostic and Statistical Manual of Mental Disorders*, ed 3, revised. Copyright American Psychiatric Association, Washington, DC, 1987. Used with permission.

The true incidence of dyspareunia is not known, but it has been estimated that *30 (not 5) percent of surgical procedures* on the female genital area result in temporary dyspareunia. In addition, 30 to 40 percent of women with this complaint who are seen in sex therapy clinics have pelvic pathology.

Organic abnormalities leading to dyspareunia and vaginismus include irritated or infected hymenal remnants, episiotomy scars, Bartholin's gland infection, various forms of vaginitis and cervicitis, endometriosis, and other pelvic disorders. The postmenopausal woman may develop dyspareunia resulting from thinning of the vaginal mucosa and lessened lubrication. Dynamic factors are often considered causative.

See Table 20.8 for the DSM-III-R diagnostic criteria for dyspareunia.

21 ||||||

Normal Sleep and Sleep Disorders

Because sleep occupies one third of a person's life and involves not one but two basic biological states of the brain and the body, many disorders of sleep are possible. The control of the body's physiological functions is decidedly different during sleep than during waking and sometimes differs even between the two major sleep states, nonrapid eye movement (NREM) sleep and rapid eye movement (REM) sleep. That difference provides an opportunity for many specific disorders of the sleep mechanisms to appear and results in the possibility of secondary disorders. Various chemical and environmental stimuli may have different effects during sleep and during waking and, thus, may unexpectedly produce sleep disorders.

A list of sleep disorders reported in recent years would be large and somewhat bewildering. And, indeed, many of the sleep disorders

listed would turn out to be merely nighttime problems associated with known medical illnesses, especially neurological illnesses, and thus of only limited interest to psychiatrists. Psychiatrists need not know all the details of those disorders, but they should at least be aware of their existence.

The student should be familiar with normal sleep architecture (including REM and the stages of NREM sleep), sleep changes observed in such mental disorders as major depression, the neurochemistry of sleep, polysomnogram findings, and the sleep disorders.

Students should review Chapter 21 of *Synopsis VI*, "Normal Sleep and Sleep Disorders," Section 1.9 of *CTP V*, "Basic Science of Sleep," and Chapter 22 of *CTP V*, "Sleep Disorders," and should then study the questions and answers below to test their knowledge of this area.

HELPFUL HINTS

The student should know and be able to define each of the terms listed below.

normal sleep
SWS
EEG
REM, NREM
K complexes
poikilothermic
L-tryptophan
melatonin
sleep deprivation, REM-deprived
dyssomnias
parasomnias
DIMS
insomnia
  transient
  persistent
  nonorganic
  organic
  primary
  secondary
hypersomnia

somnolence, hypersomnolence
narcolepsy
variable sleepers
DOES
sleep apnea
alveolar hypoventilation syndrome
sleep paralysis, sleep attacks
idiopathic CNS hypersomnolence
microsleeps
Kleine-Levin syndrome
sleep drunkenness
sleep-wake schedule disorder
delayed sleep phase syndrome
advanced sleep phase syndrome
somnambulism
somniloquy
pavor nocturnus, incubus
nightmares
dream anxiety disorder
night terrors

sleep terror
sleep-related epileptic seizures
sleep-related bruxism
sleep-related (nocturnal)
  myoclonus syndrome
dysesthesias
jactatio capitis nocturna
familial sleep paralysis
sleep-related cluster headaches
  and chronic paroxysmal
  hemicrania
sleep-related abnormal swallowing
  syndrome
sleep-related asthma
sleep-related cardiovascular
  symptoms
sleep-related gastroesophageal
  reflux
paroxysmal nocturnal
  hemoglobinuria

QUESTIONS

DIRECTIONS: Each of the incomplete statements below is followed by five suggested completions. Select the *one* that is *best* in each case.

21.1. Some patients with insomnia are treated with behavioral techniques involving the use of the bed only for sleep and their arising after five minutes if they have not fallen asleep. This approach is most useful for
A. transient insomnia
B. short-term insomnia
C. persistent insomnia
D. insomnia associated with major depression
E. insomnia associated with organic factors

21.2. An electroencephalogram (EEG) pattern showing frequent spindle-shaped tracings at 12 to 14 cycles a second and slow, triphasic waves is characteristic of
A. the waking EEG
B. stage 1
C. stage 2
D. stage 3
E. stage 4

21.3. An 11-year-old girl asked her mother to take her to a psychiatrist because she feared she might be "going crazy." Several times during the past two months she had awakened confused about where she was until she realized she was on the living room couch or in her little sister's bed, even though she went to bed in her own room. When she woke up in her older brother's bedroom, she became very concerned and felt quite guilty about it. Her younger sister said that she had seen the patient walking during the night, looking like "a zombie," that she did not answer when she called her, and that she had walked at night several times but usually went back to her bed. The patient feared she might have amnesia because she had no memory of anything happening during the night.

There was no history of seizures or of similar episodes during the day. An electroencephalogram and physical examination results were normal. The patient's mental status was unremarkable except for some anxiety about her symptoms and the usual early adolescent concerns. School and family functioning were excellent.

[From *DSM-III-R Case Book.* Used with permission.]

The most likely diagnosis of this patient's condition is
A. dream anxiety disorder
B. familial sleep paralysis
C. somniloquy
D. somnambulism
E. pavor nocturnus, incubus

21.4. Narcolepsy is associated with
A. cataplexy
B. hypnagogic hallucinations
C. sleep paralysis
D. brief awakenings during the night
E. all the above

DIRECTIONS: For each of the questions or incomplete statements below, *one or more* of the responses or completions given are correct. Choose answer

A. if only *1, 2, and 3* are correct
B. if only *1 and 3* are correct
C. if only *2 and 4* are correct
D. if only *4* is correct
E. if *all* are correct

21.5. The sleep apnea syndrome
1. may effectively be treated with barbiturates
2. can be diagnosed only with polysomnographic recordings
3. is referred to as Pickwickian syndrome in infants and children
4. is likely to occur in the elderly and in obese persons

21.6. During rapid eye movement (REM) periods
1. pulse, respiration, and blood pressure are higher than during nonrapid eye movement (NREM) periods
2. brain oxygen use increases
3. thermoregulation is altered
4. body movement is absent

21.7. Which of the following neurotransmitters are involved in sleep and waking mechanisms?
1. Dopamine
2. Norepinephrine
3. Acetylcholine
4. Serotonin

DIRECTIONS: Each group of questions below consists of lettered headings followed by a list of numbered words or statements. For each numbered word or statement, select the *one* lettered heading that is most closely associated with it. Each lettered heading may be used once, more than once, or not at all.

Questions 21.8–21.10
A. Pavor nocturnus
B. Nocturnal myoclonus
C. Jactatio capitis nocturna

21.8. Urge to move the legs

21.9. Patient wakes up screaming

21.10. Head banging

Questions 21.11–21.14
A. Transient insomnia
B. Persistent insomnia

21.11. Grief reaction

21.12. Impending job interview

21.13. Conditioned associative response

21.14. Results in impaired social or occupational functioning

Questions 21.15–21.19
A. REM sleep
B. NREM sleep

21.15. Sleepwalking

21.16. Bed-wetting (enuresis)

21.17. Paroxysmal hemicrania

21.18. Erections

Normal Sleep and Sleep Disorders

21.1. The answer is C (*Synopsis VI*, pages 470–472; *CTP V*, page 1107).

Behavioral techniques are most useful in the treatment of *persistent insomnia*. Persistent insomnia refers to a group of conditions in which the problem most often is difficulty in falling asleep, rather than remaining asleep, and involves somatized tension and anxiety. Treatment is among the most difficult problems in sleep disorders. In some patients with disorders of initiating and maintaining sleep, or insomnia, in which a conditioned component is prominent, a deconditioning technique may be useful. The conditioned component involves the patient's bed or bedroom when it is associated with activities other than sleep, such as eating and watching television. The patient is asked to use the bed for sleeping and for nothing else; if not asleep after five minutes in bed, the patient is instructed to get up and do something else. Sometimes even changing to another bed or going to another room is helpful. When somatized or muscle tension is prominent, relaxation tapes, meditation, or biofeedback is occasionally helpful.

Treatment of insomnia associated with *major depression* involves treatment of the underlying depression, rather than of the sleep problems.

Insomnia associated with *organic factors*, such as a known physical condition or medication, is addressed by treating the underlying medical condition or by altering the medication.

Specific treatment for *transient insomnia* (also known as *short-term insomnia*) is usually not required, although the practitioner should keep in mind that an acute insomnia may sometimes be the beginning of a psychotic episode or a severe depression. If necessary, hypnotic medications should be used for a short time.

21.2. The answer is C (*Synopsis VI*, pages 466–467; *CTP V*, pages 86–89).

As a person falls asleep, his or her brain waves go through certain characteristic changes, classified as stages 1, 2, 3, and 4. The *waking* electroencephalogram (EEG) is characterized by alpha waves of 8 to 12 cycles a second and low-voltage activity of mixed frequency. As the person falls asleep, alpha-activity begins to disappear. *Stage 1*, considered the lightest stage of sleep, is characterized by low-voltage, regular activity at 3 to 7 cycles a second. After a few seconds or minutes, this stage gives way to

stage 2, a pattern showing frequent spindle-shaped tracings at 12 to 14 cycles a second (sleep spindles) and slow, triphasic waves known as K complexes. Soon thereafter, delta waves—high-voltage activity at 0.5 to 2.5 cycles a second—make their appearance and occupy less than 50 percent of the tracing (*stage 3*). Eventually, in *stage 4*, delta waves occupy more than 50 percent of the record. It is common practice to describe stages 3 and 4 as delta sleep or slow-wave sleep because of their characteristic appearance on the EEG record. See Figure 21.1 for the human sleep stages.

21.3. The answer is D (*Synopsis VI*, pages 477–478; *CTP V*, pages 567 and 1037).

The most likely diagnosis of the 11-year-old girl's condition is *somnambulism*, sleepwalking disorder. Sleepwalking consists of a sequence of complex behaviors initiated in the first third of the night during deep nonrapid eye movement (NREM) sleep (stages 3 and 4). The disorder consists of arising from bed during sleep and walking about, appearing unresponsive during the episode, amnesia for the sleepwalking event on awakening, and no impairment in consciousness several minutes after awakening. Sleepwalking usually begins between ages 6 and 12 and tends to run in families.

Dream anxiety disorder is the *Diagnostic and Statistical Manual of Mental Disorders,* edition 3, revised (DSM-III-R), term for nightmare; it consists of repeated awakenings from long, frightening dreams. The awakening usually occurs during the second half of the sleep period during REM sleep. *Familial sleep paralysis* is characterized by a sudden inability to execute voluntary movements either just at the onset of sleep or on awakening during the night or in the morning. *Somniloquy*, sleep talking, occurs in all stages of sleep. The talking usually involves a few words that are difficult to distinguish, and sleep talking by itself requires no treatment. *Pavor nocturnus*, also known as incubus or sleep terror disorder, is an arousal in the first third of the night during deep NREM sleep. Night terrors are characterized by awakening in terror. There is generally no dream recall. Pavor nocturnus is inaugurated by a piercing scream and is accompanied by behavioral manifestations of intense anxiety. Most often, patients fall back to sleep and, as with sleepwalking, forget the episode.

See Table 21.1 for the DSM-III-R diagnostic criteria for sleepwalking disorder.

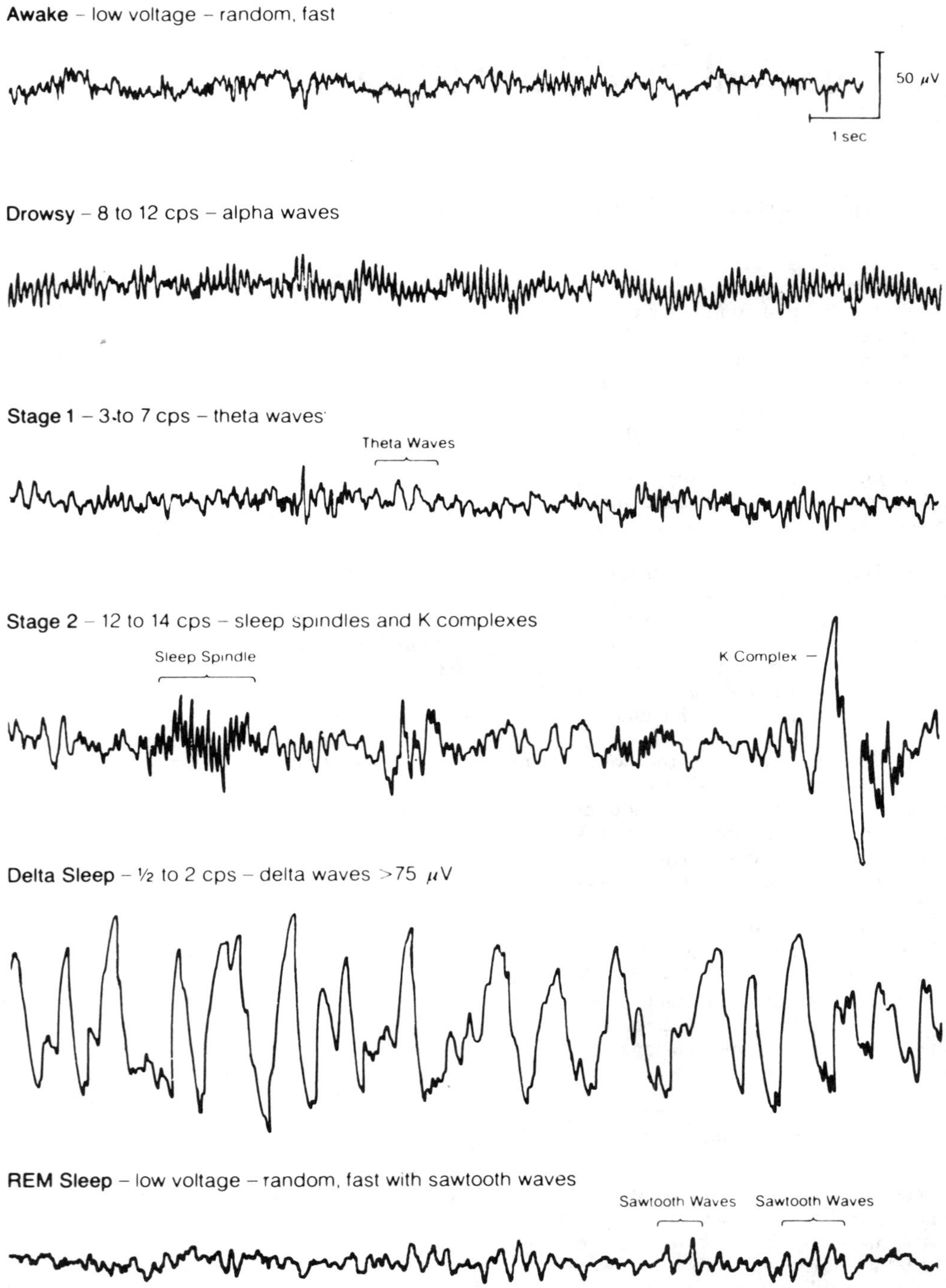

Awake – low voltage – random, fast

50 μV

1 sec

Drowsy – 8 to 12 cps – alpha waves

Stage 1 – 3 to 7 cps – theta waves

Theta Waves

Stage 2 – 12 to 14 cps – sleep spindles and K complexes

Sleep Spindle

K Complex —

Delta Sleep – ½ to 2 cps – delta waves >75 μV

REM Sleep – low voltage – random, fast with sawtooth waves

Sawtooth Waves   Sawtooth Waves

Figure 21.1. Human sleep stages. (From P Houri: *The Sleep Disorders*, p. 7. Current Concepts, Upjohn, Kalamazoo, MI, 1982, with permission.)

Table 21.1
Diagnostic Criteria for Sleepwalking Disorder

A. Repeated episodes of arising from bed during sleep and walking about, usually occurring during the first third of the major sleep period.
B. While sleepwalking, the person has a blank, staring face; is relatively unresponsive to the efforts of others to influence the sleepwalking or to communicate with him or her; and can be awakened only with great difficulty.
C. On awakening (either from the sleepwalking episode or the next morning), the person has amnesia for the episode.
D. Within several minutes after awakening from the sleepwalking episode, there is no impairment of mental activity or behavior (although there may initially be a short period of confusion or disorientation).
E. It cannot be established that an organic factor initiated and maintained the disturbance (e.g., epilepsy).

Table from DSM-III-R, *Diagnostic and Statistical Manual of Mental Disorders*, ed 3, revised. Copyright American Psychiatric Association, Washington, DC, 1987. Used with permission.

21.4. The answer is E (*Synopsis VI*, page 475; *CTP V*, pages 1116–1117).

Narcolepsy is a syndrome consisting of excessive daytime sleepiness and abnormal manifestations of rapid eye movement (REM) sleep. These manifestations include the presence of frequent sleep-onset REM periods, which may be subjectively experienced as *hypnagogic hallucinations*, hallucinations that occur just before falling asleep. Other manifestations include *cataplexy*, a temporary loss of muscle tone and weakness, and *sleep paralysis*, the sudden inability to execute voluntary movements either at the onset of sleep or on awakening.

The appearance of REM sleep within 10 minutes of sleep onset is evidence of narcolepsy. Other commonly associated symptoms are sleep attacks and a number of *brief awakenings* during the night. The patient rarely experiences blackouts associated with automatic behavior (e.g., driving miles from home without knowing how one got there).

21.5. The answer is D (4) (*Synopsis VI*, pages 473–474; *CTP V*, pages 87–88, 1111, and 1115).

Apnea is defined as the absence of breathing; sleep-induced apnea results from the failure of the respiratory center to stimulate adequate respiration during sleep. Breathing during sleep is more fragile and more easily compromised than breathing while awake. Thus, the sleep apnea syndrome is likely to occur in the *elderly* and in obese persons, even people who do not have clinical symptoms. In obese patients (not infants and children), the sleep apnea syndrome is referred to as *Pickwickian syndrome* (named after a fat character in the Charles Dickens novel *Pickwick Papers*).

Clinically, one can suspect sleep apnea and make a tentative diagnosis even without *polysomnographic recordings*. If a history is obtained from a spouse or a bed partner, reports include loud, inter- mittent snoring, at times accompanied by gasping. Sometimes observers recall apneic periods when patients appeared to be trying to breathe but were unable to do so.

When sleep apnea is established or suspected, it is important to avoid the use of *barbiturates* and other depressant medications, including alcohol. These medications can considerably exacerbate the condition and may then become life-threatening. Treatment for various forms of sleep apnea include medications to stimulate the respiratory center, a mechanical tongue-retaining device, oxygen, and, in severe obstructive apnea, surgical intervention. This is a physiological disorder, not a psychogenic disorder.

21.6. The answer is E (all) (*Synopsis VI*, pages 466–468; *CTP V*, pages 86–90).

Sleep is divided into nonrapid eye movement (NREM) and REM sleep: REM correlates most closely with the dreaming state in humans. In normal persons NREM sleep is a peaceful state relative to waking; there are no or few rapid eye movements in this sleep state, and most physiological functions are markedly reduced.

During REM periods, *pulse, respiration, and blood pressure* are higher than during NREM sleep (and quite often higher than during waking). In addition, *brain oxygen use* increases, and *body movement* is absent. During REM sleep, *thermoregulation* is altered; a poikilothermic condition (a state in which animal temperature varies with the changes in the temperature of the surrounding medium) is present. Poikilothermy results in a failure to respond to changes in the ambient temperature by shivering or sweating. During NREM sleep and wakefulness a homeothermic condition of temperature regulation is present, in which the body tends to maintain a constant temperature.

21.7. The answer is E (all) (*Synopsis VI*, pages 468–469; *CTP V*, pages 90–91).

Neurotransmitters involved in sleep and waking mechanisms include dopamine, norepinephrine, acetylcholine, and serotonin. The neurotransmitter most clearly involved in sleep and waking mechanisms is brain *serotonin*. Prevention of serotonin synthesis or destruction of the dorsal raphe nucleus of the brain stem, which contains nearly all the brain's serotonergic cell bodies, reduces sleep for a considerable time. The synthesis and the release of serotonin by serotonergic neurons are influenced by the availability of amino acid precursors of serotonin, such as L-tryptophan. Ingestion of large amounts of L-tryptophan (1 to 15 g) has been shown to reduce sleep latency and nocturnal awakenings. Conversely, L-tryptophan deficiency is associated with less time spent in rapid eye movement (REM) sleep. Thus, enhancement of serotonergic neurotransmission may be beneficial in the treatment of sleep disturbances.

Norepinephrine-containing neurons with cell bodies located in the locus ceruleus play an important role in controlling normal sleep patterns. Drugs and manipulations that increase the firing of these noradrenergic neurons produce a marked reduction in REM sleep (REM-off neurons) and an increase in wakefulness. Electrical stimulation of the locus ceruleus in humans with chronically implanted electrodes (for control of spasticity) profoundly disrupts all sleep parameters.

Brain *acetylcholine* is also involved in sleep, particularly in the production of REM sleep. In animal studies, injection of cholinergic-muscarinic agonists into pontine reticular formation neurons (REM-on neurons) results in a shift from wakefulness to REM sleep. Disturbances in central cholinergic activity are associated with the sleep changes observed in major depression. As compared with healthy subjects and nondepressed psychiatric controls, depressed patients have marked disruption of REM sleep patterns, including shortened REM latency (60 minutes or less), greater overall percentage of REM, and a shift in REM distribution from the last half to the first half of the night. The administration of a muscarinic agonist, such as arecoline, to depressed patients during the first or second NREM periods results in a rapid onset of REM sleep. It is postulated that depression is associated with an underlying supersensitivity to acetylcholine.

Another intriguing observation suggests a link between acetylcholine and depression. Drugs that reduce REM sleep, such as antidepressants, produce beneficial effects in depression. Indeed, about half of the patients with major depressions experience temporary improvement when deprived of or restricted from sleep. Conversely, reserpine (Serpasil), which is one of the few drugs that increases REM sleep, also produces depression. Narcolepsy, which is characterized by pathological manifestations of REM sleep, is aggravated by compounds that enhance or mimic cholinergic activity.

Evidence shows that *dopamine* has an alerting effect. Drugs that increase brain dopamine tend to produce arousal and wakefulness. In contrast, dopamine blockers, such as pimozide (Orap) and the phenothiazines, tend to increase sleep time.

21.8–21.10

21.8. The answer is B (*Synopsis VI*, page 478; *CTP V*, page 1111).

21.9. The answer is A (*Synopsis VI*, pages 477–478; *CTP V*, page 1122).

21.10. The answer is C (*Synopsis VI*, page 478; *CTP V*, page 1123).

Sleep-related (nocturnal) myoclonus syndrome, also known as restless legs syndrome, consists of highly stereotyped contractions of certain leg muscles during sleep. Though rarely painful, these dys-

esthesias cause an almost irresistible urge to *move the legs*, thus interfering with sleep.

In sleep terror disorder (pavor nocturnus, incubus), the patient typically sits up in bed with a frightened expression and *wakes up screaming*, often with a feeling of intense terror; patients are often amnestic for the episode. See Table 21.2 for the DSM-III-R diagnostic criteria for sleep terror disorder.

Sleep-related *head banging* (jactatio capitis nocturna) consists chiefly of rhythmic to-and-fro head rocking (less commonly, total body rocking) occurring just before or during sleep but rarely persisting into or occurring in deep nonrapid eye movement sleep.

21.11–21.14

21.11. The answer is A (*Synopsis VI*, page 470; *CTP V*, pages 1106–1112).

21.12. The answer is A (*Synopsis VI*, page 470; *CTP V*, pages 1106–1112).

21.13. The answer is B (*Synopsis VI*, page 470; *CTP V*, pages 1106–1112).

21.14. The answer is B (*Synopsis VI*, page 470; *CTP V*, pages 1106–1112).

A brief period of insomnia most often associated with anxiety, either as a sequela to an anxious experience or in anticipation of an anxiety-provoking experience (e.g., an examination or an *impending job interview*), is transient insomnia. In some persons, transient insomnia may be related to a *grief reaction*, reaction to loss, or almost any life change.

According to DSM-III-R, in the case of persistent insomnia, the disturbance occurs at least three times a week for at least one month and results in significant daytime fatigue or *impaired social or occupational functioning*. It can also be associated with anxiety concerning the loss of sleep. Persistent insomnia is fairly common, though not well understood, and

Table 21.2
Diagnostic Criteria for Sleep Terror Disorder

A. A predominant disturbance of recurrent episodes of abrupt awakening (lasting 1 to 10 minutes) from sleep, usually occurring during the first third of the major sleep period and beginning with a panicky scream.

B. Intense anxiety and signs of autonomic arousal during each episode, such as tachycardia, rapid breathing, and sweating, but no detailed dream is recalled.

C. Relative unresponsiveness to efforts of others to comfort the person during the episode and, almost invariably, at least several minutes of confusion, disorientation, and perseverative motor movements (e.g., picking at pillow).

D. It cannot be established that an organic factor initiated and maintained the disturbance (e.g., brain tumor).

Table from DSM-III-R, *Diagnostic and Statistical Manual of Mental Disorders*, ed 3, revised. Copyright American Psychiatric Association, Washington, DC, 1987. Used with permission.

refers to a group of conditions in which the problem is in falling asleep, rather than in remaining asleep. Persistent insomnia often involves the somatization of anxiety and a *conditioned associative response*. This conditioned response refers to the fact that people complaining of persistent insomnia associate nonsleep activities, such as eating, with their bed and bedrooms.

See Table 21.3 for the DSM-III-R diagnostic criteria for insomnia disorders.

Table 21.3
Diagnostic Criteria for Insomnia Disorders

A. The predominant complaint is of difficulty in initiating or maintaining sleep, or of nonrestorative sleep (sleep that is apparently adequate in amount, but leaves the person feeling unrested).
B. The disturbance in A occurs at least three times a week for at least one month and is sufficiently severe to result in either a complaint of significant daytime fatigue or the observation by others of some symptom that is attributable to the sleep disturbance (e.g., irritability or impaired daytime functioning).
C. Occurrence not exclusively during the course of sleep-wake schedule disorder or a parasomnia.

Table from DSM-III-R, *Diagnostic and Statistical Manual of Mental Disorders*, ed 3, revised. Copyright American Psychiatric Association, Washington, DC, 1987. Used with permission.

21.15–21.19

21.15. **The answer is B** (*Synopsis VI*, page 477; *CTP V*, pages 1107–1108).

21.16. **The answer is B** (*Synopsis VI*, page 467; *CTP V*, pages 1107–1108).

21.17. **The answer is A** (*Synopsis VI*, pages 478–479; *CTP V*, page 1108).

21.18. **The answer is A** (*Synopsis VI*, page 468; *CTP V*, page 1108).

Sleepwalking occurs during the first third of the night during NREM sleep, stages 3 and 4. *Bed-wetting* (enuresis), a repetitive and inappropriate passage of urine during sleep, is associated with NREM sleep, stages 3 and 4. *Paroxysmal hemicrania* is a type of unilateral vascular headache that is sleep-exacerbated and occurs only in association with REM sleep. *Erections* are associated with REM sleep. Almost every REM period is accompanied by a partial or a full penile erection (or clitoral erection in women).

22

Factitious Disorders

Physicians have used many names for factitious disorders—artifactual illness, hospital addiction, polysurgical addiction, and professional patient syndrome, among others. These terms are descriptive of the primary clinical characteristic of factitious illness—the repeated, voluntary simulation of disease for the sole purpose of assuming the patient role. Of all the labels, the eponym Munchausen syndrome remains the most widely used. This complex disorder is often difficult to recognize and even more difficult to treat.

The revised third edition of *Diagnostic and Statistical Manual of Mental Disorders* (DSM-III-R) describes three types of factitious disorder: factitious disorder with physical symptoms (the most frequently reported and the syndrome that is being described when the label Munchausen syndrome is used); factitious disorder with psychological symptoms (known in the past as Ganser's syndrome and, in DSM-III-R, classified not as a factitious disorder but as an atypical dissociative disorder); and factitious disorder not otherwise specified (a combination of the characteristics described for each of the other disorders).

The issues of volition and conscious control, although fundamental to the conceptualization of these disorders, are nonetheless the source of divergent opinions. DSM-III-R describes factitious disorder patients as having voluntary control over their behavior. However, the source of voluntary control is subjective and can only be inferred by the observer. What seems to be true of these disorders is the strength of underlying emotional factors. The behavior of

the patients has a compulsive quality, and the tenacity with which they maintain their factitious illnesses may represent an involuntary habit pattern. A striking aspect of this disorder is the fact that the patient does not seek help for the problem, even when the sham is discovered and help is offered.

Factitious disorders must be distinguished from malingering. Malingerers, unlike persons with factitious disorders, have an obvious, identifiable environmental goal in producing symptoms; malingerers may wish to be in the hospital to evade police, avoid work, or obtain financial compensation. Persons with factitious disorders make hospitalization the primary goal and being a patient the primary way of life. They are usually unable to stop their symptom production when it is no longer considered profitable (as do malingerers) or when the stakes get too high and they risk their own lives.

Psychiatrists currently believe that the factitious disorders represent a final common pathway for maladaptive behavior in certain vulnerable people. Common elements in the past history of the patients (including a history of employment as a nurse, laboratory technician, physician, or other health worker) suggest certain predisposing factors, such as physical disorders during childhood that require extensive medical treatment.

Readers should refer to Chapter 22, "Factitious Disorders," of *Synopsis VI* and to Chapter 23, "Factitious Disorders," of *CTP V* and should then study the questions and answers below to test their knowledge of this area.

HELPFUL HINTS

The student should be able to define each of the terms below.

factitious disorder
   with physical symptoms
   with psychological symptoms
   NOS
as-if personalities
regression
symbolization

Munchausen syndrome
gridiron abdomen
pseudomalingering
pseudologia fantastica
somatoform disorders
schizophrenia
malingering

drug abuse
Ganser's syndrome
approximate answers
unmasking ceremony
Briquet's syndrome

QUESTIONS

DIRECTIONS: Each of the incomplete statements below is followed by five suggested completions. Select the *one* that is *best* in each case.

Questions 22.1–22.2

A 29-year-old female laboratory technician was admitted to the medical service through the emergency room because of bloody urine. The patient said that she was being treated for lupus erythematosus by a physician in a different city. She also mentioned that she had had von Willebrand's disease (a rare hereditary blood disorder) as a child. On the third day of her hospitalization, a medical student told the resident that she had seen the patient several weeks before at a different hospital, where the patient had been admitted for the same problem. A search of the patient's belongings revealed a cache of anticoagulant medication. When confronted with this information, she refused to discuss the matter and hurriedly signed out of the hospital against medical advice. [From *DSM-III-R Case Book*. Used with permission.]

22.1. The best diagnosis in this case is
A. malingering
B. factitious disorder with psychological symptoms
C. factitious disorder with physical symptoms
D. antisocial personality disorder
E. somatoform disorder

22.2. A leading predisposing factor in the development of factitious disorder with physical symptoms is employment as a
A. teacher
B. health care worker
C. police officer
D. banker
E. waitress

22.3. Persons suffering from factitious disorders
A. simulate physical or psychological symptoms
B. practice self-mutilation
C. alter their body temperatures
D. have the sole objective of assuming the role of patient
E. all the above

22.4. All the following are synonymous with factitious disorder with physical symptoms *except*
A. professional patient syndrome
B. hospital addiction
C. Munchausen syndrome
D. Ganser's syndrome
E. polysurgical addiction

22.5. Factitious disorder with physical symptoms does not occur exclusively during the course of
A. schizophrenia
B. histrionic personality disorder
C. borderline personality disorder
D. seizure disorder
E. diabetes mellitus

22.6. Histories of persons displaying a factitious illness often reveal
A. exposure to a genuine illness in a family member
B. extensive medical treatment as a child
C. an important relationship with a physician in the past
D. early parental deprivation and rejection
E. all the above

ANSWERS

Factitious Disorders

22.1. The answer is C (*Synopsis VI*, pages 480–481; *CTP V*, pages 1136–1137).

The best diagnosis in this case is *factitious disorder with physical symptoms*. The unusual circumstances—the woman's possession of anticoagulants (taken to simulate bleeding disorders), her history of repeated hospitalizations, and her leaving the hospital when confronted—strongly suggest that her symptoms were under voluntary control and were not genuine symptoms of a physical disorder. The diagnoses to consider include malingering, somatoform disorder, and factitious disorder.

In *somatoform disorder* the production of symptoms is unconscious and involuntary, and in this case the symptom production appeared to be under voluntary control. *Malingerers* have an obvious, recognizable environmental goal in producing their symptoms, and, from what is known in this case, the patient had no understandable goal other than that of assuming the role of a patient. Since the feigned symptoms were physical (bloody urine), the diagnosis of *factitious disorder with psychological symptoms* is ruled out. Because of pathological lying, a hostile and manipulative manner, and lack of close relationships with others, many factitious disorder patients are also classified as having *antisocial personality disorder*. It is unusual, however, for antisocial persons to volunteer for invasive procedures or to resort to hospitalization as a way of life, the way this person seemed to. Not enough information is available in this case to determine whether this patient had a personality disorder. If she did, it should be coded on Axis II, with the diagnosis of factitious disorder with physical symptoms coded on Axis I.

See Table 22.1, for the DSM-III-R diagnostic criteria for factitious disorder with physical symptoms.

22.2. The answer is B (*Synopsis VI*, pages 480–481; *CTP V*, pages 1137–1138).

Employment as a *health care worker* is considered a leading predisposing factor in the development of factitious disorder with physical symptoms. Nurses make up one of the largest risk groups in the development of this disorder. In this case the patient was a laboratory technician.

22.3. The answer is E (*Synopsis VI*, page 480; *CTP V*, page 1136).

Persons suffering from factitious disorders *simulate physical or psychological symptoms* with the

Table 22.1
Diagnostic Criteria for Factitious Disorder with Physical Symptoms

A. Intentional production or feigning of physical (but not psychological) symptoms.
B. A psychological need to assume the sick role, as evidenced by the absence of external incentives for the behavior, such as economic gain, better care, or physical well-being.
C. Occurrence not exclusively during the course of another Axis I disorder, such as schizophrenia.

Table from DSM-III-R, *Diagnostic and Statistical Manual of Mental Disorders*, ed 3, revised. Copyright American Psychiatric Association, Washington, DC, 1987. Used with permission.

sole objective of assuming the role of a patient. Many of these patients make hospitalization a primary objective and often a way of life. They show a compulsive quality, and their behaviors are considered voluntary in that they are deliberate. To support their histories, these patients may feign symptoms suggestive of a disorder, or they may initiate the production of symptoms through *self-mutilation* or interference with diagnostic procedures. For example, *body temperature*, routinely recorded and presumably an objective measure, may be made to appear elevated through either manipulation or substitution of a thermometer. Similarly, urine collected for laboratory examination may be contaminated with feces or blood, obtained by self-laceration, to suggest infection or renal disease. Feigned psychological symptoms can include depression, hallucinations, dissociative and conversion symptoms, and bizarre behavior. Table 22.2 lists the DSM-III-R diagnostic criteria for factitious disorder with psychological symptoms.

22.4. The answer is D (*Synopsis VI*, page 480; *CTP V*, pages 1136–1137).

Factitious disorder with physical symptoms has been designated by a variety of labels, the best known of which is *Munchausen syndrome*, named for the Baron Münchausen. A German who lived in the 18th century, he wrote many fantastic travel and adventure stories and wandered from tavern to tavern, telling tall tales. Patients who suffer from Munchausen syndrome wander from hospital to hospital, where they manage to be admitted because of the dramatic stories they tell about being dangerously ill. Interestingly, Baron Münchausen never underwent any operations and was not known to be con-

Table 22.2
Diagnostic Criteria for Factitious Disorder
with Psychological Symptoms

A. Intentional production or feigning of psychological (but not physical) symptoms.
B. A psychological need to assume the sick role, as evidenced by the absence of external incentives for the behavior, such as economic gain, better care, or physical well-being.
C. Occurrence not exclusively during the course of another Axis I disorder, such as schizophrenia.

Table from DSM-III-R, *Diagnostic and Statistical Manual of Mental Disorders*, ed 3, revised. Copyright American Psychiatric Association, Washington, DC, 1987. Used with permission.

cerned about illness. Other names used for the disorder are *hospital addiction, polysurgical addiction,* and *professional patient syndrome*; sometimes these patients are referred to as hospital hoboes.

Ganser's syndrome is classified in DSM-III-R as an atypical dissociative disorder, as it is often associated with such dissociative phenomena as amnesia, fugue, perceptual disturbances, and conversion symptoms. A controversial condition most typically associated with prison inmates, it is characterized by the use of approximate answers. Persons with this syndrome respond to simple questions with strikingly incorrect answers. For example, when asked to give the sum of "2 plus 2," a patient may answer "5." Ganser's syndrome may be a variant of malingering in that patients avoid punishment or responsibility for their actions.

22.5. The answer is A (*Synopsis VI*, page 481; *CTP V*, page 1137).

The DSM-III-R diagnostic criteria for factitious disorder with physical symptoms are (A) intentional production or feigning of physical (but not psycho-logical) symptoms; (B) a psychological need to assume the sick role, as evidenced by the absence of external incentives for the behavior, such as economic gain, better care, or physical well-being; and (C) occurrence not exclusively during the course of another Axis I disorder, such as *schizophrenia. Histrionic and borderline personality disorders* are Axis II diagnoses and may coexist with an Axis I diagnosis of factitious disorder with physical symptoms. *Diabetes mellitus* and *seizure disorder* are Axis III medical diagnoses and can also coexist with a factitious disorder.

22.6. The answer is E (*Synopsis VI*, page 480; *CTP V*, page 1137).

Histories of persons displaying a factitious illness often reveal exposure to a *genuine illness in a family member, extensive medical treatment as a child, an important relationship with a physician,* and *parental deprivation and rejection* early in their lives. Previous or current employment as a nurse, laboratory technician, ambulance driver, physician, or other health-related worker is so common to persons displaying factitious illness that it suggests inclusion as a clinical feature and a causal factor. Consistent with the concept of poor identity formation is the observation that the patient oscillates between two roles—that of a health professional and that of a patient—with momentary confusion as to which role is being played at the time.

The physician is perceived by the patient as a potential source of the sought-for love and as a person who will fulfill the unmet dependency needs. The physician serves as a substitute father or mother figure and as the object of a parental transference. The patient uses the facsimile of genuine illness to recreate the original hoped-for parent-child interaction.

23 ||||

Impulse Control Disorders Not Elsewhere Classified

The revised third edition of *Diagnostic and Statistical Manual of Mental Disorders* (DSM-III-R) classifies five specific categories as impulse control disorders not elsewhere classified—intermittent explosive disorder, kleptomania, pathological gambling, pyromania, and trichotillomania. The student should be aware of the epidemiology, causes, clinical features, course, differential diagnosis, and treatment of these disorders, all of which have certain characteristics in common. First, the person fails to resist carrying out the particular act, and the failure to resist results in some degree of harm to that person or others. Second, an increasing source of emotional discomfort builds before the act is committed. Finally, the act itself is egosyntonic; that is, at the time the act is committed, it is associated with a conscious desire to commit it and is accompanied in some form by a mood experienced as positive by the person. Negative feelings of guilt, remorse, or shame may follow when consequences of the act are considered, but the act itself is accompanied by feelings of pleasure.

The causes of impulse control disorders are not known. Psychodynamic, psychosocial, and biological aspects have all been investigated and felt to play interacting roles.

What all categories of impulse control disorders have in common is the inability to delay gratification so as not to commit the impulsive act at all or to find alternative nonharmful methods to achieve gratification. Numerous authors have offered various dynamic explanations to specify the psychological contribution to the particular impulse control disorder patient in question, and the student should be aware of these explanations. Psychosocial factors thought to be important include violence, alcoholism, divorce, and antisocial activity in the parental home.

The reaction of many experienced clinicians is that several of the categories of impulse control disorder, especially the violent categories, have significant organic involvement. Particularly relevant is the entire limbic system, with special interest in the amygdala; certain hormones, particularly testosterone; the possible relation between temporal lobe epilepsy and certain aggressive behaviors; the effect of mixed cerebral dominance; and a reported negative correlation between violence and cerebral spinal fluid levels of 5-hydroxyindoleacetic acid, a serotonin metabolite.

Students should refer to Chapter 23 of *Synopsis VI*, "Impulse Control Disorders Not Elsewhere Classified," and to Section 24.2 of *CTP V*, "Impulse Control Disorders Not Elsewhere Classified." Students can test their knowledge by studying the questions and answers below.

HELPFUL HINTS

The terms below relate to impulse control disorders and should be defined by the student.

impulse control	testosterone	progressive-loss stage
intermittent explosive disorder	childhood MBD	desperate stage
kleptomania	epileptoid personality	enuresis
pathological and social gambling	catathymic crisis	multidetermined
pyromania	anticonvulsants	trichophagy
trichotillomania	benzodiazepines	trichomalacia
impulse control disorder NOS	lithium	alopecia
pleasure and reality principles	lust angst	hydroxyzine hydrochloride
psychodynamics	behavior therapy	biofeedback
limbic system	winning phase	hypnotherapy

QUESTIONS

DIRECTIONS: Each of the incomplete statements below is followed by five suggested completions. Select the *one* that is *best* in each case.

23.1. A compulsion to pull out one's own hair is termed
A. trichotillomania
B. trichopathia
C. trichophobia
D. trichogen
E. trichology

23.2. Pathological gambling is associated with
A. the loss of a parent before the age of 15 years
B. a family history of alcohol dependence
C. periods of stress
D. antisocial personality disorder
E. all the above

23.3. Trichotillomania
A. may be associated with a preexisting skin inflammation, such as head lice
B. usually begins in late adulthood
C. involves a superstition regarding Friday the 13th
D. is more common in females than in males
E. is more common in males than in females

23.4. General characteristics of impulse control disorders include
A. increased tension after the behavior is enacted
B. amnesia for the act
C. guilt while the behavior is enacted
D. a fear of violent confrontation
E. the inability to resist the impulse to carry out the act

DIRECTIONS: Each set of lettered headings below is followed by a list of numbered phrases. For each numbered phrase, select the one lettered heading that is *most* closely associated with it. Each lettered heading may be selected once, more than once, or not at all.

Questions 23.5–23.8
A. Trichotillomania
B. Pyromania

23.5. More common in females than in males

23.6. More common in males than in females

23.7. Treated with clomipromine (Anafranil)

23.8. Associated with truancy

Questions 23.9–23.14
A. Intermittent explosive disorder
B. Kleptomania

23.9. Greater prevalence among males than among females

23.10. Most associated with organic brain disease

23.11. Often begins in childhood

23.12. Usually begins in adulthood

23.13. Greater prevalence among females than among males

23.14. Treated with carbamazepine (Tegretol)

ANSWERS

Impulse Control Disorders Not Elsewhere Classified

23.1. The answer is A (*Synopsis VI*, pages 491–493; *CTP V*, pages 1149–1150).

Trichotillomania is defined as a compulsion to pull out one's own hair, resulting in noticeable hair loss. *Trichopathia* is the term relating to any disease of the hair. *Trichophobia* is a morbid disgust caused by the sight of loose hairs on the clothing or elsewhere. *Trichogen* is an agent that promotes hair growth. *Trichology* is the study of the hair—its anatomy, growth, and diseases. See Table 23.1 for the DSM-III-R diagnostic criteria for trichotillomania.

23.2. The answer is E (*Synopsis VI*, page 489; *CTP V*, pages 1146–1147).

As defined by DSM-III-R, pathological gambling is characterized by a chronic and progressive failure to resist impulses to gamble and gambling behavior that compromises, disrupts, or damages personal, family, or vocational pursuits. The gambling preoccupation, urge, and activity increase during *periods of stress*.

Predisposing factors for the development of the disorder include *loss of a parent* by death, separation, divorce, or desertion before the child is 15 years of age; inappropriate parental discipline; family emphasis on material and financial symbols; and a lack of family emphasis on sharing and budgeting.

Alcohol dependence is more common among the parents of pathological gamblers than among the general population, and women with the disorder are more likely than women not affected to be married to an alcoholic who is often absent from the home.

Persons with *antisocial personality disorder* may have problems with gambling. DSM-III-R suggests that, in cases in which both disorders are present, both should be diagnosed.

Estimates place the number of pathological gamblers at 2 to 3 percent of the adult U.S. population. The disorder is much more common in men than in women.

See Table 23.2 for the DSM-III-R diagnostic criteria for pathological gambling.

23.3. The answer is D (*Synopsis VI*, pages 491–493; *CTP V*, pages 1150–1151).

The essential feature of trichotillomania is the voluntary and persistent, repeated pulling out of one's hair, resulting in significant hair loss. A fear of *Friday the 13th* (also known as triskaidekaphobia) is not at all similar to trichotillomania.

The diagnosis of trichotillomania should not be made when there is a preexisting physical cause, such as *inflammation of the skin* secondary to head lice. Trichotillomania is apparently found *more in females* than in males, and, although prevalence data are unavailable, the disorder may be more common than has been believed. Trichotillomania usually begins in childhood, *not late adulthood*, although it can occur at any age. It has been reported that mainly oldest or only children are affected by the disorder.

Table 23.1
Diagnostic Criteria for Trichotillomania

A. Recurrent failure to resist impulses to pull out one's own hair, resulting in noticeable hair loss.
B. Increasing sense of tension immediately before pulling out the hair.
C. Gratification or a sense of relief when pulling out the hair.
D. No association with a preexisting inflammation of the skin, and not a response to a delusion or hallucination.

Table from DSM-III-R, *Diagnostic and Statistical Manual of Mental Disorders*, ed 3, revised. Copyright American Psychiatric Association, Washington, DC, 1987. Used with permission.

Table 23.2
Diagnostic Criteria for Pathological Gambling

Maladaptive gambling behavior, as indicated by at least four of the following:
1. frequent preoccupation with gambling or with obtaining money to gamble
2. frequent gambling of larger amounts of money or over a longer period of time than intended
3. a need to increase the size or frequency of bets to achieve the desired excitement
4. restlessness or irritability if unable to gamble
5. repeated loss of money by gambling and returning another day to win back losses ("chasing")
6. repeated efforts to reduce or stop gambling
7. frequent gambling when expected to meet social or occupational obligations
8. sacrifice of some important social, occupational, or recreational activity in order to gamble
9. continuation of gambling despite inability to pay mounting debts, or despite other significant social, occupational, or legal problems that the person knows to be exacerbated by gambling

---

Table from DSM-III-R, *Diagnostic and Statistical Manual of Mental Disorders*, ed 3, revised. Copyright American Psychiatric Association, Washington, DC, 1987. Used with permission.

There is no consensus on the best treatment for trichotillomania; it usually involves combined treatment by psychiatrists and dermatologists. When depression is present, antidepressant agents may lead to dermatological improvement. Many psychotropic agents have been used to treat dermatological manifestations, and their use testifies to the wide belief that emotional factors underlie the cause of these manifestations.

23.4. The answer is E (*Synopsis VI*, page 485; *CTP V*, page 1145).

General characteristics of impulse control disorders include *increased tension* before the behavior is enacted, not after, and pleasure or relief, not *guilt*, while the behavior is enacted.

Persons with impulse control disorders may or may not consciously plan the act, and they may or may not feel genuine regret, self-reproach, or guilt, but there is no *amnesia for the act.* By definition, the person is unable to *resist the impulse* to carry out the act.

Intermittent explosive disorder is one of the impulse control disorders. It is defined by episodes of loss of control, resulting in serious assaultive acts or destructiveness; *violent confrontation* is clearly a characteristic of this disorder, and thus a fear of confrontation is not a general characteristic of impulse control disorders.

See Table 23.3 for the DSM-III-R diagnostic criteria for intermittent explosive disorder.

23.5–23.8

23.5. The answer is A (*Synopsis VI*, pages 491–493; *CTP V*, pages 1148–1152).

23.6. The answer is B (*Synopsis VI*, pages 490–491; *CTP V*, pages 1148–1152).

23.7. The answer is A (*Synopsis VI*, pages 491–493; *CTP V*, pages 1148–1152).

Table 23.3
Diagnostic Criteria for Intermittent Explosive Disorder

A. Several discrete episodes of loss of control of aggressive impulses resulting in serious assaultive acts or destruction of property.
B. The degree of aggressiveness expressed during the episodes is grossly out of proportion to any precipitating psychosocial stressors.
C. There are no signs of generalized impulsiveness or aggressiveness between the episodes.
D. The episodes of loss of control do not occur during the course of a psychotic disorder, organic personality syndrome, antisocial or borderline personality disorder, conduct disorder, or intoxication with a psychoactive substance.

23.8. The answer is B (*Synopsis VI*, pages 490–491; *CTP V*, pages 1148–1152).

Pyromania is defined as deliberate and purposeful fire setting on more than one occasion; trichotillomania is the persistent pulling out of one's own hair. Common features for a patient with a disorder of impulse control (e.g., trichotillomania, pyromania) are (1) failure to resist an impulse to perform some action that is harmful to the self or others; (2) a sense of increased tension or arousal before committing the act; (3) gratification or release of tension while committing the act.

Pyromania is far *more common in males* than in females. Trichotillomania is apparently *more common in females* than in males. Fire setters have classically been noted to have a history of antisocial traits, such as *truancy*, running away from home, and delinquency. Trichotillomania has not been specifically associated with truancy, although its onset has been linked to stressful situations in more than one quarter of the cases.

When pyromania has its onset in adolescence or adulthood, the fire setting tends to be deliberate and destructive. The prognosis for adults is guarded because of their frequent use of denial and refusal to take responsibility. The treatment of fire setters has been notoriously difficult because of their lack of motivation, and incarceration may be the only way to prevent a recurrence. Treatment for trichotillomania is also frequently challenging, usually involving psychiatrists and dermatologists in a joint endeavor. Psychopharmacological methods that have been used to treat trichotillomania include anxiolytics, antidepressants, and antipsychotics. Most pharmacological methods of treatment of trichotillomania have not shown good results; however, the use of *clomipramine* (Anafranil), a drug approved in 1990 for the treatment of obsessive-compulsive disorder, has shown more promise in giving relief to patients with trichotillomania than have other medications. Clomipramine and fluoxetine (Prozac) are both being investigated to define their efficacy in the treatment of trichotillomania.

See Table 23.4 for the DSM-III-R diagnostic criteria for pyromania. Table 23.1 lists the diagnostic criteria for trichotillomania.

23.9–23.14

23.9. The answer is A (*Synopsis VI*, pages 486–487; *CTP V*, pages 1152–1153).

23.10. The answer is A (*Synopsis VI*, pages 486–487; *CTP V*, pages 1152–1153).

23.11. The answer is B (*Synopsis VI*, pages 487–488; *CTP V*, pages 1147–1148).

23.12. The answer is A (*Synopsis VI*, pages 486–487; *CTP V*, pages 1152–1153).

Table 23.4
Diagnostic Criteria for Pyromania

A. Deliberate and purposeful fire-setting on more than one occasion.
B. Tension or affective arousal before the act.
C. Fascination with, interest in, curiosity about, or attraction to fire and its situational context or associated characteristics (e.g., paraphernalia, uses, consequences, exposure to fires).
D. Intense pleasure, gratification, or relief when setting fires, or when witnessing or participating in their aftermath.
E. The fire-setting is not done for monetary gain, as an expression of sociopolitical ideology, to conceal criminal activity, to express anger or vengeance, to improve one's living circumstances, or in response to a delusion or hallucination.

Table from DSM-III-R, *Diagnostic and Statistical Manual of Mental Disorders*, ed 3, revised. Copyright American Psychiatric Association, Washington, DC, 1987. Used with permission.

23.13. The answer is B (*Synopsis VI*, pages 487–488; *CTP V*, pages 1147–1148).

23.14. The answer is A (*Synopsis VI*, pages 486–487; *CTP V*, pages 1152–1153).

Intermittent explosive disorder and kleptomania are among the DSM-III-R disorders of impulse control that are not elsewhere classified. Many investigators have noted a possible *association with organic brain disease* for all the impulse control disorders, especially those presenting with overtly violent behavior, such as intermittent explosive disorder. Lesions in the limbic system, for example, have been associated with violent behavior and loss of control of aggressive impulses. Profitless stealing, kleptomania, has been less strongly associated with brain disease and mental retardation.

Intermittent explosive disorder *usually begins in adulthood*. Typical patients are physically large men whose sense of masculine identity is poor. The history of these patients often reveals a childhood environment of alcoholism, physical violence, and parental instability. Most of these patients have poor work histories and have been in trouble with the law.

Intermittent explosive disorder, according to DSM-III-R, is diagnosed when there are several discrete assaultive acts or destruction of property, when the degree of aggressiveness during the episode is grossly out of proportion to any precipitating stress, and when there are no signs of generalized impulsiveness or aggressiveness between the episodes. The disorder is apparently rare and appears to have a *greater prevalence among males* than among females.

Kleptomania is also rare, and the sex ratio is unknown. However, as shoplifting itself is more common in females than in males, kleptomania-related

Table 23.5
Diagnostic Criteria for Kleptomania

A. Recurrent failure to resist impulses to steal objects not needed for personal use or their monetary value.
B. Increasing sense of tension immediately before committing the theft.
C. Pleasure or relief at the time of committing the theft.
D. The stealing is not committed to express anger or vengeance.
E. The stealing is not due to conduct disorder or antisocial personality disorder.

Table from DSM-III-R, *Diagnostic and Statistical Manual of Mental Disorders*, ed 3, revised. Copyright American Psychiatric Association, Washington, DC, 1987. Used with permission.

shoplifting is also thought to be *more common in females* than in males. It often *begins in childhood*.

Most patients with intermittent explosive disorder are treated with a combined pharmacological and psychotherapeutic approach. Psychotherapy with violent patients is exceedingly difficult because of potential problems with countertransference and limit setting. Anticonvulsants, phenothiazines, and antidepressants have all been effective in some cases of intermittent explosive disorder, and studies have shown that both *lithium* and *carbamazepine* (Tegretol) are useful in certain cases. The latter has not been used in the treatment of kleptomania.

Kleptomania is diagnosed when there is a recurrent failure to resist impulses to steal objects not needed for personal use or their monetary value. Behavior therapy has been a mainstay in the treatment of kleptomania. Systematic desensitization, aversive conditioning, and marital therapy have all been reported to be successful in treating kleptomaniacs.

Antisocial personality disorder must be considered in the differential diagnosis of both kleptomania and intermittent explosive disorder. One can differentiate intermittent explosive disorder from antisocial personality disorder by the fact that in intermittent explosive disorder there are no signs of generalized impulsiveness or aggressiveness between the episodes. In antisocial personality disorder, the aggressiveness and impulsiveness are part of the patient's character and are present between outbursts. Stealing that occurs in association with antisocial personality disorder is clearly related to the pervasive underlying disorder, unlike the stealing that occurs in kleptomania. According to the DSM-III-R criteria, neither intermittent explosive disorder nor kleptomania can be diagnosed when impulsiveness, aggressiveness, or stealing is due to antisocial personality disorder.

Table 23.5 lists the DSM-III-R diagnostic criteria for kleptomania. See Table 23.3 for the criteria for intermittent explosive disorder.

24 |||||

Adjustment Disorder

Adjustment disorder is often diagnosed when a maladaptive, exaggerated response follows a stress within the realm of ordinary life experience, such as an acute financial loss or the death of a spouse. In such cases, the person's ability to participate in the ordinary activities of everyday life is impaired, with the occurrence of such common symptoms as anxiety, depression, withdrawal, immobility, and physical complaints.

The basis of the diagnosis of adjustment disorder lies in the concept of trauma as psychic overload, with a subsequent partial or complete feeling of helplessness, accompanied by regression and inhibitions. With adjustment disorder, the stressor is a usual life event, the response is disproportionately intense, and the overload is surprising, but the impairment is moderate and temporary.

The clinician needs to exercise good judgment about what constitutes a stressor. Stressors may be single, such as a divorce or the loss of a job, or multiple, such as the death of an important person at the time of one's own physical illness and loss of a job. Stressors may be recurrent, such as seasonal business difficulties, or continuous, as in chronic illness or having to live in a poverty area. Discordant intrafamilial relationships may produce adjustment disorder with effects on the family system. Specific developmental stages—such as beginning school, leaving home, getting married, becoming a parent, failing to achieve occupational goals, the last child's leaving home, and retiring—are often associated with adjustment disorder.

Special scales describe the types and the severities of psychosocial stressors in adults and children. The student should be familiar with these scales, which are listed on pages 224 and 225 of *Synopsis VI* and on page 466 of *CTP V*.

For example, the death of a child is considered a catastrophic event in the life of an adult; similarly, the death of both parents is a catastrophic event for a child. A child's leaving home, however, is a mild stress for an adult.

Whether or not a person has an adjustment disorder after a stress depends on many factors: biological and psychological vulnerability, the presence or absence of support systems, early life experiences, personality makeup, and the age of the person, among others.

The severity of the stress does not always correlate with the severity of the adjustment disorder. The death of a loved one, for example, usually results in uncomplicated bereavement, which is a normal response associated with a temporary impairment in functioning. It is not an adjustment disorder, because the impairment during grief is within expectable bounds of behavior.

At the other end of the spectrum is a posttraumatic stress disorder (PTSD) in which the person reacts to an event outside the range of normal human experience, such as earthquakes, floods, and rape. The student should be able to distinguish a normal reaction to stress from an adjustment disorder and a PTSD.

Adjustment disorder is among the most common psychiatric disorders and has a favorable prognosis. Antianxiety agents and antidepressant drugs may be of help; however, the first approach is to enable the patient to talk about the stressful experience. This can be done with the psychiatrist individually or in a group. Allowing the patient to interact with others who may have undergone similar experiences is of great use. Groups composed of rape or incest victims, for example, can be of tremendous benefit. Most patients recover from an adjustment disorder within three months and often learn from the experience, so that they are stronger than they were before the episode occurred.

The student should refer to Chapter 24, "Adjustment Disorder," in *Synopsis VI* and to Section 24.1, "Adjustment Disorder," in *CTP V* and should then study the questions and answers below to gain an understanding of this area.

HELPFUL HINTS

The student should know the terms and types of adjustment disorders below.

maladaptive reaction	AD with disturbance of conduct	posttraumatic stress disorder
psychosocial stressor	AD with work or academic	mass catastrophes
Donald Winnicott	inhibition	catastrophic reaction
good-enough mother	AD with withdrawal	severity of stress scale
types	AD with physical complaints	secondary gain
adjustment disorder (AD) with	AD NOS	recovery rate
depressed mood	conditions not attributable to a	
AD with anxious mood	mental disorder	
AD with mixed emotional features	uncomplicated bereavement	

QUESTIONS

DIRECTIONS: Each of the incomplete statements below is followed by five suggested completions. Select the *one* that is *best* in each case.

John was a 50-year-old retired policeman who sought treatment a few weeks after his dog had been run over and died. Since that time he had felt sad and tired and had had trouble in sleeping and concentrating.

John lived alone and had for many years had virtually no conversational contacts with other human beings beyond a "Hello" or "How are you?" He preferred to be by himself, found talk a waste of time, and felt awkward when other people tried to initiate a relationship. He occasionally spent some time in a bar but always off by himself and not really following the general conversation. He read newspapers avidly and was well informed in many areas but took no particular interest in the people around him. He was employed as a security guard but was known by his fellow workers as a cold fish and a loner. They no longer even noticed or teased him, especially since he never seemed to notice or care about their teasing.

John floated through life without relationships except for that with his dog, which he dearly loved. At Christmas he would buy the dog elaborate gifts and, in return, would receive a wrapped bottle of Scotch whiskey that he bought for himself as a gift from the dog. He believed that dogs are more sensitive and loving than people, and he could, in return, express toward them a tenderness and an emotion not possible in his relationships with people. The losses of his pets were the only events in his life that caused him sadness. He had experienced the deaths of his parents without emotion and felt no regret whatever at being completely out of contact with the rest of his family. He considered himself different from other people and regarded emotionality in others with bewilderment.

24.1. The best diagnosis in this case is
A. major depression
B. dysthymia
C. adjustment disorder with depressed mood
D. adjustment disorder with anxious mood
E. interpersonal problem

24.2. For a diagnosis of adjustment disorder, the reaction to a psychosocial stressor must occur within
A. one week
B. two weeks
C. one month
D. two months
E. three months

24.3. Vulnerability to an adjustment disorder is affected by
A. early mothering experiences
B. a previous history of a personality disorder
C. adolescence
D. the severity of the stress
E. all the above

DIRECTIONS: For the incomplete statement below, *one or more* of the completions given are correct. Choose answer

     A. if only *1, 2, and 3* are correct
     B. if only *1 and 3* are correct
     C. if only *2 and 4* are correct
     D. if only *4* is correct
     E. if *all* are correct

24.4. An adjustment disorder is
1. an exacerbation of a preexisting psychiatric disorder
2. a normal response to a nonspecific stress
3. a normal response to a clearly identifiable event
4. a maladaptive reaction to adverse circumstances

ANSWERS

Adjustment Disorder

24.1. The answer is C (*Synopsis VI*, pages 494–497; *CTP V*, pages 1141–1143).

John had an intense, maladaptive reaction to the stress of the death of his dog. He sought treatment because he felt sad and tired and had had difficulty in sleeping and concentrating for several weeks. Since his predominant manifestation was consistent with depression, the diagnosis is *adjustment disorder with depressed mood. Adjustment disorder with anxious mood* is diagnosed if the patient has complaints such as palpitations, agitation, jitters, and other symptoms of anxiety.

John's long-standing self-isolative life-style indicates a schizoid personality disorder, but there is no indication that he has chronic bouts of sadness or chronic changes in appetite, sleep, or concentration, ruling out the diagnoses of *dysthymia* and *major depression.* Although *interpersonal problems* exist in John's life, his maladaptive functioning is far too pervasive for this to be the diagnosis.

24.2. The answer is E (*Synopsis VI*, pages 494–495; *CTP V*, page 1141).

According to the definition of adjustment disorder in the revised third edition of *Diagnostic and Statistical Manual of Mental Disorders* (DSM-III-R), symptoms of the disorder must occur within *three months* of the onset of the stressors, which presumes a cause-and-effect process. If a longer time (e.g., one year) intervenes between the onset of the psychiatric symptoms and an identifiable psychosocial stressor, the clinician should not make a diagnosis of adjustment disorder. See Table 24.1 for the DSM-III-R diagnostic criteria for adjustment disorder.

24.3. The answer is E (*Synopsis VI*, pages 494–495; *CTP V*, pages 1142–1143).

Vulnerability to an adjustment disorder is affected by many factors. Persons with a previous history of a *personality disorder* or an organic mental disorder are more susceptible than others. The *severity of the stress* also increases vulnerability (e.g., the loss of a young child is a greater stress than the loss of an aged parent, and the loss of a child is likely to precipitate an adjustment disorder).

Adjustment disorders are prevalent, and, although they may occur at any age, they are most

Table 24.1
Diagnostic Criteria for Adjustment Disorder

A. A reaction to an identifiable psychosocial stressor (or multiple stressors) that occurs within three months of onset of the stressor(s).
B. The maladaptive nature of the reaction is indicated by either of the following:
   1. impairment in occupational (including school) functioning or in usual social activities or relationships with others
   2. symptoms that are in excess of a normal and expectable reaction to the stressor(s)
C. The disturbance is not merely one instance of a pattern of overreaction to stress or an exacerbation of one of the mental disorders previously described.
D. The maladaptive reaction has persisted for no longer than six months.
E. The disturbance does not meet the criteria for any specific mental disorder and does not represent uncomplicated bereavement.

Table from DSM-III-R, *Diagnostic and Statistical Manual of Mental Disorders*, ed 3, revised. Copyright American Psychiatric Association, Washington, DC, 1987. Used with permission.

common during *adolescence* and young adulthood. Vulnerability is increased by poor *mothering experiences.* Providing the infant with an environment in which anxiety is attended to appropriately enables the growing child to tolerate the frustrations in life. Vulnerability is also associated with the lack of a parent during infancy and childhood.

24.4. The answer is D (4) (*Synopsis VI*, page 494; *CTP V*, page 1141).

According to DSM-III-R, an adjustment disorder is a *maladaptive reaction* to an identifiable psychosocial stressor or to adverse circumstances. The disturbance is not merely an *exacerbation of a preexisting psychiatric disorder,* but the response is to an identifiable, rather than a nonspecific, stress. The response must be identified either by impairment in occupational functioning or in usual social activities or relationships with others or by symptoms that are in excess of a normal and expectable reaction to the stressor. Thus, it is not a normal response to either a *nonspecific stress* or a *clearly identifiable event.*

Behavioral Medicine and Psychological Factors Affecting Physical Condition (Psychosomatic Disorders)

Behavioral medicine is the interdisciplinary field concerned with the development and the integration of behavioral and biomedical science knowledge and techniques relevant to health and illness and the application of this knowledge and these techniques for prevention, diagnosis, and rehabilitation. It therefore includes the field of psychosomatic medicine. The goal of both behavioral medicine techniques and psychosomatic therapeutic modalities is to favorably affect the psychosomatic equation. The interrelation of the psyche (mind) and the soma (body) has been highlighted in a group of disorders in which emotional and physical states overlap.

The psychological factors affecting physical disorders or, more succinctly, psychosomatic disorders are those in which psychologically meaningful stimuli are temporally related to the initiation or the exacerbation of a physical condition. These physical conditions have a known organic pathology or a known pathophysiological process.

Common examples listed in the revised third edition of *Diagnostic and Statistical Manual of Mental Disorders* (DSM-III-R) include obesity, tension headache, migraine headache, angina pectoris, painful menstruation, sacroiliac pain, neurodermatitis, acne, rheumatoid arthritis, asthma, tachycardia, arrhythmia, gastric ulcer, duodenal ulcer, cardiospasm, pylorospasm, nausea and vomiting, regional enteritis, ulcerative colitis, and frequency of micturition. All these conditions have either demonstrable organic pathology (e.g., rheumatoid arthritis) or a known pathophysiological process (e.g., migraine headache).

A basic concept underlying the mechanism of psychosomatic illness is that there are phys-iological concomitants of psychic conflict and trauma. Emotional arousal gives rise to profound physiological reaction. Under ordinary conditions the somatic concomitants of acute grief, rage, or anxiety do not lead to adverse physical consequences in the healthy person. However, some persons are organically vulnerable to the physiological concomitants of emotion, and psychophysiological disorders may develop as a result of emotional arousal. Organic vulnerability is a crucial but variable factor in the genesis of psychosomatic illness. Some patients are highly vulnerable to almost any type of emotional arousal, whereas others have a smaller degree of vulnerability, and symptoms develop only when the emotional reaction assumes a pathological form and is excessively severe or chronically unrelieved. In general, psychophysiological disorders are more likely to develop when there is both a high degree of organic vulnerability and a substantial emotional stress. Although they play a significant role in causing psychosomatic disorders, psychic factors are not the only causative determinant. They interact with somatic factors—such as constitution, nutritional status, and organ pathology—to produce the final disease state.

In the treatment of psychosomatic conditions, the emphasis is on the interrelation of mind and body in the genesis of symptoms and in their amelioration or cure. Close collaboration between the psychiatrist and the internist or other specialist is required in a combined treatment approach to psychosomatic illness. The internist treats the medical symptoms, and the psychiatrist helps the patient focus on his or her feelings about the symptoms and gain understanding about the conflicts, stressors, or unconscious processes that contribute to or exacerbate the illness.

The student should learn which medical problems may present with psychiatric symptoms. For example, depression may be the first symptom of hypothyroidism, and disorientation may be the first symptom of the acquired immune deficiency syndrome (AIDS). A broad knowledge of medicine and psychiatry enables the clinician to exercise sound clinical judgment in making the correct diagnosis.

This chapter also covers consultation-liaison (CL) psychiatry. The CL psychiatrist consults with regard to patients in medical or surgical settings and provides follow-up psychiatric treatment. Most CL psychiatry occurs in the general hospital, and the CL psychiatrist serves as a bridge between psychiatry and other specialties. There are many reasons for asking to have a psychiatric consultation on a patient in a general hospital, the most common of which are disorientation, agitation, a suicide attempt or threat, depression, hallucinations, sleep disorder, and noncompliance with or refusal to consent to a procedure. The student

should be familiar with each of these reasons in great detail.

As cancer treatment has advanced, so has the understanding of the psychological effects of cancer on the patient, the family, and the staff advanced. One half of all cancer patients have psychiatric disorders. The student should be familiar with the types of disorders and the treatments available for those affected.

Finally, new methods of treatment, particularly treatments involving the transplantation of organs, are associated increasingly with psychiatric problems. The attitude of the person receiving a new organ and the emotional significance of donating an organ to another person is an important new area of interest.

Students should read Chapter 25, "Behavioral Medicine and Psychological Factors Affecting Physical Condition (Psychosomatic Disorders)," in *Synopsis VI* and Chapter 25, "Psychological Factors Affecting Physical Condition (Psychosomatic Disorders)," in *CTP V* and then test their knowledge by answering the questions below and studying the explanations that follow.

HELPFUL HINTS

The terms relating to psychophysiological medicine listed below should be defined.

psychosomatic	cardiac arrhythmias	IgM and IgA
psychophysiological	psychogenic cardiac nondisease	atopic
psyche and soma	neurocirculatory asthenia	idiopathic amenorrhea
conversion disorder	Jacob DaCosta	chronic pain
somatization disorder	propranolol (Inderal)	pain threshold and perception
hypochondriasis	bronchial asthma	undermedication
dysthymia	parentectomy	behavior modification,
Holmes and Rahe	hay fever	deconditioning program
social readjustment rating scale	hyperventilation syndrome	analgesia
life-change units	peptic ulcer	pain clinics
specific versus nonspecific stress	ulcerative colitis	immune disorders
Flanders Dunbar	compulsive personality traits	immune response
Friedman and Rosenman	obesity	immediate and delayed
Franz Alexander	bulimia and anorexia nervosa	hypersensitivity
general adaptation syndrome	rheumatoid arthritis	cell-mediated immunity
alexithymia	low back pain	humoral immunity
coronary artery disease	migraine headaches	AIDS
postcardiotomy delirium	tension headaches	allergic disorders
type A and type B personalities	obsessional personalities	organ transplantation
essential hypertension	hyperthyroidism	autoimmune diseases
biofeedback	thyrotoxicosis	systemic lupus erythematosus
relaxation therapy	diabetes mellitus	skin disorders
congestive heart failure	PMS	pruritus
vasomotor syncope	LLPDD	hyperhidrosis
personality types	dysmenorrhea	CL psychiatry
specificity hypothesis	menopausal distress	myxedema madness
vasovagal attack	climacteric	Wilson's disease

pancreatic carcinoma	hemodialysis units	vasomotor syncope
command hallucination	dialysis dementia	giving up-given up complex
gun-barrel vision	surgical patients	hormonal personality factors
pheochromocytoma	crisis intervention	
ICUs	Hans Selye	

QUESTIONS

DIRECTIONS: Each of the incomplete statements below is followed by five suggested completions. Select the *one* that is *best* in each case.

25.1. A 42-year-old trial lawyer, married and the mother of two children, was referred for psychiatric consultation by her gastroenterologist after her third hospitalization for duodenal ulcer disease. Her ulcer disease was first diagnosed four years ago, but an upper gastrointestinal series at that time showed evidence of both an active ulcer and scarring secondary to previously healed ulcers. The gastroenterologist requested the consultation for help in considering the possibility of surgery, prompted by the seriousness of the bleeding episode that precipitated the patient's last admission and by the fact that she seemed to ignore pain. His referral note indicated that he saw no clear connection between the bleeding episodes and the patient's highly stressful occupation.

The patient appeared exactly on time for her appointment; she was neatly and conservatively dressed. She presented an organized, coherent account of her medical problem and denied any past or immediate family history of significant mental disorder. She appeared genuinely worried by her recent hospitalization, frightened by the prospect of surgery, and doubtful that speaking to a psychiatrist would produce any meaningful help. There seemed to be no temporal relation between her attacks and several dramatic and highly taxing court cases in which she had appeared.

Her marriage seemed sound. As she began to talk about her two sons, aged 8 and 4, the patient became noticeably more tense and appeared much more concerned and upset than usual while describing minor crises they experienced with friends or in school. With great surprise she discovered that the chronology of these crises corresponded clearly to five of her seven ulcer attacks, including all the attacks that resulted in hospitalization. She admitted that, despite being upset by her sons' problems, she found it difficult to share her concerns about parenting with her husband or friends. At the end of the session, she commented: "You would have made a good lawyer. I'm glad I'm not arguing against you." She herself suggested that some further sessions might be in order. [From *DSM-III-R Case Book*. Used with permission.]

The most likely diagnosis is
A. somatoform disorder
B. conversion disorder
C. factitious disorder with physical symptoms
D. psychological factors affecting physical condition
E. somatization disorder

25.2. The most common symptom associated with chronic headaches is
A. depression
B. hallucinations
C. altered body image
D. memory disturbance
E. perseveration

25.3. Biofeedback has not been found efficacious in the treatment of
A. peptic ulcer disease
B. low back pain
C. epilepsy
D. migraine headache
E. ulcerative colitis

25.4. The diagnostic criteria for psychological factors affecting physical condition (psychosomatic disorder) include all the following *except*
A. psychologically meaningful environmental stimuli
B. a temporal relation to the initiation or the exacerbation of a physical condition
C. the physical condition involves no demonstrable organic pathology
D. the physical condition involves a known pathophysiological process
E. the condition does not meet the criteria for a somatoform disorder

25.5. The percentage of cancer patients who later have a psychiatric disorder is
A. 20 percent
B. 30 percent
C. 50 percent
D. 60 percent
E. 75 percent

25.6. All the following statements about menopausal distress are true *except*
A. the symptoms appear to be related to both physiological and psychological factors
B. women with low self-esteem and low life satisfaction are likely to be vulnerable to menopausal distress
C. a woman's response to menopause parallels her response to other crucial physiological events in her life
D. the incidence of mental illness in women increases during menopause
E. psychotherapy should address the meaning of aging to the patient

25.7. The following statements about obesity are true *except*
A. there is a familial predisposition to obesity
B. when obesity first occurs in adulthood, it is usually hyperplastic obesity
C. among the psychodynamic factors are oral fixation, oral regression, and the overvaluation of food
D. bulimia may be present
E. the patient often has a history of poor early conditioning to food intake

DIRECTIONS: For each of the questions or incomplete statements below, *one* or *more* of the responses or completions given are correct. Choose answer

A. if only *1, 2, and 3* are correct
B. if only *1 and 3* are correct
C. if only *2 and 4* are correct
D. if only *4* is correct
E. if *all* are correct

25.8. Patients with chronic pain resulting from cancer respond best to
1. psychotropic drugs
2. analgesics
3. psychotherapy
4. nerve blocks

25.9. Which of the following statements about late luteal phase dysphoric disorder are true?
1. Symptoms occur only during the four days before the onset of menses
2. Suicidal ideation may be present
3. It is most often seen in women under 30 years of age
4. Symptoms occurred during the majority of menstrual cycles within the previous year

25.10. Behavior modification in the treatment of chronic pain patients involves
1. prescription of an analgesic at regular intervals
2. discontinuation of disability payments as the patient begins to get better
3. increased attention by the staff when the patient is displaying healthy behavior
4. hospitalization

25.11. Disorders associated with psychological factors affecting physical condition include
1. rheumatoid arthritis
2. diabetes mellitus
3. pruritis ani
4. hay fever

25.12. Stressful life experiences, particularly experiences of separation and loss, have been reported to precede the clinical onset of
1. cancer of the cervix
2. leukemia
3. lymphoma
4. cancer of the breast

DIRECTIONS: Each group of questions below consists of five lettered headings followed by a list of numbered statements. For each numbered statement, select the *one* lettered heading that is most closely associated with it. Each lettered heading may be selected once, more than once, or not at all.

Questions 25.13–25.15
A. Flanders Dunbar
B. Meyer Friedman and Ray Rosenman
C. Franz Alexander
D. T. H. Holmes and R. H. Rahe
E. Jacob DaCosta

25.13. Type A and type B personalities

25.14. Neurocirculatory asthenia

25.15. Social Readjustment Rating Scale

Questions 25.16–25.19
A. Wilson's disease
B. Pheochromocytoma
C. Systemic lupus erythematosus
D. Acquired immune deficiency syndrome (AIDS)
E. Pancreatic cancer

25.16. Dementia syndrome with global impairment and seropositivity

25.17. Resembles steroid psychosis

25.18. Explosive anger and labile mood

25.19. Symptoms of a classic panic attack

ANSWERS

Behavioral Medicine and Psychological Factors Affecting Physical Condition (Psychosomatic Disorders)

25.1. The answer is D (*Synopsis VI*, pages 498–499; *CTP V*, pages 1155–1156).

The most likely diagnosis in the case of the trial lawyer is *psychological factors affecting physical condition;* the diagnostic criteria are that psychologically meaningful environmental stimuli were significantly—albeit partially—and temporally related to the initiation or the exacerbation of a physical disorder. Although this patient's duodenal ulcer attacks were unrelated to her court appearances, she did discover that the chronology of the majority of the attacks or bleeding episodes corresponded clearly with minor crises involving her two sons.

In the past, somatic disorders deemed to be of psychological cause were known as psychosomatic or psychophysiological. Now somatic disorders with demonstrable pathophysiology in which psychological issues are considered to play a meaningful role in the course of the illness are classified as psychological factors affecting physical condition. This change shifts the importance of the psychological areas from causative to exacerbations and remissions. In addition to ulcers, common examples of such disorders include obesity, tension headache, migraine headache, and asthma.

In *somatoform disorders* there is no demonstrable pathophysiological process; they are characterized by physical symptoms that resemble medical disease but exhibit no organic pathology.

Somatization disorder and *conversion disorder* are two types of somatoform disorders. Somatization disorder is a chronic syndrome that presents with recurrent and multiple somatic complaints associated with psychosocial distress for which medical attention has been sought but that apparently are not attributable to any physical disorder. In conversion disorder there is a loss or a change in bodily functioning that results from a psychological conflict or need. Such bodily symptoms cannot be explained by any known medical disorder.

Factitious disorder with physical symptoms is a disorder in which the patient intentionally produces or feigns physical symptoms. The presentation may be total fabrication or a feigned exacerbation with an underlying minor physical ailment.

See Table 25.1 for the DSM-III-R diagnostic criteria for psychological factors affecting physical condition.

25.2. The answer is A (*Synopsis VI*, page 507; *CTP V*, pages 232–234).

The most common symptom associated with chronic headaches is *depression*. The relation between headaches and depressed mood is complex. Any chronic medical illness predisposes toward depression, and headaches are no exception. The depression apparently has no organic basis but, rather, is secondary to the stress of having to deal with a chronic illness. The converse is also true; that is, headaches may also be seen as the presenting symptom of depression. Internists and primary care physicians are often the first to see patients suffering from headaches, and they often refer their patients to psychiatrists only after an extensive and costly medical workup. After an organic illness has been ruled out, the idea of a psychological illness is entertained.

Hallucinations (false sensory perceptions) and *perseveration* (verbal repetition of words or phrases) are typically seen in psychotic illnesses and organic mental syndrome and are not associated with headaches. *Memory disturbance* is most often evidence of an organic dysfunction, toxic or otherwise, and is not typical of headaches. *Altered body image*, the idea

Table 25.1
Diagnostic Criteria for Psychological Factors Affecting Physical Condition

A. Psychologically meaningful environmental stimuli are temporally related to the initiation or exacerbation of a specific physical condition or disorder (recorded on Axis III).
B. The physical condition involves either demonstrable organic pathology (e.g., rheumatoid arthritis) or a known pathophysiologic process (e.g., migraine headache).
C. The condition does not meet the criteria for a somatoform disorder.

Table from DSM-III-R, *Diagnostic and Statistical Manual of Mental Disorders*, ed 3, revised. Copyright American Psychiatric Association, Washington, DC, 1987. Used with permission.

that one's body is shaped differently than it really is, is seen in the eating disorders anorexia nervosa and bulimia.

25.3. The answer is E (*Synopsis VI*, pages 506–507 and 524; *CTP V*, pages 1024–1025 and 1474–1475).

Biofeedback has not been found to be efficacious in the treatment of *ulcerative colitis*, a chronic disease of unknown cause characterized by ulceration and bleeding of the mucosa of the colon and the rectum. It frequently causes anemia, hypoproteinemia, and electrolyte imbalance. Biofeedback has been used with some therapeutic success in, for example, *peptic ulcer disease, low back pain, epilepsy*, and *migraine headache*, although the results are as yet inconclusive.

Biofeedback refers to information provided externally to a person about normally subthreshold biological or physiological processes. Among the most effective feedback instruments are the electromyograph, the electroencephalogram, and the galvanic skin-response gauge. Peptic ulcer disease is a circumscribed ulceration of the mucous membrane of the stomach or the duodenum, occurring in areas exposed to gastric acid and pepsin. Low back pain refers to pain in the lower lumbar, lumbosacral, and sacroiliac region. Although organic factors may clearly be involved (e.g., a ruptured intervertebral disk), some studies indicate that 95 percent of cases are psychological in origin. Epilepsy is a neurological disorder resulting from a sudden excessive, disorderly discharge of neurons in either a structurally normal or a diseased cerebral cortex. Migraine headaches are a paroxysmal disorder characterized by recurrent headaches with or without related visual and gastrointestinal disturbances.

25.4. The answer is C (*Synopsis VI*, page 499; *CTP V*, pages 1155–1156).

The diagnostic criteria in DSM-III-R for psychological factors affecting physical condition (i.e., psychosomatic disorders) are that *psychologically meaningful environmental stimuli* are *temporally related to the initiation or the exacerbation* of a specific physical condition or disorder. Such a condition involves either *demonstrable organic pathology*, such as rheumatoid arthritis, or a *known pathophysiological process*, such as migraine headache. Many believe that the DSM-III-R deletion of the nosological term "psychophysiological" (a synonym for psychosomatic) deemphasized the interaction of mind (psyche) and body (soma), a concept that emphasizes a unitary causative or holistic approach to medicine in that all diseases are influenced by psychological factors. The DSM-III-R diagnostic criteria for psychological factors affecting physical condition are presented in Table 25.1.

Excluded from this DSM-III-R classification are (1) classical psychiatric disorders presenting with physical symptoms as part of the disorder (e.g., conversion disorder, in which a physical symptom is produced by psychological conflict); (2) somatization disorders, in which there are physical symptoms not based on organic pathology; (3) hypochondriasis, in which there is an exaggerated or imagined concern with one's health; (4) physical complaints that are frequently associated with psychological disorders (e.g., dysthymia, which usually has such somatic accompaniments as muscle weakness, asthenia, fatigue, and exhaustion); (5) physical complaints associated with habit disorders (e.g., coughing associated with nicotine dependence); and (6) *somatoform disorder,* in which severe and prolonged pain has no medical explanation.

25.5. The answer is C (*Synopsis VI*, page 512; *CTP V*, page 1249).

About *50 percent* of cancer patients have psychiatric disorders; 68 percent of these disorders are adjustment disorders; 13 percent of those with psychiatric symptoms have major depression, and 8 percent have delirium associated with organic mood syndromes. Although cancer patients may express suicidal wishes, the actual suicide incidence is only 1.4 to 1.9 times that of the general population. Vulnerability to suicide is increased by the factors summarized in Table 25.2.

25.6. The answer is D (*Synopsis VI*, pages 509–510; *CTP V*, page 1337).

Menopause is a natural physiological event, most often occurring between the ages of 48 and 55. Menopause also occurs immediately after the surgical removal of the ovaries. Many psychological symptoms—including anxiety, fatigue, tension, emotional lability, and depression—have been attributed to menopause. The *symptoms* seem to be related to the rate of hormone withdrawal; the amount of hormone depletion; a woman's constitutional ability to withstand the overall aging process, including her overall health and level of activity; and the psychological meaning of aging for her.

Table 25.2
Suicide Vulnerability Factors in Cancer Patients

Depression and hopelessness
Poorly controlled pain
Mild delirium (disinhibition)
Feeling of loss of control
Exhaustion
Anxiety
Preexisting psychopathology (substance abuse, character
  pathology, major psychiatric disorder)
Acute family problems
Threats or history of prior attempts at suicide
Positive family history of suicide
Other usually described risk factors in psychiatric patients

Table adapted from W. Breitbart: "Suicide in Cancer Patients," Oncology *1*: 49, 1987. Used with permission.

Women who have previously experienced psychological difficulties, such as *low self-esteem and low life satisfaction*, are likely to be vulnerable to difficulties during menopause. A woman's response to menopause has been noted to *parallel her response* to other crucial developmental events in her life, such as puberty and pregnancy. Attempts to link the severity of menopausal distress with the premenstrual tension syndrome have been inconclusive.

Some women who have invested heavily in childbearing and child-rearing activities may suffer distress during the postmenopausal years. Concerns about aging, loss of childbearing capacity, and changes in appearance all may be focused on the social and symbolic significance attached to the physical changes of the menopause.

Although in the past it was assumed that the incidence of mental illness and depression increases during the menopause, epidemiological evidence casts doubt on this assumption. Epidemiological studies of mental illness showed no increase in symptoms of *mental illness* or in depression during the menopausal years, and studies of psychological complaints found no greater frequency in menopausal women than in younger women.

Psychological distress should be evaluated and treated primarily by appropriate psychotherapeutic and sociotherapeutic measures. Psychotherapy should include an exploration of the life stage and the *meaning of aging* and reproduction to the patient. The psychotherapist should encourage the patient to accept the menopause as a natural life event and to develop new activities, interests, and gratifications. The psychotherapist should also attend to family dynamics and enlist the family and other social support systems when necessary.

25.7. The answer is B (*Synopsis VI*, page 506; *CTP V*, pages 1179–1186).

Obesity is characterized by the excessive accumulation of fat, specifically when body weight exceeds by 20 percent the ideal weight listed on normative height-weight tables.

There is a *familial predisposition to obesity*. Obese children increase the number of their fat cells (hyperplastic obesity), which predisposes the children to obesity as adults. When obesity first occurs in adulthood, it is usually hypertrophic, an increase in fat-cell size, *not hyperplastic*. Psychological factors play a key role in obesity caused by overeating. Among the psychodynamic factors are *oral fixation, oral regression, and overvaluation of food*. Bulimia, associated with binge eating, may be present. The patient often has a history of *poor early conditioning to food intake*. The treatment of obesity should be through dietary limitation, the reduction of caloric intake, and the increase in exercise. Emotional support and behavior modification techniques are helpful, especially for the anxiety and the depression associated with the cycle of overeating and dieting.

25.8. The answer is C (2, 4) (*Synopsis VI*, page 511; *CTP V*, pages 1268–1271).

Patients with chronic pain resulting from cancer respond best to *analgesics* and *nerve blocks*. Many cancer patients may be kept relatively active, alert, and comfortable with the judicious use of morphine, thus avoiding costly and incompletely effective surgical procedures, such as peripheral nerve section, cordotomy, and stereotaxic thalamic ablations.

Patients are often undermedicated with analgesics because of lack of knowledge of the pharmacology of analgesics, an unrealistic fear of causing addiction (even in terminal patients), and the ethical judgment that only bad physicians prescribe large doses of narcotics. It is critical to separate patients with chronic benign pain (who tend to do much better with *psychotherapy* and *psychotropic drugs*) from those with chronic pain attributable to cancer and other chronic medical disorders.

25.9. The answer is C (2, 4) (*Synopsis VI*, pages 508–509; *CTP V*, pages 632 and 1333).

The essential feature of late luteal phase dysphoric disorder (LLPDD) is a pattern of clinically significant emotional and behavioral symptoms that occur during the last week of the luteal phase and remit within a few days after the onset of the follicular phase of the menstrual cycle. The occurrence of symptoms in not limited to just *four days before the onset of menses*. The diagnosis is given only if the symptoms are sufficiently severe to cause marked impairment in social or occupational functioning and have occurred during the *majority of menstrual cycles within the previous year*. Essential features include affective lability, irritability, anger, and signs and symptoms of depression. Some women may develop *suicidal ideation*. Physical symptoms such as headache, muscular skeletal pain, and edema may occur premenstrually. Although this disorder has been reported to occur at any age after menarche, it is most often seen in women *over (not under) 30 years of age*.

Similar symptoms are seen in premenstrual syndrome (PMS), which is characterized by cyclical subjective changes in mood that are correlated with the menstrual cycle; however, in LLPDD the changes in mood and other symptoms occur to a much greater degree than normal. Some symptoms of PMS are reported in 70 to 90 percent of all women of childbearing age. Symptoms may also be seen in women after hysterectomies, provided the ovaries remain intact.

25.10. The answer is B (1, 3) (*Synopsis VI*, page 511; *CTP V*, pages 1268–1271).

A behavior modification deconditioning program may be useful in the treatment of chronic pain patients. An analgesic should be *prescribed at regular intervals,* rather than only as needed. Otherwise, patients must suffer before receiving relief, which only increases their anxiety and sensitivity to pain. Standing orders dissociate experiencing pain from receiving medication. The deconditioning of needed care from experiencing increased pain should also extend to the patients' interpersonal relationships. Patients should receive as much or *more attention* when they are displaying active and healthy behavior as they receive for passive, dependent, pain-related behaviors. Their spouses, employers, friends, physicians, health care providers, and social service agencies should not reinforce chronic pain and penalize patients (including threatening to *discontinue disability payments*) if patients begin to relinquish their sick role. Patients should be assured of regular and supportive appointments that are not contingent on pain. *Hospitalization* should be avoided, if possible, to prevent further regression.

25.11. The answer is E (all) (*Synopsis VI*, page 499; *CTP V*, pages 1155–1156).

Various disorders have been considered classically psychosomatic and are now classified in DSM-III-R under psychological factors affecting physical condition. *Rheumatoid arthritis* is a disease characterized by chronic musculoskeletal pain caused by inflammatory disease of the joints. This disorder has significant hereditary, allergic, immunological, and psychological causative factors. It has been suggested that psychological stress predisposes patients to rheumatoid arthritis.

Diabetes mellitus is a disorder of metabolism and the vascular system manifested by a disturbance of the body's handling of glucose, lipids, and protein. Heredity and family history are important in the onset of diabetes. An acute onset is often associated with emotional stress, which disturbs the homeostatic balance in a predisposed patient. Psychological factors that seem relevant are those provoking feelings of frustration, loneliness, and dejection.

Pruritis ani is itching localized to the anus. The investigation of this disorder commonly yields a history of local irritation or general systemic factors. However, pruritis ani often fails to respond to therapeutic measures and acquires a life of its own. Personality deviations often precede this condition, and emotional disturbances often precipitate and maintain it.

Hay fever is the result of strong psychological factors combined with allergic elements. One factor may dominate, and the factors may alternate in importance. Considerable clinical evidence suggests that psychological factors are related to the precipitation of many allergic disorders. Emotional reactions, personality patterns, and conditioning have been reported to contribute to the onset and the course of hay fever.

25.12. The answer is A (1, 2, 3) (*Synopsis VI*, pages 512–514; *CTP V*, pages 1156–1158).

Some studies report that stressful life experiences, particularly experiences of separation and loss, frequently precede the clinical onset of various neoplasms, including *cancer of the cervix, leukemia*, and *lymphoma*. By contrast, several studies have found no association between life experience and the onset of *cancer of the breast*. In one of these studies, however, there was a relation between life events and benign breast disease.

The growing information on the immunological aspects of cancer raises the possibility that psychosocial influences are important to the mediation of immunological mechanisms in the susceptibility and the course of neoplastic disease.

25.13–25.15

25.13. The answer is B (*Synopsis VI*, page 500; *CTP V*, pages 1193–1194).

25.14. The answer is E (*Synopsis VI*, page 505; *CTP V*, page 1187).

25.15. The answer is D (*Synopsis VI*, page 501; *CTP V*, page 1157).

Most investigators agree that chronic, severe, and perceived stress may play a causative role in the development of certain somatic diseases. The character of the stress, the general underlying psychophysiological factors, and the nature of the emotional conflicts (whether specific or nonspecific) are some of the factors that produce disease. Important investigators involved in stress-related illness include Flanders Dunbar, Meyer Friedman and Ray Rosenman, Franz Alexander, T. H. Holmes and R. H. Rahe, and Jacob DaCosta.

Specific personality types were first postulated by Flanders Dunbar, who spoke of the coronary personality. Dunbar described the personality of coronary disease patients as aggressive-compulsive with a tendency to be hard-driving. Most recently, Friedman and Rosenman defined *type A and type B personalities*. Type A people show excessive ambition, a tendency to be overscheduled, overwhelming aggression, and impatience. They are particularly prone to the development of coronary artery disease and possibly other somatic disorders. This type is in contrast to the more easy-going, relaxed type B personality. Franz Alexander, rather than emphasizing the conscious personality, hypothesized specific typical unconscious conflicts associated with various somatic disorders (e.g., unconscious dependency conflicts predispose to peptic ulcers).

General types of stress leading to physical disorders have been described by T. H. Holmes and R. H. Rahe. A stressful or traumatic life situation is one that generates challenges to which the organism cannot adequately respond. Holmes and Rahe devised a *Social Readjustment Rating Scale* that lists 43 life events associated with varying amounts of stress in the average person's life (e.g., death of a spouse, 100 units; divorce, 73 units; death of a close family member, 63 units). They found that an accumulation of 200 or more life-change units in a single year increased the incidence of physical disorders.

A different type of problem is presented by patients who are free of heart disease and yet complain of symptoms suggestive of heart disease. They often exhibit a morbid concern about their hearts and an exaggerated fear of heart disease. Jacob DaCosta in 1871 first described this syndrome, which he termed *neurocirculatory asthenia*, irritable heart. It does not appear in DSM-III-R as an official diagnosis; however, psychiatrists today view it as a clinical variant of anxiety disorder.

25.16–25.19

25.16. The answer is D (*Synopsis VI*, page 517; *CTP V*, pages 1294 and 1307–1309).

25.17. The answer is C (*Synopsis VI*, page 518; *CTP V*, page 1295).

25.18. The answer is A (*Synopsis VI*, page 517; *CTP V*, page 1295).

25.19. The answer is B (*Synopsis VI*, page 518; *CTP V*, page 1295).

Wilson's disease, hepatolenticular degeneration, is a familial disease of adolescence that tends to have a chronic, rather than acute, course. The pathology is caused by defective copper metabolism, leading to excessive copper deposits in tissues. The earliest psychiatric symptoms are *explosive anger and labile mood*—sudden and rapid changes from one mood to another. As the illness progresses, eventual brain damage occurs with memory and intelligence quotient (I.Q.) loss. The lability and combativeness tend to persist even after the brain damage develops.

Pheochromocytoma is a tumor of the adrenal medulla that causes headaches, paroxysms of severe hypertension, and the physiological and psychological symptoms of a *classic pain attack*—intense anxiety, tremulousness, apprehension, dizziness, palpitations, and diaphoresis. The tumor tissue secretes catecholamines that are responsible for the symptoms. The intermittently normal blood pressure and the resemblance of these symptoms to a panic attack often result in the diagnosis of pheochromocytoma being missed.

Systemic lupus erythematosus is an autoimmune disorder in which the body makes antibodies against its own cells. These cells are then attacked by the antibodies as if they were infectious agents and, depending on which cells are being attacked, give rise to different symptoms. Frequently, the arteries in the cerebrum are affected, causing a cerebral arteritis, which alters the blood flow to various parts of the brain. The decreased blood flow can give rise to psychotic symptoms, such as a thought disorder with paranoid delusions and hallucinations. The symptoms can *resemble steroid psychosis* or schizophrenia.

The diagnosis of acquired immune deficiency syndrome (AIDS) includes a *dementia syndrome*. AIDS patients with the syndrome present with global impairment, including memory and cognitive defects and disorientation. Tests reveal the presence of antibodies to the human immunodeficiency virus (HIV), seropositivity. The dementia can be caused by the direct attack on the central nervous system by the virus or by secondary infections, such as toxoplasmosis.

Although any chronic illness can give rise to depression, some diseases, such as pancreatic carcinoma, are more likely causes than others. The depression of pancreatic cancer patients is often associated with a sense of imminent doom.

26 ||||||

Personality Disorders

Patients with personality disorders are characterized by their long-standing, deeply ingrained, inflexible, and maladaptive patterns of relating to and perceiving both the environment and themselves.

The revised third edition of *Diagnostic and Statistical Manual of Mental Disorders* (DSM-III-R) groups the personality disorders into three clusters: (A) paranoid, schizoid, schizotypal; (B) antisocial, borderline, histrionic, narcissistic; and (C) avoidant, dependent, obsessive-compulsive, passive-aggressive. The student should be familiar with the genetic and the biochemical data that suggest a biological basis for normal temperament and pathological personality types. In particular, the student should understand which of the personality disorders may be related to schizophrenia and to mood and anxiety disorders. The student should also study the psychoanalytic and sociocultural theories regarding the shaping of personality styles.

The first cluster of personality disorders includes odd and eccentric persons. Paranoid personality disorder is difficult to treat but may respond to both pharmacological and psychosocial interventions. Schizoid personality disorder may be a particularly strong indication for group psychotherapy, although schizoid personality disorder patients may be quite silent during group sessions. Schizotypal personality disorder may be the personality disorder that fits best within the broader spectrum of schizophrenia.

The second cluster includes dramatic and erratic persons. Contemporary psychoanalysis has been of great importance in the development of theoretical formulations for histrionic, narcissistic, and borderline personality disorders. The possible relations between antisocial and borderline personality disorders and alcoholism and mood disorders should be familiar to the student. The treatment of borderline personality disorder patients on inpatient wards is a common and difficult problem, and the student should be comfortable with discussing potential pharmacological interventions and individual and milieu approaches with these troubled persons.

The third cluster includes anxious and fearful persons. The student should carefully study the subtle but important distinguishing features among avoidant, dependent, and schizoid personality disorders. Although obsessive-compulsive and passive-aggressive personality disorders are particularly intractable, the possible treatment approaches involving behavioral and psychodynamic therapies should be familiar to the student.

The student should also review three additional, somewhat controversial, personality disorders—sadomasochistic, self-defeating, and sadistic personality disorders. The concept of sadomasochism has strong psychoanalytic roots. The diagnostic criteria for self-defeating and sadistic personality disorders are more generally accepted in that they are defined in the appendix of DSM-III-R. Many of the questions presented in this chapter are based on clinical case vignettes of the various personality disorders. The student should become familiar with the nuances of behavior that characterize the personality disorders and be aware of their differential diagnoses.

Readers should refer to Chapter 26, "Personality Disorders," of *Synopsis VI* and to Chapter 27, "Personality Disorders," of *CTP V*. After completing those chapters, readers can test their knowledge by studying the questions and answers below.

HELPFUL HINTS

The terms below should be defined and known to the student.

alloplastic	anal triad	Heinz Kohut
autoplastic	three Ps	mask of sanity
ego-dystonic	Wilhelm Reich	ambulatory schizophrenia
paranoid	character armor	as-if personality
schizoid	Erik Erikson	pseudoneurotic schizophrenia
schizotypal	fantasy	psychotic character
histrionic	dissociation	emotionally unstable personality
narcissistic	denied affect	micropsychotic episodes
antisocial	isolation	identity diffusion
borderline	projection	panphobia
avoidant	counterprojection	pananxiety
dependent	repression	panambivalence
obsessive-compulsive	hypochondriasis	chaotic sexuality
passive-aggressive	secondary gain	timid temperament
extroversion	splitting	inferiority complex
introversion	turning anger against the self	Sigmund Freud
Carl Jung	acting out	*folie à deux*
clusters A, B, C	*la belle indifférence*	free association
Briquet's syndrome	dependency	sadomasochistic personality
platelet MAO	Stella Chess, Alexander Thomas	Marquis de Sade
SPEM	goodness of fit	castration anxiety
saccadic movements	ideas of reference	Leopold von Sacher-Masoch
endorphins	magical thinking	self-defeating personality
object choices	macropsia	sadistic personality
oral character	hysterical personality	

QUESTIONS

DIRECTIONS: Each of the questions or incomplete statements below is followed by five suggested responses or completions. Select the *one* that is *best* in each case.

Questions 26.1–26.3

Tom, a 21-year-old man, did not look at all like a criminal type or a shifty delinquent. Tom looked and was in robust physical health. His manner and appearance were pleasing. The poised young man's immediate problem was serious but not monumental. His family and legal authorities were in hope that, if some psychiatric disorder could be discovered in him, he might escape a jail sentence for stealing.

Evidence of his maladjustment became distinct in childhood. He appeared to be a reliable and manly fellow but could never be counted on to keep at any task or to give a straight account of any situation. He was frequently truant from school. Though he was generously provided for, he stole some of his father's chickens from time to time, selling them at stores downtown. Pieces of table silver would be missed. These were sometimes recovered from those to whom he had sold them for a pittance or swapped them for odds and ends that seemed to hold no particular interest or value for him.

Often, when truant from high school classes, Tom wandered more or less aimlessly, sometimes shooting at chickens, setting fire to a rural privy on the outskirts of town, or perhaps loitering about a cigar store or a pool room, reading the comics, throwing rocks at squirrels in a park, perpetrating small thefts or swindles. He often charged things in stores to his father and stole cigarettes, candy, and cigars. He lied so plausibly and with such equanimity, devised such ingenious alibis, or simply denied all responsibility with such convincing appearances of candor that for many years his real career was poorly estimated. Though he often fell in with groups or small gangs, he never for long identified himself with others in a common cause.

At 14 or 15, having learned to drive, Tom began to steal automobiles with some regularity.

Meanwhile, Tom continued to forge his father's name to small checks and to steal change, pocketknives, and textbooks at school. Occasionally, on the pretext of ownership, he would sell a dog or a calf belonging to some member of the community.

Tom was sent to a federal institution in a distant state, where a well-organized program of rehabilitation and guidance was available. He soon impressed authorities at this place with his attitude and in the way he discussed his past mistakes and plans for a different future.

He found employment in a dry dock at a nearby port and talked modestly but convincingly of the course he would now follow, expressing aims and plans few could greatly improve. His employers found him at first energetic, bright, and apparently enthusiastic about the work. Soon, evidence of inexplicable irresponsibility emerged and accumulated. Sometimes he missed several days and brought simple but convincing excuses of illness. As the occasions multiplied, explanations so detailed and elaborate were made that it seemed only facts could have produced them. Later, he sometimes left the job, stayed away for hours, and gave no account of his behavior except to say that he did not feel like working at the time.

Reliable information indicated that he had been arrested and imprisoned 50 or 60 times. It is estimated that he would have been put in jails or police barracks for short or long periods of detention on approximately 150 other occasions if his family had not made good his small thefts and damages and paid fines for him.

Sometimes he was arrested for fomenting brawls in low resorts, provoking fights, or for such high-handed and disturbing behavior as to constitute a public nuisance. Though not a regular drinker or one who characteristically drank to sodden confusion or stupefaction, he exhibited unsociable and unprepossessing manners and conduct after taking even a few beers or highballs. In one juke-joint imbroglio he was credited with having struck a fellow reveler on the head with a piece of iron.

This young man apparently never formed a substantial attachment for another person. Sexually, he had been desultorily promiscuous under a wide variety of circumstances. A year or two earlier he had married a girl who had achieved considerable local recognition as a prostitute and as one whose fee was moderate. He had previously shared her offerings (on a commercial basis) during an evening with friends or with brief acquaintances among whom he found himself. He soon left the bride and never showed signs of shame or chagrin about the character of the woman he had espoused or any responsibility toward her.

[From *DSM-III-R Case Book.* Used with permission.]

26.1. The most likely diagnosis in this case is
A. narcissistic personality disorder
B. borderline personality disorder
C. antisocial personality disorder
D. schizoid personality disorder
E. paranoid personality disorder

26.2. True statements concerning antisocial personality disorder include all the following *except*
A. the prevalence of antisocial personality disorder is 3 percent in men and 1 percent in women
B. a familial pattern is present
C. these patients often show abnormal electroencephalograms and soft neurological signs
D. antisocial personality disorder is synonymous with criminality
E. these patients appear to lack a conscience

26.3. The symptoms of patients with personality disorders are experienced as
A. ego-dystonic
B. ego-syntonic
C. autoplastic
D. adaptive
E. flexible

Questions 26.4–26.6

An 85-year-old man was seen by a social worker at a senior citizens center for evaluation of health care needs for himself and his bedridden wife. He was apparently healthy, with no evidence of impairment in thinking or memory. He had been caring for his wife but had been reluctantly persuaded to seek help because her condition had deteriorated and his strength and energy had decreased with age.

A history was obtained from him and his daughter. He had never been treated for mental illness and, in fact, had always claimed to be "immune to psychological problems" and to act

only on the basis of rational thought. He had had a moderately successful career as a lawyer and a businessman. He had been married for 60 years, and his wife was the only person for whom he had ever expressed tender feelings and was probably the only person he had ever trusted. He had always been extremely careful about revealing anything about himself to others, assuming that they were out to take something away from him. He refused obviously sincere offers of help from acquaintances because he suspected their motives. He never revealed his identity to a caller without first questioning him as to the nature of his business. Throughout his life there had been numerous occasions on which he had displayed exaggerated suspiciousness, sometimes of almost delusional proportions (e.g., storing letters from a client in a secret safe deposit box so that he could use them as evidence in the event that the client attempted to sue him for mismanagement of an estate).

He had always involved himself in "useful work" during his waking hours and claimed never to have had time for play, even during the 20 years he had been retired. He spent many hours monitoring his stock market investments and had had altercations with his broker when he suspected that an error on a monthly statement was evidence of the broker's attempt to cover up some fraudulent deal.

[From *DSM-III-R Case Book*. Used with permission.]

26.4. The most appropriate diagnosis based on the information in this case is
A. paranoid schizophrenia
B. delusional disorder
C. borderline personality disorder
D. schizoid personality disorder
E. paranoid personality disorder

26.5. An increased incidence of paranoid personality disorder is associated with all the following *except*
A. relatives of patients with schizophrenia
B. homosexuals
C. immigrants
D. the deaf
E. minority groups

26.6. The defense mechanism most often associated with paranoid personality disorder is
A. hypochondriasis
B. splitting
C. isolation
D. projection
E. dissociation

26.7. Leon was a 45-year-old postal employee who was evaluated at a clinic specializing in the treatment of depression. He claimed to have felt constantly depressed since the first grade, without a period of "normal" mood for more than a few days at a time. His depression had been accompanied by lethargy, little or no interest or pleasure in anything, trouble in concentrating, and feelings of inadequacy, pessimism, and resentfulness. His only periods of normal mood occurred when he was home alone, listening to music or watching TV.

On further questioning, Leon revealed that he could never remember feeling comfortable socially. Even before kindergarten, if he was asked to

speak in front of a group of family friends, his mind would "go blank." He felt overwhelming anxiety at children's social functions, such as birthday parties, which he either avoided or, if he went, attended in total silence. He could answer questions in class only if he wrote down the answers in advance; even then, he frequently mumbled and couldn't get the answer out. He met new children with his eyes lowered, fearing their scrutiny, expecting to feel humiliated and embarrassed. He was convinced that everyone around him thought he was "dumb" or "a jerk."

As he grew up, Leon had a couple of neighborhood playmates, but he never had a best friend. His school grades were good but suffered when oral classroom participation was expected. As a teenager, he was terrified of girls and to this day had never gone on a date or even asked a girl for a date. This bothered him, although he was so often depressed that he felt he had little energy or interest in dating.

Leon attended college and did well for a while, then dropped out as his grades slipped. He remained self-conscious and "terrified" of meeting strangers. He had trouble finding a job because he was unable to answer questions in interviews. He worked at a few jobs for which only a written test was required. He passed a civil service exam at age 24 and was offered a job in the post office on the evening shift. He enjoyed this job, since it involved little contact with others. He was offered but refused several promotions because he feared the social pressure. Although by now he supervised a number of employees, he still found it difficult to give instructions, even to people he had known for years. He had no friends and avoided all invitations to socialize with coworkers. During the past several years, he had tried several therapies to help him get over his "shyness" and depression. Leon had never experienced sudden anxiety or a panic attack in social situations or at other times. Rather, his anxiety gradually built to a constant level in anticipation of social situations. He had never experienced any psychotic symptoms.

[From *DSM-III-R Case Book*. Used with permission.]

On the basis of this history, the best diagnosis is
A. avoidant personality disorder
B. schizoid personality disorder
C. schizotypal personality disorder
D. social phobia
E. adjustment disorder with anxious mood

26.8. A pervasive pattern of grandiosity, lack of empathy, and hypersensitivity to the evaluation of others suggests the diagnosis of which of the following personality disorders?
A. Schizotypal
B. Passive-aggressive
C. Borderline
D. Narcissistic
E. Paranoid

Questions 26.9–26.10

Matthew was a 34-year-old single man who lived with his mother and worked as an accountant. He sought treatment because he was unhappy after having just broken up with his girlfriend. His mother had disapproved of his marriage plans, ostensibly because the woman was of a different religion. Matthew felt trapped and forced to choose between his mother and his girlfriend, and, since "blood is thicker than water," he had decided not to go against his mother's wishes. Nonetheless, he was angry at himself and at his mother and believed that she would never let him marry and was possessively hanging on to him. His mother "wore the pants" in the family and was a domineering woman who was used to getting her way. Matthew was afraid of her and criticized himself for being weak but also admired his mother and respected her judgment—"Maybe Carol wasn't right for me after all." He alternated between resentment and a "Mother knows best" attitude. He felt that his own judgment was poor.

Matthew worked at a job several grades below what his education and talent would permit. On several occasions he had turned down promotions because he didn't want the responsibility of having to supervise other people or make independent decisions. He had worked for the same boss for 10 years, got on well with him, and was, in turn, highly regarded as a dependable and unobtrusive worker. He had two close friends, whom he had had since early childhood. He had lunch with one of them every workday and felt lost if his friend was sick and missed a day.

Matthew was the youngest of four children and the only boy. He was "babied and spoiled" by his mother and elder sister. He had considerable separation anxiety as a child—difficulty in falling asleep unless his mother stayed in the room, mild school refusal, and unbearable homesickness when he occasionally tried sleepovers. As a child, he was teased by other boys because of his lack of assertiveness and was often called a baby. He had lived at home his whole life except for one year of college, from which he returned because of homesickness. His heterosexual adjustment had been normal except for his inability to leave his mother in favor of another woman.

[From *DSM-III-R Case Book*. Used with permission]

26.9. This patient would most likely be classified as having
A. avoidant personality disorder
B. schizoid personality disorder
C. passive-aggressive personality disorder
D. sadomasochistic personality disorder
E. dependent personality disorder

26.10. People who may be prone to dependent personality disorder include all the following *except*
A. men
B. young children
C. persons with chronic physical illness in childhood
D. children of mothers with panic disorder
E. persons with separation anxiety disorder

26.11. The patient was a 32-year-old unmarried, unemployed woman on welfare who complained that she felt spacey. Her feelings of detachment had gradually become stronger and more uncomfortable. For many hours each day, she felt as if she were watching herself move through life, and the world around her seemed unreal. She felt especially strange when she looked into a mirror. For many years, she had felt able to read people's minds by a "kind of clairvoyance I don't understand." According to her, several people in her family apparently had this ability. She was preoccupied by the thought that she had some special mission in life but was not sure what it was; she was not particularly religious. She was self-conscious in public, often felt that people were paying special attention to her, and sometimes thought that strangers crossed the street to avoid her. She was lonely and isolated and spent much of each day lost in fantasies and watching soap operas on television. She spoke in a vague, abstract, digressive manner, generally just missing the point, but she was never incoherent. She seemed shy, suspicious, and afraid she would be criticized. She had no gross loss of reality testing, such as hallucinations or delusions. She had never had treatment for emotional problems. She worked occasionally but drifted away from her jobs because of lack of interest. [From *DSM-III-R Case Book*. Used with permission.]

The most appropriate diagnosis in this case is
A. schizophreniform disorder
B. schizophrenia
C. schizotypal personality disorder
D. schizoid personality disorder
E. none of the above

Questions 26.12–26.13

The patient was a 23-year-old veterinary assistant admitted for her first psychiatric hospitalization. She arrived late at night, referred by a local psychiatrist, saying, "I don't really need to be here."

Three months before admission, the patient learned that her mother had become pregnant. The young woman began drinking heavily, ostensibly in order to sleep nights. While drinking, she became involved in a series of one-night stands. Two weeks before her hospital admission, she began feeling panic and having experiences in which she felt as if she were removed from her body and in a trance. During one of these episodes she was stopped by the police while wandering on a bridge late at night. The next day, in response to hearing a voice repeatedly telling her to jump off a bridge, she ran to her supervisor and asked for help. Her supervisor, seeing her distraught condition and also noting scars from a recent wrist slashing, referred her to a psychiatrist, who then arranged for her immediate hospitalization.

At the time of the hospitalization, the patient appeared as a disheveled and frail but appealing waif. She was cooperative, coherent, and frightened. Although she did not feel hospitalization was needed, she welcomed the prospect of relief from her anxiety and depersonalization. She acknowledged that she had had feelings of loneliness and inadequacy and brief periods of depressed mood and anxiety since adolescence. Recently, she had been having fantasies that she was stabbing herself or a little baby with a knife. She complained that she was "just an empty shell that is transparent to everyone."

The patient's parents divorced when she was 3 years old, and for the next five years she lived with her maternal grandmother and her mother, who had a severe drinking problem. The patient had night terrors, during which she would frequently end up sleeping with her mother. At age 6 she went to a special boarding school for a year and a half, after which she was withdrawn by her mother, against the advice of the school. When she was 8, her maternal grandmother died; the patient recalled trying to conceal her grief about this from her mother. The patient spent most of the next two years living with various relatives, including a period with her father, whom she had not seen since the divorce. When she was 9, her mother was hospitalized with a diagnosis of schizophrenia. From age 10 through college, the patient lived with an aunt and an uncle but had ongoing and frequent contacts with her mother. Her school record was consistently good.

Since adolescence she had dated regularly, having an active but rarely pleasurable sex life. Her relationships with men usually ended abruptly after she became angry with them when they disappointed her in some apparently minor way. She then concluded that they were "no good to begin with." She had had several roommates but had had trouble establishing a stable living situation because of her jealousy of sharing her roommates with others and her manipulative efforts to keep them from seeing other people.

Since college she had worked steadily and well as a veterinary assistant. At the time of her hospital admission, she was working night shift in a veterinary hospital and living alone.

[From *DSM-III-R Case Book*. Used with permission.]

26.12. On the basis of the history given, the most likely diagnosis of this patient is
A. dysthymia
B. major depression
C. antisocial personality disorder
D. borderline personality disorder
E. none of the above

26.13. True statements regarding borderline personality disorder include all the following *except*
A. borderline patients have more relatives with mood disorders than do control groups
B. monoamine oxidase inhibitors are used in the treatment of borderline patients
C. borderline personality disorder and mood disorders often coexist
D. smooth pursuit eye movements are abnormal in borderline personality disorder
E. first-degree relatives of persons with borderline personality disorder show an increased prevalence of alcoholism

26.14. An association has been found between histrionic personality disorder and
A. somatization disorder
B. alcoholism
C. Briquet's syndrome
D. conversion disorder
E. all the above

DIRECTIONS: For the incomplete statement below, *one* or *more* of the completions are correct. Choose answer

    A. if only *1, 2, and 3* are correct
    B. if only *1 and 3* are correct
    C. if only *2 and 4* are correct
    D. if only *4* is correct
    E. if *all* are correct

26.15. Obsessive-compulsive personality disorder is characterized by
1. indecisiveness
2. emotional constriction
3. excessive devotion to work
4. suspiciousness

DIRECTIONS: The questions below consist of lettered headings followed by a list of numbered statements. For each numbered statement, select the *one* lettered heading that is most closely associated with it. Each lettered heading may be selected once, more than once, or not at all.

Questions 26.16–26.20
    A. Schizoid personality disorder
    B. Narcissistic personality disorder
    C. Passive-aggressive personality disorder
    D. Self-defeating personality disorder
    E. Sadistic personality disorder

26.16. Covert obstructionism, procrastination, and stubbornness

26.17. Heightened sense of self-importance and grandiose feelings

26.18. Cruel, demeaning, and aggressive behavior

26.19. Avoidance or undermining of pleasurable experiences

26.20. Pattern of social withdrawal, discomfort with human interaction, and bland, constricted affect

Questions 26.21–26.25
    A. Schizoid personality disorder
    B. Schizotypal personality disorder

26.21. Strikingly odd or eccentric behavior

26.22. Ideas of reference

26.23. Suspiciousness or paranoid ideation

26.24. Magical thinking

26.25. Formerly called simple or latent schizophrenia

ANSWERS

Personality Disorders

26.1. The answer is C (*Synopsis VI*, pages 532–533; *CTP V*, pages 1373–1377).

The most likely diagnosis in this case is *antisocial personality disorder*. Antisocial personality disorder is characterized by continual antisocial or criminal acts and an inability to conform to social norms that involve many aspects of the patient's adolescent and adult development. In the case of the 21-year-old man described, the many arrests for criminal acts, the aggressiveness, and the inability to maintain an enduring attachment to a sexual partner all suggest antisocial personality disorder. DSM-III-R requires evidence of antisocial behavior before age 15 to make the diagnosis of antisocial personality disorder, and in this case the history of truancy and thefts—all before age 15—confirms the diagnosis.

Narcissistic personality disorder is characterized by a heightened sense of self-importance and by grandiose feelings of uniqueness, lack of empathy, and hypersensitivity to the evaluation of others. *Bor-*

Table 26.1
Diagnostic Criteria for Antisocial Personality Disorder

A. Current age at least 18.
B. Evidence of conduct disorder with onset before age 15, as indicated by a history of *three* or more of the following:
1. was often truant
2. ran away from home overnight at least twice while living in parental or parental surrogate home (or once without returning)
3. often initiated physical fights
4. used a weapon in more than one fight
5. forced someone into sexual activity with him or her
6. was physically cruel to animals
7. was physically cruel to other people
8. deliberately destroyed others' property (other than by fire-setting)
9. deliberately engaged in fire-setting
10. often lied (other than to avoid physical or sexual abuse)
11. has stolen without confrontation of a victim on more than one occasion (including forgery)
12. has stolen with confrontation of a victim (e.g., mugging, purse-snatching, extortion, armed robbery)
C. A pattern of irresponsible and antisocial behavior since the age of 15, as indicated by at least *four* of the following:
1. is unable to sustain consistent work behavior, as indicated by any of the following (including similar behavior in academic settings if the person is a student):
   a. significant unemployment for six months or more within five years when expected to work and work was available
   b. repeated absences from work unexplained by illness in self or family
   c. abandonment of several jobs without realistic plans for others
2. fails to conform to social norms with respect to lawful behavior, as indicated by repeatedly performing antisocial acts that are grounds for arrest (whether arrested or not), e.g., destroying property, harassing others, stealing, pursuing an illegal occupation
3. is irritable and aggressive, as indicated by repeated physical fights or assaults (not required by one's job or to defend someone or oneself), including spouse- or child-beating
4. repeatedly fails to honor financial obligations, as indicated by defaulting on debts or failing to provide child support or support for other dependents on a regular basis
5. fails to plan ahead, or is impulsive, as indicated by one or both of the following:
   a. traveling from place to place without a prearranged job or clear goal for the period of travel or clear idea about when the travel will terminate
   b. lack of a fixed address for a month or more
6. has no regard for the truth, as indicated by repeated lying, use of aliases, or "conning" others for personal profit or pleasure
7. is reckless regarding his or her own or others' personal safety, as indicated by driving while intoxicated, or recurrent speeding
8. if a parent or guardian, lacks ability to function as a responsible parent, as indicated by one or more of the following:
   a. malnutrition of child
   b. child's illness resulting from lack of minimal hygiene
   c. failure to obtain medical care for a seriously ill child
   d. child's dependence on neighbors or nonresident relatives for food or shelter
   e. failure to arrange for a caretaker for young child when parent is away from home
   f. repeated squandering, on personal items, of money required for household necessities
9. has never sustained a totally monogamous relationship for more than one year
10. lacks remorse (feels justified in having hurt, mistreated, or stolen from another)
D. Occurrence of antisocial behavior not exclusively during the course of schizophrenia or manic episodes

Table from DSM-III-R, *Diagnostic and Statistical Manual of Mental Disorders*, ed 3, revised. Copyright American Psychiatric Association, Washington, DC, 1987. Used with permission.

derline personality disorder is characterized by severely unstable mood, affect, behavior, object relations, and self-image. Antisocial personality disorder is frequently associated with narcissistic and borderline personality disorders. *Schizoid personality disorder* is diagnosed in patients with lifelong patterns of social withdrawal. Schizoid personalities are often seen by others as eccentric, isolated, or lonely. *Paranoid personality disorder* is characterized by long-standing suspiciousness and mistrust of people in general. According to DSM-III-R, the essential feature of this disorder is a pervasive and unwarranted tendency to interpret other people's actions as deliberately demeaning or threatening. The history provided on the case does not justify the diagnosis of either schizoid or paranoid personality disorder.

See Table 26.1 for the DSM-III-R diagnostic criteria for antisocial personality disorder.

26.2. The answer is D (*Synopsis VI*, pages 532–533; *CTP V*, pages 1373–1377).

Antisocial personality disorder is characterized by continual antisocial or criminal acts, but it is *not synonymous with criminality*. Rather, it is a pattern of irresponsible and antisocial behavior that pervades the patient's adolescence and adulthood. The prevalence of antisocial personality disorder is *3 percent in men and 1 percent in women*. It is most common in poor urban areas and among mobile residents of those areas. The onset of the disorder is before the age of 15. In prison populations the prevalence of antisocial personality disorder may be as high as 75 percent. A *familial pattern* is present in that it is five times more common among first-degree relatives of males with the disorder than among controls.

Antisocial personalities demonstrate a lack of anxiety or depression that may seem grossly incongruous with their situation. Promiscuity, spouse abuse, child abuse, and drunk driving are common events in these patients' lives. A notable finding is a lack of remorse for the actions; that is, these patients appear to *lack a conscience*.

A diagnostic workup of patients with antisocial personality disorder should include a thorough neurological examination. Because these patients often show *abnormal electroencephalograms and soft neurological signs* suggestive of minimal brain damage in childhood, these findings can be used to confirm the clinical impression.

26.3. The answer is B (*Synopsis VI*, page 525; *CTP V*, pages 1352–1353).

The symptoms of patients with personality disorder are experienced as *ego-syntonic* (acceptable to the self). These patients are likely to refuse psychiatric help and to deny their problems. Their symptoms are alloplastic (the process of adapting and altering the external environment); they do not feel anxiety about their *inflexible, maladaptive* behavior. In contrast to personality disorders, the symptoms

of neurotic disorders are *autoplastic* (the process of adapting by changing the self) and *ego-dystonic* (unacceptable to the self).

26.4. The answer is E (*Synopsis VI*, pages 527–528; *CTP V*, pages 1365–1367).

The most appropriate diagnosis based on the information in the case of the 85-year-old-man is *paranoid personality disorder*. He showed a long and pervasive pattern of suspiciousness and hypersensitivity. People with this disorder almost invariably expect to be exploited or harmed in some way. Paranoid patients appear affectively constricted and unemotional. Ideas of reference—false beliefs that people's conversations and thoughts are centered on them, usually in a negative way—are common. The patient exhibited hypersensitivity to criticism, avoidance of accepting warranted blame, no sense of humor, emotional coldness, and an inability to relax.

Paranoid personality disorder can be differentiated from *delusional disorder* because fixed, prominent delusions are absent and from *paranoid schizophrenia* by the absence of hallucinations and a formal thought disorder. Paranoid personality disorder can be distinguished from *borderline personality disorder* because the paranoid patient is rarely as capable as the borderline patient of overinvolved relations with others. *Schizoid* personalities are withdrawn and aloof and do not have paranoid ideation. See Table 26.2 for the DSM-III-R diagnostic criteria for paranoid personality disorder.

26.5. The answer is B (*Synopsis VI*, page 527; *CTP V*, pages 1365–1366).

An increased incidence of paranoid personality disorder is not associated with *homosexuals*, as was once thought; it is believed to be more common among *minority groups, immigrants*, and *the deaf*. *Relatives of schizophrenia patients* exhibit a higher incidence of paranoid personalities than do controls. The disorder is more common in men than in women; it does not appear to have a familial pattern.

26.6. The answer is D (*Synopsis VI*, pages 527–528; *CTP V*, page 1365).

The defense mechanism most often associated with paranoid personality disorder is *projection*. Paranoid personalities externalize their own emotions and attribute to others the impulses and thoughts that they are unable to accept in themselves. Excessive fault finding, sensitivity to criticism, prejudice, and hypervigilance to injustice can all be understood as examples of projecting unacceptable impulses and thoughts onto others.

Hypochondriasis is used as a defense mechanism in some personality disorders, particularly in borderline, dependent, and passive-aggressive disorders. Hypochondriasis disguises reproach; that is, the hypochondriac's complaint that others do not provide help often conceals bereavement, loneliness, or unacceptable aggressive impulses. The mecha-

Table 26.2
Diagnostic Criteria for Paranoid Personality Disorder

A. A pervasive and unwarranted tendency, beginning by early adulthood and present in a variety of contexts, to interpret the actions of people as deliberately demeaning or threatening, as indicated by at least *four* of the following:
1. expects, without sufficient basis, to be exploited or harmed by others
2. questions, without justification, the loyalty or trustworthiness of friends or associates
3. reads hidden demeaning or threatening meanings into benign remarks or events, e.g., suspects that a neighbor put out trash early to annoy him
4. bears grudges or is unforgiving of insults or slights
5. is reluctant to confide in others because of unwarranted fear that the information will be used against him or her
6. is easily slighted and quick to react with anger or to counterattack
7. questions, without justification, fidelity of spouse or sexual partner
B. Occurrence not exclusively during the course of schizophrenia or a delusional disorder

Table from DSM-III-R, *Diagnostic and Statistical Manual of Mental Disorders*, ed 3, revised. Copyright American Psychiatric Association, Washington, DC, 1987. Used with permission.

nism of hypochondriasis permits covert punishment of others with the patient's own pain and discomfort.

Splitting is used by borderline patients in particular. With splitting, the patient divides ambivalently regarded people, both past and present, into all good or all bad, rather than synthesizing and assimilating less-than-perfect caretakers.

Isolation is the defense characteristic of the orderly, controlled person, often labeled a compulsive personality. Isolation allows the person to face painful situations without painful affect or emotion and thus to remain always in control.

Dissociation consists of a replacement of unpleasant affects with pleasant ones. It is most often seen in histrionic personalities.

26.7. The answer is A (*Synopsis VI*, page 535; *CTP V*, pages 1379–1380).

On the basis of the history of the 45-year-old postal employee, the best diagnosis is *avoidant personality disorder*. His lifelong chronic discomfort whenever he was away from home may be diagnosed as dysthymia because of his subjective depressed mood, low energy, pessimism, and anhedonia. Although feeling constantly depressed caused him to seek treatment, the pervasive pattern of social avoidance, fear of criticism, and lack of close peer relationships was of equal importance. Persons with avoidant personalities show an extreme sensitivity to rejection, which may lead to social withdrawal. They are not asocial but are shy and show a great desire for companionship; they need unusually strong guarantees of uncritical acceptance. In this case the patient exhibited a long-standing pattern

of difficulty in relating to others. People with *schizoid personality disorder* do not evince the same strong desire for affection and acceptance. Avoidant personalities desire social interaction, whereas schizoid personalities want to be alone. *Schizotypal personality disorder* is characterized by strikingly odd or strange behavior, magical thinking, peculiar ideas, ideas of reference, illusions, and derealization. The patient described did not exhibit these characteristics.

Social phobia is an irrational fear of a specific situation, such as public speaking or eating in public. A social phobia is anxiety concerning specific social situations, not relationships in general.

A person with a personality disorder can have a superimposed adjustment disorder but only if the current episode includes new clinical features not characteristic of his or her personality. There is no evidence in the case described that the anxiety was qualitatively different from what the patient always experienced in social situations. Thus, an additional diagnosis of *adjustment disorder with anxious mood* is not made. An adjustment disorder is a maladaptive reaction to a clearly identifiable psychosocial stressor that occurs within three months of the stressor's onset.

The DSM-III-R diagnostic criteria for avoidant personality disorder are listed in Table 26.3.

26.8. The answer is D (*Synopsis VI*, pages 531–532; *CTP V*, pages 1372–1373).

A pervasive pattern of grandiosity (in fantasy or behavior), lack of empathy, and hypersensitivity to the evaluation of others suggests the diagnosis of

Table 26.3
Diagnostic Criteria for Avoidant Personality Disorder

A pervasive pattern of social discomfort, fear of negative evaluation, and timidity, beginning by early adulthood and present in a variety of contexts, as indicated by at least *four* of the following:
1. is easily hurt by criticism or disapproval
2. has no close friends or confidants (or only one) other than first-degree relatives
3. is unwilling to get involved with people unless certain of being liked
4. avoids social or occupational activities that involve significant interpersonal contact, e.g., refuses a promotion that will increase social demands
5. is reticent in social situations because of a fear of saying something inappropriate or foolish, or of being unable to answer a question
6. fears being embarrassed by blushing, crying, or showing signs of anxiety in front of other people
7. exaggerates the potential difficulties, physical dangers, or risks involved in doing something ordinary but outside his or her usual routine, e.g., may cancel social plans because she anticipates being exhausted by the effort of getting there

Table from DSM-III-R, *Diagnostic and Statistical Manual of Mental Disorders*, ed 3, revised. Copyright American Psychiatric Association, Washington, DC, 1987. Used with permission.

narcissistic personality disorder. The fantasies of narcissistic patients are of unlimited success, power, brilliance, beauty, and ideal love; their demands are for constant attention and admiration. Narcissistic personalities are indifferent to criticism or respond to it with feelings of rage or humiliation. Other common characteristics are entitlement, surprise and anger that people do not do what the patient wants, interpersonal exploitiveness, and relationships that vacillate between the extremes of overidealization and devaluation.

Schizotypal personality disorder is characterized by various eccentricities in communication or behavior, coupled with defects in the capacity to form social relationships. The term emphasizes a possible relation with schizophrenia. The manifestation of aggressive behavior in passive ways—such as obstructionism, pouting, stubbornness, and intentional inefficiency—typify the *passive-aggressive* personality. *Borderline* personality is marked by instability of mood, interpersonal relationships, and self-image. *Paranoid* personality disorder is characterized by rigidity, hypersensitivity, unwarranted suspicion, jealousy, envy, an exaggerated sense of self-importance, and a tendency to blame and ascribe evil motives to others.

Table 26.4 lists the DSM-III-R diagnostic criteria for narcissistic personality disorder.

26.9. The answer is E (*Synopsis VI*, page 536; *CTP V*, pages 1380–1382).

The patient described in the case would most likely be classified as having a *dependent personality disorder.* This disorder is characterized by the subordination of the patient's own needs to the needs of others and getting others to assume responsibility for major areas in the patient's life; in this case, for example, the patient's mother was making the important decision regarding the patient's marriage. The patient's pervasive lack of self-confidence was reflected in his "Mother knows best" attitude. He also displayed discomfort when alone and fears of abandonment, as evidenced by his history of separation anxiety as a child and his current feelings of loss if his friend at work missed a day.

The traits of dependency are found in many psychiatric disorders. *Avoidant personality disorder* and dependent personality disorder may be similar. The dependent personality, however, tends to have a greater fear of being abandoned or not loved than does the avoidant personality. *Schizoid personality disorder* tends to be characterized by isolation, as is dependent personality disorder, but in schizoid personality disorder the patient wishes and seeks isolation, whereas the dependent person is terrified of it. *Passive-aggressive personality disorder* is characterized by procrastination, stubbornness, and inefficiency. Such behavior is a manifestation of underlying aggression, expressed passively. There is not enough information in this history to warrant this diagnosis.

Table 26.4
Diagnostic Criteria for Narcissistic Personality Disorder

A pervasive pattern of grandiosity (in fantasy or behavior), lack of empathy, and hypersensitivity to the evaluation of others, beginning by early adulthood and present in a variety of contexts, as indicated by at least *five* of the following:
1. reacts to criticism with feelings of rage, shame, or humiliation (even if not expressed)
2. is interpersonally exploitative: takes advantage of others to achieve his or her own ends
3. has a grandiose sense of self-importance, e.g., exaggerates achievements and talents, expects to be noticed as "special" without appropriate achievement
4. believes that his or her problems are unique and can be understood only by other special people
5. is preoccupied with fantasies of unlimited success, power, brilliance, beauty, or ideal love
6. has a sense of entitlement: unreasonable expectation of especially favorable treatment, e.g., assumes that he or she does not have to wait in line when others must do so
7. requires constant attention and admiration, e.g., keeps fishing for compliments
8. lack of empathy: inability to recognize and experience how others feel, e.g., annoyance and surprise when a friend who is seriously ill cancels a date
9. is preoccupied with feelings of envy

Table from DSM-III-R, *Diagnostic and Statistical Manual of Mental Disorders*, ed 3, revised. Copyright American Psychiatric Association, Washington, DC, 1987. Used with permission.

In DSM-III-R, personality disorder not otherwise specified (NOS) includes disorders of personality functioning not classified as specific personality disorders. In DSM-III, it was called mixed personality disorder. The diagnosis of personality disorder NOS can be used, for instance, when the clinician believes that a specific personality disorder is present but is not part of the official DSM-III-R nomenclature. An example is *sadomasochistic personality disorder*, which is not an official diagnostic category in DSM-III-R or its appendix.

Some personality types are characterized by elements of sadism or masochism or a combination of both. Sadism is the desire to cause others pain by being sexually, physically, or psychologically abusive. Some people can achieve sexual pleasure only through sexually sadistic behavior. Masochism is the seeking of humiliation and failure, and in the sexual realm it is the achievement of sexual gratification by inflicting pain on the self. The patient described shows no evidence of sadistic behavior; although he may be described as masochistic in certain areas of his functioning, he does not appear to achieve sexual gratification through masochistic behavior.

Table 26.5 lists the DSM-III-R diagnostic criteria for dependent personality disorder.

26.10. The answer is A (*Synopsis VI*, page 536; *CTP V*, page 1381).

People who may be prone to dependent personality disorder include *women (not men), young chil-*

Table 26.5
Diagnostic Criteria for Dependent Personality Disorder

A pervasive pattern of dependent and submissive behavior, beginning by early adulthood and present in a variety of contexts, as indicated by at least *five* of the following:
1. is unable to make everyday decisions without an excessive amount of advice or reassurance from others
2. allows others to make most of his or her important decisions, e.g., where to live, what job to take
3. agrees with people even when he or she believes they are wrong, because of fear of being rejected
4. has difficulty initiating projects or doing things on his or her own
5. volunteers to do things that are unpleasant or demeaning in order to get other people to like him or her
6. feels uncomfortable or helpless when alone, or goes to great lengths to avoid being alone
7. feels devastated or helpless when close relationships end
8. is frequently preoccupied with fears of being abandoned
9. is easily hurt by criticism or disapproval

Table from DSM-III-R, *Diagnostic and Statistical Manual of Mental Disorders*, ed 3, revised. Copyright American Psychiatric Association, Washington, DC, 1987. Used with permission.

dren, and persons who suffered *chronic physical illness during childhood*. Some workers believe that *separation anxiety disorder* predisposes to the development of dependent personality disorder. Separation anxiety disorder has its onset before the age of 18 years and is characterized by excessive anxiety concerning separation from people to whom the child is attached. Separation anxiety disorder itself may be more frequent in *children of mothers with panic disorder*, and this factor may predispose to the development of dependent personality disorder. Panic disorder is characterized by recurrent, discrete periods of intense fear or discomfort not initiated or maintained by an organic factor.

26.11. The answer is C (*Synopsis VI*, pages 529–530; *CTP V*, pages 1368–1369).

The most appropriate diagnosis in the case of the 32-year-old unmarried, unemployed woman on welfare is *schizotypal personality disorder*. Schizotypal personality disorder is characterized by a pervasive pattern of deficits in interpersonal relationships and peculiarities of ideation, appearance, and behavior. Magical thinking, peculiar ideas, ideas of reference, unusual perceptual experiences (such as illusions), and odd speech are part of schizotypal patients' everyday world. Although the patient's symptoms in the case described became more distressing to her recently, they are manifestations of a long-standing maladaptive pattern that suggests a personality disorder, rather than the new development of another major disorder. Her symptoms include depersonalization (feeling as though she were watching herself move through life), derealization (the world around her seems unreal), magical thinking (clairvoyance), ideas of references (strangers cross the street to avoid

her), isolation (she spends most of her day lost in fantasies, watching soap operas), odd speech (vague and abstract), suspiciousness, and hypersensitivity to criticism. All these symptoms are typical of schizotypal personality disorder.

In *schizophrenia* and *schizophreniform disorder*, the patient would exhibit psychotic symptoms, including frank delusions, hallucinations, and a formal thought disorder. The presentation of schizophreniform disorder is identical to that of schizophrenia except for the duration of symptoms; schizophreniform disorder is diagnosed if the clinical presentation is less than six months in duration, whereas schizophrenia is diagnosed if the presentation has lasted six months or longer. *Schizoid personality disorder* is associated with a pervasive pattern of indifference to social relationships and a restricted range of emotional experience and expression. The oddities in speech, perception, and behavior associated with schizotypal personality disorder are not characteristic of schizoid personalities. The DSM-III-R diagnostic criteria for schizotypal personality disorder are listed in Table 26.6.

26.12. The answer is D (*Synopsis VI*, pages 533–534; *CTP V*, pages 1377–1379).

On the basis of the history given by the 23-year-old woman, the most likely diagnosis is *borderline*

Table 26.6
Diagnostic Criteria for Schizotypal Personality Disorder

A. A pervasive pattern of deficits in interpersonal relatedness and peculiarities of ideation, appearance, and behavior, beginning by early adulthood and present in a variety of contexts, as indicated by at least *five* of the following:
1. ideas of reference (excluding delusions of reference)
2. excessive social anxiety, e.g., extreme discomfort in social situations involving unfamiliar people
3. odd beliefs or magical thinking, influencing behavior and inconsistent with subcultural norms, e.g., superstitiousness, belief in clairvoyance, telepathy, or "sixth sense," "others can feel my feelings" (in children and adolescents, bizarre fantasies or preoccupations)
4. unusual perceptual experiences, e.g., illusions, sensing the presence of a force or person not actually present (e.g., "I felt as if my dead mother were in the room with me")
5. odd or eccentric behavior or appearance, e.g., unkempt, unusual mannerisms, talks to self
6. no close friends or confidants (or only one) other than first-degree relatives
7. odd speech (without loosening of associations or incoherence), e.g., speech that is impoverished, digressive, vague, or inappropriately abstract
8. inappropriate or constricted affect, e.g., silly, aloof, rarely reciprocates gestures or facial expressions, such as smiles or nods
9. suspiciousness or paranoid ideation
B. Occurrence not exclusively during the course of schizophrenia or a pervasive developmental disorder

Table from DSM-III-R, *Diagnostic and Statistical Manual of Mental Disorders*, ed 3, revised. Copyright American Psychiatric Association, Washington, DC, 1987. Used with permission.

personality disorder. This disorder is marked by a pervasive pattern of severe instability of mood, interpersonal relationships, and self-image. Borderline patients may swing quickly from being argumentative to being depressed to complaining of feeling empty. Their behavior is highly unpredictable, and the painful nature of their lives is reflected in repetitive self-destructive acts, such as wrist slashing and other self-mutilations. Because they experience feelings of both dependency and hostility, often simultaneously, their interpersonal relationships tend to be chaotic. They cannot tolerate being alone and complain of a lack of a consistent sense of identity. They may experience brief psychotic episodes, in which the psychotic symptoms are circumscribed or fleeting. Borderline patients tend to distort current relations by putting every person in either an all-good or an all-bad category. This mechanism is termed splitting and results in vacillation between idealization and devaluation, often of the same person, within brief periods of time.

The patient described is classically borderline. Her functioning is characterized by impulsivity (promiscuity and self-mutilation); unstable and intense interpersonal relationships (idealization and devaluation); inappropriate, intense anger (fantasies of stabbing a baby with a knife); recurrent suicidal threats or gestures; affective instability; and brief psychotic symptoms (hearing a voice telling her to jump off a bridge).

Although this woman was suicidal, there is no description of other depressive symptoms (such as sleep or appetite disturbances, decreased libido, poor concentration, and slowed thinking and speaking) that would warrant the diagnosis of *dysthymia* or *major depression.* Dysthymia is a chronic, pervasive, low-grade depression that is not as severe as that found in major depression.

The patient described also does not exhibit the pattern of irresponsible and antisocial behavior beginning before the age of 15 that is required to make the diagnosis of *antisocial personality disorder.* Antisocial personalities, in contrast to borderline patients, often present a normal exterior, even charming and ingratiating. Lying, truancy, running away, thefts, fights, and illegal activities are typical experiences that these patients report as beginning in childhood.

Table 26.7 lists the DSM-III-R diagnostic criteria for borderline personality disorder.

26.13. The answer is D (*Synopsis VI*, pages 533–535; *CTP V*, pages 1377–1379 and 1388).

Smooth pursuit eye movements are normal in borderline patients. They are abnormal in schizophrenics and schizotypal personalities.

Borderline patients have more *relatives with mood disorders* than do control groups, and borderline personality disorder and mood disorder often *coexist.* Borderline disorder is thought to be present in about 1 or 2 percent of the population and is twice as common in women as in men. There is an *in-*

Table 26.7
Diagnostic Criteria for Borderline Personality Disorder

A pervasive pattern of instability of mood, interpersonal relationships, and self-image, beginning by early adulthood and present in a variety of contexts, as indicated by at least *five* of the following:
1. a pattern of unstable and intense interpersonal relationships characterized by alternating between extremes of overidealization and devaluation
2. impulsiveness in at least two areas that are potentially self-damaging, e.g., spending, sex, substance use, shoplifting, reckless driving, binge eating (Do not include suicidal or self-mutilating behavior covered in 5.)
3. affective instability: marked shifts from baseline mood to depression, irritability, or anxiety, usually lasting a few hours and only rarely more than a few days
4. inappropriate, intense anger or lack of control of anger, e.g., frequent displays of temper, constant anger, recurrent physical fights
5. recurrent suicidal threats, gestures, or behavior, or self-mutilating behavior
6. marked and persistent identity disturbance manifested by uncertainty about at least two of the following: self-image, sexual orientation, long-term goals or career choice, type of friends desired, preferred values
7. chronic feelings of emptiness or boredom
8. frantic efforts to avoid real or imagined abandonment (Do not include suicidal or self-mutilating behavior covered in 5.)

Table from DSM-III-R, *Diagnostic and Statistical Manual of Mental Disorders*, ed 3, revised. Copyright American Psychiatric Association, Washington, DC, 1987. Used with permission.

creased prevalence of alcoholism and substance abuse in first-degree relatives of persons with borderline personality disorder.

Psychotherapy for borderline patients is an area of intensive investigation and is the treatment of choice. Because of the apparent association of borderline personality with mood disorders, the use of antidepressants in the treatment of borderline patients is of use in some cases. *Monoamine oxidase inhibitors* have been effective in modulating affective instability and impulsivity in a number of borderline patients.

26.14. The answer is E (*Synopsis VI*, pages 530–531; *CTP V*, pages 1370–1371).

An association has been found between histrionic personality disorder and *somatization disorder* (also known as *Briquet's syndrome*), *conversion disorder*, and *alcoholism.* Histrionic personality is diagnosed much more frequently in women than in men and is more common among first-degree biological relatives of patients with the disorder than among the general population. In somatization disorder, complaints of physical illness dominate the clinical picture, although histrionic features are common. Somatization disorder is characterized by a history of many physical complaints or a belief that one is sickly, beginning before the age of 30 and persisting for several years. Conversion disorder is a loss of or an alteration in physical functioning, suggesting a physical disorder, in which psychological factors are judged to be causatively related to the symptoms. Alcoholism is diagnosed in DSM-III-R as alcohol dependence.

Table 26.8 lists the DSM-III-R diagnostic criteria for histrionic personality disorder.

26.15. The answer is A (1, 2, 3) (*Synopsis VI*, pages 537–538; *CTP V*, pages 1382–1383).

Obsessive-compulsive personality disorder is characterized by a pervasive pattern of perfectionism and inflexibility, as indicated by (1) restricted expression of affection or *emotional constriction;* (2) *indecisiveness*, in which decision making is avoided, postponed, or protracted; and (3) *excessive devotion to work* and productivity to the exclusion of leisure activities and friends. *Suspiciousness* is not associated with obsessive-compulsive personality; paranoid personality disorder, by definition, is characterized by hypervigilance and suspiciousness.

Other clinical features of obsessive-compulsive personalities are orderliness, neatness, and a preoccupation with details. These persons often lack a sense of humor, insist that rules be followed rigidly, and are unable to tolerate what they perceive to be infractions. They are inflexible, intolerant, and routinized.

Table 26.9 lists the DSM-III-R diagnostic criteria for obsessive-compulsive personality disorder.

26.16–26.20

26.16. The answer is C (*Synopsis VI*, page 538; *CTP V*, pages 1384–1385).

Table 26.8
Diagnostic Criteria for Histrionic Personality Disorder

A pervasive pattern of excessive emotionality and attention-seeking, beginning by early adulthood and present in a variety of contexts, as indicated by at least *four* of the following:
1. constantly seeks or demands reassurance, approval, or praise
2. is inappropriately sexually seductive in appearance or behavior
3. is overly concerned with physical attractiveness
4. expresses emotion with inappropriate exaggeration, e.g., embraces casual acquaintances with excessive ardor, uncontrollable sobbing on minor sentimental occasions, has temper tantrums
5. is uncomfortable in situations in which he or she is not the center of attention
6. displays rapidly shifting and shallow expression of emotions
7. is self-centered, actions being directed toward obtaining immediate satisfaction; has no tolerance for the frustration of delayed gratification
8. has a style of speech that is excessively impressionistic and lacking in detail, e.g., when asked to describe mother, can be no more specific than, "She was a beautiful person."

Table from DSM-III-R, *Diagnostic and Statistical Manual of Mental Disorders*, ed 3, revised. Copyright American Psychiatric Association, Washington, DC, 1987. Used with permission.

Table 26.9
Diagnostic Criteria for Obsessive-Compulsive Personality Disorder

A pervasive pattern of perfectionism and inflexibility, beginning by early adulthood and present in a variety of contexts, as indicated by at least *five* of the following:
1. perfectionism that interferes with task completion, e.g., inability to complete a project because own overly strict standards are not met
2. preoccupation with details, rules, lists, order, organization, or schedules to the extent that the major point of the activity is lost
3. unreasonable insistence that others submit to exactly his or her way of doing things, or unreasonable reluctance to allow others to do things because of the conviction that they will not do them correctly
4. excessive devotion to work and productivity to the exclusion of leisure activities and friendships (not accounted for by obvious economic necessity)
5. indecisiveness: decision making is either avoided, postponed, or protracted, e.g., the person cannot get assignments done on time because of ruminating about priorities (do not include if indecisiveness is due to excessive need for advice or reassurance from others)
6. overconscientiousness, scrupulousness, and inflexibility about matters of morality, ethics, or values (not accounted for by cultural or religious identification)
7. restricted expression of affection
8. lack of generosity in giving time, money, or gifts when no personal gain is likely to result
9. inability to discard worn-out or worthless objects even when they have no sentimental value

Table from DSM-III-R, *Diagnostic and Statistical Manual of Mental Disorders*, ed 3, revised. Copyright American Psychiatric Association, Washington, DC, 1987. Used with permission.

26.17. The answer is B (*Synopsis VI*, pages 531–532; *CTP V*, pages 1372–1373).

26.18. The answer is E (*Synopsis VI*, pages 539 and 542; *CTP V*, pages 1386–1387).

26.19. The answer is D (*Synopsis VI*, pages 539–540; *CTP V*, pages 1385–1386).

26.20. The answer is A (*Synopsis VI*, pages 528–529; *CTP V*, pages 1367–1368).

Passive-aggressive personality disorder is characterized by *covert obstructionism, procrastination, stubbornness*, and inefficiency. Such behavior is a manifestation of underlying aggression, which is expressed passively. Passive-aggressive persons resist demands for adequate performance, find excuses for delays, and find fault with those on whom they depend. In interpersonal relationships, passive-aggressive personalities attempt to manipulate themselves into a position of dependency, but their passive, self-detrimental behavior is often experienced by others as punitive and manipulative. The close relationships of passive-aggressive personalities are rarely tranquil or happy. Because passive-aggressive personalities are bound to their resentment more closely than to their satisfaction, they may never even formulate what they want for themselves with regard to enjoyment. According to DSM-III-R, people with this disorder lack self-confidence and are typically pessimistic about the future.

Persons with narcissistic personality disorder are characterized by a *heightened sense of self-importance and grandiose feelings* that they are unique in some way. They consider themselves special people and expect special treatment. They want their own way and are frequently ambitious, desiring fame and fortune. Aging is handled poorly, as these patients value beauty, strength, and youthful attributes, to which they cling inappropriately. Narcissistic personality disorder is chronic and difficult to treat. Narcissistic patients must renounce their narcissism if progress is to be made.

A pervasive pattern of *cruel, demeaning, and aggressive behavior* that is directed toward others typifies the sadistic personality. Physical cruelty or violence is used to inflict pain on others and not to achieve some other goal (e.g., mugging someone in order to steal). Such persons like to humiliate or demean people in front of others and usually have treated or disciplined someone unusually harshly, especially children. In general, sadistic personalities are fascinated by violence, weapons, injury, or torture. If sexual arousal is derived from their sadistic behavior, a paraphilia should be diagnosed.

The self-defeating personality may often *avoid or undermine pleasurable experiences* and be drawn to situations or relationships in which he or she will suffer. Such persons choose people and situations that lead to disappointment, failure, or mistreatment, even when better options are clearly available. They reject the attempts of others to offer help. After positive personal events (e.g., a new achievement), these persons respond with depression, guilt, or a behavior that produces pain (e.g., an accident). They also invite rejecting responses from others and then feel hurt, defeated, or humiliated (e.g., they may make fun of their spouses in public, provoking an angry retort, and then feel devastated). In general, they engage in excessive self-sacrifice that is unsolicited and discouraged by others. Self-defeating personalities do not derive any sexual pleasure from humiliation; persons who do are classified as having a paraphilia.

Sadistic personality disorder and self-defeating personality disorder are controversial additions to DSM-III-R. They are listed in the appendix for diagnostic categories requiring further study and are not considered an official part of DSM-III-R.

Schizoid personality disorder is diagnosed in patients who display a lifelong pattern of *social withdrawal, discomfort with human interaction, and bland, constricted affect.* Schizoid personalities are often seen by others as eccentric, isolated, or lonely. They give an impression of being cold and aloof and display a remote reserve and a lack of involvement with everyday events and the concerns of others. They are the last to adopt changes in popular fashion. Their sexual lives may exist exclusively in fan-

Table 26.10
Diagnostic Criteria for Passive-Aggressive Personality Disorder

A pervasive pattern of passive resistance to demands for adequate social and occupational performance, beginning by early adulthood and present in a variety of contexts, as indicated by at least *five* of the following:
1. procrastinates, i.e., puts off things that need to be done so that deadlines are not met
2. becomes sulky, irritable, or argumentative when asked to do something he or she does not want to do
3. seems to work deliberately slowly or to do a bad job on tasks that he or she really does not want to do
4. protests, without justification, that others make unreasonable demands on him or her
5. avoids obligations by claiming to have "forgotten"
6. believes that he or she is doing a much better job than others think he or she is doing
7. resents useful suggestions from others concerning how he or she could be more productive
8. obstructs the efforts of others by failing to do his or her share of the work
9. unreasonably criticizes or scorns people in positions of authority

Table from DSM-III-R, *Diagnostic and Statistical Manual of Mental Disorders*, ed 3, revised. Copyright American Psychiatric Association, Washington, DC, 1987. Used with permission.

Table 26.11
Diagnostic Criteria for Sadistic Personality Disorder

A. A pervasive pattern of cruel, demeaning, and aggressive behavior, beginning by early adulthood, as indicated by the repeated occurrence of at least four of the following:
1. has used physical cruelty or violence for the purpose of establishing dominance in a relationship (not merely to achieve some noninterpersonal goal, such as striking someone in order to rob him or her)
2. humiliates or demeans people in the presence of others
3. has treated or disciplined someone under his or her control unusually harshly, e.g., a child, student, prisoner, or patient
4. is amused by, or takes pleasure in, the psychological or physical suffering of others (including animals)
5. has lied for the purpose of harming or inflicting pain on others (not merely to achieve some other goal)
6. gets other people to do what he or she wants by frightening them (through intimidation or even terror)
7. restricts the autonomy of people with whom he or she has a close relationship, e.g., will not let spouse leave the house unaccompanied or permit teen-age daughter to attend social functions
8. is fascinated by violence, weapons, martial arts, injury, or torture
B. The behavior in A has not been directed toward only one person (e.g., spouse, one child) and has not been solely for the purpose of sexual arousal (as in sexual sadism)

Table from DSM-III-R, *Diagnostic and Statistical Manual of Mental Disorders*, ed 3, revised. Copyright American Psychiatric Association, Washington, DC, 1987. Used with permission.

tasy, and they may postpone mature sexuality indefinitely. Men may not marry because they are unable to achieve intimacy; women may passively agree to marry aggressive men. Usually, schizoid persons reveal a lifelong inability to express anger directly. They are able to invest enormous affective energy in isolated interests, such as mathematics and astronomy, and they may be attached to animals.

Tables 26.10 through 26.13 list the DSM-III-R diagnostic criteria for passive-aggressive, sadistic, self-defeating, and schizoid personality disorders, re-

Table 26.12
Diagnostic Criteria for Self-Defeating Personality Disorder

A. A pervasive pattern of self-defeating behavior, beginning by early adulthood and present in a variety of contexts. The person may often avoid or undermine pleasurable experiences, be drawn to situations or relationships in which he or she will suffer, and prevent others from helping him or her, as indicated by at least five of the following:
1. chooses people and situations that lead to disappointment, failure, or mistreatment even when better options are clearly available
2. rejects or renders ineffective the attempts of others to help him or her
3. following positive personal events (e.g., new achievement), responds with depression, guilt, or a behavior that produces pain (e.g., an accident)
4. incites angry or rejecting responses from others and then feels hurt, defeated, or humiliated (e.g., makes fun of spouse in public, provoking an angry retort, then feels devastated)
5. rejects opportunities for pleasure, or is reluctant to acknowledge enjoying himself or herself (despite having adequate social skills and the capacity for pleasure)
6. fails to accomplish tasks crucial to his or her personal objectives despite demonstrated ability to do so, e.g., helps fellow students write papers, but is unable to write his or her own
7. is uninterested in or rejects people who consistently treat him or her well, e.g., is unattracted to caring sexual partners
8. engages in excessive self-sacrifice that is unsolicited by the intended recipients of the sacrifice
B. The behaviors in A do not occur exclusively in response to, or in anticipation of, being physically, sexually, or psychologically abused
C. The behaviors in A do not occur only when the person is depressed.

Table from DSM-III-R, *Diagnostic and Statistical Manual of Mental Disorders*, ed 3, revised. Copyright American Psychiatric Association, Washington, DC, 1987. Used with permission.

Table 26.13
Diagnostic Criteria for Schizoid Personality Disorder

A. A pervasive pattern of indifference to social relationships and a restricted range of emotional experience and expression, beginning by early adulthood and present in a variety of contexts, as indicated by at least *four* of the following:
1. neither desires nor enjoys close relationships, including being part of a family
2. almost always chooses solitary activities
3. rarely, if ever, claims or appears to experience strong emotions, such as anger and joy
4. indicates little if any desire to have sexual experiences with another person (age being taken into account)
5. is indifferent to the praise and criticism of others
6. has no close friends or confidants (or only one) other than first-degree relatives
7. displays constricted affect, e.g., is aloof, cold, rarely reciprocates gestures or facial expressions, such as smiles or nods
B. Occurrence not exclusively during the course of schizophrenia or a delusional disorder

Table from DSM-III-R, *Diagnostic and Statistical Manual of Mental Disorders*, ed 3, revised. Copyright American Psychiatric Association, Washington, DC, 1987. Used with permission.

spectively. The diagnostic criteria for narcissistic personality disorder are listed in Table 26.4.

26.21–26.25

26.21. The answer is B (*Synopsis VI*, pages 528–530; *CTP V*, pages 1367–1370).

26.22. The answer is B (*Synopsis VI*, pages 528–530; *CTP V*, pages 1367–1370).

26.23. The answer is B (*Synopsis VI*, pages 528–530; *CTP V*, pages 1367–1370).

26.24. The answer is B (*Synopsis VI*, pages 528–530; *CTP V*, pages 1367–1370).

26.25. The answer is B (*Synopsis VI*, pages 528–530; *CTP V*, pages 1367–1370).

Unlike schizoid personality disorder, schizotypal personality disorder manifests with *strikingly odd or eccentric behavior. Magical thinking, ideas of reference*, illusions, and derealization are common; their presence formerly led to defining this disorder as borderline, *simple, or latent schizophrenia. Suspiciousness or paranoid ideation* occurs in schizotypal personality disorder, not schizoid personality disorder.

27 |||||

Conditions Not Attributable to a Mental Disorder

Thirteen conditions fall within this *Diagnostic and Statistical Manual of Mental Disorders,* revised third edition (DSM-III-R), category. Twelve of the 13 conditions not attributable to a mental disorder are listed on Axis I in DSM-III-R, along with clinical syndromes: academic problem, adult antisocial behavior, childhood or adolescent antisocial behavior, malingering, marital problem, noncompliance with medical treatment, occupational problem, parent-child problem, other interpersonal problem, other specified family circumstances, phase of life problem or other life circumstance problem, and uncomplicated bereavement. Borderline intellectual functioning is the one condition not attributable to a mental disorder that is coded on Axis II.

DSM-III-R states that this category is provided for conditions that are a focus of attention or treatment but are not attributable to a mental disorder. In some instances a thorough evaluation has failed to uncover any mental disorder, and in other instances a diagnostic evaluation has not been adequate to determine the presence or the absence of a mental disorder, but with further information the presence of a mental disorder may become apparent. Finally, according to DSM-III-R, a person may have a mental disorder, but the focus of attention or treatment may be on a condition that is not due to the mental disorder. For example, a person with bipolar disorder may have marital problems that are not directly related to manifestations of the mood disorder.

Students should review Chapter 27, "Conditions Not Attributable to a Mental Disorder," of *Synopsis VI* and Chapter 28, "Conditions Not Attributable to a Mental Disorder," of *CTP V* and then study the questions and answers below to assess their knowledge of this subject.

HELPFUL HINTS

The following words and terms should be known by the student.

antisocial behavior
kleptomania
adoption studies
superego lacunae
juvenile delinquency
emotional deprivation
sociopathic
academic problems
conditioning
borderline intellectual functioning
I.Q. ranges
malingering
medicolegal context of
    presentation

galvanic skin response
marital problems
noncompliance
compliance
adherence
doctor-patient match
patient contract
occupational problems
job-related stress
parent-child problems
noncustodial parent
other specified family
    circumstances
childhood chronic illness

dual-career families
stress
coping mechanisms
phase of life problems
mature defense mechanisms
cultural transition
culture shock
uncomplicated bereavement
normal grief

QUESTIONS

DIRECTIONS: Each of the questions or incomplete statements below is followed by five suggested responses or completions. Select the *one* that is *best* in each case.

27.1. Which one of the following conditions is motivated by financial gain?
A. Factitious illness
B. Conversion disorder
C. Somatoform disorder
D. Malingering
E. Body dysmorphic disorder

27.2. Adults with antisocial behavior have the most difficulty in
A. work
B. marriage
C. finances
D. arrests
E. alcohol abuse

27.3. In dual-career families
A. mothers are vulnerable to guilt and anxiety regarding their maternal role
B. both parents assume equal responsibility regarding homemaking and child care
C. mothers emphasize the importance of discipline
D. the children are likely to have academic difficulties and psychological problems
E. the divorce rate is higher than in single-career marriages

27.4. According to DSM-III-R, the category of occupational problem includes
A. job dissatisfaction
B. uncertainties about career choices
C. acceptance of essentially distasteful work
D. stressful work conditions
E. all the above

27.5. In DSM-III-R the category of marital problem can be used when the
A. marital problem is due to a mental disorder
B. presenting complaint is always vocalized by both partners
C. presenting complaint is part of a greater disturbance
D. marital problem is precipitated by the birth of a child
E. marital problem is not due to cultural pressures

DIRECTIONS: For each of the incomplete statements below, *one* or *more* of the completions given are correct. Choose answer

A. if only *1, 2, and 3* are correct
B. if only *1 and 3* are correct
C. if only *2 and 4* are correct
D. if only *4* is correct
E. if *all* are correct

27.6. Uncomplicated bereavement is characterized by
1. impaired social and occupational functioning
2. preoccupation with thoughts about the deceased
3. insomnia
4. mummification

27.7. True statements concerning compliance include
1. approximately two thirds of patients are compliant with treatment
2. medical patients are less compliant than psychiatric patients
3. severity of illness is the most important variable in determining compliance
4. an increased complexity of regimen and an increased number of behavioral changes appear to be associated with noncompliance

27.8. The term "academic problem"
1. is listed in DSM-III-R as a condition not attributable to a mental disorder
2. encompasses such problems as failing grades and underachievement in a person with adequate intellect
3. should be differentiated from adjustment disorder with academic inhibition
4. is considered a diagnosable psychiatric disorder

DIRECTIONS: The lettered headings below are followed by a list of numbered phrases. For each numbered phrase select the one best answer. Each heading may be used once, more than once, or not at all.

Questions 27.9–27.10
A. Adult antisocial behavior
B. Antisocial personality disorder

27.9. Previous diagnosis of conduct disorder with onset before age 15

27.10. Mental disorder

ANSWERS

Conditions Not Attributable to a Mental Disorder

27.1. The answer is D (*Synopsis VI*, page 548; *CTP V*, pages 1396–1399).

Malingering, characterized by the voluntary production and presentation of false or grossly exaggerated physical or psychological symptoms, always has an external motivation, such as financial gain or avoidance of responsibility. The presence of a clearly definable goal is the main factor that differentiates malingering from a *factitious illness*. Evidence of an intrapsychic need to maintain the sick role suggests factitious disorder.

Conversion and *somatoform* disorders do not show intentionality; there are no obvious, external incentives. Moreover, the symptoms in malingering are less likely to be symbolically related to an underlying emotional conflict.

Patients with *body dysmorphic disorder* believe that they are physically misshapen or defective in some way, despite an objectively normal appearance. The clinical features of this disorder are not motivated by the prospect of financial gain.

27.2. The answer is A (*Synopsis VI*, page 549; *CTP V*, pages 1400–1405).

Adults with antisocial behavior have difficulty in almost every aspect of life. The most common area of difficulty is *work*. *Marriage* problems, *financial* dependence, *arrests*, and *alcohol abuse* are also common areas of difficulty for those with antisocial behavior. Antisocial behavior is characterized by activities that are illegal or immoral or both and that violate the society's legal system. According to DSM-III-R, this diagnosis should not be made if the behavior is caused by a mental disorder (e.g., antisocial personality disorder) or an impulse control disorder (e.g. kleptomania).

27.3. The answer is A (*Synopsis VI*, pages 544–545; *CTP V*, pages 1408–1411).

A particular stress develops in dual-career families, defined as families in which both spouses have careers. Mothers are found to be particularly vulnerable to *guilt and anxiety* regarding their maternal role and their relative lack of availability to their children. These women usually accept middle-class or upper-middle-class values that emphasize the importance of psychological health and the individual development of the child, *not discipline*. They espouse sophisticated child-rearing practices that use sensitivity and communication to impart values to the child, rather than punishment. Despite the high educational levels and the intellectual sophistication

of these couples, the women generally still assume the major *responsibility* for child rearing and homemaking. The husbands do contribute more than in previous generations, but their help is frequently couched in the form of "helping out their wives," rather than as a fully shared, equal burden. No evidence suggests that the children are likely to have *academic difficulties or psychological problems* as a result of these familial arrangements. There is no evidence that the *divorce rate* is higher in dual-career marriages than in single-career marriages.

27.4. The answer is E (*Synopsis VI*, pages 544–545; *CTP V*, pages 1410–1411).

According to DSM-III-R, the category of occupational problem is used when the focus of attention or treatment is an occupational problem that is apparently not due to a mental disorder. Examples are *job dissatisfaction, uncertainties about career choices, acceptance of essentially distasteful work*, and *stressful work conditions*.

An occupational history is part of the total psychiatric interview. On occasion, dissatisfaction with work is the presenting complaint. Because some work situations can be unpleasant in themselves, because there is evidence that mental effort under such conditions can produce emotional problems, and because economic necessity may force people to accept work not of their choosing, someone with this complaint may be otherwise psychiatrically normal.

Job-related stress is most likely to develop when work objectives are not clear, when workers are pressured by conflicting demands, when they have too much or too little to do, and when they are responsible for the professional development of others. Persons who have little control over decisions that affect them in the workplace are particularly vulnerable to stress-related illnesses, such as headache, backache, and general fatigue.

27.5. The answer is D (*Synopsis VI*, pages 543–544; *CTP V*, pages 1408–1409).

According to DSM-III-R, the category of marital problem can be used when the focus of attention or treatment is a marital problem that is *not due to a mental disorder;* the clinician must determine whether the presenting complaint is engendered by the marriage or is part of a greater disturbance. The presenting complaint may be *vocalized by only one partner*. The other partner may not share that view of the problem. If the problem is *part of greater disturbance*, such as secondary to a major mood disorder, the mood disorder becomes the diagnostic focus, as opposed to the marital problem. However, a person with a major mood disorder may have marital problems that are not directly related to manifestations of the mood disorder but are the principal focus of treatment. The developmental, familial, sexual, personal, and occupational history, as well as the marital history, should be enlightening in this regard. Marriage involves many stressful situations that tax the partners' adaptive capacities. One possible problem period may be precipitated by the *birth of a child*, especially the first child, as it is a stressful time for both parents. *Cultural pressures* can cause marital problems. If the partners have different backgrounds and have been raised in different value systems, conflicts are more likely to arise than if they have similar backgrounds. Economic stresses, moves to new areas, unplanned pregnancies, and abortions may upset a seemingly healthy marriage. Differing attitudes toward religion can also present a problem.

27.6. The answer is A (1, 2, 3) (*Synopsis VI*, page 550; *CTP V*, pages 1345–1347).

Characteristic of uncomplicated bereavement are feelings of sadness, tearfulness, irritability, *insomnia, preoccupation with thoughts about the deceased*, and often temporarily *impaired social and occupational functioning*.

Uncomplicated bereavement is not considered a mental disorder, although some bereaved persons do, for a period of time, meet the criteria for depression. The differentiation between depression and uncomplicated bereavement is based on the severity and the length of the symptoms. A grief reaction is limited to a varying period of time, based on one's cultural group (usually no longer than six months). Among the symptoms seen in depressive disorder that evolve from unresolved bereavement are a morbid preoccupation with worthlessness, suicidal ideation, marked functional impairment, a particularly severe anniversary reaction, and *mummification* (keeping the deceased's belongings exactly as they were).

27.7. The answer is D (4) (*Synopsis VI*, pages 9–10 and 545; *CTP V*, pages 1409–1410).

An *increased complexity of regimen* and an increased number of required behavioral changes appear to be associated with noncompliance. A complex regimen consists of many different medications taken for different problems in different doses at different times of the day. Behavioral changes may include asking the patient to stop smoking, start exercising, lose weight, eat less cholesterol, and work fewer hours—all at the same time. Patients are generally noncompliant if they have to take more than three types of medication a day or if their medications must be taken more than four times a day. Approximately *one third (not two thirds) of patients* are felt to be consistently compliant with treat-

ment. One third are felt to be never compliant, and one third are compliant inconsistently. *Medical patients are more compliant* than psychiatric patients, not the other way around. *Severity of illness* is not always a good indicator of compliant behavior. For instance, treatment of an asymptomatic illness, such as hypertension, is associated with a lower rate of compliance than is a less severe illness, such as tension headache, that does have symptoms.

27.8. The answer is A (1, 2, 3) (*Synopsis VI*, page 547; *CTP V*, pages 1406–1407).

The term "academic problem" is listed in DSM-III-R as a condition in which the focus of attention or treatment is an academic problem that apparently is not due to a *mental disorder*. Examples of an academic problem include *failing grades and underachievement* in a person with adequate intellect. Although *not considered a diagnosable psychiatric disorder*, academic problems can often be best alleviated by psychological means. Psychotherapeutic techniques can be used successfully for scholastic difficulties, including problems related to poor motivation, poor self-concept, and underachievement. Tutoring is also an effective technique in dealing with academic problems and should be considered in all cases.

Academic problems should be differentiated from *adjustment disorder with academic inhibition*, which is characterized by a change from a previously adequate academic performance after a psychosocial stressor.

27.9–27.10

27.9. The answer is B (*Synopsis VI*, pages 532–533 and 548–550; *CTP V*, pages 1400–1401).

27.10. The answer is B (*Synopsis VI*, pages 532–533 and 548–550; *CTP V*, pages 1400–1401).

The diagnosis of antisocial personality disorder, in contrast to antisocial behavior, requires evidence of preexisting psychopathology, such as *a conduct disorder with onset before age 15*, and a longstanding pattern of irresponsible and antisocial behavior since the age of 15. Illegal behavior is not considered the equivalent of psychopathology and, without evidence of preexisting psychological disturbance, would not be deemed secondary to an antisocial personality disorder.

Adult antisocial behavior is characterized by activities that are illegal or immoral or both and that violate the society's legal system. Examples include thievery, racketeering, drug dealing, and murder. According to DSM-III-R, the diagnosis of antisocial behavior should not be made if the behavior is caused by a mental disorder. Antisocial behavior is not considered a *mental disorder*, but antisocial personality disorder is. The diagnosis of antisocial behavior should not be made if the behavior is caused by a disorder of impulse control.

It has been difficult to sort out the genetic and environmental factors in both antisocial behavior and personality disorder, but there is a consensus in some areas. There is a high incidence of abnormalities in the perinatal periods in children who subsequently develop antisocial behavior. Similar findings have been reported for several of the personality disorders, including antisocial personality disorder. Similarities also exist between antisocial behavior and antisocial personality disorder in their higher incidences in lower socioeconomic classes and their greater frequency in males than in females. Familial patterns for both these diagnostic classes have been reported as well.

28 ||||||

Psychiatric Emergencies

Among the most serious psychiatric emergencies are those that involve patients who have committed or are planning to commit bodily harm to themselves or others. Suicidal ideation is the most common of these emergencies and must be carefully assessed. Homicidal ideation, attempts, or threats, although less common, must be fully evaluated, too. Other acute situations—amnesia, psychosis, extreme anxiety, panic attacks, acute intoxication, extremes of mood—are also seen in the emergency setting and require the psychiatrist to attend to these situations in a precise and professional manner.

The assessment of suicide risk is, at best, a difficult and somewhat impressionistic process. Nevertheless, specific epidemiological facts are known about the type of person who commits suicide, and these facts need to be assessed during the interview and noted clearly in the clinical record. Such a reasoned evaluation requires that the student know these epidemiological facts well so that they can be pursued even in the most difficult interview situations. The student should know the psychodynamic formulations regarding suicidal behavior and the recent neurochemical data from suicide victims. Child and adolescent suicides are an increasing problem, and the student should know the specific warning signs in these age groups.

The student should know the general principles of emergency room psychiatry and should consider the unique qualities of the physician-patient relationship in this setting. The temptation for the clinician to judge the behavior or to be caught up in the emotional turmoil of emergency psychiatric patients must be avoided. To be effective in these settings, the physician must know what pharmacological, psychotherapeutic, and physical resources are available to administer immediate treatment. Although patients who are emotionally and behaviorally out of control may protest at the time, most of them are, in fact, relieved that someone is going to take the responsibility of bringing the situation under control.

Students should read Chapter 28 of *Synopsis VI*, "Psychiatric Emergencies," and Chapter 29 of *CTP V*, "Emergency Psychiatry," and should then study the questions and answers below to assess their understanding of the subject.

HELPFUL HINTS

The terms below relate to psychiatric emergencies and should be defined.

suicide rate	Karl Menninger	crisis listening posts
anniversary suicides	Thanatos	suicidal depression
age of suicides	Aaron Beck	adolescent suicide
chronic suicides	5-HIAA in CSF	ECT
methods	platelet MAO activity	amnesia
the suicide belt	suicidal thoughts	hypnosis
Émile Durkheim	suicidal threats	panic
drugs and suicide	copy-cat suicide	homosexual panic
egoistic, altruistic, anomic suicides	Werther syndrome	posttraumatic stress disorder
Mourning and Melancholia	prevention centers	mania

catatonic stupor	alkalosis	sedative-hypnotic withdrawal
psychotic withdrawal	grief and bereavement	nystagmus
catatonic excitement	delirium	CAS
akinetic mutism	dementia	lethal catatonia
insomnia	Wernicke's encephalopathy	delirious state
anorexia nervosa	alcoholism	hypertoxic schizophrenia
bulimia	acute intoxication	exhaustion syndrome
headache	blackouts	hyperthermia
dysmenorrhea	alcohol withdrawal	hypothermia
LLPDD	DTs	mydriasis
hyperventilation	opioids	miosis

QUESTIONS

DIRECTIONS: Each of the questions or incomplete statements below is followed by five suggested responses or completions. Select the *one* that is *best* in each case.

28.1. Which of the following patients presents the lowest statistical risk of suicide?
A. A single 60-year-old man who currently has a major depression
B. A married 45-year-old woman whose mother died one week before, who is frequently tearful, and who is now requesting medication for sleep
C. A married 60-year-old woman with terminal lung cancer who often requests pain medicine
D. A single 20-year-old man who frequently abuses alcohol
E. A single 30-year-old man with schizophrenia who is currently severely psychotic and who twice has jumped from buildings in response to command auditory hallucinations

28.2. Which of the following drugs is contraindicated in the treatment of central anticholinergic syndrome?
A. Phenothiazines
B. Chlordiazepoxide (Librium)
C. Diazepam (Valium)
D. Phenobarbital (Luminal)
E. Physostigmine (Antilirium)

28.3. Which of the following neurobiological findings is associated with suicide?
A. Increased 5-hydroxyindoleacetic acid (5-HIAA) levels in the cerebrospinal fluid (CSF)
B. Increased levels of platelet monoamine oxidase (MAO)
C. Serotonin deficiencies
D. Changes in the dopaminergic system
E. Normal findings on electroencephalograms (EEGs)

28.4. Completed suicide is most often associated with
A. antisocial personality disorder
B. alcoholism
C. borderline personality disorder
D. schizophrenia
E. opioid dependence

28.5. Which of the following statements about the predictability of suicide is true?
A. Of persons who eventually kill themselves, 50 percent give warnings of their intent
B. Of persons who eventually kill themselves, 50 percent say openly that they want to die
C. A patient who openly admits to a plan of action is at less risk for suicide than is a patient who has only vague ideas about suicide
D. A patient who has been threatening suicide who becomes quiet and less agitated is at less risk for suicide than is a patient who remains agitated
E. A previously suicidal patient who begins to demonstrate a positive response to pharmacological treatment of depression is not at risk for suicide

DIRECTIONS: For each of the questions below, *one* or *more* of the responses given are correct. Choose answer

    A. if only *1, 2, and 3* are correct
    B. if only *1 and 3* are correct
    C. if only *2 and 4* are correct
    D. if only *4* is correct
    E. if *all* are correct

28.6. Which of the following statements about suicide are true?
1. Suicide is ranked as the eighth overall cause of death in the United States
2. Historically, suicide rates among Catholic populations have been lower than rates among Protestants and Jews
3. Among occupational rankings, physicians have had the highest risk for suicide
4. Suicide increases in December or during holiday periods

28.7. Which of the following statements about child and adolescent suicide are true?
1. Suicide in children under the age of 12 is relatively common
2. About 6,000 adolescents commit suicide each year
3. There is little indication of parental physical abuse or neglect among children and adolescents who attempt or commit suicide
4. Suicide is higher in single-parent homes than in two-parent homes

DIRECTIONS: Each group of questions below consists of five lettered headings followed by a list of numbered statements. For each numbered statement, select the *one* lettered heading that is most closely associated with it. Each lettered heading may be used once, more than once, or not at all.

Questions 28.8–28.13
    A. Opioids
    B. Barbiturates
    C. Phencyclidine (PCP)
    D. Monoamine oxidase inhibitors
    E. Acetaminophen (Tylenol)

28.8. Toxic interaction with meperidine (Demerol)

28.9. Pinpoint pupils after overdose

28.10. Cross-tolerant with diazepam (Valium)

28.11. Phenothiazines are contraindicated

28.12. Hypertensive crisis can occur

28.13. Treated with propranolol (Inderal)

Questions 28.14–28.17
    A. Émile Durkheim
    B. Sigmund Freud
    C. Karl Menninger
    D. Aaron Beck
    E. Johann Wolfgang von Goethe

28.14. Werther syndrome

28.15. *Man Against Himself*

28.16. Hopelessness as indication of suicidal risk

28.17. *Mourning and Melancholia*

ANSWERS

Psychiatric Emergencies

28.1. The answer is B (*Synopsis VI*, pages 551–554; *CTP V*, pages 1414–1418).

Of the patients described, the *married 45-year-old woman* whose mother died one week ago, who is frequently tearful, and who is now requesting medication for sleep presents the lowest statistical risk of suicide. Major risk factors for suicide include age greater than 45 years for men and greater than 55 years for women. Males between the ages of 15 and 24 are also at high risk. Men, in general, are at greater risk than women. Those who are single, widowed, or divorced are at higher risk than the married. Suicide is more common in people who have a history of suicide in the family or who have attempted suicide themselves in the past. Concurrent depression, terminal disease, severe pain, chronic illness, alcohol or drug abuse, and psychosis all significantly increase the risk for suicidal behavior. Thus, the *single 60-year-old man* with a major depression, the *married 60-year-old woman* with terminal lung cancer, the *single 20-year-old alcoholic man*, and the *single 30-year-old man with schizophrenia and a past history of suicide attempts* are all at significant statistical risk for suicidal behavior.

28.2. The answer is A (*Synopsis VI*, page 565; *CTP V*, page 1646).

Phenothiazines are contraindicated in the treatment of central anticholinergic syndrome (CAS). This syndrome is characterized by agitation, confusion, seizures, fever, mydriasis, and stupor—all side effects of anticholinergic-acting drugs. Patients are intolerant of phenothiazines because of their anticholinergic effects and tend to react with more delirium and sometimes with dangerous hypotension. Instead, *chlordiazepoxide* (Librium), *diazepam* (Valium), or *phenobarbital* (Luminal) should be used.

A physician may administer *physostigmine* (Antilirium), 4 mg intramuscularly, for diagnostic purposes and swift symptomatic relief. However, CAS may also be caused by antidepressant and antipsychotic medications, in which case physostigmine is generally avoided because most of the damage from the overdose is due to cardiotoxic effects that become the primary focus of treatment.

28.3. The answer is C (*Synopsis VI*, page 557; *CTP V*, pages 1416–1417).

A *serotonin deficiency,* as measured as a decrease (not an increase) in the serotonin metabolite 5-hydroxyindoleacetic acid (*5-HIAA*) in the cerebrospinal

fluid (CSF), has been found in a subgroup of patients who attempted suicide. In addition, some postmortem studies have reported changes in the noradrenergic system (not *dopaminergic system*). Decreased (not increased) levels of *platelet monoamine oxidase* (MAO) have been discovered in some suicidal patients. When blood samples from normal volunteers were analyzed, it was found that those persons with the lowest level of MAO in their platelets had eight times the prevalence of suicide in their families. *Abnormal findings* on electroencephalograms (EEGs), not normal findings, and ventricular enlargement have been demonstrated in a few studies of suicidal patients.

28.4. The answer is B (*Synopsis VI*, pages 553–554; *CTP V*, page 1420).

The two psychiatric illnesses predominantly associated with completed suicide are depression and *alcoholism*. About 70 percent of suicides fall into one of these categories, and about 5 percent of suicides are *schizophrenic*. Suicide attempts are common among *borderline personalities* and *antisocial personalities*. *Opioid dependence* increases the risk of suicide.

Among alcoholics who commit suicide, loss of affectional relationships—divorce or separation from a spouse; death of a spouse; bereavement involving the death of another relative or close friend; and other losses, such as being left behind by a relative's move from home—plays a more important role than it does among persons with depression. During the last year preceding suicide, about one quarter of suicides suffer the loss of an affectional relationship. The high number of affectional losses among alcoholics in the last year of life may be a result of the chronicity of alcoholism and the difficulties involved in living with such chronically ill people.

28.5. The answer is B (*Synopsis VI*, page 554; *CTP V*, page 1426).

Eighty percent of people who eventually kill themselves give *warnings of their intent* (not 50 percent). Fifty percent of suicides had said openly that they *wanted to die*. A patient who openly admits to a *plan of action* is at greater (not less) risk for suicide than is a patient who has only vague ideation. A patient who has been *threatening suicide* who becomes quiet and less agitated may be at increased (not less) risk, as may be a previously suicidal patient who begins to demonstrate a *positive response to pharmacological treatment* of depression. Such patients may still harbor suicidal thoughts, and, because they are energized, they can carry out their plans. Depressed patients are most likely to commit suicide at the onset or at the end of a depressive episode. The risk of suicide also increases in the immediate period after discharge from inpatient psychiatric treatment.

28.6.   The answer is A (1, 2, 3) (*Synopsis VI*, pages 551–552; *CTP V*, pages 1414–1426).

Suicide is ranked as the *eighth overall leading cause of death* in the United States, preceded by heart disease, cancer, stroke, accidents, pneumonia, diabetes mellitus, and cirrhosis. Among adolescents, suicide is currently the second leading cause of death, preceded by accidents. Historically, suicide rates among *Catholic populations* have been lower than rates among Protestants and Jews. It may be that a person's degree of orthodoxy is a more accurate measure of risk than is simple religious affiliation.

Among occupational rankings with respect to risk for suicide, professionals, particularly *physicians*, have had the highest risk. Among physicians, psychiatrists were once considered to be at the greatest risk for suicide, followed by ophthalmologists and anesthesiologists; however, there is currently a trend toward equalization among all medical specialties. Other special at-risk populations are musicians, dentists, law enforcement officials, lawyers, and insurance agents.

Contrary to popular belief, there is no increase in suicide in *December* or during other holiday periods, and no seasonal correlation has been found, although there appears to be a slight increase in the spring and fall.

Other statistics of interest include the following:

- In the United States, approximately 28,000 deaths each year are attributed to suicide.
- The suicide rate is highest in Scandinavia and lowest in the Netherlands.
- Three times as many men commit suicide as women, but women attempt suicide four times more often than men.
- Whites commit suicide nearly two times more often than nonwhites.
- Among married persons, the rate is 11 per 100,000; among widowed persons, 24 per 100,000; among divorced men, 69 per 100,000; among divorced women, 18 per 100,000; among never-married persons, 22 per 100,000.
- Seventy percent of suicide victims had been suffering from one or more active, mostly chronic, illnesses at the time of death.
- There are eight times more suicide attempts than successful suicides.
- Annually, 1 to 2 percent of people attempting unsuccessful suicides are eventually successful.
- Thirty percent of people attempting unsuccessful suicides make subsequent attempts.

28.7.   The answer is C (2, 4) (*Synopsis VI*, pages 557–558; *CTP V*, pages 1420–1421).

About 6,000 adolescents commit suicide each year; suicide is the second leading cause of death in this age group. Suicide is *higher in single-parent homes* as a result of separation or divorce than in two-parent homes. Sixty percent of adolescent suicides live with only one parent, and the suicide risk is higher when one or more family members have a chronic illness. A child who has lost a parent before the age of 13 has an increased risk for mood disorders and suicide. Suicide in children under the age of 12 *is not relatively common* but an exceedingly rare event. The number of children under 15 who kill themselves each year, however, did increase from fewer than 40 in 1950 to 300 in 1985. Suicidal thoughts and threats are more common than successful suicides. Among children and adolescents who attempt or complete suicide, there is a high (not a low) incidence of *parental physical abuse or neglect*.

28.8–28.13

28.8.   The answer is D (*Synopsis VI*, pages 564–569 and 658; *CTP V*, page 1667).

28.9.   The answer is A (*Synopsis VI*, pages 564–569; *CTP V*, page 656).

28.10.   The answer is B (*Synopsis VI*, pages 564–569; *CTP V*, page 1435).

28.11.   The answer is C (*Synopsis VI*, pages 564–569; *CTP V*, page 1439).

28.12.   The answer is D (*Synopsis VI*, pages 564–569; *CTP V*, page 1667).

28.13.   The answer is C (*Synopsis VI*, pages 564–569; *CTP V*, page 1439).

Abuse and misuse of drugs are among the many reasons for visits to psychiatric emergency rooms. Patients who take overdoses of opioids (e.g., heroin) can be recognized by characteristic signs and symptoms. Patients who overdose on heroin tend to be pale and cyanotic (a dark bluish or purplish coloration of the skin and mucous membranes), with *pinpoint pupils* and absent reflexes. After blood is drawn for a study of drug levels, these patients should be given intravenous naloxone hydrochloride (Narcan), a narcotic antagonist that reverses the opioid effects, including respiratory depression, within two minutes of the injection.

The use of barbiturates and anxiolytics is widespread, and withdrawal from sedative hypnotic drugs is a common reason for psychiatric emergencies. The first symptom of withdrawal can start as soon as eight hours after the last pill has been taken and may consist of anxiety, confusion, and ataxia. As withdrawal progresses, the patient may have seizures; occasionally, a psychotic state erupts, with hallucinations, panic, and disorientation. Barbiturates are *cross-tolerant* with all antianxiety agents, such as diazepam (Valium). In the treatment of sedative-hypnotic withdrawal, one must take into account the usual daily drug intake.

Next to alcohol, phencyclidine (PCP or angel dust) has become the most common cause of psychotic drug-related hospital admissions. The presence of dissociative phenomena, nystagmus (ocular ataxia), muscular rigidity, and elevated blood pressure in a patient who is agitated, psychotic, or comatose strongly suggests PCP intoxication. In the treatment of PCP overdose, the patient should have gastric lavage to recover the drug, diazepam to reduce anxiety, an acidifying diuretic program consisting of ammonium chloride and furosemide (Lasix), which will enhance PCP excretion, and treatment of hypertension with *propranolol* (Inderal). Acidification is not recommended with hepatic or renal failure or when barbiturate use is suspected. Treatment of the condition with *phenothiazines is contraindicated*, because muscle rigidity and seizures are side effects of PCP and can be exacerbated by phenothiazines, as can the anticholinergic effects of PCP.

Atropine, scopalomine, belladonna, and antihistamines are active ingredients in over-the-counter or nonprescription sleeping pills. As a result of overdose or drug sensitivity, these so-called anticholinergic substances may produce an acute psychotic reaction. In addition to the psychotic symptoms, patients are characterized by fixed and dilated pupils, flushed skin, blurred vision, fever, delirium, and urinary retention. Clinicians should administer physostigmine (Antilirium) to reverse the anticholinergic syndrome. Phenothiazines should not be used to treat these psychotic reactions. Just as with PCP, patients are intolerant to major tranquilizers because of their anticholinergic effects.

Monoamine oxide inhibitors (MAOIs) are useful in treating depression, but a *hypertensive crisis* can occur if the patients have eaten food with a high tyramine content while on their medication. Hypertensive crisis is characterized by severe occipital headaches, nausea, vomiting, sweating, photophobia, and dilated pupils. When a hypertensive crisis occurs, the MAOI should be discontinued, and therapy should be instituted to reduce blood pressure. Chlorpromazine (Thorazine) and phentolamine (Regitine) have both been found useful in these hypertensive crises. There is a toxic interaction between MAOIs and meperidine hydrochloride *(Demerol)*, which can be fatal. When patients combine these two drugs, they become agitated, disoriented, cyanotic, hyperthermic, hypertensive, and tachycardic. Acetaminophen (Tylenol) is an analgesic and antipyretic. Overdose is characterized by fever, pancytopenia, hypoglycemic coma, renal failure, and liver damage. Treatment should begin with the induction of emesis or gastric lavage, followed by the administration of activated charcoal. Early treatment is critical to protect against hepatotoxicity.

28.14–28.17

28.14. The answer is E (*Synopsis VI*, pages 557–558; *CTP V*, pages 2140–2143).

28.15. The answer is C (*Synopsis VI*, pages 555–556; *CTP V*, pages 2140–2143).

28.16. The answer is D (*Synopsis VI*, page 556; *CTP V*, page 1541).

28.17. The answer is B (*Synopsis VI*, page 555; *CTP V*, page 2140).

Many of the greatest authors, sociologists, and psychiatrists in history have addressed the issues of suicide. In *The Sorrows of Young Werther*, the German novelist Johann Wolfgang von Goethe presented as the hero a man who killed himself. This book was banned in some European countries after its publication more than 200 years ago because of a rash of suicides by young men who had read it. The *Werther syndrome* describes the tendency of disturbed young persons to imitate highly publicized suicides. It is also known as copy-cat suicide and is common in adolescence.

The first major contribution to the study of suicide was made at the end of the nineteenth century by the French sociologist Émile Durkheim. Durkheim divided all suicides into three social categories: egoistic, altruistic, and anomic. Egoistic suicide applies to those people who are not strongly integrated into any social group. Lack of family integration has been used to explain why the unmarried are more vulnerable to suicide than are the married and why rural communities, which are more socially integrated than are urban areas, also have fewer suicides. Altruistic suicide describes the group whose tendency toward suicide stems from an excessive integration into a group. Durkheim had in mind the kind of suicide that some people expect of certain classes in Japanese society. Anomic suicide applies to those persons whose integration with society is disturbed, thereby depriving them of the customary norms of behavior. Anomic suicide can explain why the greatest incidence of suicide is among divorced persons, as compared with the married, and why people whose economic situation has changed drastically are more vulnerable. Anomie also refers to social instability, with a breakdown of society's standards and values.

Sigmund Freud delivered the first important psychological insight into the nature of suicide in his 1917 paper *Mourning and Melancholia*, in which he stated that the self-hatred seen in depression is caused by anger toward a love object that persons eventually turn back on themselves. Freud viewed suicide as the ultimate form of this phenomenon and expressed doubts that a suicide could be committed without an earlier repressed desire to kill someone else. Karl Menninger built on Freud's concepts in *Man Against Himself*, in which he conceived of suicide as retroflexed murder or inverted homicide as a result of the patient's anger toward another person. Menninger's formulation of the triad—to kill, to be killed, and to die—is of great practical help to clinicians in assessing their patients.

The relationship between suicide and depression has been studied extensively. Many suicidal patients use a preoccupation with suicide as a way of fighting off intolerable depression and a sense of hopelessness. In a study by Aaron Beck, *hopelessness* was found to be one of the most accurate indicators of long-term suicidal risk.

29 |||||

Psychotherapies

Psychotherapy is the art and science of making troubled people feel better. It is a method of healing that goes back to antiquity, and it is the only health science that uses words and speech as its instruments. It depends also on the unique relationship between the therapist and the patient, a relationship built on mutual trust and the empathic capacity of the therapist to place himself or herself in the patient's place.

This chapter covers a broad array of therapeutic modalities: psychoanalysis, psychoanalytic psychotherapy (including supportive psychotherapy), brief psychotherapy and crisis intervention, group psychotherapy, combined individual and group psychotherapy, psychodrama, family therapy, marital therapy, behavior therapy, biofeedback, hypnosis, and cognitive therapy. This listing is but a sample of the many therapeutic transactions between the therapist and the patient, all of which share the common goal of alleviating anxiety, depression, and other dysphoric states and allowing the person to realize his or her full potential.

A comprehensive definition of group psychotherapy might read as follows: Group psychotherapy is a broad designation for the form of therapy that is practiced by clinicians in groups formed for the specific purpose of helping people with their psychological and emotional difficulties, with the goals of such therapy depending largely on the therapist's technique.

Family therapy derives from two fundamental propositions. First, the family is conceptualized as a behavior system with unique properties, rather than as the sum of the characteristics of its individual members. Second, it is postulated that a close interrelationship exists between the psychosocial functioning of the family as a group and the emotional adaptation of its separate members. Family therapy has evolved from these propositions as an approach to the link between the disorders of family living and the disorders of individual members of a family by means of dynamically oriented interviews with the entire family population. This technique is based on the assumption that these individual emotional difficulties stem from disturbances in the overall interaction of the family. More specifically, treatment focuses on the family as a natural biosocial unit (including grandparents, extended kin, and others who are not consanguineous but who play significant roles in family life, as well as the crucial figures in the family organization).

Of all the psychotherapies, hypnosis (derived from the Greek word *hypnos*, meaning sleep) may be the oldest. Hypnotic phenomena have probably occurred in one form or another since the beginning of humankind. However, they were first mentioned as a therapeutic tool in the 18th century by Franz Anton Mesmer, who referred to hypnosis as animal magnetism. In the next century James Braid, Jean Martin Charcot, Ambroise-August Liebeault, Hippolyte-Marie Bernheim, Pierre Janet, Sigmund Freud, and many others studied hypnotic phenomena. Recently, there has been a resurgence of interest in the medical uses of hypnosis in the United States.

Students should be familiar with each modality in Chapter 29 of *Synopsis VI*, "Psychotherapies," and in Chapter 30, "Psychotherapies," in *CTP V* and know the following: theoretical basis, indications and contraindications, selection of patients, and techniques used. They should then answer the questions below to test their knowledge of the subject.

HELPFUL HINTS

The names of the workers, their theories, and the techniques of therapy should be known.

psychoanalysis
psychoanalytic psychotherapy
transference, transference
  neurosis, negative transference
Anna O.
hysteria
ego psychology
object relations
Studies on Hysteria
The Interpretation of Dreams
The Ego and the Id
parapraxes
structural theory
Otto Fenichel
tabula rasa
analyst incognito
free association
Jacques Lacan
fundamental rule of
  psychoanalysis
free-floating attention
rule of abstinence
narcissistic transference
splitting
manifest and latent dream content
day's residue
countertransference
self-analysis
therapeutic alliance
resistance
expressive therapy
insight-oriented psychotherapy
supportive therapy
relationship or superficial
  psychotherapy
Franz Alexander
confidentiality
regression
brief dynamic psychotherapy
Thomas French
Eric Lindemann
Michael Balint
Daniel Malan
James Mann
Habib Davanloo
time-limited psychotherapy
psychotherapeutic focus
STAPP
Peter Sifneos
patient-therapist encounter
early therapy
height of the treatment
evidence of change, termination
IPT

crisis theory
crisis intervention
group psychotherapy
combined individual and group
  psychotherapy
psychodrama
Eric Berne
here and now
Frederick Perls
Gestalt group therapy
Carl Rogers
transactional group therapy
behavioral group therapy
authority anxiety
dyad
peer anxiety
time-extended therapy
homogeneous versus
  heterogeneous groups
reality testing
universalization
cohesion
intellectualization, interpretation
ventilation and catharsis
abreaction
inpatient versus outpatient groups
self-help groups
AA, GA, OA
Jacob Moreno
protagonist, auxiliary ego
role reversal
double and multiple double
mirror technique
Nathan Ackerman
family therapy
family sculpting
self-observation
Murray Bowen
family systems
triangulation
genogram
structural model
indicated patient
family group therapy
Neal Miller
thermistor
the bell and the pad
thermal biofeedback
GSR
yoga, Zen
relaxation response
Jacobson's exercise
mental imagery
H. J. Eysenck

B. F. Skinner
operant conditioning
Joseph Wolpe
systematic desensitization
reciprocal inhibition
behavior therapy
relaxation training
hierarchy construction
hypnosis
flooding
assertiveness
social skills training
behavior rehearsal
implosion
reward of desired behavior
noxious stimulus
social network therapy
long-term reciprocity
psychodynamic model
experimental model
relational equitability
marriage counseling
marital therapy
  individual
  conjoint
  four-way session
  group psychotherapy
  combined therapy
behavioral medicine
disorders of self-control
graded exposure
participant modeling
aversive therapy
positive reinforcement
token economy
disulfiram (Antabuse) therapy
Jean Charcot
Hippolyte Bernheim
autogenic therapy
hypnotic capacity and induction
eye-roll sign
posthypnotic suggestion
Aaron Beck
schemas
cognitive triad of depression
testing automatic thoughts
identifying maladaptive
  assumptions
cognitive rehearsal
Paul Schilder
guided imagery
flexible schemas

QUESTIONS

DIRECTIONS: Each of the questions or incomplete statements below is followed by five suggested responses or completions. Select the *one* that is *best* in each case.

29.1. The most effective method of psychotherapeutic treatment for patients with pathological gambling disorders is
A. activity groups
B. self-help groups
C. family therapy
D. psychodrama
E. individual therapy

29.2. Cognitive therapy has been applied mainly to
A. panic attacks
B. obsessive-compulsive disorder
C. paranoid personality disorder
D. depression
E. somatoform disorder

29.3. The use of disulfiram (Antabuse) therapy in the treatment of alcoholism is an example of
A. graded exposure
B. relaxation training
C. aversion therapy
D. token economy
E. positive reinforcement

29.4. The one exclusion criterion in most brief dynamic psychotherapies is the patient who has
A. a circumscribed chief complaint
B. the ability to tolerate anxiety, guilt, and depression
C. a history of at least one meaningful relationship
D. motivation for symptom relief only
E. an above-average intelligence

29.5. A patient with a fear of heights is brought to the top of a tall building and required to remain there as long as necessary for the anxiety to dissipate. This is an example of
A. graded exposure
B. participant modeling
C. aversion therapy
D. flooding
E. systematic desensitization

29.6. Which one of the following conditions is not amenable to hypnosis?
A. Paranoia
B. Pruritus
C. Alcoholism
D. Obesity
E. Asthma

DIRECTIONS: For each of the questions and incomplete statements below, *one* or *more* of the responses or completions given are correct. Choose answer

A. if only *1, 2, and 3* are correct
B. if only *1 and 3* are correct
C. if only *2 and 4* are correct
D. if only *4* is correct
E. if *all* are correct

29.7. Easily hypnotizable people are
1. able to roll their eyes upward while the lids are closed
2. able to use visual imagery
3. willing to participate in the procedure
4. likely to have obsessive-compulsive characteristics

29.8. In group therapy
1. most therapists consider 8 to 10 members the optimal size for a group
2. membership should be as heterogeneous as possible
3. the average length of a group session is 1½ hours
4. a 20-year-old person and a 65-year-old person should be treated in separate groups

29.9. The most effective instruments used in biofeedback are
1. electromyograph
2. galvanic skin response gauge
3. electroencephalograph
4. thermistor

29.10. Systematic desensitization has been shown to be applicable in the treatment of
1. obsessive-compulsive disorders
2. sexual problems
3. stuttering
4. bronchial asthma

29.11. Which of the following statements concerning interpersonal psychotherapy are true?
1. Sessions are held weekly over a three-to-four-month period
2. It is of use mainly in the treatment of depression
3. The therapist offers direct advice to the patient
4. Little or no attention is given to the transference

29.12. A patient with a fear of snakes is encouraged by her therapist to imagine snakes crawling all over her body. This is an example of
1. flooding
2. participant modeling
3. implosion
4. aversion therapy

29.13. Therapeutic factors in group therapy include
1. cohesion
2. multiple transferences
3. universalization
4. collective transference

29.14. Biofeedback can be used to treat
1. hypertension
2. epilepsy
3. Raynaud's syndrome
4. fecal incontinence and enuresis

29.15. The cognitive therapy approach includes
1. eliciting automatic thoughts
2. testing automatic thoughts
3. identifying maladaptive underlying assumptions
4. testing the validity of maladaptive assumptions

DIRECTIONS: Each group of questions below consists of lettered headings followed by a list of numbered phrases. For each numbered phrase, select the *one* lettered heading that is most closely associated with it. Each lettered heading may be selected once, more than once, or not at all.

Questions 29.16–29.18
A. Psychoanalysis
B. Supportive therapy

29.16. Analysis of transference

29.17. Therapist actively intervenes and gives advice

29.18. Personality organization of potential patient may range from psychotic to neurotic

Questions 29.19–29.20
A. Analytically oriented group therapy
B. Supportive group therapy

29.19. Primary indications include psychotic and neurotic disorders

29.20. Challenges existing defenses

DIRECTIONS: Each of the incomplete statements below is followed by five suggested completions. Select the *one* that is *best* in each case.

29.21. All the following are characteristic of orthodox Freudian psychoanalysis *except*
A. free association
B. four or more sessions a week
C. use of a couch
D. analyst out of sight of the patient
E. frequent use of many interpretations

29.22. As defined by Freud, the fundamental rule of psychoanalysis is that the patient agree to
A. be completely candid with the analyst
B. attend three to five sessions a week
C. use the couch
D. keep the sessions confidential
E. pay the fee on time

29.23. Supportive psychotherapy uses such techniques as
A. strong leadership
B. a warm and friendly atmosphere
C. gratification of dependency needs
D. support in development of legitimate independence
E. all the above

29.24. Patients who tend to experience anxiety in a group therapy setting are likely to
A. feel anxious in the presence of authority
B. have had destructive relationships with peers
C. have no siblings
D. have limited peer relationships
E. be characterized by all the above

ANSWERS

Psychotherapies

29.1. The answer is B (*Synopsis VI*, pages 585–587; *CTP V*, pages 1146–1147).

Self-help groups are the most effective method of psychotherapeutic treatment for patients with pathological gambling disorders. Gamblers seldom come forward voluntarily for treatment. Legal difficulties, family pressures, or other psychiatric complaints are what bring the gamblers into treatment. Gamblers Anonymous (GA) was founded in 1957 and was modeled after Alcoholics Anonymous (AA); both GA and AA, as well as Overeaters Anonymous (OA), are termed self-help groups, as they are led and organized by nonprofessional group members.

A distinguishing characteristic of the self-help group is its homogeneity. Members suffer from the same disorder, and they share their experiences—good and bad, successful and unsuccessful—with one another. By so doing, they educate one another, provide mutual support, and alleviate the sense of alienation that is usually felt by the person drawn to this type of group.

Self-help groups emphasize cohesion, which is exceptionally strong in these groups; because of the shared problems and similar symptoms, a strong emotional bond develops. The groups are a form of inspirational group therapy and involve public confession, peer pressure, and the pressure of reformed gamblers, in this instance, available to help members resist the impulse to gamble.

Activity groups are a type of group therapy introduced and developed by S. R. Slavson and designed for children and young adolescents. Activity group therapy assumes that poor experiences have led to deficits in appropriate personality development of children; thus, corrective experiences in a therapeutically conditioned environment will modify them. Activity group therapy uses interview techniques, verbal explanations of fantasies, group play, work, and other communications. *Family therapy* is the treatment of more than one member of a family in the same session. Family relationships and processes are viewed as part of a family system, which has a stake in maintaining the status quo. The family believes that one or several family members are the source of all family problems. Family therapy may be helpful to pathological gamblers, in conjunction with GA. *Psychodrama* is a psychotherapy method originated by J. L. Moreno in which personality makeup, interpersonal relationships, conflicts, and emotional problems are expressed and explored through dramatization. The therapeutic dramatization of emotional problems includes the protago-

nist (patient), auxiliary egos (other group members), and the director (leader or therapist). The protagonist presents and acts out his or her emotional problems with the help of the auxiliary egos, who represent persons or things in the protagonist's experience. The auxiliary egos help account for the great range of therapeutic effects available in psychodrama. The director encourages the members of the group (members of the psychodrama and the audience) to be spontaneous and so has a catalytic function. The director must be available to meet the group's needs and not superimpose his or her values on it. Traditionally, psychodrama has not been the treatment of choice for pathological gamblers. *Individual therapy* is the traditional dyadic therapeutic technique, in which a psychotherapist treats one patient during a given therapeutic session. Individual therapy techniques are useful with some impulse disorders, but in such disorders as pathological gambling, results are better when groups are composed of other gamblers who have mastered the problem.

29.2. The answer is D (*Synopsis VI*, pages 602–604; *CTP V*, pages 1548–1549).

Cognitive therapy has been applied mainly to *depression*. Developed by Aaron Beck, cognitive therapy is short-term structured therapy that uses active collaboration between the patient and the therapist to achieve the therapeutic goals. It is also used with other conditions, such as panic attacks, obsessive-compulsive disorder, paranoid personality disorder, and somatoform disorder, but the treatment of depression is seen as the paradigm of the cognitive approach. The cognitive theory of depression holds that cognitive dysfunctions are the core of depression and that the affective and physical changes in depression are consequences of the cognitive dysfunctions. For example, apathy and low energy are the results of a person's expectation of failure in all areas.

The cognitive triad of depression consists of (1) a negative self-percept that sees oneself as defective, inadequate, deprived, worthless, and undesirable; (2) a tendency to experience the world as a negative, demanding, and defeating place and to expect failure and punishment; and (3) the expectation of continued hardship, suffering, deprivation, and failure.

Cognitive therapists also define a concept known as schemas or assumptions, which are stable cognitive patterns through which one interprets experience. Schemas of depression are analogous to viewing the world through dark glasses. Depressogenic schemas may involve viewing experiences as black or white without shades of gray, as categorical imperatives that allow no options, or as expectations that people are either all good or all bad. Cognitive errors are systematic errors in thinking that lead to the persistence of negative schemas despite contradictory evidence.

The goal of cognitive therapy is to alleviate depression and to prevent its recurrence by helping the patient (1) to identify and test negative cognitions, (2) to develop alternative and more flexible schemas, and (3) to rehearse both new cognitive and new behavioral responses. By changing the way a person thinks, cognitive therapy eventually alleviates the depressive syndrome.

Panic attacks are acute episodic events during which the patient feels overwhelmed by severe anxiety and an impending sense of doom. *Obsessive-compulsive disorder* is characterized by recurrent and intrusive mental events (obsessions) and recurrent, standardized conscious behavior (compulsions). Both the obsessions and the compulsions are severe enough to interfere markedly with functioning. *Paranoid personality disorder* is characterized by a pervasive and unwarranted tendency to interpret the actions of others as deliberately demeaning or threatening. *Somatoform disorders* are characterized by physical symptoms that resemble medical disease but that exhibit no organic pathology.

29.3. The answer is C (*Synopsis VI*, pages 597–598; *CTP V*, page 698).

The use of disulfiram (Antabuse) therapy in the treatment of alcoholism is an example of *aversion therapy*. The alcohol-free alcoholic is given a daily dose of disulfiram, which produces severe physiological consequences if alcohol is ingested while it is in the system (e.g., nausea, vomiting, hypertension, epilepsy). Another type of aversion therapy is to make the alcoholic vomit by adding an emetic to the alcoholic drink, which is then imbibed.

Relaxation training is a method in which the patient is taught to relax major muscle groups to relieve anxiety. *Graded exposure* teaches phobic patients to approach a feared object in small increments until the phobia is extinguished. *Positive reinforcement* is characterized by a desirable behavioral response being followed by a reward, such as food, avoidance of pain, or praise. The person will repeat the behavior in order to receive the reward. *Token economy* is a technique in which a patient is rewarded with a token that is used to purchase luxury items or certain privileges. It is used on inpatient hospital wards to modify behavior.

29.4. The answer is D (*Synopsis VI*, page 578; *CTP V*, pages 1564–1565).

The several types of brief dynamic psychotherapy generally have the same criteria for selecting and excluding patients. One criterion that most of these therapies consider to be an exclusion criterion is the patient who has *motivation for symptom relief only*. Those patients who are motivated only for symptom relief and who do not fulfill the other criteria are not suitable for brief dynamic psychotherapy. They may be better suited to one of the short-term behavioral approaches that treat a specific symptom, such as a phobia.

The criterion considered important in the selection process is a patient with good to excellent motivation for long-term change who has the short-term ability to *tolerate feelings of anxiety, guilt, and depression*. Other criteria used in selecting candidates for brief dynamic psychotherapy include the following: a *circumscribed chief complaint* (this implies an ability to select one out of a variety of problems to which patients assign top priority and which they want to solve as a result of the treatment); *one meaningful relationship*, especially during early childhood; the ability to interact flexibly with the therapist and to express feelings appropriately; and above-average psychological sophistication (this implies not only an *above-average intelligence* but also an ability to respond to interpretations). Brief dynamic psychotherapies generally stipulate a maximum of 12 to 40 sessions in which to do the therapeutic work.

29.5. The answer is D (*Synopsis VI*, page 597; *CTP V*, page 1465).

Flooding is a technique in which, for example, a patient with a fear of heights is brought to the top of a tall building and required to remain there as long as necessary for the anxiety to dissipate. Flooding is based on the premise that escaping from an anxiety-provoking experience reinforces the anxiety through conditioning. Thus, if the person is not allowed to escape, anxiety can be extinguished, and the conditioned avoidance behavior can be prevented. In clinical situations, flooding consists of having the patient confront the anxiety-inducing object or situation at full intensity for prolonged periods of time, resulting in the patient's being flooded with anxiety. The confrontation may be done in imagination, but results are better when real-life situations are used.

The groundless anxiety of the phobia tends to diminish to low levels after 5 to 25 minutes, depending on the patient's characteristics and the history of the disorder. In the next treatment session, preferably within a day or so, the initial anxiety is less, and less time is required to reach a state of calm. The process is repeated until there is little or no initial anxiety. Additional sessions are carried out at increasing intervals of time to avoid the spontaneous recovery of the conditioned anxiety until the frequency with which the patient encounters heights in the natural environment is sufficient to prevent relapse. The success of the procedure depends on the patient's remaining in the fear-generating situation on each trial until he or she is calm and feels a sense of mastery. Premature withdrawal from the situation or prematurely terminating the fantasized scene is tantamount to an escape, and both fear conditioning and avoidance (phobic) behavior are reinforced. Depending on some details of the particular case, as few as 5 and seldom more than 20 sessions are required.

Graded exposure is the process in which the patient is exposed over a period of time to objects that cause increasing levels of anxiety. It is similar to flooding except that the phobic object or situation is approached through a series of small steps, rather than all at once. *Participant modeling* is based on imitation, whereby patients learn to confront a fearful situation or object by modeling themselves after the therapist. *Aversion therapy* involves the presentation of a noxious stimulus immediately after a specific behavioral response, leading to the response's being inhibited and extinguished. The negative stimulus (punishment) is paired with the undesired behavior, which is thereby suppressed. *Systematic desensitization*, like graded exposure, is based on the concept that a person can overcome maladaptive anxiety elicited by a situation or object by approaching the feared situation gradually and in a psychophysiological state that inhibits anxiety. The patient attains a state of complete relaxation and then is exposed to the anxiety-producing stimulus. The negative reaction of anxiety is inhibited by the relaxed state. Systematic desensitization differs from graded exposure in two important respects: (1) systematic desensitization uses relaxation training, whereas graded exposure does not, and (2) systematic desensitization uses a graded list or hierarchy of anxiety-provoking scenes that the patient imagines, as opposed to graded exposure, in which the treatment is carried out in a real-life context.

29.6. The answer is A (*Synopsis VI*, pages 599–601; *CTP V*, pages 1504–1506 and 1514).

Paranoia is not amenable to hypnosis, simply because paranoid patients are suspicious and usually avoid or resist efforts to be hypnotized. Any patient who has difficulty with basic trust or who has problems with giving up control is not a good candidate for hypnosis. However, a variety of conditions have been treated with varying degrees of success by using hypnosis, including pruritus, alcoholism, obesity, asthma, substance-use disorders, smoking, warts, and chronic pain.

Hypnosis is a complex mental phenomenon that has been defined as a state of heightened focal concentration and receptivity to the suggestions of another person. Its essential feature is the subjective experiential alteration in perception, memory, or mood. Persons under hypnosis are said to be in a trance state. In a light trance there are motor activity changes such that muscles feel relaxed, hands can levitate, and paresthesias can be induced. A medium trance is characterized by decreased pain sensation and partial or complete amnesia. A deep trance is associated with hallucinatory experiences and deep anesthesia. In posthypnotic suggestion the

patient is instructed to perform a single act or to experience a particular sensation after awakening from a trance state. Thus, it may be used to give a bad taste to a particular food or drink, aiding in the treatment of *obesity* or *alcoholism;* to extinguish the sensation of itching, aiding in the treatment of *pruritus;* or to diminish the sense of hopelessness and anxiety that can snowball into the psychological and somatic manifestations of *asthma.*

Induction techniques vary but share the quality of having the patient concentrate his or her attention on an image, an idea, or a part of the body. Persons can also be taught self-hypnosis (also called autogenic training), in which they learn to relax.

29.7. The answer is A (1, 2, 3) (*Synopsis VI*, pages 600–601; *CTP V*, pages 1504–1506).

Hypnotizability is a person's ability to be hypnotized and to respond to suggestion. Herbert Speigel described an eye-roll sign for hypnotizability: the ability to *roll one's eyes upward* while they are closed. Other signs are the *ability to use visual imagery* and a *willingness to participate* in the procedure. Patients who have problems giving up control, such as those with *obsessive-compulsive characteristics*, are not good candidates for hypnosis. Typical obsessive-compulsive characteristics include perfectionism and inflexibility.

29.8. The answer is A (1, 2, 3) (*Synopsis VI*, page 584; *CTP V*, pages 1517–1535).

Group therapy has been successful with as few as 3 members and as many as 15, but most therapists consider *8 to 10 members* the optimal size. Most therapists conduct group sessions weekly. The average length of a group session is *1½ hours;* however, sessions may last anywhere between one and two hours. The time limit should be kept constant. Most therapists believe that the group membership should be as *heterogeneous* as possible, to ensure maximum interaction. Thus, the group can be composed of members from different diagnostic categories, with varied behavioral patterns, from all races and social levels, and of varying ages and both sexes. In general, *patients between 20 and 65* can be effectively included in the same group.

29.9. The answer is E (all) (*Synopsis VI*, page 594; *CTP V*, pages 1474–1475).

The most effective instruments used in biofeedback are the *electromyograph* (EMG), which measures the electrical potentials of muscle fibers; the *electroencephalograph*, which measures alpha waves that occur in relaxed states; the *galvanic skin response gauge* (GSR), which shows decreased skin conductivity during a relaxed state; and the *thermistor*, which measures skin temperature that drops during tension because of peripheral vasoconstriction.

Biofeedback is being used to enable a person to gain some element of voluntary control over autonomic body functions. The technique is based on the learning principle that a desired response is learned when received information (feedback) indicates that a specific thought complex or action has produced the desired response. The patient is attached to one of the measuring instruments, which measures a physiological function and translates the impulse into an audible or visual signal that the patient uses to gauge his or her responses. For example, in treating bruxism, an EMG is attached to the masseter muscle. The EMG emits a high tone when the muscle is contracted and a low tone when it is at rest. The patient can learn to alter the tone to indicate relaxation. He or she receives feedback about the masseter muscle; the tone reinforces the learning; and the condition ameliorates—all these events interacting synergistically.

29.10. The answer is E (all) (*Synopsis VI*, pages 596–597 and 771; *CTP V*, pages 999 and 1475).

Systematic desensitization has been shown to be applicable in the treatment of *obsessive-compulsive disorders, sexual problems, stuttering, bronchial asthma*, and other conditions. Joseph Wolpe first described systematic desensitization, a behavioral technique in which the patient is trained in muscle relaxation; a hierarchy of anxiety-provoking thoughts or objects is paired with the relaxed state until the anxiety is systematically decreased and eliminated.

Generally, systematic desensitization is applicable when one can identify the stimulus antecedents that elicit anxiety, which, in turn, mediate maladaptive or disruptive behavior. Often, for example, obsessive-compulsive disorder (recurrent, instrusive mental events and behavior) is mediated by the anxiety elicited by specific objects or situations. Through systematic desensitization, the patient can be conditioned not to feel anxiety when around these objects or situations and thus to diminish the intensity of the obsessive-compulsive behavior.

Desensitization has been used effectively with some stutterers by deconditioning the anxiety associated with a range of speaking situations. Certain sexual problems—such as impotence, anorgasmia, and premature ejaculation—are amenable to desensitization therapy.

29.11. The answer is E (all) (*Synopsis VI*, page 581; *CTP V*, pages 1559–1560).

A specific type of short-term psychotherapy called interpersonal psychotherapy (IPT) is used mainly to treat *depression*. Therapy consists of 45-to-50-minute sessions *held weekly over a three-to-four-month period*. It is called IPT because interpersonal behavior is emphasized as a cause of depression and as a method of cure. The therapist offers *direct advice*, aids in making decisions, and helps clarify areas of conflict. Little or no attention is paid to the *transference*. Studies have shown that, in selected cases of depression, IPT compares favorably with drug therapy with antidepressant agents.

29.12. The answer is B (1, 3) (*Synopsis VI*, pages 597–598; *CTP V*, pages 999 and 1465).

Encouraging a patient with a fear of snakes to imagine snakes crawling all over her body is an example of *implosion*, a variant of *flooding*. These techniques are based on the premise that not allowing a person to escape from an anxiety-provoking situation serves eventually to extinguish the anxiety, thus eliminating avoidance behavior. In implosion, as distinguished from flooding, the imagined or real event is made worse than it actually is (e.g., this patient not only saw a snake but saw it crawling on her body).

Participant modeling refers to having the patient learn by imitation. In phobias the patient may observe the therapist describing the feared activity in a calm manner with which the patient can identify.

Aversion therapy is characterized by a noxious stimulus presented immediately after a specific behavioral response, which is thereby eventually inhibited or extinguished (e.g., receiving a mild electric shock after smoking a cigarette).

29.13. The answer is E (all) (*Synopsis VI*, page 586; *CTP V*, pages 1520–1522).

Many factors account for therapeutic change in group therapy. *Multiple transferences* consist of a variety of group members who may stand for people significant in a patient's past or current life situation. Group members may take the roles of wife, mother, father, siblings, and employer. The patient can then work through actual or fantasized conflicts with the surrogate figures to a successful resolution.

Collective transference is a member's pathological personification of the group as a single transferential figure, generally the mother or the father, and is a phenomenon unique to group therapy. The therapist attempts to encourage the patient to respond to members of the group as individuals and to differentiate them.

Universalization is the process by which patients recognize that they are not alone in having an emotional problem. It is generally felt to be one of the most important processes in group therapy.

Cohesion is a sense of "we-ness," a sense of belonging. The members value the group, which engenders loyalty and friendliness among them. The members are willing to work together and take responsibility for one another in achieving their common goals. And they are willing to endure a certain degree of frustration to maintain the group's integrity. The more cohesion a group has, the more likely it is that it will have a successful outcome. Cohesion is considered the most important therapeutic factor in group therapy.

29.14. The answer is E (all) (*Synopsis VI*, pages 594–595; *CTP V*, pages 1474–1475).

Biofeedback can be used to treat numerous conditions, including fecal incontinence, enuresis, Raynaud's syndrome, epilepsy, and hypertension. Triple lumen rectal catheters are used to provide feedback to *incontinent* patients in order for them to reestablish normal bowel habits. The sounding of a buzzer to awake sleeping *enuretic* children at the first sign of moisture is an effective method for that condition. Cold hands and cold feet are frequent concomitants of anxiety and also occur in *Raynaud's syndrome,* which is caused by vasospasm of arterial smooth muscles. A number of studies indicate that thermal feedback from the hand is effective in about 70 percent of those cases. A variety of biofeedback procedures have been used to teach patients with *hypertension* to decrease their blood pressure. Some follow-up data indicate that these changes may persist for at least two years and often permit the reduction or elimination of antihypertensive medications. A number of electroencephalographic biofeedback procedures have been used experimentally in *epilepsy* to suppress seizure activity prophylactically in patients not responsive to anticonvulsant medication.

Other biofeedback applications include neuromuscular rehabilitation, migraine and tension headaches, cardiac arrhythmias, orthostatic hypotension, myofacial and temporomandibular joint pain, hyperactivity, and asthma.

29.15. The answer is E (all) (*Synopsis VI*, page 603; *CTP V*, pages 1541–1549).

The cognitive therapy approach includes four processes: (1) *eliciting automatic thoughts*, (2) *testing automatic thoughts*, (3) *identifying maladaptive underlying assumptions*, and (4) *testing the validity of maladaptive assumptions*.

Automatic thoughts are cognitions that intervene between external events and the person's emotional reactions to the events. An example of an automatic thought is, "Everyone is going to laugh at me when they see how badly I dance"—a thought that occurs to someone who has been asked to go dancing and declines. Another example is, "He [or she] doesn't like me" if someone passes that person in the hall without saying hello.

Assumptions, schemas, are underlying ideas, often unconscious, that trigger automatic thoughts. Assumptions are considered patterns that represent rules or maladaptive general beliefs that guide the patient's life. An example of an assumption is, "If I don't do everything perfectly, it doesn't count."

The therapist, acting as a model and teacher, helps the patient test the validity of automatic thoughts. The goal is to encourage the patient to reject inaccurate or exaggerated automatic thoughts after careful examination. Patients often blame themselves for things that go wrong that may well have been outside their control. The therapist reviews with the patient the entire situation and helps to explain the blame or the cause of the unpleasant events more accurately. Generating alternative explanations for events is another way of undermining inaccurate and distorted automatic thoughts.

Similar to the testing of the validity of automatic thoughts is the testing of the accuracy of maladaptive assumptions. For example, if a patient states that he or she should always work up to his or her potential, the therapist may challenge the patient to defend the validity of this assumption by asking, "Why is that so important to you?"

29.16–29.18

29.16. The answer is A (*Synopsis VI*, pages 571–574; *CTP V*, page 1453).

29.17. The answer is B (*Synopsis VI*, pages 575–576; *CTP V*, page 1453).

29.18. The answer is B (*Synopsis VI*, pages 575–576; *CTP V*, page 1453).

A major criterion by which psychoanalysis can be differentiated from supportive therapy is the management of the transference. Psychoanalysis has been called the *analysis of transference* to emphasize the point. Transference is a phenomenon occurring in psychoanalysis in which the patient develops a strong emotional attachment to the therapist as a symbolized familial figure. In supportive therapy the transference is not analyzed, as it is generally felt that the patients who require supportive therapy (patients in acute crises or chronically psychotic) cannot tolerate the intense emotions associated with transference analysis. In supportive therapy the therapist *actively intervenes* in the patient's life and gives advice, limit setting, and friendship; this type of relationship does not occur in classical psychoanalysis.

Both psychoanalysis and supportive therapy go on for an extended period, sometimes for years. In contrast, a limited number of interviews are used in the so-called brief therapies, which are used primarily in crisis intervention or for clearly circumscribed chief complaints. The prerequisites for patients in psychoanalysis include a relatively mature personality, a favorable life situation, and psychological mindedness. In supportive therapy the patients can range from *psychotic to neurotic*, with at least some capacity to form a therapeutic alliance. In both psychoanalysis and supportive therapy, the verbalization of unexpressed strong emotions may bring considerable relief. However, in psychoanalysis the goal of such talking out is primarily to gain insight into the unconscious dynamic patterns that may be intensifying current responses; in supportive therapy the goal may simply be to help the patient feel better and less alone.

29.19–29.20

29.19. The answer is B (*Synopsis VI*, page 583; *CTP V*, page 1523).

29.20. The answer is A (*Synopsis VI*, page 583; *CTP V*, page 1523).

At the present time, many approaches are made to the group method of treatment. Analytically oriented group therapy usually involves meeting one to three times a week, can last a year or longer, and is primarily indicated for neurotic and personality disorders. Supportive group therapy usually involves meeting once a week, generally can last from six months on, and is indicated for both *psychotic and neurotic disorders*. The analytically oriented group therapist tends to *challenge defenses*, whereas supportive group therapists are more likely to act to strengthen existing defenses. Major group processes for supportive groups include universalization and reality testing; processes for analytically oriented groups include transference and reality testing. In supportive group therapy the focus is on environmental factors that lead to emotional stress; in analytically oriented therapy, the understanding and the linking of present and past life situations are the focus. In both therapies an attempt is made to focus on the causality of specific symptoms.

29.21.   The answer is E (*Synopsis VI*, pages 571–574; *CTP V*, pages 1442–1461).

The setting of the psychoanalytic situation is little changed from Freud's day. The patient lies on a *couch* with the analyst sitting behind the patient, remaining for the most part *out of sight* of the patient and intruding as little as possible into the patient's thought processes. Sessions are usually held *four or more* times a week and have an average duration of 45 to 50 minutes. Innovators, such as Jacques Lacan from France, successfully introduced decreases in session frequency and length. Some analyses are now being conducted in this country with session lengths of from 20 to 30 minutes and frequency of one to two sessions a week. Patients are guided in their behavior by the so-called basic or fundamental rule—that they keep nothing back. The analyst endeavors to maintain an evenly suspended attention that is the counterpart to the patients' activity of *free association*, in which patients verbalize without censorship the passing contents of their minds. For the most part the analyst's activity is limited to timely interpretations of the patient's associations. Such *interpretations* are usually few in number.

29.22.   The answer is A (*Synopsis VI*, page 572; *CTP V*, page 1456).

As defined by Freud, the fundamental rule of psychoanalysis is that the patient agree to be completely *candid with the analyst*. All ideas, impulses, thoughts, and feelings are to be verbalized. Implicit in the fundamental rule of psychoanalysis are two interrelated principles: First, psychoanalysis emphasizes the value of the recognition and the verbalization of psychic contents—of ideas, impulses, conflicts, and emotions. Second, psychoanalytic technique emphasizes that action based on impulse without adequate consideration is to be avoided.

Some patients may take the fundamental rule so literally that they sabotage their treatment while giving an appearance of meticulously complying with its requirements. This is particularly likely to occur in some obsessional states, in which being completely candid with the analyst may be used as a

weapon against the analyst, rather than against the neurosis. Some analysts, therefore, do not always give their patients explicit statements about the fundamental rule, preferring, instead, to lead them to discover it for themselves through a study of the obstacles they place in the way of communication.

Other features that many analysts consider inherent in the process include the patient's agreeing to attend *three to five sessions* a week, to use *the couch*, and to *pay the fee* on time and for both the patient and the analyst to keep the sessions *confidential*.

29.23.   The answer is E (*Synopsis VI*, page 575; *CTP V*, pages 1459–1461).

Supportive psychotherapy uses such techniques as *strong leadership*, a warm and *friendly atmosphere*, gratification of *dependency needs* (if done without evoking undue shame), support in the development of *legitimate independence*, help in the development of hobbies and of pleasurable but nondestructive sublimations, the removal of excessive external strain (if a productive step), hospitalization when indicated, medication to alleviate some symptoms, and guidance and advice on current issues. Supportive psychotherapy offers support by an authority figure during a period of illness, turmoil, or temporary decompensation. It is also used as maintenance therapy for chronically disturbed patients. It uses techniques that may make the patient feel more secure, accepted, protected, encouraged, and safe and less anxious and less alone.

29.24.   The answer is E (*Synopsis VI*, pages 583–584; *CTP V*, pages 1517–1535).

Many patients experience anxiety when placed in a group or when group therapy is suggested. That anxiety often relates to the patients' past experiences. For example, patients who had *destructive relationships* with their peer groups or who had *limited peer relationships*, such as those with schizoid personality disorder, generally react negatively or with increased anxiety when placed in a group setting, as do patients, both adults and children, who *have no siblings*.

Those patients whose primary problems center on their relationships to authority and who are anxious in the presence of *authority figures* often do better in the group setting than in the dyadic one-to-one setting, even though, initially, these patients experience anxiety in group therapy. Patients with a great deal of authority anxiety may be blocked, anxious, resistant, and unwilling to verbalize their thoughts and feelings in the individual setting, generally for fear of censure or disapproval from the therapist. They may ultimately welcome the suggestion of group psychotherapy to avoid the scrutiny of the dyadic situation. Conversely, if the patient reacts negatively to the suggestion of group psychotherapy or is openly resistant to the idea, the therapist should consider the possibility of a high degree of peer anxiety and should assess the relationship to peers and to authority figures, current and past.

30 |||||

Biological Therapies

The biological therapies are among the most effective treatments for many psychiatric disorders. The reemergence of a medical model of psychiatry, the acceptance of the biological bases of many psychiatric syndromes, and the increased focus on the biological treatment of severe psychiatric disorders add further importance to the biological therapies. Parallel to the increased importance of the biological therapies is an increased complexity. Students, residents, and practicing clinicians must remain current with the ever-expanding literature on biological treatments in psychiatry. General principles of pharmacology should be studied, including the concepts of pharmacokinetics (drug absorption, distribution, metabolism, and excretion) and pharmacodynamics (receptor mechanism; dose-response curve; therapeutic index; and the development of tolerance, dependence, and withdrawal phenomena). The concepts of both pharmacokinetic and pharmacodynamic drug-drug interactions should be understood. The psychiatrist should be able to list the criteria he or she uses in choosing a particular drug for a particular patient and should be able to list the possible causes to be considered in the event that a therapeutic trial fails. Patient education, informed consent, special considerations in children and geriatric patients, and the use of drugs during pregnancy are issues that the student should be able to discuss.

The psychiatrist should know the classes of drugs traditionally referred to as the antipsychotics. These drugs have also been referred to as neuroleptics and major tranquilizers. The term "neuroleptic," however, refers more to the neurological side effects of these drugs, and the term "major tranquilizer" inaccurately implies that the primary effect of these medications is

sedation. This diverse group of drugs, with the exception of the novel compound clozapine (Clozaril), have in common the property of being dopamine-receptor antagonists. The differences among these drugs in terms of potency and adverse effects are issues about which the student should be knowledgeable. The indications for these drugs extend somewhat beyond psychosis; however, because of the long-term adverse effects associated with them, such indications must be considered carefully. The pharmacodynamic basis for both the clinical and the adverse effects are crucial for a complete appreciation of these drugs. They are associated with a wide range of adverse effects, and a prescribing psychiatrist needs to know how to address the management of each of these adverse effects, particularly tardive dyskinesia. The clinician should be aware of the pharmacological alternatives in treating psychosis, in addition to the traditional antipsychotics.

The drugs referred to as antidepressants include the tricyclic and tetracyclic antidepressants the monoamine oxidase inhibitors (MAOIs), the sympathomimetics (e.g., amphetamine), and several atypical antidepressants—trazodone (Desyrel), bupropion (Wellbutrin), and fluoxetine (Prozac). The reasons to choose among these drugs in specific clinical situations should be known to the student. These reasons include both differential clinical indications and differential adverse-effect profiles. The antidepressants are a diverse group of compounds with different adverse-effect profiles. There are many indications in addition to depression for these agents. The guidelines for the initiation and the maintenance of treatment and for the supplementation of these drugs with lithium and L-triiodothyronine (T$_3$ or liothyronine [Cytomel]) are important clinical aspects. The MAOIs are probably an underused class of drugs, partly because of a lack of knowledge about these compounds. A rational approach to the risk of tyramine-induced hypertensive crisis should be known to every clinician. Several sympathomimetics are available in the United States, and they may be the drugs of choice in several clinical situations. Finally, trazodone, bupropion, clomipramine (Anafranil), and fluoxetine are additional antidepressant drugs that offer important alternative treatment approaches.

Although lithium is the prototypical drug for the treatment of bipolar disorder, other drugs are also available—carbamazepine (Tegretol), valproic acid (Depakene), clonazepam (Klonopin), verapamil (Calan), and clonidine (Catapres). The student should still focus, however, on developing a detailed knowledge regarding the clinical use of lithium, which has many clinical indications in addition to treating bipolar disorder. The risks of and approaches to adverse effects, particularly renal and thyroid, are important knowledge for the student; and the use of other drugs, including carbamazepine and levothyroxine (T_4 or thyroxine [Levothroid]), in combination with lithium, should also be studied. Of the alternative treatments for bipolar disorder, carbamazepine should be the

drug that students emphasize in their study.

The benzodiazepines and buspirone (BuSpar) are the anxiolytic drugs on which the student should concentrate. Other drugs that should be reviewed are barbiturates, alcohols, antihistamines, and carbamates. The pharmacokinetic differences among different benzodiazepines and the common pharmacodynamic effects of these drugs should be studied. Buspirone is a novel compound that lacks many of the potential problems of the benzodiazepines.

Other organic therapies include electroconvulsive therapy (ECT), psychosurgery, light therapy, sleep deprivation and alteration of sleep schedules, and drug-assisted interviewing. The efficacy and indications for ECT are important for the student to know. The advances in and the indications for psychosurgery are of possibly increasing clinical importance. Finally, light therapy is an exciting new approach to the treatment of depression, and the theoretical basis and the indications for this treatment should be studied.

Readers should refer to Chapter 30, "Biological Therapies," of *Synopsis VI* and to Chapter 31, "Biological Therapies," of *CTP V* and should then study the questions and answers below to test their knowledge of this area.

HELPFUL HINTS

The student should know the terms listed below, in addition to specific drugs.

ECT	FDA	receptor blockade
Ugo Cerletti	DEA	noradrenergic, histaminic,
Lucio Bini	therapeutic trial	cholinergic receptors
insulin coma therapy	BPRS	cholinergic rebound
psychosurgery	SADS	idiopathic psychosis
Egas Moniz	informed consent	secondary psychosis
Julius von Wagner-Jauregg	teratogenic	drug intoxications
John Cade	Ebstein's anomaly	movement disorders
artificial hibernation	antipsychotics, major tranquilizers	anticholinergic side effects
Rauwolfia serpentina	deinstitutionalization	anticholinergic delirium
buspirone (BuSpar)	positive and negative symptoms	CNS depression
pharmacokinetics	protein binding	narrow-angle glaucoma
pharmacodynamics	distribution volume	noncompliance
biotransformation	lipid solubility	plasma levels
half-life	metabolic enzymes	megadose therapy
therapeutic index	metabolites	rapid neuroleptization
TD_{50}	potency—high and low	orthostatic (postural) hypotension
dose-response curve	D_2 receptors	drug holidays
haloperidol (Haldol)	mesolimbic	depot preparations
combination drugs	mesocortical	dystonias

parkinsonian symptoms	monoamine hypothesis	use in pregnancy
akathisia	down-regulation of receptors	tonic, clonic phases
amantadine (Symmetrel)	secondary depression	EEG, EMG
adrenergic blockade	agoraphobia with panic attacks	status epilepticus
pilocarpine	generalized anxiety	apnea
physostigmine	obsessive-compulsive disorder	ECT contraindications
atropine sulfate	clomipramine (Anafranil)	stereotactic
prolactin	eating disorders	psychosurgery
retrograde ejaculation	side-effect profiles	light therapy
allergic dermatitis	L-triiodothyronine	zeitgebers
photosensitivity	tapering	melatonin
retinitis pigmentosa	prophylactic treatment	sleep deprivation
cardiac effects	neuroendocrine tests	drug-assisted interviewing
weight gain	drug-induced mania	narcotherapy
sudden death	BPH	mute patients
hematological effects	triplicate prescriptions	catatonia
jaundice	clonazepam (Klonopin)	acupuncture and acupressure
overdoses	clonidine (Catapres)	orthomolecular therapy
epileptogenic effects	renal clearance	megavitamin therapy
oculogyric crisis	phosphatidylinositol	hemodialysis
tardive dyskinesia	bipolar disorder	carbon dioxide therapy
pill-rolling tremor	schizoaffective disorder	electrosleep therapy
rabbit syndrome	schizophrenia	continuous sleep treatment
demethylation	impulse disorders	fluoxetine (Prozac)
hydroxylation and glucuronidation	TFTs	
reuptake blockade	electrolyte screen	

QUESTIONS

DIRECTIONS: Each of the incomplete statements below is followed by five suggested completions. Select the *one* that is *best* in each case.

30.1. The benzodiazepine with the shortest half-life is
A. lorazepam (Ativan)
B. temazepam (Restoril)
C. triazolam (Halcion)
D. alprazolam (Xanax)
E. oxazepam (Serax)

30.2. The medication most commonly used in drug-assisted psychiatric interviewing is
A. meprobamate (Miltown)
B. diazepam (Valium)
C. amobarbital (Amytal)
D. phenothiazine
E. chloral hydrate (Noctec)

30.3. Of the following, the most teratogenic drug is
A. diazepam (Valium)
B. haloperidol (Haldol)
C. lithium
D. chlorpromazine (Thorazine)
E. amitriptyline (Elavil)

30.4. All the following are major classes of antipsychotic medication *except*
A. thioxanthenes
B. dibenzoxazepines
C. phenothiazines
D. sympathomimetics
E. butyrophenones

30.5. High-potency antipsychotics
A. are more efficacious than low-potency antipsychotics
B. must be given in divided doses
C. have a higher incidence of cardiac and epileptogenic effects than do low-potency medications
D. have a higher incidence of adverse neurological effects than do low-potency antipsychotics
E. are less expensive than low-potency antipsychotics

30.6. Propranolol (Inderal) is useful for the treatment of
A. akathisia
B. lithium-induced tremor
C. aggression
D. social phobia
E. all the above

30.7. Amantadine (Symmetrel) is
A. a dopamine antagonist
B. effective for the treatment of acute dystonic reactions
C. effective for the treatment of drug-induced parkinsonism
D. relatively contraindicated in patients with liver disease
E. all the above

30.8. Eosinophilia-myalgia syndrome (EMS)
A. is associated with the use of L-tryptophan
B. can cause congestive heart failure and death
C. includes symptoms of fatigue
D. includes symptoms of swelling of the extremities
E. includes all the above

DIRECTIONS: For each of the questions or incomplete statements below, *one* or *more* of the responses or completions given are correct. Choose answer

A. if only *1, 2, and 3* are correct
B. if only *1 and 3* are correct
C. if only *2 and 4* are correct
D. if only *4* is correct
E. if *all* are correct

30.9. Benzodiazepines effective in the treatment of panic disorder include
1. chlordiazepoxide (Librium)
2. diazepam (Valium)
3. lorazepam (Ativan)
4. alprazolam (Xanax)

30.10. Indications for lithium include
1. schizophrenia
2. major depression
3. impulse control disorder
4. bipolar disorder

30.11. Which of the following drugs are used in the treatment of bipolar disorder?
1. Carbamazepine (Tegretol)
2. Clonidine (Catapres)
3. Valproic acid (Depakene)
4. Levothyroxine (Levothroid)

30.12. Adverse effects of the tricyclic and tetracyclic antidepressants include
1. sedation
2. excessive salivation
3. hypotension
4. diarrhea

30.13. Which of the following statements about carbamazepine (Tegretol) are true?
1. Bipolar disorder patients who respond to carbamazepine usually have electroencephalogram abnormalities
2. The most serious adverse effect of carbamazepine is transient leukopenia
3. Carbamazepine should never be used concurrently with lithium because of the risk of synergistic neurotoxicity
4. Carbamazepine plasma levels for bipolar disorder should be maintained at 8 to 12 μg per mL

30.14. Persons most responsive to electroconvulsive therapy include those with
1. delusional or psychotic depression
2. features of melancholia
3. nonsuppression on the dexamethasone-suppression test
4. a blunted response of thyroid-stimulating hormone to thyrotropin-releasing hormone infusion

30.15. Dystonias are
1. observed in approximately 10 percent of patients receiving antipsychotic medication
2. usually observed in the first few hours or days of treatment
3. most common in young men
4. rare with thioridazine (Mellaril)

30.16. Situations in which electroconvulsive therapy poses an increased risk include
1. evolving strokes
2. recent myocardial infarction
3. severe underlying hypertension
4. intracranial masses

30.17. Medications used in the treatment of depression include
1. alprazolam (Xanax)
2. methylphenidate (Ritalin)
3. carbamazepine (Tegretol)
4. lithium

30.18. Electroconvulsive therapy
1. may provide prophylaxis against recurrences of depression
2. can be administered safely during pregnancy
3. has less cardiotoxicity than do tricyclic and tetracyclic pharmacological treatments
4. is not used to treat schizophrenia

30.19. Which of the following statements about the adverse effects of lithium are true?
1. Lithium tremor is significantly worsened by propranolol (Inderal)
2. Leukocytosis is an ominous effect and requires the discontinuation of lithium
3. Hyperthyroidism is the most common lithium-induced thyroid effect
4. Lithium-induced nephrogenic diabetes insipidus is routinely treated with diuretics, such as hydrochlorothiazide (Esidrix)

DIRECTIONS: Each group of questions below consists of lettered headings followed by a list of numbered words or statements. For each numbered word or statement, select the *one* lettered heading that is most closely associated with it. Each lettered heading may be used once, more than once, or not at all.

Questions 30.20–30.23
A. Light therapy
B. Psychosurgery
C. Amytal interview
D. Acupuncture
E. Orthomolecular therapy

30.20. Catatonia

30.21. Seasonal pattern of major depression

30.22. Chronic, severe, intractable major depression

30.23. Chemical addictions

Questions 30.24–30.28
A. Chloral hydrate (Noctec)
B. Diphenhydramine (Benadryl)
C. Meprobamate (Miltown)
D. Glutethimide (Doriden)
E. L-Tryptophan

30.24. A reasonable loading dose can be obtained from a large glass of milk

30.25. Contraindicated in acute intermittent porphyria

30.26. The major adverse effect is occasional severe gastritis or ulceration

30.27. Used as a sedative in children and the elderly

30.28. Hemoperfusion is needed to clear drug from system in overdose

Questions 30.29–30.30
    A. Benzodiazepines
    B. Barbiturates

30.29. Often lethal in overdose

30.30. Marked development of dependence

Questions 30.31–30.32
    A. Diazepam (Valium)
    B. Alprazolam (Xanax)

30.31. Withdrawal syndrome may be delayed for one to two weeks

30.32. Metabolized by hydroxylation and glucuronidation

Questions 30.33–30.36
    A. Fluoxetine (Prozac)
    B. Trazodone (Desyrel)

30.33. Long half-life

30.34. Dosage range of 200 to 600 mg a day

30.35. Associated with orthostatic hypotension

30.36. Associated with insomnia and nervousness

Questions 30.37–30.38
    A. Bupropion (Wellbutrin)
    B. Buspirone (BuSpar)

30.37. Treatment primarily of major depression

30.38. Treatment primarily of generalized anxiety disorder

Questions 30.39–30.42
    A. Clozapine (Clozaril)
    B. Clonazepam (Klonopin)

30.39. Treatment of psychotic disorders

30.40. Increased incidence of agranulocytosis

30.41. Increased incidence of seizures

30.42. Treatment of bipolar disorder

DIRECTIONS: The letters on the dose-response curves shown represent different drugs. Match the letters with the correct numbered phrases below.

Questions 30.43–30.46

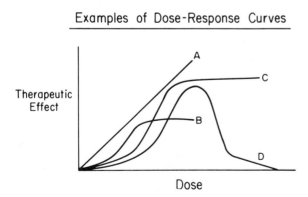

Examples of Dose-Response Curves

30.43. Therapeutic window

30.44. Linear dose response

30.45. Greater potency at small dosages

30.46. Higher maximum efficacy

ANSWERS

Biological Therapies

30.1. The answer is C (*Synopsis VI*, page 623; *CTP V*, pages 1580–1583).

Triazolam (Halcion), a triazolobenzodiazepine, has the shortest half-life (two to three hours) of all the benzodiazepines. *Alprazolam* (Xanax), also a triazolobenzodiazepine, has a half-life of 10 to 15 hours. The benzodiazepines can be subclassified as 2-keto-, 3-hydroxy-, and triazolobenzodiazepines. The metabolism of benzodiazepines differs for the three subclasses. As a result of slow metabolism, all the 2-ketobenzodiazepines have plasma half-lives of 30 to 100 hours and, therefore, are the longest-acting benzodiazepines. They include chlordiazepoxide (Librium) and diazepam (Valium). The 3-hydroxybenzodiazepines have short half-lives (10 to 30 hours) because they are directly metabolized by glucuronidation and, thus, have no active metabolites. They include *oxazepam* (Serax), *lorazepam* (Ativan), and *temazepam* (Restoril).

30.2. The answer is C (*Synopsis VI*, page 674; *CTP V*, page 1579).

Amobarbital (Amytal) is the medication most commonly used in drug-assisted psychiatric interviewing. It can be of use with patients who have difficulty in expressing themselves freely or who are suppressing anxiety-provoking material. In narcotherapy regularly scheduled interviews are conducted using Amytal as an adjunctive agent. The drug-assisted interview can also be of help in differentiating organic from psychogenic illness. For example, a patient suffering from a paralyzed right arm may move it normally during an Amytal interview and thus point to a psychogenic, rather than an organic, cause.

Meprobamate (Miltown), *diazepam* (Valium), and *chloral hydrate* (Noctec) are agents used as sedatives, hypnotics, and anxiolytics. The *phenothiazines* are antipsychotic agents used in the treatment of schizophrenia. Some workers advocate using intravenous diazepam in place of Amytal for the drug-assisted interview.

30.3. The answer is C (*Synopsis VI*, pages 654–655; *CTP V*, page 1659).

One of the most teratogenic drugs in the psychopharmacological armamentarium is *lithium*. Anticonvulsants are also associated with a high risk of teratogenic effects. Lithium administration during pregnancy is associated with a high incidence of birth abnormalities, including Ebstein's anomaly (a downward displacement of the tricuspid valve into the right ventricle), a serious abnormality in cardiac development. Other psychoactive drugs are less clearly associated with birth defects than is lithium; however, they should also be avoided during pregnancy if at all possible.

A clinician should attempt to avoid administering any drug to a woman who is pregnant, particularly during the first trimester. This rule, however, occasionally needs to be broken when the mother's psychiatric disorder is severe. The most common such clinical situation is seen when a pregnant woman becomes psychotic. If a decision is made not to terminate the pregnancy, it is preferable to administer antipsychotics such as *haloperidol* (Haldol) and *chlorpromazine* (Thorazine), rather than lithium. That holds true even if the woman has a manic episode in which lithium is considered the drug of choice. *Diazepam* (Valium) and *amitriptyline* (Elavil), although less closely associated with birth defects than is lithium, should be avoided during pregnancy if at all possible.

30.4. The answer is D (*Synopsis VI*, pages 637–638; *CTP V*, pages 1593–1594).

Sympathomimetics are not one of the classes of antipsychotic medications; they are useful in treating some patients with depression. Nine classes of drugs are grouped together as antipsychotics: (1) *phenothiazines*, (2) *thioxanthenes*, (3) dihydroindoles, (4) *butyrophenones*, (5) diphenylbutylpiperidines, (6) benzamides, (7) *dibenzoxazepines*, (8) dibenzodiazepines, and (9) Rauwolfia.

Sympathomimetics work by decreasing the release of catecholamines. Examples of sympathomimetics are dextroamphetamine (Dexedrine) and methylphenidate (Ritalin).

30.5. The answer is D (*Synopsis VI*, pages 640–646; *CTP V*, pages 1604–1606).

High-potency antipsychotics have a higher incidence of adverse *neurological effects*, such as dystonias and extrapyramidal symptoms, than do low-potency antipsychotics.

High-potency antipsychotics include haloperidol (Haldol), fluphenazine (Prolixin), and pimozide (Orap). The potency of these compounds correlates with their high affinity for the dopamine type 2 (D_2) receptor. All available antipsychotic medications are equally *efficacious* in the treatment of psychosis at equivalent doses. Although the half-lives of the antipsychotics range from 10 to 20 hours, all the dopamine-receptor antagonists can be given in one daily *dose* once a patient is in a stable condition and has adjusted to any adverse effects. Divided doses may be helpful to increase compliance with additional medications, such as anticholinergics. Low-potency antipsychotics have a higher incidence of *cardiac, epileptogenic*, sexual, and allergic side effects than do high-potency antipsychotics. There is no relation between the *expense* of a drug and its potency.

30.6. The answer is E (*Synopsis VI*, page 627; *CTP V*, page 1575).

Propranolol (Inderal), a β-adrenergic receptor antagonist, is useful for the treatment of drug-induced *tremor, aggression*, and *social phobia*. Propranolol can be effective in the treatment of antipsychotic drug-induced *akathisia*, which can be particularly recalcitrant to drug therapy. Lithium-induced tremors may occur even when lithium concentrations are within normal therapeutic levels. Propranolol is an effective treatment to decrease this tremor.

Studies have found that β-adrenergic antagonists, including propranolol, are effective in decreasing aggressivity and violent behavior associated with schizophrenia, organic brain diseases, and conduct disorders. Propranolol has also been reported to be useful in reducing the peripheral manifestations of anxiety associated with social phobias and with stage fright.

30.7. The answer is C (*Synopsis VI*, page 617; *CTP V*, page 1612).

The primary indication for amantadine (Symmetrel) in psychiatry is for the treatment of extrapyramidal disorders—such as *parkinsonism*, akinesia, and rabbit syndrome—induced by the administration of dopamine-receptor antagonist antipsychotic drugs. Amantadine is a *dopamine* agonist (not antagonist). Amantadine augments dopaminergic neurotransmissions in the central nervous system. Amantadine is not generally considered effective for the treatment of *acute dystonic reactions*. Amantadine is relatively *contraindicated* in patients with kidney disease, not liver disease. Amantadine is excreted unmetabolized in the urine. Patients with renal failure accumulate amantadine in their bodies.

30.8. The answer is E (*Synopsis VI*, page 667; *CTP V*, pages 49 and 1591).

L-*Tryptophan*, the amino acid precursor to serotonin, has been used as an adjuvant to antidepressant drugs and lithium and has also been used as a hypnotic. In 1989 L-tryptophan and L-tryptophan-containing products were recalled in the United States because of an outbreak of eosinophilia-myalgia syndrome (EMS). Evidence points to a contaminant in the manufacture of the drug that accounts for EMS. The symptoms of EMS include shortness of breath, rashes, *fatigue*, and *swelling of the extremities. Congestive heart failure* and death can also occur. Because of the danger of EMS, L-tryptophan should not be prescribed.

30.9. The answer is D (4) (*Synopsis VI*, page 624; *CTP V*, pages 1580–1581).

Alprazolam (Xanax) is the main benzodiazepine that may be effective in the treatment of panic disorders; it is approved for use in patients with mixed symptoms of anxiety and depression.

The major clinical applications for benzodiazepines—for example, *diazepam* (Valium), *lorazepam* (Ativan), and *chlordiazepoxide* (Librium)—in psychiatry is the treatment of anxiety, both idiopathic generalized anxiety disorder and anxiety associated with specific life events (e.g., adjustment disorder with anxious mood). In addition, chlordiazepoxide is used to manage the symptoms of alcohol withdrawal; intramuscular lorazepam is used to manage drug-induced (except amphetamine) and psychotic agitation in the emergency room; and diazepam has minor analgesic properties.

30.10. The answer is E (all) (*Synopsis VI*, page 651; *CTP V*, page 1575).

Indications for lithium include *schizophrenia, major depression, impulse control disorder*, and *bipolar disorder*. Lithium is the major pharmacological treatment for bipolar disorder and is effective in its acute treatment and prophylaxis in about 70 to 80 percent of patients. The symptoms of approximately one fifth to one half of all schizophrenic patients are further reduced when lithium is added to their antipsychotic drug. Some schizophrenic patients who cannot take antipsychotics may benefit from lithium treatment. Lithium is used in major depression as an adjuvant to tricyclic and tetracyclic antidepressants or monoamine oxidase inhibitors in order to convert an antidepressant nonresponder into a responder.

Lithium alone may be effective for depressed patients who actually have bipolar disorder but have not yet had their first manic episode. It is also used to treat the impulse disorders of episodic violence and rage. Such episodic outbursts in mentally retarded patients may be reduced with lithium.

30.11. The answer is E (all) (*Synopsis VI*, pages 382 and 608; *CTP V*, page 1575).

A variety of drugs are now available to treat bipolar disorder. Lithium is still the major pharmacological treatment for the disorder, but anticonvulsants such as *carbamazepine* (Tegretol) and *valproic acid* (Depakene) are also of value. *Levothyroxine* (Levothroid) is sometimes used to augment the clinical response to lithium, especially in patients with rapid cycling of manic and depressive episodes.

Studies show that calcium channel inhibitors (e.g., verapamil [Calan]), a benzodiazepine anticonvulsant (clonazepam [Klonopin]), and an α-2-adrenergic agonist (*clonidine* [Catapres]) are also effective treatments for bipolar disorder. More evidence supports the efficacy of verapamil than the efficacy of clonidine.

30.12. The answer is B (1, 3) (*Synopsis VI*, pages 665–666; *CTP V*, pages 1644–1647).

Sedation is a common effect of tricyclic and tetracyclic antidepressants. They can be of use in the treatment of depression if one of the symptoms is insomnia. The most sedating of these antidepressants are amitriptyline (Elavil), doxepin (Adapin), trimipramine (Surmontil), and trazodone (Desyrel); desipramine (Norpramin) and protriptyline (Vivactil) are the least sedating. *Hypotension* is the most common autonomic side effect of the drugs and can result in falls and injuries to patients. Patients with preexisting cardiovascular illness are most susceptible. Other possible autonomic effects are profuse sweating, palpitations, and increased blood pressure. Anticholinergic effects are quite common but often diminish over the first few weeks of treatment. The antidepressants differ in their ability to cause dry mouth (not excessive *salivation*), constipation (*not diarrhea*), blurred vision, and urinary retention.

30.13. The answer is D (4) (*Synopsis VI*, pages 632–635; *CTP V*, pages 1681–1682).

Carbamazepine (Tegretol) is recommended for use in the United States to treat temporal lobe epilepsy and trigeminal neuralgia. Studies have shown, however, that carbamazepine is also effective in treating bipolar disorder patients. The average daily dose is from 100 to 1,200 mg. Carbamazepine *plasma levels* of 8 to 12 µg per mL are the norm. Bipolar disorder patients who respond to this drug usually have completely normal *electroencephalograms*. The most serious adverse effect associated with carbamazepine is aplastic anemia (not *transient leukopenia*). The incidence of aplastic anemia is approximately 1 in 50,000, and 50 percent of the cases result in death. If a patient does not respond to lithium or carbamazepine separately, a combination of the two drugs may be effective. Because of a few cases of synergistic neurotoxicity, the dosages should be raised more slowly than when either drug is used alone, but the drugs can be used *concurrently*.

30.14. The answer is E (all) (*Synopsis VI*, pages 206, 365, and 670–671; *CTP V*, pages 1670–1678).

The most common indication for electroconvulsive therapy (ECT) is major depression. More than 80 percent of ECT patients in the United States have this diagnosis. ECT treatment yields a quicker therapeutic response and fewer adverse effects than does treatment with antidepressants. *Delusional or psychotic depression* is particularly responsive to ECT, whereas the response of this disorder to antidepressants alone is poor. Depression with *features of melancholia* (e.g., markedly severe symptoms, psychomotor retardation, early morning awakening, diurnal variation, decreased appetite and weight,

and agitation) is the type of depression most likely to respond to ECT. Patients with nonsuppression on the *dexamethasone-suppression test* (DST), called a positive test result, and a blunted response of *thyroid-stimulating hormone* (TSH) or thyrotropin-releasing hormone (TRH) infusion are also likely to respond.

The DST is used to confirm a diagnostic impression of major depression. It tests for the hypersecretion of cortisol that is present in some depressed patients. The DST finding is abnormal in approximately 50 percent of depressed patients, indicating a hyperactivity of the hypothalamic-pituitary-adrenal axis. The TRH stimulation test is indicated in patients who have marginally abnormal thyroid test results with suspected subclinical hypothyroidism, which may account for their clinical depression.

30.15. The answer is E (all) (*Synopsis VI*, pages 643–644; *CTP V*, pages 1622–1623).

Dystonias are observed in approximately *10 percent* of patients receiving antipsychotic medication. The reaction usually occurs in the *first few hours* or days of treatment. Dystonic movements result from a slow, sustained muscular contraction or spasm that can result in an involuntary movement. Dystonias can involve the eyes, neck, jaw, tongue, or entire body. They are most common in *young men* but can occur at any age in either sex. Although they are most common with intramuscular doses of high-potency antipsychotics (e.g., haloperidol [Haldol]), dystonias can occur with any antipsychotic, although they are rare with *thioridazine* (Mellaril).

30.16. The answer is E (all) (*Synopsis VI*, pages 672–673; *CTP V*, page 1677).

Electroconvulsive therapy (ECT) has no absolute contraindications, only situations in which it poses an increased risk. Patients with *intracranial masses* and *evolving strokes* are likely to deteriorate neurologically with ECT because of an ECT-associated transient breakdown of the blood-brain barrier and an increase in intracranial pressure. ECT for such patients should be carried out only in the presence of measures designed to minimize the adverse sequelae (e.g., antihypertensives, steroids, and careful monitoring). The presence of a recent *myocardial infarction* increases the risk of further cardiac decompensation with ECT because of the increased cardiovascular demands associated with the procedure. Severe *underlying hypertension* can be a concern because ECT may cause a transient increase in blood pressure. Bringing the blood pressure into the normal range at the time of each treatment is essential in such cases.

30.17. The answer is E (all) (*Synopsis VI*, page 608; *CTP V*, page 1575).

A variety of drugs have proved useful in treating depression. *Alprazolam* (Xanax) is a triazolobenzodiazepine that appears to have potent antipanic activity; however, it has also been shown to have moderate antidepressant activity. *Methylphenidate* (Ritalin), a stimulant, has been used successfully in depression, but it is generally used in a short-term manner. Many patients become readily tolerant to its antidepressant effect.

Carbamazepine (Tegretol) was initially used in the treatment of seizure disorders. It has been found to be effective in the treatment of both mania and depression. *Lithium* is successful in treating some patients with depression, although its major indication is for mania. The onset of lithium activity is quite slow and is best supplemented by tricyclic and tetracyclic antidepressants.

30.18. The answer is A (1, 2, 3) (*Synopsis VI*, pages 669–673; *CTP V*, pages 1676–1678).

Electroconvulsive therapy (ECT) is a treatment for acute episodes of depression and may also provide *prophylaxis* against its recurrences. It is probably the safest treatment in certain special circumstances, including pregnancy and old age, and in the presence of extreme symptoms that require immediate relief. Although ECT can be administered safely during *pregnancy*, in advanced pregnancy the risk to the baby of respiratory depression secondary to anesthesia must be considered. In medically ill and elderly patients, *ECT* has less *cardiotoxicity* than do currently available pharmacological treatments, such as the tricyclic and tetracyclic antidepressants. Approximately 15 to 20 percent of patients receiving ECT are being treated for *schizophrenia*. Schizophrenic patients with acute, catatonic, or affective symptoms are the most likely to respond.

30.19. The answer is D (4) (*Synopsis VI*, pages 652–655; *CTP V*, pages 1660–1662).

Lithium-induced nephrogenic diabetes insipidus is not responsive to vasopressin treatment and results in urine volumes of up to eight liters a day and difficulty in maintaining adequate lithium levels. This syndrome can be treated with *hydrochlorothiazide* (Esidrex) (50 mg a day) or amiloride (Midamor) (5 to 10 mg a day). The lithium dose should be halved and the diuretic not started for five days because the diuretic is likely to increase the retention of lithium.

Lithium tremor affects mostly the fingers and sometimes can be worse at peak levels of the drug. It can be reduced by further dividing the dose. *Propranolol* (Inderal) (30 to 160 mg a day in divided doses) reduces the tremor significantly in most patients. *Leukocytosis* is a common and not worrisome effect of lithium treatment.

Lithium also affects thyroid function, causing a generally benign and often transient diminution in the concentrations of circulating thyroid hormones. Lithium-induced *hyperthyroidism* has been reported rarely.

30.20–30.23

30.20. The answer is C (*Synopsis VI*, page 674; *CTP V*, page 1602).

30.21. The answer is A (*Synopsis VI*, pages 673–674; *CTP V*, pages 1685–1686).

30.22. The answer is B (*Synopsis VI*, page 675; *CTP V*, pages 1679–1680).

30.23. The answer is D (*Synopsis VI*, page 676; *CTP V*, pages 658 and 1686).

Light therapy, also called phototherapy, involves exposing patients to artificial light sources. The major indication for this treatment is the *seasonal pattern of major depression*, a constellation of depressive symptoms that occurs during the fall and the winter and disappears during the spring and the summer. It is also called seasonal pattern mood disorder and seasonal affective disorder (SAD).

In psychosurgery the brain is modified to reduce the symptoms of severely ill psychiatric patients who have not responded to more traditional treatments. A reasonable guideline is that the disorder should have been present for at least three years, during which a variety of alternative treatments were attempted. Chronic, severe, intractable *major depression* is one of the disorders sometimes responsive to psychosurgery, although it is a treatment of last resort and is rarely used or recommended.

The most commonly performed psychosurgical procedure is an anterior cingulotomy, thought to work by disrupting the thalamofrontal tracts. A less common technique is thalamotomy, which some workers believe to be the most useful psychosurgical procedure to treat intractable depression. This lesion destroys the dorsomedial nucleus of the thalamus. A third procedure is the lesioning of the substantia innominata. Psychosurgical procedures destroy either specific brain regions (e.g., frontal lobotomies, cingulotomies) or connecting tracts (e.g., tractotomies, leukotomies). Psychosurgery is used sparingly, if at all, to reduce the symptoms of severely ill psychiatric patients who have not responded adequately to more traditional treatments. Stereotactic neurosurgical equipment now allows the neurosurgeon to place discrete lesions in the brain. Radioactive implants, cryoprobes, electrical coagulation, proton beams, and ultrasonic waves are used to make the actual lesion. Few psychosurgical procedures are performed in the United States.

To make it easier to gather information during a psychiatric interview, some psychiatrists advocate drug-assisted interviewing. The common use of an intravenous (IV) injection of amobarbital (Amytal) led to the popular name of Amytal interview for this technique. The most common reasons for an Amytal interview are uninformative or mute patients, *catatonia*, and conversion disorder. Mute patients with a psychiatric disorder may have catatonic schizophrenia, and IV barbiturates may help in temporarily activating them.

Acupuncture is the stimulation of specific points on the body with electrical stimulation or transcutaneous needle insertion. Several American investigators have reported that acupuncture is an effective treatment of some patients with *chemical addictions* (e.g., nicotine, caffeine, cocaine, heroin).

30.24–30.28

30.24. The answer is E (*Synopsis VI*, pages 667–668; *CTP V*, pages 49 and 1591).

30.25. The answer is C (*Synopsis VI*, page 621; *CTP V*, page 1294).

30.26. The answer is A (*Synopsis VI*, pages 635–636; *CTP V*, page 2042).

30.27. The answer is B (*Synopsis VI*, pages 619–620; *CTP V*, page 1589).

30.28. The answer is D (*Synopsis VI*, page 622; *CTP V*, pages 1579–1580).

Chloral hydrate (Noctec) is a commonly used hypnotic that has an alcohol base. It is a relatively short-acting drug that is useful in treating mild complaints of initial insomnia. Its major adverse effect is occasional severe *gastritis or ulceration.*

Antihistamines have sedative effects in some adults, and one such drug, diphenhydramine (Benadryl), is used as a *sedative* in children and the elderly. Antihistamines are indicated in patients with mild symptoms or in patients who cannot tolerate other sedative-hypnotics, such as diazepam (Valium).

Meprobamate (Miltown) is a carbamate that is effective as an anxiolytic, sedative, hypnotic, and muscle relaxant. Carbamates have a lower therapeutic index and a higher abuse potential than do benzodiazepines. The carbamates may have even more abuse potential and may be more dependence-inducing than all the barbiturates. Fatal overdoses can occur with meprobamate in doses as low as 12 g (thirty 400-mg tablets) without any other sedatives ingested. It is *contraindicated* in acute intermittent porphyria.

Glutethimide (Doriden) has a slow and unpredictable absorption after oral administration. It is a class of drugs more subject to abuse and more lethal in overdose than are the barbiturates and carbamates. It is a rare patient for whom treatment with these drugs is indicated. It is highly toxic, with reports of patients' dying from a single dose as low as 5 g—ten 500-mg tablets. *Hemoperfusion* using a column containing Amberlite has demonstrated high clearance rates and has proved useful in overdoses.

L-Tryptophan is an amino acid that, when taken in a dose of 1 to 6 g, is an effective hypnotic. It is thought to work by increasing the concentrations of brain serotonin. A reasonable *loading dose* can be obtained from a large glass of milk.

30.29–30.30

30.29. The answer is B (*Synopsis VI*, pages 620–622; *CTP V*, pages 1435 and 1579–1580).

30.30. The answer is B (*Synopsis VI*, pages 620–622; *CTP V*, pages 1435 and 1579–1580).

The benzodiazepines bind to specific receptor sites that are associated with the γ-aminobutyric acid (GABA) receptor-chloride ion channel complex. Benzodiazepine binding increases the affinity of the GABA receptor for GABA, thereby increasing the flow of chloride ions into the neurons. The mechanism of action for the barbiturates is thought also to involve the GABA receptor-chloride ion channel complex. The adverse effects of barbiturates are similar to the effects of benzodiazepines, including cognitive disorganization, rare paradoxical increases in aggression, and hyperactivity. Overdoses with benzodiazepines generally have a favorable outcome unless other drugs (e.g., alcohol) have also been ingested. In that case, respiratory depression, coma, seizures, and death are much more likely.

Barbiturates are *often lethal* by themselves in overdoses because of respiratory depression, although clearly the lethality increases if the drug is combined with alcohol. The barbiturates differ from the benzodiazepines in their *marked development of dependence*, high abuse potential, and low therapeutic index. The symptoms of barbiturate withdrawal are similar to but more marked than the symptoms of benzodiazepine withdrawal.

30.31–30.32

30.31. The answer is A (*Synopsis VI*, pages 623–624; *CTP V*, pages 1580–1581).

30.32. The answer is B (*Synopsis VI*, pages 623–624; *CTP V*, pages 1580–1581).

Absorption, attainment of peak levels, and onset of action are most rapid for the following drugs in each class: 2-keto—diazepam (Valium); 3-hydroxy—lorazepam (Ativan); triazolo—both alprazolam (Xanax) and triazolam (Halcion). The rapid onset of effects for these drugs can be partly attributed to their high lipid solubility. Diazepam (Valium), as well as most other 2-ketobenzodiazepines, is metabolized first to desmethyldiazepam (Nordazepam), then to oxazepam (Serax), and finally to glucuronide. This slow metabolism leads to half-lives of 30 to 100 hours. The 3-hydroxybenzodiazepines have short half-lives because they are directly metabolized by glucuronidation and, thus, have no active metabolites. The triazolobenzodiazepines, alprazolam and triazolam, are hydroxylated before they undergo *glucuronidation*. Several benzodiazepines are available in parenteral forms for intramuscular (IM) administration, but only lorazepam (a 3-hydroxybenzodi-azepine) has rapid and reliable absorption from the IM route. The appearance of a withdrawal syndrome from benzodiazepines depends on the length of time a patient has taken the drug, the dose, the rate at which the drug is tapered, and the half-life. The development of a severe withdrawal syndrome is seen only in patients who have taken high doses for long periods of time. The appearance of the *withdrawal syndrome* may be delayed for one to two weeks in patients who have been taking 2-ketobenzodiaze-pines (e.g., diazepam) with long half-lives. Both diazepam and alprazolam are likely to produce a withdrawal syndrome; however, a number of studies have reported that patients taking alprazolam seem to have a more severe withdrawal syndrome than those taking diazepam.

30.33–30.36

30.33. The answer is A (*Synopsis VI*, pages 649–650; *CTP V*, pages 1190 and 1631).

30.34. The answer is B (*Synopsis VI*, page 661; *CTP V*, pages 1190 and 1630).

30.35. The answer is B (*Synopsis VI*, page 661; *CTP V*, pages 1190 and 1630).

30.36. The answer is A (*Synopsis VI*, pages 649–650; *CTP V*, pages 1190 and 1631).

Fluoxetine (Prozac) is an antidepressant drug that has a highly selective blockade of the reuptake of serotonin. Fluoxetine has no anticholinergic, antihistaminergic or anti-α_1-adrenergic activity, and so it has the least adverse effects of the available antidepressants.

Fluoxetine is metabolized to an active compound, norfluoxetine, in the liver. The half-life of fluoxetine is two to three days; the half-life of norfluoxetine is seven to nine days. Because of this *long half-life*, steady-state levels are not attained until after two to three weeks at a stable dosage. Although some antidepressant effects may be seen in the first three weeks, it is reasonable to wait to evaluate the antidepressant activity until the patient has been on the medication for four to six weeks. The most common adverse effects of fluoxetine, such as *insomnia and nervousness,* involve the central nervous system and the gastrointestinal system. Anorgasmia and delayed orgasm occur in about 5 percent of patients, and rashes appear in 4 percent of patients receiving fluoxetine. Fluoxetine is available in 20 mg tablets. The maximum daily dose recommended is 80 mg.

Trazodone (Desyrel) is an antidepressant that also acts as a specific inhibitor of serotonin reuptake. It has a half-life of 6 to 11 hours. Trazodone is available in tablets that can be divided into 50, 75, 100, 150, and 300 mg sizes. The usual starting dose is 50 mg by mouth the first day. The dosage can be increased to 50 mg by mouth twice a day the second day and possibly 50 mg by mouth three times a day

the third or fourth day if the patient has no problems with sedation or orthostatic hypotension. The therapeutic range for trazodone is *200–600 mg a day* in divided doses. It is reasonable practice to titrate a patient up to 300 mg a day and then evaluate the need for further dosage increases on the basis of the presence or absence of initial signs of clinical improvement.

The most common adverse effects associated with trazodone are sedation, *orthostatic hypotension*, dizziness, headaches, and nausea. Dry mouth is present in some patients as a result of adrenergic blockade. Trazodone is associated with the rare occurrence of priapism, prolonged erection in the absence of sexual stimuli. The patient should be advised that, if his erections are gradually becoming more frequent or prolonged, he should report it to his doctor, who should consider changing to another antidepressant medication.

30.37–30.38

30.37. The answer is A (*Synopsis VI*, page 628; *CTP V*, page 924).

30.38. The answer is B (*Synopsis VI*, page 630; *CTP V*, page 1665).

Bupropion (Wellbutrin) is a unicyclic antidepressant. Because seizures occur in some patients, specific guidelines concern the initiation and the maintenance dosages of bupropion. Treatment of the average adult patient should be started at 100 mg by mouth twice a day. On the fourth day of treatment, the dosage can be raised to 100 mg by mouth three times a day. Since 300 mg is the recommended daily dosage, it seems reasonable to maintain the patient on this dosage for several weeks before increasing the dosage further. Because of the risk of seizures, increases in dosage should never exceed more than 100 mg in a three-day period, a single dose of bupropion should never exceed 150 mg, and the total daily dose should not exceed 450 mg. Bupropion should not be coadministered with monoamine oxidase inhibitors. The major indication for bupropion is the treatment of *major depression.* It is as effective as the standard antidepressants and is associated with significantly fewer adverse effects than the standard antidepressants.

Buspirone (BuSpar) is an azaspirodecanedione anxiolytic drug. Buspirone does not affect the GABA-associated receptor mechanism. It acts as an agonist on serotonin type 1A receptors. The primary indication for buspirone is anxiety, particularly *generalized anxiety disorder.* Buspirone is not effective in the treatment of withdrawal from benzodiazepines, alcohol, and other sedative drugs because it does not affect the GABA-channel complex.

Buspirone has no immediate effect. It takes two to four weeks to have its full clinical effect. Buspirone is not associated with any abuse potential or withdrawal phenomenon.

30.39–30.42

30.39. The answer is A (*Synopsis VI*, pages 647–649; *CTP V*, page 1610).

30.40. The answer is A (*Synopsis VI*, pages 647–649; *CTP V*, page 1621).

30.41. The answer is A (*Synopsis VI*, pages 647–649; *CTP V*, page 1625).

30.42. The answer is B (*Synopsis VI*, page 624; *CTP V*, pages 1682–1683).

Clozapine (Clozaril) is a newly available alternative drug for the treatment of *psychotic disorders*, particularly schizophrenia. Clozapine is a dibenzodiazepine but should not be confused with the drug clonazepam (Klonopin), which is a benzodiazepine. Clozapine is unique among the antipsychotics in that it is not associated with extrapyramidal adverse effects and probably does not cause either tardive dyskinesia or neuroleptic malignant syndrome. The major disadvantage of clozapine is a 1 to 2 percent incidence of *agranulocytosis* in patients who take the drug. Agranulocytosis can appear precipitously or gradually; it most often develops in the first six months of treatment, although it can appear much later. Clozapine is also associated with the development of benign cases of leukocytosis, leukopenia, eosinophilia, and elevated erythrocyte sedimentation rates.

Clozapine is associated with the development of *seizures*. Approximately 14 percent of patients taking more than 600 mg a day of clozapine, 1.8 percent of patients taking 300 to 600 mg a day, and 0.6 percent of patients taking less than 300 mg a day have seizures. Clozapine differs from all other available antipsychotic drugs, which have their major effects as antagonists of dopamine receptors, particularly D_2 receptors. The antiserotonergic (5HT2), antiadrenergic (α_1 and α_2), anticholinergic (muscarinic), and antihistaminergic activities of clozapine are significantly more potent than its antidopaminergic activity. Moreover, its D_1 antagonist activity is much greater than its D_2 antagonist activity.

The sole indication for clozapine at this time is the treatment of psychotic patients, usually those affected with schizophrenia, who have not responded to traditional antipsychotic drugs or who cannot tolerate the adverse effects associated with those drugs. Clozapine has been shown to be as effective as the standard antipsychotics in both the short-term and the long-term management of psychosis. Clozapine has been reported to be more effective than standard drugs in reducing the negative symptoms of schizophrenia. Approximately 30 percent of patients who have not responded to standard antipsychotic treatments respond to clozapine treatment.

In the United States it is necessary to register clozapine-treated patients in the Clozaril Patient Management System (CPMS), which has specific guidelines for the hematological monitoring of patients.

Clonazepam (Klonopin) has been useful in the treatment of *bipolar disorder*. Clonazepam is effective in the treatment of acute mania. It is also used as an adjuvant to lithium in lieu of antipsychotics. As an adjuvant to lithium, clonazepam may result in a longer time between cycles and in fewer depressive episodes. Clonazepam and alprazolam (Xanax) have been shown to be useful in the treatment of panic disorder, with and without agoraphobia, and in the treatment of social phobias.

30.43–30.46

30.43. The answer is D (*Synopsis VI*, page 610; *CTP V*, pages 1598–1600).

30.44. The answer is A (*Synopsis VI*, page 610; *CTP V*, pages 1598–1600).

30.45. The answer is B (*Synopsis VI*, page 610; *CTP V*, pages 1598–1600).

30.46. The answer is C (*Synopsis VI*, page 610; *CTP V*, pages 1598–1600).

The dose-response curve plots a drug's concentration against the drug's effects. Drug A has a *linear dose response,* which means that larger doses produce a greater therapeutic effect. Drug D has a *therapeutic window,* which means that both low and high doses are less effective than are midrange doses. The potency of a drug refers to the relative dose required to achieve a certain effect. Haloperidol (Haldol), for example, is more potent than chlorpromazine (Thorazine), because only 5 mg of haloperidol is required to achieve the same therapeutic effect as 100 mg of chlorpromazine. Both haloperidol and chlorpromazine, however, are equal in their maximal efficacy; that is, they are equal in the maximum clinical response achievable by the administration of a drug. In the figure, drugs B and C have sigmoidal curves, which, in this case, means that drug B has a *greater potency* at small dosages than do equal doses of drug C. Nevertheless, drug C has a *higher maximum efficacy* than does drug B.

31 ||||||

Child Psychiatry: Assessment, Examination, and Psychological Testing

The goals of the psychiatric examination of the child are to establish a trusting relationship with the child and the parents while assessing the child's strengths and difficulties. In addition to making a formal diagnosis, the physician must assess the child's capacity to form relationships and to engage in psychotherapy. The information gained from psychological testing reflects the child's assets, as well as identifying problem areas. When reviewing the information with the parents and the child or adolescent to discuss treatment recommendations, the clinician must discuss the child's and the family's positive qualities, as well as the nature of the difficulties identified.

The psychiatric examination is based on the principle that the child's mental state in disorder, as in health, reflects biological, psychodynamic, and social forces. Transactions among these forces from birth or from before birth and at milestones during childhood or at times of unusual stress have decisive significance to the child's state of mind and have to be taken into account at the time the assessment is undertaken.

The psychiatrist needs to be aware of the feelings, thoughts, and wishes generated by the physical, psychological, and social experiences that affect the child and by the maturational changes taking place in the course of the child's growth. Healthy mental functioning in childhood is marked by evidence that the child is maintaining age-appropriate development and is, by and large, in a satisfied frame of mind.

Some of the most important information about children comes from interviews with the parents. Developmental, medical, social, and psychological histories, including relationships with peers and school adjustment, can be obtained from parental interviews. It is useful to obtain the parents' opinions about possible causes of the child's illness and to review their feelings about the disorder and about various treatments proposed.

Faced with the task of evaluating and treating a child presenting a problem such as school failure, misconduct, phobia, or aggressiveness, the psychiatrist must identify the determinants of the child's problem. Those determinants may be wholly exogenous in nature—for example, a punitive home or school environment that impels an essentially normal child to school failure or aggressive behavior—or wholly endogenous in nature—for example, a mental defect in a child experiencing school failure despite a supportive environment. More often than not, the determinants are of a mixed nature. Because of their objective and focused nature, psychological test findings may help identify the determining factors. Thus, they can be an important component of diagnostic evaluation. The test procedures are particularly useful in assessing intelligence level, probing for the presence of specific cognitive disabilities, eliciting behavioral evidence of brain dysfunction, and providing indications of the child's emotional development and personality characteristics.

Students should read the material in Chapter 31, "Child Psychiatry: Assessment, Examination, and Psychological Testing," in *Synopsis VI* and Chapter 33, "Psychiatric Examination of the Infant, Child, and Adolescent," in *CTP V*. By studying the questions and answers below, they can assess their knowledge of these areas.

HELPFUL HINTS

The terms below, which relate to child assessment, should be defined.

developmental milestones	retarded reading level	direction of cathexis
historical and factual data	fantasies	destructive symptoms
open-ended interview	developmental delay	infantile symptoms
goodness of fit	character problems	Gesell Developmental Scales
scaffolding	intelligence	Cattell Infant Scale for Intelligence
stimulus shelter	memory	Stanford-Binet test
symbolic play	affects	Binet-Simon scales
unstructured play sessions	object relations	WISC-R
temperament	drive behavior	DAT
limit setting	defense organization	STEP
confidentiality	digit-span test	improvement test
mental status examination	self-esteem	personality tests
physical appearance	adaptive capacity	CAT
separation	positive attributes	TAT
manner of relating	GAP	Blacky Pictures
CNS functions	healthy responses	Rosenzweig Picture-Frustration Study
reading and writing	Anna Freud	
language and speech	libido economy	

QUESTIONS

DIRECTIONS: Each of the incomplete statements below is followed by five suggested completions. Select the *one* that is *best* in each case.

31.1. Intelligence tests in infancy and early childhood
A. are reliable in predicting the child's intelligence in late childhood
B. are valuable only for the identification of gifted children
C. emphasize the same functions that constitute intelligence in late childhood
D. show fluctuations in I.Q. scores that are usually associated with the older child's motivation and emotional environment
E. tend to show an increased I.Q. score with age in children in socioeconomically disadvantaged environments

31.2. Countertransference phenomena include all the following *except*
A. expectations higher than the child's developmental level
B. identification with the child or adolescent
C. ambivalent feelings toward the child's siblings
D. reactions by the child to the therapist as if the therapist were a parent
E. repeated arguing with the child or adolescent

DIRECTIONS: For each of the questions or incomplete statements below, *one* or *more* of the responses or completions given are correct. Choose answer

- A. if only *1, 2, and 3* are correct
- B. if only *1 and 3* are correct
- C. if only *2 and 4* are correct
- D. if only *4* is correct
- E. if *all* are correct

31.3. In the psychiatric assessment of children and adolescents
1. adolescents should be given the choice of being seen first alone or being present during the initial interview with their parents
2. each parent should be seen in separate interviews to discern differences in their views of the child's problem
3. the clinician should ask the adolescent about the use of drugs and sexual experience
4. the younger the child is, the more information has to be shared between the psychiatrist and the parents

31.4. Which of the following statements about personality tests for children are true?
1. Personality tests and tests of ability are of equal reliability and validity
2. Both the Children's Apperception Test and the Thematic Apperception Test use pictures of people in different situations
3. The Rorschach test has not been developed for children or adolescents
4. The Mooney Problem Check List is basically a checklist of personal problems

31.5. Which of the following statements about the mental status examination of children are true?
1. Too much ease in separating from the parent may indicate superficial relationships associated with frequent separations or maternal deprivation
2. Many first-graders (6-year-olds) reverse letters
3. At age 8, children can count five digits forward and two or three digits backward
4. Hallucinations in childhood are a normal developmental phenomenon

31.6. Included in the mental status examination of children is the evaluation of
1. fantasies and inferred conflicts
2. judgment and insight
3. positive attributes
4. self-esteem

31.7. Hostility in the initial psychiatric interview by an adolescent may reflect a
1. test of how much the clinician can be trusted
2. defense against anxiety
3. transference phenomenon
4. depression

DIRECTIONS: The questions below consist of five lettered headings followed by a list of numbered statements. For each numbered statement, select the *one* lettered heading that is most closely associated with it. Each lettered heading may be used once, more than once, or not at all.

Questions 31.8–31.11
- A. Metropolitan Readiness Test
- B. Sequential Tests of Educational Progress
- C. Differential Aptitude Tests
- D. Blacky Pictures
- E. Rosenzweig Picture-Frustration Study

31.8. Scores in eight abilities and most useful in testing older children

31.9. Educational achievement battery with the main emphasis on the application of learned skills to the solution of new problems

31.10. Designed to assess a child's qualifications for schoolwork, with special emphasis placed on those abilities found to be most important in learning to read

31.11. Cartoons with blank spaces in which the child writes what he or she believes the cartoon figures are saying

ANSWERS

Child Psychiatry: Assessment, Examination, and Psychological Testing

31.1. The answer is D (*Synopsis VI*, page 683; *CTP V*, pages 516–518).

In theory, if a child's biological, social, and psychological attributes all remain stable, his or her I.Q. remains stable. However, infant tests are not *reliable in predicting* intelligence in late childhood. Infant tests are valuable only for the early detection of developmental delays and deviations, not for the identification of *gifted children*. Infant tests rely heavily on sensorimotor functions that bear little significance in the development of verbal, social and abstract skills in *late childhood*.

I.Q. scores do fluctuate to some degree. Large shifts in I.Q. scores in the older child are usually associated with the child's *motivation,* emotional independence, cultural milieu, and home *emotional environment*. The I.Q. scores of children in *socioeconomically disadvantaged* environments tend to decrease, not increase, with age.

31.2. The answer is D (*Synopsis VI*, pages 3–4, 573, and 679; *CTP V*, page 1719).

Countertransference, the phenomenon in which the therapist responds to the patient as if the patient were an important figure from the therapist's past, occurs when working with children and adolescents, as well as when working with adults. Examples of countertransference include the following: (1) the clinician's setting *expectations* higher than the child's developmental level; (2) the regressive pull experienced by the clinician, causing the clinician to *identify* with the child; (3) *ambivalent feelings* toward the child's siblings, which may be due to residual feelings from the clinician's own childhood relationships; (4) repeated *arguing with the child* or adolescent, which may suggest that the clinician has become enmeshed with the patient. *Reactions by the child* to the therapist as if the therapist were a parent is an example of transference, not countertransference.

31.3. The answer is E (all) (*Synopsis VI*, pages 678–679; *CTP V*, pages 1716–1719).

In the psychiatric assessment of children and adolescents, adolescents should be given the *choice* of being seen first alone or being present during the initial interview with their parents. In addition to seeing the parents together, the clinician should see each parent in *separate interviews* to discern differences in their views of the child's problem. Eventually, the clinician should ask the adolescent about use of *drugs and sexual experience*. The *younger the*

child is, the more information has to be shared between the psychiatrist and the parents.

31.4. The answer is D (4) (*Synopsis VI*, page 684; *CTP V*, pages 489–495).

The *Mooney Problem Check List* is basically a checklist of personal problems. It is a self-report inventory, a series of questions concerning emotional problems, worries, interests, motives, values, and interpersonal traits. The major usefulness of personality inventories is in the screening and identifying of children in need of further evaluation. Personality tests and tests of ability are not of equal *reliability and validity*. Personality tests are much less satisfactory with regard to norms, reliability, and validity. The Children's Apperception Test (CAT) is different from the adult Thematic Apperception Test (TAT) in that the TAT uses *pictures of people,* whereas the CAT uses pictures of animals on the assumption that children respond more readily to animal characters than to people. The *Rorschach test*, one of the most widely used projective techniques, has been developed for children between the ages of 2 and 10 years and for adolescents between the ages of 10 and 17.

31.5. The answer is A (1, 2, 3) (*Synopsis VI*, pages 679–680; *CTP V*, pages 1719–1726).

How and what a child plays, says, and does constitute the raw data for the mental status examination. Too much ease in *separating* from the parent may indicate superficial relationships associated with frequent separations or maternal deprivation. Excessive difficulty in separating may indicate an ambivalent parent-child relationship. Some children struggle to read or write and may spell poorly; and many normal *first-graders* (6-year-olds) reverse letters. Clinicians should look for signs of general reading backwardness, with a broadly retarded reading level (2 to 2¼ years below the predicted level) and specific reading retardation. Children exhibiting reading and writing disorders should be evaluated further by means of standardized tests. At *age 8* normal children can count five digits forward and two or three digits backward; at age 10 they can count six digits forward and four digits backward. Minor difficulties may simply reflect anxiety, but poor performance on the digit-span test may indicate brain damage (particularly left-hemisphere damage) or mental retardation. *Hallucinations* in childhood are almost always pathological and are not a normal developmental phenomenon. They may be secondary to drug intoxication, seizure disorder, metabolic disorder, infection, immaturity, stress, anxiety, mood disorder, or schizophrenia. Depending on the cause, it may be no more than a passing event and of no great consequence.

31.6. The answer is E (all) (*Synopsis VI*, pages 679–680; *CTP V*, pages 1719–1720).

Included in the mental status examination of children is the evaluation of fantasies and inferred conflicts, judgment and insight, positive attributes, and self-esteem. *Fantasies and inferred conflicts* can be assessed by direct questioning about the child's dreams, drawings, doodles, or spontaneous play. *Judgment and insight* can be assessed by exploring what the child thinks caused the presenting problem, how upset the child appears to be about the problem, what the child thinks may help solve the problem, and how the child thinks the clinician can help. *Positive attributes* include physical health, attractive appearance, normal height and weight, normal vision and hearing, even temperament, normal intelligence, appropriate emotional responses, recognition of feelings and fantasies, a good command of language, and good academic and social performance at school. Low *self-esteem* is often heralded by the child who makes such remarks as, "I can't do that" or "I'm no good at anything."

31.7. The answer is E (all) (*Synopsis VI*, page 679; *CTP V*, pages 1717–1719).

In the initial psychiatric interview many adolescents may be rejecting or even hostile toward the psychiatrist. The clinician must be patient and not jump to any conclusions. This hostility is often a *test* of how much the clinician can be trusted, a *defense* against anxiety, a *transference phenomenon*, or evidence of a *depression*. In adolescents, poor academic performance, drug abuse, antisocial behavior, sexual promiscuity, truancy, and running away from home may all be symptoms of a depression. Transference phenomena involve reactions toward the clinician that derive from unconscious feelings toward childhood authority figures, rather than from the real relationship with the clinician. That real relationship must also be examined, and the experienced clinician always asks whether the patient's reaction is justified.

31.8–31.11

31.8. The answer is C (*Synopsis VI*, page 683; *CTP V*, pages 489–495).

31.9. The answer is B (*Synopsis VI*, page 683; *CTP V*, pages 489–495).

31.10. The answer is A (*Synopsis VI*, page 683; *CTP V*, pages 489–495).

31.11. The answer is E (*Synopsis VI*, page 684; *CTP V*, pages 489–495).

Many aptitude batteries provide a profile of scores on separate tests. An example is the *Differential Aptitude Tests*, which yield scores in eight abilities and are most useful in testing older children. Achievement tests measure the effects of a course of study. An example of an educational achievement battery that cuts across subject matter specialties is the *Sequential Tests of Educational Progress* (STEP). The main emphasis in the STEP is on the application of learned skills to the solution of new problems. Readiness tests, such as the *Metropolitan Readiness Tests*, are designed to assess a child's qualification for schoolwork. Special emphasis is placed on those abilities found to be most important to learning to read. In projective tests, the subject is assigned an unstructured task that permits an almost unlimited variety of possible responses. An example is the *Blacky Pictures*, a set of cartoons showing a small dog, the dog's parents, and a sibling. Based on the psychoanalytic theory of psychosexual development, the cartoons depict situations suggesting various types of sexual conflicts. Another example of a picture test is the *Rosenzweig Picture-Frustration Study*. This test presents a series of cartoons in which one person frustrates another. In a blank space provided, the child writes what the frustrated person may be saying.

32

Mental Retardation

The role of the psychiatrist in the field of mental retardation has shifted from the diagnosis of the disorder to include also the treatment and the prevention of both mental retardation and the psychiatric disorders from which retarded persons may suffer. Recent developments in medicine, genetics, biochemistry, and behavioral sciences require that the psychiatrist collaborate with other specialists in the diagnosis of the medical and the neurological disorders associated with mental retardation.

Psychiatrists have come to realize that mentally retarded persons may have associated mental disorders of the same types as nonretarded persons and that retarded persons can benefit from the same treatment interventions as nonretarded persons. The clinician must remember that the manifestations of these psychiatric disorders may be modified by the retarded person's developmental level and that treatment modalities must, therefore, be tailored to that level of development.

The diagnostic criteria for mental retardation of both the revised third edition of *Diagnostic and Statistical Manual of Mental Disorders* (DSM-III-R) and the American Association of Mental Deficiency (AAMD) are essentially identical and require that all three of the following be simultaneously present:

1. Significant subaverage general intellectual functioning with an intelligence quotient (I.Q.) of below 70 on an individually administered I.Q. test
2. Significant deficits or impairments in adaptive functioning for chronological age and the cultural milieu in which the person is being reared
3. Onset before 18 years of age

Mental retardation is further subdivided into four degrees of severity:

Mild: I.Q. 50–55 to approximately 70
Moderate: I.Q. 35–40 to 50–55
Severe: I.Q. 20–25 to 35–40
Profound: I.Q. below 20 or 25

These subdivisions are significantly related to cause, socioeconomic status of the parents, clinical course, and prognosis.

Persons with I.Q.s below 50 are much more likely than are persons with I.Q.s above 50 to have known biological causes for their retardation, and they are distributed statistically proportionately throughout all socioeconomic classes. A specific biological cause can be identified in about 25 percent of all cases of mental retardation. The physician must be familiar with these causes in order to counsel families regarding genetic risks, maternal immunizations, amniocentesis, proper prenatal care, and the screening of newborns for inborn errors of metabolism.

The mildly mentally retarded with I.Q.s of 50 or above most frequently have idiopathic causes and are statistically overrepresented in the low socioeconomic groups. The reason may be relative sociocultural and stimulus deprivation, poor prenatal care, and adverse environmental conditions.

Mental retardation is about 1½ times more frequent in males than in females. It is estimated that only 1 percent of the general population fulfills the diagnostic criteria for mental retardation at any given time. The incidence peaks during early adolescence, when academic and sociocultural demands increase markedly.

Current functioning, clinical course, and prognosis can be roughly estimated once one knows the person's I.Q. The I.Q. is defined as mental age divided by chronological age or 16 years (whichever is less) and multiplied by 100.

Thus, multiplying a person's I.Q. by 16 and dividing by 100 provides the approximate ultimate mental age at which that person will function as an adult. The student should remember that the approximate maximum level of academic achievement can be estimated if one considers that most children begin first grade at about age 6 years. Thus, a 12-year-old with an I.Q. of 50 functions approximately like the average 6-year-old and, as an adult, will perform intellectually at about an 8-year-old or a late second-grade to early third-grade level. Actual differences between the retarded 12-year-old and the average 6-year-old are quite apparent. They result primarily from the 12-year-old's having lived twice as long, learning much through experience, and being physically larger, whereas the normal 6-year-old is more resilient, flexible, and adaptable.

During late adolescence and early adulthood, formal schooling requirements end, and social and work situations usually become stabilized. Many persons who are mildly mentally retarded and functioning at a high level may no longer satisfy the diagnostic criteria for mental retardation at that time.

The mentally retarded cover a broad behavioral spectrum. Mildly retarded persons have much more in common with nonretarded persons than they do with the profoundly or severely retarded. All subgroups of the mentally retarded, however, are at significantly greater risk than is the general population for concomitant psychiatric disorders.

The student should know the important syndromes that produce mental retardation, along with their diagnostic manifestations (e.g., craniofacial and skeletal changes). As these syndromes are genetically transmitted in many cases, the student should know whether a particular disorder is autosomal recessive or dominant, X-linked, or unknown at this time. Such knowledge plays a role in genetic counseling of patients, which is of increasing importance in the general practice of medicine and especially in the prevention of mental retardation.

Students should read Chapter 32, "Mental Retardation," of *Synopsis VI* and Chapter 34, "Mental Retardation," of *CTP V* and then study the questions and answers below to test their knowledge of the subject.

HELPFUL HINTS

The student should be able to define the terms listed below.

biomedical and sociocultural adaptational models
AAMD
general intellectual functioning
mental deficiency
WHO
feeblemindedness
oligophrenia
amentia
I.Q.
Raymond Cattell
Arnold Gesell
Down's syndrome
PKU
rubella syndrome
cytomegalic inclusion disease
microcephaly
microphthalmia
hydrocephalus
toxoplasmosis
AIDS
toxemia
placenta previa
Ebstein's anomaly

Klinefelter's syndrome
Turner's syndrome
XO
XXY
XXXY
XXYY
trisomy 21
mosaicism
translocation
amniocentesis
hypotonia
Moro's reflex
cri-du-chat syndrome (cat-cry syndrome)
phenylalanine
dihydropteridine
biopterin
fetal alcohol syndrome
Laurence-Moon-Biedl syndrome
Möbius syndrome
neurofibromatosis
Sturge-Weber syndrome
mandibulofacial dysostosis
trisomy 18

trisomy 13
tuberous sclerosis
Niemann-Pick disease
infantile Gaucher's disease
Krabbe's disease
metachromatic leukodystrophy
Fabry's disease
Hurler's syndrome
Sanfilippo's syndrome
Morquio's disease
homocystinuria
tyrosinosis
maple syrup urine disease
urea cycle disorders
Hartnup disease
galactosemia
hepatolenticular degeneration
Menkes kinky-hair disease
Lesch-Nyhan syndrome
dermatoglyphics
hypertonia
hyperreflexia
choreoathetosis
pneumoencephalogram

porencephaly	Peabody Vocabulary Test	aphasia
Goodenough Draw-a-Person Test	alexia	Heller's disease
Benton Visual Retention Test	agraphia	fragile X syndrome

DIRECTIONS: Each of the questions or incomplete statements below is followed by five suggested responses or completions. Select the *one* that is *best* in each case.

32.1. Mental retardation is caused by known biological abnormalities in approximately
A. 5 percent of cases
B. 10 percent of cases
C. 25 percent of cases
D. 40 percent of cases
E. 60 percent of cases

32.2. The incidence of Down's syndrome in the United States for mothers age 32 and above is about 1 in every
A. 25 births
B. 100 births
C. 250 births
D. 500 births
E. 700 births

32.3. Which of the following chromosomal abnormalities is most likely to cause mental retardation?
A. XO (Turner's syndrome)
B. XXYY (Klinefelter's syndrome) variation
C. XXY (Klinefelter's syndrome)
D. Extra chromosome 21 (trisomy 21)
E. Fusion of chromosomes 21 and 15

32.4. The genetic finding most closely linked to advancing maternal age is
A. mitotic nondisjunction of chromosome 21
B. nondisjunction of chromosome 21 occurring after fertilization
C. meiotic nondisjunction of chromosome 21
D. 15-21 translocation
E. none of the above

32.5. Mental retardation should be diagnosed when the intelligence quotient falls below
A. 20
B. 40
C. 70
D. 90
E. 100

32.6. Environmental and sociocultural influences in the development of mental retardation
A. are significant in the development of mild retardation
B. include up to 75 percent of the mentally retarded population
C. include factors such as multiple caretakers
D. include inadequate infant stimulation
E. include all the above

32.7. Fetal alcohol syndrome is characterized by
A. lengthened palpebral fissures
B. midfacial hypoplasia
C. renal defects
D. macrocephaly
E. tall stature

32.8. Fragile X syndrome
A. affects only males
B. usually causes severe to profound retardation
C. is associated with schizoid personality disorder in adulthood
D. has a phenotype that includes postpubertal microorchidism
E. has a phenotype that includes a large head and large ears

DIRECTIONS: For each of the questions or incomplete statements below, *one or more* of the responses or completions given are correct. Choose answer

- A.   if only *1, 2, and 3* are correct
- B.   if only *1 and 3* are correct
- C.   if only *2 and 4* are correct
- D.   if only *4* is correct
- E.   if *all* are correct

32.9. Which of the following statements about mental retardation are true?
1. Idiopathic intellectual impairment is usually severe and associated with intelligence quotients (I.Q.s) below 40
2. Psychosocial deprivation is not believed to contribute to mental retardation
3. Rubella is second only to syphilis as the major cause of congenital malformations and mental retardation attributable to maternal infection
4. Persons with profound mental retardation (I.Q. below 20 or 25) constitute 1 to 2 percent of the retarded population

32.10. Common behavioral features of moderately mentally retarded persons include
1. egocentricity
2. organicity
3. concrete thinking
4. aggressive behavior

32.11. Tay-Sachs disease
1. is transmitted as an autosomal recessive trait
2. causes macular changes
3. causes seizures and spasticity
4. is treatable

32.12. Children born to mothers affected with rubella may present with a number of abnormalities, including
1. congenital heart disease
2. deafness
3. cataracts
4. microcephaly

32.13. The hallmarks of brain damage in older children include
1. hyperactivity
2. short attention span
3. distractibility
4. low frustration tolerance

32.14. Neurofibromatosis is associated with
1. seizures
2. large skin polyps
3. café au lait spots
4. transmission in an autosomal dominant pattern

32.15. The important signs of Down's syndrome in a newborn are
1. general hypotonia
2. oblique palpebral fissures
3. protruding tongue
4. palmar transversal crease

32.16. Maple syrup urine disease is
1. usually fatal if untreated
2. usually diagnosable only after age 6 months
3. treated by a dietary regimen
4. inherited as a sex-linked trait

32.17. Profoundly retarded preschool-age children are able to
1. develop social and communicative skills
2. profit from training in self-help
3. have fair motor development
4. get by only with constant aid and supervision

32.18. Which of the following diseases in the mother can produce mental retardation in the child?
1. Toxoplasmosis
2. Cytomegalic inclusion disease
3. Hepatitis
4. Acquired immune deficiency syndrome (AIDS)

32.19. Phenylketonuria is
1. transmitted as a simple recessive autosomal Mendelian trait
2. caused by the inability to convert phenylalanine to tyrosine
3. associated with eczema
4. reported predominantly in people of north European origin

32.20. Factors of paramount importance when interviewing a mentally retarded patient include
1. use of leading questions
2. interviewer's attitude
3. patient's mental age
4. manner of communication

DIRECTIONS: Each group of questions below consists of lettered headings followed by a list of numbered words or statements. For each numbered word or statement, select the *one* lettered heading that is most closely associated with it. Each lettered heading may be selected once, more than once, or not at all.

Questions 32.21–32.23
A. Profound mental retardation
B. Severe mental retardation
C. Moderate mental retardation
D. Mild mental retardation
E. None of the above

32.21. Capable of reaching but unlikely to progress beyond second-grade level

32.22. Can talk or learn to communicate but are unable to profit from vocational training

32.23. Can learn academic skills up to approximately sixth-grade level by late teens

Questions 32.24–32.26
A. Cri-du-chat syndrome
B. Phenylketonuria

32.24. Microcephaly

32.25. Laryngeal abnormalities

32.26. Eczema, blond hair, musty odor

Questions 32.27–32.30
A. Primary prevention
B. Secondary prevention
C. Tertiary prevention

32.27. Prenatal medical care

32.28. Genetic counseling

32.29. Behavior modification therapy

32.30. Family therapy

ANSWERS

Mental Retardation

32.1. The answer is C (*Synopsis VI*, page 686; *CTP V*, pages 1738–1745).

Mental retardation is caused by known biological abnormalities in *25 percent of cases*. No specific biological causes can be identified in 75 percent of cases of mental retardation. The levels of intellectual impairment of those with no known biological cause are usually mild, with intelligence quotients between 50 and 70. It has been suggested that this group may have mental retardation secondary to poor prenatal care, adverse environmental conditions, and sociocultural deprivation. Table 32.1 lists the DSM-III-R diagnostic criteria for mental retardation.

32.2. The answer is B (*Synopsis VI*, pages 687–688; *CTP V*, pages 1739–1740).

The incidence of Down's syndrome in the United States for mothers age 32 and above is about 1 in every *100 births*. This fact is important in genetic counseling. Amniocentesis is recommended for all pregnant women over the age of 35. Amniocentesis, in which a small amount of amniotic fluid is removed from the amniotic cavity transabdominally between the 14th and the 16th weeks of gestation, has been useful in diagnosing various infant abnormalities, especially Down's syndrome. Amniotic fluid cells, mostly fetal in origin, are cultured for cytogenetic and biochemical studies. Many serious hereditary disorders can be predicted with this method, and then positive therapeutic abortion is the only method of prevention. Figure 32.1 illustrates amniocentesis.

Table 32.1
Diagnostic Criteria for Mental Retardation

A. Significantly subaverage general intellectual functioning: an IQ of 70 or below on an individually administered IQ test (for infants, a clinical judgment of significantly subaverage intellectual functioning, since available intelligence tests do not yield numerical IQ values).

B. Concurrent deficits or impairments in adaptive functioning, i.e., the person's effectiveness in meeting the standards expected for his or her age by his or her cultural group in areas such as social skills and responsibility, communication, daily living skills, personal independence, and self-sufficiency.

C. Onset before the age of 18.

Table from DSM-III-R, *Diagnostic and Statistical Manual of Mental Disorders*, ed 3, revised. Copyright American Psychiatric Association, Washington, DC, 1987. Used with permission.

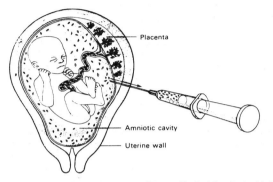

Figure 32.1. Amniocentesis. (From G B Moment, H M Haberman: *Biology: A Full Spectrum*. Williams & Wilkins, Baltimore, 1973.)

32.3. The answer is D (*Synopsis VI*, pages 687–688; *CTP V*, pages 1739–1745).

An *extra chromosome 21* (47 chromosomes) is trisomy 21, the most common genetic abnormality found in Down's syndrome and the most likely abnormality of the abnormalities listed to cause mental retardation. Abnormalities in autosomal chromosomes are, in general, associated with mental retardation. The chromosomal aberration represented by 46 chromosomes with *fusion of chromosomes 21 and 15* produces a type of Down's syndrome that, unlike trisomy 21, is usually inherited.

Aberrations in sex chromosomes are not always associated with mental retardation (e.g., Turner's syndrome with *XO* and Klinefelter's syndrome with *XXY, XXYY*, and XXXY variations). Some children with Turner's syndrome have normal to superior intelligence.

In Turner's syndrome one sex chromosome is missing (XO). The result is an absence (agenesis) or minimal development (dysgenesis) of the gonads; no significant sex hormone, male or female, is produced in fetal life or postnatally. The sexual tissues thus retain a female resting state. Because the second X chromosome, which seems responsible for full femaleness, is missing, these girls are incomplete in their sexual anatomy and, lacking adequate estrogens, develop no secondary sex characteristics without treatment. They often suffer other stigmata, such as web neck.

In Klinefelter's syndrome the person (usually XXY) has a male habitus, under the influence of the Y chromosome, but this effect is weakened by the presence of the second X chromosome. Although he is born with a penis and testes, he has small and infertile testes, and the penis may also be small. In adolescence, some of these patients begin to show gynecomastia and other feminine-appearing contours.

32.4. The answer is C (*Synopsis VI*, pages 687–688; *CTP V*, pages 1739–1741).

Meiotic nondisjunction of chromosome 21, trisomy 21, produces the majority of cases of Down's syndrome—almost 85 percent—and has been most closely linked to advancing maternal age. Paternal age has also been implicated as a factor in some studies. Nondisjunction of chromosome 21 occurring *after fertilization*—the same as *mitotic nondisjunction*—accounts for about 1 percent of Down's syndrome cases and is independent of maternal age. Translocation events constitute only 5 percent of Down's syndrome cases. Furthermore, in many cases in which an asymptomatic parent carries the aberrant chromosome in the genotype, the incidence of Down's syndrome is unrelated to parental age. If the *translocation*, for example, occurs between chromosomes 15 and 21 (15-21), the proband carries 46 chromosomes, including two normal 21s, one normal 15, and the 15-21 translocation, which carries parts of both chromosomes. Any asymptomatic parent or sibling who is a carrier of the translocation has only 45 chromosomes—missing one chromosome 21—and thus is spared the excessive genetic complement.

32.5. The answer is C (*Synopsis VI*, page 685; *CTP V*, pages 1728–1730).

Mental retardation should be diagnosed when the intelligence quotient (I.Q.) falls below 70. According to DSM-III-R, the following classification of mental retardation is used: mild (I.Q. 50–55 to approximately 70), moderate (I.Q. 35–40 to 50–55), severe (I.Q. 20–25 to 35–40), and profound (I.Q. below 20 or 25).

32.6. The answer is E (*Synopsis VI*, pages 686–687 and 692–694; *CTP V*, pages 1746–1747).

Environmental and sociocultural factors are known to influence the *development* of mental retardation. Mild retardation is significantly more prevalent among persons of culturally deprived, low socioeconomic groups than among other groups. Family members and siblings are often affected with a similar degree of retardation. Mild retardation with no known biological cause includes up to *75 percent* of the mentally retarded. Children in poor, socioculturally deprived families are subjected to potentially pathogenic and developmentally adverse conditions. The prenatal environment is compromised by poor medical care and poor maternal nutrition. Teenage pregnancies are frequent and are associated with obstetrical complications, prematurity, and low birth weight. Poor postnatal medical care, malnutrition, exposure to such toxic substances as lead, and physical traumata are frequent. Family

instability, frequent moves, and multiple but inadequate *caretakers* are common. Furthermore, the mothers in such families are often poorly educated and ill-equipped to give the infant appropriate *stimulation*. Another unresolved issue is the influence of severe parental mental illness. It has been hypothesized that such illness adversely affects the child's care and stimulation and other aspects of the environment, thus putting the child at a developmental risk.

32.7. The answer is B (*Synopsis VI*, page 687; *CTP V*, page 1743).

Fetal alcohol syndrome is caused by maternal alcohol consumption during pregnancy. The degree of retardation in the child is variable. Many children with fetal alcohol syndrome have short, not lengthened, *palpebral fissures; midfacial hypoplasia;* cardiac, not *renal*, defects; microcephaly, not *macrocephaly;* and short, not tall, *stature*.

32.8. The answer is E (*Synopsis VI*, page 688; *CTP V*, pages 1741–1742).

Fragile X syndrome is a recently discovered genetic cause of retardation. It occurs in 0.5 to 1 in every 1,000 male births. Female carriers are usually less impaired than *males* but can manifest the typical physical characteristics and mild mental retardation. The intellectual range in males is from low average intelligence to severe retardation (not *severe to profound retardation*). The typical phenotype includes a *large head* and large ears, long and narrow face, short stature, and postpubertal macroorchidism, not *microorchidism*. The syndrome is associated in adulthood with antisocial, not *schizoid*, personality disorder. Those affected by this disorder may also have attention-deficit hyperactivity disorder and specific developmental disorders.

32.9. The answer is D (4) (*Synopsis VI*, pages 685–687; *CTP V*, page 1729).

Persons with *profound mental retardation*—intelligence quotient (I.Q.) below 20–25—make up 1 to 2 percent of the retarded population; mild cases (I.Q. 50–55 to approximately 70) make up 85 percent; moderate retardation (I.Q. 35–40 to 50–55), 10 percent; and severe retardation (I.Q. 20–25 to 35–40), 3 to 4 percent. The level of intellectual impairment of persons with no known cause (e.g., *idiopathic intellectual impairment*) is usually mild, with I.Q.s between 50 and 70. No specific biological cause for mental retardation can be found in 75 percent of cases. Psychosocial (social, linguistic, intellectual) *deprivation* has been suspected as contributing to idiopathic mental retardation. *Rubella* has surpassed syphilis as the major cause of congenital malformations and mental retardation attributable to maternal infection. The children of affected mothers may present a number of abnormalities, including congenital heart disease, mental retardation, cataracts, deafness, microcephaly (abnormal smallness of the head), and microphthalmia (abnormal small-ness of one or both eyeballs).

32.10. The answer is B (1, 3) (*Synopsis VI*, page 694; *CTP V*, pages 1748–1750).

Certain behavioral patterns may be frequently associated with mental retardation because of a re-tarded person's cognitive deficits and life experi-ences. Common behavioral features of moderately mentally retarded persons include *egocentricity* and *concrete thinking*, which are related to cognitive def-icits, particularly difficulties in concept formation and abstract thinking. *Organicity*, definite neuro-logical abnormalities, usually cannot be readily linked to behavioral patterns, especially in mildly or moderately impaired persons. Such abnormalities are more common in profoundly retarded people and may be associated with hyperactivity and shortened attention span. *Aggressive behavior* is not organi-cally based and is not an especially common behav-ioral feature of retarded persons.

32.11. The answer is A (1, 2, 3) (*Synopsis VI*, page 693; *CTP V*, page 1740).

Tay-Sachs disease is caused by an inborn error of metabolism transmitted as an *autosomal recessive* trait. The disease occurs chiefly among Jewish in-fants of eastern European descent and begins between the approximate ages of 4 and 8 months. Clinical features include progressive mental deteri-oration, *spasticity, seizures*, and *macular changes*. The macular changes involve cherry-red spots in the macula lutea (or central area) of each retina, leading to the loss of visual function. The disease is pro-gressive and *untreatable;* death usually occurs within two to four years.

32.12. The answer is E (all) (*Synopsis VI*, page 687; *CTP V*, pages 214 and 1744).

The children of mothers affected with rubella may present with a number of abnormalities, including *congenital heart disease*, mental retardation, *deaf-ness, cataracts, microcephaly*, and microphthalmia. Timing is crucial, as the extent and the frequency of the complications are inversely related to the du-ration of pregnancy at the time of the maternal in-fection. When mothers are infected in the first trimester of pregnancy, 10 to 15 percent of the chil-dren are affected, but the incidence rises to almost 50 percent when the infection occurs in the first month of pregnancy. The situation is often compli-cated by subclinical forms of maternal infection, which often go undetected. Maternal rubella can be prevented by immunization.

32.13. The answer is E (all) (*Synopsis VI*, pages 695–696; *CTP V*, page 1755).

In older children *hyperactivity, short attention span, distractibility*, and a *low frustration tolerance* are often hallmarks of brain damage. The infants

with the poorest prognosis manifest a combination of inactivity, general hypotonia, and exaggerated re-sponses to stimuli. In general, the younger the child at the time of investigation, the more caution is in-dicated in predicting future ability, as the recovery potential of the infantile brain is very good. Follow-ing the child's development at regular intervals is probably the most reliable approach.

32.14. The answer is E (all) (*Synopsis VI*, page 690; *CTP V*, pages 214 and 1744).

Neurofibromatosis is associated with *seizures, large skin polyps, café au lait spots* (small, discrete, pigmented skin lesions), bone lesions, optic and acoustic tumors, and transmission in an *autosomal dominant* pattern. Also known as Recklinghausen's disease, neurofibromatosis is characterized by the development of multiple, slow-growing neurofibro-mas, usually subcutaneous, along the course of any peripheral nerve. Mental retardation may or may not occur with this disorder.

32.15. The answer is E (all) (*Synopsis VI*, page 688; *CTP V*, pages 213 and 1743).

Down's syndrome is often difficult to diagnose in newborns; the most important signs include *general hypotonia, oblique palpebral* (eyelid) *fissures*, abun-dant neck skin, a small flattened skull, high cheek bones, and a *protruding tongue*. The hands are broad and thick, with a single *palmar transversal crease*, and the little fingers are short and curved inward. Moro's reflex is weak or absent. The diagnosis of Down's syndrome is made with relative ease in an older child because of the easily identifiable physical characteristics. The children with this syndrome were originally called mongoloid because of their slanted eyes, epicanthal folds, and flat noses.

32.16. The answer is B (1, 3) (*Synopsis VI*, page 692; *CTP V*, page 1741).

Maple syrup urine disease (Menkes disease) is an enzyme-deficiency disorder, inherited as an autoso-mal recessive trait, not a *sex-linked trait*. It is *di-agnosable* within the first week of life, not only after 6 months of age. The infant deteriorates rapidly and has decerebrate rigidity, seizures, respiratory irreg-ularity, and hypoglycemia. If untreated, the disease is *usually fatal*, most infants dying in the first months of life; the infants who survive are severely retarded. Some variants have been reported, with transient ataxia and only mild retardation. Treat-ment follows the general principles established for phenylketonuria and consists of a *diet* low in the three involved amino acids—leucine, isoleucine, and valine.

32.17. The answer is D (4) (*Synopsis VI*, page 686; *CTP V*, pages 1728–1729).

Profoundly retarded preschool-age children re-quire nursing care. They are able to get by only with *constant aid and supervision*. Those children who have the capacity to develop *social and communicative skills* are considered mildly retarded. Children who are able to profit from *training in self-help* and who have *fair motor development* are categorized as moderately or mildly retarded.

32.18. The answer is E (all) (*Synopsis VI*, page 687; *CTP V*, pages 1742–1745).

Toxoplasmosis, cytomegalic inclusion disease, and acquired immune deficiency syndrome (AIDS) in the mother can produce mental retardation in the child. *Toxoplasmosis* results from the presence in various tissues of *Toxoplasma gondii*, usually acquired from the feces of cats, undercooked meat, or aerosol or mucous contamination. Except in immunologically depressed persons and in fetuses, most infections exhibit mild symptoms.

Cytomegalic inclusion disease results from a viral infection—cytomegalovirus, a member of the herpesvirus family—that causes enlargement of the cells of certain organs and the development of inclusion bodies in the nucleus and cytoplasm. It is noted in about 1 in every 200 live births and is thought to cause mental retardation in 10 percent of all cases. In many cases, cytomegalic inclusion disease remains dormant in the mother. Children with mental retardation from this disease frequently have cerebral calcification, microcephaly, or hydrocephalus.

The pregnancy of a woman who has a confirmed case of *AIDS* usually results in fetal death, stillbirth, spontaneous abortion, or death within a few years. Because the virus is known to affect the brain tissue directly, children born to such mothers show signs of brain damage with varying degrees of mental retardation.

Brain damage to the fetus from maternal *hepatitis* has also been reported.

32.19. The answer is E (all) (*Synopsis VI*, pages 688 and 692; *CTP V*, pages 214, 1739, and 1741).

Phenylketonuria (PKU) is transmitted as a *simple recessive autosomal* Mendelian trait. Although the disease is reported predominantly in people of *north European origin*, sporadic cases have been described in blacks, Yemenite Jews, and Asians. The frequency among institutionalized mentally retarded people is about 1 percent.

The basic metabolic defect in PKU is an *inability to convert phenylalanine*, an essential amino acid, to tyrosine because of the absence or inactivity of the liver enzyme phenylalanine hydroxylase, which catalyzes the conversion.

The majority of patients with PKU are severely retarded, but some patients are reported to have borderline or normal intelligence. *Eczema* and convulsions are present in about one third of all cases. Although the clinical picture varies, typical PKU children are hyperactive and exhibit erratic, unpredictable behavior that makes them difficult to manage. They have frequent temper tantrums and often

display bizarre movements of their bodies and upper extremities and twisting hand mannerisms; their behavior sometimes resembles that of autistic or schizophrenic children. Verbal and nonverbal communication is usually severely impaired or nonexistent. Coordination is poor, and the patients have many perceptual difficulties.

32.20. The answer is C (2, 4) (*Synopsis VI*, page 695; *CTP V*, pages 1753–1754).

Two factors are of paramount importance when interviewing a mentally retarded patient: the *interviewer's attitude* and the *manner of communication*. The interviewer should not be guided by the *patient's mental age*, as it cannot fully characterize the person. A mildly retarded adult with a mental age of 10 is not a 10-year-old child. When addressed as children, some retarded people become justifiably insulted, angry, and uncooperative. Others may assume the child's role because they think it is expected of them. *Leading questions* should be avoided, as retarded persons may be suggestible and wish to please others. However, subtle directiveness, structure, and reinforcements may be necessary to keep them on the task or topic.

32.21–32.23

32.21. The answer is C (*Synopsis VI*, page 686; *CTP V*, pages 1750–1752).

32.22. The answer is B (*Synopsis VI*, page 686; *CTP V*, pages 1750–1752).

32.23. The answer is D (*Synopsis VI*, page 686; *CTP V*, pages 1750–1752).

School-age children (above the age of 6) who are severely retarded *can talk or learn to communicate* but are unable to profit from vocational training. Moderately retarded school-age children are capable of reaching but unlikely to progress beyond a *second-grade level*. They can usually profit from training in social and occupational skills, although it is often difficult for them to achieve social conformity. Mildly mentally retarded school-age children can learn academic skills up to approximately *sixth-grade level* by their late teens and can be guided toward social conformity. Profoundly mentally retarded school-age children have some motor development present; they may respond to minimal or limited training in self-help.

32.24–32.26

32.24. The answer is A (*Synopsis VI*, page 688; *CTP V*, page 1743).

32.25. The answer is A (*Synopsis VI*, page 688; *CTP V*, page 1743).

32.26. The answer is B (*Synopsis VI*, pages 688 and 692–693; *CTP V*, page 1741).

Children with cat-cry (cri-du-chat) syndrome are missing part of the fifth chromosome. Phenylketonuria (PKU) is an inborn error of metabolism transmitted as a simple recessive autosomal trait. The basic metabolic defect in PKU is an inability to convert phenylalanine, an essential amino acid, to tyrosine because of the absence or inactivity of the liver enzyme phenylalanine hydroxylase, which catalyzes the conversion. Severe mental retardation is seen in both cri-du-chat syndrome and PKU. *Microcephaly* (abnormally small head), low-set ears, oblique palpebral (eyelid) fissures, hypertelorism (abnormal distance between two paired organs), micrognathia (smallness of the jaw) and the characteristic catlike cry—a result of *laryngeal abnormalities*—are all part of the cri-du-chat syndrome. PKU has been associated with *eczema, blond hair, and a musty odor.* In cases of PKU, early diagnosis is important, as a low phenylalanine diet significantly improves both behavior and developmental progress. The best results are obtained when dietary treatment is started before 6 months of age. The prognosis for cri-du-chat syndrome is poor.

32.27–32.30

32.27. The answer is A (*Synopsis VI*, page 697; *CTP V*, pages 1764–1765).

32.28. The answer is A (*Synopsis VI*, page 697; *CTP V*, pages 1764–1765).

32.29. The answer is C (*Synopsis VI*, pages 697–698; *CTP V*, pages 1764–1765).

32.30. The answer is C (*Synopsis VI*, pages 697–698; *CTP V*, pages 1764–1765).

Primary prevention refers to efforts and actions taken to eliminate or reduce the factors that lead to mental retardation. Examples of primary prevention include prenatal and postnatal *medical care, genetic counseling* for families with a history of a genetic disorder leading to mental retardation, and early childhood enrichment programs. Secondary prevention is treatment that shortens the course of an illness. Examples are thyroid medication for hypothyroidism and dietary restriction for metabolic disorders. Tertiary prevention is designed to minimize the sequelae or consequent handicaps caused by a disorder. Examples of tertiary prevention are *behavior modification therapy*, especially positive reinforcement, to reduce maladaptive behaviors in mentally retarded persons and *family therapy* if the family needs assistance in dealing with a mentally retarded family member. Parental counseling is often helpful in allowing parents to express their feelings regarding their child's disorder and future.

33

Pervasive Developmental Disorders

Pervasive developmental disorders (PDDs), the most severe psychiatric disturbances of childhood, involve impairments in social relatedness and communication and a markedly restricted repertoire of interests and activities. These disorders were previously called childhood psychoses.

The pervasive developmental disorders first entered the official diagnostic nomenclature of the American Psychiatric Association in 1980. Autistic disorder is the only subgroup recognized by the revised third edition of *Diagnostic and Statistical Manual of Mental Disorders* (DSM-III-R), with all other cases being classified as PDD not otherwise specified (NOS). The DSM-III-R diagnostic criteria for autistic disorder should be reviewed carefully; the examples accompanying them vividly illustrate many of the most characteristic behaviors of autistic children. The majority of children with PDDs have concomitant delays or quantitative developmental abnormalities as well. A reasonable estimate is that about 50 percent are moderately, severely, or profoundly retarded (intelligence quotient less than 50); about 25 percent are mildly retarded (I.Q. between 50 and 70); and about 25 percent have I.Q.s over 70. However, I.Q. is not taken into consideration in making the diagnosis of a PDD. There are great differences between severely retarded children with autistic disorders and those autistic children with approximately normal intelligence. To avoid serious diagnostic error, one must always compare the autistic child with a child of similar chronological age and intelligence (either normal or retarded) who has no additional psychiatric impairment.

Autistic disorder is rare, with a prevalence of about 4 or 5 cases per 10,000 children. It is diagnosed about three to five times more frequently in boys than in girls. The risk of autism in siblings of autistic children is increased by up to 50 times.

Three misconceptions about autism are particularly important to correct:

1. Virtually all serious investigators agree that autistic disorder is causatively heterogeneous and results from biological abnormalities affecting the central nervous system; it is not psychodynamically caused by "refrigerator mothers" or "schizophrenogenic parents," as some of the literature once suggested.
2. Autistic disorder appears to be distributed throughout all socioeconomic classes. Early studies suggesting an unusually high preponderance of cases in families of high socioeconomic status were highly influenced by referral artifacts.
3. Autistic disorder is not related to schizophrenia. It is not the earliest form of schizophrenia; it is unusual for a person with autistic disorder to later fulfil the diagnostic criteria for schizophrenia.

To date, no treatment has proved satisfactory for autistic disorder. Early identification and placement in a therapeutic nursery—stressing a psychoeducational approach and the development of language, self-care, and social skills and the decrease of behavioral symptoms—are recommended. Auxiliary treatment with an antipsychotic, such as haloperidol (Haldol), in low doses often appears to facilitate treatment.

Autistic disorder has a chronic course and a guarded prognosis. Autistic children who develop the use of communicative language by age 5 and those children with high I.Q.s have the best outcomes. Extremely few, perhaps 1 or 2 percent, may attain an appearance of relative normality, but social awkwardness and ineptness usually persist. Puberty may either exacerbate or ameliorate the condition. Up to 25 percent of all autistic children, the large majority of whom have I.Q.s of less than 50, have a seizure disorder by adulthood.

Schizophrenia with childhood onset was formally separated from autistic disorder in 1980. Evidence showed that the family history, the age of onset, clinical signs and symptoms, the course, and the prognosis were different for the two disorders. In general, schizophrenia with childhood onset is easily differentiated from au-

tistic disorder by those parameters. The student should be aware of the diagnosis, treatment, and outcome for schizophrenia with childhood onset.

Readers are referred to Chapter 33 of *Synopsis VI*, "Pervasive Developmental Disorders," and to Chapter 35 of *CTP V*, "Pervasive Developmental Disorders," and should then study the questions and answers below to assess their knowledge of the subject.

HELPFUL HINTS

The following terms relating to pervasive developmental disorders should be known.

pervasive developmental disorder	CT scans	encopresis
autistic disorder	grand mal seizures	splinter functions
Leo Kanner	EEG abnormalities	islets of precocity
extreme autistic aloneness	failed cerebral lateralization	idiot savant
echolalia	concordance rates	childhood schizophrenia
pronominal reversal	physical characteristics	developmental language disorder
monotonous repetition	dermatoglyphics	acquired aphasia
rote memory	eye contact	congenital deafness
dread of change	attachment behavior	disintegrative (regressive) psychoses
abnormal relationships	separation anxiety	psychoses
prevalence	language deviance and delay	insight-oriented psychotherapy
sex distribution	voice quality and rhythm	educational and behavioral treatments
social class	play	treatments
psychodynamic and family causation	rituals	tardive and withdrawal dyskinesias
parental rage and rejection	sterotypies	dyskinesias
perinatal complications	vestibular stimulation	fenfluramine
organic abnormalities	hyperkinesis	ego-educative approach
congenital physical anomalies	self-injurious behavior	low purine diet
	enuresis	hyperuricosuria

QUESTIONS

DIRECTIONS: Each of the questions or incomplete statements below is followed by five suggested responses or completions. Select the *one* that is *best* in each case.

33.1. Which one of the following statements about the pathogenesis of autistic disorder is true?
A. The parents of autistic children have been found in general to be preoccupied with intellectual abstractions and to show little genuine interest in their children
B. Parental rage and rejection have been found to play a role in the development of the disorder
C. Parental reinforcement of autistic symptoms plays a pivotal role in the development of the disorder
D. Parents of autistic children and parents of normal children have been shown to display significant differences in infant- and child-rearing skills
E. Perinatal stress seems to increase the risk of infantile autism

33.2. Characteristics thought to be associated with autistic children include all the following *except*
A. intelligent and attractive appearance
B. increased sensitivity to pain
C. abnormal dermatoglyphics
D. ambidextrousness
E. high incidence of upper respiratory infections

33.3. The category of pervasive developmental disorder not otherwise specified (PDDNOS) is
A. used for children who have experienced psychosocial deprivation
B. sometimes called Asperger's syndrome
C. never used with severe problems of social relatedness
D. never diagnosed in cases of mental retardation with behavioral symptoms
E. diagnosed on Axis I

33.4. Autistic disorder
A. occurs at a rate of 1 percent under ages 12 to 15
B. affects boys twice as often as girls
C. tends to be less severe in girls than in boys
D. is 50 times more likely in a sibling of an autistic child than in the general population
E. is found in families whose nonautistic members are likely to exhibit emotional problems

33.5. Unusual or precocious abilities in some autistic children are referred to as
A. Rett's syndrome
B. echolalia
C. splinter functions
D. stereotypies
E. hyperkinesis

DIRECTIONS: For each of the incomplete statements below, *one or more* of the completions given are correct. Choose answer

    A. if only *1, 2, and 3* are correct
    B. if only *1 and 3* are correct
    C. if only *2 and 4* are correct
    D. if only *4* is correct
    E. if *all* are correct

33.6. Autistic disorder is characterized by
1. a marked lack of awareness of the existence or the feelings of others
2. abnormal nonverbal communication
3. absence of play acting and fantasy
4. stereotyped body movements

33.7. In the differentiation of autistic disorder from mental retardation, autistic children
1. are better able to relate to adults
2. make little use of meaning in their memory and thought processes
3. do not show splinter functioning
4. fail to develop usual relatedness to other children

33.8. Effective treatment of autistic disorder includes
1. insight-oriented individual psychotherapy
2. phenobarbital
3. loosely structured training programs
4. haloperidol (Haldol)

33.9. Neurological-biochemical abnormalities associated with autistic disorder include
1. grand mal seizures
2. ventricular enlargement on computed tomography scans
3. electroencephalogram irregularities
4. elevated serum serotonin levels

DIRECTIONS: The lettered headings below are followed by a list of numbered phrases. For each numbered phrase, select the *best* lettered heading. Each heading may be used once, more than once or not at all.

Questions 33.10–33.14
A. Schizophrenia with onset in childhood
B. Infantile autism

33.10. Onset after 5 years of age

33.11. Family history of schizophrenia

33.12. Majority of cases show evidence of mental retardation

33.13. Male-to-female ratio is nearly equal

33.14. Hallucinations and delusions

ANSWERS

Pervasive Developmental Disorders

33.1. The answer is E (*Synopsis VI*, pages 699–701; *CTP V*, pages 1778–1780).

Perinatal stress seems to increase the risk of infantile autism. Autistic disorder is currently considered to have multiple causes. Evidence indicates that significant biological, as opposed to psychodynamic, abnormalities usually underlie the disorder. Autistic children show more evidence of perinatal complications than do comparison groups of normal children or children with other disorders. The finding that autistic children have significantly more minor congenital physical anomalies than do their siblings or normal controls suggests that complications of pregnancy in the first trimester are important in this disorder.

In his initial report Leo Kanner noted that the parents and other family members of autistic children were preoccupied with *intellectual abstractions* and showed little genuine interest in the children. This finding has not been replicated in 40 years. Other theories, such as *parental rage and rejection* and *parental reinforcement of autistic symptoms*, have also not been substantiated. Recent studies comparing parents of autistic children with parents of normal children have not shown significant differences in *infant- and child-rearing skills*. No satisfactory evidence shows that any particular kind of deviant family functioning or psychodynamic constellation of factors leads to autistic disorder.

33.2. The answer is B (*Synopsis VI*, pages 701–703; *CTP V*, pages 1778–1780).

Various characteristics are thought to be associated with autistic children. Many autistic children have a decreased (not increased) *sensitivity to pain*. These children may injure themselves severely and not cry. They may not complain of pain either verbally or by gesture and may not show the malaise of an ill child. Leo Kanner, who coined the term "infantile autism," was impressed by autistic children's *intelligent and attractive appearance*. They also tend to be shorter between the ages of 2 and 7 than is the normal population. Cerebral lateralization is not found in most autistic children; that is, they remain *ambidextrous* at an age when cerebral dominance is established in normal children. Autistic children also show a greater incidence of *abnormal dermatoglyphics* (e.g., fingerprints) than does the general population. A *higher incidence of upper respiratory infections* is found in young autistic children than in normal controls. Autistic children also show increased burping, febrile seizures, constipa-

tion, and loose bowel movements. Autistic children may not have elevated temperatures with infectious illness, and their behavior or relatedness may improve to a noticeable degree when they are ill.

33.3. The answer is B (*Synopsis VI*, pages 704–705; *CTP V*, pages 1780–1781).

The category of PDDNOS is reserved for cases that meet the general description of PDD but in which the number and the severity of the symptoms fall short of meeting the specific criteria for autistic disorder. Some children, described by Hans Asperger as having severe problems with social relatedness but less impaired language development than autistic children, are said to have *Asperger's syndrome*.

PDDNOS may be diagnosed when the child shows severe problems of *social relatedness* but the full syndrome of autistic disorder is not present. When *mental retardation with behavioral symptoms* is present, one finds that (1) mentally retarded children usually relate to adults and other children in accordance with their mental age, (2) they use the language they do have to communicate with others, and (3) they have a relatively even profile of retardedness without splinter functions. When both mental retardation and the syndrome of pervasive developmental disorder are present, both should be diagnosed. The developmental disorders, both pervasive and specific, are diagnosed on Axis II, *not Axis I*. Children who have experienced *psychosocial deprivation*, also known as failure-to-thrive children, may appear apathetic, withdrawn, and alienated, and their language and motor development may be delayed. These children, however, almost always improve rapidly when placed in an enriched, nurturing environment; that does not happen with children with pervasive developmental disorder.

See Table 33.1 for the diagnostic criteria for PDDNOS.

33.4. The answer is D (*Synopsis VI*, page 699; *CTP V*, pages 1775–1780).

Autistic disorder *occurs at a rate of* 0.04 to 0.05 percent under age 12 to 15, not 1 percent. Three to five times (not two times) more *boys* than girls are affected. When girls have autistic disorder, it tends to be more severe, not *less severe*. Between 2 and 4 percent of *siblings* of autistic children are also autistic, a rate 50 times higher than the general population. Clinical reports and studies find that nonautistic family members are likely to have language or cognitive problems, not *emotional problems*.

Table 33.1
Diagnostic Criteria for Pervasive Developmental Disorder Not Otherwise Specified

This category should be used when there is a qualitative impairment in the development of reciprocal social interaction and of verbal and nonverbal communication skills, but the criteria are not met for autistic disorder, schizophrenia, or schizotypal or schizoid personality disorder. Some people with this diagnosis will exhibit a markedly restricted repertoire of activities and interests, but others will not.

Table from DSM-III-R, *Diagnostic and Statistical Manual of Mental Disorders*, ed 3, revised. Copyright American Psychiatric Association, Washington, DC, 1987. Used with permission.

33.5. The answer is C (*Synopsis VI*, pages 701–703; *CTP V*, pages 1778–1780).

Unusual or precocious cognitive or vasomotor abilities are present in some autistic children. These abilities may exist even within the overall retarded functioning and are referred to as *splinter functions* or islets of precocity. Perhaps the most striking examples are the idiot savants who have prodigious rote memories or calculating abilities. Their specific abilities are usually beyond the capabilities of normal peers. Other precocious abilities in young autistic children include hyperlexia, early ability to read well (although they are not able to understand what they read), memorizing and reciting, and musical abilities (singing tunes or recognizing different musical pieces).

Rett's syndrome is a disorder of progressive mental retardation, accompanied by autisticlike and neurological symptoms, that occurs only in girls. *Echolalia* is the immediate or delayed repetition of words or phrases said to the person. Often, the speaker's tone and inflection are preserved. *Stereotypies* are repetitive behaviors, often performed rhythmically, that are not goal-directed. *Hyperkinesis*, overactivity, is a common behavior problem among young autistic children, as are aggressiveness and temper tantrums.

33.6. The answer is E (all) (*Synopsis VI*, pages 699–703; *CTP V*, pages 1778–1780)

Autistic disorder is characterized by behavioral abnormalities and includes three major clusters of developmental and behavioral diagnostic criteria: (1) impairments in reciprocal social interaction (such as a marked *lack of awareness* of the existence or the feelings of others); (2) impairments in communication and imaginative activity (such as markedly *abnormal nonverbal communication*, as in stiffening when being held, not looking or smiling at the person on social approach, and *absence of play acting, fantasy*, or interest in stories); (3) a markedly restricted repertoire of activities and interests (such as *stereotyped body movements*, persistent preoccupation with parts of objects, and marked distress over trivial

changes in the environment). See Table 33.2 for the diagnostic criteria for autistic disorder.

33.7. The answer is C (2, 4) (*Synopsis VI*, page 703; *CTP V*, pages 1782–1783).

Included in the differential diagnosis of infantile autism is mental retardation with behavioral symptoms. About 40 percent of autistic children are moderately, severely, or profoundly retarded, as opposed to approximately 15 to 16 percent of generally mentally retarded children. Mentally retarded children usually *relate to adults* and other children in accordance with their mental age, as opposed to autistic children, who fail to develop the usual relatedness to their parents, other adults, and *other children*. The social development of autistic children is characterized by a lack of attachment behavior and a relatively early failure of person-specific bonding. Mentally retarded children use the language they do have to communicate with others, as opposed to autistic children, who have gross deficits and deviances in language development. In contrast with normal or mentally retarded children, autistic children make little use of meaning in their *memory and thought processes*. When autistic children do learn to converse fluently, they lack social competence, and their conversations are not characterized by reciprocal responsive interchanges.

Mentally retarded children have a relatively even profile of retardedness without splinter functions, as opposed to autistic children, who do show *splinter functioning*. Splinter functions are also termed islets of precocity and are defined as unusual or precocious cognitive or visuomotor abilities in the context of an overall retarded functioning. The most striking examples are the idiot savants, who have prodigious rote memories or calculating abilities.

33.8. The answer is D (4) (*Synopsis VI*, page 704; *CTP V*, pages 1784–1786).

The goals of treatment of autistic disorder are to decrease the behavioral symptoms and to aid in the development of delayed, rudimentary, or nonexistent functions, such as language and self-care. Pharmacological treatment of autistic disorders include *haloperidol* (Haldol). The administration of haloperidol both reduces the behavioral symptoms and accelerates learning. The drug decreases hyperactivity, stereotypies, withdrawal, fidgetiness, abnormal object relations, irritability, and labile affect. *Insight-oriented individual psychotherapy* has proved ineffective as treatment. Educational and behavioral methods are currently considered the treatments of choice. Careful training and individual tutoring of parents in the concepts and the skills of behavior modification, within a problem-solving format, may yield considerable gains in the child's language, cognitive, and social areas of behavior. However, the *training programs* are rigorous and require a great deal of the parent's time. The autistic child requires as much structure as possible, and a daily

Table 33.2
Diagnostic Criteria for Autistic Disorder

At least eight of the following sixteen items are present, these to include at least two items from A, one from B, and one from C.

Note: Consider a criterion to be met *only* if the behavior is abnormal for the person's developmental level.

A. Qualitative impairment in reciprocal social interaction as manifested by the following:
   (The examples within parentheses are arranged so that those first mentioned are more likely to apply to younger or more handicapped, and the later ones, to older or less handicapped, persons with this disorder.)
   1. marked lack of awareness of the existence or feelings of others (e.g., treats a person as if he or she were a piece of furniture; does not notice another person's distress; apparently has no concept of the need of others for privacy)
   2. no or abnormal seeking of comfort at times of distress (e.g., does not come for comfort even when ill, hurt, or tired; seeks comfort in a stereotyped way, e.g., says "cheese, cheese, cheese" whenever hurt)
   3. no or impaired imitation (e.g., does not wave bye-bye; does not copy mother's domestic activities; mechanical imitation of others' actions out of context)
   4. no or abnormal social play (e.g., does not actively participate in simple games; prefers solitary play activities; involves other children in play only as "mechanical aids")
   5. gross impairment in ability to make peer friendships (e.g., no interest in making peer friendships; despite interest in making friends, demonstrates lack of understanding of conventions of social interaction, for example, reads phone book to uninterested peer)

B. Qualitative impairment in verbal and nonverbal communication, and in imaginative activity, as manifested by the following:
   (The numbered items are arranged so that those first listed are more likely to apply to younger or more handicapped, and the later ones, to older or less handicapped, persons with this disorder.)
   1. no mode of communication, such as communicative babbling, facial expression, gesture, mime, or spoken language
   2. markedly abnormal nonverbal communication, as in the use of eye-to-eye gaze, facial expression, body posture, or gestures to initiate or modulate social interaction (e.g., does not anticipate being held, stiffens when held, does not look at the person or smile when making a social approach, does not greet parents or visitors, has a fixed stare in social situations)
   3. absence of imaginative activity, such as playacting of adult roles, fantasy characters, or animals; lack of interest in stories about imaginary events
   4. marked abnormalities in the production of speech, including volume, pitch, stress, rate, rhythm, and intonation (e.g., monotonous tone, questionlike melody, or high pitch)
   5. marked abnormalities in the form or content of speech, including stereotyped and repetitive use of speech (e.g., immediate echolalia or mechanical repetition of television commercial); use of "you" when "I" is meant (e.g., using "You want cookie?" to mean "I want a cookie"); idiosyncratic use of words or phrases (e.g., "Go on green riding" to mean "I want to go on the swing"); or frequent irrelevant remarks (e.g., starts talking about train schedules during a conversation about sports)
   6. marked impairment in the ability to initiate or sustain a conversation with others, despite adequate speech (e.g., indulging in lengthy monologues on one subject regardless of interjections from others)

C. Markedly restricted repertoire of activities and interests, as manifested by the following:
   1. stereotyped body movements, e.g., hand-flicking or -twisting, spinning, head-banging, complex whole-body movements
   2. persistent preoccupation with parts of objects (e.g., sniffing or smelling objects, repetitive feeling of texture of materials, spinning wheels of toy cars) or attachment to unusual objects (e.g., insists on carrying around a piece of string)
   3. marked distress over changes in trivial aspects of environment, e.g., when a vase is moved from usual position
   4. unreasonable insistence on following routines in precise detail, e.g., insisting that exactly the same route always be followed when shopping
   5. markedly restricted range of interests and a preoccupation with one narrow interest, e.g., interested only in lining up objects, in amassing facts about meteorology, or in pretending to be a fantasy character

D. Onset during infancy or childhood.

Specify if childhood onset (after 36 months of age).

Table from DSM-III-R, *Diagnostic and Statistical Manual of Mental Disorders*, ed 3, revised. Copyright American Psychiatric Association, Washington, DC, 1987. Used with permission.

program for as many hours as feasible is desirable. *Phenobarbital* is not an effective treatment for the symptoms of autistic disorder. It is useful in the treatment of seizure disorders.

33.9. The answer is E (all) (*Synopsis VI*, pages 700–701; *CTP V*, pages 1776–1778).

Current evidence indicates that significant neurological and biochemical abnormalities are usually associated with autistic disorders. *Grand mal seizures* develop at some time in 4 to 32 percent of autistic persons, and about 20 to 25 percent of autistic persons show *ventricular enlargement* on computed tomography scans. Various *electroencephalogram (EEG)* abnormalities are found in 10 to 83 percent of autistic children; although no EEG finding is specific in infantile autism, there is some indication of failed cerebral lateralization. *Elevated serum serotonin levels* are found in about one third of autistic children; however, these levels are also raised in about one third of nonautistic children with severe mental retardation.

33.10–33.14

33.10. **The answer is A** (*Synopsis VI*, page 703; *CTP V*, pages 1778–1781).

33.11. **The answer is A** (*Synopsis VI*, page 703; *CTP V*, pages 1778–1781).

33.12. **The answer is B** (*Synopsis VI*, pages 702–703; *CTP V*, pages 1778–1781).

33.13. **The answer is A** (*Synopsis VI*, pages 699 and 703; *CTP V*, pages 1778–1781).

33.14. **The answer is A** (*Synopsis VI*, pages 700 and 703; *CTP V*, pages 1778–1781).

Infantile autism is defined as a pervasive lack of responsiveness to other people and gross deficits in language development, with an onset in children under 36 months of age. Childhood schizophrenia has an onset before puberty but *after 5 years of age.* There has been confusion about whether infantile autism is the earliest possible manifestation of schizophrenia or whether it is a discrete clinical entity. Currently, the evidence weighs heavily in the direction of distinguishing infantile autism from schizophrenia. Autism appears to be three to four times more common in males than in females; the *male-to-female ratio* in childhood schizophrenia is nearly equal. About 70 percent of autistic children have intelligence quotients (I.Q.s) that are less than or equal to 70, meaning that the majority of cases show evidence of *mental retardation.* Conversely, only 15 percent of schizophrenics have I.Q.s that are less than or equal to 70. Schizophrenic children experience the classic adult schizophrenic symptoms of *hallucinations, delusions*, and thought disorder. Autistic children do not experience hallucinations, delusions, and loosening of associations.

There is no apparent increase in the incidence of schizophrenia in the families of autistic children, whereas there is an increased evidence in the *families* of childhood schizophrenics. Infantile autism is considered rare; it occurs in 4 or 5 children in every 10,000 (0.04 to 0.05 percent). Because of the paucity of data, the occurrence of childhood schizophrenia is unknown, but it is possibly even rarer than infantile autism. Children with schizophrenia, like their adult counterparts, can be treated with antipsychotic agents, such as haloperidol (Haldol). Although no drug has proved specific to autistic disorder, the administration of haloperidol reduces the behavioral symptoms and accelerates learning. The drug decreases hyperactivity, stereotypies, withdrawal, fidgetiness, abnormal object relations, irritability, and labile affect.

34 ||||

Specific Developmental Disorders

The specific developmental disorders greatly affect all aspects of development, and many disabilities last throughout the child's life. These specific disorders also affect the skills needed in peer relations, social interactions, and family life. The full effects of a specific developmental disorder must be understood to provide the patient with appropriate remediation and treatment. Untreated, many affected children develop secondary emotional, social, and family problems. Therefore, the clinician must determine whether the emotional problems are causing academic difficulties or are the consequences of academic difficulties and of the frustrations and failures experienced.

The evaluation of the child or the adolescent requires an interdisciplinary team, and the remediation must also be multimodal. School programs and counseling the parents to assist their child within the family, with peers, and in outside activities are essential for a favorable outcome.

Specific developmental disorders include a variety of conditions: arithmetic, expressive writing, reading, articulation, language (both expressive and receptive), and coordination disorders. The inclusion of these categories in a classification of mental disorders is controversial because many children with these disorders have no other signs of psychophysiological disorder, and treatment often takes place within the educational system, rather than the mental health system.

The causes of the specific developmental disorders are multifactorial. Maturational, cognitive, emotional, educational, and socioeconomic factors account in varying degrees and combinations for all the disorders. Some disorders, such as those affecting writing, are frequent in families. Others, such as reading disorders, are more common in boys than in girls. Recent studies in neuropsychiatry suggest that various defects in processing visual-spatial stimuli contribute to many of these disorders. The diagnosis is not made, however, if gross defects in visual or hearing ability account for the symptoms or if a neurological disorder is diagnosed.

The most common developmental disorder is reading disorder, also referred to as dyslexia, which is found in up to 8 percent of school-age children in the United States. A variety of remedial training strategies have been developed to deal with this problem and have met with success. In this disorder (as in many others), school failure often occurs, and that experience contributes to low self-esteem and seems to confirm preexisting doubts that many developmentally disordered children have about themselves.

No methods of treating specific developmental disorders are universally accepted. The field is subject to faddish remedial approaches. These approaches have included motor and optometric retraining and vitamin and diet therapies.

The success of any treatment method depends to a great extent on the skill of the therapist using the method. The therapist's task includes coordinating his or her efforts with those of the teacher and other professionals. It also includes working closely with the parents, who are understandably anxious and must be apprised regularly of the child's status and rate of progress.

A great deal depends on the specialists' responsiveness to the developmental shifts within the child and on the flexibility with which they can adapt their techniques to individual characteristics and learning styles. A child's progress in overcoming and compensating for the disorder, whatever the treatment approach, is easily assessed through the periodic administration of standardized tests and through reports from the classroom teacher about the child's level of functional reading.

Finally, the likelihood of a successful outcome is enhanced by early identification of the problem and early implementation of remediation.

Readers are referred to Chapter 34, "Specific Developmental Disorders," of *Synopsis VI* and to Chapter 36, "Specific Developmental Disorders of Childhood," of *CTP V,* which cover all the developmental disorders mentioned above. Readers should then assess their knowledge by answering the questions and studying the explanations below.

HELPFUL HINTS

The specific developmental disorder terms listed below should be defined.

developmental arithmetic disorder
acalculia
Gerstmann's syndrome
congenital arithmetic syndrome
dyscalculia
linguistic, perceptual, attention, mathematical skills
attention-deficit disorders
project MATH
developmental expressive writing disorder
dyslexia
WISC-R
WAIS-R
developmental reading disorder
alexia
reading backwardness
developmental word blindness

reading retardation
cerebral palsy
psychoeducational tests
developmental articulation disorder
baby talk
lalling
dyslalia
functional speech disorder
infantile perseveration
infantile articulation
lazy speech
oral inaccuracy
lateral slip
palatal lisp
speech therapy
developmental expressive language disorder

developmental receptive language disorder
delayed language acquisition
decoding
functional enuresis
phonemes
encoding
audiogram
acquired aphasia
developmental coordination disorder
developmental hypothesis
organic hypothesis
Maria Montessori
specific developmental disorder not otherwise specified

QUESTIONS

DIRECTIONS: Each of the incomplete statements below is followed by five suggested completions. Select the *one* that is *best* in each case.

34.1. Janet, 13 years old, had a long history of school problems. She failed first grade, supposedly because her teacher was mean, and was removed from a special classroom after she kept getting into fights with the other children. Currently in a normal sixth-grade classroom, she was failing reading and barely passing English, arithmetic, and spelling but doing satisfactory work in art and sports. Her teacher described Janet as a "slow learner with a poor memory" and stated that Janet doesn't learn in a group setting and requires a great deal of individual attention.

Janet's medical history was unremarkable except for a tonsillectomy at age 5 and an early history of chronic otitis. She sat up at 6 months, walked at 12 months, and began talking at 18 months. Examination revealed an open and friendly girl who was touchy about her academic problems. She stated that she was "bossed around" at school but had good friends in the neighborhood. Intelligence testing revealed a full-scale intelligence quotient of 97. Wide-range achievement testing produced grade-level scores of 4.8 for reading, 5.3 for spelling, and 6.3 for arithmetic.

[From *DSM-III-R Case Book.* Used with permission.]

The most likely diagnosis of this girl is
A. developmental expressive writing disorder
B. developmental expressive language disorder
C. developmental articulation disorder
D. developmental reading disorder
E. none of the above

34.2. All the following statements about developmental reading disorder are true *except*
A. it has also been referred to as dyslexia
B. it affects 2 to 8 percent of school-age children
C. it is two to four times more common in boys than in girls
D. it does not appear to be more prevalent in family members than in the general population
E. it is associated with right-left confusion

34.3. Developmental reading disorder
A. is usually apparent by age 4
B. does not affect oral reading
C. does not affect comprehension
D. is associated with cerebral palsy
E. is not associated with difficulties in attention or concentration

DIRECTIONS: For each of the incomplete statements below, *one or more* of the completions given are correct. Choose answer

A. if only *1, 2, and 3* are correct
B. if only *1 and 3* are correct
C. if only *2 and 4* are correct
D. if only *4* is correct
E. if *all* are correct

34.4. Developmental arithmetic disorder has been referred to by various terms, including
1. acalculia
2. Gerstmann's syndrome
3. congenital arithmetic disability
4. dyscalculia

34.5. The prevalence of developmental coordination disorder has been estimated to be
1. higher among girls than among boys
2. higher among children with relatives with developmental coordination disorder than in the general population
3. higher among children with neurological disorders than among children without neurological disorders
4. as high as 6 percent in children between the ages of 5 and 11 years

34.6. Developmental articulation disorder
1. has a prevalence of approximately 5 percent in children below 8 years of age
2. may be recognized as early as 3 years of age
3. has a prevalence of approximately 10 percent in children above 8 years of age
4. is more common in boys than in girls

34.7. Developmental expressive writing disorder is often associated with
1. developmental reading disorder
2. developmental expressive and receptive language disorders
3. developmental coordination disorder
4. developmental arithmetic disorder

34.8. Terms used synonymously with developmental reading disorder include
1. alexia
2. dyslexia
3. word blindness
4. dyslalia

34.9. Skills that may be impaired in developmental arithmetic disorder include
1. translating written problems into mathematical symbols
2. recognizing numerical symbols
3. copying figures correctly
4. counting objects

34.10. Don, 3 years and 7 months old, had a complicated early medical history, including having been born 11 weeks prematurely with hyaline membrane disease and later having undergone bilateral hernia repairs. He began sitting up at 6 months, crawling at 10 months, walking at 13 months, and saying words at 12 months. At 3 years his parents noted that his speech seemed far less well developed than that of his many playmates, although most of them were younger than he. Don did not attend nursery school and had been subjected to a number of moves because of parental problems and divorce.

During the examination, Don was slow to warm up. He was extremely difficult to understand and had to augment most of his utterances with gestures to make himself understood. Most of his sentences consisted of single words that were mispronounced—for example, "gun" was "dub," "scissors" was "duhduh," and "fish" was "pet." The boy could follow commands, such as, "Get the red book and bring it to the table"; could point out body parts and objects in the room; and could produce drawings that seemed quite sophisticated for his age. Scores on several standardized tests of language development, such as the Carrow Elicited Language Inventory (CELI) and the Illinois Test of Psycholinguistic Abilities (ITPA), were significantly lower than expected, as was the verbal I.Q. from the Stanford-Binet Intelligence Scale. In contrast, Don's performance I.Q. was only slightly below average.

[From *DSM-III-R Case Book*. Used with permission.]

The differential diagnosis includes
1. mental retardation
2. pervasive developmental disorder
3. developmental articulation disorder
4. developmental language disorder

34.11. A high frequency of developmental articulation disorder has been found among children
1. from large families
2. from families of low socioeconomic status
3. with a family history of a similar disorder
4. who are left-handed

34.12. Spontaneous recovery is associated with
1. developmental articulation disorder
2. developmental receptive language disorder
3. developmental expressive language disorder
4. developmental coordination disorder

DIRECTIONS: Each set of lettered headings below is followed by a list of numbered phrases. For each numbered phrase, select the best lettered heading. Each heading may be used once, more than once, or not at all.

Questions 34.13–34.15
A. Articulation disorder caused by neurological abnormalities
B. Developmental articulation disorder
C. Articulation disorder caused by hearing impairment

34.13. Physical abnormalities

34.14. Slow rate of speech

34.15. The phonemes f, th, sh, and s are affected most commonly

Questions 34.16–34.19
A. Developmental expressive language disorder
B. Developmental receptive language disorder

34.16. Failure to develop comprehension (decoding)

34.17. Family history of the disorder

34.18. Underlying impairment in auditory discrimination

34.19. Less favorable prognosis

ANSWERS

Specific Developmental Disorders

34.1. The answer is D (*Synopsis VI*, pages 711–712; *CTP V*, pages 1790–1796).

The most likely diagnosis for Janet is *developmental reading disorder*. Developmental reading disorder is characterized by marked impairment in the development of word-recognition skills and reading comprehension that cannot be explained by mental retardation, inadequate schooling, visual or hearing defect, or a neurological disorder. Reading-disordered children make many errors in their oral reading, including omissions, additions, and distortions of words. In this case, Janet's difficulties were apparently limited to reading and spelling. Janet had average intelligence and normal scores on achievement tests of arithmetic but markedly low scores for spelling and reading.

Developmental *expressive writing disorder* is characterized by poor performance in writing and composition; developmental *expressive language disorder* is characterized by marked impairment in the development of age-appropriate expressive language; developmental *articulation disorder* is characterized by frequent and recurrent misarticulations of speech sounds, resulting in abnormal speech. The case described does not meet the criteria for any of these developmental disorders. Table 34.1 lists the diagnostic criteria for developmental reading disorder in the revised third edition of *Diagnostic and Statistical Manual of Mental Disorders* (DSM-III-R).

34.2. The answer is D (*Synopsis VI*, page 711; *CTP V*, page 1791).

Developmental reading disorder has also been referred to as *dyslexia*, alexia, learning disability, and

Table 34.1
Diagnostic Criteria for Developmental Reading Disorder

A. Reading achievement, as measured by a standardized individually administered test, is markedly below the expected level, given the person's schooling and intellectual capacity (as determined by an individually administered IQ test).

B. The disturbance in A significantly interferes with academic achievement or activities of daily living requiring reading skills.

C. Not due to a defect in visual or hearing acuity or neurologic disorder.

Table from DSM-III-R, *Diagnostic and Statistical Manual of Mental Disorders*, ed 3, revised. Copyright American Psychiatric Association, Washington, DC, 1987. Used with permission.

developmental word blindness. This disorder affects *2 to 8 percent* of school-age children, with *boys two to four times* more commonly affected than girls. Developmental reading disorder does tend to be *more prevalent* among family members than in the general population. Developmental reading disorder is also associated with *right-left confusion*, although not with laterality of handedness or eyedness.

34.3. The answer is D (*Synopsis VI*, pages 711–712; *CTP V*, page 1794).

Developmental reading disorder is usually apparent by *age 7, not 4*. Sometimes it is compensated for in the early grades and may not be diagnosed until later. All reading skills may be affected. *Oral reading* is characterized by errors of omission, distortion, and addition of words. Reading speed is slow, and *comprehension* is often minimal. There tends to be a high incidence of developmental reading disorder among children with *cerebral palsy* who have normal intelligence. It is also associated with histories of prenatal or perinatal complications, prematurity, and low birth weight. Children with developmental reading disorder often have more *difficulty in concentrating* and have shorter attention spans than do children of the same age without reading disorders.

34.4. The answer is E (all) (*Synopsis VI*, page 707; *CTP V*, pages 1800–1801).

Developmental arithmetic disorder has been referred to by various terms, including *acalculia* (inability to perform arithmetic operation, also known as *dyscalculia*), *Gerstmann's syndrome* (consisting in part of acalculia and left-right disorientation), *congenital arithmetic disability*, and arithmetic disorder. It is one of the academic skills disorders included in the DSM-III-R category of specific developmental disorders. In developmental arithmetic disorder the person's performance in daily activities requiring arithmetic skills is markedly below his or her intellectual capacity, and these impaired arithmetic skills and performance are confirmed by an individually administered standardized test.

Table 34.2 lists the DSM-III-R criteria for developmental arithmetic disorder.

34.5. The answer is D (4) (*Synopsis VI*, page 720; *CTP V*, pages 1818–1820).

In some studies the prevalence of developmental coordination disorder has been estimated to be as

Table 34.2
Diagnostic Criteria for Developmental Arithmetic Disorder

A. Arithmetic skills, as measured by a standardized, individually administered test, are markedly below the expected level, given the person's schooling and intellectual capacity (as determined by an individually administered IQ test).
B. The disturbance in A significantly interferes with academic achievement or activities of daily living requiring arithmetic skills.
C. Not due to a defect in visual or hearing acuity or a neurologic disorder.

Table from DSM-III-R, *Diagnostic and Statistical Manual of Mental Disorders*, ed 3, revised. Copyright American Psychiatric Association, Washington, DC, 1987. Used with permission.

high as *6 percent* in children between the ages of 5 and 11 years. The ratio between boys and girls is not known; however, as in most developmental disorders, *more boys than girls* are affected. No data suggest an increased incidence of this disorder among the *relatives* of children with developmental coordination disorder.

According to DSM-III-R, the essential feature of developmental coordination disorder is a marked impairment in the development of motor coordination that cannot be explained by mental retardation and that is not due to a known physical disorder—for example, cerebral palsy, hemiplegia, or muscular dystrophy. The diagnosis of developmental coordination disorder should be made only if the impairment significantly interferes with academic achievement or with activities of daily living and precludes no known *neurological* or neuromuscular disorders. However, slight reflex abnormalities and other soft neurological signs may occasionally be found on examination.

Table 34.3 lists the DSM-III-R diagnostic criteria for developmental coordination disorder.

Table 34.3
Diagnostic Criteria for Developmental Coordination Disorder

A. The person's performance in daily activities requiring motor coordination is markedly below the expected level, given the person's chronological age and intellectual capacity. This may be manifested by marked delays in achieving motor milestones (walking, crawling, sitting), dropping things, "clumsiness," poor performance in sports, or poor handwriting.
B. The disturbance in A significantly interferes with academic achievement or activities of daily living.
C. Not due to a known physical disorder, such as cerebral palsy, hemiplegia, or muscular dystrophy.

Table from DSM-III-R, *Diagnostic and Statistical Manual of Mental Disorders*, ed 3, revised. Copyright American Psychiatric Association, Washington, DC, 1987. Used with permission.

34.6. The answer is C (2, 4) (*Synopsis VI*, pages 713–714; *CTP V*, pages 1806–1807).

In severe cases, developmental articulation disorder may be recognized as early as *3 years of age*. In less severe cases, this disorder may not be apparent until age 6. The prevalence of developmental articulation disorder is conservatively estimated to be approximately *10 (not 5) percent* of children below 8 years of age and approximately *5 (not 10) percent* of children 8 years of age and above. The disorder is two to three times *more common in boys* than in girls.

Table 34.4 lists the DSM-III-R diagnostic criteria for developmental articulation disorder.

34.7. The answer is E (all) (*Synopsis VI*, pages 709–710; *CTP V*, pages 1796–1798).

Developmental *reading disorder*, developmental *expressive and receptive language disorders*, developmental *coordination disorder*, developmental *arithmetic disorder*, and disruptive behavior disorders are often associated with developmental expressive writing disorder.

The ability to transfer one's thoughts into written words and sentences requires multimodal sensory-motor coordination and information processing. DSM-III-R defines developmental expressive writing disorder as an academic skills disorder that first occurs during childhood and is characterized by poor performance in writing and composition (spelling words and expressing thoughts), considering the level of the person's schooling and intellectual capacity.

Children with developmental expressive writing disorder have difficulties in spelling, expressing their thoughts, grammar, word choices, and organizing paragraphs, which lead to general poor school performance, truancy, conduct disorder, frustration, and often depression. The DSM-III-R diagnostic criteria for developmental expressive writing disorder are listed in Table 34.5.

34.8. The answer is A (1, 2, 3) (*Synopsis VI*, page 711; *CTP V*, pages 1790–1791).

Terms used synonymously with developmental reading disorder, which involves delay and impair-

Table 34.4
Diagnostic Criteria for Developmental Articulation Disorder

A. Consistent failure to use developmentally expected speech sounds. For example, in a 3-year-old, failure to articulate p, b, and t, and in a 6-year-old, failure to articulate r, sh, th, f, z, and l.
B. Not due to a pervasive developmental disorder, mental retardation, defect in hearing acuity, disorders of the oral speech mechanism, or a neurologic disorder.

Table from DSM-III-R, *Diagnostic and Statistical Manual of Mental Disorders*, ed 3, revised. Copyright American Psychiatric Association, Washington, DC, 1987. Used with permission.

Table 34.5
Diagnostic Criteria for Developmental Expressive Writing Disorder

A. Writing skills, as measured by a standardized, individually administered test, are markedly below the expected level, given the person's schooling and intellectual capacity (as determined by an individually administered IQ test).
B. The disturbance in A significantly interferes with academic achievement or activities of daily living requiring the composition of written texts (spelling words and expressing thoughts in grammatically correct sentences and organized paragraphs).
C. Not due to a defect in visual or hearing acuity or a neurologic disorder.

Table from DSM-III-R, *Diagnostic and Statistical Manual of Mental Disorders*, ed 3, revised. Copyright American Psychiatric Association, Washington, DC, 1987. Used with permission.

ment of reading competence, include *alexia, dyslexia,* reading backwardness, learning disability, specific reading disability, and developmental *word blindness.* Alexia is defined as the loss of the ability to grasp the meaning of written or printed words and sentences. Dyslexia, incomplete alexia, is defined as a level of reading ability markedly below that expected on the basis of the person's level of overall intelligence or ability in skills. *Dyslalia* is a disorder of articulation caused by structural abnormalities of the articulatory organs or by impaired hearing.

34.9. The answer is E (all) (*Synopsis VI,* pages 707–708; *CTP V,* pages 1802–1803).

According to DSM-III-R, a number of different types of skills may be impaired in developmental arithmetic disorder, including linguistic skills, such as *translating written problems into mathematical symbols;* perceptual skills, such as *recognizing numerical symbols;* attention skills, such as *copying figures correctly;* and mathematical skills, such as *counting objects.*

Some investigators have classified developmental arithmetic disorder into several subcategories: (1) difficulty in learning to count meaningfully, (2) difficulty in mastering cardinal and ordinal systems, (3) difficulty in performing arithmetic operations, and (4) difficulty in envisioning clusters of objects as groups. In addition, there may be difficulties in associating auditory and visual symbols, understanding the conservation of quantity, remembering a sequence of arithmetic steps, and choosing principles for problem solving.

34.10. The answer is E (all) (*Synopsis VI,* pages 716–717; *CTP V,* pages 1815–1816).

The differential diagnosis includes four disorders in this case. *Mental retardation* should be considered as a diagnosis, but Don's normal developmental milestones and near-average performance I.Q. rule out this disorder. *Pervasive developmental disorder*

requires an impairment in social relationships. Although slow to warm up, Don did demonstrate social interaction and attempted to make himself understood. *Developmental articulation disorder* is ruled out because Don's problem is in finding the proper words to express himself, not in articulating certain speech sounds. The evidence that Don understands language indicates that he has an expressive type of *developmental language disorder.*

The DSM-III-R diagnostic criteria for developmental expressive language disorder and developmental receptive language disorder are listed in Tables 34.6 and 34.7. DSM-III-R also has a residual classification of specific developmental disorder not otherwise specified, cited in Table 34.8.

Table 34.6
Diagnostic Criteria for Developmental Expressive Language Disorder

A. The score obtained from a standardized measure of expressive language is substantially below that obtained from a standardized measure of nonverbal intellectual capacity (as determined by an individually administered IQ test).
B. The disturbance in A significantly interferes with academic achievement or activities of daily living requiring the expression of verbal (or sign) language. This may be evidenced in severe cases by use of a markedly limited vocabulary, by speaking only in simple sentences, or by speaking only in the present tense. In less severe cases, there may be hesitations or errors in recalling certain words, or errors in the production of long or complex sentences.
C. Not due to a pervasive developmental disorder, defect in hearing acuity, or a neurologic disorder (aphasia).

Table from DSM-III-R, *Diagnostic and Statistical Manual of Mental Disorders*, ed 3, revised. Copyright American Psychiatric Association, Washington, DC, 1987. Used with permission.

Table 34.7
Diagnostic Criteria for Developmental Receptive Language Disorder

A. The score obtained from a standardized measure of receptive language is substantially below that obtained from a standardized measure of nonverbal intellectual capacity (as determined by an individually administered IQ test).
B. The disturbance in A significantly interferes with academic achievement or activities of daily living requiring the comprehension of verbal (or sign) language. This may be manifested in more severe cases by an inability to understand simple words or sentences. In less severe cases, there may be difficulty in understanding only certain types of words, such as spatial terms, or an inability to comprehend longer or more complex statements.
C. Not due to a pervasive developmental disorder, defect in hearing acuity, or a neurologic disorder (aphasia).

Table from DSM-III-R, *Diagnostic and Statistical Manual of Mental Disorders*, ed 3, revised. Copyright American Psychiatric Association, Washington, DC, 1987. Used with permission.

Table 34.8
Diagnostic Criteria for Specific Developmental Disorder Not Otherwise Specified

Disorders in the development of language, speech, academic, and motor skills that do not meet the criteria for a specific developmental disorder. Examples include aphasia with epilepsy acquired in childhood ("Landau syndrome") and specific developmental difficulties in spelling.

Table from DSM-III-R, *Diagnostic and Statistical Manual of Mental Disorders*, ed 3, revised. Copyright American Psychiatric Association, Washington, DC, 1987. Used with permission.

34.11.   The answer is A (1, 2, 3) (*Synopsis VI*, page 714; *CTP V*, pages 1806–1809).

A disproportionately high frequency of developmental articulation disorder has been found among children from *large families* and from *families of low socioeconomic status*, suggesting the possible causal effects of inadequate speech stimulation and reinforcement in these families. The high proportion of children with the disorder who have a *family history of a similar disorder* suggests that the disorder may have a genetic component. Motor coordination, laterality, and right- or *left-handedness* have not been proved to contribute to developmental articulation disorder.

The essential feature of developmental articulation disorder is an articulation defect characterized by the consistent failure to use developmentally expected speech sounds of certain consonants. These defects include omissions, substitutions, and distortions of phonemes, most commonly those phonemes acquired late in the normal language acquisition process. Developmental articulation disorder is not diagnosed if there are structural or neurological abnormalities that are accompanied by normal language development. Although the cause is unknown, it is generally believed that a simple developmental lag or maturational delay in the neurological process underlying speech is at fault.

34.12.   The answer is B (1, 3) (*Synopsis VI*, pages 714, 717–718, and 720; *CTP V*, pages 1809, 1816, and 1820).

Spontaneous recovery is associated with developmental *articulation disorder* and developmental *expressive language disorder*. The child with developmental articulation disorder is not able to articulate certain phonemes correctly and may distort, substitute, or even omit the affected phoneme. In children whose misarticulations involve only a few phonemes, recovery is frequently spontaneous. However, spontaneous recovery is rare after the age of 8.

The essential feature of the child with developmental expressive language disorder is an impairment in the development of age-appropriate expressive language, which results in the use of verbal or sign language that is markedly below the expected level, considering the child's nonverbal intellectual capacity. The child's language understanding (decoding) skills remain relatively intact. As many as 50 percent of children with a mild developmental expressive language disorder recover spontaneously without any sign of language impairment, whereas children with a severe developmental expressive language disorder may later display the features of mild to moderate impairment.

Children with developmental *receptive language disorder* show a markedly delayed and below-normal ability to comprehend (decode) verbal or sign language, although they have age-appropriate nonverbal intellectual capacity. In most cases, verbal or sign expression (encoding) of language is also impaired. The overall prognosis for developmental receptive language disorder is less favorable than that for developmental expressive language disorder. In mild cases, the prognosis is fair; in severe cases with auditory perceptual problems and difficulties in sensory integration, memory recall, and sequencing, the prognosis is guarded.

The essential feature of developmental *coordination disorder* is a marked impairment in the development of motor coordination that cannot be explained by mental retardation and that is not due to a known physical disorder. Some studies suggest a favorable outcome among those children who have an average or above-average intellectual capacity because they are able to learn to compensate for their coordination deficits. In general, the clumsiness persists into adolescence and adult life.

34.13–34.15

34.13.   The answer is A (*Synopsis VI*, page 715; *CTP V*, pages 1808–1809).

34.14.   The answer is A (*Synopsis VI*, page 715; *CTP V*, pages 1808–1809).

34.15.   The answer is C (*Synopsis VI*, page 715; *CTP V*, pages 1808–1809).

Developmental articulation disorder is characterized by frequent and recurrent misarticulations of speech sounds, resulting in abnormal speech. The disorder cannot be attributed to structural or neurological abnormalities and is accompanied by normal language development. Articulation disorder caused by structural or neurological abnormalities, also called dysarthria, is by definition attributable to specific *physical abnormalities* of the lips, tongue, or palate. It is also associated with muscular weakness, incoordination, or disturbances of the vegetative functions, such as sucking and chewing. In this disorder, the findings in a physical examination are not normal, a critical factor that helps distinguish it from developmental articulation disorder. In developmental articulation disorder and in articulation disorder caused by hearing impairment, the physical examination findings are within normal limits. The *rate of speech* in developmental articulation disorder and in articulation disorder caused hearing impairment is generally within normal limits, although articulation may deteriorate with increased rate. In articulation disorder resulting from structural or neurological abnormalities, the rate of speech is slow, and articulation deteriorates markedly with increased rate.

A phoneme in linguistics is a speech sound that serves to distinguish words from one another. In articulation disorders, phonemes are affected. In developmental articulation disorder, the most commonly affected phonemes are r, sh, th, ch, dg, j, f, v, s, and z. In articulation disorder caused by hearing impairment, the *phonemes f, th, sh, and s* are affected most commonly. The child has difficulty in articulating these phonemes and may distort, substitute, or even omit them. In articulation disorder resulting from neurological abnormalities, any phonemes, even vowels, may be affected.

34.16–34.19

34.16. The answer is B (*Synopsis VI*, page 718; *CTP V*, pages 1813–1817).

34.17. The answer is A (*Synopsis VI*, pages 716 and 718; *CTP V*, pages 1813–1817).

34.18. The answer is B (*Synopsis VI*, page 718; *CTP V*, pages 1813–1817).

34.19. The answer is B (*Synopsis VI*, pages 717–718; *CTP V*, pages 1813–1817).

According to DSM-III-R, the diagnosis of either developmental expressive language disorder or developmental receptive language disorder should be made only if the impairments significantly interfere with the expression or comprehension of verbal (or sign) language. Thus, in the expressive type, the child's language comprehension (decoding) skills remain relatively intact, but there is a failure in the development of age-appropriate vocal expression (encoding), which results in the use of verbal or sign language that is markedly below the child's nonverbal intellectual capacity. Developmental receptive language disorder shows marked impairment of both language production and language *comprehension*. Children with receptive language disorder, as opposed to those with expressive language disorder, appear to have an underlying impairment in *auditory discrimination*. They are more responsive to environmental sounds than to speech sounds. An audiogram is indicated in all suspected developmental receptive language-disordered children to rule out deafness or other types of auditory deficit.

Severe forms of developmental expressive language disorder generally occur before the age of 3. Less severe forms may not take place until early adolescence, when language ordinarily becomes

Table 34.9
Differential Diagnosis of Articulation Disorders

Criteria	Articulation Disorder Due to Structural or Neurological Abnormalities (Dysarthria)	Articulation Disorder Due to Hearing Impairment	Developmental Articulation Disorder	Articulation Disorder Associated with Mental Retardation, Infantile Autism, Developmental Dysphasia, Acquired Aphasia, or Deafness
Language development	Within normal limits	Within normal limits unless hearing impairment is serious	Within normal limits	Not within normal limits
Examination	Possible abnormalities of lips, tongue, or palate; muscular weakness, incoordination, or disturbance of vegetative functions, such as sucking or chewing	Hearing impairment shown on audiometric testing	Normal	
Rate of speech	Slow; marked deterioration of articulation with increased rate	Normal	Normal; possible deterioration of articulation with increased rate	
Phonemes affected	Any phonemes, even vowels	F, th, sh, and s	R, sh, th, ch, dg, j, f, v, s, and z are most commonly affected	

Table by Lorian Baker, Ph.D., and Dennis Cantwell, M.D.

more complex. Developmental receptive language disorder typically appears before the age of 4 years. Severe forms are generally apparent before age 2 (mild forms may not become evident until age 7 or even older).

Developmental expressive language disorder is more prevalent among children who have a *family history* of developmental articulation disorder or other developmental disorders. There is no familial pattern found in developmental receptive language disorder.

In general, the prognosis for developmental lan-

guage disorder is favorable. Factors affecting the overall prognosis include timely institution of therapeutic intervention, hearing loss, and emotional state. The overall prognosis for developmental receptive language disorder is *less favorable* than for developmental expressive language disorder. The prognosis ranges from fair in mild cases to guarded in severe cases with auditory perceptual problems and difficulties in sensory integration, recall, and sequencing. See Table 34.9 for a comparison of these disorders.

35 ||||||

Disruptive Behavior Disorders

Many children have conduct problems at some time in their development, and a small number have a short-lived clinical syndrome at some point. An even smaller number of children have a persistent disorder that violates either the basic rights of others or the age-appropriate norms of behavior for a period of at least six months.

The disruptive behavior disorders are thought to be of multifactorial origin. When genetic risk factors are accompanied by environmental risk factors, the rates of antisocial behavior are at their highest.

Conduct disorder, a diagnosis made only in patients less than 18 years of age, has been associated with the development of antisocial personality disorder in adulthood. Conduct disorder accounts for a high percentage of the inpatient psychiatric admissions to many child and adolescent units. The core feature of conduct disorder is repetitive, persistent violation of the basic rights of others or of the age-appropriate societal rules. This disorder is more common in boys than in girls and is more common in the children of parents with antisocial personality disorder and alcohol dependence than in the general population. Chaotic home conditions and parental psychiatric impairments are implicated in the development of conduct disorder.

Conduct disorder of the solitary aggressive type is characterized by bullying, physical aggression, and cruelty toward peers; children and adolescents with this disorder display behavior that is unacceptable in almost any social setting. Conduct disorder of the group type usually occurs in the context of a peer group within which the patient has established friendships; behaviors range from truancy and stealing to serious acts against people and property. Ju-

venile delinquency is most often associated with conduct disorder of this type.

Attention-deficit hyperactivity disorder (ADHD) is the designation in the revised third edition of *Diagnostic and Statistical Manual of Mental Disorders* (DSM-III-R) for children who in the past were described variously as having hyperkinetic or hyperactive child syndrome and attention-deficit disorder with or without hyperactivity, among other terms. This disorder is a major cause of school failure and often coexists with specific developmental learning disabilities. Children with ADHD display a short attention span, leading to poor concentration, impulsivity, and hyperactivity; the onset of symptoms before age 7 is required for this diagnosis. The diagnosis is essential to consider in the differential diagnosis of a child with poor school performance, since stimulant medication may give the child dramatic relief of the symptoms. Although hyperactivity per se may remit after puberty, children with ADHD often have continued problems with concentration and impulsivity as adults. Low self-esteem and poor peer interactions beginning in childhood may also have long-term sequelae. In some children, attention-deficit hyperactivity disorder appears to be an important precursor to the development of conduct disorder and antisocial personality disorder.

Oppositional defiant disorder, which typically begins by age 8, is characterized by negativistic, hostile, defiant behavior, often directed toward adults or peers the child knows well. Unlike the behavioral problems in conduct disorder, the problems in oppositional defiant disorder do not include serious violations of the basic rights of others. Although oppositional, negativistic behavior is developmentally normal in early childhood, children with this disorder behave in a manner that unfavorably impinges on the normal development of interpersonal relationships and school achievement. In evaluating an oppositional child, the clinician must bear in mind the particular circumstances of that child's life. Temperament, precipitating events, and intercurrent life stresses may be contributory factors.

The reader is referred to Chapter 35 of *Synopsis VI*, "Disruptive Behavior Disorders," and to Chapter 37 of *CTP V*, "Disruptive Behavior Disorders." Studying the questions and answers below will enhance one's knowledge of this area.

HELPFUL HINTS

The student should be able to define these terms relating to behavior disorders.

disruptive behavior disorders	hyperkinetic syndrome	methylphenidate (Ritalin)
ADHD	hyperactive child syndrome	pemoline (Cylert)
conduct disorder	residual symptoms	imipramine hydrochloride
solitary aggressive type	maturational lag	(Tofranil)
group type	emotional lability	terrible twos
oppositional defiant disorder	impulsivity	developmental-stage oppositional
narcissistic orientation	visual-motor-perceptual	behavior
marital and family therapies	impairments	adult manifestation
countertransference	dextroamphetamine sulfate	
juvenile delinquency	(Dexedrine)	
hyperkinetic reaction of childhood	body anxiety	

QUESTIONS

DIRECTIONS: Each of the incomplete statements below is followed by five suggested completions. Select the *one* that is *best* in each case.

35.1. Phillip, age 12, was suspended from a small-town Iowa school and referred for psychiatric treatment by his principal. The following note came with him:

> This child has been a continual problem since coming to our school. He does not get along on the playground because he is mean to other children. He disobeys school rules, sasses the patrol children, steals from the other children, and defies all authority. Phillip keeps getting into fights with other children on the bus.
>
> He has been suspended from cafeteria privileges several times for fighting, pushing, and shoving. After he misbehaved one day at the cafeteria, the teacher told him to come up to my office to see me. He flatly refused, lay on the floor, and threw a temper tantrum, kicking and screaming.
>
> The truth is not in Phillip. When caught in actual misdeeds, he denies everything and takes upon himself an air of injured innocence. He believes we are picking on

> him. His attitude is sullen when he is refused anything. He pouts and sasses. When asked why he does these things, he points to his head and says, "Because I'm not right up here."
>
> This boy needs help badly. He does not seem to have friends. His aggressive behavior prevents the children from liking him. Our school psychologist tested Phillip, and the results indicated average intelligence, but his school achievement is only at the third- and low fourth-grade level.

The psychiatrist learned from Phillip's grandmother that he was an illegitimate child, born when his mother was a senior in high school. Her parents insisted that she keep the baby and help rear him; most of his upbringing had been by his grandparents, however.

Phillip was "three months premature" and a "blue baby," requiring oxygen for 24 hours. Shortly after his birth, Phillip's mother ran off with a man, married him, and had a second child. The marriage broke up, and she left that child with its father. Phillip had no contact with his mother after she left him.

Phillip's toilet training was not successful, and he remained a bedwetter for some years. At the age of 5 years, his maternal grandparents adopted him because they were afraid that his mother might some day claim him. He showed anxiety at separation from his grandmother when he began school.

He was then in a serious car accident, in which his grandmother was injured and one person in the other car was killed. Phillip did not appear to be injured but seemed to have some transient memory loss, probably a direct, immediate result of the impact. Subsequently, he suffered from nightmares, fear of the dark, and an exacerbation of his fear of separation from his grandmother.

Phillip's school progress was not good. He repeated third grade and then was in a special class for underachievers. His grandmother recalled that Phillip's teacher complained that he "could never stay in his seat."

A few months before the consultation, Phillip was seen in a mental health clinic and began taking some mild tranquilizers. A three-month return appointment was arranged, but the school suspended him before that date.

[From *DSM-III-R Case Book*. Used with permission.]

The most appropriate diagnosis in this case is
A. conduct disorder, solitary aggressive type
B. conduct disorder, group type
C. oppositional defiant disorder
D. antisocial personality disorder
E. none of the above

35.2. The most frequently cited characteristic among children with attention-deficit hyperactivity disorder is
A. emotional lability
B. disorders of memory and thinking
C. disorders of speech and hearing
D. hyperactivity
E. perceptual-motor impairment

35.3. In a clinical interview the child or adolescent who has conduct disorder, solitary aggressive type, may be
A. provocative and uncooperative
B. charming and apparently compliant
C. denying any problem
D. openly belligerent
E. all the above

35.4. Factors thought to contribute to the development of conduct disorders include all the following *except*
A. chaotic home conditions
B. parental alcoholism
C. maternal diabetes
D. attention-deficit hyperactivity disorder
E. socioeconomic deprivation

35.5. The first symptom of attention-deficit hyperactivity disorder to remit is usually the
A. overactivity
B. impulse-control problems
C. decreased attention span
D. learning problems
E. distractibility

DIRECTIONS: For each of the incomplete statements below, *one or more* of the completions given are correct. Choose answer

    A. if only *1, 2, and 3* are correct
    B. if only *1 and 3* are correct
    C. if only *2 and 4* are correct
    D. if only *4* is correct
    E. if *all* are correct

35.6. At their wits' end, the parents of Jordan, a 6-year-old boy, brought him to a child psychiatrist for evaluation. Their already shaky marriage was being severely tested by conflict over their son's behavior at home and at school. The mother complained bitterly that the father, frequently away from home on business, overindulged their son. In fact, the son would argue and throw temper tantrums and insist on continuing games and books whenever his father put him to bed, so that a 7:30 P.M. bedtime was delayed until 10:30, 11:00, or even 11:30 at night. Similarly, the father had been known to cook four or five different meals for his son's dinner if the son stubbornly insisted that he would not eat what had been prepared. At school, several teachers had complained that he was stubborn, often spoke out of turn, refused to comply with classroom rules, and deliberately annoyed other children. Jordan often blamed other children for his own mistakes. This pattern of behavior had persisted and increased over the preceding year.

On questioning by the psychiatrist, the parents denied that their son had ever been destructive of property, lied excessively, or stole. When interviewed, the child was observed to be able to sit quietly in his chair, listening attentively to the questions that were asked him. His answers, however, were brief, and he tended to minimize the extent of the problems he was having with his parents and teachers. [From *DSM-III-R Case Book*. Used with permission.]

The differential diagnosis of this boy includes
1. adjustment disorder
2. developmental-stage oppositional behavior
3. conduct disorder
4. oppositional defiant disorder

35.7. The mental status examination of the child with attention-deficit hyperactivity disorder may show
1. a thought disturbance
2. a secondarily depressed mood
3. impaired reality testing
4. a concrete mode of thinking

35.8. The hyperactive child is
1. accident-prone
2. explosively irritable
3. preoccupied with water play
4. fascinated by spinning objects

35.9. The treatment of conduct disorder, solitary aggressive type,
1. often requires removing the child from the home
2. is more successful with older children than with young children
3. includes the family whenever feasible
4. is futile

35.10. The pharmacological agents used in the treatment of attention-deficit hyperactivity disorder include
1. dextroamphetamine sulfate (Dexedrine)
2. chlorpromazine (Thorazine)
3. methylphenidate (Ritalin)
4. diazepam (Valium)

DIRECTIONS: The lettered headings below are followed by a list of numbered phrases. For each numbered phrase, select the heading most associated with it. Each heading may be used once, more than once, or not at all.

Questions 35.11–35.15
    A. Conduct disorder, solitary aggressive type
    B. Conduct disorder, group type

35.11. Aggressive physical or verbal behavior toward others

35.12. Adequate or excessive conformity during early childhood

35.13. Gang membership

35.14. Poor prognosis

35.15. Few youngsters remain delinquent beyond adolescence

ANSWERS

Disruptive Behavior Disorders

35.1. The answer is A (*Synopsis VI, pages 722–725 and 532–533; CTP V, pages 1821–1822*).

Phillip's stealing, fighting, lying, and disobedience, lasting for more than six months, makes the most appropriate diagnosis *conduct disorder, solitary aggressive type*. He does not have any appropriate peer relationships. As with many children with this disorder, "his aggressive behavior prevents the children from liking him." Phillip's behavior is reflective of a repetitive and persistent pattern of conduct in which the basic rights of others are violated; it is classified as a conduct disorder. The solitary aggressive type of conduct disorder is further characterized by predominant features of aggressive physical or verbal behavior. The aggressive behavior is solitary, not a group activity. The child's aggressive behavior rarely seems directed toward any definable goal and offers little pleasure, success, or even sustained advantage with peers or authority figures. Characteristically, children with this disorder lack concern for the feelings, wishes, and welfare of others. They seldom have feelings of guilt or remorse.

Conduct disorder, group type, is characterized by conduct problems occurring mainly as a group activity in the company of friends to whom the child is loyal. Children with this disorder are likely to have age-appropriate friends and to show concern for the welfare of their friends and gang members. *Oppositional defiant disorder* is characterized by a pattern of negativistic and defiant behavior but without the serious violations of the basic rights of others seen in the various conduct disorders. If this pattern of antisocial behavior persists beyond the age of 18 (as well it may), a diagnosis of *antisocial personality disorder* should be considered. Antisocial personality disorder is characterized by evidence of conduct disorder with the onset before age 15 (but the current age of the patient must be at least 18) and by a pattern of irresponsible and antisocial behavior.

See Table 35.1 for the DSM-III-R diagnostic criteria for conduct disorder.

35.2. The answer is D (*Synopsis VI, page 727; CTP V, pages 1832–1833*).

The most frequently cited characteristic among children with attention-deficit hyperactivity disorder (ADHD) is *hyperactivity*, followed by *perceptual-motor impairment, emotional lability*, general coordination deficit, disorders of attention, impulsivity, *disorders of memory and thinking*, specific learning disabilities, *disorders of speech and hearing*, and

Table 35.1
Diagnostic Criteria for Conduct Disorder

A. A disturbance of conduct lasting at least six months, during which at least three of the following have been present:
   1. has stolen without confrontation of a victim on more than one occasion (including forgery)
   2. has run away from home overnight at least twice while living in parental or parental surrogate home (or once without returning)
   3. often lies (other than to avoid physical or sexual abuse)
   4. has deliberately engaged in fire-setting
   5. is often truant from school (for older person, absent from work)
   6. has broken into someone else's house, building, or car
   7. has deliberately destroyed others' property (other than by fire-setting)
   8. has been physically cruel to animals
   9. has forced someone into sexual activity with him or her
   10. has used a weapon in more than one fight
   11. often initiates physical fights
   12. has stolen with confrontation of a victim (e.g., mugging, purse-snatching, extortion, armed robbery)
   13. has been physically cruel to people

Note: The above items are listed in descending order of discriminating power based on data from a national field trial of the DSM-III-R criteria for disruptive behavior disorders.

B. If 18 or older, does not meet criteria for antisocial personality disorder.

Table from DSM-III-R, *Diagnostic and Statistical Manual of Mental Disorders*, ed 3, revised. Copyright American Psychiatric Association, Washington, DC, 1987. Used with permission.

equivocal neurological signs and electroencephalographic irregularities.

Emotional lability refers to an excessive emotional responsiveness, characterized by unstable and rapidly changing emotions. Disorders of attention encompass short attention span, distractibility, perseveration (persisting response to a prior stimulus after a new stimulus has been presented), failure to finish things, inattention, and poor concentration. Impulsivity involves action before thought, abrupt shifts in activity, and lack of organization (e.g., jumping up in class).

The DSM-III-R diagnostic criteria for attention-deficit hyperactivity disorder and undifferentiated attention-deficit disorder are listed in Tables 35.2 and 35.3.

Table 35.2
Diagnostic Criteria for Attention-Deficit Hyperactivity Disorder

Note: Consider a criterion met only if the behavior is considerably more frequent than that of most people of the same mental age.

A. A disturbance of at least six months during which at least eight of the following are present:
   1. often fidgets with hands or feet or squirms in seat (in adolescents, may be limited to subjective feelings of restlessness)
   2. has difficulty remaining seated when required to do so
   3. is easily distracted by extraneous stimuli
   4. has difficulty awaiting turn in games or group situations
   5. often blurts out answers to questions before they have been completed
   6. has difficulty following through on instructions from others (not due to oppositional behavior or failure of comprehension), e.g., fails to finish chores
   7. has difficulty sustaining attention in tasks or play activities
   8. often shifts from one uncompleted activity to another
   9. has difficulty playing quietly
   10. often talks excessively
   11. often interrupts or intrudes on others, e.g., butts into other children's games
   12. often does not seem to listen to what is being said to him or her
   13. often loses things necessary for tasks or activities at school or at home (e.g., toys, pencils, books, assignments)
   14. often engages in physically dangerous activities without considering possible consequences (not for the purpose of thrill-seeking), e.g., runs into street without looking

Note: The above items are listed in descending order of discriminating power based on data from a national field trial of the DSM-III-R criteria for disruptive behavior disorders.

B. Onset before the age of 7.

C. Does not meet the criteria for a pervasive developmental disorder.

Table from DSM-III-R, *Diagnostic and Statistical Manual of Mental Disorders*, ed 3, revised. Copyright American Psychiatric Association, Washington, DC, 1987. Used with permission.

35.3. The answer is E (*Synopsis VI*, pages 723–724; *CTP V*, pages 1824–1825).

In a clinical interview the child or adolescent who meets the criteria for conduct disorder, solitary aggressive type, typically is *uncooperative, provocative,* and hostile. However, some may have a superficial *charm and appear compliant* until they are urged to discuss problem behaviors. Often, the conduct-disordered child or adolescent *denies any problem.* When pressed in an interview, the child may become *openly belligerent* or leave the room.

Table 35.3
Diagnostic Criteria for Undifferentiated Attention-Deficit Disorder

This is a residual category for disturbances in which the predominant feature is the persistence of developmentally inappropriate and marked inattention that is not a symptom of another disorder, such as mental retardation or attention-deficit hyperactivity disorder, or of a disorganized and chaotic environment. Some of the disturbances that in DSM-III would have been categorized as attention deficit disorder without hyperactivity would be included in this category. Research is necessary to determine if this is a valid diagnostic category and, if so, how it should be defined.

Table from DSM-III-R, *Diagnostic and Statistical Manual of Mental Disorders*, ed 3, revised. Copyright American Psychiatric Association, Washington, DC, 1987. Used with permission.

35.4. The answer is C (*Synopsis VI*, pages 722–723; *CTP V*, pages 1823–1824).

Although clear evidence links maternal diabetes to certain fetal abnormalities, such as high-birth-weight infants, no evidence links *maternal diabetes* to the development of conduct disorder.

Some parental attitudes and faulty child-rearing practices influence the development of children's maladaptive behaviors. *Chaotic home conditions* are associated with the development of conduct disorders and delinquency. Parental psychiatric impairments, particularly sociopathy and *alcoholism*, are viewed as important causal factors; recent studies suggest that many of the parents of children with conduct disorders suffer from even more serious psychopathology.

Current sociological theories suggest that *socioeconomic deprivation*, including an inability to achieve status and obtain material goods through legitimate routes, forces some children to resort to socially unacceptable means to achieve their goals.

Attention-deficit hyperactivity disorder, dysfunction of or damage to the central nervous system, parental rejection, early institutional living, inconsistent management and harsh discipline, frequent shifting of parental figures (foster parents, relatives, stepparents), and illegitimacy can predispose a child to the development of a conduct disorder.

35.5. The answer is A (*Synopsis VI*, page 728; *CTP V*, page 1834).

The *overactivity* is usually the first symptom of attention-deficit hyperactivity disorder (ADHD) to remit, and *distractibility* is the last. The course of the condition is highly variable: Symptoms may persist into adolescence or adult life, they may remit at puberty, or the hyperactivity may disappear, but the *decreased attention span* and *impulse-control problems* may persist. Remission is not likely before the age of 12. If remission does occur, it is usually between the ages of 12 and 20. Remission may be accompanied by a productive adolescence and adult life, satisfying interpersonal relationships, and few significant sequelae. The majority of patients with ADHD, however, undergo partial remission and are vulnerable to antisocial and other personality disorders and mood disorders. *Learning problems* often continue. Methylphenidate (Ritalin) is indicated with adult manifestations of ADHD.

35.6. The answer is E (all) (*Synopsis VI*, pages 731–732; *CTP V*, pages 1842–1844).

The differential diagnosis of 6-year-old Jordan includes *adjustment disorder, conduct disorder, developmental-stage oppositional behavior*, and *oppositional defiant disorder*. The most likely diagnosis in this case is oppositional defiant disorder.

Although disturbances in the functioning of this family (expressed as an already shaky marriage, the mother complaining bitterly of the father's frequent absences from home) may have contributed to this child's difficulties, Jordan now shows a pervasive pattern of maladaptive behavior that is not limited to his interaction with his parents. His temper tantrums, breaking school rules, argumentativeness, provocative behavior, and stubbornness are all part of a persistent pattern of disobedience, negativism, and opposition to authority figures. As Jordan's behavior does not involve the violation of the basic rights of others or of major age-appropriate societal norms or rules (such as physical aggression or truancy), it is not a conduct disorder. Because oppositional behavior is both normal and adaptive at specific developmental stages, these normal periods of negativism must be distinguished from the true disorder. Oppositional defiant behavior that occurs temporarily in reaction to a severe stress should be diagnosed as an adjustment disorder.

Developmental-stage oppositional behavior is of shorter duration than is oppositional defiant disorder. Jordan's oppositional defiant behavior persisted and increased over a year and is not more frequent or more intense than that of other children of the same mental age. See Table 35.4 for the DSM-III-R diagnostic criteria for oppositional defiant disorder.

35.7. The answer is C (2, 4) (*Synopsis VI*, page 728; *CTP V*, pages 1832–1833).

The mental status examination of the child with attention-deficit hyperactivity disorder may show a *secondarily depressed mood* but *no thought disturbance, impaired reality testing*, or inappropriate affect. There may be great distractibility, perseverations, and a literal and *concrete mode of thinking*. There may be indications of visual-perceptual, auditory-perceptual, language, or cognition problems. Occasionally, there is evidence of a basic, pervasive, organically based anxiety, often referred to as body anxiety.

Table 35.4
Diagnostic Criteria for Oppositional Defiant Disorder

Note: Consider a criterion met only if the behavior is considerably more frequent than that of most people of the same mental age.

A. A disturbance of at least six months during which at least five of the following are present:
1. often loses temper
2. often argues with adults
3. often actively defies or refuses adult requests or rules, e.g., refuses to do chores at home
4. often deliberately does things that annoy other people, e.g., grabs other children's hats
5. often blames others for his or her own mistakes
6. is often touchy or easily annoyed by others
7. is often angry and resentful
8. is often spiteful or vindictive
9. often swears or uses obscene language

Note: The above items are listed in descending order of discriminating power based on data from a national field trial of the DSM-III-R criteria for disruptive behavior disorders.

B. Does not meet the criteria for conduct disorder, and does not occur exclusively during the course of a psychotic disorder, dysthymia, or a major depressive, hypomanic, or manic episode.

Table from DSM-III-R, *Diagnostic and Statistical Manual of Mental Disorders*, ed 3, revised. Copyright American Psychiatric Association, Washington, DC, 1987. Used with permission.

35.8. The answer is E (all) (*Synopsis VI*, pages 727–728 and 702; *CTP V*, pages 1828–1833).

The hyperactive child is often *accident-prone, explosively irritable, fascinated by spinning objects*, and *preoccupied with water play*. In school hyperactive children may rapidly attack a test but answer only the first two question, or they may be unable to wait to be called on and respond for everyone else. At home they cannot be put off for even a minute. Irritability may be set off by relatively minor stimuli, and they may seem puzzled and dismayed over that phenomenon. These children are frequently emotionally labile and easily inspired to laughter and to tears, and their moods and performances are apt to be variable and unpredictable.

Disturbances in all the following functions and abilities may be found in the hyperactive child: left-right discrimination; internal time telling or clock time telling; visual or auditory perception; visuomotor performance and hand-eye coordination; fine motor coordination; figure-background discrimination; the abilities to abstract, conceptualize, and generalize; and the abilities to assimilate, retain, and recall.

35.9. The answer is B (1, 3) (*Synopsis VI*, page 724; *CTP V*, pages 1826–1828).

Many clinical studies report difficulties in successfully treating children with conduct disorder of the solitary aggressive type. Treatment often requires *removing the child from the home*. However, even when placed in a foster home or institution, youngsters with conduct disorders can be expected to continue their extraordinary aggressiveness, testing of limits, and provocation; this issue needs to be broached directly with the persons who are assuming care of the child.

Whenever feasible, *the family* should be included in the treatment process. Unless the parents can come to feel some acceptance of and warmth toward the youngster and provide consistent guidelines for acceptable behavior, even the most intensive work with the child will probably not be helpful. A course of conjoint family and marital therapy is demanding but essential.

Studies have found that therapeutic success is more likely in younger rather than *older children*, not only because of the tendency of this behavioral pattern to become increasingly internalized and fixed (in the face of the counterhostility that these youngsters engender in others) but also because of the relative ease with which overt aggressiveness can be managed in a young child. The prognosis is often poor, but it is by no means hopeless, and treatment is not *futile*. The prognosis for conduct disorder, group type, appears to be better than that for conduct disorder, solitary aggressive type.

35.10. The answer is B (1, 3) (*Synopsis VI*, page 729; *CTP V*, pages 1835–1836).

The pharmacological agents used in the treatment of attention-deficit hyperactivity disorder (ADHD) are the central nervous system stimulants, primarily *dextroamphetamine sulfate* (Dexedrine), *methylphenidate* (Ritalin), and pemoline (Cylert). A child may respond favorably to one of these drugs and unfavorably to the others or better to one drug than to the others; the appropriate dosage varies. The mechanism of action of the stimulants is unknown, but they have a paradoxical reaction in that they decrease motor activity and increase attention span.

Chlorpromazine (Thorazine) is an antipsychotic medication used primarily for the treatment of psychotic or extremely agitated patients, and *diazepam* (Valium) is a benzodiazepine. Neither is useful in treating ADHD.

35.11–35.15

35.11. The answer is A (*Synopsis VI*, pages 723–725; *CTP V*, pages 1821–1822).

35.12. The answer is B (*Synopsis VI*, pages 723–725; *CTP V*, pages 1821–1822).

35.13. The answer is B (*Synopsis VI*, pages 723–725; *CTP V*, pages 1821–1822).

35.14. The answer is A (*Synopsis VI*, pages 723–725; *CTP V*, pages 1821–1822).

35.15. The answer is B (*Synopsis VI*, pages 723–725; *CTP V*, pages 1821–1822).

The essential feature of conduct disorder is a repetitive and persistent pattern of conduct in which either major age-appropriate societal norms or rules or the basic rights of others are violated. (The actions in oppositional defiant disorder do not include the serious violations of the basic rights of others, although features such as disobedience and defiant oppositional behavior in response to authority figures are characteristic of both.) DSM-III-R lists three types of conduct disorders: solitary aggressive type, group type, and undifferentiated type.

Aggressive physical or verbal behavior toward others is characteristic of the solitary aggressive type of conduct disorder. In the group type, physical aggression is less commonly seen. More often, group antisocial behavior involves truancy, stealing, and relatively minor criminal or antisocial acts.

In most cases of conduct disorder, group type, the child has a history of fair to good overall functioning, including adequate or even excessive *conformity during early childhood* that ends when the youngster becomes a *gang member*, usually in preadolescence or adolescence. However, many children with this disorder show some evidence of earlier adaptive problems, such as marginal or poor school performance.

The group type of conduct disorder, as the name implies, describes a disorder in which the misdeeds generally occur in the company of a peer group. The parents often recognize the role of the peer group in the youngsters' difficulties and complain of their children's wish to spend increasing amounts of time with their friends.

The *prognosis* for conduct disorder, solitary aggressive type, is poor. Children with this disorder are difficult to engage in treatment, and, although therapeutic approaches have been attempted, expectations for more socialized behavior from the youngsters need to be initially minimal and only gradually increased. Given their pathology in this disorder—including lack of social attachments, inability to maintain peer relationships, and lack of guilt or remorse regarding their behavior—these children are at high risk to continue their antisocial behavior and to have antisocial personality disorder in adulthood. In contrast, in conduct disorder, group type, *few youngsters remain delinquent* beyond adolescence, and many even give up this behavior during adolescence. They may relinquish their delinquent behavior in response to fortuitous positive events, such as academic or athletic success and romantic attachments.

Traditional individual counseling alone has proved to be relatively ineffective, but a cognitive approach in a group setting has shown favorable results. Groups using this approach are made up of a core of reformed delinquents who understand the rationalizations, demands, and self-justifications of gang members seeking help and who vigorously confront them with the realities of their behavioral predicament and the inevitability of negative conse-quences. Occasionally, such youngsters need to be separated from their previous peer groups and trans-planted to entirely new environments (e.g., training schools and therapeutic residential programs).

36

Anxiety Disorders of Childhood or Adolescence

The concept of anxiety forms a central core for the understanding of the developmental difficulties, symptom formation, and the clinical symptoms of the anxiety disorders of childhood or adolescence. Anxiety is the term used to describe any of a large variety of affective, motor, and physiological responses to the perception of danger. These feelings of dread, discomfort, and fear that something terrible will happen are the core clinical symptoms of the three anxiety disorders diagnosed in childhood or adolescence.

In separation anxiety disorder and in avoidant disorder of childhood or adolescence, anxiety is situation-specific. In overanxious disorder, anxiety is generalized. When evaluating a child or adolescent, the clinician must assess the effect of the anxiety on the particular developmental phase the child is passing through. The earliest form of anxiety occurs when the mothering figure is unavailable to comfort, feed, or lull the infant in need of physiological gratification. Unable to master growing physiological tension, the infant reacts with a group of behaviors—including crying, writhing body movements, and increased pulse and respiratory rates—conceptualized by the term "anxiety." Thus, anxiety is a signal of impending danger or the absence of a crucial mothering figure.

In separation anxiety disorder, extreme anxiety is precipitated when a child or adolescent is separated from a major attachment figure, the home, or other familiar surroundings. The disorder occurs equally in boys and girls; it occurs as early as the preschool years but more commonly around age 11 or 12. Frequently, separation from the mother or the mothering figure is key. An example of a well-defined separation anxiety disorder in early infancy is an-

aclitic depression, resulting from the loss of the infant's mothering figure. As described by René Spitz in his studies of institutionalized infants, anaclitic depression can result in the failure to thrive and in death. A second form of separation anxiety disorder—school phobia, school refusal in its extreme form—presents as a psychiatric emergency when the child refuses to attend school for a period of weeks. The treatment is to return the child to school, if only at first to enter the building among supportive staff. A parent's conscious or unconscious wish not to be separated from the child must also be considered.

Avoidant disorder of childhood or adolescence is characterized by extreme shyness around unfamiliar people of sufficient severity to impair normal social functioning, yet the patient shows a clear desire to be around people he or she knows well. The diagnostic criteria in the revised third edition of *Diagnostic and Statistical Manual of Mental Disorders* (DSM-III-R) require that such behavior be present for at least six months and that the child be 2½ years of age, well past the normal phase of stranger anxiety, which develops at 8 months of age. Like children with separation anxiety disorder, children with avoidant disorder may have difficulty with separation from parents. The emphasis here, however, is on the child's reluctance to be in the company of a stranger.

Overanxious disorder presents a clinical picture of a child or an adolescent experiencing excessive, unrealistic, generalized anxiety for a period of at least six months. Overanxious patients tend to be self-conscious, to worry about future events, and to seem mature beyond their years because of their concerns about competence and achievement. Often highly verbal and intellectually bright, children with overanxious disorder may grow into adults with anxiety disorders. Their social skills and academic achievements may show little adverse effects but at the cost of a generalized sense of discomfort and stress.

Effective treatment of the anxiety syndromes is based on knowledge of the following concepts: (1) genetic and constitutional tendency to react to stress with anxiety, (2) the complex interactions between children and their parents, (3) overt stresses or traumas in the child's life, (4) the symbolic meaning of a particular stress, and (5) the pattern of interactions with siblings, other relatives, peers, and the educational and recreational environments.

The reader is referred to Chapter 36 of *Synopsis VI*, "Anxiety Disorders of Childhood or Adolescence," and to Chapter 38, "Anxiety Disorders," of *CTP V* and should then study the questions and answers below to assess his or her knowledge of this area.

HELPFUL HINTS

The terms below refer to anxiety disorders and should be defined.

separation anxiety disorder
avoidant disorder of childhood or adolescence
overanxious disorder
developmental fears
phobic anxiety

depression
panic reactions
clinging
shadowing
panic disorder with agoraphobia
adjustment disorder

social and simple phobias
hypermature
diazepam (Valium)
diphenhydramine (Benadryl)
insight therapy

QUESTIONS

DIRECTIONS: Each of the questions or incomplete statements below is followed by five suggested responses or completions. Select the *one* that is *best* in each case.

Questions 36.1–36.2

A 12-year-old pubertal girl came for a consultation because of a one-year history of nervousness. About a year before the consultation, her parents had separated. Their marriage apparently had been stable and outwardly satisfactory up until that time, and their child-rearing practices were unremarkable. After her parents' separation, the patient had several fears and a relatively persistent state of anxiety. She began to bite her nails and worry about the excellence of her school performance; she became afraid of the dark and appeared to live in a relatively constant state of apprehension. Her worries were mostly realistic but greatly exaggerated. She was concerned about her appearance and felt awkward, and her shyness in social situations became more pronounced. She reported relatively constant feelings of nervousness and anxiety, which seemed to be exacerbated by almost any event in her life. She experienced no panic attacks and no specific fears on separation from her parents, although she was occasionally worried about their safety without good reason.

The patient was a shy girl who often had difficulty in making friends, although she had developed lasting and close relationships with several peers. Her school performance ranged from adequate to outstanding and had not declined in the past year.

During the interview her palms were sweating, it was hard for her to look at the examiner, and she was inhibited and tense. She denied persistent feelings of sadness and lack of interest in her environment, and she said she was able to enjoy things except for the times when her anxiety peaked. When questioned about guilt, she reported with difficulty that sometimes she felt that somehow she was responsible for her parents' separation, although she could not say how. Physical examination findings were unremarkable. Specifically, she had no goiter or exophthalmos, and her thyroid indices were within normal limits. Neurological findings were unremarkable, except for a mild tremor of extended hands during the examination, but this did not interfere with fine-motor skills. [From *DSM-III-R Case Book*. Used with permission.]

36.1. The most likely diagnosis in this case is
A. generalized anxiety disorder
B. separation anxiety disorder
C. overanxious disorder
D. panic disorder
E. obsessive-compulsive disorder

36.2. Which of the following may be useful in the treatment of overanxious disorder?
A. Diazepam (Valium)
B. Diphenhydramine (Benadryl)
C. Buspirone (BuSpar)
D. Insight therapy
E. All the above

36.3. Which one of the following is not characteristic of avoidant disorder of childhood or adolescence?
A. Duration of at least six months
B. Good peer relations
C. Difficulty in falling asleep
D. Blushing
E. Body tension

DIRECTIONS: For each of the incomplete statements below, *one or more* of the completions given are correct. Choose answer

A. if only *1, 2, and 3* are correct
B. if only *1 and 3* are correct
C. if only *2 and 4* are correct
D. if only *4* is correct
E. if *all* are correct

36.4. Avoidant disorder of childhood or adolescence
1. is relatively common
2. is observed clinically more frequently in girls than in boys
3. may develop before the age of 2½ years
4. involves a clear desire for social involvement with familiar people

36.5. Characteristic personality features of children with separation anxiety disorder include
1. conscientiousness
2. eagerness to please
3. tendency toward conformity
4. intrusiveness into adult affairs

36.6. Children with separation anxiety disorder frequently have histories involving
1. loss of a parent
2. illness and hospitalization
3. illness of a parent
4. geographic relocation

36.7. Children predisposed to avoidant disorder of childhood or adolescence often have a history of
1. mothers who suffer from anxiety disorders
2. chronic medical problems
3. many geographic relocations
4. parents who support the child's shyness

36.8. Overanxious disorder appears to be most common in
1. large families
2. families of upper socioeconomic status
3. youngest children
4. urban areas

DIRECTIONS: The lettered headings below are followed by a list of numbered phrases. For each numbered phrase, select the lettered heading most associated with it. Each lettered heading may be used once, more than once, or not at all.

Questions 36.9–36.10
A. Separation anxiety disorder
B. Overanxious disorder

36.9. Anxiety is focused

36.10. Anxiety is generalized

DIRECTIONS: Each of the incomplete statements below is followed by five suggested completions. Select the *one* that is *best* in each case.

Questions 36.11–36.12

Emily was a 7-year-old girl who was brought to an outpatient mental health clinic for children by her mother because of difficulties with peer relationships. A recent telephone call from Emily's second-grade teacher convinced her mother that it was necessary to seek professional help for Emily. The teacher was becoming increasingly concerned about Emily's reluctance to interact with the other children in the class. During recess, Emily stood off to the side of the playground with her head down, looking extremely uncomfortable. In the classroom she never initiated conversations with the other children and had great difficulty responding even when approached by another child. Six months into the school year, Emily's extreme discomfort around her peers had not improved at all. Indeed, she did not have a single friend in the classroom.

Emily's discomfort in interacting with peers dated back to kindergarten. Her teachers in kindergarten and first grade had commented on her report card that she was very withdrawn and nervous with the other children. However, her second-grade teacher was the first to take an active role in trying to get Emily the help she needed.

Emily's mother had tried repeatedly to get Emily involved with other children in the neighborhood. In fact, she would take Emily by the hand and lead her to neighbors' homes where there were children of the same age to try to make friends for her child. Unfortunately, when she did this, Emily would start to shake or cry and would not be able to say a word to the neighbor's child. Emily had never been asked to attend a birthday party for another child.

Her behavior at home was quite different. Emily was warm and outgoing with her family, in marked contrast to the withdrawn and anxious child observed by her teachers and peers.

[From *DSM-III-R Case Book.* Used with permission.]

36.11. The best diagnosis for this 7-year-old girl is
A. generalized anxiety disorder
B. separation anxiety disorder
C. overanxious disorder
D. avoidant disorder of childhood or adolescence
E. social phobia

36.12. The treatment for this disorder may include
A. individual psychotherapy
B. family therapy
C. antianxiety medication
D. environmental modification
E. all the above

Questions 36.13–36.14

Tina—a small, sweet-faced, freckled 10-year-old—had been referred by a pediatrician who was unsuccessful in treating her for refusing to go to school. Her difficulties began on the first day of school one year ago, when she cried and hid in the basement. She agreed to go to school only when her mother promised to go with her and stay to have lunch with her at the school. For the next three months, on school days Tina had a variety of somatic complaints, such as headaches and "tummy aches," and each day she would go to school only reluctantly, after much cajoling by her parents. Soon thereafter she could be gotten to school only if her parents lifted her out of bed, dressed and fed her, and drove her to school. Finally, in the spring, the school social worker consulted Tina's pediatrician, who instituted a behavior-modification program with the help of her parents. Because this program was of only limited help, the pediatrician had now, at the beginning of the school year, referred Tina to a psychiatrist.

According to her mother, despite Tina's absences from school last year, she performed well. During this time she also happily participated in all other activities, including Girl Scout meetings, sleepovers at friends' houses (usually with her sister), and family outings. Her mother wondered if taking a part-time bookkeeping job two years ago, plus the sudden death of a maternal grandmother to whom Tina was particularly close, might have been responsible for the child's difficulties.

When Tina was interviewed, she at first minimized any problems about school, insisting that "everything [was] okay" and that she got good grades and liked all the teachers. When this subject was pursued, she became angry and gave a lot of "I don't know" responses as to why, then, she often refused to go to school. Eventually, she said that kids teased her about her size, calling her "Shrimp" and "Shorty"; but she gave the impression, as well as actually stated, that she liked school and her teachers. She finally admitted that what bothered her was leaving home. She could not specify why but hinted that she was afraid something would happen, though to whom or to what she did not say; but she confessed that she felt uncomfortable when all her family were out of sight.

On the Rorschach there was evidence of obsessive rumination about catastrophic events involving injury to members of her family and themes concerning family disruption.

[From *DSM-III-R Case Book*. Used with permission.]

36.13. The best diagnosis for Tina's problem is
A. generalized anxiety disorder
B. separation anxiety disorder
C. overanxious disorder
D. avoidant disorder
E. social phobia

36.14. The treatment of this disorder may include
A. behavior modification
B. individual psychotherapy
C. family therapy
D. antidepressant medication
E. all the above

ANSWERS

Anxiety Disorders of Childhood or Adolescence

36.1. **The answer is C** (*Synopsis VI*, pages 733–738; *CTP V*, pages 1849–1850).

In the case of the 12-year-old girl with a one-year history of nervousness, the most likely diagnosis is *overanxious disorder*. According to DSM-III-R, the essential feature of overanxious disorder is excessive and unrealistic anxiety for a period of six months or longer. Children with this disorder tend to be extremely self-conscious (she is concerned about her appearance, feeling awkward and shy), to worry about future events (she worries about the excellence of her school performance, which continues to range from adequate to outstanding) or about meeting expectations (her feelings of nervousness and anxiety were exacerbated by almost any event in her life), and to be concerned about the discomfort or the dangers of a variety of situations (she worries about her parents' safety without good reason).

Although characteristically similar, the diagnosis of *generalized anxiety disorder* is not made because of the age criterion—generalized anxiety disorder is diagnosed when the patient is older than 18 years of age, whereas overanxious disorder is an anxiety disorder specific to childhood or adolescence. The precipitating stress associated with *separation anxiety disorder* involves separation from a familiar person, rather than this patient's anxiety, which is generalized to a variety of situations. *Panic disorder* is characterized by recurrent panic attacks and a fear of future attacks, which were not part of this patient's history. *Obsessive-compulsive disorder* has more highly structured obsessions and compulsions than does overanxious disorder.

See Table 36.1 for the DSM-III-R diagnostic criteria for overanxious disorder.

36.2. **The answer is E** (*Synopsis VI*, page 739; *CTP V*, page 1852).

Diazepam (Valium), *diphenhydramine* (Benadryl), *buspirone* (BuSpar), and *insight therapy* may all be useful in the treatment of anxiety disorders. Antianxiety medications, such as diazepam, may be useful in acute situations when accompanied by a discussion of their use and the concomitant psychotherapeutic involvement of the parents. Acute anxiety accompanied by insomnia can be effectively treated by the use of such anxiolytics as buspirone, a nonbenzodiazepine anxiolytic. Diphenhydramine can also be used as a short-term anxiety-reducing agent because it has sedative effects. When overanxious children complain of psychophysiological symptoms, they should be given the benefit of a thor-

Table 36.1
Diagnostic Criteria for Overanxious Disorder

A. Excessive or unrealistic anxiety or worry, for a period of six months or longer, as indicated by the frequent occurrence of at least *four* of the following:
1. excessive or unrealistic worry about future events
2. excessive or unrealistic concern about the appropriateness of past behavior
3. excessive or unrealistic concern about competence in one or more areas, e.g., athletic, academic, social
4. somatic complaints, such as headaches or stomachaches, for which no physical basis can be established
5. marked self-consciousness
6. excessive need for reassurance about a variety of concerns
7. marked feelings of tension or inability to relax

B. If another Axis I disorder is present (e.g., separation anxiety disorder, phobic disorder, obsessive-compulsive disorder), the focus of the symptoms in A is not limited to it. For example, if separation anxiety disorder is present, the symptoms in A are not exclusively related to anxiety about separation. In addition, the disturbance does not occur only during the course of a psychotic disorder or a mood disorder.

C. If 18 or older, does not meet the criteria for generalized anxiety disorder.

D. Occurrence not exclusively during the course of a pervasive developmental disorder, schizophrenia, or any other psychotic disorder.

Table from DSM-III-R, *Diagnostic and Statistical Manual of Mental Disorders*, ed 3, revised. Copyright American Psychiatric Association, Washington, DC, 1987. Used with permission.

ough medical or pediatric examination. If the findings of the examination are normal, their symptoms should be discussed and treated as somatic equivalents of anxiety. The patient should be assured that such symptoms will disappear when the basis for anxiety is resolved.

These children are excellent candidates for insight therapy, either individually or with their families. Many believe this therapy to be the treatment of choice. Themes of sibling rivalry, wishes to excel, and oedipal struggles tend to emerge. The prognosis in such children is usually excellent with treatment.

36.3. **The answer is B** (*Synopsis VI*, pages 736–737; *CTP V*, pages 1850–1851).

Characteristic of avoidant disorder of childhood or adolescence are tentative, overly inhibited (*not good*) *peer relations*, duration of at least *six months* to establish the diagnosis, *difficulty in falling asleep, blushing,* and *body tension.*

Children with avoidant disorder of childhood or adolescence hold back excessively from establishing interpersonal contacts or satisfactory relationships with strangers to an extent that noticeably interferes with their peer functioning. Typically, these children relate warmly and naturally in their home situations. However, they may be clinging, whining, and overly demanding with caretakers, making great demands on persons who are with them. Blushing, difficulties in speech, body tension, and easy embarrassment are characteristic. Underneath these behaviors and often expressed in close relationships are anger, sullen resentment, rage, or grandiosity.

See Table 36.2 for the DSM-III-R diagnostic criteria for avoidant disorder of childhood or adolescence.

36.4. The answer is D (4) (*Synopsis VI*, page 736; *CTP V*, pages 1850–1851).

Avoidant disorder of childhood or adolescence is characterized by a persistent and excessive shrinking from contact with unfamiliar people that is of sufficient severity to interfere with social functioning in peer relationships, is of at least six months' duration, and is coupled with a clear desire for *social involvement with familiar people,* such as family members and peers the person knows well. Avoidant disorder of childhood or adolescence *is not common;* it is observed clinically *more frequently in boys than in girls,* possibly because of the socially sanctioned role models of passivity in girls. The age of onset must be at least (not before) *2½ years,* after stranger anxiety as a normal developmental phenomenon should have disappeared.

36.5. The answer is E (all) (*Synopsis VI*, pages 734–735; *CTP V*, pages 1847–1848).

Characteristic personality features of children with separation anxiety disorder include *conscientiousness, eagerness to please,* a tendency toward *conformity,* and *intrusiveness into adult affairs.* Families of such children tend to be closely knit and caring, and the children often seem to be spoiled or the objects of parental overconcern. Many of these children are demanding and require constant attention to allay their anxieties. Separation anxiety disorder is a clinical syndrome whose predominant feature is excessive anxiety of separation from the major attachment figures or from home or other familiar surroundings. When so separated, the children may experience anxiety to the point of panic, beyond that expected at their developmental level.

Table 36.3 lists the DSM-III-R diagnostic criteria for separation anxiety disorder.

36.6. The answer is E (all) (*Synopsis VI*, pages 733–735; *CTP V*, pages 1847–1848).

Children with separation anxiety disorder often have histories showing important episodes of sepa-

Table 36.2
Diagnostic Criteria for Avoidant Disorder of Childhood or Adolescence

A. Excessive shrinking from contact with unfamiliar people, for a period of six months or longer, sufficiently severe to interfere with social functioning in peer relationships.

B. Desire for social involvement with familiar people (family members and peers the person knows well), and generally warm and satisfying relations with family members and other familial figures.

C. Age at least 2½ years.

D. The disturbance is not sufficiently pervasive and persistent to warrant the diagnosis of avoidant personality disorder.

Table from DSM-III-R, *Diagnostic and Statistical Manual of Mental Disorders,* ed 3, revised. Copyright American Psychiatric Association, Washington, DC, 1987. Used with permission.

Table 36.3
Diagnostic Criteria for Separation Anxiety Disorder

A. Excessive anxiety concerning separation from those to whom the child is attached, as evidenced by at least three of the following:
  1. unrealistic and persistent worry about possible harm befalling major attachment figures or fear that they will leave and not return
  2. unrealistic and persistent worry that an untoward calamitous event will separate the child from a major attachment figure, e.g., the child will be lost, kidnapped, killed, or be the victim of an accident
  3. persistent reluctance or refusal to go to school in order to stay with major attachment figures or at home
  4. persistent reluctance or refusal to go to sleep without being near a major attachment figure or to go to sleep away from home
  5. persistent avoidance of being alone, including "clinging" to and "shadowing" major attachment figures
  6. repeated nightmares involving the theme of separation
  7. complaints of physical symptoms, e.g., headaches, stomachaches, nausea, or vomiting, on many school days or on other occasions when anticipating separation from major attachment figures
  8. recurrent signs or complaints of excessive distress in anticipation of separation from home or major attachment figures, e.g., temper tantrums or crying, pleading with parents not to leave
  9. recurrent signs of complaints of excessive distress when separated from home or major attachment figures, e.g., wants to return home, needs to call parents when they are absent or when child is away from home

B. Duration of disturbance of at least two weeks.

C. Onset before the age of 18.

D. Occurrence not exclusively during the course of a pervasive developmental disorder, schizophrenia, or any other psychotic disorder.

Table from DSM-III-R, *Diagnostic and Statistical Manual of Mental Disorders,* ed 3, revised. Copyright American Psychiatric Association, Washington, DC, 1987. Used with permission.

ration, such as *illness and hospitalization, illness of a parent, loss of a parent*, and *geographic relocation*. The period of infancy should be scrutinized for evidence of separation-individuation disorders or lack of an adequate mothering figure.

36.7. The answer is E (all) (*Synopsis VI*, page 736; *CTP V*, pages 1850–1851).

Children predisposed to avoidant disorder of childhood or adolescence often have a history of *mothers* who suffer from anxiety disorders, chronic *medical problems, many geographic relocations*, and parents who *support the child's shyness*. Anxiety disorders are more common in the mothers of children with avoidant disorder than in the general population. Devastating losses early in childhood, sexual traumas, and other kinds of physical abuse or neglect may also contribute to avoidant disorder. Children who have chronic medical problems in childhood, such as rheumatic fever and orthopedic handicaps, may not learn the age-related social skills shared by their peers because they have not been involved in typical social interactions with their age mates. Likewise, children who have grown up in other countries or have had many relocations may not learn the necessary social skills that allow them to integrate effectively. Temperamental differences may account for some of the predisposition to avoidant disorder, particularly if a parent supports the child's shyness and withdrawal. Modeling of a shy, retiring parent is frequently noted in the histories of children with the disorder.

36.8. The answer is C (2, 4) (*Synopsis VI*, page 738; *CTP V*, page 1849).

Overanxious disorder, characterized by excessive worry and fearful behavior, appears to be most common in *small (not large) families of upper socioeconomic status* and in *firstborn (not youngest) children*. It may also be more common in *urban* areas than in rural areas. Some workers believe that overanxious disorder is more common in boys than in girls; however, DSM-III-R describes the disorder as equally common in the two sexes.

36.9–36.10

36.9. The answer is A (*Synopsis VI*, pages 733–734; *CTP V*, pages 1847–1848).

36.10. The answer is B (*Synopsis VI*, pages 737–738; *CTP V*, pages 1849–1850).

Separation anxiety disorder is distinguished from overanxious disorder in that the anxiety in separation anxiety disorder is *focused* on a specific situation. On separation, children with this disorder may experience anxiety to the point of panic, beyond that expected at their developmental level. In overanxious disorder, the anxiety is *generalized* to a variety of situations. Children with overanxious disorder excessively worry about future events or about meeting expectations. They are greatly concerned about performance and competence and about being judged negatively. Although these two disorders evolve from different causative factors, they share many clinical features. For example, sleep difficulties, including insomnia and nightmares, are typical of both. School phobias may develop in separation anxiety disorder at the thought of travel away from home or in overanxious disorder as a result of performance anxiety. Somatic complaints, such as headaches and respiratory and gastrointestinal symptoms, are also typical of both disorders. There is evidence of a familial pattern in both disorders; afflicted children with either disorder are likely to have mothers who also suffer from anxiety disorders.

Table 36.4 lists the common characteristics of the anxiety disorders of childhood or adolescence.

36.11. The answer is D (*Synopsis VI*, pages 733–738; *CTP V*, page 1851).

Emily demonstrates *avoidant disorder* of childhood or adolescence. For more than six months Emily has shown excessive shrinking from contact with unfamiliar people that interferes with her social functioning. Emily also has warm and satisfying relations with her family members at home. *Generalized anxiety disorder* is diagnosed only if the patient is 18 or older. Before 18 years of age, generalized anxiety disorder is called *overanxious disorder*. It is characterized by excessive and unrealistic anxiety for more than six months. *Social phobia*, generalized type, is also characterized by excessive shrinking from unfamiliar people, usually because of a fear of embarrassment or humiliation. In children under 18, this diagnosis is made only if the patient does not meet the criteria for avoidant disorder of childhood or adolescence. *Separation anxiety disorder* is marked by severe anxiety that occurs when the person is separated from an attachment figure.

36.12. The answer is E (*Synopsis VI*, page 737; *CTP V*, page 1852).

Individual psychotherapy with the explicit approval of the parent figure is the treatment of choice at the start. A great deal of work is directed toward helping the child separate from the parent and recognize that independent activity can be safe and fulfilling. In working with the parents, the therapist should show empathically and sensitively how the child is controlling the parent by means of shyness. The parent can then give the child opportunities to experience manageable anxiety and thus be able to give up some of the secondary gains of shyness. The development of skills in dancing, music performance, singing, or writing may be valuable ego supports for children with this disorder.

On occasion, *antianxiety medication* on a short-term basis may decrease anxiety enough to overcome the avoidant behavior. What is most needed, however, is a restructuring of relationships in a suppor-

Table 36.4
Common Characteristics of Anxiety Disorders of Childhood or Adolescence

Criteria	Separation Anxiety Disorder	Avoidant Disorder	Overanxious Disorder
Minimum duration to establish diagnosis	More than two weeks	At least six months	Not specified
Age of onset	Preschool to 18 years	2½ to 18 years	3 years or older
Precipitating stresses	Separation from significant parental figure, other losses, travel	Pressure for social participation	Unusual pressure for performance, damage to self-esteem, feelings of lack of competence
Peer relations	Good when no separation is involved	Tentative, overly inhibited	Overly eager to please, peers sought out and dependent relationship established
Sleep	Difficulty in falling asleep, fear of dark, nightmares	Difficulty in falling asleep at times	Difficulty in falling asleep
Psychophysiological symptoms	Stomachaches, nausea, vomiting, flulike symptoms, headaches, palpitations, dizziness, faintness	Blushing, body tension	Stomachaches, nausea, vomiting, lump in the throat, shortness of breath, dizziness, palpitations
Differential diagnosis	Overanxious disorder, schizophrenia, depressive disorder, conduct disorders, pervasive developmental disorder, major depression, panic disorder with agoraphobia	Adjustment disorder with withdrawal, overanxious disorder, separation anxiety disorder, major depression, dysthymia, avoidant personality disorder, borderline personality disorder	Separation anxiety disorder, attention-deficit hyperactivity disorder, avoidant disorder, adjustment disorder with anxious mood, obsessive-compulsive disorder, psychotic disorder, mood disorder

Adapted from table by Sidney Werkman, M.D.

tive therapeutic environment (*environmental modification*) that directs the child toward facing new situations and mastering anxiety in order to achieve a higher level of independent functioning.

Parents often require *family therapy* because they may be unwilling to support the newly assertive child, especially if shyness fulfilled unconscious needs in the parents to keep the child infantalized.

36.13. The answer is B (*Synopsis VI*, pages 733–738; *CTP V*, page 1848).

Tina's problems involve a fear of going to school. Tina stated that what was troubling her was the fear that something bad would happen when her family were out of sight. Having greater than two weeks' duration, this symptom merits the diagnosis of *separation anxiety disorder*. *Generalized anxiety disorder* for those over age 18 and *overanxious disorder* for those under age 18 are diagnosed when excessive and unrealistic anxiety persists for more than six months about more than one area. For example, the child may be anxious about school, the future, and the appropriateness of past behaviors. *Avoidant disorder* is not warranted, as Tina does not shrink from contact with all unfamiliar people, nor have her problems interfered with peer relations, as evidenced by her participation in the Girl Scouts and sleepovers. *Social phobia*, usually caused by a fear of embarrassment or humiliation when in a social context, may also be ruled out because of these extracurricular activities.

36.14. The answer is E (*Synopsis VI*, page 736; *CTP V*, page 1849).

The treatment of separation anxiety disorder requires a comprehensive treatment plan that involves the child, the parents, peers, and school. The child should be encouraged to attend school, if only to be in a nonthreatening setting or to be with peers in nonacademic situations. Graded contact with the object of anxiety should be encouraged under the tutelage of a benevolent adult. This form of *behavior modification* can be applied to any type of separation anxiety.

Anxiety disorders in general respond to *individual psychotherapy* directed toward increasing the child's autonomy by exploring the unconscious meaning of the symptoms. *Family therapy* helps the parents understand the need for consistent, supportive love and the importance of preparing for any important change in life, such as illness, surgery, or geographic relocation.

Pharmacotherapy is useful for panic and separation anxiety. The *antidepressants*, such as imipramine (Tofranil), are usually begun in doses of 25 mg daily, increased by additional 25 mg doses up to a total of 150 to 200 mg daily until a therapeutic effect is noted. If no effect is noted with 200 mg daily, the plasma levels of imipramine and its active metabolite, desmethylimipramine, should be studied to determine whether a therapeutic blood level has been attained. Aside from its antidepressant effect, imipramine has been postulated to yield results that reduce panic and fear related to separation. Diphenhydramine (Benadryl) can be used to break a dangerous cycle of sleep disturbances.

37 |||||

Eating Disorders

Disorders of eating, particularly the syndromes of anorexia nervosa and bulimia nervosa, have attracted increasing attention in the psychiatric community and the general public in recent years. This interest has greatly accelerated the pace of investigation into eating disorders. Despite this large increase in research, questions about the causes, the pathology, and the treatment of eating disorders remain.

Four serious eating disorders are of concern to physicians. Pica and rumination disorder of infancy occur primarily in young children; anorexia nervosa and bulimia nervosa occur in adolescents and young adults, with striking predominance among females. All four disorders carry the risk of significant sequelae. They are included among the disorders of childhood or adolescence in the revised third edition of *Diagnostic and Statistical Manual of Mental Disorders* (DSM-III-R) because of their onset early in life.

Pica is defined as the repeated eating of nonnutritive substances, such as dirt, paint, hair, and paper. Although rare in adults, the disorder may be seen in pregnant women and in mentally retarded persons. More commonly, young children display this behavior, ingesting substances according to what is accessible and how mobile the child is. A baby in an old crib may chew on railings; a toddler may pick up objects from the floor or ground. Potential dangers include lead poisoning, iron deficiency, parasites, and intestinal obstruction.

Rumination is rare. This disorder, usually in infants 3 to 12 months of age, is characterized by the repeated regurgitation of food into the mouth, followed by spitting out or reswallowing the food. Infants consequently fail to thrive, with the risk not only of physical growth delay but also of failure to attain normal development. Death has been reported to occur in up to 25 percent of cases.

Students should recognize the differences between anorexia nervosa and bulimia nervosa. Anorexia nervosa presents a dramatic picture of self-starvation, peculiar attitudes toward and handling of food, weight loss (leading to maintenance of body weight at least 15 percent below that expected), and intense fear of weight gain. Although early reports pointed toward a correlation between anorexia and schizophrenia, patients with anorexia nervosa generally are not psychotic; they do, however, display body-image distortion to a psychotic degree, claiming to be fat even when emaciated. Anorexia occurs most often in 13- to 20-year-olds and is associated with a significant risk of death.

Bulimia nervosa involves recurrent episodes of binge eating, followed by resources to prevent weight gain: self-induced vomiting, use of laxatives or diuretics, fasting, and vigorous exercise. Unlike anorexic patients, bulimic patients may appear to be of normal weight in that some food is absorbed before purging. Bulimic patients may never come to medical attention, although dehydration, electrolyte imbalance, and damage to the dental enamel from acidic vomiting may occur. This hidden disorder may be indicated by a careful dietary history, although patients with bulimia nervosa are often reluctant to divulge their reliance on these methods of weight control.

Readers should refer to Chapter 37 of *Synopsis VI*, "Eating Disorders," and to Chapter 39 of *CTP V*, "Eating Disorders." After completing those chapters, readers can test their knowledge by studying the questions and answers below.

HELPFUL HINTS

The student should know and be able to define the terms below.

anorexia nervosa	obsessive-compulsive disorder	binge eating
bulimia nervosa	lanugo	postbinge anguish
pica	edema	Klüver-Bucy-like syndrome
rumination disorder of infancy	hypothermia	hypersexuality
geophasia	LH	hyperphagia
Argo starch	ACTH	borderline personality
Kleine-Levin syndrome	MHPG	disorder
psychosocial dwarfism	T waves	hypersomnia
ruminate	denial	imipramine (Tofranil)
merycism	hypokalemic alkalosis	eating disorder not otherwise
pyloric stenosis	ST segment depression	specified
aversive conditioning	gastric dilation	cyproheptadine (Periactin)
amenorrhea	ECT	self-stimulation

QUESTIONS

DIRECTIONS: The incomplete statement below is followed by five suggested completions. Select the *one* that is *best*.

37.1. All the following are frequently described in patients with anorexia nervosa *except*
A. amenorrhea
B. parental history of a weight phobia
C. above-average scholastic achievement
D. good sexual adjustment
E. ritualistic exercising

DIRECTIONS: For each of the incomplete statements below, *one or more* of the completions given are correct. Choose answer

A. if only *1, 2, and 3* are correct
B. if only *1 and 3* are correct
C. if only *2 and 4* are correct
D. if only *4* is correct
E. if *all* are correct

37.2. George—a thin, pale 5-year-old—was admitted to the hospital for a nutritional anemia that seemed to be due to his ingestion of paint, dirt, wood, and paste. He had had numerous hospitalizations under similar circumstances, beginning at 19 months of age, when he had ingested lighter fluid.

George's parents subsisted on welfare and were described as immature and dependent. He was the product of an unplanned but normal pregnancy. His mother began eating dirt when she was pregnant, at 16 years of age. His father

periodically abused drugs and alcohol. [From *DSM-III-R Case Book*. Used with permission.]

Epidemiological features associated with the disorder described in this case include the fact that it is
1. rarely seen in adults
2. seen in up to 32 percent of children between the ages of 1 and 6 years
3. increased in incidence among pregnant women in certain subcultures
4. more frequently seen in males than in females.

Questions 37.3–37.4

Mary was a gaunt 15-year-old high school student evaluated at the insistence of her parents, who were concerned about her weight loss. She was 5 feet 3 inches tall and had obtained her greatest weight of 100 pounds a year earlier. Shortly thereafter she decided to lose weight to be more attractive. She felt chubby and thought she would be more appealing if she were thinner. She first eliminated all carbohydrate-rich foods and gradually increased her dieting until she was eating only a few vegetables a day. She also started a vigorous exercise program. Within six months, she was down to 80 pounds. She then became preoccupied with food and started to collect recipes from magazines to prepare gourmet meals for her family. She had difficulty in sleeping and was irritable and depressed, having several crying spells every day. Her menses had started last year, but she had had only a few normal periods.

Mary had always obtained high grades in school and had spent a great deal of time studying. She had never been active socially and had never dated. She was conscientious and perfectionistic in everything she undertook. She had never been away from home as long as a week. Her father was a business manager. Her mother was a housewife who for the past two years had had a problem with hypoglycemia and had been on a low-carbohydrate diet.

During the interview, Mary said she felt fat, even though she weighed only 80 pounds, and she described a fear of losing control and eating so much food that she would become obese. She did not feel she was ill and thought hospitalization unnecessary. [From *DSM-III-R Case Book*. Used with permission.]

37.3. In this case the diagnosis of anorexia nervosa can be made on the basis of Mary's
1. 20-pound weight loss
2. feeling fat at a weight of 80 pounds at a height of 5 feet 3 inches
3. having had only a few normal periods
4. fear of becoming obese

37.4. Features associated with the disorder described in this case include
1. onset between the ages of 10 and 30
2. lanugo
3. mortality rates from 5 to 18 percent
4. the fact that 4 to 6 percent of those affected are male

37.5. Susan was admitted to the hospital at 6 months of age by an aunt for evaluation of failure to gain weight. She had been born into an impoverished family after an unplanned, uncomplicated pregnancy. During the first four months of her life, she gained weight steadily. Regurgitation was noted during the fifth month and increased in severity until she was regurgitating after every feeding. After each feeding Susan would engage in one of two behaviors: (1) she would open her mouth, elevate her tongue rapidly, and thrust it back and forward, after which milk would appear at the back of her mouth and slowly trickle out, or (2) she would vigorously suck her thumb and place her fingers in her mouth, after which milk would slowly flow out of the corner of her mouth.

In the past two months, Susan had been cared for by a number of people, including her aunt and her paternal grandmother. Her parents were making a marginal marital adjustment. [From *DSM-III-R Case Book*. Used with permission.]

Features in this case associated with the diagnosis are
1. its development after a period of normal functioning
2. failure to gain expected weight
3. having a parent engaged in marital conflict
4. the age at which the symptoms were first noted

37.6. Complications associated with pica include
1. iron deficiency
2. lead poisoning
3. zinc deficiency
4. intestinal obstruction

37.7. Proposed causes of rumination disorder of infancy include
1. disturbances in the mother-child relationship
2. overstimulation and tension
3. a dysfunctional autonomic nervous system
4. the positive reinforcement of self-stimulation

DIRECTIONS: The lettered headings below are followed by a list of numbered words or phrases. For each numbered word or phrase, select the *one* lettered heading that is most closely associated with it. Each lettered heading may be selected once, more than once, or not at all.

Questions 37.8–37.15
A. Bulimia nervosa
B. Anorexia nervosa

37.8. Associated with significant mortality rates

37.9. Severe weight loss

37.10. Amenorrhea

37.11. Sexually active

37.12. Rigid and perfectionistic

37.13. Impulsive and emotionally labile

37.14. Behavior ego-dystonic

37.15. Benefits from treatment with cyproheptadine (Periactin)

ANSWERS

Eating Disorders

37.1. The answer is D (*Synopsis VI*, pages 743–745; *CTP V*, pages 1859–1860).

Poor (not good) sexual adjustment is frequently described in patients with anorexia nervosa. Many adolescent anorexics have delayed psychosocial sexual development, and adults often have a markedly decreased interest in sex that accompanies the onset of illness. Many female anorexics come to medical attention because of *amenorrhea* (absence of menses), which often appears before their weight loss is noticeable. Often, mothers or fathers of anorexics have had an explicit history of significantly low adolescent weight or a *weight phobia*, but the available evidence does not permit any conclusions about the role of heredity in the development of anorexia.

Above-average scholastic achievement, model perfectionism, and an unrealistic fear of failure are often characteristics of anorexics. Obsessive-compulsive behavior, depression, anxiety, and somatization are psychiatric symptoms in anorexia nervosa frequently noted in the literature. *Ritualistic exercising*, extensive cycling, walking, jogging, and running are common activities.

Table 37.1 lists the DSM-III-R diagnostic criteria for anorexia nervosa.

37.2. The answer is A (1, 2, 3) (*Synopsis VI*, pages 740–741; *CTP V*, page 1861).

The boy described is suffering from pica—the repeated ingestion of nonnutritive substances, such as dirt, clay, plaster, and paper. Pica is *rarely seen in adults*, although clay eating and starch eating appear to have an increased incidence among *pregnant women* in certain subcultures. In one study, 55 percent of pregnant women in Georgia had a history of clay eating. Several studies report that between 10 and *32 percent of children* between the ages of 1 and 6 years have pica; its onset is usually between the ages of 12 and 24 months. The incidence of the disorder decreases with age (usually remitting by adolescence), and it is *equally frequent* in the two sexes (not more frequent in males).

Table 37.2 lists the DSM-III-R diagnostic criteria for pica.

37.3. The answer is E (all) (*Synopsis VI*, page 745; *CTP V*, pages 1854–1855).

The diagnosis of anorexia nervosa can be made in the case of Mary, a gaunt 15-year-old high school student, on the basis of her *20-pound weight loss*, her *feeling fat* at 80 pounds and 5 feet 3 inches, her having had only a *few normal periods*, and her *fear of becoming obese*.

The DSM-III-R diagnostic criteria for anorexia nervosa include a weight loss leading to maintenance of body weight 15 percent below that expected. In Mary's case, her weight loss of 20 pounds represents 20 percent. Another example in the diagnostic criteria is that the person claims to feel fat even when emaciated, which Mary stated. According to DSM-III-R, the absence of at least three consecutive menstrual cycles when otherwise expected to occur (primary or secondary amenorrhea) is a diagnostic feature of anorexia nervosa. Although Mary's menses started last year, she has had only a

Table 37.1
Diagnostic Criteria for Anorexia Nervosa

A. Refusal to maintain body weight over a minimal normal weight for age and height, e.g., weight loss leading to maintenance of body weight 15% below that expected; or failure to make expected weight gain during period of growth, leading to body weight 15% below that expected.

B. Intense fear of gaining weight or becoming fat, even though underweight.

C. Disturbance in the way in which one's body weight, size, or shape is experienced, e.g., the person claims to "feel fat" even when emaciated, believes that one area of the body is "too fat" even when obviously underweight.

D. In females, absence of at least three consecutive menstrual cycles when otherwise expected to occur (primary or secondary amenorrhea). (A woman is considered to have amenorrhea if her periods occur only following hormone, e.g., estrogen, administration.)

Table from DSM-III-R, *Diagnostic and Statistical Manual of Mental Disorders*, ed 3, revised. Copyright American Psychiatric Association, Washington, DC, 1987. Used with permission.

Table 37.2
Diagnostic Criteria for Pica

A. Repeated eating of nonnutritive substance for at least one month.

B. Does not meet the criteria for either autistic disorder, schizophrenia, or Kleine-Levin syndrome.

Table from DSM-III-R, *Diagnostic and Statistical Manual of Mental Disorders*, ed 3, revised. Copyright American Psychiatric Association, Washington, DC, 1987. Used with permission.

few normal periods. And fulfilling the criteria for anorexia is the patient's intense fear of gaining weight or becoming fat, even though underweight, which Mary stated as fear of losing control and eating so much food that she would become obese.

37.4. The answer is E (all) (*Synopsis VI*, pages 743–745; *CTP V*, pages 1854–1862).

Features associated with anorexia nervosa include *onset between the ages of 10 and 30, lanugo* (neonatallike body hair), *mortality rates from 5 to 18 percent*, and the fact that *4 to 6 percent of those affected are male*. Recent prevalence studies have shown anorexia nervosa to be a common disorder in the age group most at risk, especially in the high socioeconomic classes. As many as 1 in 100 and as few as 1 in 800 girls between the ages of 12 and 18 years may have the disorder.

Anorexia nervosa is an eating disorder characterized by self-imposed dietary limitations, peculiar patterns of handling food, significant weight loss, and an intense fear of obesity and gaining weight. There is a significant disturbance in body image (anorexics claim to feel fat even when emaciated), and there must be a weight loss leading to the maintenance of body weight at least 15 percent below that expected. The onset of anorexia nervosa is uncommon before the age of 10 and after age 30; in about 85 percent of all anorexic patients, the illness develops between the ages of 13 and 20 years. Patients usually come to medical attention when their weight loss becomes apparent. As the weight loss becomes profound, physical signs such as hypothermia (low body temperature), edema (swelling), bradycardia (slow heart rate), hypotension (low blood pressure), and lanugo appear.

The course of anorexia nervosa varies greatly from spontaneous recovery without treatment, recovery after a variety of treatments, and a fluctuating course of weight gains followed by relapses to a gradually deteriorating course resulting in death from the complications of starvation.

37.5. The answer is E (all) (*Synopsis VI*, pages 741–742; *CTP V*, pages 1855 and 1861).

The disorder described in this case is rumination disorder of infancy, characterized by repeated regurgitation of food. Associated features include weight loss or *failure to gain expected weight* that develops after a *period of normal functioning* and having a parent engaged in *marital conflict* at the age at which the *symptoms were first noted* (Susan at 4 months old). The disorder is rare, is most common among infants between 3 months and 1 year of age, is associated with severe secondary complications, and is often treated by using behavioral techniques.

In this disorder, partially digested food is brought up into the mouth without nausea or associated gastrointestinal disorder. The food is then ejected from the mouth or reswallowed. The infant makes sucking movements of the tongue and gives the impression of gaining considerable satisfaction from the activity.

Although spontaneous remissions are common, severe secondary complications may develop, such as progressive malnutrition, dehydration, and lowered disease resistance. Failure to thrive, with growth failure and developmental delays in all areas, may occur. Mortality as high as 25 percent has been reported in severe cases.

Treatments include improvement of the child's psychological environment, more tender loving care, and psychotherapy for the parents. Behavioral techniques have also been used effectively. Aversive conditioning appears to be the most rapidly effective treatment and can involve squirting an unpleasant substance (e.g., lemon juice) in the mouth whenever the rumination occurs; if successful, this technique sometimes eliminates rumination in three to five days.

The diagnostic criteria for rumination disorder of infancy are listed in Table 37.3.

37.6. The answer is E (all) (*Synopsis VI*, pages 740–741; *CTP V*, page 1861).

Complications associated with pica include severe *iron deficiency* after the ingestion of large quantities of starch; *lead poisoning*, usually from lead-based paint; anemia and *zinc deficiency* after the ingestion of clay; *intestinal obstruction* from the ingestion of hair balls, stones, or gravel; and intestinal parasites after the ingestion of soil or feces. Clinical implications, clearly, may be benign or life-threatening, according to the objects ingested.

37.7. The answer is E (all) (*Synopsis VI*, page 742; *CTP V*, pages 1857–1858).

Proposed causes of rumination disorder of infancy include various disturbances in the *mother-child relationship, overstimulation and tension*, a *dysfunctional autonomic nervous system*, and the *positive reinforcement* of the pleasurable self-stimulation and the attention that the baby receives from others as a consequence of the disorder. A substantial number of children classified as ruminators may also have gastroesophogeal reflux or a hiatal hernia.

Psychodynamic theories hypothesize that the caretakers of infants with this disorder are usually

Table 37.3
Diagnostic Criteria for Rumination Disorder of Infancy

A. Repeated regurgitation, without nausea or associated gastrointestinal illness, for at least one month following a period of normal functioning.

B. Weight loss or failure to make expected weight gain.

Table from DSM-III-R, *Diagnostic and Statistical Manual of Mental Disorders*, ed 3, revised. Copyright American Psychiatric Association, Washington, DC, 1987. Used with permission.

immature, involved in marital conflict, and unable to give much attention to the baby. This lack of attention results in insufficient emotional gratification and stimulation for the infant, who seeks gratification from within.

37.8–37.15

37.8. The answer is B (*Synopsis VI*, pages 743–748; *CTP V*, pages 1854–1863).

37.9. The answer is B (*Synopsis VI*, pages 743–748; *CTP V*, pages 1854–1863).

37.10. The answer is B (*Synopsis VI*, pages 743–748; *CTP V*, pages 1854–1863).

37.11. The answer is A (*Synopsis VI*, pages 743–748; *CTP V*, pages 1854–1863).

37.12. The answer is B (*Synopsis VI*, pages 743–748; *CTP V*, pages 1854–1863).

37.13. The answer is A (*Synopsis VI*, pages 743–748; *CTP V*, pages 1854–1863).

37.14. The answer is A (*Synopsis VI*, pages 743–748; *CTP V*, pages 1854–1863).

37.15. The answer is B (*Synopsis VI*, pages 743–748; *CTP V*, pages 1854–1863).

Bulimia nervosa is an episodic, uncontrolled, compulsive, and rapid ingestion of large quantities of food over a short period of time (binge eating). The person also regularly uses laxatives or diuretics or induces vomiting or other extreme means of purging. Vomiting does not always have to be present to make the diagnosis. Anorexia nervosa is an eating disorder characterized by self-imposed dietary limitations, peculiar patterns of handling food, significant weight loss, and an intense fear of obesity and gaining weight. The appetite is maintained in the disorder.

Pharmacological agents have been effective adjuncts to treatment in both anorexia and bulimia nervosa. Antidepressants, such as amitriptyline (Elavil) and imipramine (Tofranil), have been used with favorable results in bulimia nervosa, as have monoamine oxidase inhibitors. Fluoxetine (Prozac) also appears to be a promising treatment for bulimics.

As yet, no one class of drugs is beneficial to many anorexics. The most promising medication is *cyproheptadine* (Periactin). Cyproheptadine is both an antihistamine and a serotonin antagonist. Some nonbinging anorexics gain weight on cyproheptadine. Antidepressants have not been shown to be of much help to anorexics.

In the descriptive literature of both disorders, several stressful adolescent life situations (e.g., going away to school, getting a job) have been noted to occur shortly before the onset of the disorders. Anorexia nervosa is one of the few psychiatric illnesses that may have a course that leads to death; *mortality* rates are significant and have been reported to range between 5 and 18 percent. Bulimia nervosa is usually a chronic condition present over a period of many years and is rarely incapacitating or fatal. In both anorexia and bulimia nervosa much of the aberrant eating behavior takes place in secret. Anorexic patients often refuse to eat with their families or in public places. Some anorexic patients cannot continuously control the self-imposed restriction of food and so have binges, which are generally secret and take place at night. While eating meals, anorexics may try to dispose of food in their napkins or hide it in their pockets. During eating binges, bulimic patients eat food that is sweet, high in calories, and generally of smooth texture or soft, such as cakes and pastry. The food is eaten secretly and rapidly. The self-induced vomiting and use of laxatives or diuretics, typical of bulimics, are behaviors also carried out secretly and accompanied by feelings of guilt, depression, or self-disgust.

Anorexics are *rigid and perfectionistic*. The incidence of anorexia nervosa is high among high-achieving females. Anorexics appear to respond to the demands of adolescence by substituting the preoccupations with eating and weight control for normal adolescent pursuits. Psychologically, bulimics, like anorexics, have problems with the demands of adolescence. Bulimics are more *impulsive and emotionally labile* than anorexics. Suicide attempts, alcohol abuse, and shoplifting are associated with bulimia nervosa. Most anorexics are disinterested in psychiatric treatment. Bulimics, in general, experience their symptoms as *ego-dystonic* and are more likely than anorexics to seek help.

Anorexia nervosa is associated with significant and sometimes *severe weight loss;* one of the DSM-III-R criteria for this disorder is weight loss leading to the maintenance of body weight at least 15 percent below that expected. Bulimia nervosa does not lead to severe weight loss, and most bulimic patients are within their normal weight range. *Amenorrhea* is one of the DSM-III-R criteria for making the diagnosis of anorexia nervosa (in DSM-III-R, the absence of at least three consecutive menstrual cycles when otherwise expected to occur); amenorrhea is rare in patients with bulimia nervosa. An example of an eating disorder not otherwise specified is a female with all the features of anorexia except the absence of menses. Both anorexic and bulimic patients may indulge in episodic binge eating with self-induced vomiting. For bulimic patients, this clinical feature often defines the disorder, whereas for anorexic patients it has been related to poor outcome in some studies. Most bulimics are concerned about their sexual attractiveness and remain *sexually active*. Anorexics frequently have poor sexual adjustment, delayed psychosocial sexual development, and a markedly decreased interest in sex accompanying the onset of the illness.

The term "anorectic" is defined as lacking appetite, which is paradoxical in that anorexics are, in fact, hungry but deny themselves food. The hunger ceases only late in the illness.

Tables 37.4 and 37.5 list the DSM-III-R diagnostic criteria for bulimia nervosa and eating disorders not otherwise specified (NOS), respectively.

Table 37.4
Diagnostic Criteria for Bulimia Nervosa

A. Recurrent episodes of binge eating (rapid consumption of a large amount of food in a discrete period of time).

B. A feeling of lack of control over eating behavior during the eating binges.

C. The person regularly engages in either self-induced vomiting, use of laxatives or diuretics, strict dieting or fasting, or vigorous exercise in order to prevent weight gain.

D. A minimum average of two binge eating episodes a week for at least three months.

E. Persistent overconcern with body shape and weight.

Table from DSM-III-R, *Diagnostic and Statistical Manual of Mental Disorders,* ed 3, revised. Copyright American Psychiatric Association, Washington, DC, 1987. Used with permission.

Table 37.5
Diagnostic Criteria for Eating Disorder Not Otherwise Specified

Disorders of eating that do not meet the criteria for a specific eating disorder.
Examples:
1. a person of average weight who does not have binge eating episodes, but frequently engages in self-induced vomiting for fear of gaining weight
2. all of the features of anorexia nervosa in a female except absence of menses
3. all of the features of bulimia nervosa except the frequency of binge eating episodes

Table from DSM-III-R, *Diagnostic and Statistical Manual of Mental Disorders*, ed 3, revised. Copyright American Psychiatric Association, Washington, DC, 1987. Used with permission.

38 ||||

Gender Identity Disorders

Even though patients may present with gender identity problems at any age, most cases begin in childhood and adolescence. The gender identity disorders are postulated to be at the end of a continuum of difficulties that many children have in reconciling their sex of rearing with their gender identity. The complexities of gender identity evolve during the life cycle, and the pathologies of gender identity assume different forms over the course of the life cycle. Clinicians are alerted to the gender identity disorders by patients who demonstrate or verbalize discomfort with living as members of their own sex at any age.

Most of the time, gender identity, the sense of self as male or female, and gender role, the behavioral aspect of gender identity, match one's anatomical sex. The most significant factor influencing gender identity, however, is not anatomical sex but the sex of rearing, assigned sex. Hence, in the care of a newborn with ambiguous genitalia, sex assignment and surgical and hormonal treatment are most likely to be successful, from a psychological standpoint, if performed early in life, before the development of gender identity. Clarification of the infant's assigned sex also inevitably influences how his or her parents approach rearing the infant.

The three gender identity disorders in the revised third edition of *Diagnostic and Statistical Manual of Mental Disorders* (DSM-III-R) with which the student should become acquainted are (1) gender identity disorder of childhood, (2) transsexualism, and (3) gender identity disorder of adolescence or adulthood, nontranssexual type (GIDAANT). Gender identity disorder of childhood, occurring in prepubertal children, is marked by the child's experiencing persistent, intense distress about his or her assigned sex and a desire to be or insistence that he or she is a member of the opposite sex. The prevalence of this disorder is unknown; boys much more frequently than girls come to professional attention. The identification of patients having a true disorder is blurred by the wide spectrum of presenting complaints and by varying cultural and parental expectations for boys and girls: a tomboyish girl, for example, may be viewed with less parental alarm than an effeminate boy or vice versa. Cross-dressing, sometimes associated with this disorder, tends to appear early; 75 percent of boys displaying this behavior do so before age 4. Homosexuality is said to develop in one third to two thirds of patients with childhood gender disorder, less often in girls than in boys. As always in the assessment of children, one should evaluate such presenting behaviors as cross-dressing in the context of the child's overall development, with attention to whether or not the behavior is having an adverse effect on the child's functioning at home, in school, and among peers.

The diagnosis of transsexualism is reserved for postpubertal patients, but the disorder usually begins in childhood. By DSM-III-R criteria, patients with this disorder experience persistent discomfort and a sense of inappropriateness about their assigned sex and a preoccupation, of at least two years' duration, with obtaining a sex change. Although a transsexual patient's sexual orientation may be asexual or homosexual, most transsexuals view themselves as heterosexual, based on attraction to the sex opposite to their gender, not anatomical, identity. Anatomically, a male patient feels a sense of being a "woman trapped in a man's body"; anatomically, a female patient experiences the reverse. Transsexual patients may avidly seek sex-reassignment surgery. By contrast, patients with GIDAANT do not seek to change their anatomical sex.

Intersexual disorders—such as Turner's and Klinefelter's syndromes, congenital virilizing adrenal hyperplasia, pseudohermaphroditism, and androgen insensitivity syndrome—are physical conditions affecting patients' anatomical and physiological sexual characteristics. Patients with intersexual disorders may present with psychological sequelae, such as impaired self-esteem, depression, and mourning of the absence of a normal body.

Students are referred to Chapter 38, "Gender Identity Disorders," of *Synopsis VI* and to Section 21.2, "Gender Identity Disorders of Childhood, Adolescence, and Adulthood," of *CTP V* for further discussion of the gender identity disorders. Studying the questions and answers below will enhance their understanding of these disorders.

HELPFUL HINTS

The student should know the gender identity syndromes and terms listed below.

gender identity	intersexual disorders	gender confusion
gender role	Turner's syndrome	sex of rearing
gender identity disorder not otherwise specified	dysgenesis	homosexual orientation
	Klinefelter's syndrome	agenesis
transsexualism	adrenogenital syndrome	dysgenesis
GIDAANT	pseudohermaphroditism	male habitus
cross-gender	hermaphroditism	ambiguous genitals
cross-dressing	androgen insensitivity syndrome	virilized genitals
assigned sex	testicular feminization syndrome	cryptorchid testis
transvestic fetishism	sex steroids	buccal smear
homosexuality	genotype	Barr body
SRS	phenotype	
asexual	X-linked	

QUESTIONS

DIRECTIONS: For each of the questions or incomplete statements below, *one or more* of the responses or completions given are correct. Choose answer

- A. if only *1, 2, and 3* are correct
- B. if only *1 and 3* are correct
- C. if only *2 and 4* are correct
- D. if only *4* is correct
- E. if *all* are correct

38.1. A 25-year-old patient, who called herself Charles, requested a sex-change operation. She had for three years lived socially and been employed as a man. For the last two of these years, she had been the housemate, economic provider, and husband-equivalent of a bisexual woman who had fled from a bad marriage. That woman's two young children regarded Charles as their stepfather, and there was a strong affectionate bond between them.

In social appearance the patient passed as a not very virile man whose sexual development in puberty might be conjectured to have been extremely delayed or hormonally deficient. Her voice was pitched low but not baritone. Her shirt and jacket were bulky and successfully camouflaged tightly bound, flattened breasts. A strap-on penis produced a masculine-looking bulge in the pants; it was so constructed that, in case of a social necessity, it could be used as a urinary conduit in the standing position. Without success, the patient had tried to obtain a mastectomy so that in summer she could wear only a T-shirt while working outdoors as a heavy construction machine operator. She had also been unsuccessful in trying to get a prescription for testosterone to produce male secondary sex characteristics and suppress menses. The patient wanted a hysterectomy and oophorectomy and, as a long-term goal, looked forward to obtaining a successful phalloplasty.

The history was straightforward in its account of progressive recognition in adolescence of being able to fall in love only with a woman after a tomboyish childhood that had finally consolidated into the transsexual role and identity.

Physical examination revealed normal female anatomy, which the patient found personally repulsive, incongruous, and a source of continual distress. The endocrine laboratory results were within normal limits for a woman. [From *DSM-III-R Case Book*. Used with permission.]

In this case the diagnosis of transsexualism can be made on the basis of the patient's
1. persistent discomfort and sense of inappropriateness about assigned sex
2. persistent preoccupation with getting rid of primary and secondary sex characteristics
3. age
4. persistent request for sex-reassignment surgery

38.2. Which of the following statements about boys with gender identity disorder are true?
1. Gender identity disorder begins to develop before age 4
2. A boy with the disorder rarely claims that his penis or testes are disgusting
3. Boys who cross-dress begin to do so before age 4
4. Transsexualism is the usual adolescent outcome

38.3. Persons with gender identity disorder of adolescence or adulthood, nontranssexual type,
1. take hormones to acquire characteristics of the other sex
2. are involved in cross-dressing in the role of the opposite sex
3. have intense sexual urges and sexually arousing fantasies involving cross-dressing
4. often are female impersonators

38.4. Girls with gender identity disorder of childhood
1. regularly have male companions
2. may refuse to urinate in a sitting position
3. may assert that they have or will grow a penis
4. maintain masculine behavior through adolescence

38.5. Transsexualism
1. usually begins in childhood
2. is most often transient
3. is more common in males than in females
4. may be diagnosed in persons without the desire to acquire sex characteristics of the other sex

DIRECTIONS: Each group of questions below consist of lettered headings followed by a list of numbered statements. For each numbered statement, select the *one* lettered heading that is most closely associated with it. Each lettered heading may be selected once, more than once, or not at all.

Questions 38.6–38.10
A. Turner's syndrome
B. Klinefelter's syndrome
C. Adrenogenital syndrome
D. Hermaphroditism
E. Androgen insensitivity syndrome

38.6. Also known as testicular feminization syndrome

38.7. Genotype is XXY

38.8. Most common female intersex disorder

38.9. Associated with web neck, dwarfism, and cubitus valgus

38.10. Also known as virilizing adrenal hyperplasia

Questions 38.11–38.12
A. Gender
B. Gender identity
C. Gender role

38.11. Sense of oneself as being male or female

38.12. The public expression that indicates the view of oneself as male or female

ANSWERS

Gender Identity Disorders

38.1. The answer is E (all) (*Synopsis VI*, pages 752–753; *CTP V*, pages 1061–1062).

The diagnosis of transsexualism is suggested by the patient's persistent requests for *sex-reassignment surgery* from female to male. In addition, the DSM-III-R diagnostic criteria are met for transsexualism. They include (1) *persistent discomfort* and sense of inappropriateness about one's assigned sex (e.g., recognition in adolescence of being able to fall in love only with a woman, followed by a transsexual role and identity); (2) persistent preoccupation for at least two years with getting rid of one's *primary and secondary sex characteristics* and acquiring the sex characteristics of the other sex (e.g., camouflaging the breasts, strapping on a penis, requesting a mastectomy); and (3) the person has achieved puberty (Charles is 25 years of *age*).

In addition, the homosexual type is specified, based on Charles's sexual preferences (i.e., a biological female who prefers another female). The clinician, however, should be aware that the overwhelming majority of transsexuals believe themselves to be heterosexual. The common statement of people like Charles is, "I am a man trapped in a woman's body." Transsexual women do not deny their anatomical sex but are preoccupied with the sense of really being men who are attracted to women.

See Table 38.1 for the DSM-III-R diagnostic criteria for transsexualism.

38.2. The answer is B (1, 3) (*Synopsis VI*, pages 751–752; *CTP V*, pages 1063–1064).

Gender identity disorder begins in boys *before age 4*, and peer conflict develops during the early school years, at about the ages of 7 and 8. Grossly feminine

Table 38.1
Diagnostic Criteria for Transsexualism

A. Persistent discomfort and sense of inappropriateness about one's assigned sex.

B. Persistent preoccupation for at least two years with getting rid of one's primary and secondary sex characteristics and acquiring the sex characteristics of the other sex.

C. The person has reached puberty.

Specify history of sexual orientation: **asexual, homosexual, heterosexual,** or **unspecified.**

Table from DSM-III-R, *Diagnostic and Statistical Manual of Mental Disorders*, ed 3, revised. Copyright American Psychiatric Association, Washington, DC, 1987. Used with permission.

mannerisms may lessen as the child grows older, especially if attempts are made to discourage such behavior. Cross-dressing may be part of the disorder, and 75 percent of *boys who cross-dress* begin to do so before age 4.

Follow-up studies of gender-disturbed boys consistently indicate that *homosexual orientation, not transsexualism*, is the usual adolescent outcome. Transsexualism occurs in less than 10 percent of cases. In both sexes, homosexuality is likely to develop in one third to two thirds of cases, although fewer girls than boys become homosexual, for reasons that are not clear.

A boy with this disorder asserts that he wants to grow up to become a woman and often claims that his *penis or testes are disgusting*. The prognosis for gender identity disorder depends on the age of onset and the intensity of the symptoms.

Table 38.2 lists the DSM-III-R diagnostic criteria for gender identity disorder of childhood.

38.3. The answer is C (2, 4) (*Synopsis VI*, pages 753–754; *CTP V*, pages 1062–1063).

Persons with gender identity disorder of adolescence or adulthood, nontranssexual type (GIDAANT), are *involved in cross-dressing* in the role of the opposite sex, either in fantasy or in reality. This disorder is often found among *female impersonators*. Unlike transsexualism, GIDAANT describes persons who are not interested in acquiring the *characteristics of the other sex* or changing their sex, although these persons are uncomfortable with their assigned sex. GIDAANT differs from transvestism (transvestic fetishism) in that there are no *sexual urges and sexually arousing fantasies* involved in the cross-dressing. Some people with this disorder once had transvestic fetishism but no longer become aroused by cross-dressing.

See Table 38.3, which lists the DSM-III-R diagnostic criteria for GIDAANT.

38.4. The answer is A (1, 2, 3) (*Synopsis VI*, pages 751–752; *CTP V*, pages 1064–1066).

Girls with gender identity disorder of childhood regularly have *male companions* and an avid interest in sports and rough-and-tumble play; they show no interest in dolls and playing house. In a few cases a girl with this disorder may *refuse to urinate in a sitting position*, may assert that she has or will grow a *penis*, does not want to grow breasts or menstruate, and asserts that she will grow up to become a man. The girl has a stated desire to be a boy, which is not

Table 38.2
Diagnostic Criteria for Gender Identity Disorder of Childhood

For Females:
A. Persistent and intense distress about being a girl, and a stated desire to be a boy (not merely a desire for any perceived cultural advantages from being a boy), or insistence that she is a boy.

B. Either 1 or 2:
  1. persistent marked aversion to normative feminine clothing and insistence on wearing stereotypical masculine clothing, e.g., boys' underwear and other accessories
  2. persistent repudiation of female anatomic structures, as evidenced by at least one of the following:
     a. an assertion that she has, or will grow, a penis
     b. rejection of urinating in a sitting position
     c. assertion that she does not want to grow breasts or menstruate

C. The girl has not yet reached puberty.

For Males:
A. Persistent and intense distress about being a boy and an intense desire to be a girl or, more rarely, insistence that he is a girl.

B. Either 1 or 2:
  1. preoccupation with female stereotypical activities, as shown by a preference for either cross-dressing or simulating female attire, or by an intense desire to participate in the games and pastimes of girls and rejection of male stereotypical toys, games, and activities
  2. persistent repudiation of male anatomic structures, as indicated by at least one of the following repeated assertions:
     a. that he will grow up to become a woman (not merely in role)
     b. that his penis or testes are disgusting or will disappear
     c. that it would be better not to have a penis or testes

C. The boy has not yet reached puberty.

Table from DSM-III-R, *Diagnostic and Statistical Manual of Mental Disorders,* ed 3, revised. Copyright American Psychiatric Association, Washington, DC, 1987. Used with permission.

merely a desire for any perceived cultural advantages of being a boy. Most girls give up *masculine behavior* by adolescence.

38.5. The answer is B (1, 3) (*Synopsis VI*, pages 752–753; *CTP V*, pages 1061–1066).

Transsexualism, which *usually begins in childhood,* is usually chronic in nature and not *transient.* It is much more common in *males (1 per 30,000)* than in *females (1 per 100,000).* Included in the DSM-III-R criteria for transsexualism is the persistent preoccupation for at least two years of getting rid of one's primary and secondary sex characteristics (e.g., breasts). Such persons wish to acquire the *sex characteristics* of the opposite sex.

An example of gender identity disorder not otherwise specified (NOS) is people who have a persistent preoccupation with castration (penectomy) without a desire to acquire the sex characteristics of the other sex.

Table 38.4 lists the DSM-III-R diagnostic criteria for gender identity disorder NOS.

Table 38.3
Diagnostic Criteria for Gender Identity Disorder of Adolescence or Adulthood, Nontranssexual Type (GIDAANT)

A. Persistent or recurrent discomfort and sense of inappropriateness about one's assigned sex.

B. Persistent or recurrent cross-dressing in the role of the other sex, either in fantasy or actuality, but not for the purpose of sexual excitement (as in transvestic fetishism).

C. No persistent preoccupation (for at least two years) with getting rid of one's primary and secondary sex characteristics and acquiring the sex characteristics of the other sex (as in transsexualism).

D. The person has reached puberty.

Specify history of sexual orientation: **asexual, homosexual, heterosexual,** or **unspecified.**

Table from DSM-III-R, *Diagnostic and Statistical Manual of Mental Disorders,* ed 3, revised. Copyright American Psychiatric Association, Washington, DC, 1987. Used with permission.

Table 38.4
Diagnostic Criteria for Gender Identity Disorder Not Otherwise Specified

Disorders in gender identity that are not classifiable as a specific gender identity disorder.
Examples:
  1. children with persistent cross-dressing without the other criteria for gender identity disorder of childhood
  2. adults with transient, stress-related cross-dressing behavior
  3. adults with the clinical features of transsexualism of less than two years' duration
  4. people who have a persistent preoccupation with castration or peotomy without a desire to acquire the sex characteristics of the other sex

Table from DSM-III-R, *Diagnostic and Statistical Manual of Mental Disorders,* ed 3, revised. Copyright American Psychiatric Association, Washington, DC, 1987. Used with permission.

Table 38.5
Intersexual Disorders

Adrenogenital syndrome (*virilizing adrenal hyperplasia*)	Results from excess androgens in fetus with XX genotype; *most common female intersex disorder;* associated with enlarged clitoris, labia, hirsutism in adolescence.
Turner's syndrome	Results from absence of second female sex chromosome (XO); associated with *web neck, dwarfism, cubitis valgus;* no sex hormones produced; infertile. Usually assigned as female because of female-looking genitals.
Klinefelter's syndrome	*Genotype is XXY;* male habitus present with small penis and rudimentary testes because of low androgen production; weak libido. Usually assigned as male.
Androgen insensitivity syndrome *(testicular feminization syndrome)*	Congenital X-linked recessive disorder that results in inability of tissues to respond to androgens; external genitals look female, and cryptorchid testes present. Assigned as female, even though patient has XY genotype. In extreme form, patient has breasts, normal female external genitals, short blind vagina, and absence of pubic and axillary hair.
Hermaphroditism	True hermaphroditism is rare and characterized by both testes and ovaries in same person (may be 46 XX or 46 XY).
Pseudohermaphroditism	Usually the result of endocrine or enzymatic defect (e.g., adrenal hyperplasia) in persons with normal chromosomes. Female pseudohermaphrodites have masculine-looking genitals but are XX. Male pseudohermaphrodites have rudimentary testes and external genitals and are XY. Assigned as male or female, depending on morphology of genitals.

38.6–38.10

38.6. The answer is E (*Synopsis VI*, pages 754–755; *CTP V*, page 1068).

38.7. The answer is B (*Synopsis VI*, pages 754–755; *CTP V*, page 1068).

38.8. The answer is C (*Synopsis VI*, pages 439 and 754–755; *CTP V*, page 1068).

38.9. The answer is A (*Synopsis VI*, pages 754–755; *CTP V*, page 1068).

38.10. The answer is C (*Synopsis VI*, pages 754–755; *CTP V*, page 1068).

Intersexual disorders are conditions in which persons have characteristics of both males and females that may be genetic, anatomical, or physiological in nature. The appearance of the genitalia in these conditions is ambiguous or incongruent with the genetic or chromosomal makeup of the person. This group of disorders is not part of the official DSM-III-R nosology; the disorders are known to clinicians, however, and should be classified on Axis III in DSM-III-R, which relates to physical disorders and conditions.

Intersexual patients may have gender identity problems based on sex of assignment. The genital appearance at birth determines the sex assignment, and gender identity is male or female, depending on the parents' conviction as to the child's sex and their subsequent rearing practices. Usually, a panel of experts determines the sex of assignment on the basis of a clinical examination, urological studies, buccal smears, chromosome studies, and parental wishes.

Assignment should be agreed on as early as possible, so that the parents can adapt accordingly. If surgery is necessary to correct a genital deformity, it is generally done before the age of 3 years. It is easier to assign the patient to be female in ambiguous cases, especially if surgical intervention is necessary. Male-to-female surgical procedures are far more advanced than female-to-male procedures.

Table 38.5 outlines some types of intersexual disorders.

38.11–38.12

38.11. The answer is B (*Synopsis VI*, page 750; *CTP V*, page 1061).

38.12. The answer is C (*Synopsis VI*, page 750; *CTP V*, page 1061).

Gender refers to the assigned sex, based on the anatomical appearance at birth. Gender identity refers to the *sense of oneself* as being male or female. Most children develop a gender identity consonant with their assigned sex. Gender role is the *public expression* of gender identity. It is what a person does to convey the view of oneself as male or female. Children learn culturally acceptable gender roles through dress, play, and expectations conveyed to them by their caretakers and peers, among others. Gender identity disorders occur when children have difficulty in reconciling their anatomical sex with their gender identity.

Tic Disorders

Tic disorders were attributed to demonic possession in the Middle Ages. Because of evidence of a familial pattern and of a positive response to dopamine-blocking medications for those with chronic tic disorders, psychiatrists now think that these disorders have an organic basis.

Tics are relatively common in childhood, with 5 to 24 percent of school-age children reporting past or present tics. These involuntary, sudden, recurrent motor movements or vocal productions are experienced by the patient as irresistible but can be suppressed voluntarily for varying periods of time. Any muscle or muscle group may be involved; most often, muscles of the face are affected, as in eye blinking, facial twitching, and grimacing. Both motor and vocal tics may be either simple or complex.

In approaching a patient with a chief complaint of tics, one should bear in mind the importance of excluding underlying neurological diseases that can manifest as tics. The examiner should make careful note of the pattern of muscles involved and of the reported duration of the tics, remembering that a child may suppress tics in the examiner's presence. Maneuvers to distract the patient's attention may elicit tics not otherwise shown.

The three main tic disorders described in the revised third edition of *Diagnostic and Statistical Manual of Mental Disorders* (DSM-III-R) are transient tic disorder, chronic motor or vocal tic disorder, and Tourette's disorder. All have in common the occurrence of tics many times a day nearly every day, occurrences not exclusively in association with psychoactive substance intoxication or known central nervous system disease, and onset before age 21. Hence, by this classification, tics with onset

after age 21 are diagnosed in a fourth category, tic disorder not otherwise specified.

Duration is the distinguishing factor between transient tic disorder (at least two weeks but no longer than 12 consecutive months) and chronic motor or vocal tic disorder (for more than one year). Tourette's disorder is distinguished from chronic motor or vocal tick disorder by the occurrence at some time of both motor and vocal elements, although not necessarily concurrently. Tourette's disorder is also distinguished by a favorable response to pharmacological agents. Haloperidol (Haldol) has been the pharmacological treatment of choice, with significant initial improvement in up to 80 percent of patients; newer agents receiving attention are pimozide (Orap) and clonidine (Catapres).

Controversy continues about the role of psychostimulants in the onset or the exacerbation of tic disorders. Most children who develop tics while receiving stimulant medication for the treatment of attention-deficit hyperactivity disorder (ADHD) either have a family history of tics or had evidence of abnormal movements before the initiation of medication. It is prudent, therefore, to use alternative classes of medications for those children with ADHD who have a family history of tic disorders or who have any evidence of movement disorders at the time of the initial assessment. The clinician should consider discontinuing stimulant medication if a child shows any evidence of a movement disorder during the course of treatment for ADHD.

Although most children presenting with new onset of a tic disorder experience remission of their symptoms, this outcome cannot be predicted with certainly for an individual child.

Even transiently, tics can create discomfort and prove anxiety-provoking to children and their parents. Patients with chronic tics, particularly those with Tourette's disorder, may suffer significant social embarrassment, anxiety, and depression. They often benefit not only from therapeutic approaches to enhance symptom relief but also from ongoing therapy to enhance

their ability to cope with the stress of a chronic disorder.

Students are referred to Chapter 39 of *Synopsis VI*, "Tic Disorders," and to Chapter 40 of *CTP V*, "Tic Disorders," for more detailed discussion. Studying the questions and answers below will enhance their understanding of these problems.

HELPFUL HINTS

The terms below relate to tic disorders and should be known by the student.

Tourette's disorder	palilalia	Pelizaeus-Merzbacher disease
motor tic	echolalia	status dysmyelinisatus
vocal tic	echokinesis	Sydenham's chorea
transient tic disorder	dystonia	Wilson's disease
simple or complex tics	hemiballism	Lesch-Nyhan syndrome
eye blinking	stereotypy	Gilles de la Tourette
neck jerking	compulsions	Jean Charcot
shoulder shrugging	hyperdopaminergia	benztropine (Cogentin)
facial grimacing	encephalitis lethargica	tardive dyskinesia
grunting	tremor	pimozide (Orap)
barking	Hallervorden-Spatz disease	clonidine (Catapres)
coprolalia	Huntington's chorea	torsion dystonia

QUESTIONS

DIRECTIONS: Each of the questions or incomplete statements below is followed by five suggested responses or completions. Select the *one* that is *best* in each case.

39.1. Which one of the following distinguishes transient tic disorder from chronic motor or vocal tic disorder and Tourette's disorder?
A. Age of onset
B. Motor tics only
C. Vocal tics only
D. Both motor and vocal tics
E. Progression of the tic symptoms over time

39.2. All the following statements about tic disorders are true *except*
A. dysregulation of the neurochemical systems of the central nervous system (CNS) is probably the most important causative factor in the majority of tics
B. tics are experienced as irresistible but can be voluntarily suppressed for varying lengths of time, from minutes to hours
C. CNS stimulants may exacerbate existing tics or cause new tics
D. tics occur at equal rates in males and females
E. head trauma may precipitate the onset of a tic disorder

39.3. All the following statements about tic disorders are true *except*
A. 5 to 24 percent of school-age children have a history of a transient tic
B. the average age of onset in transient tic disorder is 7 years
C. most transient tic disorders do not progress to a chronic disorder
D. most tics disappear during sleep
E. tics are about 10 times more common in males than in females

DIRECTIONS: For each of the questions or incomplete statements below, *one or more* of the responses or completions given are correct. Choose answer

    A. if only *1, 2, and 3* are correct
    B. if only *1 and 3* are correct
    C. if only *2 and 4* are correct
    D. if only *4* is correct
    E. if *all* are correct

Questions 39.4–39.5

Alan, a 10-year-old boy, was brought for a consultation by his mother because of "severe compulsions." The mother reported that the child at various times had to run and clear his throat, touch the doorknob twice before entering any door, tilt his head from side to side, rapidly blink his eyes, and touch the ground with his hands suddenly by flexing his whole body. These "compulsions" began two years ago. The first was the eye blinking, and then the others followed, with a waxing and waning course. The movements occurred most frequently when the patient was anxious or under stress. The last symptom to appear was the repetitive touching of doorknobs. The consultation was scheduled after the child began to make the middle-finger sign while saying profanities.

When examined, Alan reported that he did not know most of the time when the movements were going to occur except for the touching of doorknobs. On questioning, he said that, before he felt he had to touch a doorknob, he got the thought of doing it and tried to push it out of his head, but he couldn't because it kept coming back until he touched the doorknob several times; then he felt better. When asked what would happen if someone would not let him touch the doorknob, he said that he would just get mad; when his father tried to stop him, the boy had had a temper tantrum.

During the interview the child grunted, cleared his throat, turned his head, and rapidly blinked his eyes several times. At other times he tried to make it appear that he had voluntarily been performing these movements.

Past history and physical and neurological examinations were totally unremarkable except for the abnormal movements and sounds. The mother reported that her youngest uncle had had similar symptoms when he was an adolescent, but she could not elaborate any further.

[From *DSM-III-R Case Book.* Used with permission.]

39.4. In this case the diagnosis is made on the basis of
1. onset before age 21
2. the presence of vocal tics
3. coprolalia
4. no known central nervous system disease

39.5. Improvements in Tourette's disorder have been demonstrated with haloperidol (Haldol) and
1. pimozide (Orap)
2. benztropine (Cogentin)
3. clonidine (Catapres)
4. amphetamine

39.6. If the onset is after age 21, which of the following tic disorders may be diagnosed?
1. Transient tic disorder
2. Chronic motor or vocal tic disorder
3. Tourette's disorder
4. Tic disorder not otherwise specified

DIRECTIONS: Each set of lettered headings below is followed by a list of numbered phrases. For each numbered phrase, select the lettered heading most associated with it. Each heading may be used once, more than once, or not at all.

Questions 39.7–39.9

A. Tic disorder
B. Stereotypy and habit disorder

39.7. Voluntary nonspasmodic movements

39.8. Affected person is not distressed by the symptoms

39.9. Occurrence not exclusively during psychoactive substance intoxication

Questions 39.10–39.12

A. Coprolalia
B. Palilalia
C. Echolalia
D. Echokinesis

39.10. Imitation of observed movements

39.11. Repetition of socially unacceptable, frequently obscene words

39.12. Repetition of one's own sounds or words

ANSWERS

Tic Disorders

39.1. The answer is E (*Synopsis VI*, pages 757–763; *CTP V*, pages 1867–1869).

Transient tic disorder can be distinguished from chronic motor or vocal tic disorder and Tourette's disorder only by following the *progression of the tic symptoms* over time. DSM-III-R emphasizes precise and specific symptom patterns, time framework, and age of onset in classifying the tic disorders.

Tables 39.1 through 39.3 list the diagnostic criteria for transient tic disorder, chronic motor or vocal tic disorder, and Tourette's disorder.

39.2. The answer is D (*Synopsis VI*, page 756; *CTP V*, page 1869).

Tics do not occur at *equal rates in males and females*, being about three times more frequent in males. *Dysregulation of the neurochemical systems* of the central nervous system (CNS) is probably the most important causative factor in the majority of tics. *Head trauma* may also precipitate the onset of a tic disorder. Tics are involuntary, sudden, rapid, recurrent, nonrhythmic, stereotyped motor movements or vocal productions. They are *experienced as irresistible* but can be voluntarily suppressed for varying lengths of time, from minutes to hours. CNS *stimulants* may exacerbate existing tics or cause new ones, probably as a result of the release of dopamine from nigrostriatal dopaminergic nerve terminals.

Table 39.1
Diagnostic Criteria for Transient Tic Disorder

A. Single or multiple motor and/or vocal tics.

B. The tics occur many times a day, nearly every day for at least two weeks, but for no longer than 12 consecutive months.

C. No history of Tourette's or chronic motor or vocal tic disorder.

D. Onset before age 21.

E. Occurrence not exclusively during psychoactive substance intoxication or known central nervous system disease, such as Huntington's chorea and postviral encephalitis.

Specify: single episode or **recurrent.**

Table 39.2
Diagnostic Criteria for Chronic Motor or Vocal Tic Disorder

A. Either motor or vocal tics, but not both, have been present at some time during the illness.

B. The tics occur many times a day, nearly every day, or intermittently throughout a period of more than one year.

C. Onset before age 21.

D. Occurrence not exclusively during psychoactive substance intoxication or known central nervous system disease, such as Huntington's chorea and postviral encephalitis.

Table 39.3
Diagnostic Criteria for Tourette's Disorder

A. Both multiple motor and one or more vocal tics have been present at some time during the illness, although not necessarily concurrently.

B. The tics occur many times a day (usually in bouts) nearly every day or intermittently throughout a period of more than one year.

C. The anatomic location, number, frequency, complexity, and severity of the tics change over time.

D. Onset before age 21.

E. Occurrence not exclusively during psychoactive substance intoxication or known central nervous system disease, such as Huntington's chorea and postviral encephalitis.

39.3. The answer is E (*Synopsis VI*, pages 756–757; *CTP V*, page 1869).

Tic disorders are common in children; *5 to 24 percent* of school-age children have a history of tics. The average *age of onset of tics is 7 years*, but tics may occur as early as 2 years of age. The most common tics affect the face and the neck, with a descending gradient of frequency to the feet. Most transient tic disorders *do not progress* to a more serious, chronic disorder. Only a small percentage of patients have chronic symptoms. Most tics *disappear during sleep* and are exacerbated by stress. Tics are about 3 times, not 10 times, *more common in males than in females.*

39.4. The answer is E (all) (*Synopsis VI*, pages 760–761; *CTP V*, page 1867).

In the case of this 10-year-old boy, the correct diagnosis is Tourette's disorder. He has both chronic motor tics and *vocal tics*, including *coprolalia*. The tics have occurred for more than one year. The disorder started well under *age 21*. He also has *no known central nervous system disease.*

Obsessions and compulsions are often seen, as in Alan's case, in persons with Tourette's disorder. His obsessions and compulsions are not persistent and disruptive enough, however, to meet the diagnosis of obsessive-compulsive disorder. See Table 39.3 for the DSM-III-R criteria for Tourette's disorder.

39.5. The answer is B (1, 3) (*Synopsis VI*, page 762; *CTP V*, page 1876).

In addition to haloperidol (Haldol), which is now the standard treatment against which other proposed treatments should be judged, improvements in Tourette's disorder have been demonstrated with *pimozide* (Orap) and *clonidine* (Catapres). Pimozide, an inhibitor of postsynaptic dopamine receptors, has been approved to treat Tourette's disorder and is used in patients with severe symptoms who fail to respond to haloperidol. Although not currently approved for use in Tourette's disorder, clonidine, a presynaptic α-adrenergic blocking agent, has been reported in several studies to be efficacious, with 40 to 70 percent of patients benefiting from it.

Immediate and long-term adverse effects of haloperidol are possible, including acute dystonic reactions and parkinsonian symptoms. Although prophylactic use of an anticholinergic agent is not recommended, it is appropriate to prescribe diphenhydramine (Benadryl) or *benztropine* (Cogentin) for the patient, should adverse reactions occur, not as a treatment for Tourette's disorder. Stimulant medications (e.g., methylphenidate [Ritalin], *amphetamine*, and pemoline [Cylert]) have been reported to exacerbate preexisting tics and to precipitate the development of new tics and Tourette's disorder.

Table 39.4 lists the differential diagnosis of tic disorders.

39.6. The answer is D (4) (*Synopsis VI*, page 763; *CTP V*, pages 1868–1869).

All tic disorders with onset after age 21 must be diagnosed as *tic disorder not otherwise specified* (NOS), a residual category for tics that do not meet the criteria for a specific tic disorder. *Transient tic disorder, chronic motor or vocal tic disorder*, and *Tourette's disorder* all specify onset before age 21.

Table 39.5 lists the DSM-III-R diagnostic criteria for tic disorder NOS.

39.7–39.9

39.7. The answer is B (*Synopsis VI*, page 757; *CTP V*, pages 1874 and 1903–1908).

39.8. The answer is B (*Synopsis VI*, page 757; *CTP V*, pages 1874 and 1903–1908).

39.9. The answer is A (*Synopsis VI*, page 759; *CTP V*, pages 1866–1867 and 1874).

Stereotypy and habit disorder are distinguishable from tics in that they consist of *voluntary nonspasmodic movements;* tics are involuntary, spasmodic movements. Moreover, unlike children with a tic disorder, children with a stereotypy and habit disorder are *not distressed by the symptoms*. Both autistic and mentally retarded children may exhibit symptoms similar to the symptoms seen in the tic disorders, including Tourette's disorder. Likewise, it is possible in stereotypy and habit disorder for the patient to be mentally retarded. Both tic disorders and stereotypy and habit disorder are more prevalent in males than in females. DSM-III-R specifies that, in a diagnosis of tic disorder, its occurrence should not be exclusively during *psychoactive substance intoxication* or known central nervous system (CNS) disease, such as Huntington's chorea and postviral encephalitis. Stereotypy and habit disorder, though, may be diagnosed concurrently with organic mental disorder induced by a psychoactive substance (e.g., amphetamine), severe sensory impairments, CNS and degenerative disorders (e.g., Lesch-Nyhan syndrome), severe schizophrenia, or obsessive-compulsive disorder.

DSM-III-R notes that both motor and vocal tics may be classified as either simple or complex, although the boundaries are not well defined. Common simple motor tics are eye blinking, neck jerking, shoulder shrugging, and facial grimacing. Common simple vocal tics are coughing, throat clearing, grunting, sniffing, snorting, and barking. Common complex motor tics are facial gestures, grooming behaviors, hitting or biting self, jumping, touching, stamping, and smelling an object. Common complex vocal tics are repeating words or phrases out of context, coprolalia (use of socially unacceptable words, frequently obscene), palilalia (repeating one's own sounds or words), and echolalia (repeating the last heard sound, word, or phrase of another person or other last heard sound). Other complex tics include echokinesis (imitation of the movements of someone who is being observed).

Stereotypy and habit disorder involves intentional, repetitive, nonfunctional behaviors (such as hand shaking or waving, body rocking, head banging, mouthing of objects, nail biting, and picking at the nose or skin). The behaviors are so severe as to cause physical injury to the child or to markedly interfere with normal activities.

Table 39.4
Differential Diagnosis of Tic Disorders

Disease or Syndrome	Age at Onset	Associated Features	Course	Predominant Type of Movement
Hallervorden-Spatz	Childhood–adolescence	May be associated with optic atrophy, club feet, retinitis pigmentosa, dysarthria, dementia, ataxia, emotional lability, spasticity, autosomal recessive inheritance	Progressive to death in 5 to 20 years	Choreic, athetoid, myoclonic
Dystonia muscularum deformans	Childhood–adolescence	Autosomal recessive inheritance commonly, primarily among Ashkenazi Jews; a more benign autosomal dominant form also occurs	Variable course, often progressive but rare remissions	Dystonia
Sydenham's chorea	Childhood, usually 5–15 years	More common in females, usually associated with rheumatic fever (carditis elevated ASLO titers)	Usually self-limited	Choreiform
Huntington's chorea	Usually 30–50 years, but childhood forms are known	Autosomal dominant inheritance, dementia, caudate atrophy on CT scan	Progressive to death in 10 to 15 years after onset	Choreiform
Wilson's disease (hepatolenticular degeneration)	Usually 10–25 years	Kayser-Fleischer rings, liver dysfunction, inborn error of copper metabolism; autosomal recessive inheritance	Progressive to death without chelating therapy	Wing-beating tremor, dystonia
Hyperekplexias (including latah, myriachit, jumping Frenchman of Maine)	Generally in childhood (dominant inheritance)	Familial; may have generalized rigidity and autosomal inheritance	Nonprogressive	Excessive startle response; may have echolalia, coprolalia, and forced obedience
Myoclonic disorders	Any age	Numerous causes, some familial, usually no vocalizations	Variable, depending on cause	Myoclonus
Myoclonic dystonia	5–47 years	Nonfamilial, no vocalizations	Nonprogressive	Torsion dystonia with myoclonic jerks
Paroxysmal myoclonic dystonia with vocalization	Childhood	Attention, hyperactive, and learning disorders; movements interfere with ongoing activity	Nonprogressive	Bursts of regular, repetitive clonic (less tonic) movements and vocalizations
Tardive Tourette's disorder syndromes	Variable (after antipsychotic medication use)	Reported to be precipitated by discontinuation or reduction of medication	May terminate after increase or decrease of dosage	Orofacial dyskinesias, choreoathetosis, tics, vocalization

(Continued)

Table 39.4
Continued

Disease or Syndrome	Age at Onset	Associated Features	Course	Predominant Type of Movement
Neuroacanthocytosis	Third or fourth decade	Acanthocytosis, muscle wasting, parkinsonism, autosomal recessive inheritance	Variable	Orofacial dyskinesia and limb chorea, tics, vocalization
Encephalitis lethargica	Variable	Shouting fits, bizarre behavior, psychosis, Parkinson's syndrome	Variable	Simple and complex motor and vocal tics, coprolalia, echolalia, echopraxia, palilalia
Gasoline inhalation	Variable	Abnormal EEG; symmetrical theta and theta bursts frontocentrally	Variable	Simple motor and vocal tics
Postangiographic complications	Variable	Emotional lability, amnestic syndrome	Variable	Simple motor and complex vocal tics, palilalia
Postinfectious	Variable	EEG: occasional asymmetrical theta bursts before movements, elevated ASLO titers	Variable	Simple motor and vocal tics, echopraxia
Posttraumatic	Variable	Asymmetrical tic distribution	Variable	Complex motor tics
Carbon monoxide poisoning	Variable	Inappropriate sexual behavior	Variable	Simple and complex motor and vocal tics, coprolalia, echolalia, palilalia
XYY genetic disorder	Infancy	Aggressive behavior	Static	Simple motor, vocal tics
XXY and 9$_p$ mosaicism	Infancy	Multiple physical anomalies, mental retardation	Static	Simple motor, vocal tics
Duchenne muscular dystrophy (X-linked recessive)	Childhood	Mild mental retardation	Progressive	Motor, vocal tics
Fragile X syndrome	Childhood	Mental retardation, facial dysmorphism, seizures, autistic features	Static	Simple motor, vocal tics, coprolalia
Developmental and perinatal disorders	Infancy, childhood	Seizures, EEG and CT abnormalities, psychosis, agressivity, hyperactivity, Ganser syndrome, compulsivity, torticollis	Variable	Motor and vocal tics, echolalia

Table adapted from A K Shapiro, E Shapiro, J G Young, T E Feinberg: *Gilles de la Tourette Syndrome,* ed 2. Raven Press, New York, 1987, with permission.

Table 39.5
Diagnostic Criteria for Tic Disorder
Not Otherwise Specified

Tics that do not meet the criteria for a specific tic disorder. An example is a tic disorder with onset in adulthood.

Table from DSM-III-R, *Diagnostic and Statistical Manual of Mental Disorders,* ed 3, revised. Copyright American Psychiatric Association, Washington, DC, 1987. Used with permission.

39.10–39.12

39.10. The answer is D (*Synopsis VI*, page 756; *CTP V*, page 1867).

39.11. The answer is A (*Synopsis VI*, page 756; *CTP V*, page 1867).

39.12. The answer is B (*Synopsis VI*, page 756; *CTP V*, page 1866).

Vocal tics may be simple. For example, coughing and barking are simple vocal tics. Complex vocal tics consist of repeating words or phrases out of context. Coprolalia is the repetition of *socially unacceptable, frequently obscene words*. Palilalia is the repetition of *one's own words*. Echolalia is the repetition of the last heard word, phrase, or sound of another person. Echokinesis is a complex motor tic consisting of the repetition of *observed movements*.

40 ||||| Elimination Disorders

The elimination disorders, functional enuresis and functional encopresis, have been subject to interpretations paralleling the prevalent psychological theories of the era. In the 1930s rigid toilet training was common, following theories derived from behavioral psychology. As psychoanalytic theory became widely known, it led to a permissive, laissez-faire attitude of toilet training. At this time, maturation delays are thought to play a role in the development of elimination disorders. No unitary theory of causes or treatment has withstood the accumulation of new data, emphasizing the complexity of seemingly simple symptoms.

The two elimination disorders described in the revised third edition of *Diagnostic and Statistical Manual of Mental Disorders* (DSM-III-R), encopresis and enuresis, generally create harried parents and unhappy children. Toilet training in the course of a normal child's development is laden with struggles for autonomy and control. Children failing to attain bowel and bladder control when expected to do so are at risk of suffering impaired self-esteem, teasing, and ostracism by peers and parental disappointment or anger.

Functional encopresis is defined as the repeated passage of feces into inappropriate places; functional enuresis is the repeated voiding of urine during the day or the night into a child's clothing or bed. Both disorders comprise both involuntary and voluntary behaviors and are designated as either primary or secondary in type. Both also necessitate the exclusion of causative or contributory physical conditions and, hence, are optimally evaluated by a pediatrician and child psychiatrist working closely together.

Functional encopresis, occurring in about 1 percent of 5-year-olds, is rarer than functional enuresis, which at age 5 affects about 7 percent of boys and 3 percent of girls. Diagnosis of functional encopresis requires a chronological and mental age of 4; diagnosis of functional enuresis requires a chronological age of 5 and a mental age of 4.

Encopresis is more distasteful to others than is enuresis and generally leads to more severe social ostracism. Children who have successfully attained physical bowel control but persist in placing their feces in inappropriate locations, such as their bedrooms, often have an associated psychiatric disorder warranting psychotherapy. Behavioral techniques, using tangible rewards for positive reinforcement of appropriate behavior, and parent counseling to reduce stress at home are also useful therapeutically.

Functional enuresis shows some evidence of genetic influence; about 75 percent of enuretic children have a first-degree relative who is or was enuretic. Concomitant psychiatric problems are seen in about 20 percent of enuretic children. Among successful treatment approaches are behavioral techniques, including the use of a pad and a buzzer, and, for some children, imipramine (Tofranil).

Students should read Chapter 40 in *Synopsis VI*, "Elimination Disorders," and Chapter 41 in *CTP V*, "Elimination Disorders," and then study the questions and answers below to assess their knowledge of this area.

HELPFUL HINTS

These terms relating to enuresis and encropesis should be understood.

functional encopresis
primary and secondary encopresis
psychogenic megacolon
aganglionic megacolon
Hirschsprung's disease
star charts

functional enuresis
primary and secondary enuresis
diurnal enuresis
spina bifida occulta
cystitis
somnambulism

thioridazine (Mellaril)
appropriate toilet training
bell (or buzzer) and pad
bladder training
symptom substitution
cardiotoxicity

QUESTIONS

DIRECTIONS: Each of the incomplete statements below is followed by five suggested completions. Select the *one* that is *best* in each case.

40.1. All the following statements about functional enuresis are true *except*
A. males are more frequently enuretic than females
B. diurnal enuresis is much less common than nocturnal enuresis
C. functional enuresis is usually self-limited
D. psychiatric problems are present in about 20 percent of enuretic children
E. psychotherapy alone is an effective treatment of enuresis

40.2. In the treatment of enuresis in children
A. drug treatment should be given a trial in all cases
B. imipramine (Tofranil) is an effective long-term medication
C. relapses seldom occur after discontinuation of medication
D. desmopressin is effective in some cases
E. a star chart is of little or no use

DIRECTIONS: For each of the questions below, *one or more* of the responses given are correct. Choose answer

A. if only *1, 2, and 3* are correct
B. if only *1 and 3* are correct
C. if only *2 and 4* are correct
D. if only *4* is correct
E. if *all* are correct

40.3. Which of the following statements about functional enuresis are true?
1. A minimum chronological age of 5 years is required to make the diagnosis
2. It is not diagnosed when the voiding is done intentionally
3. About 75 percent of enuretic children have a first-degree relative who is or was enuretic
4. Enuretic children are no more likely than normal children to have concomitant developmental delays

40.4. Which of the following statements about functional encopresis are true?
1. The primary type is diagnosed only if there has been a proper period of fecal continence lasting at least one year
2. Nocturnal encopresis has a better prognosis than encopresis that occurs during waking hours
3. In psychogenic megacolon, the encopretic child becomes hypersensitive to rectal pressure and of the need to defecate
4. It may be associated with short attention span and hyperactivity

40.5. Which of the following statements about functional enuresis are true?
1. Enuretic children feel an urge to void with less urine in the bladder than do normal children
2. About 80 percent of enuretics have the primary type of enuresis
3. Secondary enuresis in children is more frequently associated with a concomitant psychiatric difficulty than is primary enuresis
4. Enuresis occurs exclusively during rapid-eye-movement sleep

ANSWERS

Elimination Disorders

40.1. The answer is E (*Synopsis VI*, pages 765–767; *CTP V*, pages 1879–1881).

Controlled studies have found that *psychotherapy alone* is not an effective treatment of enuresis. However, psychotherapy is useful in dealing with emotional and family difficulties that arise because of enuresis or with coexisting psychiatric problems.

Psychiatric problems are present in only about 20 percent of enuretic children, and they are most common in enuretic girls and in children who wet both day and night.

Classical conditioning with the bell (or buzzer) and pad apparatus is the most effective and generally safe treatment for enuresis. Dryness results in more than 50 percent of cases. *Males* are more frequently enuretic than females. Prevalence is estimated to be 7 percent of boys and 3 percent of girls at age 5, 3 percent of boys and 2 percent of girls at age 10, and 1 percent of boys and almost no girls at age 18.

Diurnal enuresis (occurring during the day) is much less common than nocturnal enuresis (occurring at nighttime). Only about 2 percent of 5-year-olds have diurnal enuresis at least weekly. Unlike nocturnal enuresis, diurnal enuresis is more common in girls than in boys. Functional enuresis (as opposed to enuresis of organic cause) is *usually self-limited*. The child can eventually remain dry with virtually no psychiatric sequelae. Although an organic cause precludes a diagnosis of functional enuresis, the correction of an anatomical defect or the cure of an infection does not always cure the enuresis, which suggests that the cause may still be at least partially functional in some of these cases.

Enuresis is manifested as a repetitive and inappropriate passage of urine; the voiding may be voluntary or involuntary. Enuretics are categorized as primary if they have never been continent for a minimum of one year and secondary if their enuresis began after one year of dryness.

Table 40.1 lists the DSM-III-R diagnostic criteria for functional enuresis.

40.2. The answer is D (*Synopsis VI*, pages 766–767; *CTP V*, pages 1881–1882).

Desmopressin (DDAVP), an antidiuretic administered intranasally, has been shown in initial studies to be effective in reducing enuresis in some cases. *Drugs* should rarely be used in treating enuresis and then only as a last resort in intractable cases that cause serious socioemotional difficulties for the sufferer. *Imipramine (Tofranil)* is efficacious and has

Table 40.1
Diagnostic Criteria for Functional Enuresis

A. Repeated voiding of urine during the day or night into bed or clothes, whether involuntary or intentional.

B. At least two such events per month for children between the ages of 5 and 6, and at least one event per month for older children.

C. Chronologic age at least 5 and mental age at least 4.

D. Not due to a physical disorder, such as diabetes, urinary tract infection, or a seizure disorder.

Specify primary or secondary type.
    Primary type: the disturbance was not preceded by a period of urinary continence lasting at least one year.
    Secondary type: the disturbance was preceded by a period of urinary continence lasting at least one year.

Specify nocturnal only, diurnal only, or **nocturnal and diurnal.**

Table from DSM-III-R, *Diagnostic and Statistical Manual of Mental Disorders*, ed 3, revised. Copyright American Psychiatric Association, Washington, DC, 1987. Used with permission.

been approved for use, primarily on a short-term basis, in treating childhood enuresis. Initially, up to 30 percent of enuretics may stay dry, and up to 85 percent may wet less frequently than before taking the medication. This effect, however, does not often last. Tolerance often develops after six weeks of therapy; once the drug is discontinued, *relapses* and enuresis at former frequencies usually occur within a few months. A more serious problem is the drug's adverse effects, which include cardiotoxicity; therefore, the drug should not be used on a long-term basis. A *star chart*, a record-keeping device that rewards the child, is helpful in many cases.

40.3. The answer is B (1, 3) (*Synopsis VI*, pages 765–767; *CTP V*, pages 1879–1881).

Functional enuresis requires a *minimum chronological age of 5 years* and a minimum mental age of 4 years to make the diagnosis. About *75 percent* of enuretic children have a first-degree relative who is or was enuretic, and the concordance rate is higher in monozygotic twins than in dizygotic twins. However, a genetic component to enuresis is difficult to separate from psychosocial factors. The voiding may be unintentional or *intentional*. For instance, persons with daytime enuresis may intentionally fail to inhibit the reflex to pass urine, and some persons admit to being awake and choosing to urinate in bed, rather than get up and go to the toilet. In a longitudinal study of child development, those children who are enuretic were about twice as likely to have *concomitant developmental delays.*

40.4. The anwer is D (4) (*Synopsis VI*, pages 764–765; *CTP V*, pages 1883–1885).

Functional encopresis may be associated with other neurodevelopmental problems, including easy distractibility, *short attention span, hyperactivity*, low frustration tolerance, and poor coordination. DSM-III-R specifies two types of functional encopresis. In the primary type the disturbance is not preceded by a *period of fecal continence* lasting at least one year, whereas in the secondary type the disturbance follows at least one year of fecal continence. Most encopresis occurs during waking hours; cases associated with *nocturnal encopresis* have a poorer (not better) prognosis. In psychogenic megacolon, which may be part of the functional encopretic picture, chronic constipation leads to rectal distention, loss of rectal wall muscle tone, and *desensitization (not hypersensitization) to pressure.* Thus, many children are also desensitized to the need to defecate. See Table 40.2 for the DSM-III-R criteria for functional encopresis.

40.5. The answer is A (1, 2, 3) (*Synopsis VI*, pages 765–767; *CTP V*, pages 1883–1885).

Enuresis does not take place exclusively during *rapid-eye-movement (REM) sleep;* it does not appear to be related to a specific stage of sleep or time of night; rather, bedwetting appears randomly. Some workers believe that, if any stage is more predominant, it is most likely to be the stage of nonREM sleep. In most cases the quality of sleep is normal. Little evidence indicates that enuretics sleep more soundly than do other children.

Table 40.2
Diagnostic Criteria for Functional Encopresis

A. Repeated passage of feces into places not appropriate for that purpose (e.g., clothing, floor), whether involuntary or intentional. (The disorder may be overflow incontinence secondary to functional fecal retention.)

B. At least one such event a month for at least six months.

C. Chronologic and mental age, at least 4 years.

D. Not due to a physical disorder, such as aganglionic megacolon.

Specify primary or secondary type.
    Primary type: the disturbance was not preceded by a period of fecal continence lasting at least one year.
    Secondary type: the disturbance was preceded by a period of fecal continence lasting at least one year.

Table from DSM-III-R, *Diagnostic and Statistical Manual of Mental Disorders*, ed 3, revised. Copyright American Psychiatric Association, Washington, DC, 1987. Used with permission.

Most enuretics have a bladder with a normal anatomical capacity; however, they feel an urge to void with *less urine in the bladder* than do normal children. They also urinate more frequently and in smaller quantities than do normal children. DSM-III-R describes two types of enuresis: (1) In the primary type the disturbance was not preceded by a period of urinary continence lasting at least one year. (2) In the secondary type the disturbance was preceded by a period of continence lasting at least one year. About *80 percent* of enuretics have the primary type of enuresis, never having achieved a yearlong period of dryness. Some evidence indicates that secondary enuresis in children is more frequently associated with a *concomitant psychiatric difficulty* than is primary enuresis.

41 ||||||

Speech Disorders
Not Elsewhere Classified

Stuttering, the frequent repetition or prolongation of sounds that markedly impair the fluency of speech, and cluttering, the erratic and dysrhythmic speech that usually involves faulty phrasing patterns, are the speech disorders not elsewhere classified in the revised third edition of *Diagnostic and Statistical Manual of Mental Disorders* (DSM-III-R). Both disorders impede intelligibility.

The current conceptualization of the child at risk of becoming a stutterer is one of a youngster with tenuous systems involved in speech production. Stuttering is a universal disorder, appearing in all cultures across recorded history. Cluttering is characterized as a central language imbalance; it is rarer than stuttering and is associated with academic skills disorders and with other speech disorders. Cluttering may describe the speech characteristics of a subgroup of children with language and learning disorders.

Speech production refers to fluency, articulation, and voice volume. Disturbances of these factors lead to phenomena that are often incorrectly diagnosed as psychogenic. Generally, other features of the neurological examination establish the organic diagnosis; however, several conditions have no known organic pathophysiological mechanism, which does not mean that they are due to psychological disturbances.

Throughout childhood and later, communicative speech takes on more and more importance in the person's experiences and behavior patterns. Speech also greatly facilitates the syntaxic mode of experience in which consensual validation is predominant and that enables reality testing to occur. Thus, speech contributes greatly to the elaboration and the refinement of the ever-growing self-esteem.

The person affected by stuttering is painfully aware of the speech disorder; impairment of social and academic functioning may ensue, the result of associated anxiety, frustration, or low self-esteem. In cluttering, however, the person is generally unaware of any communicative impairment.

The treatment of stuttering focuses on the restructuring of fluency. The entire pattern of speech production is shaped. The success of relatively brief treatment periods for young children has encouraged clinicians to recommend early treatment for stuttering. The treatment of cluttering includes speech therapy to increase the patient's sensory awareness of speech feedback. Therapy may be hampered by the relatively low motivation of clutterers because of their unawareness of their altered fluency.

The student must be able to distinguish cluttering and stuttering from each other, from normal childhood dysfluency, and from spastic dysphonia. The student must also be able to choose from among the variety of psychotherapeutic modalities and remedial approaches in formulating the best treatment plan, according to each individual case.

Students should review Chapter 41 in *Synopsis VI*, "Speech Disorders Not Elsewhere Classified," and Section 36.3b in *CTP V*, "Speech Disorders Not Elsewhere Classified," and then study the questions, answers, and explanations below to assess their understanding of this area.

HELPFUL HINTS

The student should be able to define the speech disorder terms listed below.

cluttering	semantogenic	spastic dysphonia
dysrhythmic	theory of cerebral dominance	distraction
stuttering	breakdown theory	suggestion
stammering	repressed-need theory	relaxation
cybernetic model	anticipatory-struggle theory	self-therapy
genogenic	stimulus-response theories	desensitization
psychogenic		

QUESTIONS

DIRECTIONS: Each question or incomplete statement below is followed by five suggested responses or completions. Select the *one* that is *best* in each case.

41.1. A worried psychiatrist and his wife were referred to a speech therapist for a consultation on their 3-year-old son, Aaron. The psychiatrist explained that several months previously he and his wife had first noticed that at times Aaron had been stuttering. When this happened, he would get stuck on words or initial syllables, often repeating them many times until he was finally able to finish the sentence. Sometimes he was unable to finish the sentence and just gave up. Initially, these periods were rare; but in the last few weeks they had become much more frequent, and now Aaron was visibly upset when they occurred. A few days earlier he had become so frustrated that he began striking his head with his fist in an effort to get the words out.

Aaron's parents knew that transient stuttering, particularly among boys, was common. However, they now wondered if something needed to be done to make sure that the problem did not become chronic. They had consulted their pediatrician, who tried to reassure them; but the pediatrician's own slight but noticeable stuttering was disconcerting, to say the least.

The speech therapist told the parents that it was important to maintain their own composure during Aaron's episodes of distress and not to complete his sentences for him. She sympathized with their concern but said that most likely the stuttering would go away and would not leave any permanent emotional scars. [From *DSM-III-R Case Book*. Used with permission.]

On the basis of this history, the most likely diagnosis is

A. spastic dysphonia
B. cluttering
C. stuttering
D. developmental expressive language disorder
E. dysarthria

41.2. Which of the following statements about stuttering is *not* true?
A. Stuttering has an abrupt onset
B. Approximately 3 percent of all children have a persistent problem with stuttering
C. Stuttering usually appears before the age of 12
D. Fifty to 80 percent of children with mild cases of stuttering recover spontaneously
E. Frustration, anxiety, and depression are common associated features of stuttering

DIRECTIONS: For the incomplete statement below, *one or more* of the completions given are correct. Choose answer

A. if only *1, 2, and 3* are correct
B. if only *1 and 3* are correct
C. if only *2 and 4* are correct
D. if only *4* is correct
E. if *all* are correct

41.3. Cluttering is a disorder of speech
1. fluency
2. rate
3. rhythm
4. volume

DIRECTIONS: The lettered headings below are followed by a list of numbered phrases. For each numbered phrase, select the *one* lettered heading that is most closely associated with it. Each lettered heading may be selected once, more than once, or not at all.

Questions 41.4–41.10
A. Cluttering
B. Stuttering

41.4. Frequent repetition or prolongation of sounds

41.5. Rapid, jerky spurts

41.6. Affected person is usually unaware of the speech disturbance

41.7. Less associated with social isolation and depression

41.8. Synonymous with "stammering"

41.9. Associated features include tics

41.10. Less common disorder

ANSWERS

Speech Disorders Not Elsewhere Classified

41.1. The answer is C (*Synopsis VI*, pages 768–771 and 716; *CTP V*, pages 1810–1811).

On the basis of the history, 3-year-old Aaron's diagnosis is *stuttering*. *Spastic dysphonia*, a stutteringlike speech disorder, is differentiated from stuttering by the presence of an abnormal breathing pattern and may be ruled out here. *Cluttering* is ruled out by the normal rate of speech Aaron displays. In addition, characteristic of stuttering but not of cluttering is the painful awareness of the speech disorder, as evidenced by Aaron's striking himself in frustration. There is no evidence at this time of marked impairment in Aaron's speech, and *developmental expressive language disorder* may be ruled out. *Dysarthria* is a disorder of articulation resulting from structural or neurological abnormalities and is not applicable here. Table 41.1 lists the DSM-III-R diagnostic criteria for stuttering.

41.2. The answer is A (*Synopsis VI*, pages 769–771; *CTP V*, pages 1810–1811).

Stuttering does not have an *abrupt onset;* it typically occurs over a period of weeks or months with a repetition of initial consonants, whole words that are usually first words of a phrase, or long words. As the disorder progresses, the repetitions become more frequent, with consistent stuttering on the most important words or phrases, although it may be absent during oral reading, singing, or talking to pets or inanimate objects. Approximately 3 percent of all children have a *persistent problem* with stuttering that continues into adolescence. Stuttering usually *appears before the age of 12*, is about three times more common in boys than in girls, and persists longer in boys. Fifty to 80 percent of children with mild cases *recover spontaneously*. *Frustration, anxiety, and depression* are common associated features of stuttering. In chronic cases of school-age children academic difficulties and impairment in peer relationships may result, which may subsequently affect occupational choice or advancement.

Four gradually evolving phases in the development of stuttering have been identified.

Phase 1 (during the preschool period): Initially, the difficulty tends to be episodic; there is a high percentage of recovery. Children stutter most often when excited or upset, when they seem to have a great deal to say, and under other conditions of communicative pressure.

Phase 2 (in the elementary school years): The disorder is chronic with few, if any, intervals of normal speech. Children become aware of their speech difficulty and regard themselves as stutterers, with the stuttering occurring mainly on the major parts of speech—nouns, verbs, adjectives, and adverbs.

Phase 3 (after age 8 and up to adulthood—most often in late childhood and early adolescence): The stuttering comes and goes largely in response to specific situations, such as reciting in class, speaking to strangers, making purchases in stores, and using the telephone; certain words and sounds are regarded as more difficult than others.

Phase 4 (late adolescence and adulthood): Stutterers show a vivid, fearful anticipation of stuttering. They fear words, sounds, and situations; word substitutions and circumlocutions are common; and the stutterers avoid situations requiring speech and show other evidence of fear and embarrassment.

41.3. The answer is A (1, 2, 3) (*Synopsis VI*, page 768; *CTP V*, page 1811).

Cluttering is a disorder of speech *fluency* involving both the *rate* and the *rhythm* of speech, which results in impaired speech and intelligibility. Speech *volume* dysregulation is not included among the DSM-III-R diagnostic criteria for cluttering, which are listed in Table 41.2.

Table 41.1
Diagnostic Criteria for Stuttering

Frequent repetitions or prolongations of sounds or syllables that markedly impair the fluency of speech.

Table from DSM-III-R, *Diagnostic and Statistical Manual of Mental Disorders,* ed 3, revised. Copyright American Psychiatric Association, Washington, DC, 1987. Used with permission.

Table 41.2
Diagnostic Criteria for Cluttering

A disorder of speech fluency involving both the rate and the rhythm of speech and resulting in impaired speech intelligibility. Speech is erratic and dysrhythmic, consisting of rapid and jerky spurts that usually involve faulty phrasing patterns (e.g., alternating pauses and bursts of speech that produce groups of words unrelated to the grammatical structure of the sentence).

Table from DSM-III-R, *Diagnostic and Statistical Manual of Mental Disorders,* ed 3, revised. Copyright American Psychiatric Association, Washington, DC, 1987. Used with permission.

41.4–41.10

41.4. **The answer is B** (*Synopsis VI*, pages 769–771; *CTP V*, pages 1810–1812).

41.5. **The answer is A** (*Synopsis VI*, page 768; *CTP V*, pages 1810–1812).

41.6. **The answer is A** (*Synopsis VI*, page 768; *CTP V*, pages 1810–1812).

41.7. **The answer is A** (*Synopsis VI*, page 768; *CTP V*, pages 1810–1812).

41.8. **The answer is B** (*Synopsis VI*, pages 769–771; *CTP V*, pages 1810–1812).

41.9. **The answer is B** (*Synopsis VI*, pages 769–771; *CTP V*, pages 1810–1812).

41.10. **The answer is A** (*Synopsis VI*, page 768; *CTP V*, pages 1810–1812).

Stuttering is characterized by *frequent repetition or prolongation of sounds* or syllables, thereby mark-edly impairing the fluency of speech, whereas cluttering results in erratic and dysrhythmic speech, consisting of *rapid and jerky spurts* that usually involve faulty phrasing patterns. A major differential diagnostic feature is that in cluttering the affected person is *usually unaware* of the disturbance, whereas, after the initial phase of stuttering, the person is painfully aware of the speech disorder.

Although research on cluttering is sparse, it appears to be slightly more common in boys than in girls. It is estimated that cluttering is *less common* than stuttering, which is about three times more common in boys than in girls. The term *"stammering"* is used synonymously with stuttering.

Stutterers may develop certain associated features, including depression, eye blinks, *tics,* and tremors of the jaw. Cluttering is less associated than is stuttering with such features as *social isolation and depression.* In a few severe cases of cluttering, secondary emotional disorders may ensue as a result of poor peer interaction or inadequate family support for the child.

42 ||||

Other Disorders of Infancy, Childhood, or Adolescence

Elective mutism, identity disorder, reactive attachment disorder of infancy or early childhood, stereotypy and habit disorder, and undifferentiated attention-deficit disorder make up the other disorders of infancy, childhood, or adolescence in the revised third edition of *Diagnostic and Statistical Manual of Mental Disorders* (DSM-III-R).

Elective mutism, by definition, does not have a biological cause. Two types of psychologically based mutism have been described. The first, called traumatic mutism, occurs immediately after a psychological or physical shock. The second, generally referred to as elective mutism, develops with no apparent precipitant, and talking may occur in a familiar situation or with a small group of intimates.

Elective mutism is apparently rare; it is found in fewer than 1 percent of child-guidance, clinical, and school social casework referrals.

The student must be able to distinguish elective mutism from transient adaptational shyness and refusal to speak, which is common, for example, on entering school. The student must also be able to differentiate elective mutism from organic and developmental disabilities, in which the child may have an inability to speak, rather than a refusal to do so—such as severe or profound mental retardation, pervasive developmental disorders, and developmental expressive language disorder.

Identity disorder is thought to occur when adolescents are unable to perform the normal intrapsychic and interpersonal tasks necessary to attain a core sense of self, an ego identity. The essential feature of identity disorder is a severe subjective distress regarding an inability to integrate aspects of the self into a relatively coherent and acceptable sense of self, the symptoms of which result in impairments in social, academic, or occupational functioning. The student must be able to differentiate identity disorder from the more pervasive and persistent disturbances associated with borderline personality disorder. Identity disorder should not be diagnosed if the identity problems are secondary to another mental disorder (e.g., a mood disorder, schizophrenia, or schizophreniform disorder).

Reactive attachment disorder of infancy or early childhood is characterized by marked disturbances in the relatedness of the young child and is caused by grossly pathogenic care by the primary caretakers. Separating a normal child from the adequate mother may result in the child's failure to thrive because of the inadequacies in the new environment and caretaker. When the caretaker-child relationship itself is hostile, serious physical and psychological symptoms may arise in the infant or child. The student must know the primary considerations in the differential diagnosis of reactive attachment disorder of infancy or early childhood— the pervasive developmental disorders, various severe neurological abnormalities, and psychosocial dwarfism. Children who are psychosocially, physically, or sexually abused or who are neglected may react in a variety of ways. If the reaction constitutes a mental disorder, the student must also consider posttraumatic stress disorder (generally for the older child) and adjustment disorder.

The overriding consideration in the choice of treatment—to hospitalize the infant or child or attempt treatment while the child remains in the home—must be the child's safety. Except in extreme cases of neglect—including starvation, dehydration, and other intercurrent physical conditions that can cause death before therapeutic measures can take effect—the clinical picture can substantially improve. Such a therapeutic response is the ultimate confirmation of the diagnosis.

The diagnosis of stereotypy and habit disorder is given only when the disturbance either causes physical injury to the child or markedly interferes with normal activities; the disturbance is intentional and involves repetitive nonfunctional behavior (e.g., nail biting, body rocking, head banging, skin picking, teeth grinding, noncommunicative and repetitive vocalizations, breath holding, hyperventilation, and aerophagia). DSM-III-R notes that these symptoms cannot be caused by a more pervasive disorder, such as autistic disorder, which is likely to be the most difficult differential diagnosis among moderately, severely, and profoundly retarded children who have associated autistic symptoms. The stereotyped behavior present in tic disorders is involuntary, even though it can be suppressed for varying periods of time, and must be distinguished from stereotypy and habit disorder. When the behavior

is induced by psychoactive substances, the diagnoses of both stereotypy and habit disorder and psychoactive substance-induced organic mental disorder should be made.

In undifferentiated attention-deficit disorder, the predominant feature is the persistence of developmentally inappropriate and marked inattention that is not a symptom of another disorder, such as mental retardation or attention-deficit hyperactivity disorder, or of a disorganized and chaotic environment. Some of the disturbances that DSM-III would have categorized as attention-deficit disorder without hyperactivity are included in this category in DSM-III-R.

After completing Chapter 42 of *Synopsis VI*, "Other Disorders of Infancy, Childhood, or Adolescence," and Chapter 42 of *CTP V*, "Other Disorders of Infancy, Childhood, and Adolescence," students should answer the questions below. A review of the answers and the explanations will help them assess their knowledge in this area.

HELPFUL HINTS

The student should know and be able to define the following terms.

traumatic mutism	affectionless character	pervasive developmental disorder
elective mutism	psychosocial dwarfism	marasmus
negativism	stereotypy	malnutrition
hysteria	habit	attachment disorder
identity disorder	Lesch-Nyhan syndrome	John Bowlby
identity crisis	attention-deficit	parenting skills
abulia	hyperactivity disorder	repetitive hand mover
Erik Erikson	obsessive-compulsive disorder	head banging
reactive disorder		

QUESTIONS

DIRECTIONS: Each of the incomplete statements below is followed by five suggested completions. Select the *one* that is *best* in each case.

42.1. A 16-year-old high school junior was referred by a teacher to the mental health clinic with the complaint that she was unable to make any verbal contributions in her classes. Her inability to speak had begun one year previously, after the death of her mother. It took school personnel some time to realize that she did not

speak in any of her classes. She had kept up with her assignments, handing in all her written work and receiving better than average grades on tests.

The patient's father was a janitor in a large apartment building. Because of his work, he usually came home late and was rather passive and indifferent toward the patient and her six younger siblings. He had never responded to school requests for visits to discuss his daughter's problems. Since her mother's death, the patient had assumed the mothering of the siblings: cooking the meals, cleaning, and listening to their requests and complaints.

When seen, the patient was a thin, neatly dressed girl who was alert but responded only with brief nods of her head at first. With reassurance, she began to whisper monosyllabic answers to questions. Her responses were rational and logical, but she denied that her failure to speak was much of a problem. A younger sibling reported that the patient had no difficulty in speaking at home. [From *DSM-III-R Case Book*. Used with permission.]

As described, the patient's symptoms characteristic of elective mutism include all the following *except*

A. no difficulty in speaking at home
B. she refuses to speak in school
C. she communicates by nodding
D. she performs satisfactorily in school
E. the onset followed an emotional trauma

42.2. All the following signs and symptoms occur in stereotypy and habit disorder *except*

A. nail biting
B. head banging
C. finger sucking
D. skin picking
E. hallucinations

42.3. Alice was a 20-year-old single white junior in a Southern college. She came to a student health clinic with complaints of turbulence in her life, which she experienced as vague feelings of anxiety, depression, and worries about the uncertainty of her future. She felt confused and directionless, and these feelings often interfered with her ability to concentrate on her schoolwork.

Alice had looked forward to attending college and, when she arrived, was excited by the diversity of people she met. Sometimes she enjoyed being with her "arty, more way-out and kind of radical" friends, and at other times she felt more comfortable with her "traditional, more moderate preppie" friends. In the past year, however, she had increasingly had the feeling that she did not fit into any one group of friends and was confused about who she really was. She experienced this indecision not only with regard to her friends but in her academic studies as well: A second-semester junior, she still did not have a clear idea of what she really wanted to study or, in a larger sense, what she wanted to do with her life after finishing college. At the end of her sophomore year, she had decided on chemistry but then had changed to sociology at the beginning of her junior year. More recently, she had changed to art history but still was not completely happy with her choice—"It's as if I want to do everything and yet I don't really want to do anything in particular." [From *DSM-III-R Case Book*. Used with permission.]

The features in this case that confirm the diagnosis are

A. her uncertainty about career choice
B. her ambivalence about friendships
C. the duration of the disturbance
D. her decreased ability to concentrate on schoolwork
E. all the above

Questions 42.4–42.5

Ten-month-old Molly was brought by her mother, at the suggestion of her pediatrician, for a consultation with a specialist in infant development. Her mother was most concerned because "Molly is not responding to me. She often won't look at me. She looks in the opposite direction. She won't smile, won't play, and bangs her hand on the table, looking angry. She throws toys on the floor. When I talk to her, she closes her eyes." Her mother also reported that her little girl was waking up three or four times each night and refusing to go back to sleep unless she stayed with her in the room, either holding her or stroking her back.

The current problems seemed to begin two months earlier, when Molly's mother, a busy attorney, went back to work full-time. The father, also an attorney, was quite angry at her for returning to work. He had wanted her to give up her career and stay at home. For the first month

after she returned to work, Molly was cared for by a baby-sitter, who eventually was fired after a neighbor reported that the baby-sitter was frequently drunk and left Molly in her crib, with a bottle of formula, ignoring her cries. Although Molly's mother had suspected that the baby-sitter was far from ideal, she did not realize how bad she was until she heard about it from the neighbor. For the past month, Molly's care had been arranged on a day-to-day basis, and she had had six different baby-sitters.

During the last two months, because of sleepless nights and feeling overwhelmingly guilty about Molly's distress, yet at the same time feeling compelled to return to work or else "lose my status in my firm," Molly's mother had been " a nervous wreck." Now she blamed herself for all Molly's difficulties, saying, "I've done a terrible thing. Now, not only my husband doesn't love me, but Molly doesn't love me either."

Molly weighed eight pounds at birth and was in good health. The pregnancy had been unremarkable. The pediatrician's report revealed that Molly had slightly increased motor tone bilaterally, with no asymmetries, and tended to be overly sensitive to touch. For example, her mother reported that, when she tried to bathe Molly, the child would often scream and that she had to hold her with soft cotton blankets in order for her to feel comfortable. Molly was also very sensitive to loud noises, turning red and becoming rigid. She often cried if lights were too bright.

Molly had displayed social responsiveness by the fourth month but only if her parents worked hard and found just the right rhythm of sound and "funny faces." By age 6 months she was able to reach for objects, but her parents reported that, if they handed her something, she would often try to knock it out of their hands, rather than grab it.

Molly had always been a fussy eater but nonetheless was gaining adequate weight and was in the 80th percentile for size and weight. Her pediatrician said that her overall physical health was good and that, in terms of motor milestones, she was doing fine.

During the evaluation, the impression of Molly as physically healthy was confirmed. Her gross and fine motor functioning were age-appropriate. Observation of parent-infant interaction revealed an infant who held her body stiffly, looked away from her parents' eyes, and reacted to their vocalization by arching her back. When offered interesting objects, she would usually grab another object or knock the offered object away. Her facial expression was angry and tense. Her mother appeared depressed, and her interaction with Molly had a mechanical quality. Molly's father was impatient and abrupt with her.

[From *DSM-III-R Case Book*. Used with permission.]

42.4. The features of Molly's disorder include
A. mental retardation
B. stranger anxiety
C. grossly pathogenic care
D. excessive response to social stimulation
E. extreme interest in the environment

42.5. The primary considerations in the differential diagnosis of reactive attachment disorder of infancy or early childhood are
A. autistic disorder
B. mental retardation
C. psychosocial dwarfism
D. severe neurological abnormalities
E. all the above

DIRECTIONS: For each of the incomplete statements below, *one or more* of the completions given are correct. Choose answer

A. if only *1, 2, and 3* are correct
B. if only *1 and 3* are correct
C. if only *2 and 4* are correct
D. if only *4* is correct
E. if *all* are correct

42.6. Identity disorder
1. is believed to have a strong biological basis
2. may be manifested by sleep difficulties
3. usually resolves by the mid-30s
4. is more common in modern society than in earlier times

42.7. Elective mutism
1. occurs in about 5 percent of children
2. usually lasts only a few weeks or months
3. is more common in boys than in girls
4. is a psychologically determined disorder

ANSWERS

Other Disorders of Infancy, Childhood, or Adolescence

42.1. The answer is D (*Synopsis VI*, page 772; *CTP V*, pages 1887–1889).

As described, the one symptom of the 16-year-old high school junior not typically characteristic of elective mutism is her *school performance*. She kept up with her assignments, handed in all her written work, and received better than average grades. Children with elective mutism generally have no difficulty in *speaking at home*, but they do have difficulty elsewhere, especially at *school*. Consequently, they often have significant academic difficulties and even failure. Some children with elective mutism communicate with gestures, such as *nodding,* or saying "umm-hum," which may be their initial responses to a therapist. Some children seem predisposed to elective mutism after early physical or *emotional trauma*. As in this case, the inability to speak can begin after the death of a parent. Table 42.1 lists the DSM-III-R diagnostic criteria for elective mutism.

42.2. The answer is E (*Synopsis VI*, page 778; *CTP V*, pages 1903–1908).

Stereotypy and habit disorder includes *nail biting*, thumb or *finger sucking*, nose or *skin picking*, and *head banging. Hallucinations* are not part of this disorder. They are false sensory perceptions that in children are most commonly caused by fever, delirium, or the ingestion of toxic substances. Stereotypy and habit disorder usually causes physical injury or markedly interferes with the child's normal activities. Because stereotypies are especially prevalent among the mentally retarded and persons with pervasive developmental disorder, the two diagnoses frequently coexist. Stereotypy and habit disorder may be diagnosed concurrently with a psychoactive substance-induced organic mental disorder (e.g., amphetamine-induced organic mental disorder) and with severe sensory impairments, central nervous system disorders, schizophrenia, and obsessive-compulsive disorder. Table 42.2 lists the DSM-III-R diagnostic criteria for stereotypy and habit disorder.

Table 42.1
Diagnostic Criteria for Elective Mutism

A. Persistent refusal to talk in one or more major situations (including at school).

B. Ability to comprehend spoken language and to speak.

Table from DSM-III-R, *Diagnostic and Statistical Manual of Mental Disorders,* ed 3, revised. Copyright American Psychiatric Association, Washington, DC, 1987. Used with permission.

Table 42.2
Diagnostic Criteria for Stereotypy and Habit Disorder

A. Intentional, repetitive, nonfunctional behaviors, such as hand-shaking, or -waving, body-rocking, head-banging, mouthing of objects, nail-biting, picking at nose or skin.

B. The disturbance either causes physical injury to the child or markedly interferes with normal activities, e.g., injury to head from head-banging; inability to fall asleep because of constant rocking.

C. Does not meet the criteria for either a pervasive developmental disorder or a tic disorder.

Table from DSM-III-R, *Diagnostic and Statistical Manual of Mental Disorders,* ed 3, revised. Copyright American Psychiatric Association, Washington, DC, 1987. Used with permission.

42.3. The answer is E (*Synopsis VI*, page 773; *CTP V*, pages 1889–1890).

In the case of Alice, the 20-year-old college junior, the features that confirm the diagnosis of identity disorder, in which there is severe subjective distress over an inability to reconcile aspects of the self into a relatively coherent and acceptable sense of self, are her uncertainties about *career choice*, her ambivalence about *friendship* patterns, and the *duration of the disturbance*, which DSM-III-R requires to be at least three months and in this case lasted over the past year. Alice's impairment in academic functioning, reported by her as a *decreased ability to concentrate* on her schoolwork, further confirms the diagnosis.

Many adolescents and young adults are troubled about the choices they must make about careers, lifestyles, group loyalties, and other issues relating to a sense of identity. Alice's uncertainty about issues relating to identity is sufficiently severe to cause not only subjective distress but also impairment in functioning. As this disturbance is not due to another mental disorder—a mood disorder or a psychotic disorder, such as schizophrenia—the diagnosis of identity disorder is made.

In young adults (over age 18), the diagnosis of borderline personality disorder may be considered in the differential diagnosis. However, Alice showed no evidence of this more pervasive disorder, such as affective instability, impulsivity, and intense and unstable interpersonal relationships.

The complete DSM-III-R diagnostic criteria for identity disorder are listed in Table 42.3.

Table 42.3
Diagnostic Criteria for Identity Disorder

A. Severe subjective distress regarding uncertainty about a variety of issues relating to identity, including three or more of the following:
   1. long-term goals
   2. career choice
   3. friendship patterns
   4. sexual orientation and behavior
   5. religious identification
   6. moral value systems
   7. group loyalties

B. Impairment in social or occupational (including academic) functioning as a result of the symptoms in A.

C. Duration of the disturbance of at least three months.

D. Occurrence not exclusively during the course of a mood disorder or of a psychotic disorder, such as schizophrenia.

E. The disturbance is not sufficiently pervasive and persistent to warrant the diagnosis of borderline personality disorder.

Table from DSM-III-R, *Diagnostic and Statistical Manual of Mental Disorders,* ed 3, revised. Copyright American Psychiatric Association, Washington, DC, 1987. Used with permission.

42.4. The answer is C (*Synopsis VI*, pages 774–775; *CTP V*, pages 1898–1899).

Molly's disorder is reactive attachment disorder of infancy or early childhood. This disorder is characterized by persistent failure to initiate or respond to most social interactions, not *excessive response* to social stimulation; indiscriminate sociability, not *stranger anxiety*; and *grossly pathogenic care*. Children with this disorder often demonstrate listlessness and disinterest in the environment, not *extreme interest*.

The disturbance in relatedness in reactive attachment disorder of infancy or early childhood is not a symptom of *mental retardation* or a pervasive developmental disorder. See Table 42.4 for the DSM-III-R criteria for this disorder.

42.5. The answer is E (*Synopsis VI*, page 777; *CTP V*, page 1902).

The primary considerations in the differential diagnosis of reactive attachment disorder of infancy or early childhood are autistic disorder, mental retardation, psychosocial dwarfism, and severe neurological abnormalities.

Autistic disorder in children with onset before they are 5 years of age is manifested by severe impairment in reciprocal social interaction, significant impairment in communication (both verbal and through gestures), and a markedly restricted repertoire of activities and interests. These difficulties are typically present from birth or become evident at the mental age at which specific behaviors should develop. Moderate, severe, and profound *mental re-*

Table 42.4
Diagnostic Criteria for Reactive Attachment Disorder of Infancy or Early Childhood

A. Markedly disturbed social relatedness in most contexts, beginning before the age of 5, as evidenced by either 1 or 2:
   1. persistent failure ot initiate or respond to most social interactions (e.g., in infants, absence of visual tracking and reciprocal play, lack of vocal imitation or playfulness, apathy, little or no spontaneity; at later ages, lack of or little curiosity and social interest)
   2. indiscriminate sociability, e.g., excessive familiarity with relative strangers by making requests and displaying affection

B. The disturbance in A is not a symptom of either mental retardation or a pervasive developmental disorder, such as autistic disorder

C. Grossly pathogenic care, as evidenced by at least one of the following:
   1. persistent disregard of the child's basic emotional needs for comfort, stimulation, and affection. *Examples:* overly harsh punishment by caregiver; consistent neglect by caregiver
   2. persistent disregard of the child's basic physical needs, including nutrition, adequate housing, and protection from physical danger and assault (including sexual abuse)
   3. repeated change of primary caregiver so that stable attachments are not possible, e.g., frequent changes in foster parents

D. There is a presumption that the care described in C is responsible for the disturbed behavior in A; this presumption is warranted if the disturbance in A began following the pathogenic care in C.

Note: If failure to thrive is present, code it on Axis III.

Table from DSM-III-R, *Diagnostic and Statistical Manual of Mental Disorders,* ed 3, revised. Copyright American Psychiatric Association, Washington, DC, 1987. Used with permission.

tardation are present in about 50 percent of these children, whereas most children with reactive attachment disorder are mildly retarded or have normal intelligence. No evidence shows that autism is caused by parental pathology, and most parents of autistic children do not differ significantly from the parents of normal children. Unlike children with reactive attachment disorder, autistic children do not frequently improve rapidly when removed from their homes and placed in a hospital or other more favorable environment.

Mentally retarded children may evidence delay in all social skills. These children may be differentiated from children with reactive attachment disorder, as the social relatedness of retarded children should be appropriate to their mental age and they should show a sequence of development similar to that seen in normal children.

Classic *psychosocial dwarfism* or psychosocially determined short stature is a syndrome usually first manifested in children 2 to 3 years of age. These children typically are unusually short and have growth-hormone abnormalities and severe behavioral disturbances. All these symptoms are the result of an inadequate caretaker-child relationship and resolve without any medical or psychiatric treatment when the child is removed from the home and placed in a more favorable domicile.

Neurological abnormalities and sensory deficits should be ruled out. If such deficits are responsible for the children's impaired relatedness, caretakers may need to be shown how to give appropriate stimulation and how to facilitate communication, which will usually ameliorate difficulties secondary to the sensory deficit.

42.6.   The answer is C (2, 4) (*Synopsis VI*, pages 773–774; *CTP V*, pages 1889–1890).

The onset of identity disorder is most frequently in adolescence and is usually manifested by a gradual increase in anxiety, depression, regressive phenomena (such as loss of interest in friends, school, or activities), irritability, *sleep difficulties*, and changes in eating habits. There is no reliable information on predisposing factors, familial pattern, sex ratio, or prevalence. However, identity disorder appears to be *more common in modern society* than in earlier times, perhaps because of exposure through the media and education to more moral, behavioral, and life-style possibilities and because of increased conflicts between adolescent peer values and the values of parents and society. The cause of identity disorder is hypothesized to be psychological, *not biological*. The course is usually relatively brief and generally resolves by the mid-20s, not the *mid-30s*. If it persists, the person may be unable to make career commitments or lasting attachments.

42.7.   The answer is C (2, 4) (*Synopsis VI*, page 772; *CTP V*, pages 1887–1888).

Elective mutism usually lasts only a *few weeks or months*, although some cases may persist for years. The disorder is a *psychologically determined* inhibition or refusal to speak. Maternal overprotection may predispose to its development. Elective mutism is uncommon, being present in less than 1 percent (not *5 percent*) of patients referred to child mental-health-related services. Although most childhood psychiatric disorders are more prevalent in boys than in girls, elective mutism is equally common or slightly *more common* in girls.

Child Psychiatry: Special Areas of Interest

Special areas of interest in child psychiatry include mood disorders of childhood and adolescence and child abuse and neglect. Mood disorders occur in all age groups, including childhood and adolescence, although the manifestations of the disorder may change at different stages of development. The recent rise in suicide in the young has highlighted the need for more attention to be focused on the mood disorders, previously underdiagnosed in this age group. Child abuse and neglect include emotional deprivation, malnutrition, sexual abuse, and physical maltreatment. Ten to 15 percent of all childhood accidents treated in emergency rooms are due to physical abuse. Sexual abuse is likely to escape detection because it usually does not result in visible physical injury. Physical and sexual abuse have serious sequelae.

The student needs to be aware of how childhood and adolescent mood disorders are both similar to and different from the adult disorders and to be familiar with childhood and adolescent depressive and manic equivalents, such as truancy, substance abuse, impaired school performance, and promiscuity. Most often in these covert clinical presentations, the underlying mood disorder is inferred from the presence of depressive or manic fantasy and periodic displays of overt depressive and manic affects. The student also needs to be aware of recent investigations into the biology of mood disorders in children and adolescents, how biology corresponds to the adult picture, and the differences in treatment modalities, including the use of antidepressant medications.

Violence is a social disease of epidemic and endemic proportions that is increasingly entrenched in the population. The abuse of children, both physically and sexually, is one aspect of this social violence, and this generation's battered and abused children will be, if they survive, the next generation's battering and abusing parents. Today, estimates are that almost 2 million children are abused each year and that the number of deaths from child abuse has reached 2,000 to 4,000 annually.

The maltreatment of children can include both emotional and physical deprivation and may range from inadequate nutrition and parental neglect to actual physical battering, sexual exploitation (including incest and child pornography), and ultimately death. Child abuse is currently regarded as the leading cause of death in young children. The student must be able to recognize and diagnose cases of child abuse, must be familiar with the legal and medical responsibilities in cases of child abuse, and must be aware of the issues involved in preventing it. To understand these issues fully, the student must be familiar with the most common family dynamics and constellations leading to incest and physical abuse.

After reading Chapter 43 in *Synopsis VI*, "Child Psychiatry: Special Areas of Interest," and Chapter 44 in *CTP V*, "Child Psychiatry: Special Areas of Interest," students should answer the questions below to assess their knowledge in these areas.

HELPFUL HINTS

Each of the terms below should be defined by the student as they relate to the different disorders.

mood disorders	polysomnographic findings	annual deaths
major depression	REM latency	low-birth-weight children
dysthymia	secondary complications	premature children
irritable versus depressed mood	functional impairment	family characteristics
mania	learning disabilities	diagnosis of child abuse
hypomania	psychotic symptoms	incest
cyclothymia	suicide	child pornography
schizoaffective	differential diagnosis	father-daughter and mother-son
genetic factors	hospitalization	incest
environmental factors	psychotherapy	physician's responsibility
psychobiology	psychopharmacology	treatment
GH	imipramine (Tofranil)	prevention
cortisol	child abuse	

QUESTIONS

DIRECTIONS: Each of the incomplete statements below is followed by five suggested completions. Select the *one* that is *best* in each case.

43.1. The approximate number of deaths annually in the United States attributable to child abuse and neglect is
A. under 500
B. 500 to 1,000
C. 1,000 to 1,500
D. 2,000 to 4,000
E. more than 5,000

43.2. The percentage of allegations of sexual abuse that are false is
A. less than 1 percent
B. less than 10 percent
C. about 30 percent
D. between 50 and 60 percent
E. more than 70 percent

DIRECTIONS: For each of the questions or incomplete statements below, *one or more* of the responses or completions given are correct. Choose answer.

A. if only *1, 2, and 3* are correct
B. if only *1 and 3* are correct
C. if only *2 and 4* are correct
D. if only *4* is correct
E. if *all* are correct

43.3. Mood disorders in children
1. have an increased incidence in children of mood-disordered parents
2. may be manifested by somatic complaints
3. may be manifested by changes in academic performance
4. occur at a rate of approximately 2 to 5 percent

43.4. Which of the following disorders in adults have the same diagnostic criteria as in children?
1. Manic episode
2. Cyclothymia
3. Schizoaffective disorder
4. Dysthymia

43.5. Which of the following statements about the sexual abuse of children are true?
1. Sexually abused children tend to be hyperalert to external aggression
2. Mother-son and father-daughter incest occur at about the same frequency
3. High-risk factors include a passive or absent mother
4. Approximately 10 percent of sexual abuse is by family members

43.6. Mood disorders with childhood or adolescent onset
1. are not likely to recur
2. often contribute to learning disabilities that persist even after recovery
3. usually involve mood-incongruent psychotic themes
4. do not show classic depressive polysomnographic abnormalities during a major episode

43.7. In cases of suspected child abuse and neglect, the physician should
1. obtain permission from the parents to take X-rays of the child
2. confer with members of the hospital child abuse committee within 72 hours
3. obtain permission from the legal guardians to admit the child into the hospital
4. report the case to the appropriate department of social services or child protection unit

43.8. Which of the following statements about abused or neglected children are true?
1. More than 50 percent of abused or neglected children were born prematurely or had low birth weight
2. Many abused children are perceived by their parents as slow in development or mentally retarded
3. More than 80 percent are living with married parents at the time of abuse
4. Ninety percent of abusing parents were abused as children by their own mothers or fathers

ANSWERS

Child Psychiatry: Special Areas of Interest

43.1. The answer is D (*Synopsis VI*, page 784; *CTP V*, page 1963).

An estimated *2,000 to 4,000 deaths* annually in the United States are attributable to child abuse and neglect. The National Center on Child Abuse and Neglect in Washington, D.C., has estimated that each year 1 million children are maltreated and that about 125,000 are victims of sexual abuse. The actual occurrence rates are likely to be higher than these estimates because many maltreated children go unrecognized.

43.2. The answer is B (*Synopsis VI*, page 785; *CTP V*, pages 1966–1968).

Although most cases of sexual abuse of children are not revealed, the incidence of sexual abuse is much higher than what was previously assumed. Approximately 150,000 to 200,000 cases of sexual abuse are reported each year. *Less than 10 percent* of the allegations of sexual abuse are estimated to be false. Allegations of sexual abuse require careful and patient evaluation by experienced clinicians.

43.3. The answer is E (all) (*Synopsis VI*, pages 781–782; *CTP V*, pages 1982–1985).

Mood disorders in children are rare. They occur at a rate of approximately *2 to 5 percent*. An increased incidence of mood disorders is found in the children of *mood-disordered parents* and relatives. Having one depressed parent may double the risk to the child of having a mood disorder, and having two depressed parents may quadruple the risk, when compared with children with unaffected parents.

The onset of a mood disorder in children may be insidious and difficult to pinpoint. A major depressive syndrome in children may be manifested by *somatic complaints*, decreased *academic performance*, psychomotor agitation, or mood-congruent hallucinations or delusions. Children can be reliable reporters about their behavior and emotions, but they refer to their symptoms by many names. The examiner must ask about feelings by using a range of words that takes into account the child's developmental level. For example, when asking about dysphoria, the clinician should ask about feeling sad, low, like crying, and like feeling bad inside. Mood-disordered children often identify one or more of these terms to describe their feelings.

43.4. The answer is B (1, 3) (*Synopsis VI*, pages 780–781; *CTP V*, pages 1983–1984).

The diagnostic criteria in the revised third edition of *Diagnostic and Statistical Manual of Mental Disorders* (DSM-III-R) for a *manic episode* and manic and hypomanic syndromes in children and adolescents are identical to those in adults. The DSM-III-R criteria for *schizoaffective disorder* in children, adolescents, and adults are also identical.

The DSM-III-R criteria for *cyclothymia* and *dysthymia* in children and adolescents are different from the criteria used for adults. The only DSM-III-R criterion for cyclothymia that is different is the duration of the illness. Rather than a period of two years of alternating hypomanic and depressed mood (i.e., cyclothymia), only one year is required in children. In the diagnostic criteria for dysthymia in children and adolescents and those for adults, there are two significant differences. Children and adolescents may exhibit an irritable mood, instead of or in addition to the depressed mood that is required to make the diagnosis in adults. And the mood disturbance in children and adolescents needs to be present for only one year, rather than two years.

Table 43.1 lists the DSM-III-R diagnostic criteria for symptoms of depression.

43.5. The answer is B (1, 3) (*Synopsis VI*, pages 784–785; *CTP V*, pages 1966–1968).

Sexually abused children tend to be *hyperalert to external aggression*, as shown by an inability to deal with their own aggressive impulses toward others or with others' hostility directed toward them. High-risk factors for sexual abuse of children include a *passive, absent*, sick, or in any way incapacitated mother; a daughter who takes on the maternal role in the family; alcohol abuse in the father: and overcrowding.

Approximately *50 (not 10) percent* of abuse is by family members. The most common abuse is by fathers, stepfathers, uncles, and older siblings. *Father-daughter incest* occurs much more frequently than mother-son incest. Mother-son incest is associated with more overtly severe maternal psychopathology than is father-daughter incest. In many cases, incestuous mothers are clearly suffering from schizophrenia.

Statistics on the sexual abuse of children are listed in Table 43.2.

Table 43.1
Symptoms of Depression

1. depressed mood (or can be irritable mood in children and adolescents) most of the day, nearly every day, as indicated either by subjective account or observation by others

2. markedly diminished intererst or pleasure in all, or almost all, activities most of the day, nearly every day (as indicated either by subjective account or observation by others of apathy most of the time)

3. significant weight loss or weight gain when not dieting (e.g., more than 5% of body weight in a month), or decrease or increase in appetite nearly every day (in children, consider failure to make expected weight gains)

4. insomnia or hypersomnia nearly every day

5. psychomotor agitation or retardation nearly every day (observable by others, not merely subjective feelings of restlessness or being slowed down)

6. fatigue or loss of energy nearly every day

7. feelings of worthlessness or excessive or inappropriate guilt (which may be delusional) nearly every day (not merely self-reproach or guilt about being sick)

8. diminished ability to think or concentrate, or indecisiveness, nearly every day (either by subjective account or as observed by others)

9. recurrent thoughts of death (not just fear of dying), recurrent suicidal ideation without a specific plan, or a suicide attempt or a specific plan for committing suicide

Table from DSM-III-R, *Diagnostic and Statistical Manual of Mental Disorders*, ed 3, revised. Copyright American Psychiatric Association, Washington, DC, 1987. Used with permission.

43.6. The answer is D (4) (*Synopsis VI*, pages 782–783; *CTP V*, pages 1987–1992).

Despite frequent subjective sleep complaints, prepubertal children do not show *classic depressive polysomnographic abnormalities* during a major depressive episode. In adolescents and adults, rapid eye movement latency is shortened during major depressive episodes.

Mood disorders with childhood or adolescent onset are *likely to recur* and, if not successfully treated, will produce considerable short- and long-term difficulties and complications. Depression in a child may be misdiagnosed as a learning disability. Learning problems secondary to depression, even when long-standing, *do not persist* but correct themselves rapidly after recovery from the depressive episode.

Children and adolescents with major depressive syndromes may have psychotic features. Most frequently, these psychotic symptoms are *mood-congruent* (not incongruent), which means that they are thematically consistent with the depressed mood.

43.7. The answer is C (2, 4) (*Synopsis VI*, page 785; *CTP V*, pages 1962–1963).

In cases of suspected child abuse and neglect, the physician should confer with members of the hospital child abuse committee *within 72 hours* and *report the case* to the appropriate department of social service, child protection unit, or central registry. Physicians should also diagnose the suspected maltreatment, intervene and admit the child into the hospital, and perform a physical examination and skeletal *X-rays*, even *without* the permission of the

Table 43.2
Sexual Abuse of Children

Reported cases in U.S., 1985	123,000
Prevalence of male abuse	3–31 percent
Prevalence of female abuse	6–62 percent
Perpetrators	
Father/stepfather	7–8 percent
Uncles/older siblings	16–42 percent
Friends	32–60 percent
Strangers	1 percent
Sexual activity	
Coitus	16–29 percent
Oral sex and intercourse	3–11 percent
Touching genitals	13–33 percent
Ages	Peak between ages 9 and 12 25 percent below age 8
High-risk factors	Child living in single-parent home Marital conflict History of physical abuse
Reported motivation of abuser	Pedophilic impulses No other sexual object Inability to delay gratification

Data from D Finklehor: The sexual abuse of children: Current research reviewed. Psychiatr Ann *17*: 4, 1987. Figures may total more than 100 percent because of overlapping studies.

parents. Other responsibilities include requesting a social worker's report and appropriate surgical and medical consultation and arranging a program of care for the child and the parents for social service follow-up. In a medical emergency, the child may be *admitted to the hospital without the consent* of the legal guardian or parent.

43.8.   The answer is E (all) (*Synopsis VI*, page 784; *CTP V*, pages 1963–1964).

More than 50 percent of abused or neglected children were born prematurely or had low birth weight. Many abused children are perceived by their parents as being difficult, *slow in development or mentally*

retarded, bad, selfish, or hard to discipline. The perpetrator of the battered-child syndrome is more often the woman than the man. One parent is usually the active batterer, and the other passively accepts the battering. Of the perpetrators studied, 80 percent were regularly living in the homes of the children they abused. More than 80 percent of children studied were *living with married parents* at the time of abuse; approximately 20 percent were living with a single parent. Ninety percent of abusing parents were severely *abused by their own mothers or fathers.*

Sexual abuse is usually by men, although women acting alone or in concert with men have also been involved, especially in child pornography.

Psychiatric Treatment of Children and Adolescents

Adult treatment and child and adolescent treatment are different in several ways. First, the child or the adolescent rarely requests therapy. The request for treatment is outside the child's control. Although children and adolescents may be aware that problems exist, they often view the parents' or the school's motivation to be to punish them or to enforce demands, not to aid them. Dealing with parental and school demands for improvement while attempting to establish a therapeutic alliance with the patient is in striking contrast to psychotherapy with most adults. Second, the parents must be engaged in the therapeutic process to assist in constructively altering the child's environment. The therapist must determine the degree of their participation. Finally, the therapist must be more active in therapy with children and adolescents than with adults. The therapist must select activities and set limits and must incorporate information that comes from outside the patient-therapist relationship.

Matching the category of a child's psychiatric disturbance, not to mention the individual child, with a specific psychiatric treatment is an important but difficult task. There is no single effective therapeutic element in treatment. Unfortunately, some therapists are handicapped by a tradition of mutual exclusivity of different therapeutic modalities, so that they see value in combining only some modes of treatment and excluding others.

Many types of psychotherapy for children are useful, among which are intensive individual therapy, brief therapy, family therapy, behavior therapy, play therapy, and symptom-focused remediation, such as tutoring and speech therapy. The use of these approaches singly or in combination should stem not from the therapist's preferences but from the assessment of the patient and from a broad-based background of knowledge about available treatments.

Certain elements in psychotherapy induce complications that militate against a particular form of psychotherapy for a given child. For instance, for many disturbed children a form of exploratory-interpretive psychotherapy aimed at uncovering intrapsychic conflicts is indicated. But if the youngster's ego functioning, particularly in the area of reality testing, is borderline, such an approach calls for considerable caution, lest it induce destructive ego regression. To treat a young patient effectively, a clinician needs to be firmly aware of the indications and contraindications for the various psychotherapies and organic therapies and the potential benefits, risks, and side effects of specific treatments.

Pharmacotherapy is of increasing use in children. A specific psychopharmacology for childhood disorders was developed in 1937 with the report on the beneficial effects of amphetamine sulfate on the mood or the behavior or both of a heterogeneous group of institutionalized, behavior-disordered children. The administration of similarly acting psychostimulants to children and adolescents has continued since then with the addition of dextroamphetamine (Dexedrine) and methylphenidate (Ritalin). Today these drugs are of great use in attention-deficit hyperactivity disorder.

Integrating and coordinating the techniques of various therapeutic modalities often includes the consideration of pharmacotherapy. The clinician must be aware of the relevant biological and neurophysiological factors and the psychodynamic issues surrounding the use of medication. The manner in which the child, the caretakers, and the school personnel perceive medication significantly influences the child's

389

response to medication and to the other therapies being used at the time. Medication may be a catalyst for positive change, shortening the duration of therapy and increasing compliance with treatment. The judicious choice is to use supportive therapy as an adjunct to any pharmacological treatment of a disorder in childhood or adolescence. Supportive therapy may include family members. The practice of instituting psychotherapy when using medication reduces the resistance to the needed pharmacological treatment.

No one drug is effective in all children. Medication is most helpful when there is a clear indication or target symptom for a particular drug. Sometimes a drug is a useful additional measure during the initial period of stress or, later, at times of crisis. It may be particularly helpful on a maintenance basis for certain borderline and psychotic children.

The last decade witnessed a virtual explosion in both the quantity and the diversity of drug usage reported in childhood disorders. That increase was concomitant with the upsurging interest in, research on, and knowledge about the biological contributions to mental illness.

Antidepressant medications, primarily the tricyclics and less so the monoamine oxidase inhibitors, were introduced into the treatment of children with various types of disorders.

Psychiatrists have shown an increasing concern about the problems with and the importance of more precise diagnostic classification and reliable rating instruments as necessary prerequisites to adequate methods of drug studies. Awareness of the adverse effects attendant on the use of psychoactive drugs has increased. Attention has increasingly been directed at not only those effects attributable directly to the drug itself but also the possible adverse interactions between drug effects and the developmental process. As a result, organic therapy in child psychiatry has been gradually differentiating itself from adult psychiatry. In addition, the attention to cognitive variables and the results of extensive psychostimulant research with children have begun to influence and contribute to the field of adult psychiatry.

Similarly, the recognition and the treatment of disorders such as major depression have extended conceptions from adult psychiatry to the pediatric area. This crossover has had a major effect in the area of suicidology, for example. Suicide in children and adolescents is reaching epidemic proportions, and the student should be especially aware of how to recognize and treat depression and substance abuse, which are two of the most common diagnoses associated with suicide in this age group.

After reading Chapter 44 of *Synopsis VI,* "Psychiatric Treatment of Children and Adolescents," and Chapter 43 of *CTP V,* "Child Psychiatry: Psychiatric Treatment," students should study the questions and answers below to test their knowledge in these areas.

HELPFUL HINTS

The terms below should be known and defined by the student.

psychoanalytic theories	externalization	modeling theory
developmental orientation	acting out	behavioral contracting
sequential psychosocial capacities	self-observation	group living
learning-behavioral theories	regression	milieu therapy
classical and operant conditioning	therapeutic playroom	organic therapies
family systems theory	therapeutic interventions	parental attitudes
relationship therapy	child guidance clinics	pharmacokinetics
remedial and educational	confidentiality	renal clearance
psychotherapy	group therapy	liver-to-body-weight ratio
supportive therapy	play group therapy	ADHD
release therapy	group selection criteria	psychostimulants
filial therapy	activity group therapy	tardive dyskinesia
psychoanalytically oriented	monosexual groups	Tourette's disorder
therapy	combined therapy	haloperidol (Haldol)
child psychoanalysis	parent groups	infantile autism
cognitive therapy	residential and day treatment	fenfluramine (Pondimin)

schizophrenia	sleep terror	atypical puberty
mood disorders	obsessive-compulsive disorder	substance abuse
tricyclic antidepressants	specific developmental disorders	suicide
MAOIs	eating disorders	action-oriented defenses
ECT	cardiovascular effects	masked depression
lithium	growth suppression	depressive equivalents
conduct disorder	dietary manipulation	violence
anticonvulsants	puberty and adolescence	compliance
enuresis	(differentiation)	
bell-and-pad conditioning	interview techniques	

QUESTIONS

DIRECTIONS: Each of the questions or incomplete statements below is followed by five suggested responses or completions. Select the *one* that is *best* in each case.

44.1. Traditional items in a therapeutic playroom include all the following *except*
A. multigenerational doll families
B. blocks
C. crayons
D. television set
E. rubber hammers

44.2. Group therapy is useful for all the following childhood problems *except*
A. phobias
B. male effeminate behavior
C. withdrawal and social isolation
D. extreme aggression
E. primary behavior disturbances

44.3. Which one of the following statements about children referred for residential treatment is *not* true?
A. Outpatient treatment often precedes residential treatment
B. More boys than girls are referred
C. Severe learning disabilities are a frequent concomitant secondary diagnosis
D. Most children referred are between 5 and 15 years of age
E. Suicidal behavior is among the most common referral diagnoses

44.4. Group therapy is
A. not useful for mentally ill children
B. largely unfocused with young children
C. useful in the treatment of substance-abuse problems
D. more viable with adolescents when the group is composed of mixed-sex, rather than same-sex, members
E. most effective when parents oppose it

44.5. "Symptom bearer," "distracter," "scapegoat," and "rescuer" are terms used in
A. behavioral theory
B. supportive therapy
C. psychoanalytic psychotherapy
D. family systems therapy
E. relationship therapy

44.6. Childhood illnesses in which medication is the mainstay of treatment include
A. attention-deficit hyperactivity disorder
B. Tourette's disorder
C. schizophrenia
D. obsessive-compulsive disorder
E. all the above

DIRECTIONS: For each of the questions or incomplete statements below, *one or more* of the responses or completions given are correct. Choose answer

A. if only *1, 2, and 3* are correct
B. if only *1 and 3* are correct
C. if only *2 and 4* are correct
D. if only *4* is correct
E. if *all* are correct

44.7. When compared with adults, children show what differences in the pharmacokinetics of psychotropic drug therapy?
1. The therapeutic plasma levels for antidepressant medications are higher in children
2. A higher drug tolerance may reflect greater renal clearance in children
3. Stimulants have a longer half-life in children
4. A higher drug tolerance may be due to a greater liver-to-body-weight ratio in children

44.8. Which of the following statements about the treatment of mental retardation with antipsychotic medication are true?
1. A small percentage of mentally retarded patients are currently receiving antipsychotics
2. Intelligence quotient deficits have been found to respond dramatically to phenothiazines
3. There is no risk of tardive dyskinesia when using antipsychotic medications
4. Hyperactivity and stereotypies associated with mental retardation have been found to respond to antipsychotic medications

44.9. Medications used in the treatment of attention-deficit hyperactivity disorder include
1. methylphenidate (Ritalin)
2. diazepam (Valium)
3. dextroamphetamine (Dexedrine)
4. phenytoin (Dilantin)

44.10. The side effects of antidepressant medications in children include
1. dry mouth
2. blurry vision
3. tachycardia
4. palpitations

44.11. Imipramine (Tofranil) is useful in the treatment of childhood
1. enuresis
2. school phobia
3. depressive disorders
4. autism

44.12. Pharmacological treatment of conduct disorder may include
1. haloperidol (Haldol)
2. lithium
3. carbamazepine (Tegretol)
4. propranolol (Inderal)

44.13. The use of diazepam (Valium) in children has been well established for the treatment of
1. enuresis
2. obsessive-compulsive disorder
3. attention-deficit hyperactivity disorder
4. sleep terrors

ANSWERS

Psychiatric Treatments of Children and Adolescents

44.1. The answer is D (*Synopsis VI*, page 790; *CTP V*, pages 1911–1912).

Traditional items in a therapeutic playroom do not include a *television set*. The goal is not for the child to be entertained. Television puts the child in a passive, noninteractive mode and so is generally not considered useful therapeutically.

The purpose of the therapeutic playroom is to create an environment in which the child feels comfortable enough to play freely and to express a wide range of feelings. The goal is for the child to engage in symbolic play—that is, play that expresses the child's unconscious feelings.

Multigenerational doll families are dolls from three generations and include young children, parents, and grandparents. This concept allows the child to use the dolls to express intrafamilial interactions. *Blocks* are therapeutically useful because they allow the child room to create and to project fantasies onto the creations. The use of blocks may also allow for the ventilation of aggressive impulses, as when a child builds a stack of blocks and then crashes it to the floor. Drawings with *crayons* allow the expression of creative impulses and provide access to the child's fantasy life when the child explains or tells a story about what is drawn. Play tools, such as *rubber hammers*, are also useful, enabling the child to demonstrate identification with a parental figure, to build, and to destroy.

44.2. The answer is D (*Synopsis VI*, page 792; *CTP V*, page 1931).

Group therapy is not useful for *extreme aggression*. In children, extreme aggression may indicate a diminished need or ability to be accepted by peers, and peer acceptance is felt by many therapists to be a prerequisite for group membership and treatment. Extremely aggressive children are also potentially disruptive to group functioning and intimidating to other group members, two features that severely impair their capacity for group involvement. Extremely aggressive children may engender such negative reactions from a group that group membership serves only to reinforce an already lowered self-esteem. Finally, extreme aggression in children may at least intially require the primary use of medication and limit setting as the essential therapeutic interventions.

Indications for group therapy that have been investigated include *phobias, male effeminate behavior, withdrawal and social isolation,* and *primary behavior disturbances*.

44.3. The answer is E (*Synopsis VI*, pages 794–795; *CTP V*, pages 1944–1945).

Suicidal behavior is not among the most common referral diagnoses; in fact, among the reasons to exclude children are behaviors that are likely to be destructive to the children themselves or to others under the treatment conditions. Thus, some children who threaten to run away, set fires, hurt others, or attempt suicide may not be suitable for residential treatment.

Although the age range of children referred for residential treatment varies from institution to institution, most children are *between 5 and 15 years* of age. *Boys* are referred more frequently than girls. Most, if not all, children referred for residential treatment have *severe learning disabilities* and have been seen previously by one or more professional persons, such as a school psychologist or a pediatrician, or by members of a child guidance clinic, juvenile court, or state welfare agency. Unsuccessful attempts at less drastic *outpatient treatment* and foster home or other custodial placement often precede residential treatment.

44.4. The answer is C (*Synopsis VI*, page 783; *CTP V*, pages 1928–1932).

Group therapy has been found to be useful in the treatment of *substance-abuse problems*, which are more commonly encountered in latency and pubertal-age children than in younger children. Group therapy is useful for *mentally ill children*, as well as healthier children. Young children (preschool and early school age) generally require a *focused* group, as they cannot provide this for themselves. Work with the group is usually structured by the therapist through the use of a particular technique, such as puppets or art. Play group therapy emphasizes the interactional qualities among the children and with the therapist in the permissive playroom setting. Group therapy is more viable in adolescence if the group is composed of *same-sex members*, as opposed to mixed-sex members—presumably because the upsurge of sexual energy and interest at this stage interferes, in a group setting, with the psychotherapeutic exploration necessary for psychotherapy. Group therapy is not *effective when parents oppose it;* no treatment is enhanced by opposition from significant family members, especially any therapy involving children.

44.5. The answer is D (*Synopsis VI*, pages 588–593 and 787–789; *CTP V*, pages 1539–1541 and 1931–1932).

"Symptom bearer," "distracter," "scapegoat," and "rescuer" are terms used for roles that family members play in *family systems therapy*. In this therapy the family system is viewed as a constantly evolving, self-regulating structure. The dynamic interactions between the family members are examined by family therapists to identify the roles the family members are "assigned" and to assess the boundaries and the subsystems within the family. Appreciation of the family system sometimes explains why a minute therapeutic input at a critical junction results in far-reaching changes, whereas in other situations huge quantities of therapeutic effort are absorbed with minimal evidence of change.

Behavioral theories, based on the concepts of classical (Pavlovian) conditioning or operant (Skinnerian) conditioning, hold that abnormal behavior is due to a failure to learn or is due to learning maladaptive behavior through conditioning. Appropriate behaviors are highlighted and rewarded in behaviorally oriented therapy.

Supportive therapy offers support by an authority figure. Supportive psychotherapy is particularly helpful in enabling a well-adjusted youngster to cope with the emotional turmoil engendered in a crisis. It is also used with those disturbed youngsters whose less-than-adequate ego functioning is seriously disrupted by an expressive-exploratory mode or by other forms of therapeutic intervention. At the beginning of most psychotherapy, regardless of the patient's age or the nature of the therapeutic interventions, the principal therapeutic elements perceived by the patient tend to be supportive ones, a consequence of therapists' universal efforts to be reliably and sensitively responsive. In fact, some therapy may never proceed beyond this supportive level, whereas other therapies develop an expressive-exploratory or behavioral modification flavor on top of the supportive foundation.

Psychoanalytic psychotherapy is a modified form of psychotherapy that is expressive and exploratory and that endeavors to reverse the evolution of the emotional disturbance through a reenactment and a desensitization of the traumatic events by the free expression of thoughts and feelings in an interview-play situation. Ultimately, the therapist helps the patient understand the warded-off feelings, fears, and wishes that have beset him or her.

In *relationship therapy* a positive, friendly, helpful relationship is viewed as the primary, if not the sole, therapeutic ingredient. One of the best examples of pure relationship therapy is found outside the clinical setting in the work of the Big Brother Organization.

44.6. The answer is E (*Synopsis VI*, pages 798–802; *CTP V*, pages 1934–1937).

Childhood illnesses in which medication is the mainstay of treatment include *attention-deficit hy-*peractivity disorder (ADHD), Tourette's disorder, schizophrenia, and obsessive-compulsive disorder.

ADHD provides the clearest indication for psychopharmacological treatment. The symptoms usually prompting therapy are developmentally inappropriate inattention and impulsivity that do not respond to social contact. The first choice among the organic therapies is a stimulant, of which there are three: methylphenidate (Ritalin), dextroamphetamine (Dexedrine), and pemoline (Cylert). Tourette's disorder, characterized by multiple motor and vocal tics, is also a clear indication for pharmacotherapy. Haloperidol (Haldol) is the standard treatment against which all proposed treatments of Tourette's disorder are now measured. Schizophrenia in childhood is rare, but, when such symptoms as hallucinations and delusions are present, antipsychotic medications are indicated. The same toxic side effects that adults experience—in particular, tardive dyskinesia—can occur in children, so caution must be exercised.

Clomipramine (Anafranil), an antidepressant medication used to treat adults with obsessive-compulsive disorder, has been shown to be effective in the treatment of childhood obsessive-compulsive disorder. Fluoxetine (Prozac) has also been used with some success to treat obsessive-compulsive disorder in children.

Table 44.1 covers the psychoactive drugs in use with children and adolescents. The student should know this table well, especially the dosage ranges.

44.7. The answer is C (2, 4) (*Synopsis VI*, page 797; *CTP V*, pages 1938–1939).

In children, when compared with adults, a higher drug tolerance may reflect both *greater renal clearance* and a *greater liver-to-body-weight ratio* (e.g., 30 percent greater for a 6-year-old than for an adult). Children appear to be more effective metabolizers of psychoactive drugs than are adults. Children may require or tolerate slightly higher doses on a milligram-per-kilogram-of-body-weight basis than adults—clearly the case with lithium, which may reflect the greater renal clearance seen in children. Stimulants seem to have a somewhat shorter (not longer) *half-life* in children than in adults. Depressed children require the same (not higher) therapeutic *plasma levels* of antidepressant medications as adults to achieve a response.

44.8. The answer is D (4) (*Synopsis VI*, page 799; *CTP V*, pages 1936–1937).

Mental retardation in itself is not an indication for psychotropic drug use, although some associated behaviors may respond to medication. *Hyperactivity* and the repetitive, unconscious movements known as stereotypies have been found to respond to either antipsychotics or stimulants. Approximately *50 percent* of mentally retarded patients living in institutions are receiving antipsychotics, despite the lack of any clear indications. The *intelligence quotient*

Table 44.1
Common Psychoactive Drugs for Children and Adolescents

Drugs	Indications	Dosage	Adverse Reactions and Monitoring
Antipsychotics Also known as major tranquilizers, neuroleptics Divided into (1) high-potency, low-dosage, e.g., haloperidol (Haldol), trifluoperazine (Stelazine), thiothixene (Navane) and (2) low-potency, high-dosage (more sedating), e.g., chlorpromazine (Thorazine), thioridazine (Mellaril)	In general, for agitated, aggressive, self-injurious behaviors in MR, PDD, CD, and schizophrenia Studies support following specific indications: haloperidol—PDD, CD with severe aggression, Tourette's disorder	All can be given in 2–4 divided doses or combined into one dose after gradual buildup Haloperidol—0.5–16 mg/day Thiothixene—5–42 mg/day Chlorprimazine and thioridazine—10–400 mg/day	Sedation, weight gain, hypotension, lowered seizure threshold, constipation, extrapyramidal symptoms, jaundice, agranulocytosis, dystonic reaction, tardive dyskinesia Monitor: blood pressure, CBC, LFT, EEG if indicated. With thioridazine, pigmentary retinopathy is rare but dictates celling of 800 mg in adults and proportionately lower in children
Stimulants Dextroamphetamine (Dexedrine)—FDA-approved for children 3 years and older Methylphenidate (Ritalin) and pemoline (Cylert)—FDA-approved for children 6 years and older	In ADHD for hyperactivity, impulsivity, and inattentiveness	Dextroamphetamine and methylphenidate are generally given at 8 AM and noon (the usefulness of sustained release preparations is not proved) Dextroamphetamine—2.5–40 mg/day up to 0.5 mg/kg/day Methylphenidate—10–60 mg/day up to 1.0 mg/kg/day Pemoline—37.5–112.5 mg at 8 AM	Insomnia, anorexia, weight loss (and possible growth delay), tachycardia, precipitation or exacerbation of tic disorders With pemoline, monitor LFT, as hepatotoxicity is possible
Lithium Considered an antipsychotic drug, also has antiaggressive properties	Studies support use in MR and CD for aggressive and self-injurious behaviors; can be used for same in PDD; also indicated for early-onset bipolar disorder	600–2,100 mg in 2–3 divided doses; keep blood levels to 0.4–1.2 mEq/L	Nausea, vomiting, headache, tremor, weight gain Experience with adults suggests thyroid and renal function monitoring
Antidepressants Imipramine (Tofranil) has been used in most child studies Clomipramine (Anafranil) is effective in child OCD; also fluoxetine (Prozac)	Major depression, separation anxiety disorder, bulimia nervosa, functional enuresis Sometimes used in ADHD, anorexia nervosa, somnambulism, and sleep terror disorder Clomipramine and fluoxetine used in OCD	Imipramine—start with dosage of about 1.5 mg/kg/day; can build up to not more than 5 mg/kg/day Start with 2–3 divided doses; can eventually combine in one dose Not FDA-approved for children except for functional enuresis, in which dosage is usually between 50 and 100 mg before sleep Clomipramine—start at 50 mg/day; can raise to not more than 3 mg/kg/day or 200 mg/day Prozac—dosage not established in children	Dry mouth, constipation, tachycardia, drowsiness, postural hypotension ECG monitoring is needed because of risk of cardiac conduction slowing; consider lowering dosage if PR interval > 0.20 sec or QRS interval > 0.12 sec; baseline EEG is advised as drugs can lower seizure threshold; blood levels of drug are sometimes useful
Carbamazepine (Tegretol) An anticonvulsant	Aggression or dyscontrol in MR and CD	Start with 10 mg/kg/day and can build to 20–30 mg/kg/day Therapeutic blood level range appears to be 4–12 mg/L	Drowsiness, nausea, rash, vertigo, irritability Monitor: CBC and LFT for possible blood dyscrasias and hepatotoxicity; blood levels are necessary

(Continued)

Table 44.1
Continued

Drugs	Indications	Dosage	Adverse Reactions and Monitoring
Anxiolytics Have been insufficiently studied in childhood and adolescence	Sometimes effective in parasomnias: somnambulism or sleep terror disorder; can be tried in overanxious disorder	Parasomnias: diazepam (Valium) 2–10 mg before bedtime	Benzodiazepines can cause drowsiness and dyscontrol and can be abused
Fenfluramine (Pondimin) An amphetamine congener	Well studied in autistic disorder; generally ineffective, but some show improvement	Gradually increase to between 1.0 and 1.5 mg/kg/day in divided doses	Weight loss, drowsiness, irritability, loose bowel movements
Propranolol (Inderal) A β-adrenergic blocker	Aggression in MR, PDD, and organic brain dysfunction; awaits controlled studies.	Effective dosage in children and adolescents not yet established; range is probably 40–320 mg/day	Bradycardia, hypotension, nausea, hypoglycemia, depression; avoid in asthma
Clonidine (Catapres) A presynaptic α-adrenergic blocking agent	Tourette's disorder	0.1–0.3 mg/day; 3–5.5 μg/kg/day	Orthostatic hypotension, nausea, vomiting, sedation, elevated blood glucose
Cyproheptadine (Periactin)	Anorexia nervosa	Dosages up to 8 mg q.i.d.	Antihistaminic side effects, including sedation and dryness of the mouth
Naltrexone (Trexan)	Self-injurious behaviors in MR and PDD; currently being studied in PDD	0.5–2.0 mg/kg/day	Sleepiness, aggressivity Monitor LFT, as hepatotoxicity has been reported in adults at high dosages

Table by Richard Perry, M.D.
ADHD = attention-deficit hyperactivity disorder
CBC   = complete blood count
CD   = conduct disorder
ECG   = electrocardiogram
EEG   = electroencephalogram
LFT   = liver function test
MR   = mental retardation
OCD   = obsessive-compulsive disorder
PDD   = pervasive developmental disorder
q.i.d. = four times a day

deficits that define mental retardation do not respond to phenothiazines or to any pharmacological agent yet tested. There is at least the same *risk of tardive dyskinesia* in this population, and some studies show an increased risk, perhaps as a result of the underlying central nervous system impairment.

Some psychotropic drugs may improve cognitive tests of learning functions. For example, amphetamine improves performance on a variety of tasks (see Table 44.2).

44.9.   The answer is B (1, 3) (*Synopsis VI*, pages 797–798; *CTP V*, page 1934).

Medications used in the treatment of attention-deficit hyperactivity disorder (ADHD) include *methylphenidate* (Ritalin), *dextroamphetamine* (Dexedrine), and pemoline (Cylert). Of these three drugs, methylphenidate has the shortest half-life (2½ hours). Dextroamphetamine has a somewhat longer half-life (about 6 to 8 hours), and the half-life of

pemoline is the longest (about 12 hours). The hallmarks of treatment response are decreased restlessness and impulsivity, increased attention span and concentration, and compliance with commands. *Diazepam* (Valium) is not useful in the treatment of ADHD, nor is *phenytoin* (Dilantin), an anticonvulsant agent.

44.10.   The answer is E (all) (*Synopsis VI*, page 800; *CTP V*, pages 1937–1938).

The potential side effects of antidepressant medications in children are usually similar to the side effects in adults. They include *dry mouth, blurry vision* (loss of accommodation), *tachycardia* (rapid heart rate), *palpitations* (sensation of the heart's pounding in the chest), constipation, and sweating. These side effects result primarily from the anticholinergic properties of the tricyclic antidepressants. Postural hypotension (a drop in blood pressure when changing from a sitting to a standing position), a

Table 44.2
Effects of Psychotropic Drugs on Cognitive Tests of Learning Functions

Drug Class	Continuous Performance Test (Attention)	Matching Familiar Figures (Impulsivity)	Test Function			
			Paired Associates (Verbal Learning)	Porteus Maze (Planning Capacity)	Short-Term Memory†	WISC (Intelligence)
Stimulant	↑	↑	↑	↑	↑	↑
Antidepressants	↑	0		0	0	0
Antipsychotics	↑ ↓		↓	↓	↓	0

Adapted from M G Aman: Drugs, learning, and the psychotherapies. In *Pediatric Psychopharmacology: The Use of Behavior Modifying Drugs in Children*, J S Werry, editor, Brunner/Mazel, New York, 1978.
↑ Improved, ↑ ↓ inconsistent, ↓ worse, and 0 no effect
† Various tests: digit span, word recall, etc.

common side effect in adults that frequently interferes with treatment, is less common in children, who more often have diastolic hypertension.

44.11. The answer is A (1, 2, 3) (*Synopsis VI*, pages 736 and 801–802; *CTP V*, pages 1935–1938).

Imipramine (Tofranil), the tricyclic antidepressant most frequently used with children, is useful in the treatment of *enuresis, school phobia*, and *depressive disorders*. It is usually better to try a non-pharmacological treatment (bell-and-pad conditioning for enuresis, desensitization for school phobias, psychotherapy for depression) before using medication. *Autism* does not respond to imipramine or other antidepressant medications, although haloperidol (Haldol) and fenfluramine (Pondimin, a sympathomimetic amine) have proved useful in the treatment of certain autistic symptoms.

44.12. The answer is E (all) (*Synopsis VI*, page 799; *CTP V*, pages 1935–1936).

Behavioral and verbal therapies are the mainstays of treatment of conduct disorder. In severe cases, when these treatments have failed, medication may be used to decrease the severity of the aggression. For these children *haloperidol* (Haldol) and *lithium* are the drugs of choice. Both have been effective in treating hospitalized assaultive conduct-disordered children. Recently, some researchers have claimed that *carbamazepine* (Tegretol) and *propranolol* (Inderal) are effective in decreasing the aggressivity of conduct-disordered children. The use of these medications needs further study, but they may be helpful in the treatment of some conduct-disordered children.

44.13. The answer is D (4) (*Synopsis VI*, page 802; *CTP V*, pages 1934–1938).

The use of diazepam (Valium) in children has been well established for the treatment of *sleep terrors*. It is not of use in the treatment of *enuresis, obsessive-compulsive disorder*, or *attention-deficit hyperactivity disorder* (ADHD). Diazepam is an anxiolytic from the general class of drugs called benzodiazepines. There are few indications for these drugs in the treatment of children, and they are frequently overprescribed. Sleep terror disorder consists of repeated episodes of abrupt awakening with intense anxiety marked by autonomic arousal. It occurs during stage IV sleep. Diazepam interferes with stage IV sleep and, in so doing, prevents the sleep terrors from occurring. Enuresis, nocturnal bed wetting, is treated either behaviorally with bell-and-pad conditioning or with imipramine (Tofranil), a tricyclic antidepressant. Obsessive-compulsive disorder is rare in children and is marked by recurrent thoughts (obsessions) and ritualistic behaviors (compulsions) that, if interfered with, cause the patient tremendous anxiety. Clomipramine (Anafranil, chlorinated imipramine) has been found to be successful in several studies. ADHD is generally treated with a stimulant, such as methylphenidate (Ritalin) or dextroamphetamine (Dexedrine). If stimulants are not effective or if the side effects are severe, a second line of drugs is the tricyclic antidepressants. Antipsychotics such as haloperidol (Haldol) have also been tried, but the risk of tardive dyskinesia must be considered.

45 ||||

Geriatric Psychiatry

Old age is defined in our culture as age 65 or older. By the year 2000, 35 million people will be over age 65. The needs of this increasing population will be great financially, physically, and emotionally. One reflection of the need for services to the elderly is the formation in 1991 of geriatric psychiatry as an official psychiatric subspecialty by the American Psychiatric Association.

The geriatric psychiatrist is aware of the psychophysiological aspects of old age and treats the emotional and mental disorders of the aged. The geriatric psychiatrist may also aid in the coordination of the multiple medical specialists required to care for the old person with many physical complaints.

Physicians who work with the aged must become aware of ageism, the negative stereotypes that society holds about old age, and of their own attitudes toward aging and the elderly. The physician's feeling about aging affect the transference and the countertransference. If a physician holds a negative view of aging, patients may fulfill the prophecy of a poor outcome and lose confidence in their own abilities and strengths.

The goals of all treatments are to help the patient recover from any psychiatric disorder, to minimize any adverse effects from those treatments, and to establish a living situation that is most appropriate to the individual patient.

In view of the fact that the aged population is the fastest growing demographic group in the United States, it behooves the student to become familiar with every aspect of their lives. Readers are referred to several sections and chapters in *Synopsis VI*— in addition to Chapter 45, "Geriatric Psychiatry"— to gain a full understanding of these issues. They include Section 2.6, "Late Adulthood and Old Age"; Section 2.7, "Thanatology: Death and Bereavement"; Chapter 5, "Psychology and Psychiatry: Psychometric and Neuropsychological Testing"; Chapter 21, "Normal Sleep and Sleep Disorders"; and Chapter 30, "Biological Therapies." Alzheimer's disease and organic mental disorders are fully discussed in Chapter 10. Readers are also referred to Chapter 46 in *CTP V*, "Geriatric Psychiatry."

Students should study the questions and answers below to test their knowledge of this area.

HELPFUL HINTS

Each of the following terms relating to geriatric issues should be defined.

developmental phases	loss of mastery	toxins
nutritional deficiencies	role of anxiety	uremia
ideational paucity	ritualistic behavior	diabetes
cognitive functioning	adaptational capacity	hepatic failure
organic mental disorder	social capacity	cerebral anoxia
orientation	drug-blood level	emphysema
sensorium	toxic confusional state	anoxic confusion
delirium	paradoxical reaction	overt behavior
dementia	agedness	mood disorder
late-onset schizophrenia	theory of aging	Alzheimer's disease
paraphrenia	disorders of awareness	transdermal scopolamine

levodopa (Larodopa)	hypochondriasis	remotivation techniques
trazodone (Desyrel)	anxiety disorder	psychotropic danger
rantidine	norepinephrine	akathisia
depression	serotonin	presbyopia
manic disorder	obsessive-compulsive disorder	FSH
hypomanic disorder	conversion disorder	LH
lithium	sleep disturbances	dementing disorder
neurosis	insomnia	fluoxetine (Prozac)

QUESTIONS

DIRECTIONS: Each of the incomplete statements below is followed by five suggested completions. Select the *one* that is *best* in each case.

45.1. The most common psychiatric disorder of the elderly is
A. depression
B. manic disorder
C. hypochondriasis
D. obsessive-compulsive disorder
E. conversion disorder

45.2. All the following statements about the biology of aging are true *except*
A. each cell of the body has a genetically determined life span
B. the optic lens thins
C. T-cell response to antigens is altered
D. decrease in melanin occurs
E. brain weight decreases

45.3. All the following statements about sleep disturbances in the elderly are true *except*
A. complaints about sleeplessness are common
B. catnaps may interfere with a good night's sleep
C. frequent visits to the bathroom may lead to problems in resuming sleep
D. tricyclics often induce sleep when insomnia is accompanied by a depressive reaction
E. the elderly do not need as much sleep as they did in their earlier mature years

45.4. Abnormalities of cognitive functioning in the aged are most often due to
A. depressive disturbances
B. schizophrenia
C. medication
D. cerebral dysfunctioning or deterioration
E. hypochondriasis

45.5. In the physical assessment of the aged, all the following statements are true *except*
A. toxins of bacterial origin are common
B. uremia is the most common metabolic intoxication causing mental symptoms
C. cerebral anoxia often precipitates mental syndromes
D. vitamin deficiencies are common
E. nutritional deficiencies may cause mental symptoms

45.6. All the following statements about learning and memory in the elderly are true *except*
A. complete learning of new material still occurs
B. recognition of right anwsers on multiple-choice tests remains intact
C. simple recall remains intact
D. I.Q. remains stable until age 80
E. memory-encoding ability diminishes

45.7. All the following statements about the pharmacological treatment of the elderly are true *except*
A. the elderly use more medications than any other age group
B. 25 percent of all prescriptions are for those over age 65
C. adverse medication reactions result in the hospitalization of nearly 250,000 people a year in the United States
D. 25 percent of all hypnotics dispensed in the United States each year are to those over age 65
E. 70 percent of the elderly use over-the-counter medications

45.8. Changes in the ratio of lean to fat body mass affect the distribution of all the following *except*
A. imipramine
B. diazepam
C. chlorpromazine
D. lithium
E. fluoxetine

45.9. The elderly patient is at increased risk of all the following antipsychotic side effects *except*
A. tardive dyskinesia
B. akathisia
C. neuroleptic malignant syndrome
D. orthostatic hypotension
E. rabbit syndrome

DIRECTIONS: For each of the questions and incomplete statements below, *one or more* of the responses or completions given are correct. Choose answer

A. if only *1, 2, and 3* are correct
B. if only *1 and 3* are correct
C. if only *2 and 4* are correct
D. if only *4* is correct
E. if *all* are correct

45.10. Sexual activity in persons over age 60
1. occurs in less than 10 percent of women
2. occurs in more than 70 percent of men
3. is often accompanied by guilt feelings
4. may increase in some persons, compared with earlier functioning

45.11. Alzheimer's disease is
1. the primary diagnosis in 50 percent of the 1.3 million people in nursing homes
2. a common type of senile brain disorder
3. diagnosable in millions of people throughout the world
4. associated with more than 100,000 deaths annually in the United States

45.12. Elderly persons taking antipsychotics are especially susceptible to side effects, including
1. tardive dyskinesia
2. akathisia
3. a toxic confusional state
4. paresthesias

45.13. Which of the following drugs have been implicated in producing psychiatric symptoms in the elderly?
1. Ibuprofen (Motrin, Advil)
2. Trazodone (Desyrel)
3. Cimetidine (Tagamet)
4. Levodopa (Larodopa)

45.14. Which of the following statements about the treatment of geriatric patients with psychotherapeutic drugs are true?
1. Elderly persons may be more susceptible than younger adults to adverse effects
2. The elderly patient may metabolize drugs more slowly than do other adult patients
3. Most psychotropic drugs should be given in equally divided doses
4. The most reasonable practice is to begin with a small dose

45.15. Alzheimer's disease is associated with
1. an accumulation of abnormal protein structures in neuronal cells
2. an unusually large amount of acetylcholine in the brain
3. damage in the hippocampal region of the brain
4. an abrupt onset

ANSWERS

Geriatric Psychiatry

45.1. The answer is A (*Synopsis VI*, pages 810–812; *CTP V*, pages 2017–2018).

Depression is the most common psychiatric disorder of the elderly; indeed, white elderly men have the highest suicidal rate of any group. Depressions in late life are usually precipitated by some traumatic event. *Manic* and hypomanic disorders are less frequent than depressions, although they do appear in late life. *Hypochondriasis*, an inordinate preoccupation with one's bodily functions, is especially common among the aged. With fewer worthwhile things than in the past to divert one from self-concern, it becomes easy to notice and talk about minor ailments and accidents. *Obsessive-compulsive disorders* and patterns in late life are similar to such disorders and patterns in earlier years. Compulsive characteristics—such as overconscientiousness, perfectionism, and orderliness—may be considered praiseworthy, but they eventually undermine one's efficiency and cause immobilization.

Not common among the elderly is *conversion disorder*, the giving up of the function of a bodily part—as in hysterical paralysis, blindness, and deafness—so that the rest of the organism can continue to function unimpaired. What is often seen among geriatric patients is an exaggeration of minor physical conditions.

45.2. The answer is B (*Synopsis VI*, pages 50–51; *CTP V*, pages 2037–2040).

The process of aging is known as senescence, and it results from a complex interaction of genetic, metabolic, hormonal, immunological, and structural factors acting on molecular, cellular, histological, and organ levels. The most commonly held theory is that each cell has a *genetically determined life span* during which replication occurs a limited number of times before the cell dies. Structural changes in cells take place with age. In the central nervous system, for example, age-related cell changes occur in neurons, which show signs of degeneration.

Changes in the structure of deoxyribonucleic acid (DNA) and ribonucleic acid (RNA) are also found in aging cells; the cause has been attributed to genotypic programming, X-rays, chemicals, and food products, among others. Aging probably has no single cause. All areas of the body are affected to some degree, and changes vary from person to person.

A progressive decline in many bodily functions includes a *decrease in melanin* and decreases in cardiac output and stroke volume, glomerular filtration rate, oxygen consumption, cerebral blood flow, and vital capacity. *The optic lens* thickens (not thins) in association with an inability to accommodate (presbyopia), and hearing loss is progressive, particularly at the high frequencies.

Many immune mechanisms are altered, with impaired *T-cell response to antigens* and an increase in the formation of autoimmune antibodies. These altered immune responses probably play a role in aged persons' susceptibility to infection and possibly even to neoplastic disease. Some neoplasms show a steadily increasing incidence with age, most notably cancers of the colon, prostate, stomach, and skin.

Variable changes are seen in endocrine function. For example, postmenopausal estrogen levels decrease, producing breast tissue evolution and vaginal epithelial atrophy. Testosterone levels begin to decline in the sixth decade; however, follicle-stimulating hormone and luteinizing hormone increase.

In the central nervous system, there is a decrease in *brain weight,* ventricular enlargement, and neuronal loss of approximately 50,000 a day, with some reduction in cerebral blood flow and oxygenation.

45.3. The answer is E (*Synopsis VI*, page 813; *CTP V*, page 2041).

Contrary to the popular myth, most elderly persons *need as much sleep* as they did in their earlier mature years. However, *complaints about sleeplessness* are common. To some extent these complaints can be traced to sleep disturbances, rather than to sleeplessness. The sleep disturbances may be due to the need for more *frequent visits to the bathroom,* with resulting problems in again falling asleep. Furthermore, many of the elderly—retired, unemployed, inactive, and noninvolved—succumb to the practice of taking *catnaps* during their waking hours, a habit that may interfere with what they describe as a good night's sleep.

When insomnia does occur and is unaccompanied by delirium or a psychotic disorder, it usually responds to standard hypnotics. When insomnia is accompanied by a psychotic or depressive reaction, phenothiazines or *tricyclics* often induce sleep.

45.4. The answer is D (*Synopsis VI*, page 810; *CTP V*, pages 2022 and 2028).

Abnormalities of cognitive functioning in the elderly are most often due to some *cerebral dysfunctioning or deterioration,* although they may also be the result of *depressive disturbances, schizophrenia,* or *medication* effects. In many instances, intellectual difficulties are not obvious, and a searching evaluation is necessary to detect them. The elderly are sensitive to the effects of medication; in some instances, cognitive impairment may occur as a result of overmedication. *Hypochondriasis,* the fear that one has a disease or preoccupation with one's health, is not the cause of an abnormality of cognitive functioning.

45.5.   The answer is D (*Synopsis VI,* pages 807–810; *CTP V,* pages 2037–2040).

Vitamin deficiencies in the aged are uncommon. However, a number of conditions and deficiencies are typical and should be considered in the physical assessment of the aged. *Toxins of bacterial* and metabolic origins are common in old age. Bacterial toxins usually originate in occult or inconspicuous foci of infection, such as suspected pneumonic conditions and urinary infections. The most common metabolic intoxication causing mental symptoms in the aged is *uremia,* which is an excess of urea and other nitrogenous waste products in the blood. Mild diabetes, hepatic failure, and gout are also known to cause mental symptoms in the aged and may easily be missed unless they are actively investigated. Alcohol and drug misuse may cause many mental disturbances in late life, but these abuses, with their characteristic effects, are usually easily determined by taking a history.

Cerebral anoxia resulting from cardiac insufficiency or emphysema or both often precipitates mental symptoms in old people. Anoxic confusion may follow surgery, a cardiac infarct, gastrointestinal bleeding, or occlusion or stenosis of the carotid arteries. *Nutritional deficiencies* not only may be symptomatic of emotional illness but may also cause mental symptoms.

45.6.   The answer is C (*Synopsis VI,* page 51; *CTP V,* pages 2022–2023 and 2037–2039).

Areas of difficulty for the elderly include tasks that require shifting attention, *memory-encoding ability,* and *simple recall.* These functions decline with age. However, many cognitive abilities are retained in old age. Although the elderly take longer than young persons to learn new material, *complete learning* still occurs. Old adults maintain their verbal abilities, and their *I.Q.s* remain stable until age 80. On *multiple-choice tests,* recognition of the right answers persists.

45.7.   The answer is D (*Synopsis VI,* page 814; *CTP V,* pages 2034 and 2041–2043).

Psychotropic drugs are among those most commonly prescribed for the elderly; 40 (not 25) percent of all *hypnotics* dispensed in the United States each year are to those over age 65. The elderly use *more medications than any other age group.* Indeed, *25 percent of all prescriptions* are written for those over age 65. Many old persons have adverse drug reactions, as evidenced by the fact that in the United States 250,000 people a year are hospitalized be-

cause of *adverse medication reactions.* The physician must remember that 70 percent of the elderly use *over-the-counter* (OTC) medications. These preparations can interact with prescribed drugs and lead to dangerous side effects. The physician should include the use of OTC medications when taking a patient's drug history.

45.8.   The answer is D (*Synopsis VI,* pages 814–816; *CTP V,* pages 2039–2040 and 2044–2045).

As a person ages, the ratio of lean to fat body mass changes. With normal aging, lean body mass decreases, and body fat increases. Because of that and because of decreases in plasma volume, total body water, and total plasma, the volume of distribution (Vd) for lipophilic drugs is increased. Increases in the Vd of the lipophilic drugs *imipramine, diazepam, chlorpromazine,* and *fluoxetine* may reduce their efficacy if the drugs are given in single or as-needed doses. The increased Vd also contributes to drug accumulation. *Lithium,* a hydrophilic drug, is excreted by the kidneys. The elderly person's decrease in renal clearance may cause an accumulation of lithium.

45.9.   The answer is C (*Synopsis VI,* pages 814–816; *CTP V,* pages 2046–2047).

The elderly appear to be at reduced risk of *neuroleptic malignant syndrome,* a life-threatening complication of antipsychotic treatment. This syndrome is characterized by high fever, generalized rigidity, delirium, and increased abnormal behavior.

However, the elderly patient is more sensitive than younger patients to many other side effects of antipsychotic medication. *Tardive dyskinesia*—characterized by disfiguring, involuntary buccal and lingual masticatory movements—is noted in the elderly patient most commonly after many years of antipsychotic treatment. The use of depot antipsychotics may also increase the aged person's risk of tardive dyskinesia. Extrapyramidal symptoms, including *akathisia* and the *rabbit syndrome* are more common in elderly patients than in young patients. Akathisia is the subjective feeling of muscular discomfort that causes a patient to pace or move constantly. Rabbit syndrome is a focal perioral tremor. *Orthostatic hypotension,* caused by α_1-adrenergic blockade, is problematic in the elderly. The patient's blood pressure, lying and standing, should be taken regularly during the first days of treatment.

45.10.   The answer is C (2, 4) (*Synopsis VI,* page 54; *CTP V,* page 2018).

Sexual activity continues well into old age, with William Masters and Virginia Johnson reporting sexual functioning of people in their 80s. Among women, at least *20 percent (not less than 10 percent)* over age 60 are still sexually active; among men, more than *70 percent* are still active past the age of 60. There is no indication that such activity is accompanied by *guilt feelings* that are related to age alone. In fact, as some persons get older, they resolve feelings of guilt about sex that may have existed when they were younger. It is this resolution that may account, in part, for the fact that sexual activity (e.g., masturbation, coitus) may actually *increase,* as compared with earlier levels of functioning in this area.

45.11. The answer is E (all) (*Synopsis VI*, page 810; *CTP V*, pages 2028–2029).

Alzheimer's disease is the *primary diagnosis* in 50 percent of the 1.3 million people in nursing homes. It is a common type of *senile brain disorder* that affects *millions of people* throughout the world. Alzheimer's disease is associated with more than *100,000 deaths annually* in the United States.

A primary, progressive dementia, Alzheimer's disease is characterized in its early phase by recent memory and attention deficits, general failure of efficiency, and defects in sensory perception leading to episodes of disorientation to time and place. In the later phase, disorientation become complete, rigidity of muscles becomes apparent, and the patient shows purposeless hyperactivity, confusion, and agitation and appears dull and apathetic. In the terminal phase, dementia is profound, and the patient declines to a vegetative existence. The pathology consists of generalized brain atrophy with neurofibrillary whorls, senile plaques, and granulovascular degeneration in the hippocampal pyramidal neurons. The disorder has no known treatment; once the symptoms appear, the average duration of life is 6½ years.

45.12. The answer is A (1, 2, 3) (*Synopsis VI*, page 816; *CTP V*, pages 2046–2047).

Elderly persons, particularly if they have an organic brain disease, are especially susceptible to the side effects of antipsychotics, including *tardive dyskinesia, akathisia,* and a *toxic confusional state.* Tardive dyskinesia is characterized by disfiguring and involuntary buccal and lingual masticatory movements; akathisia is a restlessness marked by a compelling need for constant motion. Choreiform body movements, which are spasmodic and involuntary movements of the limbs and the face, and rhythmic extension and flexion movements of the fingers may also be noticeable. Examination of the patient's protruded tongue for fine tremors and vermicular (wormlike) movements is a useful diagnostic procedure. A toxic confusional state, also referred to as a central anticholinergic syndrome, is characterized by a marked disturbance in short-term memory, impaired attention, disorientation, anxiety, visual and auditory hallucinations, increased psychotic thinking, and peripheral anticholinergic side effects. *Paresthesias,* which are spontaneous tingling sensations, are not a side effect of antipsychotics.

45.13. The answer is E (all) (*Synopsis VI*, pages 810–817; *CTP V*, page 2052).

Ibuprofen (Motrin, Advil), *trazodone* (Desyrel), *cimetedine* (Tagamet), and *levodopa* (Larodopa) have been implicated in the production in the elderly of psychiatric symptoms, such as depression, confusion, disorientation, and delirium. These symptoms usually cease after the drug is withdrawn, but the clinician must be alert to withdrawal reactions to a drug, especially if it is stopped abruptly.

Various drugs used in medicine can cause psychiatric symptoms in all classes of patients, especially among old patients. These symptoms may result if the drug is prescribed in too large a dose, if the patient is particularly sensitive to the medication, or if the patient does not follow instructions for its use.

45.14. The answer is E (all) (*Synopsis VI*, page 814; *CTP V*, pages 2040–2041 and 2051–2053).

Elderly persons may be *more susceptible* than younger adults to the adverse side effects of psychotherapeutic drugs (particularly adverse cardiac effects) and may *metabolize drugs more slowly.* Most psychotropic drugs should be given in *equally divided doses* three or four times over a 24-hour period, because geriatric patients may not be able to tolerate the sudden rise in drug-blood level that results from one large dose. The most reasonable clinical practice is to *begin with a small dose,* increase it slowly, and watch for possible side effects. A common concern is that geriatric patients are often taking other medications, and thus psychiatrists must carefully consider the possible drug interactions.

45.15. The answer is B (1, 3) (*Synopsis VI*, page 810; *CTP V*, pages 614–617 and 2028).

The most serious symptom of Alzheimer's disease (i.e., dementia) closely correlates with the accumulation within neuronal cells of *abnormal protein structures* known as neurofibrillary tangles. These structures are destroyed and replaced by neuritic (or senile) plaques. The damage is confined to the hippocampus, according to the most recent evidence. Experimental destruction of the *hippocampus* has been linked to a profound and lasting memory impairment that affects all types of learning. Progressive impairment in recent memory is a hallmark of Alzheimer's disease.

An unusually small (not large) amount of *acetylcholine* has been found in the brains of Alzheimer's disease patients. A reduction in brain choline acetyltransferase, the enzyme needed to synthesize acetylcholine, has been proposed to account for that finding. Alzheimer's disease *begins insidiously, not abruptly;* the patient shows impaired memory or subtle personality changes that are usually first noticed by the family, rather than by the patient.

46 |||||

Forensic Psychiatry

Few of the forces that confound communication between law and psychiatry are as profound as the difference in the basic paradigms of these two disciplines. The law operates in an adversarial model: in every case there are two opposing sides. Psychiatry operates according to the concept of the therapeutic alliance: in each case the clinician attempts to work in collaboration with the healthy side of the patient in order to make positive change.

In a judicial proceeding the psychiatrist may be called on to be a witness of fact, functioning similarly to laypersons, or to be an expert witness. The term "expert" has a particular legal meaning independent of the expertise of the clinician; expert witnesses are those who may draw conclusions from data.

Forensic psychiatry is the interface between psychiatry and the law, representing that branch of medicine concerned with the legal aspects of mental illness.

At various stages psychiatry and law have converged. Both psychiatry and law are concerned with social deviants, persons who have violated the rules of society and whose behavior presents a problem, not only because their deviance has diminished their ability to function effectively but also because it affects the functioning of the community adversely. Traditionally, the psychiatrist's efforts are directed toward elucidation of the causes and, through prevention and treatment, reduction of the self-destructive elements of harmful behavior. The lawyer, as the agent of society, is concerned with the fact that the social deviant presents a potential threat to the safety and security of other people in the environment. Both psychiatry and law seek to implement their respective goals through the application of pragmatic techniques based on empirical observations.

Psychiatrists may be asked to be consultants to the court to evaluate a patient's mental status, including the patient's competence to stand trial, to make a will, and to be executed.

A major area of concern for psychiatrists is the duty to disclose confidential information in order to safeguard the patient or others. Students should be familiar with the definitions of privilege and confidentiality and should be aware of the circumstances that cause these concepts to be superseded by judicial order or by the physician's exercise of good judgment.

Laws governing hospitalization in psychiatric facilities have safeguards to protect the patient's civil liberties. Students should know the four procedures of admission and the rights that patients retain while hospitalized voluntarily or involuntarily. These rights include both the right to treatment and the right to refuse treatment.

The premise that allows treatment is informed consent, not effectiveness, timeliness, or need. The doctrine of informed consent evolved as society moved from the concept of paternalism in medical care to the concept of the patient's right to self-determination. In general, informed consent requires that there be (1) an understanding of the nature and the foreseeable risks and benefits of a procedure, (2) a knowledge of alternative procedures, (3) awareness of the consequences of withholding consent, and (4) the recognition that consent is voluntary.

The student should study the evolution of criminal law, criminal responsibility, and the role of psychiatry in this arena. The concept of criminal responsibility has evolved from precedents first set forth in 1843 in the British courts. The M'Naghten rule held then that a person is not guilty by reason of insanity if the person had a mental disease that made the person unaware of the nature, the quality, and the consequences of the act or if the person was incapable of realizing that the act was wrong. Since 1843 there have been changes in the law to test criminal responsibility. Physicians should be aware of the current concepts and controversies about reforms of the tests for criminal responsibility.

Malpractice is the term used to refer to professional negligence. The clinician and the student should be aware of the elements necessary to claim malpractice: dereliction of duty directly causing damages (the four Ds). The current malpractice crisis requires that the student be aware of the common forms of malpractice and of the preventive measures that have proved valuable in clinical practice. Sexual relations with patients, although not a common form of malpractice, is a serious issue. The consensus from case law and medical codes of practice dictates that sexual intercourse with a patient under any circumstances is an unethical deviation from the standard of care.

The psychiatrist is neither a legal agent nor a legal expert. The responsibility for the resolution of questions of law belongs to the judge, the jury, and the contending attorneys. The psychiatrist can present his or her observations, but only the judicial process can resolve issues of guilt, innocence, competency, wills, and other matters of law.

Students should read Chapter 46 of *Synopsis VI*, "Forensic Psychiatry," and Section 49.1 of *CTP V*, "Legal Issues in Psychiatry," and then answer the questions below to test their knowledge in this area.

HELPFUL HINTS

The student should be able to define each of the terms and know each of the cases listed below.

credibility of witnesses
culpability
competency
probationary status
rules of evidence
leading questions
medical expert
pretrial conference
hearsay
plea bargaining
court-mandated evaluations
testimonial privilege
confidentiality
discriminate disclosure
disclose to safeguard
duty to warn
civil commitment
informal admission
voluntary admission
temporary admission
involuntary admission
parens patriae
mental-health information service

habeas corpus
abandonment
alliance threat
documentation
going the extra mile
emergency exception
Tarasoff v. Regents of University of California (I and II)
Rouse v. Cameron
Judge David Bazelon
civil commitment
right to treatment
Wyatt v. Stickney
state training school standards
peonage
O'Connor v. Donaldson
Thomas Szasz
forced confinement
seclusion and restraint
informed consent
classical tort
battery

mature minor rule
Gault decision
emancipated minor
consent form
custody
task-specific competence
testamentary capacity
testator
judgment
competence to inform
conservator
actus reus
mens rea
M'Naghten rule
right-wrong test
irresistible impulse
Durham rule
model penal code
antisocial behavior
insanity defense
malpractice
the four Ds

QUESTIONS

DIRECTIONS: Each of the questions or incomplete statements below is followed by five suggested responses or completions. Select the *one* that is *best* in each case.

46.1. Of the following, which is the least common cause of malpractice claims against psychiatrists by patients?
A. Suicide attempts
B. Improper use of restraints
C. Failure to treat psychosis
D. Sexual involvement
E. Drug addiction

46.2. The Gault decision refers to
A. children
B. *habeas corpus*
C. torts
D. informed consent
E. none of the above

46.3. During a court-mandated evaluation a patient always has
A. the right of patient privilege
B. the right of confidentiality
C. the right to informed consent
D. the obligation to be examined for credibility
E. all the above

46.4. In a court proceeding a psychiatrist may be called as an expert witness. Qualification as an expert
A. consists of certification in one's clinical field
B. depends on the actual expertise the clinician has in the area, as demonstrated by recognition in his or her clinical field
C. permits the clinician to draw conclusions from data
D. is not given to residents in training
E. is determined by the psychiatrist's personal opinion of his or her qualifications

46.5. Child-custody court actions are based on
A. the wishes of the child
B. the rights of the previously recognized custodial parent
C. the best interests of the child
D. the rights of the mother in the case of a young child
E. all the above

DIRECTIONS: For each question or incomplete statement below, *one or more* of the responses or completions given are correct. Choose answer

A. if only *1, 2, and 3* are correct
B. if only *1 and 3* are correct
C. if only *2 and 4* are correct
D. if only *4* is correct
E. if *all* are correct

46.6. According to the model penal code, criminal responsibility requires that the
1. person have a diagnosed mental illness
2. criminal act result from a mental illness
3. person not be able to appreciate the act of criminality
4. person not be able to control his or her conduct

46.7. A person is declared to be incompetent
1. if there is a diagnosed mental disorder
2. on the basis of psychiatrist's opinion
3. on admission to a mental hospital
4. if the person's judgment is impaired by a mental disorder

46.8. To reduce the risk of malpractice, a psychiatrist should
1. document good care
2. provide only the kind of care the psychiatrist is qualified to deliver
3. get informed consent
4. obtain a second opinion

46.9. Psychiatric malpractice suits
1. rank highest among medical specialties in frequency of occurrence
2. are not common in cases of suicide
3. are easily validated by linking injury to treatment
4. are usually associated with tangible physical injury

46.10. Which of the following are considered when evaluating a person's competence to make a will?
1. The person must know the nature and the extent of his or her property
2. The person must know that he or she is making a will
3. The person must know who the natural beneficiaries are
4. The person must not have a mental disorder

DIRECTIONS: Each group of questions below consists of five lettered headings followed by a list of numbered statements. For each numbered statement, select the *one* lettered heading that is most closely associated with it. Each lettered heading may be used once, more than once, or not at all.

Questions 46.11–46.15

A. *O'Connor v. Donaldson*
B. *Wyatt v. Stickney*
C. *Tarasoff v. Regents of University of California* (Tarasoff I)
D. *Tarasoff v. Regents of University of California* (Tarasoff II)
E. *Rouse v. Cameron*

46.11. The purpose of involuntary hospitalization is treatment

46.12. Sets out minimum requirements for staffing

46.13. Sets forth the psychiatrist's duty to protect potential victims from danger to life by a patient

46.14. Sets forth the psychiatrist's duty to warn potential victims of danger to life by a patient

46.15. Harmless mental patients cannot be confined against their will

Questions 46.16–46.19

A. Informal admission
B. One-physician certificate
C. Two-physician certificate
D. Voluntary admission
E. *Parens patriae*

46.16. Temporary admission for 15 days

46.17. The patient enters a general hospital and is free to leave against medical advice

46.18. Involuntary admission for 60 days

46.19. Power of the state to hospitalize a person involuntarily

ANSWERS

Forensic Psychiatry

46.1. **The answer is D** (*Synopsis VI*, pages 829–831; *CTP V*, pages 2109–2111).

Sexual involvement with patients accounts for 6 percent of all malpractice claims against psychiatrists and is the least common cause of malpractice litigation. This fact does not, however, minimize its importance as a significant problem. Sexual intimacy with patients is both illegal and unethical. There are also serious legal and ethical questions about a psychotherapist's dating or marrying a patient even after discharging the patient from therapy. Some psychiatrists believe in the adage "Once a patient, always a patient." Other psychiatrists hold the view that a period of two years after discharge is sufficient time to terminate prohibitions against personal involvement.

For other malpractice claims, the following figures are given: failure to manage *suicide attempts*, 21 percent; *improper use of restraints*, 7 percent; and *failure to treat psychosis*, 14 percent. *Drug addiction* accounts for about 10 percent of claims and refers to the patient's having developed a substance-abuse disorder as a result of a psychiatrist's not monitoring carefully the prescribing of potentially addicting drugs.

46.2. **The answer is A** (*Synopsis VI*, page 825; *CTP V*, pages 2107–2123).

The Gault decision refers to rights given to *children*, who, as a result of the decision, (1) must be represented by counsel, (2) must be able to confront witnesses, and (3) must be given proper notice of charges.

Habeas corpus is a legal procedure that may be proclaimed on behalf of anyone who believes he or she is being deprived of liberty illegally. For mental patients it requires that the patient be brought before a judge who will determine whether or not the patient can be detained involuntarily.

A *tort* is a legal term for a wrongful act. In psychiatry the administration of medication or electroconvulsive therapy can be considered a tort if it is done without consent.

Informed consent requires that there be an understanding of the risks involved in any psychiatric procedure to which a patient is subjected.

46.3. **The answer is C** (*Synopsis VI*, page 821; *CTP V*, pages 2111–2112 and 2120).

During a court-mandated evaluation, the patient has the *right to informed consent*—that is, the right to be informed that the information obtained may be revealed to the court. Indeed, the clinician is under an ethical and in some cases a legal obligation to inform a patient at the onset that the results of the evaluation may be revealed in court and to make certain that the patient understands this circumstance.

Patient privilege is the patient's right to have confidentiality maintained in the face of a subpoena. Currently, 38 of the 50 states have statutes that recognize some kind of physician-patient privilege. Numerous exceptions to privilege exist, including court-mandated evaluations; neither federal cases nor military court proceedings recognize psychotherapist-patient privilege.

Confidentiality binds the physician to hold secret all the information given by a patient. Apart from statutory disclosure requirements and judicial compulsion, the physician has no legal obligation to furnish information, even to law enforcement officials. In a court-mandated evaluation, however, the examination does not function under the principle of confidentiality.

Evaluation of *credibility* may be ordered by a trial judge to establish the presence or the absence of pathology in a complaining witness. Before ordering such an examination, the trial judge asks for evidence showing that such an examination is necessary to determine the merits of the case and that the imposition on the witness does not outweigh the examination's value.

46.4. **The answer is C** (*Synopsis VI*, pages 820–821; *CTP V*, pages 2120–2123).

In the context of the courtroom, an expert witness is one who may *draw conclusions from data*—for example, that a patient meets the required criteria for hospitalization or for an insanity defense under the standards of a jurisdiction. The qualifying process consists not of *certification in one's clinical field* but of being accepted by the court and both sides of the case as suitable to perform expert functions. Thus, the term "expert" has a particular legal meaning and is independent of any actual or presumed *expertise* the clinician may have in a given area. Under certain circumstances even *residents in training* may be accepted as expert witnesses to draw conclusions about, say, a patient's committability, as it is understood in many courts that residents function with supervision in such matters.

Usually, when a psychiatrist is asked to serve as an expert, he or she is asked to do it for one side in a case; rarely is a clinician an independent examiner reporting directly to the court. The implication is that the material offered is brought out by the hiring attorney during the direct examination. The other attorney then draws out additional material during the cross-examination. The psychiatrist's *personal opinions* about his or her qualifications in an area is not a determining factor in being declared an expert witness.

46.5. The answer is C (*Synopsis VI*, page 825; *CTP V*, page 2119).

The action of a court in a child-custody dispute is predicated on the *best interests of the child* and not on the *wishes of the child*. A natural parent does not have an inherent right to be named the custodial parent, but the presumption, although a bit eroded, remains in favor of the *mother* in the case of a young child. By a rule of thumb, the courts presume that the welfare of a child of tender years is generally best served by maternal custody when the mother is a good and fit parent. The best interests of the mother may be served by naming her the custodial parent, as a mother may never resolve the effects of the loss of a child, but her best interests are not to be equated *ipso facto* with the best interests of the child. In care and protection proceedings the court intervenes in the welfare of a child when the parents are unable to do so.

More and more fathers are now asserting custodial claims. In about 5 percent of child-custody cases, fathers are named the custodians. The movement supporting women's rights is also enhancing the chances of paternal custody; with more and more women going outside the home to work, the traditional rationale for maternal custody has less force now than it did in the past.

Every state today has a statute allowing a court, usually a juvenile court, to assume jurisdiction over a neglected or abused child and to remove the child from parental custody. Most states provide several grounds for assuming jurisdiction, such as parental abuse, an environment injurious to the child's welfare, and the danger of the child's being brought up to lead an idle, dissolute, or immoral life. If the court removes the child from parental custody, it usually orders that the care and custody of the child be supervised by a welfare or probation department. The *rights of the previously recognized custodial parent* do not take precedence over the best interests of the child in determining new child-custody court actions.

46.6. The answer is E (all) (*Synopsis VI*, pages 828–829; *CTP V*, pages 2121–2122).

The model penal code (MPC) is used in the federal courts to determine criminal responsibility. It requires that (1) the person have a *diagnosed mental illness*, (2) the criminal act *result from a mental illness*, (3) the person *not be able to appreciate the act*, and (4) the person *not be able to control* his or her conduct to conform to the requirements of the law.

The MPC states that repeated criminal or antisocial acts are not, by themselves, to be taken as signs of mental illness. In fact, according to DSM-III-R, antisocial behavior is not classified as a mental disorder.

46.7. The answer is D (4) (*Synopsis VI*, page 826; *CTP V*, pages 2112–2114 and 2120–2121).

A person is declared to be incompetent only if, as a result of a mental disorder, he or she has *impaired judgment* regarding the specific issues involved. A *diagnosed mental disorder* or *admission to a mental hospital* does not automatically mean the person is incompetent.

The concept of competence has meaning in terms of the task, decision, or procedure that the person is facing. Although psychiatrists often give *opinions* on competence, only a judge's ruling converts the opinion into a finding; that is, a patient is not competent or incompetent until the court says so.

46.8. The answer is E (all) (*Synopsis VI*, page 831; *CTP V*, pages 2108–2111).

Although it is impossible to eliminate malpractice completely, some preventive approaches have been invaluable in clinical practice. The *documentation of good care* is a strong deterrent to liability. Such documentation should include the decision-making process, the clinician's rationale for treatment, and an evaluation of costs and benefits. Psychiatrists should provide only the kind of care that they are *qualified to deliver*. They should never overload their practices or overstretch their abilities, and they should take reasonable care of themselves. The *informed consent* process refers to a discussion between the doctor and the patient about the treatment proposed, the side effects of drugs, and the uncertainty of psychiatric practice. Such a dialogue helps prevent a liability suit. A consultation also affords protection against liability because it allows the clinician to obtain information about his or her peer group's standard of practice. It provides a *second opinion*, enabling the clinician to submit his or her judgment to the scrutiny of the peer. The clinician who takes the trouble to obtain a consultation in a difficult and complex case is unlikely to be viewed by a jury as careless and negligent.

46.9. The answer is D (4) (*Synopsis VI*, pages 829–831; *CTP V*, pages 2108–2111).

In relative frequency of malpractice suits, psychiatry *ranks* eighth (not highest) among the medical specialties. In almost every suit in which liability was imposed, *tangible physical injury* was demonstrated. The number of suits against psychiatrists is small because patients are often reluctant to expose a psychiatric history. Psychiatrists are generally skilled in dealing with patients' negative feelings, and most liability cases arise when there are negative relationships between doctor and patient. There is also difficulty in *linking injury to treatment* in psychiatric cases.

In general, psychiatrists have been sued for malpractice for faulty diagnosis or screening, improper certification in commitment, harmful effects of convulsive and psychotropic drug treatments, improper divulgence of information, and sexual intimacy with patients. *Suicide* is a common cause of litigation.

46.10. The answer is A (1, 2, 3) (*Synopsis VI*, pages 825–827; *CTP V*, page 2114).

Three demonstrable psychological capacities must be considered when evaluating a person's competence to make a will. The person must know (1) the *nature and the extent* of his or her bounty (property), (2) that he or she is *making a will*, and (3) who the *natural beneficiaries* are (spouse, children, relatives). If any one of these capacities is damaged, the will may be invalidated.

Competence is determined on the basis of a person's ability to exercise good judgment. The diagnosis of a *mental disorder* is not in itself sufficient to warrant a finding of incompetence. The ability to make a will is called testamentary capacity.

46.11–46.15

46.11. The answer is E (*Synopsis VI*, page 824; *CTP V*, page 2116).

46.12. The answer if B (*Synopsis VI*, page 824; *CTP V*, page 2116).

46.13. The answer is D (*Synopsis VI*, page 822; *CTP V*, pages 2119–2120).

46.14. The answer is C (*Synopsis VI*, page 822; *CTP V*, pages 2119–2120).

46.15. The answer is A (*Synopsis VI*, page 824; *CTP V*, page 2116).

Various landmark legal cases have affected psychiatry and the law over the years. In the 1976 case of *O'Connor v. Donaldson*, the United States Supreme Court ruled that *harmless mental patients* cannot be confined against their will without treatment if they can survive outside. According to the Court, a finding of mental illness alone cannot justify a state's confining persons in a hospital against their will; patients must be considered dangerous to themselves or others before they are confined against their will. Many homeless persons are mentally ill and are unable to care for themselves adequately. Thus, a homeless person with pneumonia would do better in a hospital where he or she can obtain proper treatment.

In 1971, in *Wyatt v. Stickney* in Alabama Federal District Court, it was decided that persons civilly committed to a mental institution have a constitutional right to receive adequate treatment, and standards were established for *staffing,* nutrition, physical facilities, and treatment.

In 1966, in *Rouse v. Cameron* in the District of Columbia, it was ruled that the *purpose of invol-*

untary hospitalization is treatment and that a patient who is not receiving treatment has a constitutional right to be discharged from the hospital.

In the case of *Tarasoff v. Regents of University of California* (Tarasoff I), in 1974, it was ruled that a physician or psychotherapist who has reason to believe that a patient may injure or kill someone must notify the potential victim, his or her relatives or friends, or the authorities. The Tarasoff I ruling does not require therapists to report fantasies; rather, it means that, when they are convinced that a homicide is likely, they have a *duty to warn*. The Tarasoff I decision has not drastically affected psychiatrists, as it has long been their practice to warn the appropriate persons or law enforcement authorities when a patient presents a distinct and immediate threat to someone. According to the American Psychiatric Association, confidentiality may, with careful judgment, be broken in the following circumstances: (1) A patient will probably commit murder, and the act can be stopped only by the psychiatrist's notification of the police. (2) A patient will probably commit suicide, and the act can be stopped only by the psychiatrist's notification of the police. (3) A patient, such as a bus driver or an airline pilot, who has potentially life-threatening responsibilities shows marked impairment of judgment.

In 1976 the California Supreme Court issued a second ruling in the case of *Tarasoff v. Regents of University of California* (Tarasoff II). It broadened its earlier ruling, the duty to warn, to include the *duty to protect*. The Tarasoff II ruling has stimulated perhaps the most intense debates in the medicolegal field. Lawyers, judges, and expert witnesses argue the definition of prevention, the nature of the relationship between therapist and patient, and the balance between public safety and individual privacy. Clinicians argue that the duty to protect may hinder treatment because the patient may not trust the doctor if confidentiality is not maintained. Furthermore, it is not always easy to determine if a patient is dangerous enough to justify long-term incarceration because of defensive practices. As a result of such debates in the medicolegal field since 1976, state courts have not come up with a uniform interpretation of the Tarasoff II ruling, the concept of the duty to protect.

46.16–46.19

46.16. The answer is B (*Synopsis VI*, page 823; *CTP V*, pages 2114–2115).

46.17. The answer is A (*Synopsis VI*, page 823; *CTP V*, pages 2114–2115).

46.18. The answer is C (*Synopsis VI*, page 823; *CTP V*, pages 2114–2115).

46.19. The answer is E (*Synopsis VI*, page 823; *CTP V*, page 2114).

Several laws govern hospitalization of the mentally ill; all have been endorsed by both the legal and the psychiatric professions to ensure that civil liberties are secured and that no person can be railroaded into a mental hospital.

In informal admission to a general hospital, the patient applies for admission on the same basis as a medical or surgical patient and is *free to leave* the hospital at any time, even against medical advice.

A one-physician certificate, also known as temporary or emergency *admission for 15 days*, is used for patients who are unable to make a decision on their own because they have a mental illness that impairs their judgment (e.g., Alzheimer's disease). Such patients may be admitted on an emergency basis to a psychiatric hospital on the written recommendation of one physician, provided the need for hospitalization is confirmed by a psychiatrist on the hospital staff.

A two-physician certificate is used for *involuntary admission* for 60 days when patients are a danger to themselves (suicidal patients) or to others (homicidal patients). Two physicians must make independent examinations of the patient, and the next of kin must be notified if a decision is made to hospitalize the patient. The patient may be hospitalized for up to 60 days; however, during that time the patient has a right to see a judge, who determines whether such involuntary hospitalization may continue. After 60 days, if the patient is to remain hospitalized, the case must be reviewed by a board consisting of psychiatrists, other physicians, lawyers, and other citizens not connected with the institution.

Voluntary admission operates only in psychiatric hospitals and requires that patients apply in writing for admission. They come to the hospital on the advice of their personal physician or on their own. In either case, a psychiatrist on the staff of the hospital must determine that hospitalization is indicated. Voluntary admission may be converted to involuntary admission if the two-physician certificate procedure is invoked; however, the patient may immediately ask to see a judge if he or she does not agree with the decision.

Parens patriae, a legal term, means police power given to the *state* that allows mentally ill persons who are dangerous to themselves or others to be admitted to a psychiatric hospital against their will (provided two psychiatrists agree). Patients may request that a judge rule on the decision under a writ of *habeas corpus*.

47 |||||

Ethics in Psychiatry

Physicians bring personal and social values to their work and encounter the values and the standards of their patients and colleagues. Ethical dimensions are pervasive in psychiatry and become prominent when values conflict. Questions about which values take priority in a particular clinical situation must be resolved in the light of the ethical, moral, medical, and legal nuances of the situation. An appreciation of ethics in psychiatry aids the clinician in finding responsible techniques for managing these conflicts. Students should be familiar with the theoretical principles guiding ethics within a psychiatric context.

Utilitarian theory holds that our fundamental obligation in decision making is to produce the greatest possible good for the greatest number of people. Paternalism, the traditional model for the physician-patient relationship, holds that the physician has a duty to act in the best interests of the patient as the parent would act toward a child. Autonomy theory presumes that the normal adult patient is self-governing and has the right to self-determination. The right to informed consent, the right to refuse treatment, and the limitations on the ability of psychiatrists to involuntarily hospitalize and treat persons are examples of the societal belief in the person's fundamental right to self-determination.

Informed consent is a legal doctrine that upholds the rights of patients to be informed and to make treatment choices. The law does not, however, provide guidance about the complex and subtle ethical responsibility to respect the choices of one's patients, especially when their competence is to some degree compromised by illness. Informed consent calls attention to the ethics of therapeutic modality choice. This involves the right of patients not only to be informed of the benefits and the risks of treatment alternatives but also to choose among them.

The concept of the right to refuse treatment includes the right to forgo life-sustaining measures. Students should be aware of the controversy in this area of patients' rights. Living wills have evolved as a way for patients to continue to have their choices and beliefs upheld after they are no longer able to express their wishes.

Ethical issues in psychiatry continue to be complex. The general acceptance of the autonomy theory as the guideline for the physician-patient relationship creates a special problem for psychiatrists. Many patients come to treatment or are brought by others because their ability to be autonomous is in question. Furthermore, the goal of psychiatric treatment is to restore a patient to autonomous function. Involuntary hospitalization requires that psychiatrists divide their loyalties between the rights of patients and the protection of society. The clinician must understand the underlying ethical principles when deciding what psychiatric interventions to make.

Perhaps the most frequent ethical questions in psychiatry concern privacy, confidentiality, and privilege. Privacy refers to the limiting of access of others to one's body or mind. Confidentiality refers to the communication of information in a private setting with the expectation that the information will not be disclosed to a third party. Privilege refers to the right of patients or of psychiatrists on their behalf to assert that certain confidential information may not be discussed in a judicial setting. These rights of privacy, confidentiality, and privilege are both supported and limited by ethical and legal considerations.

Physicians must deal with the ethical conflicts that arise because of the intimacy of the physician-patient relationship. The emotionally laden treatment and the patient's vulnerability make it imperative that the patient never be abused or exploited by sexual contact.

Students are advised to study Chapter 47, "Ethics in Psychiatry," in *Synopsis VI* and Section 49.2, "Ethics in Psychiatry," in *CTP V* and to test their knowledge by answering the questions below.

HELPFUL HINTS

The student should be able to define each of the terms and know each of the cases listed below.

utilitarian theory	right to die	duty to protect
autonomy theory	surrogate decision-making	professional standards
individual paternalism	substituted-judgment principle	right to health care
state paternalism	best-interests principle	*Roe v. Wade*
duty of beneficence	decisional capacity	*Cruzan v. Missouri*
informed consent	confidentiality	

QUESTIONS

DIRECTIONS: The lettered headings below are followed by a list of numbered phrases. For each numbered phrase, select the lettered heading most associated with it. Each lettered heading may be used once, more than once, or not at all.

Questions 47.1–47.4
    A. Utilitarian theory
    B. Paternalism
    C. Autonomy theory

47.1. The basis for making decisions about the allocation of society's resources for treatment and medical research

47.2. The traditional model of the physician-patient relationship

47.3. The physician's duty of beneficence

47.4. The right to informed consent

DIRECTIONS: The question below is followed by five suggested responses. Select the *one* that is *best*.

47.5. The physician's obligation to refrain from sexual contact with a patient is based on which of the following principles?
A. A patient in the physician-patient relationship is too vulnerable to make fully voluntary choices
B. The focus should be on the treatment of the patient
C. Transference issues make voluntary choices about sexual contact almost impossible
D. The physician has an obligation to uphold the reputation of the profession
E. All the above

ANSWERS

Ethics in Psychiatry

47.1–47.4

47.1. The answer is A (*Synopsis VI*, page 832; *CTP V*, page 2125).

47.2. The answer is B (*Synopsis VI*, page 832; *CTP V*, page 2126).

47.3. The answer is B (*Synopsis VI*, page 832; *CTP V*, page 2126).

47.4. The answer is C (*Synopsis VI*, pages 832–833; *CTP V*, pages 2127–2128).

Utilitarian theory holds that our fundamental obligation when making decisions is to try to produce the greatest possible happiness for the greatest number of people. Sometimes the choices available are dismal. In that case one should act in ways that produce the least pain. Utilitarian theory is still used as the basis for making decisions about the *allocation of society's resources* for treatment and medical research.

Paternalism may be defined as a system in which someone acts for another's benefit without that person's consent. The requirement that health care practitioners be licensed is an example of state paternalism. Individual paternalism was the *traditional model* of the physician-patient relationship. In this model the physician is supposed to treat the patient as a caring parent would treat a child. The parent is assumed to know what is best for the child and has no obligation to ask the child for permission to perform actions that may benefit the child. The *physician's duty of beneficence*, the principle of doing good and avoiding harm, is a paternalistic principle. The physician is presumed to have knowledge that the patient may not understand or, in certain instances, is better off not knowing.

Autonomy theory presumes that the normal adult patient has the ability and the right to make rational and responsible decisions. The patient is self-governing (autonomous) and has rights to self-determination. The relationship between physician and patient is perceived as a relationship between two responsible adults. The patient's right to *informed consent*, the right to refuse treatment, and the assumption of competence are examples of the person's right to self-determination.

47.5. The answer is E (*Synopsis VI*, pages 829–831 and 833; *CTP V*, pages 2110–2111).

Physicians have an obligation to refrain from sexual contact with their patients. A number of principles underlie this obligation. A patient in the physician-patient relationship is generally too *vulnerable* to make a fully voluntary choice about sexual contact. The physician's *focus* should be on the treatment of the patient. A change in that focus to include sexual contact will compromise the physician's ability to treat the patient appropriately. In the psychiatrist-patient relationship *transference issues* make voluntary choices about sexual contact almost impossible for the patient. In addition, the physician has an obligation to uphold the standards and the *reputation of the profession*.

48 |||||

History of Psychiatry

Psychiatry is the branch of medicine that deals with the healing of mental disorders, the manifestations of which are primarily behavioral and psychological. The history of psychiatry is, at the same time, the history of civilization. As humans increased their knowledge of the world around them, they also increased their knowledge of the world within.

Psychiatry was incorporated into the field of medicine about a century and a half ago. Earlier, mental diseases had been considered the province of philosophy; and in the Middle Ages the mentally ill, when not ignored, were usually taken care of—sheltered, punished, or exorcized—by medicine men and the clergy. This history is easily understandable; diseases of the mind, whether one considers the mind as dis-

tinct from the body or as united with it, had always appeared puzzling and difficult to treat. The confusion is diminishing, however, as new knowledge from the basic behavioral sciences finds important applications in understanding the causes of mental illness and in developing more effective treatments.

The major workers in the field of psychiatry, their contributions, and important events are described in a comprehensive table in *Synopsis VI*, Chapter 48, "History of Psychiatry," and in *CTP V*, Section 50.1, "History of Psychiatry." Students should review Chapter 48 and Section 50.1 and then test their knowledge of the subject by studying the questions and answers below.

HELPFUL HINTS

The student should know the following names and the contributions of each.

Franz Anton Mesmer	Emil Kraepelin	Helene Deutsch
Philippe Pinel	Sigmund Freud	Melanie Klein
Benjamin Rush	Clifford Beers	John Cade
William Tuke	Pierre Janet	Erik Erikson
Samuel Tuke	Alfred Adler	Jean Delay
Daniel Hack Tuke	Heinz Kohut	Maxwell Jones
Franz Joseph Gall	Hermann Rorschach	Harry Stack Sullivan
Jean Esquirol	Ivan Pavlov	Carl Jung
Isaac Ray	Karen Horney	Adolf Meyer
Jean-Martin Charcot	Ugo Cerletti	William Masters
Karl Kahlbaum	Leo Kanner	Virginia Johnson

QUESTIONS

DIRECTIONS: Each group of questions below consists of five lettered headings followed by a list of numbered statements. For each numbered statement, select the *one* lettered heading that is most closely associated with it. Each lettered heading may be used once, more than once, or not at all.

Questions 48.1–48.5
A. Emil Kraepelin
B. Jean-Martin Charcot
C. Eugen Bleuler
D. Alfred Adler
E. Leo Kanner

48.1. Described hysterical symptoms in both men and women

48.2. Coined the term "schizophrenia"

48.3. Divided psychoses into dementia precox and manic-depressive insanity

48.4. Described infantile autism

48.5. Developed the term "inferiority complex"

Questions 48.6–48.10
A. Helene Deutsch
B. Erik Erikson
C. Carl Gustav Jung
D. Heinz Kohut
E. Karen Horney

48.6. Concept of the collective unconscious

48.7. Described the concept of identity crisis

48.8. Originated the school of self-psychology

48.9. Focused on sociocultural determinants of neuroses

48.10. Psychology of the as-if personality

ANSWERS

History of Psychiatry

48.1–48.5

48.1. The answer is B (*Synopsis VI*, page 841; *CTP V*, pages 2137–2140).

48.2. The answer is C (*Synopsis VI*, page 841; *CTP V*, pages 2137–2140).

48.3. The answer is A (*Synopsis VI*, page 841; *CTP V*, pages 2137–2140).

48.4. The answer is E (*Synopsis VI*, page 843; *CTP V*, pages 2137–2140).

48.5. The answer is D (*Synopsis VI*, page 842; *CTP V*, pages 2137–2140).

Jean-Martin Charcot (1825–1893) was a French neurologist and psychiatrist who greatly impressed Sigmund Freud with his live case presentations of male and female patients with *hysterical symptoms.* He repeatedly demonstrated that under hypnosis the symptoms of hysteria could be produced or removed at the will of the hypnotist and that patients responded to and acted on ideas introduced into their trains of thought.

Eugen Bleuler (1857–1939), a Swiss psychiatrist, coined the term *"schizophrenia"* to replace the term "dementia precox." His book *Dementia Praecox or The Group of Schizophrenias* (1911) differentiated between fundamental and accessory symptoms of schizophrenia. To Bleuler the primary symptoms included disturbances of affect, association, autism, and ambivalence (the four A's); secondary symptoms included hallucinations, delusions, negativism, and stupor.

Emil Kraepelin (1856–1926) was a German physician who, although he was Freud's contemporary, can be considered the last representative of the pre-dynamic school of psychiatry. He attempted to sort out definite disease entities by following their signs, courses, and outcomes. By using a prognostic approach, correlating basic symptoms with illness course, he differentiated between the chronic deteriorating *dementia precox* (schizophrenia) and the episodic, nondeteriorating *manic-depressive insanity* (now called bipolar disorder).

Leo Kanner (1894–1981), an American child psychiatrist, wrote the first account of *infantile autism* (1943), which he described as the child's inability to relate in the ordinary way to people and situations from the beginning of life. Kanner believed that many autistic children were confused with children suffering from schizophrenia or mental retardation.

Alfred Adler (1870–1937), an Austrian psychiatrist, broke with Freud over the concept of infantile sexuality. Adler founded the school of individual psychology. This personality theory included the idea of the *inferiority complex*, the sense of weakness and inadequacy with which each person is born. Everyone strives to move from a feeling of inferiority to a feeling of superiority. Normal inferiority feelings cause improvement in life, as each person tries to overcome those feelings. The abnormal person tries, instead, to raise self-esteem by depreciating others.

48.6–48.10

48.6. The answer is C (*Synopsis VI*, page 844; *CTP V*, pages 2150–2153).

48.7. The answer is B (*Synopsis VI*, page 843; *CTP V*, pages 2150–2153).

48.8. The answer is D (*Synopsis VI*, page 846; *CTP V*, pages 2150–2153).

48.9. The answer is E (*Synopsis VI*, page 842; *CTP V*, pages 2150–2153).

48.10. The answer is A (*Synopsis VI*, page 843; *CTP V*, pages 2150–2153).

Carl Gustav Jung (1875–1961), a Swiss psychoanalyst who was originally associated with Freud, developed new concepts of the unconscious. In particular, Jung described the *collective unconscious*, which he believed incorporated all those psychic contents peculiar not to one person but to many at the same time (i.e., to a society, a people, or mankind in general). He introduced the concepts of archetypes, introversion, extroversion, persona, anima, animus, and complex.

Erik Erikson (1902–   ), a Danish-American psychoanalyst, in *Childhood and Society* (1950) identified a conflict for each stage of emotional development in the human life cycle. The adolescent stage is focused on resolving the *identity crisis*. A positive resolution gives the adolescent a core sense of his or her identity; a negative resolution leaves the adolescent without a sense of self or of his or her place in the world.

Heinz Kohut (1913–1981), an Austrian-American psychoanalyst, originated the *school of self-psychology*, which requires that the patient become aware of excessive needs for approval and narcissistic gratification. He also introduced the concepts of mirroring, idealizing, and the alter ego.

Karen Horney (1885–1952), an American psychiatrist of German descent, emphasized environmental, *social, and cultural* factors in the genesis of neurosis. She challenged the universality of the Oedipus complex on cultural grounds and also challenged classic psychoanalytic theory in general, including the concepts of fixed biological phases of development and the sexual nature of child-parent relationships. Her theory is known as holistic psychology. She also introduced the concepts of actual self, real self, idealized self, and self-realization.

Helene Deutsch (1884–1982), an Austrian-American psychoanalyst, was responsible for the two-volume work *The Psychology of Women*, which for several decades presented the most comprehensive Freudian view extant of women's psychological development. She also named and described the *as-if personality*—a person who has a defective capacity for love and assumes pseudoaffective relationships through identification with others. This personality represents a behavioral adaptation to external reality through the mimicry of others without appreciation for their own real emotions. It was portrayed accurately by Woody Allen in the movie *Zelig*.

Index

Page numbers followed by t and f indicate tables and figures, respectively.